MW01009593

Case Studies
in
Modern Corporate Finance

CASE STUDIES

IN

MODERN CORPORATE FINANCE

ROBERT W. WHITE

Western Business School

Prentice Hall, Englewood Cliffs, NJ 07632

1-800-567-3806
- 850-5813

Library of Congress Cataloging-in-Publication Data

White, Robert W.
  Case studies in modern corporate finance / Robert W. White.
     p.   cm.
  ISBN 0-13-288341-4
    1. Corporations--Finance--Case studies. 2. International business
enterprises--Finance--Case studies.   I. Title.
HG4026.W483 1994
658.15'2--dc20   93-46877
                                                            CIP

Acquisition Editor   Leah Jewell
Production Editor   Maureen Wilson
Cover Designer   Design Source
Prepress Buyer   Patrice Fraccio
Editorial Assistant   Eileen Deguzman

 © 1994 by Prentice-Hall, Inc.
A Paramount Communications Company
Englewood Cliffs, New Jersey 07632

Printed in the United States of America
10 9 8 7 6 5 4 3 2 1

ISBN 0-13-288341-4

Prentice-Hall International (UK) Limited, *London*
Prentice-Hall of Australia Pty. Limited, *Sydney*
Prentice-Hall Canada Inc., *Toronto*
Prentice-Hall Hispanoamericana, S.A., *Mexico*
Prentice-Hall of India Private Limited, *New Delhi*
Prentice-Hall of Japan, Inc., *Tokyo*
Simon & Schuster Asia Pte. Ltd., *Singapore*
Editora Prentice Hall do Brasil, Ltda., *Rio de Janiero*

CONTENTS

Preface   *ix*

I. THE ASSESSMENT OF A FIRM'S PERFORMANCE AND FINANCING NEEDS AND LOAN GRANTING DECISIONS   1

1. John Labatt Limited   *2*

2. Kitchen Helper Inc.   *14*

3. Morley Industries, Inc.   *20*

4. Cambridge Nutrition Limited Financing Growth (A)   *25*

5. Note on Value-Added Taxes   *39*

6. Sophisticated Petites   *45*

7. Atlantic Lumber Traders   *57*

8. Columbia River Pulp Company Inc.—Recapitalization   *66*

v

II. SHORT TERM FINANCING VEHICLES AND DECISIONS   83

9. Warner-Lambert Canada Inc.   *84*

10. Lawson Mardon Group Limited   *94*

11. Fantastic Manufacturing, Inc.   *109*

12. Maschinenbau Arrau A. G. (A)   *116*

13. Dow Europe   *124*

III. FINANCIAL MARKETS   147

14. Anheuser-Busch and Campbell Taggart   *148*

15. Note on Insider Trading   *159*

16. Finning Tractor and Equipment Company Ltd.   *172*

17. Nesbitt Thomson Deacon Inc.—The Sceptre Resources Debenture   *190*

18. The RTZ Corporation PLC—Rio Algom Limited   *203*

IV. COST OF CAPITAL AND INVESTMENT DECISIONS   221

19. Procter & Gamble: Cost of Capital   *222*

20. The Consumers' Gas Company Ltd.   *235*

21. Lawson Mardon Group Limited—Corporate Asset Funding Facility   *258*

22. Tanzi Pump Corporation   *272*

23. Minnova Inc.—Lac Shortt Mine   *277*

24. Gold Industry Note   *285*

V. LONG TERM FINANCING VEHICLES AND DECISIONS   291

25. The Redhook Ale Brewery   *292*

26. Tri-tech Computer   *313*

27. Bell Canada   *327*

28. Rogers Communications Inc.   *351*

29. The Multi-Jurisdictional Disclosure System   *375*

30. Robotics, Inc.   *383*

31. Columbia River Pulp Company Inc.—Interest Rate Hedging Strategy   *388*

32. Export Development Corporation—Protected Index Notes (PINS)   *403*

33. American Barrick Resources Corporation   *421*

34. Citibank Canada Ltd.—Monetization of Future Oil Production   *439*

35. Columbia Pine Pulp Company, Inc.   *452*

VI. MEASURING THE VALUE GAP AND UNLOCKING VALUE TO CLOSE THE GAP   461

36. The Goodyear Tire & Rubber Company   *462*

37. Note on the North American Tire Industry   *479*

38. The Acquisition of Martell   *484*

39. Blue Jay Energy & Chemical Corporation   *498*

40. Ocelot Industries Ltd.   *520*

41. Union Enterprises Ltd.   *535*

42. Unicorp Canada Corporation   *559*

43. Sherritt Gordon Ltd.—Proxy Contest   *572*

44. Saskatchewan Oil and Gas Corporation   *594*

45. Sealed Air Corporation's Leveraged Recapitalization   *622*

Index of Cases   *644*

PREFACE

The materials in *Case Studies in Modern Corporate Finance* draw on the work of many individuals and institutions. The casebook contains cases from Leland Stanford Junior University, Harvard Business School, The International Institute for Management Development, Darden Graduate Business School, INSEAD, Dalhousie University, The Stern School of Business, and the Western Business School, and although a significant number of the cases are U.S. based, the results are substantially international and global. The book contains current cases that focus on the major financial decisions made in a corporation, including such current issues as: globalization; corporate governance; ethics; privatization; securitization; risk management; option pricing; pricing of complex securities; structured financing; value-added taxes; and so on. A detailed categorization of the cases by topic is contained in the preface to the instructor's manual. It has a balanced perspective on the role of commercial banks, their lending practices and financial markets (money markets, capital markets, foreign exchange markets, and derivative securities markets) in financing decisions. The casebook contains forty cases and five notes, and is divided into six parts, each of which builds on the previous parts. The book commences with corporate decisions involving the current portion of the balance sheet and progresses down the balance sheet to decisions with a longer term focus.

Part I, consisting of seven cases and one note, provides students with a framework for analysing cases, the assessment of a firm's performance, and financing needs and loan granting decisions. With the exception of the first case, "John Labatt," the remaining cases have full-fledged computer models to accompany them, enabling the student to develop model building skills.

Part II, consisting of five cases, focuses on short-term financing instruments and decisions: accounts receivable, commercial paper, sophisticated bank facilities, import/export financing, and foreign exchange exposure and management. It provides the student with an introduction to options and forward contracts.

Part III consists of four cases and one note dealing with financial markets. This section starts off by introducing students to the equity markets, the value of information, the efficient markets hypothesis, and ethics via a case on insider trading. The subsequent cases focus on dividend policy, the pricing of securities, the risk return trade-off, option pricing, and the process of bringing securities to market. An innovative financial instrument, instalment receipts, is introduced.

Part IV, consisting of five cases and one note, focuses on the estimation of the cost of capital and investment decisions (capital budgeting). A recent development, the securitization of accounts receivable, is introduced.

Part V, consisting of ten cases and one note, focuses on long-term financing instruments and decisions. The section starts with cases dealing with the attributes of various securities and develops the criteria for selecting between them. This is followed by cases on optimal capital structure and leasing. The section turns to decisions using the financial markets to manage risk: interest rate swaps, commodity swaps, gold options, forwards, and so on. The section ends with a comprehensive case in which students have to formulate a strategy to finance a greenfield (from scratch) pulp mill. Innovative financial instruments, protected index notes, and liquid yield option notes are introduced.

Part VI, consisting of nine cases and one note, covers special topics and integrates material by focusing on measuring the value gap and unlocking value to close the gap. In the process, students are exposed to the role of the board of directors and issues surrounding corporate governance. The first case deals with a fairness opinion for a proposed going private transaction. The perspective of the case is that of a member of the independent committee of the board of directors. Four of the next five cases are merger and acquisition decisions. The last three cases deal with a proxy contest, a privatization, and a post-leveraged recapitalization. The duties and responsibilities of management are important aspects of each of these cases.

Even though the book contains new cases, they have been taught several times to both introductory and advanced students. No matter how well a case is crafted, it is difficult to bring out the "chemistry" of a deal. To supplement the student's learning experience, videos (20 minutes in length) of remarks by the central decision makers, who attended the class when the case was taught for the first time, are available from Western Business School, (519) 661-5267, for a number of the cases.

The care and detail in writing the instructor's manual is a significant strength of the book. Thirty-eight out of the forty teaching notes were written by one person; consequently, they are consistent and follow the same framework. The remaining two teaching notes were consistent with the framework. The teaching notes provide suggested discussion questions. The case analyses are discussion question-based and follow a recommended teaching plan. In today's complex environment issues of corporate governance, the role of the board of directors and constituent groups are particularly important. The cases and teaching notes reflect the philosophy that financial decisions must reflect the corporation as a whole and its environment, i.e., integrate across functional lines and examine all aspects of the decision, both internal and external. A detailed cross-classification of the materials is contained in the preface to the instructor's manual.

The cases and computer models have been classroom tested at both the introductory and advanced course levels. The instructor's manual contains suggested outlines for a number of potential courses. Both the cases and casebook are multi-dimensional, i.e., students at all levels of abilities get involved and are challenged. To illustrate, the Nesbitt Thomson case can be taught at multiple levels: to introduce the valuation of coupon bonds and the risk-return relationship; to introduce the concept that embedded options and securities are bundles of characteristics (convertible debenture); and/or to discuss the valuation of a callable, convertible debenture. Each part of the book starts with a "single" issue case and each subsequent case gets more complex.

Case Studies in Modern Corporate Finance has a unique strategy for developing computer-based model building skills. Where applicable, cases have professionally written computer models to accompany them, included in the instructor's manual. They have been classroom tested and debugged. The strategy is to have the students learn the modelling by example. The intent is to use a "cookbook" approach to develop the students' ability to construct computer-based financial models. Note that these are full-fledged models, *not* templates. The use of these models has the additional benefits of developing the students' analytical skills, depth of understanding of theoretical concepts, and decision making skills.

In sum, this book has a number of distinctive features:

- The cases and casebook are multi-layered, so students at all levels of ability get involved and are challenged.
- The cases are current and focus on the major financial decisions made in a corporation.
- The cases deal with current issues: globalization; corporate governance; ethics; privatization; securitization; risk management; pricing of complex securities; structured financing; value-added taxes; and so on.
- The cases are drawn from a number of international locations.
- The cases and teaching notes reflect the philosophy that financial decisions must reflect both the corporation as a whole and its environment, i.e., integrate across functional lines and examine all aspects of the decision, both internal and external.
- There is a balanced perspective on the role of commercial banks and financial markets (money markets, capital markets, foreign exchange markets, and derivative securities markets) in financing decisions.
- A common theme is the process of deal making: origination; structuring; and placement. In part, the focus is to teach entrepreneurship via examples from one of the most creative fields, investment banking.
- Computer-based financial modelling is integrated into the decision-making process.
- Teaching aids exist for several cases: videos of decision makers, and LOTUS models.
- It includes cases that reflect advances in the theory of finance such as option pricing.
- There is a full spectrum of firm sizes, from the small entrepreneurship to the large multinational corporation.

- A comprehensive instructor's manual is available with detailed discussion question-format teaching notes.

ACKNOWLEDGMENTS

Many people have played a part in the creation of this book and the instructor's manual. Critical to the success of this project has been the participation of business executives who contributed time, insights, and material, much of which is cutting edge and proprietary. To these individuals and their organizations I would like to express my sincere gratitude.

I would like to thank the institutions, authors, and supervisors of the cases from the Western Business School (WBS), Leland Stanford Junior University, Harvard Business School, The International Institute for Management Development, Darden Graduate Business School, INSEAD, The Stern School of Business, and Dalhousie University. The comments and suggestions by several anonymous reviewers and the staff at Prentice Hall were very helpful. I would particularly like to thank Paul Bishop (WBS), Raymond Chan (WBS doctoral candidate), Mark Griffiths (University of Wisconsin at Milwaukee), Leah Jewell (editor at Prentice Hall), Richard Nason (WBS doctoral candidate), Rick Robertson (WBS), Don Thain (WBS), Alasdair Turnbull (WBS doctoral candidate), Maureen Wilson (editor at Prentice Hall), and Ron Wirick (WBS). Mark read both the casebook and the instructor's manual and had a number of good ideas on how they could be improved. Alasdair, a constant source of insights and encouragement, wrote most of the computer models.

The students in the Executive MBA, MBA, and HBA programs at the Western Business School have provided a forum for critical feedback and have been a constant source of encouragement. In addition to the students noted above and/or in individual cases, the following students provided assistance: John Ashby, Michel Bruyere, Vanessa Cato, Scott Dodd, Glen Farrow, Jeff Hawkins, Tom Johnston, Angela Kovich, Katie Nelson, Lani Martin, Bill McLarty and John O'Sullivan.

I would like to thank Bob Merton (then at M.I.T.), Stewart Myers (M.I.T.), Myron Scholes (then at M.I.T.), and Mary Wattum for their generous support at critical times. Last but not least I would like to thank my daughter Alicia. She has had to bear the brunt of the countless hours I spent putting it all together!

PART ONE · The Assessment of a Firm's Performance and Financing Needs and Loan Granting Decisions

1. JOHN LABATT LIMITED
2. KITCHEN HELPER INC.
3. MORLEY INDUSTRIES, INC.
4. CAMBRIDGE NUTRITION LIMITED FINANCING GROWTH (A)
5. NOTE ON VALUE-ADDED TAXES
6. SOPHISTICATED PETITES
7. ATLANTIC LUMBER TRADERS
8. COLUMBIA RIVER PULP COMPANY INC.—RECAPITALIZATION

1

JOHN LABATT LIMITED

On September 10, 1992, John Labatt Limited (Labatt) announced a major restructuring with the intention of realizing "hidden value" for shareholders. Under the plan—which would have to be approved by shareholders and various regulatory agencies—Labatt-owned Ault Foods Limited in Canada and Johanna Dairies Inc. in the United States would be spun off into a separate entity run by a separate management team. Labatt's $2 billion dairy operations, built up through several acquisitions in the mid-1980s, accounted for about 48% of its net sales in fiscal 1992. By shedding its dairy operations and focusing on beer and entertainment, Labatt had virtually cut itself in half and closed the book on its spate of acquisitions in the 1980s.

Part of the motivation for this restructuring was to address the poor returns on Labatt's large cash position of about 3% after tax when Labatt's cost of capital exceeded 10%. Other possible reasons were the changing business environment and tough economic times which had made it harder to compete in so many industries without any focus. The company's management finally realized that Labatt's brewing and dairy operations were different businesses with different operational needs. They decided to focus on beer and entertainment, because that's where they thought Labatt could prosper. Indeed, Labatt's dairy operations were the least profitable among its

This case was prepared by Ping Wang under the supervision of Professor Robert W. White for the sole purpose of providing material for class discussion at the Western Business School. Certain names and other identifying information may have been disguised to protect confidentiality. It is not intended to illustrate either effective or ineffective handling of a managerial situation. Any reproduction, in any form, of the material in this case is prohibited except with the written consent of the School. This case was prepared from publicly available information.
Copyright 1993 © The University of Western Ontario.

three business segments (Exhibit 1). Segmented earnings as a percent of net assets employed in 1992 for Dairy, Brewing and Entertainment were 9.9%, 22.7% and 41.4%, respectively. Dairy sales had been nearly stagnant over the period 1987 to 1992, whereas revenue from the entertainment segment was up sharply and Labatt's brewing sales were growing both domestically and abroad.

Speculation, which had started in 1991, about Labatt being up for sale by Brascan Ltd., which had a 37% controlling interest in Labatt, was still going on. By repackaging the company, Labatt, comprised of brewing business, entertainment business and liquid assets, would be more attractive to a number of foreign brewers seeking to establish a foothold in North America. Anheuser-Busch Cos. Inc. (A-B) of St. Louis, U.S., the world's largest beer maker, was at the top of a list of companies that might be counted on to bid for Labatt. A-B had announced a number of management and organizational changes that appeared to position A-B to make foreign acquisitions. A-B and Labatt had long been viewed as an almost perfect fit, because they were both in the beer and entertainment businesses. Labatt had interests in sports broadcasting, entertainment promotions companies and the Toronto Blue Jays baseball team, while A-B owned the St. Louis Cardinals baseball team and operated theme parks in the U.S. and other countries. In addition, the two companies already had established relationships—Labatt produced Budweiser under license from A-B. On the other hand, some analysts believed that A-B did not have to spend $1.5 billion to gain access to the Canadian markets because free trade in beer would sooner or later become a reality.

Labatt's management stated the following rationale for selecting this alternative among others to increase shareholder value:

1. It allowed the direct valuation by the market of its business segments, with better interpretation of the operating results.
2. An organizational layer could be removed in the process.
3. It would increase accountability for the respective company's management, which is useful for senior management motivation and compensation.
4. It might result in greater capital market discipline (perhaps even lead to reducing the net cost of capital).
5. It would provide greater focus.
6. This alternative was more tax efficient than selling these assets.

From a shareholder's perspective, how well had Labatt performed and what were Labatt's prospects?

BACKGROUND ON THE COMPANY

In 1847, Messrs. Labatt and Eccles purchased from John Balkwill a small brewery located in London, Ontario. The business was incorporated on December 20, 1930 under the name of John Labatt Limited. From 1946 to the early 1960s, the company, by making a number of acquisitions of breweries in Toronto, Winnipeg, Montreal, Vancouver, and St. John's, established its presence across Canada. A more complete corporate re-organization was effected during 1964 because of the broadening of the company's operations. After the change, Labatt became a holding company for its subsidiaries. The company entered into the pharmaceutical field, but subsequently abandoned it in 1967. Labatt started its interest in the food sector in 1968 when it bought Ogilvie Mills Ltd., which produces flour and starch products. During the 1980s, the company aggressively increased its portfolio of food products through acquisitions in Canada and the U.S. It was not until the mid-'80s that the company began to invest in the entertainment business. As of September 1992, Labatt consisted of three segments: Brewing, Dairy, and Entertainment.

BREWING GROUP

This group produced and marketed 35 different brands of lager and ale for sale in Canada, U.S., U.K., Italy and 17 other countries. Its most popular brands included Labatt Blue, Blue Light, 50, Genuine Draft and Budweiser (brewed under license from Anheuser-Busch). Group sales amounted to $1,564MM or 39% of 1992 total sales of Labatt. Segmented earnings were $181MM or 60% of Labatt's earnings.

There were three divisions in this group: (1) Labatt Breweries of Canada operated 11 breweries across Canada with an aggregate annual capacity of approximately 10.6 million hectolitres. During fiscal 1992, Labatt Canada's sales accounted for 42.3% of the national market share. (2) Labatt's USA operated in the high-quality segment of the U.S. beer business. The division produced and marketed the Rolling Rock brand from its Latrobe Brewing plant. The division also imported and marketed selected Labatt brands from Canada, the Birra Moretti brands from Labatt's Italian breweries and other international brands. (3) Labatt Breweries of Europe had two operating components: Labatt U.K., which operated in the United Kingdom, and Birra Moretti, which was based in Italy. Labatt U.K. distributed the Labatt's Canadian Lager and Rolling Rock brands within the United Kingdom through Maple Leaf Inn Ltd., a joint venture with Pubmaster, an independent pub retailer. Birra Moretti brewed several beer brands for sale in Italy and for export to other countries.

DAIRY GROUP

This group was named "Food Group" in fiscal 1991. During fiscal 1992, the company disposed of all of its non-dairy businesses and raised its stake in dairies. In August 1991, JL Food, a major frozen soup and pizza supplier to the hotel and restaurant industry based in Eugene, Oregon, was sold to H.J. Heinz Co. of Pittsburgh for about $600MM. In January 1992, Labatt sold its Everfresh fruit juice and drinks business to a group of U.S. investors. Three months later, Ogilvie Mills companies, which produced and distributed flour, starch, pizza and livestock feed, were sold separately to Canadian and U.S. investors. After these divestitures, the operations that remained were two main divisions in the dairy industry: Ault Foods and Johanna

Dairies. In fiscal 1992, the group's sales totalled $2,110MM or 52% of Labatt's sales. Segmented earnings were $62MM or 21% of Labatt's earnings.

Ault Foods was one of Canada's largest integrated dairy operations. It produced and marketed a full line of dairy and industrial milk products, including cheese, butter, skim milk, yogurt and ice cream, primarily in Ontario and Quebec.

Johanna Dairies was the largest table milk processor in the north eastern United States. Its customers included supermarket and convenience store chains, wholesalers, independent grocery stores and many food service accounts. The primary distribution areas were Metropolitan New York, New Jersey, Pennsylvania, Maryland and the District of Columbia.

ENTERTAINMENT GROUP

This segment comprised three divisions: the JLL Broadcast Group, the Toronto Blue Jays Baseball Club and the John Labatt Entertainment Group. In fiscal 1992, group sales were $374MM or 9% of Labatt's total sales. Segmented earnings were $58MM or 19% of Labatt's earnings.

The JLL Broadcast Group was a television broadcasting and production operation. Its business included TSN, an all-sports television service; RDS, a French-language counterpart to TSN; TSN Enterprises, a supplier of broadcast support and ancillary services; Dome Productions, a television production and video post-production facility; and Skyvision Entertainment, a television program producer.

In fiscal 1992, Labatt acquired an additional 45% interest in the Toronto Blue Jays, an American League baseball club, bringing its ownership to 90%.

John Labatt Entertainment Group comprised both marketing and entertainment services business. Supercorp Entertainment provided services to the advertising industry, primarily in the areas of commercial film productions, media planning and buying, animation, audio recording and post-production. JLL Entertainment was a live-event promoter and a merchandiser of related apparel.

THE BUSINESS ENVIRONMENT

Since Labatt owned such a diverse portfolio of businesses, each sector was being affected differently by the environment and faced different challenges from its competitors.

The Brewing Industry

The brewing industry in Canada was operating in a nearly saturated market. Gains on market share were usually obtained through introducing new products. In the past, cutting costs and lowering prices had been constrained by interprovincial barriers which prohibited the sale of beer produced in other provinces. The big breweries had to set up relatively small plants in each of the provinces. Recently, however, under the pressure of the Free Trade Agreement and GATT talks, several provinces had started phasing out regulations requiring breweries to brew beer in the province in which it was sold. This movement provided an excellent opportunity for breweries to consolidate their operations.

Internationally, beer produced in the U.S. would start to flow over the border duty-free by the end of 1993. This put substantial pressures on Canadian breweries to further reduce the cost of operations, as American breweries were operating at a much lower cost, capitalizing on a much larger market and enjoying significant economies of scale in production. In early 1992, Labatt announced the closure of its brewery in Waterloo, Ontario, and its head office in London, Ontario. At the time of this announcement, Labatt employed about 4,000 people in 12 plants, but made two-thirds as much beer as its competitor, Molson, with about 5,000 employees in 9 plants. Through its consolidation efforts, Labatt could remove some excess capacity and personnel from its operations and was expecting some $150 million or $1.50 per share savings on operating costs. This would place Labatt in a better position to compete in Canada and even to compete in the United States, because, despite the possible inroads into Canada by international breweries, especially the U.S. breweries, the Free Trade Agreement also opened up access to the huge U.S. beer market, in which the import market was about the size of the total Canadian market. The long-term significance of more equal access might be greater for both Labatt and Molson.

The Dairy Industry

For many years, the dairy business continued to operate in a sluggish market and faced aggressive competition mainly in the form of price cutting. The GATT talks were also putting pressure on the Canadian dairy industry. The talks would possibly result in the replacement of Canada's milk supply-management system with an import tariff system, although this was being vigorously opposed by the Canadian Dairy Farm Industry. Since the raw milk cost in Canada was much higher than it was in the U.S., if the replacement did take place, the Canadian dairy processors would be hit hard by the flood of cheap U.S. yogurt and ice cream products. Fortunately, Ault Foods owned a number of well-known brands such as Black Diamond Cheese, Lactantia Butter, Sealtest Dairies, Parlour 1%, Premiere Quark and Haagen-Dazs ice cream. Its survival strategy was to upgrade its products, concentrating on the brand name and developing low-fat, healthy products. In addition, Ault foods also had a very strong management team. During the 1980s, under Labatt's goal of becoming one of the largest food companies in North America, Ault Food management pursued many aggressive acquisitions and collected a number of famous brands in its portfolio. Through these products, it controlled, in 1992, about 50% of the Ontario market for milk.

In the U.S., however, Johanna Dairies continued to be a problem. It was bought in the mid-'80s, after Ault Foods had been considered a success. Soon after the acquisition, the New Jersey State Government deregulated the industry and opened the door to low-cost milk for New Jersey. The business was barely profitable. In

1992, Johanna lost a major contract and volumes were down substantially in its fluid milk business. As of September 1992, it still needed to dispose of certain products and rationalize some of its facilities before it could get into shape. Even if Labatt wanted to sell it, there would be few interested buyers.

Entertainment Industry

Most entertainment businesses were experiencing strong sales growth as demand for their various services increased. In the first quarter of 1992, this segment reported a 36% increase in profits.

THE ISSUE

Clearly, the business environment of Labatt's three segments was very different. Most entertainment businesses were positioned in a rapidly growing market; the beer business was experiencing both challenges and opportunities; and the dairy business was facing a tougher situation.

From a shareholder's perspective, how well had Labatt performed and what were Labatt's prospects? In assessing the long-term health of a firm, the analyst must consider the corporate goals, product market strategies, human resources, the environment/industry and financial strength. All the aspects that could have an impact on the firm's cash flows should be taken into consideration.

Financial statements are presented in Exhibits 2 and 3. Exhibit 4 contains condensed Dun & Bradstreet business ratios on companies in Beverages, Dairy and Entertainment industries with sales over $1 million.

EXHIBIT 1

JOHN LABATT LIMITED
Selected Segmented Information
As At December 31
($ millions)

	1992	1991	1990	1989	1988
Dairy					
Net sales	2,110	2,080	2,115	2,216	2,130
Depreciation and amortization	50	43	40	40	37
Segmented earnings	62	44	31	33	56
Capital expenditures	45	43	57	82	48
Net assets employed	629	656	600	486	545
Brewing					
Net sales	1,564	1,474	1,376	1,229	1,117
Depreciation and amortization	64	59	52	42	37
Segmented earnings	181	139	170	145	134
Capital expenditures	122	104	97	75	75
Net assets employed	799	733	752	552	483

(continued)

EXHIBIT 1 (cont.)

	1992	1991	1990	1989	1988
Entertainment					
Total net sales	494	666	698	332	163
Labatt share of net sales	374	387	369	177	93
Depreciation and amortization	11	5	6	2	1
Segmented earnings	58	47	35	17	6
Capital expenditures	5	2	11	13	1
Net assets employed	140	96	89	59	26

EXHIBIT 2

JOHN LABATT LIMITED
Consolidated Statement of Earnings
Year ended April 30
($ millions)

	1992	1991	1990	1989	1988
Net Sales	3,837	4,760	4,681	4,857	4,611
Costs and Expenses					
Cost of sales, selling &					
administration expenses	3,415	4,350	4,283	4,467	4,209
Depreciation & amortization	125	150	134	127	114
Interest expense	22	41	33	69	67
	3,562	4,541	4,450	4,663	4,390
Earnings	275	219	231	194	221
(Non-recurring charges)/other income	(145)	(61)	—	(9)	7
Earnings before income taxes	130	158	231	185	228
Income Taxes					
Current	97	57	91	54	64
Deferred	(60)	(7)	(19)	3	22
	37	50	72	57	86
Earnings before partly owned business	93	108	159	128	142
Share of net earnings (losses) in					
partly owned business	(8)	1	10	7	1
Earnings from continuing operations	85	109	169	135	141
Earnings from discontinued operations	16	—	—	—	—
Net Earnings	101	109	169	135	141

EXHIBIT 3

JOHN LABATT LIMITED
Consolidated Balance Sheets
As at April 30
($ millions)

	1992	1991	1990	1989	1988
Assets					
Current Assets					
Cash receivable on divestitures				315	

(continued)

EXHIBIT 3 (cont.)

	1992	1991	1990	1989	1988
Cash and securities	766	300	300	200	200
Accounts receivable	406	409	418	307	302
Inventories	359	444	397	345	408
Prepaid expenses	103	81	69	60	55
	1634	1254	1184	912	964
Fixed Assets	1027	1257	1181	1002	992
Other Assets	520	647	581	528	582
Net assets of discontinued operations	139	—	—	—	—
	3320	3138	2946	2757	2538
Liabilities					
Current Liabilities					
Bank advances & short-term notes	—	244	45	155	288
Accounts payable & accrued charges	759	519	473	468	427
Taxes payable	36	27	84	44	10
Long-term debt due within 1 year	41	123	26	16	11
	836	913	628	683	736
Non-convertible long-term debt	646	416	544	532	482
Deferred income taxes	90	133	130	143	162
	1572	1462	1302	1358	1380
Convertible Debentures &					
Shareholders' Equity					
Convertible Debentures	255	272	277	289	291
Shareholders' Equity					
Share Capital					
Preferred Shares	300	300	300	150	—
Common Shares	337	308	295	273	258
Retained earnings	844	826	801	707	622
Cumulative translation adjustment	12	(30)	(29)	(20)	(12)
	1493	1404	1367	1109	868
	1748	1676	1644	1398	1158
	3320	3138	2946	2757	2538

EXHIBIT 4

Industry Norms

SIC: 2080 BEVERAGES
ASSETS OVER $1,000,000

	1991 (0014) ESTAB.		1990 (0048) ESTAB.		1989 (0045) ESTAB.	
	$	%	$	%	$	%
Cash	216,868	8.2	282,589	7.7	493,614	12.0
Accounts Receivable	237,660	9.0	485,950	13.3	501,410	12.2
Notes Receivable	0	0.0	253,745	7.0	245,781	6.0

(continued)

EXHIBIT 4 (cont.)

SIC: 2080 BEVERAGES
ASSETS OVER $1,000,000

	1991 (0014) ESTAB.		1990 (0048) ESTAB.		1989 (0045) ESTAB.	
	$	%	$	%	$	%
Inventory	972,750	37.0	1,027,032	28.1	1,158,742	28.2
Other Current Assets	142,385	5.4	255,571	7.0	159,614	3.9
Total Current Assets	1,434,911	54.5	1,889,768	51.8	2,213,263	53.9
Fixed Assets	961,696	36.5	1,421,707	38.9	1,556,752	37.9
Other Non-Current	328,461	12.5	451,266	12.4	487,870	11.9
Total Assets	2,631,900	100.0	3,651,021	100.0	4,103,196	100.0
Accounts Payable	328,461	12.5	503,840	13.8	505,924	12.3
Bank Loans	488,480	18.6	495,443	13.6	644,201	15.7
Notes Payable	0	0.0	107,340	2.9	394,317	9.6
Other Payables	209,236	8.0	264,699	7.3	335,231	8.2
Total Current	906,952	34.5	1,055,145	28.9	1,299,892	31.7
Other Long Term Debt	603,494	22.9	898,516	24.6	956,454	23.3
Deferred Credit	450,318	17.1	₊ 524,286	14.4	476,791	11.6
Net Worth	1,024,598	38.9	1,524,666	41.8	1,779,966	43.4
Total Liab. & Net Worth	2,631,900	100.0	3,651,021	100.0	4,103,196	100.0
Net Sales	4,263,904	100.0	4,640,825	100.0	5,693,533	100.0
Gross Profit	0	0.0	1,365,330	29.4	0	0.0
Net Profit After Tax	−163,307	−3.8	83,534	1.8	159,988	2.8
Working Capital	527,959	—	834,623	—	913,371	—

Source: Dun & Bradstreet Canada Limited.

Key Business Ratios

SIC: 2080 BEVERAGES
ASSETS OVER $1,000,000

	1991			1990			1989		
	UQ	MED	LQ	UQ	MED	LQ	UQ	MED	LQ
SOLVENCY									
Quick Ratio (X)	0.6	0.3	0.2	0.8	0.5	0.3	1.5	0.5	0.3
Current Ratio (X)	2.0	1.3	1.2	2.6	1.6	1.1	3.7	1.7	1.1
Curr. Liab/N.Worth (%)	17.3	74.8	167.5	16.9	69.1	119.6	24.7	77.1	172.8
Curr. Liab/Inv. (%)	57.4	90.0	105.7	60.8	112.6	194.0	53.1	101.0	198.5
Total Liab/N.Worth (%)	23.6	111.4	259.1	28.7	147.3	284.9	51.0	302.0	366.4
Fixed Assets/N.W. (%)	50.0	82.1	208.2	36.6	75.9	153.7	33.4	112.6	286.4
EFFICIENCY									
Coll. Period (days)	11.8	25.5	44.2	24.4	39.2	53.2	27.2	38.3	46.1
Sales/Inventory (X)	4.4	3.3	1.7	7.4	5.2	2.0	8.6	4.4	2.5

(continued)

EXHIBIT 4 (cont.)

SIC: 2080 BEVERAGES
ASSETS OVER $1,000,000

	1991			1990			1989		
	UQ	MED	LQ	UQ	MED	LQ	UQ	MED	LQ
Assets/Sales (%)	67.6	73.3	134.2	65.6	89.3	130.6	53.6	87.5	125.6
Sales/N.W.Capital (X)	8.8	5.0	1.3	6.1	2.7	1.2	8.8	3.2	0.7
Acc.Pay.to Sales (%)	4.3	10.1	17.0	6.9	9.9	16.7	6.4	9.3	15.5
PROFITABILITY									
Return on Sales (%)	2.5	0.7	−12.9	6.7	2.0	0.7	7.7	3.5	0.9
Ret.on N.Assets (%)	2.0	0.9	−8.0	8.9	1.7	0.5	8.6	4.5	1.1
Ret.on N.Worth (%)	15.7	4.1	−16.9	14.7	10.6	1.9	21.1	9.8	2.5

Source: Dun & Bradstreet Canada Limited.

Industry Norms

SIC: 5143 WHOLESALES-DAIRY PRODUCTS
ASSETS $250,000–$1,000,000

	1991 (0000) ESTAB.		1990 (0014) ESTAB.		1989 (0018) ESTAB.	
	$	%	$	%	$	%
Cash	0	0.0	34,445	5.6	71,410	12.9
Accounts Receivable	0	0.0	173,338	28.1	181,993	32.8
Notes Receivable	0	0.0	0	0.0	0	0.0
Inventory	0	0.0	78,627	12.8	85,980	15.5
Other Current Assets	0	0.0	49,912	8.1	21,772	3.9
Total Current Assets	0	0.0	298,797	48.5	311,680	56.3
Fixed Assets	0	0.0	280,250	45.5	194,343	35.1
Other Non-Current	0	0.0	74,067	12.0	61,494	11.1
Total Assets	0	0.0	616,205	100.0	554,000	100.0
Accounts Payable	0	0.0	152,818	24.8	148,084	26.7
Bank Loans	0	0.0	114,490	18.6	108,030	19.5
Notes Payable	0	0.0	46,276	7.5	0	0.0
Other Payables	0	0.0	81,832	13.3	37,395	6.8
Total Current	0	0.0	284,933	46.2	229,633	41.5
Other Long Term Debt	0	0.0	167,731	27.2	155,397	28.1
Deferred Credit	0	0.0	75,423	12.2	43,932	7.9
Net Worth	0	0.0	166,991	27.1	192,459	34.7
Total Liab. & Net Worth	0	0.0	616,205	100.0	554,000	100.0
Net Sales	0	—	1,576,000	100.0	2,010,000	100.0
Gross Profit	0	0.0	0	0.0	0	0.0
Net Profit After Tax	0	0.0	22,694	1.4	−33,768	−1.7
Working Capital	0	—	13,864	—	82,047	—

Source: Dun & Bradstreet Canada Limited.

EXHIBIT 4 (cont.)

Key Business Ratios

SIC 5143: WHOLESALES-DAIRY PRODUCTS
ASSETS $250,000–$1,000,000

	1991			1990			1989		
	UQ	MED	LQ	UQ	MED	LQ	UQ	MED	LQ
SOLVENCY									
Quick Ratio (X)	0.0	0.0	0.0	0.7	0.4	0.2	1.3	0.8	0.5
Current Ratio (X)	0.0	0.0	0.0	1.5	0.8	0.6	2.1	1.2	0.7
Curr. Liab/N.Worth (%)	0.0	0.0	0.0	−60.8	31.5	92.6	7.2	27.8	173.4
Curr. Liab/Inv. (%)	0.0	0.0	0.0	169.7	240.8	249.6	75.2	158.5	203.7
Total Liab/N.Worth (%)	0.0	0.0	0.0	−233.6	36.7	128.0	7.2	52.7	274.6
Fixed Assets/N.W. (%)	0.0	0.0	0.0	−92.2	56.6	157.2	5.0	45.5	112.9
EFFICIENCY									
Coll. Period (days)	0.0	0.0	0.0	12.8	19.5	38.0	17.0	37.7	48.2
Sales/Inventory (X)	0.0	0.0	0.0	45.2	39.3	16.6	131.3	35.5	24.0
Assets/Sales (%)	0.0	0.0	0.0	19.8	31.0	43.7	14.7	22.6	30.8
Sales/N.W.Capital (X)	0.0	0.0	0.0	8.8	−7.9	−20.9	23.6	6.7	−7.9
Acc.Pay.to Sales (%)	0.0	0.0	0.0	2.3	6.9	8.3	3.9	6.4	7.6
PROFITABILITY									
Return on Sales (%)	0.0	0.0	0.0	2.8	0.5	−0.6	2.3	1.0	−0.8
Ret.on N.Assets (%)	0.0	0.0	0.0	5.2	2.5	−1.5	14.1	4.3	−4.8
Ret.on N.Worth (%)	0.0	0.0	0.0	24.8	7.0	1.3	27.1	15.9	0.3

Source: Dun & Bradstreet Canada Limited.

Industry Norms

SIC: 79 AMUSEMENT AND RECREATION SERVICES
ASSETS OVER $1,000,000

	1991 (0044) ESTAB.		1990 (0189) ESTAB.		1989 (0165) ESTAB.	
	$	%	$	%	$	%
Cash	658,966	21.1	333,004	13.5	386,133	15.1
Accounts Receivable	236,903	7.6	185,112	7.5	206,346	8.1
Notes Receivable	95,385	3.1	133,596	5.4	138,415	5.4
Inventory	119,387	3.8	72,713	3.0	90,659	3.6
Other Current Assets	217,265	7.0	158,984	6.5	127,944	5.0
Total Current Assets	1,044,247	33.5	663,544	26.9	703,314	27.5
Fixed Assets	2,076,026	66.6	1,802,070	73.1	1,845,369	72.3
Other Non-Current	718,504	23.1	349,519	14.2	526,591	20.6
Total Assets	3,117,157	100.0	2,464,876	100.0	2,553,791	100.0
Accounts Payable	320,755	10.3	220,852	9.0	213,496	8.4
Bank Loans	310,468	10.0	238,107	9.7	269,424	10.6
Notes Payable	275,868	8.9	126,694	5.1	174,423	6.8
Other Payables	706,659	22.7	418,289	17.0	413,714	16.2
Total Current	1,094,745	35.1	720,236	29.2	706,633	27.7

(continued)

EXHIBIT 4 (cont.)

SIC: 79 AMUSEMENT AND RECREATION SERVICES
ASSETS OVER $1,000,000

	1991 (0044) ESTAB.		1990 (0189) ESTAB.		1989 (0165) ESTAB.	
	$	%	$	%	$	%
Other Long Term Debt	1,202,910	38.6	746,117	30.3	889,230	34.8
Deferred Credit	419,881	13.5	346,068	14.0	425,972	16.7
Net Worth	1,300,166	41.7	1,114,616	45.2	1,199,004	47.0
Total Liab. & Net Worth	3,117,157	100.0	2,464,876	100.0	2,553,791	100.0
Net Sales	1,965,572	100.0	1,849,879	100.0	1,543,704	100.0
Gross Profit	0	0.0	0	0.0	0	0.0
Net Profit After Tax	150,562	7.7	71,960	3.9	136,926	8.9
Working Capital	−50,498	—	−56,692	–	−3,319	—

Source: Dun & Bradstreet Canada Limited.

Key Business Ratios

SIC: 0079 AMUSEMENT AND RECREATION SERVICES
ASSETS OVER $1,000,000

	1991			1990			1989		
	UQ	MED	LQ	UQ	MED	LQ	UQ	MED	LQ
SOLVENCY									
Quick Ratio (X)	1.4	0.8	0.2	1.1	0.5	0.2	1.3	0.7	0.2
Current Ratio (X)	1.7	1.0	0.5	1.6	0.9	0.4	1.7	1.0	0.5
Curr. Liab/N.Worth (%)	9.3	26.0	91.3	7.8	26.2	71.6	8.6	19.2	63.1
Curr. Liab/Inv. (%)	263.1	409.5	499.1	264.2	383.5	635.3	259.8	430.4	613.7
Total Liab/N.Worth (%)	19.4	96.6	152.1	18.2	60.9	158.1	15.4	53.2	166.8
Fixed Assets/N.W. (%)	79.5	115.9	200.8	90.1	126.5	197.1	77.5	104.5	185.4
EFFICIENCY									
Coll. Period (days)	5.9	18.8	38.9	7.7	17.6	36.8	5.8	19.0	42.6
Sales/Inventory (X)	88.9	38.8	21.7	113.4	48.1	22.8	90.9	39.5	18.0
Assets/Sales (%)	50.4	153.9	256.8	74.7	155.1	268.0	86.6	140.8	286.3
Sales/N.W.Capital (X)	9.9	1.2	−4.9	5.8	−1.7	−8.7	6.0	−0.7	−7.4
Acc.Pay.to Sales (%)	3.8	8.7	12.1	4.5	8.4	13.7	4.7	8.2	13.3
PROFITABILITY									
Return on Sales (%)	10.2	3.9	−2.8	8.7	2.9	−1.3	11.5	4.3	−0.5
Ret.on N.Assets (%)	13.8	3.8	−0.9	7.2	1.4	−1.0	9.8	2.4	−0.1
Ret.on N.Worth (%)	16.5	5.6	−3.8	17.4	4.3	−1.0	21.9	6.2	−1.0

Source: Dun & Bradstreet Canada Limited.

2

KITCHEN HELPER INC.

Ken Lanzetta, president of Kitchen Helper Inc., required funding to start manufacturing and marketing his new invention, a pasta server. He was uncertain how much funding he would need since the amount was dependent on sales. He wanted to start production in two weeks, on August 1, 1989. Since his distribution system was already arranged, he believed he could start selling as soon as the units were produced. He approached several venture capitalists after being turned down by the Confederation Bank, a Detroit-based bank, but was reluctant to agree to what he considered excessive demands for their capital investment. He had just returned from a meeting with Arthur Cohen, a private investor from Chicago, who had expressed an interest in the firm. In order to evaluate his potential investment, Mr. Cohen asked Lanzetta to produce projected income statements, balance sheets, and cash flow statements for Kitchen Helper Inc. up to July 31, 1990.

HISTORY

Kitchen Helper Inc., founded in May 1989, was owned jointly by Ken and Mary Lanzetta. The company was formed to design, develop, manufacture and market a unique household utensil, a pasta server. The specially curved patented plastic

This case is based on "Pasta Chef, Inc." and was prepared by Jeff Hawkins under the supervision of Professor John Humphrey for the sole purpose of providing material for class discussion at the Western Business School. Certain names and other identifying information may have been disguised to protect confidentiality. It is not intended to illustrate either effective or ineffective handling of a managerial situation. Any reproduction, in any form, of the material in this case is prohibited except with the written consent of the School.
Copyright 1993 © The University of Western Ontario.

apparatus, to be sold retail for $3.75, could be used to stir, pick up and serve all varieties of pasta.

Ken, who was 35, had conceived the idea for the device while working for the Food and Drug Administration as a research biologist. As a recent M.B.A. graduate, he was confident that he could bring his idea to fruition. His enthusiasm was echoed by his wife, Mary, aged 30, who, after having worked as a professional teacher, was to enter an M.B.A. program in September. In addition to her studies, she planned to act as vice-president and secretary of Kitchen Helper, while Ken would be president and treasurer.

The Lanzettas had already spent $10,500 before incorporation on obtaining patent approval for their invention in the United States and Canada. Patents were also being processed in Italy, Germany, France and the United Kingdom. With initial capital of $18,000 raised from personal loans of $10,500 from the Confederation Bank and $7,500 from Best Finance Ltd., the Lanzettas had established an office at their home in Ann Arbor, Michigan, and purchased production equipment. Capital expenditures consisted of $750 for office equipment, $20,250 for a single cavity production mould, $3,750 for tools and dies and $3,750 for a blister pack mould. Development costs incurred on the moulds were included in these amounts.

By July, Kitchen Helper Inc. was ready to begin production. An agreement was made with Perfect Plastics, Inc. in Ypsilanti to manufacture the utensil under contract, using Kitchen Helper moulds, at a cost of $.60 per unit. Packaging arrangements were concluded with B. Crawford & Sons Lithographic Ltd. of Ann Arbor to package the products the same month that they were produced. Distribution agreements were made with Household Ware Sales, Inc., Cooker Ltd., and Firenzo Sales Ltd.

Unfortunately, by this time, initial funds had been exhausted on capital expenditures and $10,500 was due in August on the production mould. Cash was also required for monthly administrative expenses of $3,750 for salaries, office expenses, insurance, telephone, utilities, automobile expenses, and miscellaneous supplies once production started. Perfect Plastics would not begin production without a 50 percent deposit and the remainder was due before any units would be released for sale. The packaging company also required cash payments on delivery. Without additional funding, the Lanzettas could not start production or distribution.

PRODUCTION

The pasta server would be manufactured by an injection moulding process. The process made possible the rapid production of highly finished and detailed plastic units. Plastic was melted and then injected under thousands of kilograms of pressure into a mould which was held closed by a clamping mechanism. The devices were formed into a cavity; the two halves of the mould separated, allowing the formed part to fall free. In injection moulding, parts could be formed in either single or multiple cavity moulds, depending on total production, production rate, size and weight of the part, size of machine available and the mould cost. Kitchen Helper

Inc. initially planned to use a single cavity production mould (one device per cycle). Since four cycles could be completed per minute, monthly production capacity was about 40,000 units.

Ken feared a stock-out and planned an initial production run of 40,000 units. His production strategy was to order sufficient units to replace units sold, and to maintain a minimum of 10,000 units inventory. Perfect Plastics required production runs of at least 5,000 units. Ken planned initially to store inventory in the basement and garage of his home, but if inventory exceeded 10,000 units he would have to rent warehouse space at a cost of $200 per month. The warehouse space, with a capacity of 35,000 units, could be leased on a monthly basis and no annual lease was required. Lease payments were due the month following the actual lease.

Ken had also discussed with his accountant the problem of depreciation of the production mould. The life of a mould depended on the type of steel used, the number of cycles, the type of material to be moulded and the complexity of the part to be manufactured. Handled properly, moulds used to manufacture devices similar to the pasta server lasted for millions of units. However, from a practical viewpoint, Ken recognized that his single cavity mould could be obsolete after producing only 162,000 units if he decided to buy the new two-cavity mould. His accountant suggested that a depreciation charge of $.125 per unit be used in pro forma statements to account for wear and tear and obsolescence of the mould. A combined depreciation charge of $.015 per unit was recommended for the package mould and tool and dies. In addition, $10 per month was allowed for depreciation of office equipment, which was to be considered as an administrative expense.

The products would be blister packaged on an attractive backing which would clearly show the consumer various applications for the device. Products would be packaged the same month that they were produced. Packaging costs for the product were $0.375 per unit. Material costs were included in these prices. Kitchen Helper Inc. would pay for shipping expenses of $.075 per unit, incurred when units were sold.

MARKETING

The Lanzettas suggested that every family in North America was a potential purchaser, since they believed all families ate some variety of pasta. The United States population consisted of 88.39 million families (1980 Census data, Exhibit 1). Similar data were provided for Michigan, Detroit and Ann Arbor. The Canadian market was about one-tenth the size of the U.S. market.

Household Wares, Inc. would handle the accounts of J.C. Penney and K-Mart. Cooker Ltd. was to handle WalMart, Sears and independent boutiques. Firenzo Sales Ltd. would handle grocery outlets such as Kroger, Tops and A&P.

The wholesale price by Kitchen Helper to the distributors was $1.58 per unit, net 30 days. Ken believed 50 percent of receipts would be paid the month following the sale and the remainder within the second month. Wholesalers would sell the product to retail outlets for $1.88. Kitchen Helper Inc. was also considering expanding distribution to Canada and, once patents were approved, to Europe.

Although no identical products used specifically for pasta were on the market, similar plastic kitchen utensils were occasionally used for pasta serving. These devices sold for $2.98 to $4.49, with retailers generally receiving a 100 percent markup.

Promotion by Kitchen Helper would consist of an attractive blister package for the product and free guest appearances on television talk and cooking shows such as "Good Morning America" and "Live with Regis and Kathie Lee". Free press exposure was anticipated through editorial statements and consumer goods articles. Retail stores would be encouraged to conduct in-store promotions and display the device with pasta products. Consumer questionnaires would be made available to ascertain public reaction.

Considerable reliance was placed on the distributors to promote the product. The Lanzettas anticipated that 500 units would be given away monthly for the first four months for promotional purposes. Ken's accountant suggested that these should be counted as sales expenses at their cost of $1.115 per unit ($.60 for mould manufacturing, $.375 for packaging, plus $.14 for depreciation), the same amount that would be used to value inventory. The other suggestion was to delay amortization of the patent until Kitchen Helper had two profitable years.

FINANCIAL IMPLICATIONS

Exhibit 2 shows the balance sheet for Kitchen Helper as of July 15, 1989. Arthur Cohen was considering investing up to $75,000 for a 50 percent share of the equity and profits of the new company. Cohen stated that he might be willing to settle for a smaller ownership stake but his investment would be disproportionately lower. He would not consider investing an amount greater than $75,000 unless the Lanzettas increased their investment in the company significantly. However, before he made any commitments, he wanted to examine very carefully a set of pro forma statements for the venture.

The Lanzettas did not believe that they could invest any more personal funds in the company since their personal assets of $39,300 were tied up in their home and personal possessions (Exhibit 3). Cohen suggested that the Lanzettas calculate the amount of financing required each month and from those calculations determine the total amount of financing that he would need to invest.

Monthly sales of the pasta serving devices were difficult to project. Ken's reasonable expectation was 10,000 units and he had prepared a production schedule based on this sales level (Exhibit 4). His most pessimistic and optimistic monthly sales forecasts were 5,000 units and 30,000 units, respectively. If sales were 30,000 units or more per month for two consecutive months, he planned to order a larger two-cavity production mould (two devices per cycle). The capital cost, including development, would be $54,000, payable in three monthly instalments, starting the month the equipment was ordered. A three-month lead time, from the time of ordering, was required before this mould would be operational. When operational, the mould would not only double production capacity, but also cut costs in half to $.30 per unit. Ken's accountant suggested a depreciation allowance of $.054 per unit for the two-cavity mould. With the reduction in material and depreciation costs, inventory would be costed at $0.744 per unit.

Ken believed that the first twelve months of sales were critical for the success of Kitchen Helper. He required forecasted cash flow, income statements, and balance sheets for his three different sales projections. Ken planned to use a 20 percent tax rate. If taxes were payable, they would be due 45 days after Kitchen Helper year end of July 31, 1990.

The Lanzettas wished to limit the amount of money required from Mr. Cohen. They wanted to retain as much control over the business as possible. However they recognized the danger of being underfinanced. Once they decided what amount they would request from Mr. Cohen, they would complete a formal information package and drop in to see Mr. Cohen with their completed pro forma financial statements.

EXHIBIT 1

Population and Households in the United States
(1980 Census Data)

AREA	POPULATION	NUMBER OF HOUSEHOLDS	AVERAGE NUMBER OF PEOPLE PER HOUSEHOLD
United States	226,545,805	80,389,673	2.75
Michigan	9,262,078	3,195,213	2.84
Detroit	4,618,161	1,185,025	2.84
Ann Arbor	264,748	59,424	2.62

EXHIBIT 2

KITCHEN HELPER INC.
Balance Sheet
As at July 15, 1989

Assets		Liabilities	
Current	0	Current Accounts Payable	10,500
Total Current Assets	0		
Equipment			
Single-Cavity Mould	20,250		
Tools and Dies	3,750	**Equity**	
Blister Package Mould	3,750		
Office Equipment	750	Common Stock	28,500
	28,500		
Other			
Patent	10,500		
	39,000		39,000

EXHIBIT 3

KITCHER HELPER· INC.
Lanzetta's Personal Balance Sheet
As at July 15, 1989

Assets		Liabilities	
Cash	300	Bank Loans	18,000
Real Estate	60,000	Mortgages	45,000
Automobile	10,500	Other Liabilities	6,000
Stocks, Bonds, etc.	0		
Household & Personal Effects	37,500	Total Liabilities	69,000
		Net Worth	39,300
Total Assets	108,300	Total Liabilities & Net Worth	108,300

EXHIBIT 4

KITCHEN HELPER INC.
Production Schedule (in units)
(10,000 units/month sales)

| MONTH | PRODUCTION | | | | INVENTORY | |
	MOULDED	PACKAGED	SALES	PROMOTION	HOME	WAREHOUSE
August	40,000	40,000	10,000	500	10,000	19,500
September	0	10,000	500	10,000	10,000	9,000
October	5,000	5,000	10,000	500	10,000	3,500
November	7,000	7,000	10,000	500	10,000	0
December	10,000	10,000	10,000	0	10,000	0
January	10,000	10,000	10,000	0	10,000	0
February	10,000	10,000	10,000	0	10,000	0
March	10,000	10,000	10,000	0	10,000	0
April	10,000	10,000	10,000	0	10,000	0
May	10,000	10,000	10,000	0	10,000	0
June	10,000	10,000	10,000	0	10,000	0
July	10,000	10,000	10,000	0	10,000	0

3

MORLEY INDUSTRIES, INC.

In January 1990, Sarah Fullerton, Vice President and Treasurer of Morley Industries, was working on a loan request to be presented to the company's bank of account, First Security Bank. Ms. Fullerton had to determine how large a loan to request, as well as the length and type of loan, and to appraise the likelihood of the bank's granting the loan.

Morley Industries was a manufacturer of architectural aluminum products and a major producer of aluminum frame windows. Founded in 1965, the company had experienced considerable growth in sales. Operations had been consistently profitable, except for three years when small losses were incurred. Recent balance sheets and income statements are shown in Exhibits 1 and 2. Morley Industries sold most of its products directly to construction firms, although an increasing portion of its sales were to distributors of construction products and to distributors to home building centers.

During the past three years, Morley had undertaken a major expansion and modernization program aimed at providing the efficient production facilities its management considered vital to the company's survival in a competitive environment. In anticipation of growth in the demand for aluminum products, plant capacity had been increased to a point sufficient to handle a volume of $75 million per year. It was anticipated that the company's expansion program would be completed in March 1990 with the installation of new equipment costing $2.5 million.

The expansion had been timely because Morley was hoping to increase its market share in 1990 with an all-out marketing and selling effort. Management estimated the company would reach $54 million in sales in 1990. Further sales growth of $5 to $7 million per year was expected in 1991–93.

The company's sales, like those of the industry as a whole, were highly seasonal. Over two-thirds of annual sales usually came during the first six months of the year. Exhibit 3 shows forecasted monthly sales for 1990; the pattern is similar to that of previous years. On the other hand, production was held relatively steady through the year. This policy was necessary to give employment to and thereby retain the skilled work force required in the company's manufacturing operation. Additional economies came in better utilization of equipment. In 1989, the company had been able to maintain production at nearly an even rate through the year.

Morley Industries had borrowed seasonally from First Security Bank for six years. These loans occurred under a line of credit arranged annually in January. The bank required that the loan be completely repaid and "off the books" for two months during the year. In previous years, Morley had not experienced difficulty in obtaining seasonal loans and meeting loan requirements. First Security Bank had always granted the company's seasonal needs, which in 1989 had amounted to $8.1 million at the peak.

Normally, the company began borrowing in early January and repaid its loans by mid-June. However, in 1989 the company had been unable to liquidate its loan until mid-September and by early November had again required a bank loan. At the end of 1989, the bank loan outstanding amounted to $4,260,000. Although the bank had not hesitated to extend the credit, its officers expressed disappointment at not being given greater forewarning of the continued need, particularly at a time when the federal bank examiners were conducting an examination and were critical of aberrations of any sort. They suggested that it would be helpful if Ms. Fullerton could plan Morley's requirements more carefully for 1990.

Ms. Fullerton also was disturbed by the unexpected increase in borrowing and what it might mean in terms of future requirements. Therefore, she began collecting data that might be helpful in making plans for 1990. These plans would need to be cleared with the company's founder and president, Roger Morley, before presentation to the bank.

The company's nominal terms of sales were net 30 days. However, for competitive reasons, these terms were not strictly enforced, and the average collection period had recently slipped to around 40 days. All sales were credit sales and Ms. Fullerton felt that a 40-day average period to collection was a reasonable estimate for 1990. There had been a deterioration in collection experience through 1989, but she was confident the downtrend had been arrested. (Of November 1989 sales of $1,683,000, $1,122,000 was collected in December; none of the December sales were collected in that month. All of October and earlier sales had been collected by December 31, 1989.)

Production was scheduled to be level throughout 1990 except for two weeks beginning Monday, August 6, when it was planned to shut down the plant for the annual paid vacation period. Material purchases at $1,720,000 per month were scheduled except for August, when purchases of $1,120,000 were scheduled. The company purchased its materials on varying terms, depending on the supplier, but on average paid for them in 30 days. Depreciation of $2.5 million was forecast for the year. Expenses related to labor and overhead (including depreciation) were planned at $1,480,000 per month throughout 1990. General and administrative expenses were estimated to total $10,632,000 in 1990. Disbursements for these expenses were expected to run fairly evenly through the year. Twenty-five percent of the estimated income taxes for 1990 were to be paid quarterly in March, June, September and December.

New equipment costing $2.5 million was to be delivered in March. It would be paid for in five equal monthly instalments, beginning in March. Advertising and promotion expenditures, not included elsewhere, were forecast at $50,000 per month in January and February, at $30,000 per month in March through August, and at $65,000 per month in September through December, 1990.

In 1987, Morley Industries had borrowed $12 million from a life insurance company under a 16-year mortgage loan, secured by the entire plant and certain equipment. The loan was repayable in equal semiannual principal instalments in June and December each year. Interest at the rate of 10 percent per annum on the unpaid balance was also payable on these dates. In her financial forecasting, Ms. Fullerton planned to treat differently the interest payments on the mortgage loan and on the bank loan. The two mortgage interest payments due in 1990 would be shown separately in the cash flow and income projections. In contrast, bank loan interest payments had been roughly estimated and included in the total general and administrative expenses estimate of $10,632,000.

In 1990, sales were forecast at $54 million, costs of goods sold at 70 percent, and general and administrative expenses at $10,632,000. Advertising and promotion expenses (not included elsewhere) totalled $540,000. Additional expenses of $1,031,000 (rounded to the nearest thousand) for mortgage interest resulted in an estimated profit before taxes of $3,997,000. The effective tax rate for 1990 was estimated at 35 percent.

In 1989, the company had raised its common stock dividend to $0.40 per share, payable quarterly in March, June, September and December. Ms. Fullerton knew that the directors of Morley Industries would be reluctant to raise the dividend in 1990. However, maintenance of the present dividend was essential. The company was not well-known, and directors hoped that with another several years of profitable operations and stable dividends an equity issue might be feasible.

As chief financial officer of Morley Industries, Ms. Fullerton had given considerable thought to the optimum cash position of the company. She had concluded that cash and cash equivalents of at least $1.5 million should be maintained at all times. This would take care of transactions needs, and provide a moderate amount of liquidity for emergencies.

On the basis of the plans outlined above, Ms. Fullerton asked her Assistant Treasurer to prepare a monthly cash budget for 1990, which she hoped would indicate the amount and timing of the bank credit that Morley Industries would require. She also asked the Assistant Treasurer to prepare a pro forma income statement for the year and a pro forma balance sheet for December 31, 1990. She suggested that the assistant assume no change in "other assets" or in "accruals" from the amounts shown at year-end, 1989.

EXHIBIT 1

MORLEY INDUSTRIES, INC.
Balance Sheets
As at December 31, 1987–89
(dollar figures in thousands)

	1987	1988	1989
Assets			
Cash & cash equivalents	$9,564	$2,187	$1,524
Accounts receivable	2,633	2,908	3,779
Inventories	4,632	5,547	7,280
Total Current Assets	$16,829	$10,642	$12,583
Plant and equipment (net)	18,207	24,300	26,979
Other assets	806	1,065	1,110
Total Assets	$35,842	$36,007	$40,672
Liabilities and Shareholders' Equity			
Bank loan	$0	$0	$4,260
Accounts payable	1,470	1,560	1,740
Accruals	837	963	1,014
Mortgage, current	750	750	750
Total Current Liabilities	$3,057	$3,273	$7,764
Mortgage payable	$11,250	$10,500	$9,750
Common stock (3,000,000 shares @ $2.00 par value)	6,000	6,000	6,000
Retained earnings	15,535	16,234	17,158
Total Liabilities & Equity	$35,842	$36,007	$40,672

EXHIBIT 2

MORLEY INDUSTRIES, INC.
Income Statements
Years Ended, December 31
(dollar figures in thousands)

	1987	1988	1989
Net sales	$34,788	$38,373	$44,466
Cost of goods sold[a]	24,838	27,175	30,930
Gross profit	9,950	11,198	13,536
General & admin. expenses	6,555	7,433	9,147
Mortgage interest	1,256	1,181	1,106
Profit before taxes	2,139	2,584	3,283
Income taxes	813	925	1,159
Net profit	$1,326	$1,659	$2,124
Common dividends	960	960	1,200
Change in retained earnings	$366	$699	$924

[a]Includes depreciation of $1,657, $2,223, and $2,469.

EXHIBIT 3

MORLEY INDUSTRIES, INC.
Estimated Monthly Sales for 1990
(dollar figures in thousands)

	Net Sales
November, 1989 actual	$1,683
December, 1989 actual	3,218
January, 1990	3,720
February	5,250
March	7,410
April	7,650
May	8,550
June	4,830
July	4,020
August	3,360
September	1,920
October	1,800
November	1,890
December	3,600
Total, 1990	$54,000

4

CAMBRIDGE NUTRITION LIMITED
FINANCING GROWTH (A)

In April 1985, Cambridge Nutrition Limited, a U.K.-based company established to sell a new diet product, reached a monthly sales level of almost £1 million[1] for the first time. The Cambridge Diet, its revolutionary new low calorie slimming product, had been developed in Cambridge, England, by Dr. Alan N. Howard. The formula was the result of eight years of research and clinical testing, started in 1970 by a team of British research scientists under Dr. Howard.

The diet had been a breakthrough in the field of nutrition and obesity (see Exhibit 1). It was a powder, with low-fat milk solids as the primary source of protein, which contained all the daily nutrients considered essential for health in just 300 calories. Before this development, virtually no diet below 1,000 calories could provide all these requirements without supplementation. The original product was available in a number of flavored powders which, when mixed with water, created a type of "milkshake."

Sales growth for this start-up company had been exceptional (see Exhibit 2). Sales for the fiscal year ending March 1985, the company's first year, had been

---

[1]In 1985, £1 = US$1.30.

This case was prepared by Research Associate Michael W. Birchard under the supervision of Professor Paul Strebel as a basis for class discussion rather than to illustrate either effective or ineffective handling of an administrative situation. This case is based on the Cambridge Nutrition case series written by Research Associate Juliet Taylor and Professor Christopher Parker.

£1.54 million (see Exhibits 3 and 4 for Income Statement and Balance Sheet). With Dr. Howard's new book, *The Cambridge Diet*, due to be published in May, a significant further increase in sales was expected.

Dr. Roger Howard, Managing Director of Cambridge Nutrition and brother of Dr. Alan Howard, felt that the small management team had done an incredible job handling the past year's growth. However, he also knew that, in trying to keep up with the demands of the business, no one was paying close enough attention to the company's financial picture.

Roger Howard was convinced that Cambridge needed some professional help with the company's financial management. Alan P. Howard (CA, MBA), a second cousin to Roger and Alan N., was a partner with a big eight accounting firm who was just returning to England from an assignment in Africa. After reviewing the situation in mid-April 1985, Alan P. Howard agreed to join Cambridge Nutrition Limited as the company's Director of Finance effective July 1st. He saw the position as an opportunity to apply his financial skills in a rapidly growing company. As he reviewed the financial results that Roger Howard had given him, he was impressed with the growth, but he was concerned that there were no systems in place to monitor the company's cash position on a timely basis. His first step was to produce a forecasted cash flow (based on company sales estimates) for April–September 1985 (see Exhibit 5).

THE LAUNCH OF CAMBRIDGE IN THE U.K.

In 1978, Dr. Alan N. Howard had granted a license to an American entrepreneur to produce and market Cambridge Diet in the U.S.A. under the name Cambridge Plan International (see Appendix A).

In the spring of 1984, Dr. Howard decided to launch the diet in the U.K. He formed a new company called Cambridge Nutrition Limited, which was completely independent from the American company. Cambridge Nutrition Limited was wholly owned by a British charity, the Howard Foundation, formed by Dr. Howard to assist bio-medical research on obesity, coronary heart disease, diabetes, multiple sclerosis and Third World nutrition (see Exhibit 6). Royalties from the U.S. company and Cambridge Nutrition Limited were paid to the Foundation. Cambridge Nutrition was required by company deed of covenant to pay on a monthly basis 14% of its gross sales to the Foundation. Dr. Howard and his son, Jonathan L. Howard, trustees of the foundation, managed company donations. Jonathan L. Howard also acted as legal counsel for Cambridge Nutrition.

Roger Howard, a bio-chemist by profession, had been working in several university research centers in the United States over a period of 18 years. He agreed to take the position of Managing Director when the candidate selected was unable to join the company. Starting in February 1984, Roger Howard ran the company from his mother's house in Norwich (2½ hours northeast of London), with the help of several relatives and close friends who acted as the first Cambridge Diet counsellors.

Dr. Alan N. Howard handled the production arrangements. Manufacturing was contracted to a pharmaceutical company, which produced the diet powder according to his formula and packaged it in tins ready for delivery. Sales in April 1984 were £7,000; after a steady increase, sales reached £82,000 for the month of December 1984.

The counsellor-based distribution system used by the U.K. company was a system of multi-level selling, not to be confused with pyramid selling. (See Exhibit 7 for details.) In the two years before his return to England, Roger and his wife had also been acting as counsellors, selling the Cambridge diet for the U.S. company. The U.K. distribution system was thus based on the counsellor system developed in the U.S.A.

The Cambridge counsellor was an independent agent who purchased the product from the company at a basic wholesale price and sold it to customers for a profit. A hierarchy developed whereby counsellors, who had sponsored a certain number of clients (users), received titles such as "Group Leader" along with increased bonuses for growth. These bonuses helped push sales of the diet. This method also ensured that new users were monitored and encouraged by their sponsors to stay with the diet. This support feature helped differentiate the Cambridge Diet from other diets that could be purchased from a store.

The counsellor system was the backbone of the company; therefore, Roger Howard felt that this area should be his primary management concern. In addition to the psychological benefits of helping other people to lose weight, the multi-level selling system with its high bonuses promoted rapid growth. As long as sales were increasing, the counsellors were being rewarded handsomely. In turn, the counsellors depended on a timely supply of good quality diet product.

SUDDEN GROWTH

Little by little, the English press started taking notice of the company. In November 1984, when Dr. Howard donated £850,000 (from royalties on sales in the U.S.) to Downing College, Cambridge University, for the construction of a cultural centre, press coverage was widespread. Believing that a little publicity would be good for the company, the Howards agreed that *News of the World*, the most popular Sunday newspaper in Britain, could write an article. The newspaper put four people on the diet as guinea pigs for two weeks and then presented the results to their readers. The weight losses of these four people were phenomenal and, when the article appeared in January 1985, it changed the life of Cambridge Nutrition. It was thought that as many as 10 million people may have read the article in *News of the World*.

When the newspaper article appeared, the dramatic effect on the obese population of the country gave Cambridge Nutrition its first serious shock. They inundated the company with phone calls and letters. The City of Norwich's central phone lines were jammed for days until British Telecom (the phone company) persuaded Cambridge Nutrition to install a larger phone system. The post office delivered 26 sacks of mail in the first week, many containing money to buy the diet.

Fortunately, the company was able to move into larger temporary offices. Even so, 30 to 40 people spent months dealing with the backlog of inquiries. Cambridge management and permanent and temporary staff struggled to cope with the onslaught from the millions of overweight people who, believing the diet to be a miracle, clamoured for it. Many people, unable to reach Cambridge Nutrition by phone, drove to Norwich from all over the country, anxious not to miss an opportunity to get the product.

GROWING PAINS

Since the company did not have the technical expertise to mix and package the diet, all production was subcontracted. Because of the company's short time in business, suppliers required Cambridge Nutrition to pay cash or place money in the bank as a guarantee when ordering. By January 1985, Roger had had to contract with four different suppliers in order to meet the demand. The situation was not ideal. In turn, there were three different sizes of tins. The product density varied with each supplier, confusing the users with regard to dosage amounts. Lead times for delivery were over six weeks and many orders were not produced on time. Counsellors reacted by increasing orders to meet their individual projections of demand.

The small management team was just able to keep up with the unexpected demand. Roger's family members, together with local counsellors and friends, joined the Cambridge Nutrition staff to answer inquiries, supply information and, when possible, send out the product. Living rooms became mail sorting centers and everyone helped fill envelopes with product information for the next day's mail. In Cambridge Nutrition's small warehouse, packers moved boxes of the diet product out into the snow during the day so they would have room to work and moved them inside again at night. The building bulged.

The Cambridge team, overwhelmed by demands for the product, rallied to support Roger. A sense of urgency gripped the company that was becoming a victim of its own success. The result was an 800% increase in sales (£674,000 in January 1985, up from £82,764 the previous month). Cambridge Nutrition was barely able to meet the demand. In February 1985, sales were £702,000 and in March, £772,973. In April, when sales had reached almost £1 million (£941,350), the strain of keeping up the pace began to tell. Although morale among the group was high, everyone knew that growth could not continue without improving the systems to manage it.

COMPETITION

The only serious competitor was a U.K.-based company called Univite. The company, which sold a product similar to the Cambridge Diet, had been set up about a year before Cambridge Nutrition. Univite sold its product in pre-measured sachets rather than the multiple service tins used by Cambridge. It was thought that consumers preferred the sachets. Cambridge Nutrition was especially troubled to learn that a former senior counsellor from Cambridge in the U.S.A. had joined

Univite to establish the counsellor based selling system with a significant bonus system to promote sales.

Cambridge Nutrition realized that market share depended on which company had promoted the most during any given period. Roger also knew that whatever Cambridge could not supply, Univite would. Although no one could match the service and efficiency of the Cambridge counsellors, inability to supply enough product could jeopardize everything. In early 1985, Univite held the major share of the U.K. market.

THE MANAGEMENT TEAM

By April 1985, the management team at Cambridge had grown to seven people: Roger Howard as Managing Director, and the respective managers for warehousing, stock control, finance, personnel, communications, and counsellor liaison. Permanent staff included several people in the office and the two warehouses, supported by some temporary workers, 30 employees in all.

In mid-April, Roger Howard met with senior management to assess the situation and decide how to meet the challenge of growth. It was announced that Alan P. Howard would be joining Cambridge on July 1st. Dr. Alan Wallace, a marketing expert in the food industry, had agreed to join the company in June as Marketing Director. His first responsibilities were to improve the supply situation and manage the company's advertising strategy.

In response to Roger's questions, the managers felt generally optimistic about the company's outlook, but did have reservations about its ability to handle more growth. Sufficient supply of the product continued to be a vital question. After the sales surge in April, there was only £1,000 worth of stock left in the warehouse. Although 450,000 tins of the diet, worth £1 million, were ordered to support the sales projections, first deliveries of the increased volumes would take at least six weeks.

According to the stock manager, the product was ready for shipment; the counsellor liaison manager, however, felt that more people were needed to support the counsellors and improve their service level. The personnel manager noted proudly that the company had moved into a new 8,000 sq. ft. office space after only one year in business.

As Roger was wondering how to keep up with the fantastic growth that had already occurred, his brother, Dr. Alan N. Howard, was preparing a book for publication. *The Cambridge Diet* contained stories of successful dieters as well as full details of the product and its nutritional benefits. Because of Cambridge Plan International's downfall in the United States (see Appendix A), Dr. Howard's book included the important role of public relations, particularly the media's power when criticizing a company ill-prepared to defend itself. Cambridge management felt that the book would push sales even higher than April's record level. Another rapid increase, like what followed the *News of the World* article, would be difficult to handle. Planning for this growth became the focus of the management group.

EXHIBIT 1

The Cambridge Diet

FACTS ABOUT THE CAMBRIDGE DIET

1. The Cambridge Diet is a unique breakthrough in the fields of nutrition and obesity. It is a powder which contains all the essential nutrients considered necessary for health in just 330 calories. Before this development, virtually no diet below 1000 calories could provide all these requirements without additional supplementation.

2. The formula of the Cambridge Diet was developed after $8\frac{1}{2}$ years of research and clinical testing by a team of British research scientists led by Alan N. Howard, M.A., Ph.D., F.R.I.C.

3. The clinical testing of the Cambridge Diet was carried out at Addenbrooke's Hospital, Cambridge, and a London hospital. The efficiency and safety of the Cambridge Diet has been confirmed by other doctors and scientists at University Medical Schools in the United States at Atlanta, Colorado, and West Virginia and in Europe at Copenhagen, Rotterdam, Dublin, Naples, and Gothenburg.

4. Clinical tests have shown that 15 lbs can be lost in one week and up to 35 lbs in four weeks, with an average weight loss of 16–20 lbs in four weeks with patients who were unable to lose weight with any other low calorie programme.

5. The product is so formulated as to protect the lean body mass and so ensures the body primarily utilizes fatty tissue for its energy requirement without harmful side-effects.

6. When taken as directed, the daily intake contains 34 grams of protein, 3 grams of fat and 44 grams of carbohydrate, 100% of the U.K. and U.S.A. recommended daily allowance of vitamins and minerals, and all trace elements and electrolytes specified as essential by the National Academy of Sciences, U.S.A.

7. The primary sources of protein are soya flour, low-fat milk solids and sodium caseinate which provide 100% of the daily requirements of essential amino acids. Lactose is the primary carbohydrate. Fat is added mainly as linoleic acid with lesser amounts of linolenic acid. Dietary fibre is added for bulk.

8. Weight loss is comparable to that achieved by complete starvation or gastroplasty (stomach stapling).

9. Clinical studies have shown that serum cholesterol is decreased by 20% and idglycerides by 45%. There is also a reduction in hypertension.

10. The Cambridge Diet may be used not only to lose weight but also to permanently control weight, to gain weight, and to ensure complete nutritional balance each day.

THE INVENTOR OF THE CAMBRIDGE DIET

Alan N. Howard, M.A., Ph.D., F.R.I.C., who led the team which developed the Cambridge Diet is an internationally acknowledged authority on obesity and coronary heart disease from a nutritional point of view, and has edited several books and published over 200 papers on these subjects. Dr. Howard received all of his academic degrees from the University of Cambridge. He has served on the Scientific Staff of the Medical Research Council, Dunn Nutritional Laboratories, Cambridge, and on the External Scientific Staff, Medical Research Council, Department of Pathology, University of Cambridge. He has been associated with the Department of Medicine at the University of Cambridge since 1969 and began the formulation of the diet there in 1970. He is currently Lecturer in Nutritional Research at Downing College. Dr. Howard is Chairman of the British Food Education Society and has served as secretary of the European

(continued)

EXHIBIT 1 (cont.)

Atherosclerosis Group and as Editor of the *International Journal of Obesity*. Dr. Howard was asked by BBC-TV to participate in its 10 part 1973 series, "Don't Just Sit There."

WEIGHT LOSS PROGRAMME

No calories to count. Just mix one sachet of diet powder with water three times a day. There's no other food to consider. You only have to drink an additional 6–8 glasses of water throughout the day. The unique balance of nutrients means that your appetite is curbed so that you do not feel hungry.

Moreover, since you receive your daily requirements of all essential nutrients you will not only feel but also look well.

You may stay on this regimen for four weeks before adding solid food. However, if you are under strict medical supervision you may take the Cambridge Diet as your sole source of nutrition for several months until your target weight is achieved.

WEIGHT MAINTENANCE PROGRAMME

When you have reached your target weight you will feel healthier and fitter than you have for years. You will want to continue to feel this way. You will want to maintain your weight and retain your new, slim figure. Those who have lost their weight on the Cambridge Diet have a good chance of doing so. Studies have shown that though 95% of those who lose weight on other diets regain it during the following year, only 41% of those who have lost weight on Cambridge regain it, and then usually only a fraction of what they have taken off. 33% maintain their new weight and 26% actually lose more weight.

This is where the weight-maintenance programme comes in.

First, continue to take three helpings of the Cambridge Diet each day but add two 400K calorie meals. Weigh yourself daily. If you continue to lose weight, add more calories to your meals. Alternatively, if you gain weight, reduce the number of calories consumed per day. In this way you should be able to maintain your desired weight permanently.

Don't feel guilty, however, if you cannot always stick strictly to your weight-maintenance programme. There will be times when this is difficult, in particular on special occasions such as Christmas, New Years and other celebrations. You may gain two or three pounds. That is the time to go back to using the Cambridge Diet as your sole source of nutrition until those gained pounds have been lost. This is one of the beauties of the Cambridge Diet. You are in control of your weight.

NUTRITIONAL BALANCE

Although many of us eat plenty of food, we eat the wrong foods. This is particularly true in these modern times when we grab snacks here and there throughout the day. Consequently many of us, although even over weight, are malnourished. Our bodies are not as healthy as they should be.

It should be realized, therefore, that the Cambridge Diet powder is not only a product for weight-loss, but also provides a balanced, nutritious food low in calories. When taken three times a day along with conventional solid food, sufficient to provide our daily energy requirements, we can guarantee that our bodies receive their recommended daily allowance of essential nutrients, vitamins, minerals and trace elements.

People who can benefit particularly from a daily consumption of the Cambridge Diet along with their conventional food, even though they do not need to lose weight, are the very elderly, children, adolescents, the athlete, and the underweight.

(continued)

EXHIBIT 1 (cont.)

The very elderly are usually not very interested in food. They have poor appetites and may not have the energy to prepare nutritious meals. Furthermore, since digestive systems tend to become less efficient with old age, they have greater difficulty in assimilating adequate amounts of certain nutrients from conventional foods.

Children can be very particular about food and quite often reject the very foods they need to supply their bodies with for their daily nutritional requirements. They may find the taste of the Cambridge Diet much more to their liking.

EXHIBIT 2

CAMBRIDGE NUTRITION LIMITED
Monthly Sales February 1984–April 1985
(£000s)

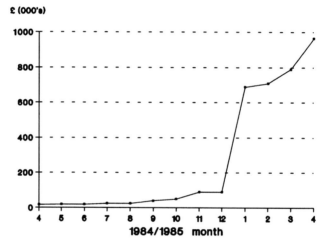

EXHIBIT 3

CAMBRIDGE NUTRITION LIMITED
Income Statement
(£000s)

	SEPTEMBER 1984 (6 MONTHS)	MARCH 1985 (12 MONTHS)
Net Sales	139.0	1,545.6
Cost of goods sold		
Diet ingredients (net of VAT refunds)	49.6	655.2
Packaging	2.9	48.6
Bonus payments to counsellors	9.7	288.7
Total	**62.2**	**992.5**
Distribution & selling expenses	4.2	67.8
Administrative expenses		
Salaries	15.0	114.5

(continued)

EXHIBIT 3 (cont.)

	SEPTEMBER 1984 (6 MONTHS)	MARCH 1985 (12 MONTHS)
Administrative expenses	27.8	99.9
Depreciation	2.0	10.1
Covenanted donations to the Howard foundation[a]	8.9	354.8
Patent royalties & medical consulting fees	0.0	26.9
Total	**53.7**	**606.2**
Operating profit (loss)	18.9	(120.9)
Interest received	0.0	5.2
Interest payable	0.0	63.0
Loss on activities before taxes	18.9	(178.7)
Taxes[b]	5.3	45.0
Net profit (loss) after taxes	**13.6**	**(223.7)**

[a]Approximately 14% of gross sales was donated to the Howard Foundation. March included some accrued payments for product shipped in April.

[b]Withholding taxes were paid when donations were made. As a charitable organization in the U.K., the foundation could reclaim the tax.

EXHIBIT 4

CAMBRIDGE NUTRITION LIMITED
Balance Sheet
(£000s)

	APRIL 1, 1984	SEPTEMBER 30, 1984	MARCH 31, 1985
Assets			
Fixed Assets	0.0	15.4	35.4
Current Assets			
Finished Goods Inventory	0.0	31.9	131.7
Accounts Receivable[a]	0.0	3.2	329.3
Cash	50.0	47.2	836.7
Total Current Assets	50.0	82.3	1,297.7
Total Assets	50.0	97.7	1,333.1
Liabilities			
Shareholders Loans	0.0	28.8	1,433.8
Interest Payable	0.0	0.0	63.0
Provision for Liabilities	0.0	5.3	10.0
Total Liabilities	0.0	34.1	1,443.8
Capital and Reserves			
Share Capital	50.0	50.0	50.0
Accrued Income	0.0	13.6	(223.7)
Total Capital and Reserves	50.0	63.6	(110.7)
Total Liabilities and Capital	50.0	97.7	1,333.1

[a]Accounts receivable are comprised mostly of VAT prepayments that are refunded by the government. Some prepayments to suppliers are also included. Sales to counsellors are on a cash basis.

EXHIBIT 5

CAMBRIDGE NUTRITION LIMITED
Cash Flow Projection April–September 1985
(£)

SALES PRICE £8
PURCHASE PRICE £2.5

MONTH	APRIL	MAY	JUNE	JULY	AUGUST	SEPTEMBER
Sales units (tins)	100,000	200,000	500,000	500,000	500,000	500,000
INCOME						
Sales	800,000	1,600,000	4,000,000	4,000,000	4,000,000	4,000,000
Handling charges	500	500	500	500	500	500
Sundry	100	100	100	100	100	100
Starter kits	1,000	1,000	1,000	1,000	1,000	1,000
Total income	801,600	1,601,600	4,001,600	4,001,600	4,001,600	4,001,600
Expenditure						
Purchases	250,000	500,000	1,250,000	1,250,000	1,250,000	1,250,000
Bonus payments	132,000	160,000	320,000	800,000	800,000	800,000
Advertising	2,000	2,000	2,000	2,000	2,000	2,000
Bank charges	50	50	50	50	50	50
Cartons, labels	4,000	8,000	20,000	20,000	20,000	20,000
Carriage	8,000	16,000	40,000	40,000	40,000	40,000
Insurance	2,000					
Light & heat	200	200	200	200	200	200
Legal & professional	2,000	2,000	2,000	2,000	2,000	2,000
Motor expenses	2,000	2,000	2,000	2,000	2,000	2,000
Printing & stat	2,000	4,000	10,000	10,000	10,000	10,000
Rent & rates	3,500	28,500	6,000	6,000	6,000	6,000
Repairs to premises	200	200	200	200	200	200
Sundry	200	200	200	200	200	200
Travel & subs	750	1,500	2,000	2,000	2,000	2,000
Telephone	2,000	10,000	3,000	3,000	3,000	3,000
Salaries	8,000	8,000	11,000	11,000	11,000	11,000
Wages	6,000	8,000	12,000	12,000	12,000	12,000
Howard Foundation	80,000	160,000	400,000	400,000	400,000	400,000
Vehicle leases	2,000	2,000	3,000	3,000	3,000	3,000
Office furniture		14,000				
Office equipment		8,000	25,000	5,000		
Total expenditure	506,900	934,650	2,108,650	2,568,650	2,563,650	2,563,650
Excess of income over exp.	294,700	666,950	1,892,950	1,432,950	1,437,950	1,437,950
Cash at start of month	120,000	414,700	1,081,650	2,974,600	4,407,550	5,845,500
Cash at end of month	414,700	1,081,650	2,974,600	4,407,550	5,845,500	7,283,450

Source: Company spreadsheet.

EXHIBIT 6

The Howard Foundation

THE FOUNDATION

The Trust was founded by Dr. Alan N. Howard, MA PhD, on 24th October 1982 by the establishment of a Trust Fund for charitable purposes.
REGD. CHARITY No. 285822

OBJECTS

General charitable purposes although the Trust Deed provides in particular for:

1. biomedical research at the University of Cambridge and other Universities in England and Wales.
2. construction and maintenance of a building or buildings at Downing College, Cambridge.
3. the establishment of a cultural centre in the city of Cambridge for the promotion of public education and the appreciation of the arts and crafts amongst the inhabitants.
4. research into the means of relieving malnutrition especially in underdeveloped countries and in particular use of the "Cambridge Diet" and other know how and technology in the possession of the Trustees and the Trust companies for this purpose.

CURRENT RESEARCH PROGRAMMES

1. University of Cambridge, research into Obesity and Multiple Sclerosis;
2. University of Wales Institute of Science and Technology, research into longevity;
3. Imperial College, London, research into Diabetes and Atherosclerosis;

THE FUTURE

The Trustees hope to continue and extend their programme of support for scientific research particularly in the areas of obesity, coronary heart disease, diabetes and multiple sclerosis.

The Trust hopes to launch a journal on the problems of malnutrition in underdeveloped countries.

In the long term the Trustees hope income will extend to some of the more ambitious objects of the Foundation such as the creation of a courtyard adjacent to the new Howard Building at Downing College to comprise mainly residential accommodation.

PROPERTY

1. Investments
2. Patents. The Foundation, jointly with a sister charitable trust, is the beneficiary of the William Harvey Foundation for Research and Education which owns the "Cambridge Diet" patents with 15 patents and patent applications in 11 countries including the United Kingdom and the United States.

   The Foundation wholly owns patents and patent foundations for the use of bran in snack foods (so-called "BranKrisps") in 22 countries including the United Kingdom and the United States.

(continued)

EXHIBIT 6 (cont.)

3. Company Shareholdings. The Foundation wholly owns Cambridge Nutrition Limited formed in April 1984 to promote the "Cambridge Diet" and health education in the United Kingdom and Eire.

   The Foundation is also the controlling shareholder in Health Foods (International) Limited formed to promote "BranKrisps" and other health products locally and internationally and also to promote the "Cambridge Diet" abroad.

   It also has a programme to create and invest in overseas health food companies.

ACHIEVEMENTS

Since its foundation the trust has supported the following:

1. University of Cambridge, Department of Medicine;
2. University of Wales Institute of Science and Technology, Department of Applied Biology;
3. Imperial College of Science and Technology, London;
4. Downing College, Cambridge for the construction of the new Howard Building. On 6th November 1984 the Trustees presented the Master and Fellows of the college with a draft for £850,000 under the terms of a Deed of Gift to build and equip a multi-purpose centre consisting of a lecture/reception hall, and a recreational lobby and basement. The building, due for completion during 1987, is to be constructed of Ketton Stone and is designed by the architect Mr. Quinlan Terry in a Palladian style to conform with existing buildings at the College.

THE TRUSTEES

ALAN N. HOWARD MA PhD is a Research Scientist based at the Department of Medicine at the University of Cambridge where he is also College Lecturer in Nutritional Research at Downing College.

From 1970 onwards he led research into a very low calorie diet subsequently called the "Cambridge Diet" and is now an acknowledged authority on the interrelated fields of nutrition, obesity and coronary heart disease, having published over 200 papers and edited several books on the subject.

Dr. Howard's book *The Cambridge Diet* was published on 1st May 1985 by Jonathan Cape Ltd.

JONATHAN L. HOWARD MA LLB is the Founder's son and was also educated at Downing College where he read law. Subsequently he was articled to Hepworth & Chadwick (Solicitors) and he now practices as a Solicitor in Leeds as Secretary to the Foundation and its companies and as a group leader of Cambridge Diet Counsellors. He is also Secretary of the Victorian Society (West Yorkshire Group).

EXHIBIT 7

Multi-Level Selling; De-coding the Pyramid

What is pyramid selling?

It is a way of selling goods and services through a trading scheme which operates on *more than one level*. People who join a pyramid selling scheme **buy goods and services from other persons or company** running the scheme or *from other participants* and then sell them to the general public in their homes. Apart from the profit they make on selling, participants are offered other rewards which they can earn including:

a. bonuses for recruiting new participants.

b. commission on sales made by other participants.

c. bonuses or higher commissions or extra discount on goods when the participant is promoted to a higher level in the scheme.

The pyramid **works like a chain letter,** where you pay out money to people already in the system in the hope that other people will eventually pay you. It is not even necessary to have a product for the pyramid to grow.

The dynamic from pyramid selling comes **from establishing a network of dealerships rather than from a sustained level of retail sales and customer satisfaction.** Individuals have to buy themselves into the company, paying a fee and placing a large stock order.

Pyramid selling gained a dreadful reputation in the past because the people who joined such schemes lost a lot of money and were left without legal redress.

How is multi-level marketing different?

There are many pyramid selling schemes which call themselves multi-level marketing organizations.

Multi-level marketing uses **direct selling.** The salesperson only orders products to sell directly to known customers. Success depends on the quality of the product, good service and a high level of re-ordering. The kind of products, best suited to direct selling are those for personal use, although double glazing and kitchen equipment are sold in this way in the U.K. The advice and service provided by the agent or counsellor are very important elements in this kind of business.

The Cambridge Diet is marketed directly because it **combines the emotional and practical support of counselling** with an economic way of distributing the product. Dr. Roger Howard explains, "If ever a product was made for multi-level marketing, this is it. It is a perfect combination; they complement each other."

Source: Company literature.

APPENDIX A
The Launch of Cambridge Diet in the U.S.A.

In 1978, Dr. Alan N. Howard was approached by an American entrepreneur, Jack Feather, who had developed a successful mail order business and a chain of health clubs in California. Mr. Feather had read about Dr. Howard's diet and wanted to offer it to his fitness club clients as a safe way to lose or maintain weight.

Although previously used only under medical supervision in U.K. hospital and obesity clinics, the diet was made ready for sale to the general public. Dr. Howard and Mr. Feather negotiated a royalty agreement to manufacture and market the product in the U.S.A. Dr. Howard maintained the patent rights but would not be involved in the U.S. business except occasionally as a consultant on nutrition. The timing of this commercialization agreement was significant to Dr. Howard. In 1978 a similar product, developed with funds from a large Swiss pharmaceutical company, was being introduced in several European markets.

Mr. Feather established Cambridge Plan International (CPI) and immediately launched the diet nationwide, using an extensive advertising campaign. Initially, the product was sold through the mail order business, but the sales strategy was soon modified to a multi-level selling system using counsellors (the system used later in the U.K.).

After introducing the multi-level system, sales spiralled upward. As the counsellor base multiplied and orders rolled in, the company had to expand quickly to meet the demand. CPI management could barely install systems fast enough. The need to step up production meant more and more investment in stock diet ingredients, factories, warehouses and distribution centers. After less than two years in business, CPI had sales of $50 million per month. During this time, the company also increased its headquarters staff to 1,000 people and had, in addition, about 250,000 counsellors and 5,000 group leaders.

On the surface, the growth of the U.S. company seemed assured. However, a certain segment of the medical profession, echoed by the media, raised questions about the diet's risks and benefits. The company did not defend itself adequately against the media attacks nor did it effectively present the medical benefits proven in U.K. clinical testing. In the summer of 1983, a particularly aggressive TV documentary program, "Monitor," claimed that the diet caused loss of lean body mass as well as fat, thus increasing the risk of heart problems. While this claim was untrue, the effect on the public was substantial.

The company, geared up to sell $50 million in July, sold only $10 million. It was left with overstocked warehouses and heavy investments in new plants, raw materials and packaging. Financial resources had been stretched beyond the limit. CPI, now bankrupt, filed for Chapter 11 protection from its creditors in the summer of 1983. Cash flow information was weeks out of date; debts had reached $35 million. Observers blamed a major portion of the company's decline on poor planning and financial management. CPI did remain in business but on a much smaller scale.

5

NOTE ON VALUE-ADDED TAXES

Value-added tax (VAT) is a multi-level consumption tax which is imposed at each stage of the production and distribution chain. The final consumer bears the burden of the tax. Since corporations do not bear the financial burden, the tax generally has no income statement impact. The tax generally shows up as a payable or receivable on the balance sheet.

Value-added taxes are a major form of taxation in Europe. All EEC countries have a VAT. Over 50 countries in the world use this type of taxation. Canada implemented a VAT (Goods and Services Tax (GST)) on January 1, 1991. There is speculation that the United States will also implement a consumption tax.

This paper's purpose is to provide a general background on how VATs work, describing the common features of VATs. An example is used to illustrate the multi-level structure of the tax. Some specific features of the Canadian and United Kingdom systems are then discussed. This paper is not intended to provide knowledge on the treatment of detailed VAT questions as VAT legislation is technical and complex. VAT legislation or professional advice should be consulted for specific transactional questions.

THE PAYMENT OF THE VAT

Virtually all countries use the "invoice method" of taxation. This means that VAT is charged and collected based on invoice amounts. This method provides simple verification, a good audit trail and low administrative burden.

The multi-stage structure of the VAT, with tax paid and input tax credits (ITCs) claimed at each stage of the production and distribution chain is illustrated in Exhibit 1. The example follows the manufacture of a cabinet from the raw material stage through to the sale to the consumer. A tax rate of 7% has been used in the example, which is the same as the Canadian GST.

At the first stage, the sawmill sells the rough timber to the lumber dealer for $200 plus $14 tax. This example assumes that the sawmill has no taxable purchases; therefore, the sawmill remits the $14 it has collected on the sale to the government. After the lumber dealer has processed the timber, it sells it to the cabinet-maker for $300 plus $21 tax. The lumber dealer then remits $7 to the government—the difference between the tax collected, $21, and the tax paid out, $14.

The cabinet-maker manufactures a cabinet and sells it to the retailer for $800 plus $56 tax. The cabinet-maker then remits $35, $56 minus $21, to the government. At the last stage, the end product is sold to the consumer for $1,000 plus $70 tax. The retailer remits $14 tax to the government. Note that the total remitted to the government by the production chain is $70 which is the same amount of tax that the consumer pays on the end product. Hence, the final consumer bears the cost of the tax while the VAT is a flow-through for the production and distribution chain.

TREATMENT OF CAPITAL EXPENDITURES

The treatment of VAT on capital expenditures differs depending on the country. The three types of systems used are as follows:

- Full refund for VAT on capital expenditure
- Amortizing of VAT refund over life of asset
- No refund

In Canada, for example, 100% of the GST paid on the purchase of a capital expenditure can be claimed immediately as an ITC. This is consistent with system 1 above.

VAT RATES AND STRUCTURES

The most uncomplicated VAT system would be a one-rate system where all goods and services are taxable at the single rate. This simplistic structure is politically difficult to achieve since the VAT is a regressive tax. That is, if one rate were applied to all goods, the tax would take a disproportionate amount of income from lower income earners.

To avoid the regressive nature of the tax, most countries apply lower rates on necessities such as food and medical services and higher rates on luxury items. Exemption and zero-rating systems are also sometimes used to address the regressive nature of the tax. To understand the exemption and zero-rating systems, the three types of supplies (sales) must be reviewed. Supplies can be categorized as taxable, zero-rated and tax-exempt.

Taxable Supplies

VAT is levied on the sale of taxable supplies. The vendor is entitled to claim an ITC on the VAT the vendor has paid on its supplies. Therefore, vendors of taxable supplies act as agents of the government by collecting tax and remitting the net difference between the total amount collected and the total paid out in a period. Taxable supplies can be taxed at a range of rates depending on the type of taxable supply. In the more simplistic systems such as the GST, the rate can either be 7% or 0%. On the other hand, the U.K. system has ranges of rates depending on the products.

Zero-rated Supplies

It is important to note that zero-rated supplies are included in the category of taxable supplies. Therefore, zero-rated supplies are taxed at zero percent and the vendor can claim ITCs on its purchases.

Tax-Exempt Supplies

No tax is payable by the consumer on tax-exempt supplies. The important distinction between these supplies and zero-rated supplies is that the vendor cannot claim ITCs for VAT paid on inputs used in the production of tax-exempt supplies. This increases the real costs of these vendors.

At the cash register the consumer may see no difference between a zero-rated and a tax-exempt supply. There likely is a difference though. The supplier of the tax-exempt product has a higher real cost of inputs since the VAT cannot be claimed back and, therefore, the end product cost probably reflects this higher cost of doing business of the tax-exempt supplier.

SPECIFICS OF THE CANADIAN GOODS AND SERVICES TAX (GST)

GST legislation took effect in Canada on January 1, 1991. The tax is a broadly based multi-stage value-added tax. The tax rate is 7% on taxable supplies. A narrow range of goods is zero-rated and tax-exempt. In addition, most provinces in Canada have a sales tax which is levied on the sale of retail goods. In Ontario, the sales tax rate is 8%.

The major categories of zero-rated goods and services include:

- prescription drugs
- medical devices
- basic groceries

- agricultural and fishery products
- exports

All exports are zero-rated. A number of rules exist to determine whether a good or service has been exported. No tax will apply to goods that are delivered outside of Canada by the supplier or are delivered to a third party carrier for delivery outside of Canada. Not taxing exports ensures that products produced in Canada and sold abroad can compete on a level playing field with global competition. Not only is there no tax on the sale but, since exports are zero-rated, the supply does not have tax built into the price. The export vendor can claim back all GST paid on the product's inputs.

Conversely, all imports into Canada are taxable. For goods crossing the border, tax is collected at the point of entry based upon the value for customs purposes. The importer of record is responsible for paying the GST. Imports of goods which are zero-rated will not attract GST upon importation.

Imported services cannot practically be taxed at the border. Registrants importing services for use exclusively in a commercial activity neither pay nor receive a credit for GST. This can be done since the tax collected and the ITC would net out so that the administrative burden to collect a net nil balance does not make sense. If, on the other hand, the services are imported for use in a tax-exempt activity, the importer is required to self-assess and pay the GST within specific deadlines.

The major categories of tax-exempt goods are:

- day-care services
- legal aid services
- health and dental services
- most educational services
- most goods and services provided by charities, non-profit organizations and governments
- most domestic financial services

Institutions providing these goods and services cannot claim back GST paid on their inputs. There are exceptions to this rule. Municipalities, universities, schools and hospitals, known as the MUSH sector, can claim back a portion of the GST they pay out on inputs. The percentages are in the neighbourhood of 60%–70% depending on the type of institution. Also, registered charities can claim a rebate for 50% of the GST paid.

Capital Expenditures

The GST paid on capital expenditures may be claimed at the earlier of the tax being paid or becoming payable. Generally, GST on capital expenditures can be claimed back immediately. If the capital item is purchased through a capital lease, the GST is claimed as the lease payments are made.

Registering and Reporting Requirements

All commercial activities doing business in Canada with over $30,000 a year in world wide sales must register for the GST. Therefore, a proprietor with over $30,000 in sales must register with Revenue Canada and collect the GST. Commercial activities with less than $30,000 sales have their choice of whether they want to register or not. The advantage of registering is that they can claim back the GST on their expenses.

Commercial activities with under $500,000 in annual sales can report annually but they must pay instalments on a quarterly basis. If a commercial activity's sales are over $6,000,000, it must file monthly (including payment with the return) and entities that fall between these two thresholds file quarterly. Refunds are usually paid out within a month. Interest is paid on outstanding refunds 21 days after the return is received.

UNITED KINGDOM VAT

VAT was introduced in the United Kingdom in 1973. VAT is imposed on the supply of goods and services by a taxable person (annual sales over £10,000) at a maximum rate of 17.5%. The U.K. system has a sliding scale of rates based upon the type of product being sold. Note that the maximum rate is not necessarily out of line with taxes charged in Canada. In the U.K., they do not have provincial sales taxes. Considering that GST plus provincial sales tax in Ontario adds up to 15%, the U.K. rate is not as excessive as it appears on the surface.

The mechanics of the U.K. system are essentially the same as the Canadian system. In the U.K., they have taxable, zero-rated and tax-exempt products.

Tax exempt items include:

- land
- insurance
- postal services
- financial transactions
- educational services
- health services

Zero-rated supplies include:

- food
- books, etc.
- news services
- drugs and medicines
- building and civil engineering

Filing is done on a quarterly basis with returns due one month after the quarter. Certain traders may be permitted to file on a monthly basis since they may generally be in a credit position.

SUMMARY

As presented here, VAT is conceptually very easy to follow. Tax is collected and claimed back at each stage of the production chain and the final consumer bears the burden of the tax. It is important to recognize, however, that VAT legislation is extremely complex and there are many specific regulations for different industries and transactions.

For example, the underwriting of securities by investment bankers is considered tax-exempt and, therefore, ITCs relating to these activities will be denied. On the other hand, investment counselling services and advice on mergers and acquisitions are taxable and, therefore, ITCs can be claimed for expenditures on these activities. Underwriting for non-resident issuers is zero-rated since this is considered an export.

While a good general knowledge of VATs is essential, in many cases detailed industry knowledge of VAT treatment is also needed in order to comprehend the specific business implications of a VAT.

EXHIBIT 1

Tax Effect on Production Chain

SAWMILL		LUMBER DEALER		CABINET-MAKER		RETAILER		CONSUMER
Invoice		Invoice		Invoice		Invoice		
								Consumer pays
Lumber	$200	Lumber	$300	Furniture	$800	Furniture	$1,000	$70 VAT/GST
VAT/GST	14	VAT/GST	21	VAT/GST	56	VAT/GST	70	on end product.
	$214		$321		$856		$1,070	
VAT/GST Ret.		VAT/GST Ret.		VAT/GST Ret.		VAT/GST Ret.		
Tax on Sale	$14	Tax on Sale	$21	Tax on Sale	$56	Tax on Sale	$70	
Less tax on		Less tax on		Less tax on		Less tax on		
Purchases	0	Purchases	14	Purchases	21	Purchases	56	
Tax to pay	$14	Tax to pay	$ 7	Tax to pay	$35	Tax to pay	$14	

Total tax payable to government by production chain:
$14 + $7 + $35 + $14 = $70

6

SOPHISTICATED PETITES

On February 24, 1990, Ann Moore, an account manager in a London, Ontario, branch of the Confederation Bank of Canada, was considering the account file of Betty and Edwin Wong. Having just completed her Account Manager Training Course, she was determined to use the skills she had learned to provide a thorough analysis for her manager.

The Wongs had just asked to increase their loan by $70,000, from $35,950 to $105,950, in order to finance the opening of a third store in London. Excited by the improved profitability in their existing stores, they were anxious to have the new store operating in time for the spring season. The money would be used to finance leasehold improvements and furniture purchases.

COMPANY BACKGROUND

The idea for Sophisticated Petites came to Betty Wong in 1986 after one of many frustrating shopping trips. Most boutiques and department stores catered to women between 5'5" and 5'10" tall. Women not in this size range had either of two choices: have their clothes custom-made or pay for extensive re-tailoring of off-the-rack

This case was prepared by Arati Chervu under the supervision of Professor Jim Hatch for the sole purpose of providing material for class discussion at the Western Business School. Certain names and other identifying information may have been disguised to protect confidentiality. It is not intended to illustrate either effective or ineffective handling of a managerial situation. Any reproduction, in any form, of the material in this case is prohibited except with the written consent of the School.

clothes. The few stores that specialized in petite clothing[1] seemed to concentrate on the price-conscious segment of the market, emphasizing clothes for women over 50 years of age. Betty felt that there was untapped market potential for a line of medium to high priced off-the-rack petite casual and professional clothing for women executives.

Although neither of the Wongs had owned businesses before, they had always planned to do so and Sophisticated Petites seemed like an ideal opportunity to capitalize on their skills. Both Betty and Edwin had university degrees: Betty in Science and Edwin in Fine Arts. Edwin had worked for five years as a buyer of men's fashion merchandise at a major national department store chain after receiving his degree and before his current position as Assistant Advertising Manager at the same firm. Betty's job as a senior supervisor for a major credit card company gave her valuable experience at managing a substantial staff of full-time and part-time employees.

After deciding that the market potential was strong in London, they scouted out suitable locations for the boutique. The clientele that they targeted was women between the ages of 25 and 55 earning incomes above $30,000. Since field research showed that a large proportion of these women shopped on Richmond Row, Sophisticated Petites began operations in January 1987 in this neighbourhood in a 1,000 square foot retail space. The store featured a line of executive clothing for the petite female professional.

Sophisticated Petites began with $75,000 equity capital and $10,500 in shareholders' loans. Betty and Edwin had savings of $50,000 and had borrowed $25,000 from Betty's parents. No terms of repayment were negotiated for this loan. In addition, they had borrowed $19,000 from Edwin's parents to be repaid in five years.

While ownership of the business was joint, Betty was responsible for the day-to-day operations. She worked an average of 70 hours per week but did not draw a salary. It was agreed that Edwin would maintain his advertising job and help out with the store only on weekends. Edwin's primary responsibility at Sophisticated Petites was to determine appropriate levels of advertising and promotions.

Betty ordered goods in specified quantities and sizes directly from Canadian manufacturers or from merchandising representatives who operated out of suites in Toronto and Montreal hotels. Purchase commitments were made about nine months in advance of each selling season. Normal industry purchase terms were 2%,10; net 30 and new businesses starting out were often sold on a C.O.D. basis. If a supplier wanted the business very badly, terms of 3%,10; net, 60 were sometimes available. Purchases had to be managed carefully since as much as 65% of sales could occur during the September to December selling season.

Sales were encouraging during 1987, which was the first year of operations. Traffic through the store was high and Betty had begun to notice repeat customers.

---

[1]Petite refers to the length of the garment and the bodice, not the general sizing. A petite woman is one who is quite short but could range from a small size to a large size. In an ordinary store the sizes may range from 4–16. Petite stores have a similar size range.

A survey of customers done in January 1988 indicated general satisfaction with the selection of clothes available; however, a number of customers indicated that the prices were higher than what they would normally be willing to pay. Betty dismissed these responses, noting that the quality of merchandise that Sophisticated Petites provided was higher than had been previously offered in this area. In both Edwin and Betty's estimation, the store was a success.

Determined to maintain momentum, the Wongs decided to open a bigger store in the newly built Masonville Mall. This opening, which occurred in January 1989, allowed them to expand their line to include casual clothing for the petite professional woman. As with the first store, sales were encouraging.

With the business demanding more managerial time than Betty could provide, Edwin had to quit his job in early 1989 to work full time at Sophisticated Petites. They also hired a total of 12 part-time employees.

During the 1989 fiscal year, Edwin and Betty drew a combined salary of $31,250. They were also able to charge a significant part of their living expenses to the business, including their car, a number of meals, and part of their rent since they used one room in their home as an office. They expected to draw a salary of $40,000 in fiscal 1990. Both Edwin and Betty felt that they had a firm grasp of the finances of the business.

THE SETBACK

During fiscal 1989, the Wongs decided to launch a menswear line within the store at Masonville Mall. Like their ladies line of clothing, the men's line was targeted at a niche market—men under 5'6".

In order to help finance the launch of the menswear line, the Wongs had taken out a Small Business Loan of $25,000 from the Confederation Bank. This loan was repayable in monthly payments of $350 plus interest at prime plus 1%. They also took out a Confederation Bank Term Loan of $18,750 repayable in monthly instalments of $300 plus interest at prime plus 2.5%. The loans were being repaid on schedule.

The new business was a complete failure. Men did not feel comfortable shopping in a store called Sophisticated Petites. In addition, they did not perceive the need for a specialized shop since most menswear stores included free alterations with suit purchases—a service which Sophisticated Petites did not offer. The menswear inventory had to be sold off at a deep discount. Furthermore, Sophisticated Petites incurred an extraordinary loss of $20,450 due to the write-off of leasehold improvements in 1989 as shown in the financial statements in Exhibit 1.

Recognizing the need for advice, the Wongs obtained the service of a chartered accountant, Joan Brunelle, who specialized in serving the retail trade. Subsequently, she played an important role in almost all major decisions regarding Sophisticated Petites. Acting on the advice of Joan Brunelle, Edwin and Betty decided to focus only on women's wear.

THE RECOVERY

Under the guidance of Joan Brunelle, business improved. By the end of February 1990, the Wongs felt that the business had turned around. High sales during the fourth quarter of 1989 and favourable feedback from their customers contributed to their optimism. The Wongs estimated a profit of $30,000 during the fourth quarter.

Expansions undertaken to date had been partially trade-financed. Sophisticated Petites had a good relationship with one of its key suppliers and often took advantage of extremely favourable credit terms, sometimes up to 90 days. The Wongs had been told by their suppliers that they would receive such favourable terms until they had completed their startup phase but that they would have to pay under normal terms once they were established. The Wongs realized that they could have to begin paying within at least 60 days if economic conditions began putting pressure on their suppliers. The business rarely had accounts receivable since most customers paid by cheque or credit card, both of which were treated as cash payments. The firm tried to maintain a minimum cash balance of $15,000. An operating line of credit for $10,000 with the Confederation Bank was seldom utilized.

THE CURRENT OPPORTUNITY

Excited by the recovery and anxious to maintain the momentum, the Wongs planned to open a third store in April in the Galleria, a major mall in downtown London. The timing of the decision was especially important because there were rumours that a competitor was considering the opening of a petites store in the mall and the Wongs felt that if they opened their store first, competitors would withdraw from the market.

Sophisticated Petites had tentatively arranged a seven year lease for a location on the first floor of the mall beginning in March with a monthly rental of $5,000 or 6% of gross sales, whichever was larger. They planned to spend $86,000 on such leasehold improvements as a storefront, signage, acoustical ceiling, electrical wiring, mannequins, and furnishings. A cash down payment of $16,000 had been made, leaving a balance of $70,000 to be raised. Edwin and Betty wanted to borrow this money through a term loan.

The Wongs were confident that a store in the Galleria had huge potential. The mall had 165 stores located on two stories. The upscale clothing stores such as Harry Rosen, Heritage, Liptons, and Susan J were located on the second floor. With popular national stores like The Gap, Eatons, and The Bay, traffic through the mall was high. In addition, London had excess commercial real estate capacity and property management firms were enticing retailers with generous leasing terms.

The store would be opened for business in April but hiring would begin immediately. The Wongs planned to hire one full time employee as an assistant manager at $30,000 per annum. They also budgeted for an additional 8 part-time employees at $8,000 per annum. Benefits would cost an additional 25% of employee salaries.

PROJECTIONS

The Wongs were optimistic about the success of Sophisticated Petites. The Richmond Row store had shown a consistent profit since its start-up. According to them, this performance would have been repeated by the Masonville store had it not been for the menswear debacle. Betty, Edwin, and Joan Brunelle felt particularly positive about the potential of the proposed Galleria store.

This confidence was reflected in their financial projections. The Wongs predicted that their gross profit margin would stabilize at 40%, the standard in the industry. Management of inventory would be critical and the Wongs expected inventory turnover (using year end inventory rather than average inventory) would be consistent with the local industry standard of three times. The average age of payables was expected to be 75 days. In addition, they expected that the new store would add $20,000 to the fixed General and Administrative Expenses and $5,000 to the Advertising Expense. The Wongs believed that the wages and benefits expenses for the Richmond and Masonville stores would be about the same in 1990 as in 1989. In 1989, of $77,513 General and Administrative Expenses, $45,000 was fixed and the rest was variable with sales.

The Wongs were not overly concerned about the tax implications of their business decisions. The effective small business tax rate was 25%. They used the same schedule for depreciation and CCA.

Joan Brunelle's projection for the Galleria store for the year ending December 1990 was for sales of $550,000. She anticipated that monthly sales for this store would ultimately be slightly higher than that for either the Richmond Row ($62,500) or Masonville ($58,333) stores because of its excellent location. Sales for all three stores combined was anticipated to reach $2,000,000.

CURRENT ECONOMIC CONDITIONS

Anxious to do a comprehensive analysis, Ann Moore reviewed topical economic and business information. The Bank Rate had shown a steady upward trend during the past $2\frac{1}{2}$ years and was currently pegged at 13.25%, reflecting the Bank of Canada's war on inflation. Inflation however was persistent and had averaged 5.33% per annum during the first two months of the year. The prime rate was currently set at 14.25%.

The persistent high interest rates had begun to slow consumer spending. Analysts were predicting real Gross Domestic Product to show its first decline in 6 years during the first quarter of 1990.

The government expected the proposed Goods and Services Tax (GST), scheduled to take effect January 1 1991, to add another 1.25% to the inflation rate at that time. Lack of confidence in the government's current policies, however, had lead economists to forecast even higher inflation rates.

The retail trade was nervous about the impact of the GST. Currently, there was no federal sales tax on clothing. The GST, therefore, would be an entirely new tax on this item. Many retailers expected to see a decline in sales during the first few months of 1991 until customers became accustomed to the new prices. Some analysts had forecast that the economic slowdown combined with the impact of the GST could result in retail sales in some sectors falling as much as 10%.

Competition within the retail sector was intensifying. Consumers were becoming more discriminating and more sensitive to price–value relationships. Combined with slow growth in real personal disposable income and the emergence of new store formats, these factors were forcing stores to focus their marketing and planning to meet special needs.

The elimination of tariffs and other trade barriers under the Free Trade Agreement was expected to provide North American retailers (Canadian and U.S.) with broader North American sourcing opportunities. It could also encourage cross-border investment. This was expected to increase overall economic activity by facilitating the flow of new retail concepts and intensifying competition.

While American retail giants had not rushed into the Canadian market, the successes of the few that had, like The Gap, were notable. There was even talk that Robert Campeau would open a Bloomingdales in Toronto. The flagship store in New York carried an extensive petite women's line.

In the long term, despite slow population growth in Canada, a significant increase in the number of people in the high-spending (35–49 year old) age group was expected. This augured well for the retail sector, which was expected to outperform the economy in the period to the mid-1990s.

Ann Moore also referred to Dun & Bradstreet International's Key Business Ratios—1990 Edition (shown in Exhibit 2) to compare key ratios for Sophisticated Petites with those in the industry. She understood that the ratios presented in this publication were averages based on an analysis of a composite sample of Canadian audited financial statements. The statements of both profitable and unprofitable concerns were included in the Dun & Bradstreet analysis.

THE DECISION AT HAND

It was clear to Ann Moore that the Wongs were extremely dedicated and anxious to succeed. During the interview with the Wongs, Ann had put together a crude personal statement of affairs for the couple (Exhibit 3) and noted that their personal assets were not very large. However, she knew that the Wongs had a number of well-to-do relatives in town.

The Wongs had been longstanding Confederation Bank clients. Until the launch of the menswear line, they had only taken advantage of the Confederation's deposit services. The two outstanding loans were being repaid on schedule. Ann also noted that the current account balance was normally in the $20,000 range, but there had been a few times when the balance had reached a small overdraft situation.

EXHIBIT 1

SOPHISTICATED PETITES
Balance Sheet
As at December 31

	1988	1989
Assets		
Current Assets		
Cash	$ 20,778	$ 19,518
Inventory	120,022	268,494
Prepaids	2,750	2,750
Total Current Assets	143,550	290,762
Fixed Assets		
Furniture and Fixtures	2,000	5,000
Leasehold Improvements	59,546	105,540
Fixed Assets	61,546	110,540
Less Accumulated Depreciation	6,155	17,209
Net Fixed Assets	55,391	93,331
Total Assets	198,941	384,093
Liabilities		
Current Liabilities		
Accounts Payable & Accrued Liabilities	79,000	206,176
Current Share of L.T. Liabilities		7,800
Total Current Liabilities	79,000	213,976
Long Term Liabilities		
Due to Shareholders	19,000	19,000
Bank Loans		43,750
Less Current Portion		(7,800)
Total Long Term Liabilities	19,000	54,950
Total Liabilities	98,000	268,926
Shareholders' Equity		
Capital Stock		
Authorized: 1,000,000 common shares		
Issued & Fully Paid 7,500 common shares	75,000	75,000
Surplus	25,941	40,167
Total Shareholders' Equity	100,941	115,167
Total Liabilities & Shareholders' Equity	$198,941	$384,093

(continued)

EXHIBIT 1 (cont.)

SOPHISTICATED PETITES
Income Statement
For the Year Ending December 31

	1988	1989
Sales	$600,110	$1,300,518
Cost of Goods Sold		
Beginning Inventory		120,022
Purchases	479,130	965,840
Freight	958	1,959
	480,088	1,087,821
Ending Inventory	120,022	268,494
Cost of Goods	360,066	819,327
Gross Profit	240,044	481,191
Expenses		
Advertising	10,000	15,000
General & Admin. Expense	45,000	77,513
Bad Debts	600	1,301
Bank Charges & Interest	8,101	22,563
Depreciation	6,155	11,054
Loss Due to Theft	6,001	13,005
Owner's Salary		31,250
Promotion	18,003	39,016
Rent	72,050	141,038
Wages and Benefits	39,543	90,034
Total Expenses	205,456	441,773
Extraordinary Loss		20,450
Income before Taxes	34,588	18,968
Taxes	8,647	4,742
Net Income	$ 25,941	$ 14,226

(continued)

EXHIBIT 1 (cont.)

SOPHISTICATED PETITES
Notes to the Financial Statements
For the Year Ending December 31, 1989

1. Significant Accounting Policy
Depreciation is calculated by using the straight line method. Assets have an estimated life of 10 years.

2. Long Term Liabilities

	December 31/89	Current Portion
Bank Loans		
$25,000 repayable in 72 monthly payments of $350.00 plus interest at prime plus 1%	$20,800	$4,200
$18,750 Term Loan repayable in 60 monthly payments of $300.00 plus interest at prime plus 2.5%	$15,150	$3,600
Shareholders Loans		
no specified repayment schedule	$19,000	
Total	$54,950	$7,800

3. Comparative Figures
In January 1989, the company opened a second retail store in Masonville Mall.

4. Bank Interest and Charges
Bank charges generally averaged $600 per annum. Also included in this item are credit card discounts. Typically, these discounts would equal 2.5% of credit sales. 50% of total sales were made on credit card, 20% with cash, and 30% with cheque.

EXHIBIT 2

Dun & Bradstreet Canada
Key Business Ratios—1990 Edition

LINE OF BUSINESS (and number of concerns reporting) DOMAINE D'EXPLOITATION (et nombre d'entreprises étudiées)	Cost of Goods Sold Coût des marchandises vendues Percent Pourcent	Gross Margin Marge bénéficiaire brute Percent Pourcent	Current Assets to Current Debt Coefficient du fonds de roulement Times Fois	Profits on Sales Coefficient du profit sur les ventes Percent Pourcent	Profits on Equity Coefficient du profit sur l'avoir Percent Pourcent	Sales to Equity Coefficient des ventes sur l'avoir Times Fois	Collection Period Période de recouvrement Days Jours	Sales to Inventory Coefficient des ventes sur les stocks Times Fois	Fixed Assets Equity Coefficient des immobilisations sur l'avoir Percent Pourcent	Current Debt Equity Coefficient des exigibilités sur l'avoir Percent Pourcent	Total Debt Equity Coefficient de la dette totale sur l'avoir Percent Pourcent
ALL COMPANIES TOUTES LES COMPAGNIES*	606,562	66.9%	33.1%	1.0	7.1%	11.3%	1.6		7.6	65.0%	124.5%	223.1%
RETAIL TRADE COMMERCE DE DÉTAIL	90,373	74.3%	25.7%	1.4	2.5%	20.9%	8.2		6.4	66.4%	142.5%	217.2%
Auto Acc. & Parts Pièces et accessoires d'automobiles	3,136	70.9%	29.1%	1.5	2.2%	20.6%	9.3		5.4	61.3%	174.8%	257.6%
Book & Stat. Stores Livres et papeterie	1,221	62.6%	37.4%	1.3	2.3%	22.0%	9.4		5.0	90.3%	216.9%	304.7%
Clothing, Men's Vêtements pour hommes	1,914	58.9%	41.1%	1.6	3.5%	12.9%	3.7		4.8	25.7%	79.4%	115.5%
Clothing, Women's Vêtements pour femmes	3,706	57.0%	43.0%	1.5	1.9%	12.8%	6.6		5.6	74.4%	139.8%	206.4%
Dept. Stores Magasins à rayons	45	69.0%	31.0%	1.7	1.4%	5.0%	3.6		5.0	29.0%	74.0%	112.5%
Drug Stores Pharmacies	3,788	72.6%	27.4%	1.5	2.2%	20.7%	9.2		5.3	41.3%	161.6%	215.6%
Dry Goods Merceries	2,798	60.6%	39.4%	1.6	1.3%	9.8%	7.3		4.4	77.2%	144.1%	246.1%
Elec. Appliances Repair Appareils électriques, réparation	1,042	57.0%	43.0%	1.7	1.9%	11.9%	6.2		8.3	45.6%	126.7%	179.5%
Florists Fleuristes	1,405	46.4%	53.6%	1.2	2.6%	24.0%	9.2		10.6	115.4%	166.7%	270.9%

Food Stores Magasins d'alimentation	13,460	77.7%	22.3%	1.1	1.0%	10.8%	10.9		15.4	95.9%	113.1%	203.6%
Fuel Dealers Vendeurs d'huile	371	79.3%	20.7%	1.5	3.9%	21.1%	5.4		14.4	72.3%	84.6%	114.8%
Furniture & Appliance Ameublement et appareils ménagers	9,344	69.3%	30.7%	1.5	1.9%	13.0%	6.7		4.7	38.1%	150.8%	200.0%
Gas. Serv. Stns. Stations-service	7,214	81.4%	18.6%	1.2	1.4%	23.1%	16.3		27.3	145.9%	133.9%	277.6%
General Mdse. Marchandises générales	1,195	79.1%	20.9%	1.3	1.7%	13.6%	8.0		7.6	77.5%	117.1%	197.7%
Hardware Quincaillerie	3,371	68.5%	31.5%	1.8	2.6%	14.5%	5.7		4.2	47.1%	110.2%	177.9%
Jewellery Store Bijouterie	2,378	54.0%	46.0%	1.8	2.9%	8.3%	2.9		2.2	25.1%	105.0%	168.0%
Motor Veh. Dealers Concessionnaires automobiles	6,405	88.0%	12.0%	1.2	-0.7%	-11.7%	16.9		5.5	125.5%	337.6%	466.9%
Motor Vehicle Repairs Réparation des véhicules	9,179	58.8%	41.2%	1.3	2.9%	21.6%	7.4		11.0	109.1%	123.7%	221.1%
Shoe Stores Magasins de chaussures	1,333	57.1%	42.9%	1.5	1.8%	8.1%	4.6		3.5	44.3%	112.8%	139.5%
Tobacconists Tabagies	398	61.0%	39.0%	2.1	-2.0%	-21.4%	10.6		8.3	162.1%	103.8%	1668.6%
Variety Stores Magasins d'articles variés	1,008	71.9%	28.1%	1.6	1.8%	12.1%	6.9		4.9	47.1%	121.8%	158.2%
WHOLESALE TRADE COMMERCE DE GROS	53,026	81.8%	18.2%	1.3	1.9%	14.0%	7.3	39	7.4	39.9%	171.0%	219.0%
App. & Dry Goods Mercerie et habillement	2,608	79.6%	20.4%	1.4	2.0%	15.3%	7.6	49	6.2	23.3%	189.6%	236.4%
Coal & Coke Charbon et coke	19	-103.8%	203.8%	2.2	-0.2%	1.2%	(4.8)	-38	(4.6)	1.2%	80.2%	77.9%
Drug & Toilet Prep. Pharmacie et produits de beauté	770	79.7%	20.3%	1.5	2.0%	15.4%	7.9	45	7.4	30.1%	159.6%	190.2%
Food Alimentation	4,211	87.3%	12.7%	1.3	1.9%	21.4%	11.4	20	16.6	40.4%	137.1%	183.7%
Furn. & Furnishings Meubles et ameublement	1,083	76.5%	23.5%	1.6	1.9%	14.2%	7.5	48	5.8	22.3%	162.0%	205.3%

EXHIBIT 3

Personal Statement of Net Worth—The Wongs

Assets		Liabilities and Equity	
Cash	$5,450	Confederation Car Loan[a]	$4,799
Value of Company	115,000	Loan from Chen Family	25,000
Shareholder's Loan	19,000	Loan from Wong Family	19,000
Nissan '87 Micra	5,500	Student Loans[b]	9,841
Jewellery & Collectibles	6,250		
Total Assets	$151,200	Subtotal	58,640
		Surplus	92,560
		Total Liabilities & Equity	$151,200

[a]Monthly payments of $140.98
[b]Monthly payments of $228.23

7

ATLANTIC LUMBER TRADERS

On April 20, 1989, Lynn Thomas put down the phone and looked at the notes before her. Gail Hall, one of the owners of Atlantic Lumber Traders, had just given Lynn the final details she needed. As credit assistant to Harry Sarson of the Maritime Bank in Saint John, New Brunswick, Lynn had been asked to review the file of Atlantic Lumber Traders. Her job was to decide if Gail Hall's explanation of what had gone wrong was plausible, then to predict risks to the bank under various projections of the company's future. Finally, Lynn was to make recommendations for action by the bank. In the worst instance, if a turnaround was not possible, it was Lynn Thomas's job to recommend the best course for the orderly wind-up of Atlantic Lumber Traders.

The file indicated that Atlantic Lumber Traders had been established in 1983 in Saint John to wholesale lumber in the Atlantic provinces. Major shareholders were brother and sister Edward and Gail Hall, members of a wealthy and respected family with a long entrepreneurial history in New Brunswick.

After four years of profitable operations, the company showed an operating loss of $219,666 and a net loss of $174,216 on sales of $17 million for the year

This case was prepared by Gordon S. Roberts, Bank of Montreal Professor of Finance and Linda P. Hendry, Finance Lecturer at Dalhousie University for the Atlantic Entrepreneurial Institute as a basis for classroom discussion and is not meant to illustrate either effective or ineffective management. Some elements of this case have been disguised.

ending December 31, 1988. This loss was an urgent concern to the Halls and to the Maritime Bank which had extended the company a $1.3 million revolving line of credit (at prime plus 1%).

When the third quarter results were in, Gail Hall felt she needed to personally take charge of the company. In October of 1988 she therefore put aside her lucrative law practice (she had netted $140,000 in 1988) to devote her full attention to the company. She first had to identify its main problems, then take corrective action.

COMPANY HISTORY

Edward and Gail Hall, both lawyers in their mid-thirties, had set up Atlantic Lumber Traders in 1983 to wholesale lumber. Atlantic Lumber Traders had sales territories in the four Atlantic Provinces, Quebec, and Ontario and, secondarily, in the United States. Approximately 80% of sales were generated in the Atlantic Provinces, 19% in Quebec and Ontario, and 1% in the United States. Shares were owned by Edward and Gail, and also by David Lawson, who had managed the company until October 1988 (see Exhibit 1 for balance sheet). At that time he was released and Edward and Gail had purchased his shares for one dollar. Lawson was blamed for the company's poor performance in late 1987 and 1988. The Halls, however, admitted they should have been more involved.

With the exception of 1988, the operation had enjoyed significant sales increases from $3 million for the first year of operation (1984), to $19 million for fiscal 1987 (Exhibit 2). Net income had reached a high of $128,000 (after a $48,000 loss from a rental operation). The rental operation consisted of two sixteen-unit apartment buildings acquired by the company in 1987. The rental operation loss was intended to offset income from the lumber operation. During 1988, due in part to the poor performance of Atlantic Lumber Traders, the rental property was sold (at book value) to another company operated by the Halls. According to Gail, the rental operation now broke even because she stepped in, did some refurbishing, changed property managers and thus increased occupancy.

The lumber operation was straightforward. At the end of 1988, Atlantic Lumber Traders had a sales team of four—three full-time traders and a general manager who did some selling—to wholesale lumber to a customer base of 50–100 large retailers. The sales staff were paid a commission of 1.8% and the mark-up ranged between 4.5% and 5.5%. No inventory for the bulk of sales was required, as orders were placed with the mills as received and wood was transported from the mill directly to the purchaser. Atlantic Lumber Traders had a small administrative staff of two to three people to handle accounting. Terms with most mills were net 10 days, with an average collection period on receivables of 22 days in 1987 (37 days for the industry, see Exhibit 3). The company thus needed to finance about 40 days' sales on average, which required a large capital base. A small inventory of uncommon lengths was maintained for special orders; approximate inventory value was $200,000.

During 1988, David Lawson had speculated on purchases both for resale and inventory, which at one point exceeded $600,000. In making these purchases, for which there was no firm order, Lawson had attempted to take advantage of swings in market prices.

During 1987 and 1988 the number of employees had reached a high of eleven, with the office staff of six exceeding the sales force of five. To satisfy customers, Lawson had sold lumber in irregular lots, rather than follow the industry practice of requiring customers to buy full lots. As a result, the company was left with a considerable stock of less popular lengths, which required a write-down in inventory once this practice was discovered.

According to Gail Hall, these practices ended when she took over the day-to-day operation of the company. Her efforts produced a small profit of $16,000 for the first quarter of 1989. According to her, this showed that the company had turned around because the first quarter of the year was traditionally the company's worst.

THE PRINCIPALS IN THE COMPANY

Although Atlantic Lumber Traders was founded in 1983, the Hall family had been involved in the wood/lumber industry for more than half a century. Hall Investments Ltd., a holding company set up in 1984 by Edward and Gail, had two wholly owned subsidiaries, one in transportation and the other in a lumber-related business. The companies dealt with all the major banks. The Halls felt they knew the lumber industry, and that they had the required contacts to generate substantial sales. Edward Hall had never taken an active role in the business and Gail agreed she neglected it in favour of her law practice. Gail appeared knowledgeable and was prepared to assist in a sales effort if necessary.

Because the Halls were very influential in the New Brunswick marketplace, Lynn knew that her boss, Harry Sarson, wished to maintain their goodwill. However, he also wanted to ensure the safety of the bank's investment.

THE BANKER'S RISK ASSESSMENT OF THE COMPANY IN APRIL 1989

Lynn Thomas identified four areas where the company significantly risked the bank's capital: (1) operating losses sustained to date; (2) debt to equity at 17:1 for year-end 1988, down to 4:1 when subordinated loans[1] and liquid security were included for the first quarter of 1989; (3) competition; and (4) inability to sustain any further losses.

According to Lynn, there were mitigating circumstances for each risk factor. The improvement in performance since year-end 1988 seemed to indicate that problem areas had been identified and corrected. In-house financial statements were monitored closely by Gail Hall. Lynn did not consider the Canada–US Free Trade

---

[1]Subordinate to the bank debt. Also called a postponement of shareholder's claims. In this case the Halls' had injected $200,000 (a subordinated shareholders' loan) into the company since year-end 1988.

Agreement a significant risk; Gail assured her it would have little impact on the 1% of company sales to the US.

Personal guarantees in the amount of $316,000 from the Halls partly offset the debt to equity position.

Atlantic Lumber Traders had an established client base; the Hall name had been synonymous with lumber for over fifty years. Lynn felt that reluctance to tarnish the Hall family name would prompt Gail to cooperate with the bank. Gail had indicated that to forestall losses, she would close down operations if there was any sign of a downturn.

ECONOMIC FORECAST

As part of her background analysis of the business, Lynn had reviewed the economic forecast prepared by the bank's Economics Department in early 1989. The forecast surveyed leading economic indicators, and showed that the economy would begin to slow down during the second quarter. The bank's economists believed that interest rates would remain high as long as John Crow, Governor of the Bank of Canada, tried to reduce inflation.

The economic report argued that the Canadian dollar was overvalued relative to the US dollar as a result of high interest rates, and the unusually wide spread in interest rates between the two currencies. The Canadian dollar was expected to fall to around 81 cents US by the end of 1989.

An economic slowdown was also forecast for the Atlantic region. This would have a negative effect on Atlantic Lumber Traders' sales. The Goods and Services Tax (GST) was to come into effect in January 1991, and, because of additional record keeping costs, was expected to have a significant impact on this low margin industry.

INDUSTRY SCAN

Lumber traders' customers were usually independent supply stores, general contractors working on large projects (cutting out the middleman), or large end users such as mobile home manufacturers.

Without the service that a lumber trader provided, the customer (wholesaler or retailer) would have to go through a time consuming process to purchase lumber. Wholesalers and retailers avoided the time necessary to purchase directly from the sawmill or to purchase partial loads by giving up a percentage of gross margin (usually 5% to 6%) to have the purchasing done by lumber traders.

Lumber traders needed experience to buy at low cost and to know which sawmills were producing given species, dimensions and grades of lumber at any given time. It was also important to know the reputation for quality and reliability of each mill. The trader also had to arrange for transportation of lumber from the mill to its destination. If a purchaser did not want a full load, as was often the case, the cost of transporting a partial load could make the order uneconomical. Low cost was a critical factor in the lumber business because it operated on low margins.

There were risks inherent in the lumber trading business; the most significant was bad debts. The trader was responsible for paying the mill regardless of whether the customer paid on time, late or not at all. If the customer did not pay, the resulting loss could bankrupt the trader. The trader also had the responsibility to deliver the stated quantity and quality of product on time. Buying off-grade lumber or having late deliveries could hurt customer relations and affect receivables collection.

The Atlantic provinces constituted the major market of Atlantic Lumber Traders; this market consumed approximately 1.2 billion board feet of lumber per year. The company's market share was about 5% in a fiercely competitive industry where they competed with other well-established families and interests such as the Irvings, another influential New Brunswick family. Atlantic Lumber Traders had to recover quickly if they were to maintain their competitive position.

Environmental factors could negatively affect the supply of lumber. Spruce budworm damage and the controversial forest spraying program had hurt the public image of the forestry industry and the profits of individual companies. Also, sawmills recognized the need to control pollution and the costs of doing so would be passed on to customers. This would put additional pressure on lumber traders' margins, and might cause some customers to deal directly with mills to reduce costs.

THE SITUATION IN APRIL 1989

Since year-end 1988 the Halls had injected an additional $200,000 into Atlantic Lumber Traders and the bank had reduced the available line of credit from $1.3 to $1 million. The availability of funds under the operating line of credit was subject to a maximum of 75% of the bank's valuation of assigned accounts receivable after deducting receivables 60 days or more past due, plus 50% of the bank's valuation of free and clear assigned inventory to a maximum value of $125,000. The bank asked for, and received, a Section 178 lien over inventory in March 1989. The lien effectively meant that if the company failed, the goods covered by the lien could be liquidated only against the debt owed by the company to the bank, and not to other creditors. The bank also had an assignment of book debts (accounts receivable).

Action taken by Gail Hall included reducing staff from eleven to six. The inefficient in-house accounting system was replaced by a simple, effective computer program. Sales personnel were put on commission only and lost their commission on accounts unpaid after 60 days. Inventory levels were cut from the $500,000–$850,000 range to below $150,000. According to Gail, these changes went a long way toward reestablishing profitability.

With its reduced staff, the company expected to sell about $10 million of lumber in 1989, compared to $16.9 million in 1988. A gross margin of 5% was expected for 1989. Based on past performance, on the company's budget for 1989 and on industry benchmarks, Lynn projected variable costs for a wholesale lumber company at about 3% of sales. She also estimated that fixed costs for the company were between $14,000 and $15,000 per month. She used her estimates to calculate breakeven sales levels and then prepared a spreadsheet to determine the combined effect (on breakeven sales and net income) of changing each of her estimates in turn—recalculating with gross margin, variable costs, and fixed costs above and below the expected values.

THE ALTERNATIVES FOR MANAGEMENT AND THE BANK

At their last meeting, Gail had given Lynn a proposal. Based on the improvements since year end, Gail hoped to negotiate an increase in the line of credit from $1 million to $1.4 million. This would allow for increased sales to about $14.5 million rather than the $10 million expected. Based on historical sales and the improvements in the first quarter, Gail felt this figure more clearly reflected the ability of the company. According to Gail, there was space available in the office for another trader, and the administrative capacity to support the added business. She pointed out that past history had shown the market could support the higher sales. Therefore, if the main constraint of working capital was overcome, Gail felt that Atlantic Lumber Traders was a viable operation.

A more conservative plan, already in the back of Lynn's mind, consisted of two parts: (1) increase the interest rate[2] by 1% (cost to the company $10,000 per year) to cover additional monitoring costs, and (2) eliminate the margin available on inventory (50% up to $125,000). Besides covering the additional costs incurred in monitoring the account, this plan would reduce the bank's exposure. The lost margin on inventory would have a direct effect on the sales potential for Atlantic Lumber Traders.

Lynn knew that at worst she could recommend that the Halls close down their operations in an orderly fashion, one sales territory at a time, so that they and the bank would recover their investments.

FINAL PREPARATIONS

Lynn took a mouthful of coffee and turned to her computer to prepare the report Harry needed before tomorrow morning's meeting with Gail Hall. She knew that since Gail Hall's efforts had resulted in some improvement in company performance in the first quarter of 1989, and Gail had cooperated with the bank in its review, calling the loan was not an option at this point.

---

[2]The bank prime rate on April 20, 1989 was 13.50%.

EXHIBIT 1

ATLANTIC LUMBER TRADERS
Balance Sheet
December 31
($000s)

	1985[a]	1986[b]	1987[b]	1988[b]
Assets				
Current				
Cash	$ 0	$ 0	$ 0	$ 0
Trade Receivables (Net)	645	938	1,174	688
Other Receivables (Net)	2	39	79	101
Inventory	99	184	570	262
Prepaid Expenses	0	0	12	5
Due from Shareholders	0	33	0	0
Income Tax Refund	0	0	1	71
Total Current Assets	746	1,194	1,836	1,127
Fixed Assets				
Land & Buildings	0	0	1,150	0
Equipment & Machinery	6	6	58	19
Leasehold Improvements	9	9	10	13
Accumulated Depreciation	(4)	(6)	(69)	(20)
Total Fixed Assets	11	9	1,149	12
Other Assets				
Intangible Assets	18	0	0	0
Investments in/Due from	0	60	180	0
Deferred Gtee Charges	0	0	11	0
Notes Receivable	0	0	0	328
Total Other Assets	18	60	191	328
Total Assets	$ 775	$1,263	$3,176	$1,467
Liabilities & Shareholders' Equity				
Current Liabilities				
Bank	$ 471	$ 668	$ 985	$ 886
Trade Payables	207	425	933	467
Income Tax Payable	14	11	0	0
Current Portion LTD	12	12	44	0
Total Current Liabilities	704	1,116	1,962	1,353
Long Term Liabilities				
Bank LTD	29	17	501	0
Other LTD to related Co. 1	0	0	225	0
Other LTD to related Co. 2	0	0	0	0
Due to Shareholders[c]	0	0	30	30
Total LT Liabilities	29	17	956	30
Total Liabilities	733	1,133	2,918	1,383

(continued)

EXHIBIT 1 (cont.)

	1985ᵃ	1986ᵇ	1987ᵇ	1988ᵇ
Shareholders' Equity				
Common Shares	1	1	1	1
Retained Earnings	41	129	257	83
Total Shareholders' Equity	42	130	258	84
Total Liabilities & Shareholders' Equity	$ 775	$1,263	$3,176	$1,467

ᵃUnaudited.
ᵇAudited.
ᶜDeferred.
Source: Company records and bank files.

EXHIBIT 2

ATLANTIC LUMBER TRADERS
Income Statement
Years Ended December 31
($000s)

	1985ᵃ	1986ᵇ	1987ᵇ	1988ᵇ
Sales	$7,507	$12,540	$19,049	$16,853
Cost of Goods Sold	7,148	11,936	18,121	16,095
Gross Profit	359	604	928	758
Operating Expenses				
Depreciation	2	2	4	9
Bad Debt Expense	12	3	2	16
Interest Expense	31	54	82	130
Salaries	102	237	419	489
Telephone	42	60	94	100
Travel	25	46	80	66
Rent	12	16	18	20
Start-up Costs (Amortization)	18	0	0	0
Otherᶜ	29	76	85	46
Total Operating Expenses	273	494	784	876
Operating Income (Loss)	86	110	144	(118)
Other Income (Expenses)				
Rental Division Loss	0	0	(48)	(102)
Affiliated Company	0	0	54	22
Miscellaneous	4	0	0	0
Income (Loss) Before Tax	90	110	150	(198)
Income Taxes (Recovery)	14	22	32	(46)
Extraordinary Gain (Loss)	0	0	10	(22)
Net Income (Loss)	$ 76	$ 88	$ 128	$ (174)

(continued)

EXHIBIT 2 (cont.)

	1985[a]	1986[b]	1987[b]	1988[b]
Opening Retained Earnings	(35)	41	129	257
Closing Retained Earnings	$ 41	$ 129	$ 257	$ 83

FINANCIAL STATEMENT COMMENTS: Sales down $2,200M from previous year due to internal management problems and restructuring. Loss incurred ($174M), after Income Tax recovery ($46M) and extraordinary loss on sale of investment in associated company ($22M). This loss attributed to drop in gross margin of 0.4% ($75M) due to inefficient purchasing by previous manager, i.e., inventory purchased on speculation, then disposed at less than normal margin. This area now under control of owners, who now manage. Total expenses up 1.1% ($185M) due to excessive spending on non-essential items (expense accounts, administration staff, etc.). Since year end, five staff released and all expense items reduced to essential (sales do not seem to have suffered to date).

[a]Unaudited.
[b]Audited.
[c]Selling, general and administrative expenses.
Source: Company records and bank files.

EXHIBIT 3

Selected Industry Ratios

	INDUSTRY RATIOS, 1987
Liquidity	
Current Ratio	1.50
Quick Ratio	0.70
Average Collection Period	36.80
Average Payment Period	10.55
Sales/Working Capital	14.90
Leverage Ratios	
Debt to Equity	2.10
Debt to Tangible Net Worth	2.10
Net Fixed Assets/TNW	0.51
Coverage Ratios	
EBIT/Interest	2.50
Profitability Ratios (%)	
Gross Profit/Sales	5.00
Gross Cash Profit/Sales	3.00
Profit Pre-Tax/Sales	2.58
Net Profit/Sales	2.30
Profit Pre-Tax/Total Assets	5.30

Source: Bank files.

8

COLUMBIA RIVER PULP COMPANY INC.— RECAPITALIZATION

In early March 1988, Derek Cathcart, Corporate Finance Manager in the Toronto–Dominion (TD) Bank's Forest Products Group, was reviewing a refinancing request for $200MM from the Columbia River Pulp Company (CRP). In addition, CRP had requested a $25MM operating facility. CRP owns and operates a world class kraft market pulp mill located in Longview, Washington.

BACKGROUND ON THE COMPANY

CRP was a wholly owned subsidiary of Whitney & Zeigler Inc. (W&Z). W&Z and its affiliated companies owned and operated North American pulp mills. Through its affiliate, W&Z operated an engineering and consulting group specializing in turnkey projects for pulp, paper and sawmill production complexes. The W&Z organization had constructed approximately thirty mill projects in ten countries throughout North and South America, Europe, and Asia.

Then a small trading firm, W&Z was purchased during the second World War by British immigrant Frank Tharle. When Frank died in 1976, ownership was passed

This case was prepared by Patrick Brady under the supervision of Professor Robert W. White for the sole purpose of providing material for class discussion at the Western Business School. Certain names and other identifying information may have been disguised to protect confidentiality. It is not intended to illustrate either effective or ineffective handling of a managerial situation. Any reproduction, in any form, of the material in this case is prohibited except with the written consent of the School.

The writers of the case would like to acknowledge the assistance of Derek Cathcart, Toronto–Dominion Bank.

Copyright 1990 © The University of Western Ontario.

to the sons, Arthur and Andrew; Andrew Tharle, CRP Chairman of the Board, impressed Cathcart with his energy, principles and intelligence. Andrew Tharle had been with W&Z for 25 years.

In 1978, a group of large U.S. insurance companies financed the capital leasing costs for W&Z's new pulp mill subsidiary, CRP. CRP began production of its bleached kraft market pulp in 1980 after a two year construction period.

In March 1988, W&Z was ready to announce a $320MM joint venture to build and operate a newsprint facility at the CRP location. This venture would be managed independently from CRP.

KRAFT MARKET PULP INDUSTRY

Kraft market pulp was a principal input in the manufacturing of high quality paper products, including writing paper and envelopes, boxboard and tissue. The "kraft" process involved cooking or "digesting" wood chips in a chemical solution at high temperature and pressure. The resulting pulp was then bleached.

Kraft market pulp producers, such as CRP, sold their output on the open market, as compared to integrated producers who shipped output to affiliated paper mills. The largest U.S. kraft market pulp producers were Weyerhaeuser, Georgia-Pacific, and International Paper. In the U.S. and Japan, the production of paper and paperboard is approximately 90 percent integrated in to pulp supply by affiliated companies. In Europe, however, paper mills were basically non-integrated in to pulp. As a result, Western Europe continued to be the largest market for kraft market pulp.

Kraft market pulp was a global commodity with price being a function of economic cycles, industry capacity, the amount of output "dumped" on the market by integrated producers, and foreign exchange rates. Price levels for kraft market pulp were extremely volatile and caused dramatic swings in the earnings and cash flow of industry participants.

In 1986 the world market was over 30MM metric tonnes (mts), or $12 billion. The North American and Scandinavian mills (the Norscan region) supplied about 18MM mts. In 1987 U.S. shipment estimates totalled 6.3MM mts. At the end of 1987, U.S. exports had grown by almost 44 percent since the beginning of 1985. In 1987, exports accounted for 59 percent of total U.S. shipments (Exhibit 1).

The escalation of the U.S. dollar during 1984–85 temporarily jeopardized the historically low cost position of U.S. kraft market pulp producers at a time of oversupply of kraft market pulp. Consequently, kraft market pulp prices hit a 10-year low of $390 per tonne in 1985. However, the U.S. dollar then declined and restored the U.S. producers to a low cost position. Pulp customers in Europe and Japan were paying less in their local currencies for U.S. kraft market pulp in 1987 than during 1984 and early 1985 (Exhibit 2).

In the U.S., after the 1985 recession, the rise in demand for kraft market pulp translated into appreciable price increases. This wave of price increases intensified with additional supply pressures from increased export demand. Kraft market pulp prices were up every quarter between late 1985 and early 1988. U.S. kraft pulp prices for 1988 were estimated to be $760 per mts (Table 1).

TABLE 1
Kraft Market Pulp Prices
(US$ per metric tonne)

	1983	1984	1985	1986	1987	1988e	1989e
Year-End Price	$450	$510	$390	$500	$610	$760	$745

U.S. production grew at an average rate of 6.6 percent over the last 5 years. Overall, U.S. producers operated at higher rates of capacity in 1986 and 1987 as compared to the Norscan region overall (Exhibit 3). The industry had been cautious to add capacity during the current cycle because of the huge costs associated with building new mills. The only announced capacity were two mills being built in Canada. The usual elapsed period between the announcement of a pulp mill and its operational start-up is 3 to 4 years. Companies had skirted high start up costs through mergers and acquisitions (M&As). Virtually every major paper company had been involved in merger and acquisition activity since 1985.

World capacity for kraft market pulp was expected to grow 0.9 percent in 1988. Brazil and North America appeared to be the likely candidates for additional pulp capacity in the future. Many parts of the world lacked timber resources and would continue to depend, perhaps increasingly so, on purchased pulp. These areas included several countries, such as Japan and China, who exhibited a relatively rapid growth rate in paper and paperboard consumption.

MARKETING

CRP estimated that the ultimate products in which its pulp was used were divided evenly between fine paper and tissues. Output from the mill was sold to paper products manufacturers in the U.S., Mexico, Europe and Japan.

By 1987, over 50 percent of CRP's sales were to North American customers (Exhibit 4). The majority of the U.S. tonnage was sold to Fortune 500 companies. CRP estimated that sales to Japanese customers would continue to account for one-third of its sales. In Europe, when the dollar was extremely strong CRP found it difficult to compete against the Scandinavians. Nevertheless, CRP maintained a core of West German customers as well as a relatively stable presence in Italy. Essentially all of CRP's output was sold to long term customers.

CRP marketed its pulp output exclusively through a sister company in Vancouver, Canada, Fraser Pulp Sales Ltd. (FPS). FPS also marketed the entire output of CRP's sister company, West Fraser Pulp & Paper Co. (British Columbia), and other third party pulp. FPS was one of the largest marketers in terms of volume and overall market coverage in the world.

Kraft market pulp prices included transportation to the customer. CRP's mill site was well situated to control freight costs by utilizing various modes of transportation including rail, trucking or shipping. Furthermore, FPS was the largest single supplier of foreign pulps to Japan, and a large exporter to Europe, thereby gaining advantageous freight arrangements.

PRODUCTION

In April 1987, a major consulting firm to the forest products industry estimated the CRP mill replacement value at $400MM, based on the depreciated value of a 10 year old facility. (A new mill would cost approximately $800MM.) The mill far exceeded 1987 environmental standards. CRP had invested heavily in emerging technology, including high pressure boilers. In August 1985, these boilers required extensive repairs, removing them from full production for 2½ years. CRP spent $37MM on repairs as well as incurring cash flow losses from reduced production efficiency and lost sales. By 1988, the boilers were repaired and CRP's annual capacity was rated at 385,000 mts.

From 1989–92, CRP planned for $20MM capital expenditures to increase output. These "optimization" expenditures were expected to increase annual production by 15,000 mts in fiscal year 1991 and reach the full impact of 25,000 mts per year by fiscal 1992 (see Table 2). The mill site was also chosen for its proximity to available wood and water supply. The company owned no timberlands. The timberlands were owned by W&Z. Fibre was supplied by 30–35 local dealers with no single supplier accounting for more than 8 percent of CRP's needs. Supplier relationships were positive. CRP was one of the few mills in the industry which operated on both hardwood and softwood fibre. This gave CRP flexibility to respond to changing market demands and wood costs.

Of all the variable costs, those for pulpwood, energy, chemicals and labour played a critical role. The forest products group at TD conducted a detailed analysis of the CRP operation, and concluded that relative to its competitors (domestic and foreign), CRP was indeed a low cost producer of kraft market pulp. Estimates of CRP's average variable costs for fiscal year 1988 were $263.00 per metric tonne produced. The mill operated with a stable non-union labour force and had virtually no turnover. Three previous attempts by unions to organize within the mill had failed.

TABLE 2
CRP's Production History

FISCAL YEARS ENDING MARCH 31	METRIC TONNES PRODUCED TOTAL
1981	304,810
1982	291,811
1983	313,768
1984	349,565
1985	344,952
1986	311,146
1987	355,666
1988 (estimated)	382,516

FINANCIAL PERFORMANCE

CRP's operating income and cash flows are shown in Exhibit 5. CRP's income statements for 1982–87 are shown in Exhibit 6. CRP had been hard hit by the significant downturn in pulp prices. From 1982–86, CRP's cumulative operating losses totalled $39.1MM. In fiscal 1983, CRP defaulted on the interest and principal payments required under the capital lease loans held by the insurance companies.

In December 1984, CRP negotiated a deferral of certain capital lease obligations and interest thereon. CRP also obtained a $15MM bank line of credit which expired on December 31, 1988. The agreement provided for interest at 120 percent of the prime rate. The loan was collateralized by inventory and certain accounts receivable and was guaranteed by W&Z. Furthermore, W&Z agreed to defer receipt of its intercompany indebtedness from CRP until the deferred capital lease obligations were paid in full. Additionally, W&Z committed to selling its investment in CRP. This action stalled the insurance companies from accelerating their loans. Consequently, all the debt was classified as a current liability. However, until late 1987 CRP continued to default on its loan payments. The following details (Table 3) illustrate the major components of CRP's current and long-term liabilities as at March 31, 1987:

TABLE 3
Current and Long-Term Liabilities
(US$ millions)

9.25% Capital Lease	29.165
Deferred Interest	119.796
Total Lease Obligations	340.706
Bank Loan	5.686
8% Note Due to an Affiliate	6.069
W&Z Intercompany Debt	9.234
Deferred Compensation[a]	8.867
Total	370.562
Less Debt—Current	(37.126)
Total Long Term Debt	333.436

[a]The deferred compensation is with a former W&Z officer, minimum payment is $250,000.

As of February 1988, CRP had paid $43.5MM of the outstanding $340.7MM principal and deferred interest payments owed to the insurance companies. CRP's deferral of interest payments were as follows:

TABLE 4
Deferred Interest Payments
(Years Ended March 31, in Millions US$)

	1982	1983	1984	1985	1986	1987
Interest Deferred	0.0	12.1	23.8	13.9	33.7	38.2

Georgia-Pacific declined to purchase CRP due to their concerns over whether the labour force would work for them. In fiscal 1987, W&Z's management decided to discontinue seeking a buyer for CRP. They convinced the insurance companies to restructure certain callable long-term obligations, and to defer debt acceleration through April 15, 1988. The restructuring was based on a proposed subordination agreement between CRP and an intermediary party who was willing to buy a portion of CRP's capital lease and deferred interest payment obligations. The portion would amount to $97.2MM, taken from CRP's $297.2MM outstanding debt to the insurance companies as at the end of February 1988. The proposed agreement was contingent on CRP's ability to refinance $200MM of the debt externally. If CRP succeeded with the refinancing, CRP would then subordinate the $97.2MM intermediary party debt. CRP's balance sheets for the years ending March 31, 1982–87 are shown in Exhibit 7.

CRP provided Derek Cathcart with their financial projections for 1989–95 (Exhibit 8). Note that the tax loss carry forwards were no longer available. Tonnage sold included the production optimization effect of planned capital expenditures. Kraft market pulp prices were CRP's forecasted values. The projections assumed a $200MM floating rate term loan with a current rate of 11 percent and mandatory prepayments of 50 percent of net cash flow from operations. Other long-term debt obligations included the intermediary party's subordinated debt of $97.2MM at 11.5 percent (interest and principal payments are deferred for 12 years, interest payments are capitalized) and the unsecured debt of $11MM at 8 percent. Production variable costs were assumed to increase at a rate of 4 percent annually.

THE DECISION

The insurance companies were very nervous about the quality of their capital lease loans and by 1988 they wanted out of the CRP deal. The principals of W&Z had invested significant sums of money outside the forest products area and suffered enormous losses; consequently they were unable to invest additional equity in CRP. Derek had to decide whether to recommend that the TD extend credit to CRP. Furthermore, if he recommended that credit be extended to CRP, Derek must decide on how to structure a refinancing loan package.

TD was one of two non-regional banks in North America that was accorded an AAA rating by Moody's Investor Service. TD's emphasis was on markets in North America, with 92 percent of its major assets located in Canada and the U.S. Furthermore, TD's focus in the U.S. was on corporate banking. In fact, their U.S. corporate lending business had grown as large as their Canadian counterpart. TD was one of the leading banks in providing financing to the forest products industry in a global context. TD had led 7 of the last 12 major project financing deals in the forest products industry.

Exhibit 9 shows the historical U.S. money market rates versus loan rates from 1970 to early 1988. LIBOR[1] rates were usually between CD[2] and Prime[3] Loan rates.[4] In the first quarter of 1988, U.S. Prime was hovering near the 8.35 percent level.

To explore the possibilities of syndicating a loan, [5] Derek solicited the advice of Michael Mueller, Senior Manager of TD's New York loan syndication department. After several years of lethargic activity, world syndicated loan volume had increased. In 1988, first quarter bank syndicated loans were US$116 billion versus US$71 billion in the first quarter of 1987. Leveraged buyouts, acquisition and project financing had dominated the market for syndicated financing in the U.S. TD's syndicated loan activity had actually dropped since 1985. In 1987, TD made 6 loans totalling US$670.42MM versus 39 loans totalling US$4,977.6MM made in 1985. Michael Mueller felt that the market would be receptive to US$225MM loan if the terms and conditions were commensurate with risks.

A variant of the traditional syndicated loan is the "bought deal." (In a bought deal, a bank[6] underwrites the entire loan[7] and then sells part or all of it off through private placement or short-form prospectus as per a syndicated loan. The selling of loans enables the bank to expand its aggregate financing to any individual customer. The amount of any single loan allowed on a Canadian chartered bank's book is limited to 50 percent of their equity base.) TD's equity position in early 1988, was over CA$3 billion. It also permitted the bank to diversify credit risk.[8] The lead bank must be willing to take the risk of giving the borrower a firm price, as much as a month before the bank could sell the issue in the secondary market. By dealing with one bank the borrower could speed up the lending process considerably.

The market for bought deals in the U.S. exploded to about US$240 billion by first quarter 1988, compared with US$26.7 billion in 1983. U.S. banks tended to sell off most of their loans once a deal has been struck, but Canadian banks preferred to keep a larger share, at least 20 percent, of the loans that they eventually put on the selling block. TD's philosophy was to hold the largest piece of the loan when they were the lead bank. TD had been Canada's most active player in the bought deal market.

---

[1]LIBOR is the acronym for London Interbank Offered Rate and represents a series of borrowing rates available in London by major banks from around the world. LIBORs may be quoted in various currencies and for different time periods. LIBOR is a base rate for comparison in most financial markets for short term rates.

[2]CDs, certificates of deposit, are non-redeemable, registered, transferable, interest bearing notes.

[3]Rate at which commercial banks lend to their most favoured customers.

[4]In the U.S., typical LIBOR loan spreads range from 50 basis points (bps) for high quality corporate revolving credit, to 150–250 bps for leveraged buyout (LBO) financing. Loan spreads for CDs are typically 10–15 bps higher than LIBOR loan spreads and Prime loan spreads can be as much as 50 bps lower than LIBOR loan spreads.

[5]Underwriting fees for a high quality loan are as low as 25 bps and for lower quality loans are as high as 200 bps.

[6]There may be more than one bank involved.

[7]The total size of a syndicated loan usually runs to hundreds of millions of dollars. A typical minimum level of participation in a syndicated loan for any one bank is US$25 million.

[8]Loan syndication and sales also have an impact on how a bank's revenues are generated, that is, revenues are transformed to a fee based structure.

EXHIBIT 1

Paper Grade Market Pulp
U.S. Exports
(metric tonnes, in thousands)

YEAR	U.S. EXPORTS	PERCENT CHANGE	PERCENT OF U.S. SHIPMENTS
1983	2,470	+10.3	52
1984	2,559	+ 3.6	52
1985	2,828	+10.5	55
1986	3,404	+20.4	58
1987	3,671	+ 7.8	59
1988[a]	3,777	+ 2.9	59

[a]Two months annualized.

Paper Grade Market Pulp
U.S. Exports by Region
(nine months 1987, metric tonnes, in thousands)

	1987	PERCENT
U.S. Shipments to:		
Western Europe	1,155	25
Japan	705	11
Other (Including Nordic)	1,411	23
Total Exports	3,671	59
Domestic Market	2,556	41
Total U.S. Shipment	6,227	100

EXHIBIT 2

Market Pulp Price Indexed to Local Currency
(Q4 1979 = 100)

	MAJOR EXPORTING COUNTRIES			MAJOR IMPORTING COUNTRIES				
	USA	CANADA	SWEDEN	ITALY	FRANCE	FED. REP. GERMANY	U.K.	JAPAN
1984								
Q1	104	111	198	211	209	160	157	101
Q2	117	129	223	240	236	180	181	113
Q3	115	129	230	253	249	190	192	118
Q4	111	124	229	255	251	192	197	114
Year	112	123	220	240	236	181	182	112
1985								
Q1	98	113	216	241	235	180	189	106
Q2	92	108	196	222	210	162	159	97
Q3	90	104	179	207	188	145	141	90
Q4	87	102	162	185	166	127	131	75
Year	92	107	188	214	200	154	155	92

(continued)

EXHIBIT 2 (cont.)

| | MAJOR EXPORTING COUNTRIES | | | MAJOR IMPORTING COUNTRIES | | | | |
	USA	CANADA	SWEDEN	ITALY	FRANCE	FED. REP. GERMANY	U.K.	JAPAN
1986								
Q1	89	107	157	174	155	118	134	70
Q2	98	115	167	183	169	124	140	70
Q3	104	123	173	183	171	123	151	68
Q4	109	128	179	184	173	124	164	73
Year	100	118	169	181	167	122	147	70
1987								
Q1	120	136	185	190	177	125	107	77
Q2	125	142	187	198	182	128	164	75
Q3	125	141	191	203	185	130	167	77
Q4	133	148[a]	189[a]	199[a]	181	125[a]	159[a]	74[a]

[a]As of December 4, 1987.

EXHIBIT 3

Norscan Shipments and Operating Rates

	SHIPMENTS METRIC TONNES (000s)	OPERATING RATE
1983	16,002	88%
1984	16,222	91
1985	16,210	86
1986	17,730	93
1987	18,460	98
1988[a]	18,432	98

[a]Two months annualized.

U.S. Shipments and Operating Rates

	SHIPMENTS METRIC TONNES (000s)	OPERATING RATE
1983	4,771	89%
1984	4,912	93
1985	5,178	86
1986	5,901	99
1987	6,227	100
1988[a]	6,426	103

[a]Two months annualized.

EXHIBIT 4

COLUMBIA RIVER PULP COMPANY INC.
Sales by Location of Customer
(fiscal year ending, metric tonnes)

	80/81	81/82	82/83	83/84	84/85	85/86	86/87
US/Mexico	41,607	55,546	112,954	152,015	164,339	155,619	187,222
Japan/Korea	102,612	81,736	80,610	95,202	96,037	96,565	105,056
W. Germany	42,272	41,704	34,852	30,404	13,168	31,438	29,153
Europe	100,548	94,176	89,975	80,527	46,638	27,801	22,306
Other	13,271	1,956	7,738	896	5,801	10,091	17,015
Total	300,310	275,118	326,129	359,044	325,983	321,514	360,752

COLUMBIA RIVER PULP COMPANY INC.
Proportion of Tonnage Sold by Location of Customer
(fiscal year ending)

	80/81	81/82	82/83	83/84	84/85	85/86	86/87
US/Mexico	13.8	20.2	34.6	42.3	50.4	48.4	51.9
Japan/Korea	34.2	29.7	24.7	26.5	29.5	30.0	29.1
W. Germany	14.1	15.2	10.7	8.5	4.0	9.8	8.1
Europe	33.5	34.2	27.6	22.4	14.3	8.7	6.2
Other	4.4	0.7	2.4	0.3	1.8	3.1	4.7
Total	100.0	100.0	100.0	100.0	100.0	100.0	100.0

EXHIBIT 5

COLUMBIA RIVER PULP COMPANY INC.
Statement of Operations and Cash Flow
Years ended March 31
(US$ millions)

	1983	1984	1985	1986	1987	1988E
Sales	$121,800	$139,600	$153,100	$107,500	$159,700	$206,400
Operating Income (loss)[a]	(15.000)	(7,000)	4,000	(21,000)	23,000	58,000
Cash Flow from Operations[b]	13,000	5,000	18,000	(4,000)	31,700	60,000

[a]Pre-tax and pre-interest expense.
[b]Pre-tax and pre-debt service. Reflects working capital and capital expenditures.

EXHIBIT 6

COLUMBIA RIVER PULP COMPANY INC.ᵃ
Income Statement
March 31, 1982–87
(US$000's)

	1982	1983	1984	1985	1986	1987
Sales	$137,798	$121,776	$139,626	$153,093	$107,502	$159,684
Costs & Expenses						
Cost of Pulp Sold	79,906	85,380	90,997	91,650	81,581	85,570
Selling, G & A	30,680	29,091	31,931	33,672	26,785	29,288
Interest	27,032	28,233	30,109	34,567	36,663	40,190
Depreciation	23,226	22,592	23,654	23,597	20,182	21,821
	160,844	165,296	176,691	183,486	165,211	176,869
	(23,046)	(43,520)	(37,065)	(30,393)	(57,709)	(17,185)
Tax Credit Adj.	10,601	20,019		(32,811)		
Net Loss	(12,445)	(23,501)	(37,065)	(63,204)	(57,709)	(17,185)

ᵃAs of March 31, 1987, CRP had tax net operating loss carryforwards of approximately $100 million which expire beginning in 1995. In addition, approximately $19 million of unused investment tax credits relating to the construction of the pulp mill are available through 1995.

EXHIBIT 7

COLUMBIA RIVER PULP COMPANY INC.
Balance Sheet
As at March 31, 1982–87
(US$000's)

	1982	1983	1984	1985	1986	1987
Assets						
Current Assets						
Cash	$289	$981	$993	$528	$659	$17,302
Accounts Rec.	5,041	6,834	12,706	7,895	9,563	15,614
Inventories	14,188	7,668	8,889	10,784	9,755	9,486
Prepaid expenses	1,130	886	759	721	1,147	1,408
Total Current Assets	20,648	15,369	23,347	19,928	12,124	43,810
Land, Plant & Equip.						
Land	2,714	2,719	2,736	2,743	2,671	2,671
Buildings	26,935	26,989	27,139	27,904	27,904	27,904
Machines & Equip.	266,756	268,742	270,662	275,323	284,156	287,237
	296,405	298,450	300,537	305,970	314,732	317,812
Less: Accum. Depr.	43,168	62,502	82,191	101,643	120,744	141,130
	253,237	235,948	218,346	204,327	193,987	176,682

(continued)

EXHIBIT 7 (cont.)

	1982	1983	1984	1985	1986	1987
Construction in Prog.	303	95	2,751	7,163	39	274
	253,540	236,043	221,097	211,490	194,026	176,956
Due From Affiliate	12,792	32,811	32,811			
Deferred Charges	12,033	8,977	5,922	4,161	3,717	3,273
Total Assets	$299,013	$294,200	$283,177	$235,579	$218,867	$224,039
Liabilities and Equity (Deficit)						
Current Liabilities						
Bank loan	$9,026	$10,028	$0	$0	$0	$0
Accounts payable	9,419	10,084	12,555	11,366	11,962	9,005
Due to affiliate		7,310	250	484	821	883
Current maturities of long term debt	5,268	244	6,980	935	250	37,126
	23,713	27,666	19,785	12,785	13,033	47,014
Callable debt				284,182	325,032	
Total Current Liab.	23,713	27,666	19,785	296,967	338,065	47,014
Long Term Debt	233,047	247,782	281,705	20,129	20,028	333,436
Equity (Deficit)						
Common stock	2	2	2	2	2	2
Additional capital	57,299	57,299	57,299	57,299	57,299	57,299
Deficit	(15,048)	(38,549)	(75,614)	(138,818)	(196,527)	(213,712)
	42,253	18,752	(18,313)	(81,517)	(139,226)	(156,411)
Total Liabilities and Equity (Deficit)	$299,013	$294,200	$283,177	$235,579	$218,867	$224,039

EXHIBIT 8

COLUMBIA RIVER PULP COMPANY INC.
Projections of Net Income and Cash Flow
Fiscal Years Ended March 31, 1989–1995
(US$000s)

	1989	1990	1991	1992	1993	1994	1995
Tons sold (ADMT)	386,210	386,210	401,177	411,155	411,155	411,155	411,155
Price per ADMT (AVG)	609.84	609.84	559.84	559.84	644.16	709.84	709.84
Gross sales	235,526	235,526	224,597	230,182	264,851	291,856	291,855
Less: Selling expenses	26,359	27,019	27,934	29,389	31,902	33,591	34,442
Net sales	209,168	208,508	196,663	200,793	232,949	258,265	257,413
Cost of sales	105,715	110,044	116,926	123,354	128,444	133,770	139,309
Depreciation/amort.	23,145	24,230	25,350	26,505	27,345	28,220	29,130
Operating profit	80,308	74,234	54,387	50,934	77,160	96,275	88,975
Less: Interest–LTD	33,149	29,997	26,465	23,465	20,489	14,097	11,181
Interest income	100	505	1,102	1,544	1,979	2,847	4,034
Pre-tax income	47,259	44,742	29,024	29,013	58,650	85,025	81,828
Applicable taxes	16,068	15,212	9,868	9,864	19,941	28,909	27,822
Net income	31,191	29,530	19,156	19,149	38,709	56,116	54,006
Cash flow							
Net income	31,191	29,530	19,156	19,149	38,709	56,116	54,006
Add: Depreciation	23,145	24,230	25,350	26,505	27,345	28,220	29,130
Deferred interest	11,181	11,181	11,181	11,181	11,181	11,181	11,181
Working capital change	(9,218)	(346)	159	(878)	(2,659)	(2,183)	(443)
Cash flow from oper.	56,299	64,595	55,846	55,957	74,576	93,334	93,874

(continued)

EXHIBIT 8 (cont.)

	1989	1990	1991	1992	1993	1994	1995
Less: Cap. exp. – Reg.	10,000	10,500	11,000	11,500	12,000	12,500	13,000
Cap. exp. – Opt.	5,000	5,000	5,000	5,000	0	0	0
Principal – TD	14,000	14,000	14,000	14,000	14,000	40,000	0
Prepayment – TD	11,025	15,923	11,798	11,604	23,145	16,505	0
Other permitted debt	5,000	3,000	2,000	2,000	2,037	0	0
Other liabilities	250	250	250	250	250	250	250
Available cash	11,024	15,992	11,798	11,603	23,144	24,079	80,624
Beginning cash balance	1,221	6,732	14,692	20,591	26,382	37,968	53,795
Less: Dividends	5,513	7,962	5,889	5,802	11,573	8,253	80,812
Cumulative cash after dividends	6,732	14,692	20,597	26,400	37,968	53,795	53,607

COLUMBIA RIVER PULP COMPANY
Projected Balance Sheets
Fiscal Years Ended March 31, 1989–1995
(US$000s)

	1989	1990	1991	1992	1993	1994	1995
Assets							
Cash and equivalents	6,732	14,692	20,591	26,392	37,963	53,789	53,601
Accounts receivables	15,309	15,309	14,599	14,962	17,215	18,971	18,971
Inventories	14,800	15,406	16,370	17,270	17,982	18,728	19,503
Prepaid expenses & other assets	2,481	2,481	2,481	2,481	2,481	2,481	2,481
Total current assets	39,322	47,888	54,041	61,105	75,641	93,969	94,556

(continued)

EXHIBIT 8 (cont.)

	1989	1990	1991	1992	1993	1994	1995
Fixed assets	339,791	355,291	371,291	387,791	399,791	412,291	425,291
Less allowances for Depre./Amort.	(183,703)	(207,993)	(233,283)	(259,788)	(287,133)	(315,353)	(344,483)
Net property & equipment	156,088	147,358	138,008	128,003	112,658	96,938	80,808
Total assets	195,410	195,246	192,049	189,108	188,304	190,912	175,369
Liabilities							
Accounts payable	6,343	6,603	7,016	7,401	7,707	8,026	8,358
Curr. portion–long term oblig.	17,250	16,250	16,250	16,287	40,250	250	250
Total current liabilities	23,593	22,853	23,266	23,688	47,957	8,276	8,608
Other permitted debt	6,037	4,037	2,037	0	0	0	0
LTD–Toronto-Dominion	160,975	131,052	105,254	79,650	16,505	0	0
Subordinated debt–Brian Smith	108,409	119,590	130,771	141,952	153,133	164,314	175,495
Other liabilities	8,063	7,813	7,563	7,313	7,063	6,813	6,563
Total long term debt	283,484	262,492	245,625	228,915	176,701	171,127	182,058
Equity							
Common stock	2	2	2	2	2	2	2
Capital surplus	57,299	57,299	57,299	57,299	57,299	57,299	57,299
Retained earnings	(168,968)	(147,400)	(134,143)	(120,796)	(93,654)	(45,792)	(72,598)
Total equity	(111,667)	(90,099)	(76,842)	(63,495)	(36,353)	11,509	(15,297)
Total liabilities and equity	195,410	195,246	192,049	189,108	188,304	190,912	175,369

EXHIBIT 9
MONEY RATES VS. LOAN RATES (in percent)

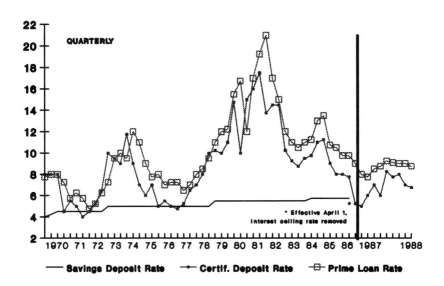

Source: Federal Reserve Board.

PART TWO • Short Term Financing Vehicles and Decisions

9. WARNER-LAMBERT CANADA INC.
10. LAWSON MARDON GROUP LIMITED
11. FANTASTIC MANUFACTURING, INC.
12. MASCHINENBAU ARRAU A.G. (A)
13. DOW EUROPE

9

WARNER-LAMBERT CANADA INC.

On September 17, 1982, Bob Serenbetz, President of Warner-Lambert Canada Inc. (Warner-Lambert) emerged from a meeting with his credit manager, Joe Champagne, and the principals of Coast Distributors Limited (Coast), Warner-Lambert's exclusive wholesale distributor for Vancouver Island. The meeting was called to review Coast's most recent financial statements in light of Warner-Lambert's outstanding account receivable of $1.2 million. Coast's profits and equity had fallen to the point where both were now negative. Champagne recommended in August that shipments to Coast be discontinued, but Serenbetz had decided against such drastic action, pending the review of financial statements and Coast's operating plan. Serenbetz now had to decide what action to take regarding the account and the sales of products in the region.

WARNER-LAMBERT CANADA INC.

Warner-Lambert Canada Inc., a wholly-owned subsidiary of Warner-Lambert Company in the United States, marketed a wide range of consumer and health care products. These products were distributed nationally through all the major food and drug chains, department stores, wholesalers, hospitals and laboratories. The company

This case was prepared by John G. Harris under the supervision of Professor David Shaw for the sole purpose of providing material for class discussion at the Western Business School. Certain names and other identifying information may have been disguised to protect confidentiality. It is not intended to illustrate either effective or ineffective handling of a managerial situation. Any reproduction, in any form, of the material in this case is prohibited except with the written consent of the School.

was organized in five divisions consisting of Adams Brands, Parke-Davis, Personal Products, Diagnostics, and Deseret (Exhibit 1). Sales for all divisions were approximately $190 million in 1982. Competition came from other large firms such as Wrigley Canada Inc., Gillette of Canada Limited, and Hoechst Canada, which sold similar products through the same distribution channels. Management believed stable growth was important to the continued success of the company. Emphasis was placed on marketing and distribution functions to achieve a strong market position in all product lines. Product research and development was considered necessary for sustained future growth.

COAST DISTRIBUTORS LIMITED

Coast Distributors Limited acted as a manufacturer's agent and distributor for wholesale and retail distribution in patent medicines, confectionery, and grocery products. The company acted for over 50 firms including Warner-Lambert. Sales of approximately $11 million in 1981 were handled through one major warehouse location and a smaller branch warehouse in the region. Coast employed 55 people. Credit sales accounted for 95 percent of the total on terms of net 30 days. During its years in business, the company had built and maintained a large and loyal customer base throughout the island.

Coast's common stock had been acquired by David Campbell Limited from the original Bromley family interests in 1978. David Campbell Limited was a holding company owned by David Campbell, a prominent lawyer in Nanaimo, and his family. Campbell had acted for the estate of Charles Bromley, the founder of Coast, who had died in 1975. David Campbell was well regarded in the community as a lawyer and businessman.

The acquisition of Coast by David Campbell Limited had been financed by bank borrowings. In 1980, the two companies were merged under the Coast Distributors name. At this time Campbell named Earl Keith as President and Chief Executive Officer. Keith had run Coast for over 20 years and had extensive experience in the distribution business on Vancouver Island. David Campbell became a Director and Chairman of the Board of Coast Distributors.

Coast had distributed Warner-Lambert products for 56 years, acting as a distribution centre by taking title to the merchandise and carrying a full product line. Good relations evolved because of the quality of service provided by Coast in distribution, credit management, and credit risk assumption. Coast kept its own account with Warner-Lambert current.

The current exclusive agency agreement between Coast and Warner-Lambert for the region of Vancouver Island was negotiated in 1966. Under this arrangement, all Warner-Lambert Divisions sold to Coast at list price less any discounts specific to a particular division. This was termed the best wholesale price. Warner-Lambert would then pay Coast 10 percent of the best wholesale price for the distribution and warehousing services it provided. The payments were made quarterly by cheque to Coast. Shipments were made once per week F.O.B destination with payment terms of net 60 days. However, the agreement also granted an extended dating program because of the logistical problems of selling in this market (i.e., isolated towns) that went as follows:

Adams and Parke-Davis Divisions
May 1–Oct. 31   60 days
Nov. 1–Apr. 30   120 days

Personal Products Divisions
May 1–Oct. 31   1%, 75 days; net 120
Nov. 1–Apr. 30   1%, 135 days; net 180

These terms were effective from the due date of the original invoice and additional dating might be allowed for special promotions. Coast was encouraged to submit tenders for government and hospital contracts at prices quoted by Warner-Lambert. However, no allowance would be paid on these orders.

The credit limit granted to Coast had risen to $1.2 million by 1981. This credit limit was reviewed and adjusted annually, based on information from financial statements submitted as requested by Warner-Lambert's credit manager. The determination of the credit limit was based on a formula tested extensively by major corporations. The formula incorporates the overall financial condition of the firm, including working capital and long term viability. Credit limits were built up under the formula by adding assigned percentages of the amount of a customer's working capital, net income, and net worth, while reductions were made under the same system of assigned percentages for long term debt and net losses. The formula was modified for quick and pledged assets. A discretionary assignment by the credit manager accounted for past performance and future prospects, trade and bank references, general reputation, or any other factors which may have been unique to the business. This discretionary factor could adjust the credit limit by plus or minus 25 percent, or possibly suspend credit altogether. A table of company statistics included in the evaluation provided client history and the degree of exposure the creditor faced. The purpose of the formula was to have a structure from which consistent decisions could be made. At Warner-Lambert, the level of authority required for approval of credit limits depended on the amount requested. The Credit Manager had authority up to $100,000, the Treasurer to $300,000, the V.P. Finance to $500,000, while the President had unlimited discretion. The credit limits established for Coast and the calculations based on the formula are presented in Exhibit 2.

EVENTS LEADING TO THE MEETING

Relations between the two companies had been good in the past, with Coast generally supplying an appropriate level of service for the compensation it received. However, in April 1981, Champagne requested audited financial statements for the year ended December 31, 1980, but received one for the year ended March 31, 1980. After reviewing this statement, he found several items of concern. Directors' remuneration had increased $123,000 in 1979 following the appointment of two additional directors, namely, the wives of David Campbell and Earl Keith. At the same time, dividends to shareholders were substantial at $94,000 in cash and $400,000 in stock. Coast's bank loan increased during this period by $400,000. From March 1979 to 1980, net profit after tax was halved. With rising interest rates and bank loans and falling profits, Champagne recommended a reduction of Coast's credit limit until he could get answers for recent organizational changes and company behavior. He suggested lowering the amount to correspond with Warner-Lambert's credit criteria of about $194,000 (Exhibit 2), using 1980 data. Several requests for more current financial information followed over the next few months but were refused by Coast. A personal visit by a member of the credit department was made in September 1981 to examine Coast's operations and find out what was happening within the company. The company restructuring was explained, as was the recent expansion and increased bank debt. The Warner-Lambert representative felt positive about the future of Coast. Current financial statements were to have been forwarded to Warner-Lambert. The statements never arrived.

In August of 1982, Champagne again tried to secure recent audited statements and once again was refused. Concerned about a significant deterioration in the financial position of Coast and the considerable risk exposure confronting Warner-Lambert, he recommended suspension of credit as a means of acquiring the information requested.

A profitability analysis of the account to Warner-Lambert was prepared as part of the annual credit review. The last profitability standing of the Coast account occurred at the end of November 1981. The results are presented in Exhibit 3. The study compared Coast's account to Warner-Lambert's average. Average days sales outstanding (DSO) of Warner-Lambert accounts receivable was 59 days, excluding Coast sales. Coast's account was 125 DSO, but was not past due. Coast's own accounts receivable DSO was only 68 days, which suggested that Warner-Lambert was contributing substantially to the short term financing requirements of Coast. Warner-Lambert products amounted to 25 percent of Coast's sales but represented 50 percent of Coast's accounts payable. Warner-Lambert's cost of carrying the excess receivables over the average was estimated at $58,000 annually, using a 15 percent interest rate. At that time, the excess in receivables above the average was $43,000 for Parke-Davis, $322,000 for Adams Brands, and $31,000 for Personal Products. These varied with interest rates. This coincided with the fact that Warner-Lambert's own credit limit evaluation indicated that Coast did not deserve any credit. The results of this analysis suggested several things to Warner-Lambert. There was a need to review both the size of Coast's credit line and the payment terms which were negotiated 16 years previously.

Coast management finally agreed to a meeting with Warner-Lambert in September 1982. At the meeting Coast supplied audited financial statements for the year ended December 31, 1981, and unaudited results for the first eight months of 1982. These statements are presented in Exhibits 4 and 5.

Serenbetz now had several alternatives to consider. With Coast's actual financial position much worse than anyone at Warner-Lambert anticipated, and with the credit limit formula showing a negative amount, Serenbetz knew that a tough decision concerning Coast was a real possibility. He would have to develop options and consider each one carefully.

The first option was to restructure the present credit arrangements with Coast and work with the firm to improve the business. The major advantage would be to use Coast's well established distribution network and client base. This would eliminate the time and cost incurred to set-up alternate distribution channels, should the Coast account be suspended. At the same time, by reducing Coast's credit terms and limit, Warner-Lambert's risk exposure would be reduced.

Serenbetz wondered if improving the efficiency of Coast's inventory of Warner-Lambert products would help to solve the problem. Inventory would turn over faster if shipments were smaller and more frequent. Merchandise would always be current and no slow-moving stock would accumulate. Although higher shipping costs would be incurred by Warner-Lambert, a lower inventory amount for Coast would reduce the investment in the account by Warner-Lambert. Currently, Coast carried $300,000 of Warner-Lambert products in inventory. In addition, reducing the credit terms to Coast, possibly through cash discount offerings, would further reduce exposure. A proposal to establish a bonded warehouse and place Coast on a consignment basis with separate inventories was discussed. Coast's collections on these products, when sold, would be kept in a separate account. Frequent audits would have to be conducted to verify the records. However, with the availability of such records, the movement of products and funds could be closely supervised. If more sales representatives were employed by Warner-Lambert on the island, they would be able to conduct the audits in addition to their duties of product promotion.

A second alternative would be to suspend all credit to Coast and attempt to collect the present outstanding balance. The account represented a substantial amount of business for Warner-Lambert. The exclusive agreement left Warner-Lambert totally dependent on Coast for sales on Vancouver Island and susceptible to Coast's credit problem. If Warner-Lambert's credit to Coast was suspended, an alternative means of distribution had to be found for the region.

About 60 wholesalers operated in the area; however, most were small jobbers—only eight to ten could replace Coast. Merchandise could be sold to them on regular credit terms and with existing compensation rates. Upon further investigation, it became apparent that these firms were smaller than Coast and were not so centrally located. The number of shipments to the alternate distributors would increase. Supplies were shipped by sea once per week from the Vancouver distribution centre. Increasing the number of shipments would raise freight costs to Warner-Lambert. Merchandise was currently shipped in container loads. If smaller wholesalers could not purchase full loads, Warner-Lambert would lose the cost efficiencies container lots provided. Poorer service and lost sales could also result from reduced coverage and the loss of a loyal customer base.

Although additional credit accounts would also have to be supervised because of an increased number of distributors, the risk would be spread around, reducing Warner-Lambert's exposure. Serenbetz thought that sales might drop by as much as 10 percent on the island if other wholesalers were used because of the strong relationship established between Coast and its customers. But he was uncertain whether the sales decline would be permanent or temporary. More frequent shipments to Vancouver Island and servicing more wholesale accounts might push Warner-Lambert's costs up by 2 percent.

Warner-Lambert could also set up its own distribution centre on Vancouver Island and sell directly to wholesalers and retailers. This would entail a large capital outlay and take time to establish. As well, many more credit accounts would have to be serviced and more salesmen hired. But the control gained over these functions might contribute to a more efficient operation.

A third alternative was to leave the account as it was and continue the extended dating terms for all divisions. Though the Coast account was over the acceptable line of credit, the firm still abided by the terms of the credit agreement. According to a recent Dun and Bradstreet report, Coast's payment record varied from prompt to 30 days slow, which was acceptable performance in this industry. Apparently the other suppliers were not concerned with Coast's account and, in all likelihood, had not received the 1981 statements. Coast's financial position had not affected its sales performance—Coast sold $2.3 million of Warner-Lambert merchandise in 1981.

Serenbetz knew that a good distribution system was the key to achieving and maintaining market share. But increased risk exposure due to Coast's deteriorating financial position could put Warner-Lambert in a high loss situation. Although Coast's operating profit for the first eight months of 1982 was better than 1981, interest costs had offset this—causing a net loss which further reduced the company's net worth. Serenbetz knew he must make a decision soon and communicated this to the departments concerned.

EXHIBIT 1

WARNER-LAMBERT CANADA INC.
Major Brands

ADAMS BRANDS	Chiclets, Dentyne, Certs, Clorets, Trident Sugarless Gum, Halls, Rolaids, Dynamints, Bubbaloo, Bubbilicious, Freshen-Up Gum, Blue Diamond Almonds
PARKE-DAVIS	Agarol, Anusol, Benylin, Benadryl, Caladryl, Gelusil, Sinutab, Strepsils, Pardec, Chloromycetin, Coly-Mycin, Choledyl, Dilantin, Peritrate, Pyridium, Mandelamine, LoEstrin
PERSONAL PRODUCTS	Listerine Antiseptic, Listermint with Fluoride, Listerine Lozenges, Bromo-Seltzer, Efferdent, Schick, Topol Tooth Polish, Porcelana Medicated Cream, Softsoap
DIAGNOSTICS	Simplastin, Verify, Coag-A-Mates, Sure-Sep, Blood G.A.S., Wellcome Reagents, Blood Bank Reagents, Micro I.D., Radioimmuno-Assay Reagents, Chemistry Reagents, Reagants, Microbiology Reagents, Chemistry Quality Control Products, Antimicrobial Disks
DESERET	Angiocath, E-Z Serubs, Filter Masks, Ground-It, Hemodialysis E.Z. Sets, Minicaths, Unigard, E.K.G.

EXHIBIT 2

COAST DISTRIBUTORS LIMITED
Credit Line Evaluation

ITEM	ALLOWANCE	1979	1980	1981
Working Capital	10%	113	115	49
Quick Assets	Max 5%			
	(50% of W/C Credit)	56	57	25
Pledged Rec/Inv.	(10%)	(28)	(33)	(37)
Long Term Debt	(3%)	(2)	(11)	(48)
Net Worth	2%	34	35	(22)
Net Income	10% or (20%)	50	31	(78)
Other[a]				
Credit Line		223	194	(111)
Credit Line Requested		1,000	1,000	1,200
Credit Line Approved				
Date				
[a]Comment:				

(continued)

EXHIBIT 2 (cont.)

ITEM	ALLOWANCE		1979	1980	1981
APPROVAL					
	MGR./SUPER.	CR. MGR.	TREAS.	V.P. FIN.	PRES.
DATE					

Statistics					
Working Capital Ratio			1.68	1.54	1.15
Quick Asset Ratio			.73	.71	.50
L/T Debt % Wkg. Cap.			5.30	31.48	331.34
L/T Debt % Net Worth			3.54	20.44	1,434.82
*Cr. Line % Wkg. Cap.			88.26	86.96	247.42
*Cr. Line % Net Worth			59.07	56.47	1,071.43
*Cr. Line % Curr. Debt			60.39	47.30	36.16

EXHIBIT 3

WARNER-LAMBERT CANADA INC.
Accounts Receivable Data
($000s)

	PARKE-DAVIS	ADAMS	PERSONAL PRODUCTS	TOTAL
Coast Accounts Receivable Balance Outstanding at 30/11/81	$243	$467	$64	$744
Coast Days Sales Outstanding	120 days	129 days	119 days	125 days
Warner-Lambert D.S.O. excluding Coast at 30/11/81	99 days	40 days	60 days	59 days
D.S.O. difference converted to dollars	$43	$322	$31	$396
Cost of carrying excess Coast Receivables at 15% per annum	$6	$48	$4	$58
Sales of Warner-Lambert products to Coast, 1981	$738	$1,322	$197	$2,257
Commissions paid to Coast	$74	$132	$20	$226
Contribution to Warner-Lambert from sales to Coast	$297	$592	$65	$954

(continued)

EXHIBIT 4

COAST DISTRIBUTORS LIMITED
Income Statement
for the Periods Described
($000s)

	8 MONTHS TO AUGUST 31, 1982	YEAR ENDED DECEMBER 31, 1981	9 MONTHS ENDED DECEMBER 31, 1980[a]	YEAR ENDED MARCH 31, 1980
Net Sales	$7,308	$11,020	$8,166	$9,545
Less: Cost of Goods Sold	6,079	9,169	6,757	7,807
Gross Profit	1,229	1,851	1,409	1,738
Deduct Expenses				
Selling, Warehouse & Delivery	416	899	697	647
Admin. and General	521	817	620	782
Subtotal	937	1,716	1,317	1,429
Operating Profit	292	135	92	309
Excess (Deficiency) of Other Income Over Charges[b]	(311)	(547)	(70)	4
Net Income Before Tax	(19)	(412)	22	313
Current Tax	—	(20)	5	(150)
Net Income	$ (19)	$ (392)	$ 17	$ 163

[a]Fiscal year end December 31, 1980, was only nine months long due to amalgamation of Coast Distributors Limited and David Campbell Ltd.

[b]Other Income includes: net cash discounts, gain on disposal of property and equipment, rent, and miscellaneous. Other charges include: long term interest and other interest charges of $337,000 August 31, 1982, $555,573 December 31, 1981, $11,968 December 31, 1980, $69,962 March 31, 1980, and excess of premiums paid over increase in cash surrender value of life insurance.

Ratios (Percentage of Net Sales)

	1982	1981	1980	1980
Gross Profit	16.81	16.79	17.26	18.21
Operating Profit	3.99	1.21	1.13	3.24
Net Income	(.25)	(3.57)	.21	1.71

EXHIBIT 5

COAST DISTRIBUTORS LIMITED
Balance Sheet
December 31, 1980, 1981 and August 31, 1982
($000s)

	AUG. 31, 1982	DEC. 31, 1981	DEC. 31, 1980
Assets			
Current Assets			
Cash	$ 1	$ 1	$ 4
Receivables (Net)	1,627	1,644	1,982
Inventories at Lower of Cost or Replacement Cost	2,322	2,136	2,456
Prepaid Expenses	81	22	19
Total Current Assets	4,031	3,803	4,462
Investments, Loans and Advances	142	113	106
Property, Plant and Equipment	1,240	1,204	1,238
Less: Accumulated Depreciation	519	453	387
	721	751	851
Land	184	146	146
Net Property, Plant, and Equipment	905	897	997
Total Assets	$5,078	$4,813	$5,565
Liabilities and Equity			
Current Liabilities			
Outstanding Cheques Less Cash	228	59	382
Demand Loan	1,103	1,250	800
Current Portion of Long Term Debt	32	96	72
Subtotal	1,363	1,405	1,254
Accounts Payable	2,216	1,912	2,163
Income Taxes Payable	0	0	29
Total Current Liabilities	3,579	3,317	3,446
Long Term Debt	1,629	1,608	1,722
Deferred Income Taxes	0	0	20
Shareholders' Equity			
Class A Preferreds	36	36	36
Class B Preferreds	47	47	142
Common Shares	5	5	5
Retained (Deficit) Earnings Beginning	(199)	194	1,246
Add: Net Income	(19)	(392)	17
Adjustment (Note 1)	—	—	1,069
Retained (Deficit) Earnings Ending	(218)	(199)	194
Total Liabilities and Equity	$5,078	$4,813	$5,565

Note 1: During 1980, Coast Distributors Ltd. and David Campbell Limited were merged. The new company, Coast Distributors Limited, adopted a December 31 year end, whereas the company previously had a March 31 year end. As a result, the financial statements for the year ended December 31, 1980, only represent nine months operations. When the accounts of the two companies were consolidated, the purchase price of the equity on David Campbell Limited's accounts was offset against the book value of the equity in Coast Distributors Limited's accounts, resulting in a write-down of $1,069 thousand.

10

LAWSON MARDON GROUP LIMITED

It was March 1989, and Carl Galloway, Treasurer of Lawson Mardon Group Ltd. (LMG), was collecting his thoughts on the company's current financial structure with a view to recommending a future strategy to his immediate boss, Ralph Steedman, Executive Vice President Corporate and Chief Financial Officer. Carl's objective was to continue to pursue a financial strategy that provided the maximum flexibility for the company in terms of ability to raise funds in all financial markets under the most favourable terms. In part, because of LMG's presence in the U.K., Carl was interested in exploring the Euro-Commercial Paper Market (ECP) and the Sterling Commercial Paper Market (SCP) as possible alternatives to its current banking facility.

BACKGROUND ON THE COMPANY

LMG was formed on August 30, 1985, when LMG acquired the predecessor to Lawson Mardon and Lawson and Jones in a leveraged buyout (LBO) acquisition from BAT Industries, plc, for an aggregate amount of $559.1 million. The acquisition was financed by $28.5 million of common equity, $98.3 million of subordinated debt and $432.3 million of secured bank debt. Approximately $80 million of the

This case was prepared by Ed Giacomelli under the supervision of Professor Robert W. White for the sole purpose of providing material for class discussion at the Western Business School. Certain names and other identifying information may have been disguised to protect confidentiality. It is not intended to illustrate either effective or ineffective handling of a managerial situation. Any reproduction, in any form, of the material in this case is prohibited except with the written consent of the School.

bank debt was hedged with an interest rate swap. The ownership of the company included management (20%), Roman Corporation (49%), the Lawson family (12%), Prudential Insurance (17%) and the Bank of Nova Scotia (2%).

LMG was an international company with manufacturing facilities in Canada, United Kingdom, United States, France, West Germany and Ireland. It should be noted that approximately 73% of LMG's revenues originated in the U.K. and Europe and 27% in North America. The company's corporate head office was located in Mississauga, Ontario. A fundamental aspect of LMG's strategy was to organize into five business groups: Flexible Packaging—Europe; Rigid Plastics and Metals—Europe; Folding Cartons—Europe; Graphics—North America; and Packaging—North America. LMG was a major supplier of packaging to the consumers good industry in the U.K. and Canada. A sample of the company's major customers is included in Exhibit 1. All businesses that did not fit with the core business were divested, with LMG divesting assets of $92.8 million within 15 months of completing the LBO and a further $22 million in fiscal year 1987.

The initial secured bank loan, a two-year term facility, was renegotiated. LMG's successful divestiture program allowed it to renegotiate its banking lines on more favourable terms. In December 1986, LMG agreed to a new 5-year revolving term facility. Key improvements were in rates (LIBOR[1] and Bankers' Acceptances margins were reduced by approximately 75 bp to 75 bp) and in the release of all security previously held by the Banks. An additional feature negotiated by LMG was a Multi-Option Facility (MOF) to be utilized in the United Kingdom.

In May 1987, taking advantage of its improved balance sheet and profit levels as noted in Exhibit 2, LMG raised $216 million ($205 million net of fees and commissions) through an initial public offering of 49.46% of its equity. The stock offering included tranches in Canada, the United States and the United Kingdom. Through the use of multiple voting shares, the original shareholders retained over 80% voting control of the company. The stock was listed initially on the Toronto Stock Exchange (TSE), the Montreal Stock Exchange (MSE) and the American Stock Exchange (AMEX). In the spring of 1988, the stock was listed in London.

The improved balance sheet position allowed LMG to approach its bankers in December 1987 for further concessions. The loan margins were reduced by a further 25 bp and the per annum standby fee on the unused portion of the loan was reduced to 0.125% p.a. from 0.25% p.a. This pricing was consistent with the pricing received by companies of similar risk in the U.K. market. LMG also renegotiated that certain restrictive covenants be removed and that the sterling tranche be increased by £15 million to £100 million while the Canadian dollar tranche remained at $75 million. Hence, LMG was provided with greater flexibility to make significant acquisitions conditional on the financial covenant pattern being adhered to. This was important to the company, as LMG had hoped to make acquisitions in the U.S. to balance its

---

[1]LIBOR is the acronym for London Interbank Offered Rate and represents a series of borrowing rates available in London by major banks from around the world. LIBORs may be quoted in various currencies and for different time periods. LIBOR is a base rate for comparison in most financial markets for short term rates.

revenue between North America and Europe. Potential acquisitions in the $100–300 million range were being contemplated. It was the view of management that an unrestricted and significant debt capacity would assist the company if an opportunity presented itself.

The flexibility accorded LMG by its bankers reflected a confidence in both the strength of management and the underlying fundamentals of its businesses. LMG works hard at keeping its bankers informed and at building long term relationships. The various banks included in the syndicate, led by The Bank of Nova Scotia, reflected LMG's geographic diversification. Exhibit 3 outlines the banks that participated in the December 1986 syndicate. The services provided by the banks were diversified and these banks were chosen to provide the maximum benefit to LMG. In 1988, Chase Manhattan Bank and Mellon Bank were added to the syndicate. This was done with a view to venturing into the U.S. market. To the extent possible, LMG attempted to achieve symmetry in terms of the lenders in the Canadian and U.K. tranches, and with few exceptions, there was symmetry between Canadian and U.K. syndicate members. It was believed that having the same lenders on either side of the Atlantic would facilitate any renegotiations or amendments to the credit facility at a later date. In fact, recent changes to the credit agreement substantiated this belief.

Despite the favourable reception LMG had received from its bankers, the stock market had not progressed in the same light (see Exhibit 4).

MULTI-OPTION FACILITY (MOF)

As the name suggests, the MOF provided a borrower with multiple financing options. In the case of LMG, borrowings might be denominated in dollars, sterling, and other major European currencies. Also, borrowings might be based on either LIBOR or Bills of Exchange[2] (similar to Canadian Bankers' Acceptances). A third feature of the MOF was called a "tender panel." The tender panel was comprised of a group of financial institutions, including syndicate members, that bids on an uncommitted basis for unrated LMG short term notes on terms usually less than 6 months. Exhibit 3 lists the tender panel members as of 1989. The number of members had increased since the tender panel was arranged to broaden the placement capability of the group.

The purpose of the tender panel was to provide the issuer with access to a lower cost of funds while giving investors the opportunity to bid at their indifference rate based on the perceived quality of the paper, their ability to sell it in the secondary market and their current book position. Any one of these factors might have caused a tender panel member to have either bid aggressively or not to have bid at all.

The committed bank facility component was a backstop for the tender panel in the event tender panel members did not wish to hold the paper at a given point in time. However, since LMG established the tender panel, it has used it extensively

---

[2] A Bill of Exchange is a short term promissory note issued by a corporation accompanied by an unconditional guarantee of payment by a commercial bank. The notes are issued on a discounted basis and typically have maturities of up to 90 days.

and achieved savings of 20–30 bp below the loan rate that would otherwise be charged on the committed facility. Furthermore, at no time had LMG experienced an overall lack of interest from the tender panel members.

The MOF with a tender panel was essentially a hybrid of a traditional syndicated bank loan, a commercial paper program and note issuance facility (NIF).[3] In the case of LMG, because the company required a five year committed facility, a traditional bank loan would be priced to include a risk premium for the term of the loan and a standby fee to make the facility available on a revolving basis. In other words, LMG could draw upon or repay its credit at any time and the syndicate guaranteed availability subject to LMG adhering to certain covenants. On an uncommitted basis only the commercial paper (CP) market would have provided the flexibility to draw down and repay advances. A NIF allowed a borrower like LMG to tap short term markets by issuing notes. However, the borrower was not entitled to repay advances. It should be noted that these restrictions are driven by the investors or purchasers of the paper.

The tender panel allowed investors (tender panel members) to bid on terms of less than 6 months. The pricing reflected the short term nature and inherently lower risk of the paper than a bank loan. Because the tender panel consisted of a closed group of bidders, rates were not as attractive as those available on either the ECP or SCP markets. Under a tender panel the distribution of the loans was effectively restricted to financial institutions, the tender panel members and institutions to whom they may sell the loans. A disadvantage of the tender panel was that the same small subgroup of the tender panel might continually win bids, while others continually bid to lose. The issuer was willing to pay a higher rate because the tender panel members will bid for the paper on a consistent basis whereas this was not necessarily the case for either ECP or SCP programs. As recently as August 1988, LMG was paying a weighted average cost of LIBOR + 22 bp on tender panel advances. CP would have cost approximately LIBOR + 5 bp. In addition, the issuer continued to pay a standby fee of 0.125% p.a. on the unused portion of the committed facility. The standby fee can be viewed as an insurance premium on maintaining availability of the facility.

Finally, the rate structure on the MOF was comprised of four types of rates or fees:

1. A fee paid to the Agent or arranger of the facility. This fee was quoted as a percent of the face value of the facility and was payable at closing.
2. A standby fee on the uncancelled or unused portion of the committed facility and was payable in arrears either semi-annually or quarterly.
3. An agency fee, or administration fee, paid to the Agent bank who acted as an intermediary among syndicate, tender panel members and the borrower.
4. A margin quoted above LIBOR.

---

[3]Note issuance facilities (NIFs) are Eurodollar market arrangements which give the borrower the ability to continually issue short term notes, in varying amounts not to exceed the total facility amount, over the life of the facility at a rate which would not exceed a specified maximum spread over a floating rate benchmark.

EURO-COMMERCIAL PAPER AND STERLING COMMERCIAL PAPER

ECP traced its origins back to the early 1970s.[4] The ECP market evolved for two main reasons. First, U.S. corporations and institutions that issued CP domestically were locating in London in greater numbers. Although these U.S. firms were also engaging in either Eurobonds or NIFs to satisfy long term and medium term needs, the short term market continued to be dominated by LIBOR based bank lines of credit. Thus, U.S. companies were anxious to see a CP program develop as it had in North America. Second, during the 70s as the quality of bank deposits began to deteriorate, investors began to diversify credit risk by investing in comparable risk non-bank money market investments.

While the ECP became a complement to a corporation's U.S. dollar funding, the SCP market did not begin until May 1986 and was aimed at those corporations that borrowed sterling in the U.K. Prior to 1986, this market was well served by the "acceptance" market. However, with investor's preference moving away from bank risk, a SCP market began to evolve. At the end of 1987, the SCP market totalled £2.5 billion, while the ECP and acceptance markets totalled approximately US$54 billion and £18 billion respectively.[5]

Although both SCP and ECP were based on the U.S. CP market, there were some distinct differences. The U.S. market was strictly a ratings market. In other words Moody's or Standard & Poor's rated the commercial paper in terms of credit worthiness and only those companies with a threshold of A1 (Standard & Poor's) or Prime 1 (Moody's) had access to these markets. The ECP market was moving towards a ratings system for borrowers not based in continental Europe. However, it remained a name recognition market for well known European borrowers.

A second major difference was that the "Dealers" (the initial purchasers of CP) were paid an explicit commission in the U.S., while in the SCP and ECP market borrowers were quoted an all-in rate that included an implicit commission. The last major difference was that the U.S. CP was quoted at its discount yield[6], while ECP and SCP were typically quoted as Money Market Yields (MMY) and were priced at a premium or discount to LIBOR and calculated on a 360 day basis.[7] This was a technical difference that borrowers and investors must be aware of if making rate comparisons among the three programs.

A key success factor in the CP markets was the consistent availability of product to dealers and investors alike. In order for a program to be successful, a program of £20,000,000 was considered to be the smallest possible amount that a borrower should expect to be in the market for at all times. Similarly, there must be consistency of yields to investors. Major ECP players such as the Canadian Export Development Corporation and PepsiCo posted rates daily with dealers and issued significant

---

[4]Bullock, Gareth R., *Euronotes and Euro-Commercial Paper*, 1987, Butterworth.
[5]*The Treasurer*, May 1988.
[6]Discount Rate = (((Face Value − Purchase Price)/Face Value) × 360/days to maturity).
[7]To convert from a discount yield (in decimal form) to a money market yield: Money Market Yield = Discount Yield/(1 − Discount Yield × Days to Maturity/360).

volume each day for a range of maturities.[8] Typically these two features, yield and availability, were common to all successful programs.

Another key success factor was the dealer group that was chosen to issue and distribute the paper. The size of the group varied but generally included 2–3 dealers for programs up to £100,000,000, 3–4 from amounts of £100,000,000 to £250,000,000, and 4–5 for amounts greater than £250,000,000.[9] The leading dealers in both SCP and ECP market are included in Exhibit 5. A dealer's presence in the markets was critical in choosing group members. However, significant consideration was also given to relationship bankers.

It should also be noted that borrowers were required to issue an Information Memorandum that specified the size of the program, the dealer group, the intended use of the proceeds, summary financial statements and general corporate information.[10] The SCP program must be registered with the Bank of England because notes were denominated in sterling. However, this was not expected to pose any significant restrictions on the SCP program.

LMG'S DECISION

Carl Galloway realized that either the ECP or SCP market would provide him with a 10–15 bp interest savings as compared to tender panel advances. For the past three years, however, money market conditions in the U.K. had resulted in the relative rate on bills of exchange being 10–15 bp lower than normal. He was also aware that each market would lead to a broader investor group holding LMG paper. LMG's ability to increase name recognition would assist any effort to float future issues.

The Treasury-Eurodollar (TED) spread[11], a widely used indicator of short term credit spreads, jumped from its post-October 1987 crash low in mid-February to its highest level since the summer of 1988 (see Exhibit 6). The combination of widening spreads and the high level of the short term yield curve made short term issues costly.

Spreads for longer-maturity, high-grade new issues widened slightly, but at a much slower pace than shorter issues. Spreads on long term junk bonds narrowed, as the anticipated deluge of paper from much publicized mega-LBOs had failed to materialize yet.

Access to the ECP market required a rating from Moody's or Standard & Poor's. Because of LMG's presence in the U.K. it was considered possible to participate in the SCP market without a rating. Rating fees were additional costs of an ECP program. The annual rating fees would be approximately 9 bp[12] on a CP program

---

[8]Bullock, Gareth R., *Euronotes and Euro-Commercial Paper*, 1987, Butterworth.

[9]*Ibid.*

[10]A Euro-commercial paper information memorandum is typically very brief, approximately three pages in length. The note is typically two pages in length.

[11]The Treasury-Eurodollar (TED) spread is the spread between the money market yield on three month U.S. Treasury bills and the yield on three month Eurodollars, or LIBOR. The TED spread provides a general indication of the level of credit spreads on short term loans.

[12]S&P charges 0.0005 per million (0.0005 × amount of program). Moody's charges $5000+(.00006 × average outstanding/quarter × 4). *Source: Techniques & Products*, The Globecon Group, Ltd.

of the size to be considered by LMG. Other costs that would be incurred were start up costs (legal and printing fees) of £25,000, administration fees of £3,000–£5,000 per year and manpower of £7,000 per year.

Carl Galloway was concerned that once rated it would be difficult to convince the rating agencies to upgrade a rating. This was of significant concern to Carl because LMG was continuing its evolution out of the LBO and its target capital structure (long term debt to long term capitalization of less than 50%, net of goodwill) might not be achieved for 2-3 years. The financial characteristics and statistics for industrial firms are summarized in Exhibit 7. The number of rating changes by Moody's and Standard & Poor's is illustrated in Exhibit 8. Special events (mergers, acquisitions, leveraged buyouts, share repurchases, etc.) were again the largest cause of industrial downgrades in 1987. Moody's reported that 34% of all industrial downgrades in 1987 were special-event related, as compared with 32% in 1986.

LMG's corporate strategy was growth via acquisitions. LMG's ability to respond quickly to potential acquisitions was dictated, in part, by its financial capacity. Also, the company had hopes of making significant acquisitions and was prepared to use leverage to achieve this end. The company was anxious to make an acquisition in the U.S. as it believed that proprietary technologies developed for the U.K. market could be best introduced through an existing U.S. based firm, thus enabling LMG to expand into a large market where they had little presence.

Ralph Steedman was expecting a recommendation on a financial strategy from Carl Galloway by March 31, 1989. Carl had to decide which markets and instruments to pursue and when. If he were to choose commercial paper, he would then have to decide which program to pursue and when, and the size and composition of the dealer group; and make a decision on a rating as well as an assessment of the downside risk should the program fail.

EXHIBIT 1
LAWSON MARDON GROUP LIMITED
Sample Customer List

NORTH AMERICA

Kraft	Chesebrough-Ponds
J.E. Seagram & Sons	Avon Canada
John Labatt	Imperial Tobasco
General Foods	Lowney's Nabisco
Playtex	Smith & Nephew
Brooke Bond	Johnson & Johnson
Sulton Canada	Charles of the Ritz
Canada Starch	Warner-Lambert
RJR MacDonald	Rothmans
Brown & Williamson	Eaton's

(continued)

EXHIBIT 1 (cont.)

NORTH AMERICA

Woolco	Hudson's Bay
Robert Simpson	Paul Masson
Coca-Cola	Nestlè
Carnation	Quaker Oats
Consumers Distributing	Procter & Gamble

U.K.

Mars	British Tissues
Imperial Group	Beecham
United Biscuits	Gallaher
Nabisco Brands	Tate & Lyle
Dalgety Spillers	Bass
R.H.M.	Davies Brook
Reckitt & Colman	Allied Lyons
Unilever	ICI
Rowntree Mackintosh	Nestlè/Findus
Assoc. British Foods	Reed International
Grand Metropolitan	Hiram Walker
B.A.T. Industries	St. Regis Packaging
Cadbury Schweppes	Paterson Zachonis
HM Government Distillers	General Foods
Kellogg	

EXHIBIT 2

LAWSON MARDON GROUP LIMITED
Financial Statements
Years Ended December 31
($000s)

	1988	1987	1986	1985
Assets				
Current Assets				
Cash	$ 533	$ 6,848	$ 3,709	$ 2,928
Accounts Receivable	171,513	174,853	137,492	127,036
Inventory	129,800	137,241	104,964	99,720
Prepaid Expenses	6,617	5,681	8,752	5,751
Due from Associated Companies	2,331			
	310,794	324,615	257,917	235,435
Long Term Assets				
Fixed Assets	278,530	286,137	219,985	211,490
Investments	16,663		12,898	20,534
Other	6,235	6,728	10,822	48,400
Pension Excess	52,277	32,408	14,244	
Goodwill	165,191	181,817	169,805	173,726
Total Assets	$829,690	$831,705	$679,004	$689,585

(continued)

EXHIBIT 2 (cont.)

	1988	1987	1986	1985
Liabilities				
Current Liabilities				
Bank Indebtedness	$ 11,983	$ 7,414	$ 10,003	$ 8,736
Accounts Payable and Accruals	204,619	233,657	185,381	150,765
Dividends Payable		5,769		
Income Taxes Payable	7,851	15,816	1,281	5,554
Current Portion of Long Term Debt	8,444	3,520	4,089	3,557
	232,897	266,176	200,757	168,612
Long Term Liabilities				
Income Taxes Payable	1,178	3,593	7,894	650
Long Term Debt	129,848	118,316	197,014	258,207
Subordinated Debt	98,164	104,042	164,569	170,591
Deferred Taxes	41,590	42,954	42,198	48,379
	270,780	268,905	411,675	477,827
Shareholders' Equity				
Share Capital	250,072	250,080	43,700	35,771
Retained Earnings	74,424	41,127	19,235	4,794
Cumulative Translation	1,517	5,057	3,657	2,581
	326,013	296,264	66,592	43,146
Total Liabilities and Equity	$829,690	$831,705	$679,004	$689,585

LAWSON MARDON GROUP LIMITED
Income Statement
Years Ended December 31
($000s)

	1988	1987	1986
Sales	$1,110,533	$1,034,699	$890,974
Operating Expenses			
Cost of Sales and Operating Expenses	855,601	810,808	703,210
Selling and General Expenses	132,814	103,973	85,066
Depreciation	38,969	33,050	29,111
	1,027,384	947,831	817,387
Earnings From Operations	83,149	86,868	73,587
Other Income (Expenses)			
Interest Expense	(33,608)	(37,390)	(48,737)
Amortization of Goodwill	(4,649)	(4,511)	(4,537)
Income from Associated Companies	(97)	1,652	
Unusual Items	8,750	(3,073)	—
Earnings Before Taxes	53,545	41,894	22,145
Income Taxes	11,597	14,233	7,704
Earnings	$ 41,948	$ 27,661	$ 14,441
Earning per share	$1.45	$1.20	$0.94
Weighted average number of shares outstanding (000s)	28,838	22,978	15,295

EXHIBIT 3

LAWSON MARDON GROUP LIMITED
Multi-Option Facility Members[a]

LENDERS

C$75,000,000	£100,000,000
The Bank of Nova Scotia	The Bank of Nova Scotia
Royal Trust Corporation	National Westminster Bank
Swiss Bank Corporation (Canada)	Canadian Imperial Bank of Commerce
Canadian Imperial Bank of Commerce	Societe Generale (London)
Credit Suisse Canada	Credit Suisse
Dresdner Bank Canada	Dresdner Bank, AG
Societe Generale (Canada)	Royal Trust Bank
National Westminster Bank of Canada	Credits Lyonnais
	Chase Manhattan Bank N.A.
	Mellon Bank N.A.
	Lloyds Bank plc

TENDER PANEL MEMBERS

The Bank of Nova Scotia	Dresdner Bank AG, London
Banque Francaise Du Commerce Exterieur, London	Hill Samuel & Co. Limited
Canadian Imperial Bank of Commerce	International Westminster Bank Group
Credit Lyonnais	Merrill Lynch Capital Markets
Credit Suisse	Royal Trust Bank
Credit Suisse First Boston	Security Pacific Hoare
Lloyds Bank plc	Govett Limited
Mellon Bank N.A.	Societe Generale (London)
Chase Manhattan Bank N.A.	Kredietbank
Allied Irish Bank	Credit du Nord
Sumitomo Bank	

[a]Chase Manhattan Bank S.A. and Mellon Bank S.A. were added to the sterling tranche in May 1988.

EXHIBIT 4

Capital Market Data
May 1987–Feb. 1989

	LAWSON MARDON GROUP LIMITED[a]			TSE300 COMPOSITE INDEX		
MONTH	CLOSING PRICE	P/E	RATE OF RETURN	INDEX	P/E	RATE OF RETURN
1987 May[b]	$16.000	N/A	N/A	3685.24	20.34	−0.85%
Jun	16.750	15.2	4.69%	3740.19	20.95	1.49
July	17.375	15.8	3.73	4030.35	21.63	7.76
Aug	17.625	14.8	1.44	3993.60	20.25	−0.91
Sept	17.375	14.6	−1.42	3902.37	14.54	−2.28
Oct	12.250	10.6	−29.50	3019.27	14.83	−22.63
Nov	10.750	8.9	−12.25	2978.34	13.89	−1.36
Dec	12.625	10.4	19.30	3160.05	14.38	6.10

(continued)

EXHIBIT 4 (cont.)

	LAWSON MARDON GROUP LIMITED[a]			TSE300 COMPOSITE INDEX		
MONTH	CLOSING PRICE	P/E	RATE OF RETURN	INDEX	P/E	RATE OF RETURN
1988 Jan	11.750	9.7	−6.93	3057.22	13.42	−3.25
Feb	14.250	11.9	21.28	3204.83	12.87	4.82
Mar	14.000	11.7	−1.75	3313.79	13.21	3.40
Apr	15.000	12.5	7.86	3339.77	12.54	0.78
May	13.125	10.9	−12.50	3249.22	12.03	−2.71
Jun	14.125	11.4	7.62	3441.48	12.75	5.92
July	12.125	10.6	−7.08	3376.73	12.05	−1.88
Aug	13.250	10.7	2.48	3285.82	11.38	−2.69
Sept	13.375	11.7	0.94	3283.71	11.12	−0.06
Oct	12.125	12.4	5.61	3395.52	11.24	3.41
Nov	12.375	8.8	−11.68	3294.68	10.71	−2.97
Dec	12.625	9.0	2.02	3389.99	10.86	2.89
1989 Jan	12.750	9.0	0.99	3616.64	11.63	6.69
Feb	12.875	8.9	1.76	3572.12	11.35	−1.23

Beta = 1.408
Standard Deviation (LMG rate of return) = 38% per annum.

[a]Ticker symbol, LMP.A.
[b]Listed on the TSE, May 29, 1987.

EXHIBIT 5

Leading ECP and SCP Dealers

STERLING COMMERCIAL PAPER[a]		EURO-COMMERCIAL PAPER AND EURO CDs[b]	
INSTITUTION	NO. OF DEALERSHIPS	INSTITUTION	NO. OF DEALERSHIPS
1. County Nat-West	56	1. Citicorp	147
2. Barlays de Zoete Wedd	52	2. SBCI	142
3. S.G. Warburg & Co.	38	3. Merrill Lynch	117
4. Morgan Grenfel & Co.	34	4. Morgan Guaranty	117
5. Midland Montagu	31	5. Shearson Lehman	101
6. Lloyds	21	6. CSFB	97
7. Kelinworth Benson	20	7. S.G. Warburg	86
8. SBCI	18	8. Morgan Stanley	74
9. Citicorp	13	9. Chase Manhattan	71
10. Morgan Guaranty	8	10. Bankers Trust	50

[a]*Source: IFR*, Issue 706, January 9, 1988.
[b]*Source: The Treasurer*, May 1988.

EXHIBIT 6

U.S. Treasury Yields

U.S. Treasury Yield Curves

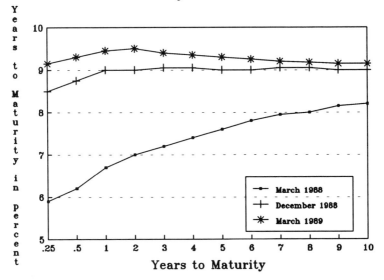

TED Spread

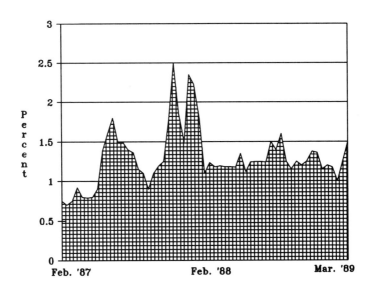

EXHIBIT 7

Summary of Industrial Bond Rating Classifications
Financial Measurement and Statistics
Median Values 1987

MEASUREMENTS	Aaa/AAA	Aa/AA	A/A	Baa/BBB	Ba/BB	B/B
Coverage						
Interest Coverage	14.70x	8.44x	5.61x	3.64x	2.07x	1.73x
Interest Coverage (Inc. Rents)	8.17x	5.59x	3.49x	2.41x	1.70x	1.41x
After Tax Coverage	10.05x	5.81x	3.87x	2.54x	1.85x	1.40x
After Tax Coverage (Inc. Rents)	6.46x	3.98x	2.53x	1.85x	1.51x	1.27x
LTD/LT Capitalization	10.73%	20.36%	29.35%	34.35%	48.10%	48.72%
Total Debt/Total Capital	19.80%	31.24%	35.03%	38.64%	50.71%	51.85%
Long Term Debt/Net Plant	16.99%	29.39%	47.14%	54.96%	69.10%	102.21%
Net Tangible Assets/Ltd	767.54%	431.27%	285.08%	242.63%	178.80%	191.84%
Net Tang. Assets/Total Debt	420.93%	299.39%	232.79%	202.62%	172.30%	170.00%
Total Liabilities/Stock Equity	78.31%	127.35%	119.03%	147.75%	186.89%	181.23%
Cash Flow/Short Term Debt	343.09%	318.43%	382.65%	418.62%	425.58%	218.83%
Cash Flow/Total Debt	103.10%	70.88%	48.65%	35.37%	30.55%	14.77%

Working Capit./LTD	348.89%	122.92%	78.01%	70.00%	50.24%	83.69%
Current Ratio	2.00x	1.45x	1.67x	1.54x	1.81x	2.04x
Cash Flow/Current Liabilities	64.24%	45.00%	48.52%	42.81%	48.97%	32.19%
Net Cash Flow/Capital Expend	149.65%	149.46%	125.51%	117.04%	123.40%	74.03%
Return on Equity	18.46%	18.63%	14.67%	11.68%	10.69%	9.11%
Return on Assets	17.78%	15.53%	12.99%	10.72%	10.03%	7.19%
Return on Permanent Capital	14.83%	20.35%	16.79%	14.21%	13.86%	9.31%
Statistics						
Cash and Equivalents	1148.20M	519.93M	112.00M	72.60M	48.36M	36.88M
Net Plant	1948.00M	2554.00M	891.20M	531.90M	397.00M	102.16M
Total Assets	6922.60M	6181.00M	2398.24M	1599.08M	1123.60M	385.41M
Long Term Debt	435.00M	762.60M	473.02M	347.49M	315.40M	140.17M
Stockholders Equity	3882.40M	2629.07M	1008.51M	588.24M	308.76M	101.56M
Net Sales	6170.30M	8258.40M	2898.06M	1703.53M	1514.43M	328.93M
Net Income	906.40M	480.00M	148.16M	52.44M	35.00M	8.21M
Capital Expenditure	344.10M	486.63M	179.75M	99.49M	79.30M	20.38M
Funds from Operations (FFO)	1049.80M	796.79M	305.47M	140.84M	116.95M	20.60M
Number of Companies	11	36	109	64	41	66

[a]*Source: 1987 Financial Measurement Handbook for Industrial Companies, First Boston, 1988.*

EXHIBIT 8

Number of Rating Changes

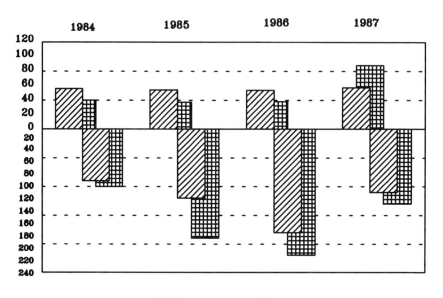

Source: 1987 Financial Measurement Handbook for Industrial Companies, First Boston, 1988.

11

FANTASTIC MANUFACTURING, INC.

In late October 1980, David Rose and Pierce Turner, principals of Fantastic Manufacturing, Inc., were preparing forecasts for their rapidly growing business assembling and marketing ceiling fans. A product many had thought of as a fad, ceiling fans had instead been accepted by consumers as energy conservers, and new-home builders and homeowners were installing them in record numbers.

Fantastic Manufacturing was incorporated in late 1976 by Mr. Rose and Mr. Turner in Charleston, South Carolina. Mr. Rose had his own manufacturers' representative, Rose Sales, Inc., with annual sales of approximately $40 million to accounts around the world. He specialized in sales of building materials to mass-merchandisers.

In 1976, Mr. Rose had found many of his accounts interested in ceiling fans, and at the end of that year he approached Mr. Turner, a tax attorney by training and head of his own manufacturing company, to discuss the possibility of importing and assembling ceiling fans. Agreeing with the idea, Mr. Turner accompanied Mr. Rose to Taiwan and Hong Kong to find parts suppliers for a new, low-priced, assemble-it-yourself fan. The men took their specifications to all the fan factories they could find in Taiwan and Hong Kong and selected exclusive suppliers.

Fantastic's first order for fans was placed in September 1977 and arrived in late November. After assembly, the fans were shipped to customers in December. By the end of the first fiscal year, which ended January 31, 1978, total sales were approximately $230,000.

Fantastic had begun operations by emphasizing sales of low-priced fans to the do-it-yourself market, selling largely through small stores. Initially, Mr. Rose and

Mr. Turner had viewed the product as appealing to nostalgia, and they expected limited growth potential. The initial objective of the business was to get the product on the shelf, and the company encouraged retailers to advertise heavily. Many stores used the product initially as a faddish draw.

Studies had shown, however, that ceiling fans were economically beneficial, reducing both cooling costs in summer and heating costs in winter. As consumers began viewing ceiling fans as energy-saving devices, the growth prospects for the industry improved. Much of this improvement was expected to come from the upper end of the market, for which Fantastic Manufacturing had positioned its recently introduced Cotillion line. Their major premium-line competition came from two domestic lines, Hunter and Casablanca, both produced by Emerson Electric. Emerson had done little to promote its products.

Not much public information was available about fan sales in general, so Mr. Rose and Mr. Turner had little to go on in estimating the potential for competition. They did know that Fantastic held a cost advantage because of its overseas sourcing. Customers were pleased with Fantastic's products and had commented positively on the high level of service and timeliness of delivery. The company's 7-year warranty on the fans had also encouraged consumer acceptance.

Fantastic's revenues increased rapidly from the beginning. In fiscal 1979 and 1980, the first two full years of operations, Fantastic had sales of $3.1 million and $9.9 million, respectively. Net profits in those years were $73,000 and $108,000, as shown in Exhibit 1. Although 1980 revenues had increased 213 percent from the prior year, net income rose only 48 percent because of substantially higher costs. Increased rent, advertising, bad debts, and interest costs had caused selling, general, and administrative costs to increase over 250 percent.

Fan sales were seasonal, with over 65 percent of revenues coming between April and September, as shown in Exhibit 2. Sales were made by salespeople working exclusively on commission. Commissions were paid in the same month the sales were made. The company served more than 100 customers, including many small accounts as well as mass-merchandisers and home center stores such as Kmart, J.C. Penney, Zayre, Ace Hardware, Best Products, and 84 Lumber. Two customers, however, had accounted for approximately 40 percent of total sales in 1980.

Salespeople wrote and confirmed the orders, with no penalty for cancellation. Customers typically paid between 60 and 90 days after Fantastic shipped the merchandise. Accounts receivable were of good quality, although the bad debts/sales ratio was 2.1 percent in 1980 because of unpaid accounts from some small stores. Balance sheets for the period are shown in Exhibit 3.

The lead time for Fantastic's orders was 60 days—30 days for their suppliers to manufacture the fan parts once the order had been received and 30 days for shipping. Because the manufacturers had limited capacity, they could not supply highly variable quantities on short notice. As a result, Fantastic management had decided to place regular fan component orders, assemble the fans, and hold them in inventory until they were sold.

To finance the parts orders, their suppliers in Taiwan and Hong Kong required that letters of credit (L/C) be issued at the time the merchandise was ordered. A typical L/C was for 30 days, the time required to manufacture the goods and prepare them for shipment. The L/Cs were submitted for payment by the supplier when the merchandise was shipped. Because growth had been rapid, Fantastic did not keep cash available to pay for the goods when the L/C documents arrived at the bank. Thus, the company typically drew a 60-day draft on the bank in the amount of the needed funds. The bank would accept the draft under an arrangement already established with Fantastic and extend the loan for a discounted amount of the draft. All Fantastic's current financing arrangements are summarized in Exhibit 4, along with representative short-term borrowing costs for 1978 to 1980.

The cost of the fans delivered at the Charleston plant had averaged 63 percent of Fantastic's final selling price. This cost varied with exchange rates, shown in Exhibit 5. So far about half of the fans had been sourced from Hong Kong and half from Taiwan. Mr. Rose and Mr. Turner were satisfied with their suppliers and expected the relationships to continue.

The company's warehouse was located near Charleston in a building that had been purchased in July 1979 by a partnership owned by Mr. Rose and Mr. Turner and subsequently leased back to Fantastic. The term of the lease was 15 years, with annual payments of $185,000. The 116,000-square-foot facility was sufficient to support a sales volume of approximately $100 million. Most of the operations were simple; the company used the facility for unloading, inspecting, processing, repacking, and shipping the imported goods. The trickiest part of the operation was weighing and balancing the fan blades.

For the first half of fiscal 1981, sales were $15.8 million and profits $1 million. By year-end, Mr. Rose and Mr. Turner expected sales to reach $30 million. Mr. Rose believed sales for 1982 would be over $71 million. He knew that this represented substantial growth in demand that far outstripped forecasts[1], but with Fantastic's $40-million order backlog, the forecast seemed reasonable. Furthermore, he believed that a return on sales of 9.8 percent was likely.

Up to now Fantastic had grown more rapidly than had been expected and planning had been lacking. Orders to suppliers had been based on forecasts of sales with a lead time of two months, and Fantastic's creditors had been willing to satisfy the growing company's capital needs on demand. Mr. Rose and Mr. Turner believed that, to continue good relations with these two critical groups, longer range forecasts would be useful. As sales grew, suppliers would have to arrange for ways to produce more, and Fantastic would have increasing needs for funds.

Mr. Rose and Mr. Turner looked at the company's brief history, considered their forecasts for the expected demand for ceiling fans, and decided their first decision would be for how long to forecast. So far demand had grown so rapidly that forecasts for even a few months would be rapidly outdated. On the other hand, some order needed to be brought to their relationships with their parts and capital suppliers. Good forecasts would help.

[1]The U.S. Department of Commerce had forecast little growth in retail sales of home appliances through mid-1982 and a slight decline in sales in the second half of that year.

EXHIBIT 1

FANTASTIC MANUFACTURING, INC.
Income Statements
(in thousands)

	YEAR ENDING		THREE MONTHS ENDING	SIX MONTHS ENDING
	JANUARY 31, 1979	JANUARY 31, 1980	APRIL 31, 1980	JULY 31, 1980
Net revenues	$3,155	$9,860	$6,693	$15,818
Cost of goods sold	2,263	7,306	4,543	10,310
Gross profit	892	2,554	2,150	5,508
Salaries and payroll taxes	252	308		
Commissions	149	487		
Freight	19	62		
Rent	0	128		
Bad debts	24	209		
Interest[a]	78	496		
Other selling, general, and administrative	278	709		
Total operating expenses	800	2,399	1,615	3,428
Income before taxes	92	155	535	2,080
Taxes	19	47	239	998
Net income before extraordinary item	73	108	296	1,082
Extraordinary item (net of income tax credit)	0	0	0	(94)
Net income	$ 73	$ 108	$ 296	$ 988

[a]Includes line-of-credit charges.

EXHIBIT 2

FANTASTIC MANUFACTURING, INC.
Monthly Pattern of Sales, 1979 and 1980

	PROPORTION OF ANNUAL SALES
January	2.8%
February	5.9
March	7.8
April	9.8
May	10.8
June	11.2
July	11.7
August	12.7
September	9.8
October	7.8
November	5.8
December	3.9
	100.0%

EXHIBIT 3

FANTASTIC MANUFACTURING, INC.
Balance Sheet
(in thousands of dollars)

	JANUARY 31, 1979	JANUARY 31, 1980	APRIL 30, 1980	JULY 31, 1980
Assets				
Cash	$ 3	$ 1	$ 1	$ 1
Accounts receivable	387	2,045	3,898	4,568
Due from affiliates	0	160	70	317
Collateral on letters of credit	97	83	171	249
Inventory	928	2,092	2,761	1,536
Inventory in transit	478	2,690	1,414	1,864
Prepaid expenses	26	78	155	112
Insurance claims receivable	0	0	0	756
Income tax refund receivable	0	0	0	134
Note receivable	0	0	0	53
Total current assets	1,919	7,149	8,470	9,590
Net property and equipment	384	241	402	614
Deposits	0	57	65	61
Total assets	$ 2,303	$ 7,447	$ 8,937	$ 10,265
Liabilities and Shareholders' Equity				
Accounts payable	$ 294	$ 613	$ 774	$ 628
Bank overdraft		312	445	51
Due to banks				
Receivable financing	252	2,046	2,682	4,493
Inventory financing	1,127	3,531	3,518	1,716
Other	0	100	100	0
Current portion of long-term debt	22	31	44	74
Due to affiliates and shareholders	43	533	719	1,161
Taxes payable	8	23	85	891
Total current liabilities	1,746	7,189	8,367	9,014
Long-term debt	360	36	53	43
Notes payable, shareholders	85	0	0	0
Total liabilities	2,191	7,225	8,420	9,057
Shareholders' equity[a]	1	1	1	1
Retained earnings	111	221	516	1,207
Net worth	112	222	517	1,208
Total liabilities and shareholders' equity	$ 2,303	$ 7,447	$ 8,937	$ 10,265
Net of allowance for doubtful accounts	$23,126	$121,821	$300,000	$336,447

[a]Common stock, $5 par; authorized, issued, and outstanding, 100 shares.

EXHIBIT 4

FANTASTIC MANUFACTURING, INC.
Summary of Financing Arrangements

LENDER	AMOUNT	USE	RATE	COLLATERAL
Congress Financial Corp.	Varied	Direct loan on eligible accounts receivable	Prime + 6%	All accounts receivable Personal guarantees Deposits by stock-holders
Standard Chartered	$6 million	Letters of credit Banker's acceptances ($4.5 million limit)	Prime + 1½% Banker's accept-ances + 2%	All inventory and personal guarantees Deposits by stock-holders Partial guarantee by Congress Financial 10% deposit on L/Cs
Capital Bank	$1 million	Letters of credit	Prime + 1½%	Unsecured

Recent Prime and Banker's Acceptance Rates

YEAR/ QUARTER	AVERAGE PRIME RATE	BANKER'S ACCEPTANCE, ANNUAL AVERAGE RATE (90 DAYS)
1978		
1	8.0%	6.8%
2	8.5	7.3
3	9.5	8.2
4	10.5	10.1
1979		
1	11.0	10.1
2	11.5	9.9
3	12.6	10.1
4	14.9	13.4
1980		
1	17.6	14.9
2	16.0	11.8
3	11.8	9.9

EXHIBIT 5

Recent Exchange Rates

HONG KONG DOLLARS (HK$) PER U.S. DOLLAR (US$)

March 31, 1978	4.6202	February 6, 1980	4.8616
June 30	4.6505	February 13	4.8668
July 31	4.6396	February 20	4.9221
August 30	4.7102	February 27	4.9421
December 29	4.7869	March 26	5.0751
March 30, 1979	4.9927	March 30	4.9059
June 29	5.0690	May 28	4.8898
July 26	5.1814	June 9	4.9179
September 28	4.9784	June 30	4.9300
October 17	4.9468	July 30	4.9564
December 31	4.9516	August 27	4.9481
January 30, 1980	4.8011	September 29	4.9916

NEW TAIWAN DOLLARS (NT$) PER U.S. DOLLAR (US$)[a]

June 18, 1980	36.1312	September 3, 1980	35.8680
July 2	35.9703	September 17	36.0711
July 16	36.0590	October 1	35.9891
July 30	35.5765	October 8	36.0685
August 6	35.5158	October 13	36.0000

[a]In July 1978, the NT$ was allowed to float around its fixed exchange rate of NT$38 = US$1.

Source: National Westminster Bank.

12

MASCHINENBAU ARRAU A.G. (A)

On 24 October 1986, Herren Peter Muller, Chairman of the Executive Board, and Walter Angst, Finance Director, respectively of Maschinenbau Arrau A.G. (MAG), a Swiss machine tool manufacturer, were faced with the decision of how to manage the foreign exchange risk and funding needs arising from a potential $100 million contract with the Soviet Union. The company had been negotiating this order with the Soviet Committee for Science and Technology (SCST) in Moscow. The equivalent of CHF 165 million at current exchange rates, it would be the largest single contract that this firm had ever considered undertaking.

THE COMPANY

MAG was founded in 1895 by Heinz Baumann in Arrau and had remained under family ownership until 1955 when it obtained a listing on the Zurich stock exchange. Following several increases of capital where family members elected not to fully subscribe, the majority of the company's shares were traded publicly by 1986. The company manufactured a complete range of single and multiple spindle lathes, including numerically controlled models, and various other types of machine tools. The major portion of sales was to the automotive industry, and its products were used by every major automobile manufacturer in the world. The latest pro forma balance sheet and income statement appear on Exhibit 1.

This case was written by H. Lee Remmers, Professor at INSEAD. It is intended to be used as a basis for class discussion rather than to illustrate either effective or ineffective handling of an administrative situation. Reprinted with the permission of INSEAD.

Sales volume had increased from CHF 380 million in 1975 to CHF 480 million for the most recent fiscal year. However, sales had suffered considerably during the 1979–1982 years as the automobile industry in the OECD member countries went through a severe restructuring. Although sales had more than recovered, competition in the machine tool industry was fierce, and profit margins were tiny. Profits were especially sensitive to changes in sales volume since, with the exception of materials and components, virtually all costs were fixed. MAG had five principal competitors, one each in the United States, France, Germany, Italy, and Japan. The German, American, and Japanese firms were all larger, although none enjoyed MAG's reputation for high quality of product and customer service. The American competitor was beginning to enjoy the benefits of the recent depreciation of the dollar, allowing it, in effect, to cut prices. It was for these reasons that the company's management had been particularly anxious to diversify its markets and obtain a part of the $400 million order for machine tools needed in the modernization of the major automobile manufacturer in the Soviet Union.

FINANCIAL POLICY

MAG had long pursued very conservative policies in managing its finances and foreign exchange positions. Funds were raised only in Swiss francs which had almost always been the cheapest obtainable. Foreign exchange risk was covered by entering into forward contracts taken to mature on the machine purchase contract payment dates, or, in the case of purchases, on the date the order was placed with their supplier. MAG usually found that its clients would not agree to be invoiced in Swiss francs, especially during the past 18 months. Machine purchase contracts were normally priced using the forward rate (quoted in Zurich) for that maturity which corresponded to the specified payment dates.

Whenever it became apparent that the actual payment date would deviate from the date specified in the machine purchase contract (and, therefore, from the maturity of the forward contracts), it was strict company policy to prolong the original forward contract, usually by means of a swap, regardless of the cost. The finance director, Herr Angst, believed that the higher the cost of prolonging a forward contract (in terms of the forward discount), the more essential it was to do so. He maintained that short-term interest rate differentials were influenced by speculative capital flows. Therefore, this would be reflected in the forward discount or premium. Herr Angst's view on this was founded on a painful experience suffered the previous year when a two-week late payment by a major British client cost MAG nearly CHF 100,000 for prolonging the forward cover. They decided not to press the client for recovery of the loss for fear of jeopardizing future orders.

THE SOVIET CONTRACT

Under the terms of the agreement being discussed with the SCST, a small team of Soviet technicians would come to the company's plant to verify the performance of each group of machines prior to their shipment. After acceptance by the Soviet team, payment in dollars would be made within one week. The SCST had always been considered in Swiss industrial circles to be fair in its dealings and a reliable payer; hence any delay in payment from the original specified dates would most likely be caused by engineering or production problems encountered by MAG.

On 10 October 1986, a four-man MAG negotiating team in Moscow reported that there was a reasonably good chance for the firm to sell up to $100 million worth of machine tools to the Soviets for delivery beginning December 1987.

A tender would have to be submitted by 27 October. The bid would be binding, at a fixed dollar price, and be accompanied by a performance guarantee provided by a major Swiss or German bank. The SCST would announce its decision on 26 November, 30 days later. The MAG sales team had met frequently with representatives from the SCST during early October, and had survived long meetings with them consuming prodigious quantities of food and drink. Nevertheless, by the 10th of October when the report was sent, it remained very uncertain how much, if any, of the $100 million contract they could expect. They were able to learn that the toughest competition would come from the American machine tool manufacturer referred to above; this firm would have the advantage of bidding in its own currency, thus avoiding any exchange risk.

In order to improve the chances of being awarded all or a major part of the contract, Herren Muller and Angst decided to modify their usual pricing policy. The bid would be based on the minimum catalog price less 5% and would not include any allowance for potential cost increases. They believed that the economies of scale gained from such a large contract would offset any unexpected cost increases. Minimum catalog prices were calculated on total cost at full plant capacity plus a 10% markup. Roughly one-third of total costs would be for materials and components. About 40% of these, mostly electronic equipment, represented dollar purchases—mainly from the United States. The exchange rate used for the bid would be the average of the high and low spot rates quoted by their principal Zurich bank on 23 October—CHF 1.65 per U.S. dollar.

Assuming that MAG would receive the entire amount of the tender—$100 million, and that it would be able to make delivery as specified in the contract, payment dates and amounts would be as follows:

1 December 1987	$25 million
1 March 1988	$25 million
1 June 1988	$25 million
1 September 1988	$25 million

DECISION ALTERNATIVES

The U.S. dollar had depreciated nearly 45% against the Swiss franc between mid-March 1985 and October 1986 (see Exhibit 2). During the first part of October, it had fallen as low as CHF 1.60 and had traded in the CHF 1.60 to 1.675 range since then. The economic forecasting unit at MAG's principal bank, Credit Helvetia, was very cautious about predicting how the dollar might move over the next 12 to 18 months. A currency newsletter service subscribed to by Herr Angst predicted a trading range from CHF 1.50 to 2.00 depending on which political/economic scenario the reader chose to accept. Most views circulating around financial circles in Zurich agreed that exchange rates would be volatile, especially in the short term. Hence, Herren Muller and Angst decided that the prospective contract should be hedged during the bid period and also subsequently from the contract award date to each payment—assuming the contract would be won.

One way to protect themselves during the bid period was to take a one-month forward contract to mature on 24 November at the 0.0035 CHF per dollar forward discount. In considering this, Herr Angst pointed out this would cost the company about CHF 350,000 on a $100 million forward contract. Moreover, he argued, it would be completely lost in the event that they were not awarded any of the contract. As an alternative, he suggested that the expected dollar payments specified in the purchase contract (see above) be covered at the time of the tender by forward contracts of the same amounts and maturities. If the contract were not received or only partially received, he believed he would be able to reduce or unwind the exposed positions with relatively little risk or loss.

Herr Muller believed a better way to obtain the necessary foreign exchange protection while at the same time provide working capital finance would be to borrow Eurodollars and convert them to Swiss francs. He estimated that the equivalent of about $20 million on average during the construction period would be needed to finance inventories including work-in-progress—if the bid were accepted in its entirety. In addition, the overdraft could be repaid saving interest expense, and the remainder of the proceeds from the dollar loans placed on deposit.

In discussing this alternative with his Chairman, Herr Angst was convinced that its cost would be practically identical to that of the forward contracts, but agreed to consider it carefully. After some further thought, he came up with yet another variation in which they would borrow Eurodollars in amounts and maturities to match the expected dollar payments by the Soviets, and invest the proceeds in long term Swiss corporate bonds. Since they were yielding substantially more than short term money market instruments, this approach should result in lower costs of covering the dollar position.

Debating the pros and cons of the above alternatives over lunch, Herren Muller and Angst decided they should ask the advice of their banker, Dr. Jurg Sprungli, before coming to a decision. Meeting with them later that afternoon and after listening to their arguments, Dr. Sprungli suggested that they divide the risk into two parts—the bid period and the post-bid period.

For the post-bid period of exposure, once the amount and timing of the contract were known with reasonable certainty, the different alternatives Herren Muller and Angst had been discussing were all suitable, depending on the financing needs and position of MAG. This, he offered, would have to be looked at in terms of cost and risk by Herr Angst.

However, Dr. Sprungli argued that during the bid period, none of the methods they had discussed was entirely suitable since one side of the hedge (the Soviet contract) was uncertain. The ideal instrument, according to Dr. Sprungli, was an option to sell dollars at a pre-arranged rate—or exercise price. His bank would be willing to sell MAG a one-month option that would give MAG the right to sell dollars against Swiss francs at the present spot rate (CHF 1.65) for a premium of CHF 0.0375 per dollar. If they did not want to sell dollars in one month's time, the option could be discarded; if the dollar weakened, they could buy dollars spot and sell them to the bank at the exercise price, thus making a profit. The option could only be exercised at maturity, i.e., a "European" option; the bank would not buy it back from MAG prior to expiration or exercise.

Before leaving the MAG executive offices, Dr. Sprungli brought up two other points for his clients to consider. Dollar interest rates had fallen considerably during the past months, with considerable effect on the differential between them and Swiss franc rates (see Exhibit 3). As a result, the discount on forward contracts had fallen. When and if they did cover the dollar exposure from the sale to the Soviets with either a forward contract or a Eurodollar loan, they needed to decide on whether the cover should be "long" (i.e., their standard policy to cover from the signing of a firm contract to the specified payment dates), or a series of "short" positions which would be rolled-over until the Soviets paid. This latter approach would implicitly anticipate a further narrowing of the interest rate differential. Secondly, Dr. Sprungli suggested they check carefully their existing currency positions before deciding on a particular method of covering.

The banker left Herren Muller and Angst with a number of new ideas, but also with more doubts about the best course of action. Both of them had read about options, but never thought they had any application in their type of operations. They were both concerned about the cost of an option—over $2\frac{1}{4}\%$ of the Swiss franc/dollar spot rate would amount to a premium of CHF 3.75 million!!! What if they did not get the contract? They doubted if they could add much of the cost of the option premium to their bid price without seeing the contract rejected by the Russians. At this point the forward looked definitely cheaper at only CHF 350,000. Besides, the other members of the Board and the major shareholders no doubt all understood what was implied by a forward contract. Herr Muller had always regarded them as a very conservative group; a currency option would probably be considered speculative by them.

Both executives agreed to spend the weekend to work out the advantages and disadvantages of each method of managing their foreign exchange risk and financing requirements implied by the Soviet tender.

EXHIBIT 1

MASCHINENBAU ARRAU A.G.
Pro Forma Balance Sheet
30 September 1986
(millions of Swiss francs)

Assets		Capital & Liabilities	
Fixed assets (net)	155	Owners' equity	175
		Long term debt	85
Current Assets		Current Liabilities	
Inventories	170	Notes payable	20
Receivables	85	Overdraft	36
Cash & bank	5	Payables & accruals[a]	99
	260		155
Total	415	Total	415

[a]Firm orders totalling $12 million had been placed with American suppliers, but, exceptionally, were currently uncovered. All other exposed positions were covered by forward contracts.

Pro Forma Income Statement
Year Ending 30 September 1986
(millions of Swiss francs)

Sales revenues	480
Cost of sales & services	358
Administrative, selling & research expenses	90
EBIT	32
Interest expense	11
Earnings before tax	21
Corporate taxes	7
Earnings after tax	14

EXHIBIT 2

Exchange Rates—Swiss Francs/U.S. Dollars

FORWARD RATES – 3 MONTH MATURITIES
USD VS. CHF – DISCOUNT FROM SPOT

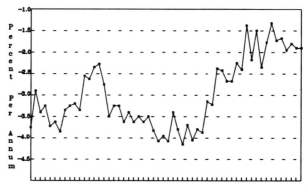

Weekly Data – 1/1/85 to 24/10/86

Foreign Exchange°
24 October, 1986

FORWARD OUTRIGHT RATES

Spot rate	1-month	3-month	6-month	12-month	18-month
1.6500	1.6465	1.6420	1.6340	1.6170	1.5985

Option Prices:		1 month maturity	
Exercise price	1.6500	Premium .0375	
Exercise price	1.6465	Premium .0355	

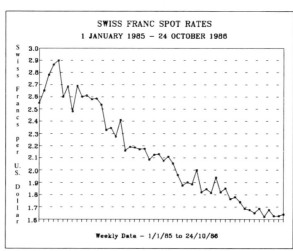

Source: Credit Helvetia, Zurich.

EXHIBIT 3

Interest Rates

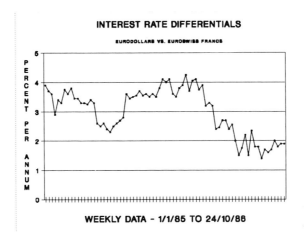

INTEREST RATE DIFFERENTIALS

EURODOLLARS VS. EUROSWISS FRANCS

WEEKLY DATA - 1/1/85 TO 24/10/86

Selected Interest Rates
24 October 1986

	MATURITIES				
LIBOR	1-month	3-month	6-month	12-month	18-month
Euro$[a]	6 1/16%	6 1/16%	6 1/8%	6 1/4%	6 3/8%
EuroCHF	3 1/2	4 1/8	4 1/8	4 1/8	4 3/16

Overdraft rate applicable to MAG: 6%

Swiss corporate bond yields (average top "names"): 4 3/4%

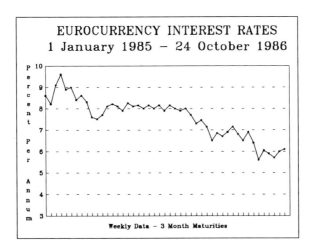

EUROCURRENCY INTEREST RATES
1 January 1985 — 24 October 1986

Weekly Data – 3 Month Maturities

---

[a]Spread over LIBOR on loans to MAG: 25 basis points.
Source: Reuters.

13

DOW EUROPE

In January 1990, Mr. Gaston Cevallos, Assistant Treasurer of Dow Europe, the European management unit of Dow Chemical Company, reflected on the effectiveness of modifications made to the company's foreign exchange management systems during the previous year. On January 1, 1989, Dow Europe had (a) switched from the United States dollar (USD) to the Ecu (European Currency Unit) as a basis for intercompany transactions, (b) changed to the local currency as the "functional currency" when translating foreign subsidiary financial statements to the USD, and (c) implemented a system for projecting the sensitivity of cash-flows to foreign currency movements. The three measures were intended to provide more efficient and representative management of the transaction, translation, and economic exposure faced by Dow.

For Dow, efficient foreign exchange (forex) management was exceedingly important. The company's two primary product areas, chemicals and plastics, were global industries characterized by low margins and dominated by large multinational corporations. Both industries were extremely cyclical, vulnerable to changes in the price of oil and fluctuations in economic growth. The characteristics of the industries placed a premium on efficient financial management of which foreign exchange management was an integral part. Dow had always taken a very aggressive approach

This case was prepared by Research Associate David H. Hover, under the supervision of Professor John J. Pringle, as a basis for class discussion rather than to illustrate either effective or ineffective handling of a business situation.

to forex management and had developed a wide reputation within the industry as a company unwilling to rest on its laurels.

Responsibility for forex management was held primarily by the treasury department. A number of foreign exchange management systems had been in place at Dow, but the need for adjustments to the systems had become apparent during the 1980s as strong growth in Dow Europe's operations and fluctuations in the USD exposed weaknesses.

Further, managers of the treasury department felt that certain exposures to foreign currency movements were not accurately identified and a more integrated approach would directly benefit the company. The question Mr. Cevallos asked himself was whether the changes made were really worthwhile, or had Dow Europe merely substituted one set of problems for another.

COMPANY BACKGROUND

The Dow Chemical Company

The Dow Chemical Company was founded in 1897 by Herbert Dow in Midland, Michigan, to produce chlorine extracted from local brine deposits. Following World War II, the company began developing petroleum-based chemicals and plastics as the demand for these products increased. By 1989 Dow Chemical had grown to be the sixth largest chemical company in the world with sales of $17,600 million and profits of $2,487 million. (Exhibits 1a and 1b are summary financial statements of the Dow Chemical Company.) The five largest chemical companies ranked in order by sales in 1989 were: BASF (West Germany), Hoechst (West Germany), Bayer (West Germany), Imperial Chemical Industries (United Kingdom), and Du Pont (USA).

Dow Chemical had traditionally focused on the production of bulk chemicals, used largely as raw materials in a wide variety of industrial processes, and industrial plastics for everything from car bumpers to compact disks. These commodity chemicals and plastics businesses typically had a low value-added component as the technology required was readily available and the large number of companies in the industry assured competition. A further complication was that chemical and plastic plants were extremely expensive to build and, once completed, difficult to convert to a different type of product. The primary feedstocks for the chemicals and plastics produced by the industry were naphtha, a petroleum derivative, and natural gas. Both products were widely traded on various markets. Dow concentrated on process technology, believing it was the best way to achieve and maintain a competitive advantage in the industry.

The 1980s were a tumultuous period for the large chemical giants. The second oil shock in 1979 and the 1982 recession reduced profits at most of the multinational chemical manufacturers. Straddled with excess capacity and very high raw material costs, there was little any of the companies could do but wait and hope for a recovery.

Beginning in 1983, demand gradually began to recover and to absorb excess capacity. Falling oil prices helped prolong the recovery through the end of the decade.

The Dow Organization

Dow Chemical had developed a three-dimensional organizational structure. The three axes were product line, geographical region, and functional area.

Preliminary work had also begun on an additional reporting line based on certain industries, such as automobiles, where customers purchased a wide variety of products throughout the world. The importance of any individual line of authority varied according to specific conditions. The treasury group, for example, was organized with very strong functional lines although individual treasurers were geographically based. Generally, however, the most cohesive lines of authority were based on geographical regions. Although complex, the organization was seen as effective given the nature of the company and the operating environment.

Dow maintained four primary product groups: chemicals (31%), plastics (41%), consumer specialties and pharmaceuticals (18%), and hydrocarbons and miscellaneous (10%). (Product group sales as a percentage of total company sales are indicated in parentheses.) Geographically, the company was organized as five areas: U.S., Canada, Latin America, Pacific, and Europe. Each area was further subdivided into regions. The regional subsidiaries were responsible for operations in either a group of countries or a single country, depending on the importance of the market.

Dow Europe

Dow Europe managed Dow Chemical Company's operations in Europe, the Middle East, and Africa from its offices in Horgen, Switzerland, an idyllic village 15 kilometers south of Zurich. The European management structure was further broken down into eight regional units: Germany, France, Italy, Iberica, United Kingdom, Benelux, Nordic, and MEAF (Middle East, Africa, Eastern Europe, Austria and Switzerland). The regional management units reported to Dow Europe headquarters.

Manufacturing operations were located in each of the regions. The most important production sites were located in Holland, Germany, and Spain. (Dow Holland operated the largest production facility in Dow Europe and the third largest for Dow worldwide.) Other regionals had production sites which varied in size, although most were relatively small. The MEAF regional, which had the highest sales volume, had virtually no production.

Treasury Organization

Treasury department operations at Dow reflected the company's philosophy of keeping decision-making responsibility centered at the lowest possible level. In Midland, the corporate treasury department focused its operations on long term finance and global functional responsibilities. The balance of the corporate treasury office's efforts were directed at enhancing the performance of the subsidiaries' treasuries through policy development and leadership.

The Dow Europe treasury office in Horgen, one of the five Dow area offices, was responsible for financial planning and strategy for the treasury unit, mergers and acquisitions operations, and funding coordination for the company's European area operations. The Horgen office also developed bank relationships and the necessary financial vehicles to insure that regional units had access to financing.

It was at the area level that Dow also centered most of its foreign exchange management. (Exhibit 2 is an organizational chart of the treasury department of Dow Europe.)

Regional treasuries were where operational activities, including credit, collections, cash management, project financing, and legal entity monitoring, took place. (Exhibit 3 shows areas of responsibility within Dow Treasury.) Regional treasurers had direct reporting responsibility both to the general manager of the region and the Treasurer of Dow Europe. Dow Europe's Treasurer reported to both the Treasurer of Dow Chemical in Midland and the President of Dow Europe.

DOW'S APPROACH TO FOREIGN EXCHANGE EXPOSURE

Three types of foreign exchange exposure were generally defined: transaction, translation, and economic. *Transaction* exposure occurred between the time a transaction, denominated in a foreign currency, was initiated and the time payment was received. During this period the relative values of each of the currencies could change, changing the value of the transaction. *Translation* exposure occurred from one period to the next, when a subsidiary's financial statements, denominated in a currency other than that of the consolidating company's, were restated in the reporting currency of the parent company. *Economic* exposure was the long range exposure of cash flows to changes in exchange rates.[1]

Dow's System for Managing Transaction Exposure

In the mid-1960s, when 100% of Dow's European sales were sourced in the U.S., the related foreign exchange management issues were limited. Dow would sell, for example, 100 cubic meters of Styrofoam to a French packaging company which would pay for the transaction in FFR (French francs). Dow would then convert the FFR to USD using one of the company's U.S. banks. Dow had foreign exchange transaction exposure between the time the contract was made and the time payment was received, but the exposure was easily managed. The local Dow sales offices were not overly concerned with exchange rates; foreign exchange management was Midland's responsibility.

As local operations and production sites proliferated, the currency issues faced by the company became more pronounced. By the mid-1980s, local production accounted for 95% of Dow Europe's sales, of which 30% were denominated in

[1]Consult the appendix for more detailed definitions.

currencies other than the local currency of the particular subsidiary involved. Dow needed a system for managing the large volume of foreign currencies generated by the company's sales structure (sales were denominated in 14 different currencies on a regular basis).

Sales transactions were generally one of four types, three of which generated transaction exposure for the subsidiaries. Differences in the characteristics of each type required special methods of handling the resulting exposure. The four types, with examples, were:

1. Transactions with local customers in local currencies: a German company purchased Styrofoam from Dow Germany and paid in DM, Dow Germany's operating currency. (No transaction exposure.)

2. Transactions between Dow subsidiaries with different operating currencies (Dow referred to this type of transaction as intercompany rather than intracompany): Dow Germany, which used DM as its operating currency, purchased agrichemicals for resale from Dow UK, which used pounds sterling as the operating currency.

3. Local customers paying with non-local currencies: similar to situation (1) except the customer made payments in French francs to reduce its excess balances in that currency. (For competitive reasons Dow's policy was to permit the customer to choose the currency.)

4. Non-local customers paying with non-local currencies: customers from other countries occasionally approached Dow units outside their usual territories for purchases of specialized products. This was discouraged by Dow but was occasionally necessary.

For Dow subsidiaries, transactions of types (2), (3), and (4) generated transaction exposure between the subsidiary's operating currency and the currency used in the transaction. For intercompany transactions (type 2), Dow Europe had established a clearing system which allowed the company to offset some currency exposures. The intercompany clearing system was not suited to third-party transactions (types 3 and 4) and, for these, an in-house factoring procedure had been devised.

Dow's Internal Factoring System

When Dow first initiated foreign currency sales, the company established a reinvoicing system to centralize the management of foreign exchange. Under the reinvoicing system adopted by Dow, as with other reinvoicing systems, after a sale, the sales unit sent an invoice to the reinvoicing center. The reinvoicing center then issued a new invoice to the customer and at the same time assumed responsibility for collection of the receivable. The sales unit received payment from the reinvoicing center in its local currency. Postal delays, excessive paper work (reinvoicing required two sets of invoices to be produced), and separation between the customer and the vendor created problems and led Dow to abandon the system in the early 1980s.

After the reinvoicing system was abandoned, Dow operated for a short while without centralized intercompany transactions. Instead, all sales to third parties were handled by the regions as was any related foreign exchange management. The lack of a centralized foreign exchange system was not entirely out of character with the goals of the Dow company. Dow tried to push decision-making responsibility as far down the corporate hierarchy as feasible.

Centralized forex management had a number of advantages including funding of receivables and easier collection of cross border receivables, which eventually enticed Dow to develop a new internal factoring system. Under the new system, regions sold their third-party receivables denominated in non-local currencies to Dow Factoring, a wholly owned subsidiary of Dow Europe. Dow Factoring purchased the receivables at a discount to face value and assumed responsibility for both collection and managing the forex risk.

Centralized forex management also permitted netting. Netting occurred, for example, when FFR, received from a FFR paying customer, were used to pay the factored receivables of Dow France. Dow Factoring maintained a cash pool which consisted of balances in a number of the currencies in which Dow had significant sales. NGL (Dutch guilders), DM (West German marks), GBP (British pounds), and FFR were the primary currencies Dow paid out because of the extensive operations in those countries. Frequently, to meet the needs of the netting system, Dow had to purchase Belgian francs, Spanish pesetas, and Dutch guilders as these currencies did not generally enter the system through normal transactions. Other currencies were generally available within the system and excess balances were sold in bulk for USD. Because of the size of the transactions, Dow was able to command meaningful price reductions.

By 1988, most of Dow Europe's USD 6 billion in sales to external customers were local sales. Only one-fourth of total sales were factored, approximately half of which were denominated in dollars. Geographically, 45% of the factored sales were from the MEAF region.

Dow's Clearing System for Intercompany Transactions

The internal factoring system described above was used only for third-party transactions (sales transactions types (3) and (4) above). Intercompany transactions between Dow units in Europe (type (2) transactions) were handled via an internal clearing system.

Prior to January 1, 1989, transactions within the internal clearing system between Dow units were invoiced in USD. Corresponding receivables and payables were denominated on subsidiary balance sheets in USD. For convenience, a company-wide exchange rate, or bookrate as it was known, was established for each currency at the beginning of every month. The bookrate was used for accounting conversions, including intercompany transactions, factoring, translations, etc., throughout the company during the month.

All intercompany transactions were managed through a special Dow Europe subsidiary. The settling of system accounts occurred once monthly, at which time cumulative transactions for the month were processed. After establishing the net positions of each subsidiary, positive net intercompany balances were paid to the subsidiaries in a currency of their choice, usually their local operating currency. Negative net positions with the clearing system were also usually paid by the subsidiary in its local currency. The exchange rate used to determine payments was set on the morning of the day of the clearing, after which Dow entered the spot market to buy and sell the necessary currencies.

Transaction exposure between the time of the intercompany sale and the clearing date was hedged by the individual subsidiaries. The subsidiaries needed only to hedge their USD denominated receivables or payables within the system against their local currency until the next clearing. The USD was selected for intercompany invoicing because it was the operating currency of Dow Europe and the currency of the parent company, Dow Chemical.

Netting of debits and credits in individual currencies was the primary benefit of the clearing system and had been the original objective of the system when developed in the 1960s. Netting occurred, for example, when FFR received from one transaction were used to settle FFR obligations arising from other transactions. Other advantages of the centralized clearing systems further reduced costs and facilitated management.

In 1988, the clearing system handled USD 6 billion in intercompany transactions, USD 2.5 billion of which was netted.

PROBLEMS WITH THE SYSTEM.   By the late 1980s, the intercompany clearing system had been operational for many years, and senior managers in Midland were generally satisfied with its performance. The only significant problem with the existing system was that receivables and payables associated with the clearing system were denominated in USD on the balance sheets of the subsidiaries. While many of the subsidiaries' positions were netted out as the month progressed, some subsidiaries were chronically long or short relative to the USD. Dow Holland, for example, was a major recipient of intercompany transfers and had large USD receivables on the books at any particular time. The value of this balance in NGL terms, Dow Holland's operating currency, was dependent on the value of the USD. Depreciation of the USD relative to the NGL reduced the value of Dow Holland. These unrealized losses, for Dow Holland and other subsidiaries, were frequently enough to wipe out the subsidiary's accounting income as reported in the local currency for the period.[2]

From the U.S. perspective, however, the USD results after consolidation were generally unaffected. The transaction loss on receivables for one subsidiary would usually be offset by an equal gain for another subsidiary able to pay its obligations to the clearing center with its more valuable local currency as the USD devalued.

---

[2]The accounting rules required that unrealized gains/losses in financial assets such as accounts receivable be treated as *transaction* gains/losses. (See the appendix for an explanation.)

The transaction losses and gains for individual subsidiaries typically evened out over the month in USD terms, and Dow Chemical in Midland was largely unconcerned with the issue; the value of the subsidiary as measured in the local currency was not an issue for Dow Midland.

The subsidiaries, however, were concerned about the impact of fluctuations in the USD on their net worth. For tax purposes, local funding requests and, in a few isolated cases, profit sharing, Dow subsidiaries were required to produce financial statements denominated in the local (operating) currency. The recipients of the subsidiary financial statements who used the profit figures to calculate tax liabilities and credit ratings were understandably distressed to see wide swings in profits due to currency fluctuations.

The magnitude of the problem was dramatic at times. Between November 1979 and January 1984, the USD appreciated against the DM almost 100%. Over the next two years the trend reversed and by August 1987, the USD had fallen below the November 1979 rate. The USD relative to other European currencies was equally variable. (Refer to Exhibit 4.) The increase in the number of companies using the clearing system, from 8 in 1972 to 90 subsidiaries 15 years later (including some non-European companies), increased the pressure on the treasury group to correct the problem. The most promising alternative to the USD for an intercompany invoicing currency was the Ecu, especially given its relation to the major European currencies. (Refer to Exhibit 5.)

THE ECU.   The Ecu was created as part of the European Monetary system (EMS) established on March 13, 1979. The EMS was a system of managing the exchange rates between the currencies of member nations. Closely tied to the European Economic Community, the EMS was intended to help draw the member nations towards eventual monetary union. The Ecu was created as the monetary unit of EMS. Instead of choosing an existing currency, a basket currency was chosen, as it would be insulated from fluctuations in any one of the component currencies and would avoid the political complications of choosing an existing national currency. All the currencies represented in the Ecu, except the British pound, Greek drachma and Portuguese escudo, were managed relative to each other within certain limits under the terms of the EMS, providing an additional stabilizing effect on the value of the Ecu. (The composition of the Ecu in 1986 and 1989, before and after the inclusion of the Spanish peseta and the Portuguese escudo, is shown in Table 1.)

Each currency's participation in the Ecu was determined by the strength of the country's economy and currency. Since its inception, the Ecu had been used increasingly. In 1989, it was the fifth most popular currency for Eurobonds; the USD was the most popular, followed by the deutschemark, British pound, and Japanese yen.

---

[3]"Ecu" had a double significance as it was both an acronym for the European Currency Unit and the name of a coin used in Europe during the Middle Ages.

TABLE 1
COMPOSITION OF THE ECU
BY PERCENTAGE WEIGHT OF NATIONAL CURRENCY

22.8.86	20.9.89	
34.2	30.1	Deutschemarks
19.0	19.0	French francs
12.8	13.0	British pounds[a]
10.8	9.4	Dutch guilders
9.6	10.1	Italian lira
8.8	7.9	Belgian/Lux. francs
2.8	2.4	Danish kroner
1.2	1.1	Irish pounds
0.8	0.8	Greek drachma[a]
—	5.3	Spanish peseta
—	0.8	Portuguese escudo[a]
100%	100%	Total

[a]These countries did not participate in the exchange rate management system of the EMS.
Source: Euromoney.

THE STUDY.   At Dow Europe the concept of using the Ecu as the base currency for intercompany transactions had developed over an extended period. The treasury department managers had been aware of the Ecu and, at least theoretically, the potential benefits which its use would give. The study pointed out that the Ecu would be advantageous for two main reasons: (1) it was an average and, therefore, fluctuated less than any single currency; and (2) fluctuations of its components were managed. Most of the currencies Dow Europe handled were included in the Ecu, making it attractive for Dow's intercompany invoicing system. Additionally, Dow observed the success other companies had using the Ecu and saw the increasing liquidity of the Ecu in international financial markets. The idea, however, was dependent on achieving support within the organization. Support materialized with the appointment in Midland of a new corporate treasurer, Pedro Reinhard, formerly the Treasurer of Dow Europe. Under the new treasurer, a study was made analyzing the potential savings of the Ecu as the intercompany invoicing currency.

As part of the study, simulations of the clearing process with the Ecu instead of the USD were conducted, using the transactions from the previous year. Results from this trial showed substantially reduced gains and losses from foreign exchange movements. Responses from the subsidiaries also favored the proposed modifications. (See letter from Dow UK, Exhibit 6.)

Before adopting the Ecu, however, Dow had to request special permission from certain countries, including Spain, Germany, and Italy, allowing subsidiaries in those countries to participate. Turkey was the only country not to grant permission. It prohibited companies from using the Ecu for any reason, forcing Dow's Turkish subsidiaries to remain with USD. In all countries, sales handled through the clearing center had to be recorded in full (unnetted) on the companies' books for tax purposes.

Dow began using the Ecu for intercompany transactions on January 1, 1989. The need for change was clear, and, although some regional treasurers had supported the continued use of the USD or a switch to the more liquid deutschemark, the advantages of the Ecu over the USD were overwhelming.

With the switch to the Ecu for intercompany invoicing, Dow subsidiaries still had large non-local currency items on their balance sheets. However, because these positions were denominated in the more stable Ecu rather than the USD, fluctuations in value were minimized. The subsidiaries were still exposed on a transaction between one bookrate and another, but this exposure was manageable. The change to the Ecu was initially only considered for the European area, although some non-European based subsidiaries began to show interest after seeing its effectiveness.

Change of the Functional Currency

At the time Dow began studying the currency used in intercompany invoicing, the treasury department was also aware of a related problem concerning the use of the USD as the functional currency.[4] Translation under the rules then in place required fixed assets of foreign subsidiaries to be translated into USD using the historical (rather than current) exchange rate.

Translating at historical rates, however, masked any potential changes in the value of the assets resulting from changes in the exchange rate. (See the appendix for a detailed discussion of this point and an example.) In reality, the USD value of foreign fixed assets changed with the exchange rate, but under the rules of FAS No. 8 these changes were reflected in the financial statements. Furthermore, under FAS No. 8, transaction and translation results were not separated. The gain or loss from the combined result was taken through the income statement, mixing the two exposures and making them difficult to manage independently.

Switching to the local currency as the functional currency under FAS No. 52 had two advantages for Dow: (1) it permitted the use of the current exchange rate rather than historical rates for the translation of fixed assets, and (2) it separated transaction results from translation results. With the local currency as the functional currency, transaction gains and losses went to the income statement as before, but translation results bypassed the income statement and went directly to a "special equity" account on the balance sheet, reflecting the change in value of the underlying assets caused by changes in the exchange rates.

---

[4]The U.S. Internal Revenue System had developed the concept of the functional currency to identify the relevant currency when a company translated its books for tax purposes. In 1983, U.S.-based multinational companies were required to choose a functional currency for translation purposes under the rules of FAS No. 52. Dow chose the U.S. dollar as the functional currency for its foreign subsidiaries. If a company chose the dollar as functional currency, the FAS No. 52 translation rules were the same as under FAS No. 8, which required the use of historical rates for translating fixed assets.

Using the current rate for translating fixed assets at Dow's European subsidiaries revealed a USD 1.6 billion exposure that had been unrecorded. The new translation method under FAS No. 52 did not alter Dow's exposure nor affect the local books of the subsidiaries stated in local currencies. The exposure had existed all along. The current rate method simply made the equity exposure explicit and separate from the company's transaction exposure. With the value of the two exposures known, they could then be managed separately.

MANAGING THE EQUITY EXPOSURE

Dow actively managed its USD 1.6 billion in equity exposure. Some of the exposure was neutralized by local borrowing, counter-balancing assets with liabilities on a currency by currency basis at the subsidiary level. The remaining exposure was hedged primarily with forward currency contracts when necessary. The company was aware that the system was not perfect. Balance sheet numbers were based on historical costs and were potentially inaccurate measures of an asset's underlying value. A Dow executive explained, "The exposure is real, we manage it. We know the numbers are wrong, but we have to work with what we have, and that's the balance sheet."

Dow's System for Managing Cash Flow Exposure

"A lot of people talk about economic exposure to foreign exchange risk," commented Gaston Cevallos. "Academics and others give advice about it. But very few companies actually do anything. Like most multinationals, we have large cash flows in many different currencies. We wanted to take the additional steps of (a) measuring the exposure, and (b) doing something about it."[5]

Dow Europe's system for managing cash flow exposure began with a projection of cash flows over the next year in each of the eight regions. The next step in the process was to determine the "economic currency" for each product group and each major cost element. Sales were invoiced in various European currencies, but the currency of the invoice was not necessarily the currency to which the selling price was most sensitive, i.e., the "economic currency."

Determining the Economic Currency

Determination of the economic currency was made by researching product price sensitivities through market data and interviews with product managers. Questions to the managers concerned the general characteristics of the market, who the competitors were, how prices were determined, and what factors influenced price trends

---

[5]Dow defined economic exposure as the long term exposure of cash flows to changes in the exchange rate.

Based on these interviews, a rating between 0 and 100 was given to each product group depending on the product's price sensitivity to changes in the U.S. dollar exchange rate. A rating of "0" meant that the product's price was dollar-sensitive: European prices would move in union with the USD exchange rate. A rating of "100" meant that the product was European-currency sensitive: the European price of a product would be completely unaffected by changes in the USD exchange rate. Similar ratings were determined for costs.

In effect, the rating system was a measure of Dow's ability to pass on changes in the U.S. dollar exchange rate to European customers. If a product were completely dollar-sensitive (rating of 0), Dow could adjust prices in line with changes in the exchange rate. If insensitive (rating 100), Dow was unable to change the European prices of its products when the U.S. dollar changed in value.

CASH FLOW ADJUSTMENT.   The projected cash flows were transformed into "economic" cash flows by multiplying them by the ratings described above. This procedure split the flows into two components: an exposed component (European currencies); and a non-exposed component (dollar). The dollar component was considered not exposed because the USD was the parent company's home currency. For example, a rating of 40 indicated that 40% of the price would not change with the dollar exchange rate (the non-dollar component), whereas the balance would change (the dollar component).

Economic exposure was calculated for each region and product line. The regional results were then aggregated to determine the overall cash flow sensitivity for Dow Europe.

The results showed Dow Europe to be short some currencies and long others relative to the US dollar: the net position was long European currencies relative to the USD. According to Mr. Cevallos, if the estimated long position were correct and the USD weakened against European currencies by 1%, Dow Europe would see its profits increase by 1% of the net exposure. The additional profit from the movement in the exchange rate would show up in improved profit margins, rather than as a gain in foreign exchange results.

Once the cash flow exposure was determined, hedging simulations were carried out to determine the results of alternative hedging strategies. Two primary strategies were tested: (1) using hedges with individual European currencies; and (2) using a proxy currency such as the Ecu or the deutschemark. According to Cevallos, results using the Ecu were "close enough to those achieved using individual currencies" to justify using it as a proxy for the individual currencies.

Implementation and Accounting Difficulties

In 1989, Dow Europe's management had enough confidence in the methodology and results to give permission to the treasury department to develop a hedging strategy based on the estimated exposure. To hedge the long position, Dow Europe sold Ecu forward against the dollar for one year in the amount of the position. The policy adopted was to hedge when there was a clear consensus within the treasury unit that the dollar was likely to strengthen. If it were felt that the odds favored a weaker dollar, no hedge was implemented.

Not all of Dow had as much confidence in the system. According to Luciano Respini, Vice President for Finance and Treasurer of Dow Europe, Dow's board in Midland limited the amount of the estimated exposure that could be managed in the first year. In subsequent years, the limit was gradually lifted. "If the accountants would let us relate the gains and losses," commented Respini, "the board would let us manage the entire amount. Top management doesn't want to have to explain 'forex loss' to shareholders and financial analysts, even when it was one side of a hedge with a gain on the other side."

Cevallos explained, "Accounting treats forex gains and losses in isolation. To some, a hedge looks like speculation. If we show a loss on a hedge, we have a difficult time convincing people that it was one side of a hedge the other side of which was an offsetting gain somewhere in operations. We can't point to the offsetting gain but it is there." Respini concluded, "If it weren't for the accounting treatment, we'd have authority to manage the whole thing."

The results in 1989 were mixed. The dollar strengthened against the Ecu during the first half of the year and weakened during the second half, finishing the year at about the same level at which it started. Unhedged, according to Cevallos, Dow would have had a cumulative loss through July, but essentially a wash for the year. On the hedge, there was a gain during the first half, a loss during the second, and a small gain for the year.

RESULTS OF THE CHANGES

The use of the Ecu for intercompany transactions, the change to the local currency as the functional currency, and the cash flow exposure system generated extensive benefits for Dow. Dow believed its decisions regarding foreign exchange management were more realistic as a result of the increased awareness. Additionally, the changes improved security and reduced costs.

Regarding the system for managing cash flow exposure, Mr. Cevallos recalled: "Initially there was some skepticism, especially from the manufacturing and commercial people. They thought the system was an excuse to speculate."

He continued, "In our system, the numbers may be wrong, but the direction is right. The program is still very experimental, but we are doing something about economic exposure, in a cautious way." The questions Mr. Cevallos and Dow faced were: Are the new systems effective in identifying the exposures? And, if so, are the management techniques used effective?

EXHIBIT 1a

DOW CHEMICAL COMPANY, MIDLAND MICHIGAN
Selected Financial Results
(all figures in millions)

INCOME STATEMENT	1989	1988	1987	1986
Net Sales	$17,600	$16,682	$13,377	$11,113
Operating costs and expenses				
Cost of sales	10,478	9,806	8,660	7,727
Insurance and finance company				
operations, net exposure (income)	(59)	(28)	20	(57)
Research and development expenses	873	772	670	605
Sales, Marketing and other	2,298	2,083	1,762	2,104
Total operating costs and expenses	13,590	12,633	11,112	9,774
Operating Income	4,010	4,049	2,265	1,339
Other income (expense)				
Equity in earnings of 20%–50% owned				
companies	138	89	43	(6)
U.S. interest and other	(271)	(288)	(220)	(127)
Gains on foreign currency transactions	58	5	39	30
Income before provision for taxes on				
income and minorities	3,935	3,855	2,127	1,236
Provision for taxes on income	1,436	1,450	882	495
Minority interests' share in income	12	7	5	0
Net income	2,487	2,398	1,240	732
Net income available for common stockholders	$2,487	$2,398	$1,240	$732
Earnings per common share	$9.20	$8.51	$4.31	$3.82

Source: Annual Reports.

EXHIBIT 1b

DOW CHEMICAL COMPANY, MIDLAND MICHIGAN
Selected Financial Results
(all figures in millions)

BALANCE SHEET	1989	1988	1987	1986
Assets				
Current Assets				
Cash and cash equivalents	$117	$225	$21	$17
Marketable securities	172	0	397	348
Accounts and notes receivable	4,219	3,768	3,229	2,381
Inventories	2,832	2,370	2,105	1,940
Total current assets	7,340	6,363	5,752	4,686

(continued)

EXHIBIT 1b (cont.)

BALANCE SHEET	1989	1988	1987	1986
Investments				
Capital stock in accumulated earnings of				
20%–50% owned companies	1,111	1,053	1,064	952
Other investments	1,089	903	684	493
Noncurrent receivables	487	267	399	378
Total investments	2,687	2,223	2,147	1,823
Plant properties				
Plant properties	17,334	15,360	13,502	12,715
Less: Accumulated depreciation	9,692	8,784	7,951	7,368
Net plant properties	7,642	6,576	5,551	5,347
Other				
Goodwill	3,997	691	485	303
Deferred charges and other assets	500	386	421	394
Total	$22,166	$16,239	$14,356	$12,553

Liabilities and Stockholders' Equity

	1989	1988	1987	1986
Current liabilities				
Notes payable	$2,206	$328	$129	$221
Long term debt due within one year	80	104	50	58
Accounts payable	2,274	1,873	1,583	1,177
United States and foreign taxes on income	263	605	511	346
Accrued and other current liabilities	1,661	1,265	1,182	1,135
Total current liabilities	6,484	4,175	3,455	2,937
Long term debt	3,855	3,338	3,779	3,404
Deferred taxes and other liabilities				
Deferred income taxes	642	567	527	441
Other noncurrent obligations	1,119	857	790	563
Total deferred taxes and other liabilities	1,761	1,424	1,317	1,004
Minority interest in subsidiary companies	595	47	36	30
Stockholders' Equity				
Common stock	818	545	541	535
Additional paid-in capital	621	923	817	725
Misc. equity	761	—	—	—
Retained earnings	8,999	7,167	5,226	4,436
Cumulative translation adjustments	205	182	95	37
Treasury stock, at cost	(1,933)	(1,562)	(910)	(555)
Net stockholder's equity	8,718	7,255	5,769	5,178
Total	$22,166	$16,239	$14,356	$12,553

Source: Annual Reports.

EXHIBIT 2

DOW EUROPE TREASURY DEPT.
Organizational Chart

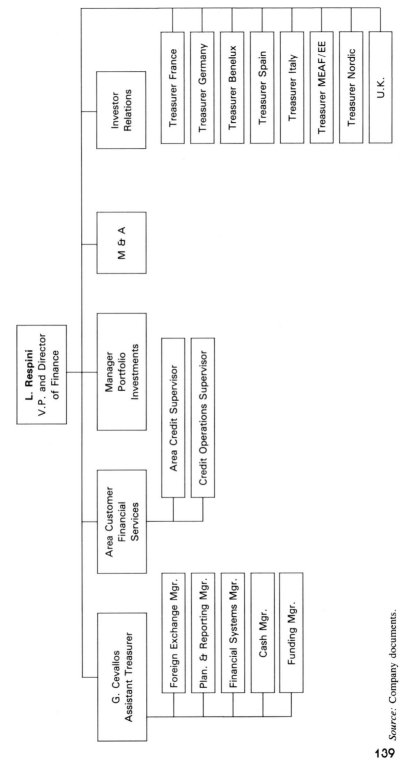

Source: Company documents.

EXHIBIT 3

Dow Treasury Organization

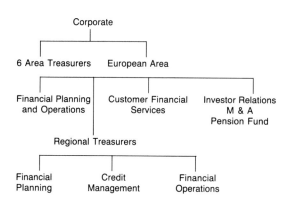

- Long term finance
- Policies
- Global functional
- Leadership

- Planning and area strategy
- Area funding coordination
- Forex and interest rates
  exposure management
- Bank relationships
- Special financial vehicles

- Short term financing
  and planning
- Cash management
- Credit and collections
- Project financing
- Legal entities monitoring

Source: Company documents.

EXHIBIT 4

Deutschemark per U.S. Dollar
11/17/1979–11/17/1989

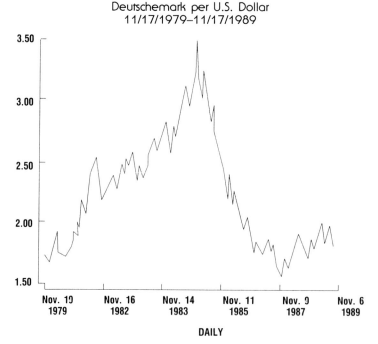

DAILY

Source: Morgan Stanley Foreign Exchange.

EXHIBIT 5

Value of 1 Ecu in Terms of US$, DM, and FF over Past 5 Years
From 6/5/83 to 6/5/88 Weekly Rebased

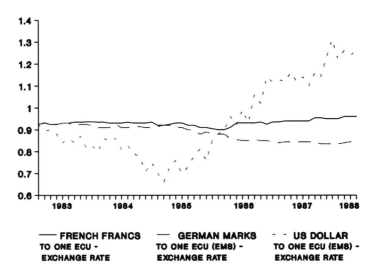

FRENCH FRANCS
TO ONE ECU -
EXCHANGE RATE

GERMAN MARKS
TO ONE ECU (EMS) -
EXCHANGE RATE

US DOLLAR
TO ONE ECU (EMS) -
EXCHANGE RATE

Source: Company document.

EXHIBIT 6

Letter from Dow UK as Part of Study
Regarding Adoption of Ecu

We basically see no reason not to shift to the Ecu as intercompany currency. Our controllers are fully supportive of the move and assure us that the transition would occur without pain.

It is obvious that on the positive side the Ecu/£ exchange rate would be less volatile than the $/£ exchange rate and, in any case, since over 80% of our intercompany trade is with Ecu countries, the Ecu would more closely reflect the underlying reality.

It can, of course, be argued that the choice of intercompany currency does not really matter from an overall company point of view since the gains in one Dow company are mirror-imaged by losses in another Dow company. This is only true from a before tax point of view.

The main advantage of the Ecu as intercompany currency would come if hedging had to be done locally, as it would facilitate defending hedging cost allowance in front of local tax authorities.

LOCAL REGULATIONS

There are no permits required or restrictions of any kind in the U.K.

SETTLEMENT OF INVOICES

Settlement of invoices can be done in Ecu via all the major U.K. banks: Barclays, Midland, Nat West, Lloyd, Bank of Scotland, etc.

LEGAL ENTITY RESULTS

Since the $ went down in 1987 and the U.K. is a net intercompany importer, it is obvious that to have the $ as intercompany currency increased local profit. The currency gains (being trade related) are added to our trading income which is taxed at 35%. So our tax bill increased by 35% of $5.5MM or about $2MM.

BUSINESS CONSIDERATIONS

Besides hedging and related tax allowances (which in my view are as much "business" as anything else), we should mention that using the Ecu as intercompany currency would facilitate discussions with the Health Authorities regarding the pricing of our pharma business in the U.K. It is hard to quantify the impact but it would certainly help.

Source: Dow Europe.

APPENDIX
Foreign Exchange Exposure

Foreign exchange exposure normally is broken down into three types: transaction exposure, translation exposure, and economic (operating) exposure.[6]

TRANSACTION EXPOSURE

Transaction exposure occurs when one currency must be exchanged for another and when a change in foreign exchange rates occurs between the time a transaction is executed and the time it is settled. For example, suppose Dow sells product to the U.K. subsidiary of a German company. The customer wishes to transact in DM. The sale is made on May 1, 1990, on 30-day terms. Dow UK receives the DM on June 1 and converts them to British pounds (GBP). If the GBP/DM exchange rate changes during May, Dow UK receives more or fewer GBP than anticipated at the time of the transaction. The amount ultimately to be received is thus subject to uncertainty. This risk involves a specific identifiable cash flow and is referred to as transaction exposure because it involves an actual gain or loss due to conversion of one currency into another.

It is possible for transaction gain or loss to occur with no conversion of currencies. Such a situation can occur when a firm has long-maturity assets or liabilities denominated in a foreign currency. Suppose a U.S. firm has a bank deposit (or a certificate of deposit) denominated in DM. A change in the DM/USD exchange rate changes the value of the deposit in USD. Such a change during an accounting period must be reported as a transaction gain or loss even though no currency conversion has yet taken place[7]. Conversion will take place eventually, so this

---

[6]For a more detailed discussion of these issues, see David K. Eiteman and Arthur I. Stonehill, *Multinational Business Finance*, 5th ed., Addison-Wesley, 1989, chapters 7–9.

[7]Whether the gain or loss is taxable depends on the rules of the country having tax jurisdiction.

approach in effect "marks the asset to market" in each accounting period with respect to currency exchange rates. Liabilities would be treated similarly.

TRANSLATION EXPOSURE

Translation exposure arises in multinational firms because of the necessity to produce consolidated financial statements. Subsidiaries of multinational companies operating in different countries typically transact in local currencies. Local currency normally is the unit used for accounting, performance measurement, and taxation at the local level. The operating financial statements of subsidiaries thus are denominated in local currencies.

Periodically, often quarterly, but at least annually, these subsidiary statements must be summed up in consolidated statements for the entire multinational enterprise, denominated in the home currency of the firm. In Dow's case, this means consolidating statements denominated in a wide variety of currencies around the globe and then expressing them in USD equivalents.

Thus financial statements denominated in foreign currencies must be *translated* into USD statements. There is no actual conversion of one currency into another; translation merely involves a *restatement* in a different currency. So translation is necessary to produce consolidated financial statements and thereby measure performance in the home currency.

What exchange rate should be used in making the translation? There lies the difficulty, the subject of a long controversy among accountants and financial officers. Should it be the *current* exchange rate at the time the translation is done? Or the historical rate at the time the asset or liability went on the books? It can make a big difference, especially in the case of long-lived items such as fixed assets. Financial Accounting Standard No. 8, promulgated in the U.S. in 1975, mandated the so-called *temporal* method, calling for the rate at the time the asset or liability was booked. This meant different rates for different items. FAS No. 8 was widely criticized and gave way to FAS No. 52 in 1981, which mandates the *current rate* method. Under the current rate method, all assets and liabilities are translated at the current exchange rate at the time of the translation, equity accounts at historical rates, and income statement items at a weighted average rate for the period.[8]

Translation *exposure* arises because changes in exchange rates change the USD equivalents of foreign currencies. A profit of FFR 10 million in Dow France would translate into USD 1,754,386 at an exchange rate of FFR 5.7 per USD. If the USD

[8]FAS No. 52 was promulgated in 1981 and made mandatory for U.S. multinational companies in 1983. It required the selection of a "functional currency" for foreign subsidiaries, defined as the currency of the "primary economic environment." If the USD were selected as the functional currency, the translation rules were identical to those of FAS No. 8. If the local currency were selected, FAS No. 52 permitted two important changes: (1) it mandated the current rate method in place of the temporal method, thus permitting the use of the current forex rate for translating fixed assets, and (2) it allowed firms to separate transaction and translation exposures, and to charge translation gains and losses to a special equity account rather than run them through the profit and loss statement, as had been required under FAS No. 8. Transaction gains continued to go through the P&L as before.

strengthens to FFR 6.0 per USD, the same FFR 10 million becomes only USD 1,666,667. An asset worth FFR 25 million translates to USD 4.386 million at an exchange rate of FFR 5.7 per USD, but to only USD 4.167 million at 6.0. Hence, the USD representation of the asset's value depends on the exchange rate.

And so it should. The shareholders of the parent company, Dow Chemical, are ultimately interested in having results in USD terms. Hence, Dow Chemical's profits and assets are *exposed* to changes in the FFR/USD exchange rate. There is no impact on the subsidiary's financial statements in FFR terms; the impact is only in the USD equivalents. Note that in this case there is no conversion of FFR into USD; we have merely expressed or translated FFR into USD equivalents. Whereas transaction exposure normally results from the actual conversion of one currency into another, translation exposure involves only a restatement.

Since balance sheet items are carried at historical values, the translation process can seriously distort forex gains and losses. Take the case of a fixed asset such as a building located in a foreign country. Suppose, over time, inflation is higher in the foreign country than in the home country and foreign exchange rates adjust so that purchasing power parity is maintained. The nominal exchange rate changes, but the real exchange rate remains constant. Assume also that the market value of the building rises with the general price level. In this case, the increase in the market value of the building in local currency terms is offset by the change in the exchange rate, so there is no change in the true market value of the building in home currency terms. However, on the foreign balance sheet, the building remains recorded at historical cost in home currency terms. A translation loss is recorded, when in fact none occurred. The distortion is due to the use of historical cost to represent the value of the building. Under FAS No. 52 the translation loss is not charged against current income, but rather is cumulated in a special equity account for translation adjustments.

The current rate method measures exposure in terms of nominal exchange rates only. If the nominal rate changes, the home currency value changes irrespective of changes in the real exchange rate. Hence the current rate method can show a value at a point in time either higher or lower than true market, and can understate or overstate the change in true value between two balance sheets that are stated in historical terms.

If translated under the temporal method of FAS No. 8, the building would be translated at the historical exchange rate. Since both the historical cost of the asset and the translation rate remain fixed, the home-currency value of the asset remains the same regardless of changes in forex rates. In this sense the translated result is consistent with the principles of historical cost accounting. But since the translated value is invariant to forex movements, the temporal method masks the fact that the asset in fact is exposed.

Thus the temporal method is misleading in that it ignores exposure of foreign assets to forex movements over time. The current rate method takes account of the exposure and then proceeds to mismeasure it. The distortion lies not in the use of the current rate for translation, but rather in the use of historical cost as the measure of value.

Although translation involves only a restatement, it is not correct to dismiss translation exposure as "merely accounting." To parent-company shareholders, what counts ultimately is performance in the home currency. Profits from foreign countries ultimately must be repatriated, and their buying power in the home country is the final measure of performance. Likewise, asset values ultimately must be measured in home currency terms. Hence the objective of translation should be to measure the true economic position in home currency terms. Unfortunately, as noted above, the historical-cost focus of GAAP accounting creates distortions in translation just as it does in purely domestic accounting applications. Translated balance sheets suffer from all the shortcomings of the originals. Market value, rather than book value, is the appropriate measure, and a proper system of measuring exposure should focus on the impact of forex changes on market value. This impact is known as economic exposure.

ECONOMIC EXPOSURE

Economic exposure to foreign exchange movements is the impact on revenues, costs, profits, cash flows, assets and liabilities and, ultimately, on value. Whereas transaction exposure focuses on cash flow effects in the very short term, economic exposure involves cumulative effects over longer time periods. Transaction and translation exposure appear in financial statements as explicitly identifiable forex gains and losses, while economic exposure appears in operating profit margins and cannot be explicitly identified as forex-related.

Since it focuses on the impact on operating cash flows, economic exposure also is called *operating* exposure. Economic exposure broadly defined also includes exposure of assets and liabilities to changes in value due to forex movements. Over the long run, asset/liability values will be reflected in cash flows one way or another, so economic exposure can be defined in terms of cash flow effects over all future periods.

In assessing the impact of changes in forex rates over time, a critical issue is inflation. If a change in the exchange rate between the two currencies over a given period is offset by a change in price levels, then there is no change in *relative* prices. Purchasing power parity (relative buying power in two countries) is maintained. The nominal exchange rate changes, but not the real exchange rate. Under these circumstances there is no impact on operating cash flows or on value expressed in home currency terms. Alternatively, if a change in nominal exchange rates is not offset by inflation, the real exchange rate changes, PPP is not maintained, and operating cash flows in home-currency terms are affected. Thus economic exposure exists if and only if there is a departure from PPP. Furthermore, since it is changes in real exchange rates that are important, traditional financial instruments such as forward contracts used to manage accounting exposure are not as effective in hedging economic exposure. Such contracts hedge nominal rather than real exposure.

The impact of forex movements on operating flows can be indirect as well as direct. A firm's products may become more or less competitive in international markets as real exchange rates change. Forex movements also make an impact on competitors, so the impact on pricing depends in part on how those competitors react. A company's suppliers also may be affected, passing along the impact through their prices. The impact on suppliers depends on the competitive structure in their respective industries, impacts on their (the suppliers') competitors and suppliers, and so on. Customers too may be affected. The full economic impact of forex changes thus depends on who the company's competitors are, where the product is sold, who the price leaders are, where the company sources its raw materials, where its competitors source, and who the low-cost producers are.[9]

So the full impact of forex changes on cash flows depends not only on first order price effects, but also on indirect effects via impact on customers, competitors, suppliers, their competitors and suppliers, and so on. Forex movements thus can make an impact on the full range of factors that affect a firm's competitive position. We must now modify the earlier statement regarding economic exposure and PPP: the necessary condition for no economic exposure is that PPP must be maintained for the company, its customers, competitors, suppliers, its competitors' suppliers, suppliers' competitors and suppliers, and so on through the entire chain of relationships.

HOW THE THREE TYPES OF EXPOSURE ARE RELATED

Economic exposure, transaction exposure, and translation exposure are all related. Economic exposure includes the present value of the firm's future transaction exposure as one component, whereas the other components relate to second-order effects on customers, competitors, etc.

Translation exposure likewise is related to economic exposure. Translation is the accounting attempt to measure the economic position of foreign units in home-currency terms. A properly designed method of translation should yield a result equal to true economic value. In such a system, the translation gain/loss during any accounting period should equal the economic gain/loss.

This statement can be made about accounting systems in general: the profit and loss statement is to measure the change in economic wealth resulting from the company's operations during the accounting period. The balance sheet is to measure true economic position. Unfortunately, present-day accounting systems only crudely approximate this ideal, and departures are often significant. One of the biggest difficulties, as noted earlier, results from stating balance sheets in historical rather than market value terms. As long as financial statements are historical-cost based, translation will continue to produce distorted measures of economic position and economic gain and loss.

---

[9]For an in-depth discussion of economic exposure, see Eugene Flood and Donald Lessard, "On the Measurement of Operating Exposure to Exchange Rates: A Conceptual Approach," *Financial Management*, Spring 1986. For a discussion of foreign exchange exposure in the broader context of corporate strategy, see Lessard, "Finance and Global Competition" in *New Developments in International Finance*, Stern and Chew (eds.), Oxford and New York: Basil Blackwell, 1988.

PART THREE · Financial Markets

14. ANHEUSER-BUSCH AND CAMPBELL TAGGART
15. NOTE ON INSIDER TRADING
16. FINNING TRACTOR AND EQUIPMENT COMPANY LTD.
17. NESBITT THOMSON DEACON INC.—THE SCEPTRE
    RESOURCES DEBENTURE
18. THE RTZ CORPORATION PLC—RIO ALGOM LIMITED

14

ANHEUSER-BUSCH AND CAMPBELL TAGGART

In mid-May 1984, Walter Suhre put the rapidly yellowing newspaper clipping (see Exhibit 1) back into a stack of related items and closed his file. Suhre, vice president and general counsel of St. Louis-based Anheuser-Busch, believed that his company might have suffered losses during its acquisition of Campbell Taggart. As far as Suhre could tell, Paul Thayer, who in 1982 was a director of Anheuser-Busch, had leaked confidential information to his friends about the impending Campbell Taggart acquisition. Thayer's friends and others then purchased shares of Campbell Taggart in the open market (see Exhibits 2, 3, and 4).[1] Suhre had learned about the details of this alleged insider trading in January 1984 from a legal complaint filed by the Securities and Exchange Commission (SEC) against Thayer and his friends.

Five months later, in October 1984, the SEC complaint was delayed in court. For the moment, Anheuser-Busch and Thayer had reached a "standstill agreement" under which Anheuser-Busch would not sue Thayer for as long as the SEC complaint remained unsettled. The agreement benefitted both parties and was terminable by either Anheuser-Busch or Thayer. Anheuser-Busch gained more time to sue, because the statute of limitations was suspended for the duration of the standstill. In addition,

---

[1]In all, 38 insiders and "tippees" purchased a total of 265,600 shares of Campbell Taggart. The figures reported in Exhibit 1 aggregate the trades of all 38 insiders and tippees.

Copyright © 1991 by the President and Fellows of Harvard College.
Harvard Business School case 9-921-020.
This case was prepared by Research Associate Jonathan Shakes and Professor Erik Sirri as the basis for class discussion rather than to illustrate either effective or ineffective handling of an administrative situation. Reprinted by permission of the Harvard Business School.

the company could use any evidence that emerged from the SEC proceedings against Thayer. As for Thayer, he gained the advantage of defending himself against one set of charges at a time. As soon as the standstill agreement lapsed, the statute of limitations would go back into effect and Anheuser-Busch would have to file suit within a short time period.

Suhre realized there was a possibility he would have to present his recommendations on the matter to Anheuser-Busch senior management. But before he could make a proposal, he wanted to assure himself that the company could demonstrate in court that it had been damaged by the alleged insider trading. On a more basic level, Suhre needed both to confirm the company's stated intention to sue Thayer and to decide if it should sue any parties other than Thayer.

REASONS FOR THE ACQUISITION

At the time of the acquisition in 1982, popular Anheuser-Busch brands such as Budweiser had allowed the company to achieve a dominant 32% share of the market for beer. (See Exhibits 5 and 6 for financial statements.) Anheuser-Busch's market strength was reflected in its stock performance, which remained good despite a traditionally low dividend yield.[2] Management believed this performance was due to the company's successful growth-based strategy, which stock analysts appreciated and rewarded with consistent "buy" recommendations. However, because management also believed that breweries had little room for continued growth, it was searching for routes to diversify.

The first such effort led to the internal development of Eagle brand snack foods, which were sold through bars, airports, and other distribution channels originally established for beer sales. By 1982, Anheuser-Busch was considering acquisitions such as Campbell Taggart as well. During this period, Campbell Taggart was regarded as the bakery industry's low-cost producer. Its market share was second only to that of the ITT Continental Baking Company. Sales were strongest in the rapidly growing southern and southwestern states, where Campbell Taggart breads, rolls, and cakes could be found in most supermarkets. Company stock had performed particularly well in the weeks preceding the merger announcement. In light of the rapid increase in Campbell Taggart's price, Anheuser-Busch made a public statement on August 2, 1982, about its interest in Campbell Taggart.

When the merger proposal was first announced publicly, industry analysts noted that by acquiring a bakery company externally, Anheuser-Busch was taking a new approach to its diversification goals, which previously had been met internally. To justify this shift, the company looked to the benefits of a distribution network that Campbell Taggart had established at restaurants and supermarkets, where the brewer had traditionally been weak.

[2]The average dividend yield on an S&P 500 stock in 1981 was about 5.1%.

THE ACQUISITION PROCESS

Anheuser-Busch decided to pursue Campbell Taggart through a negotiated merger. In this kind of transaction, also known as a "friendly takeover," the acquiring company negotiates a set of merger terms with the target company's board of directors. These terms usually specify the price to be paid for the target, and often cover operating, employment, and seniority concerns as well. If the negotiations succeed, the board then asks its shareholders to approve the merger in a proxy vote.

An acquiring firm generally offers to pay a "premium," or greater-than-market price, for a target's shares. One explanation for this premium is that the bidder must offer existing shareholders an incentive to sell shares they would normally retain. Another possible reason is that investors believe the target company will have an intrinsically higher value when and if it falls under control of the new owner. Thus, their "reservation" or "indifference" price rises in anticipation. In either instance, the prospect of receiving a premium for their shares usually causes target shareholders to support merger proposals. It is generally believed that without a reasonable premium, a merger proposal would fail.

The takeover premium that a bidder typically offers ranges from 20% to 40% more than the target's pre-merger stock price.[3] The premium is defined as the percentage increase that the final negotiated offer price represents over the target stock price one month before the merger announcement. Curiously, the price of a target firm often begins a run-up before any official announcement of a takeover attempt is made. During the weeks before a merger announcement, the target's price rises an average of 40% of the takeover premium.[4] Although the existence of a takeover premium is fairly common for a target stock, a bidding company's stock price tends to remain unchanged or to fall slightly.[5]

PAUL THAYER

Throughout his life, Paul Thayer enjoyed being a daredevil and adventurer. In World War II, he was a successful Air Force fighter pilot. After the war, he continued flying, first as a commercial pilot for TWA and later as a test pilot for Chance Vought Aircraft. Not only did Thayer survive this risky career, he advanced rapidly. By 1955 he had become a director of Vought, and after Vought merged with Ling-Temco to become LTV Aerospace, he was elected chairman, CEO and president of the new conglomerate. Thayer's stellar career and personal investments made him a multimillionaire. He began taking positions of civic leadership and was invited to join several corporate boards, including the Anheuser-Busch board which he joined in January 1982. In April 1982, he became chairman of the U.S. Chamber

[3]Michael Jensen and Richard Ruback, "The Market for Corporate Control," *Journal of Financial Economics*, (Vol. 11, 1983), 5–50.

[4]G. Jarrell and A. Poulson, "Stock Trading Before the Announcement of Tender Offers," *Journal of Law, Economics, and Organization*, (no. 5, 1989), 225–248.

[5]Jensen and Ruback (1983).

of Commerce, where he caused bitter divisions by supporting a controversial tax increase proposed by President Reagan. Later in 1982, Reagan appointed Thayer Deputy Secretary of Defense, causing him to resign his position on the Anheuser-Busch board. Once again, he showed his strong will, this time by spearheading a major campaign to reduce military waste. In his spare time, the 62-year-old Thayer continued to scuba dive, ride motorcycles through the Rocky Mountains, and perform death-defying stunts in a vintage World War II fighter plane.[6]

THE SEC COMPLAINT

Apparently, Paul Thayer took his taste for adventure too far. According to an SEC complaint filed in January 1984, he illegally disclosed stock-related information to friends, repeatedly tipping them off about the planned acquisitions, profits, and dividends of the three companies for which he served as a director. One of these companies was Anheuser-Busch.

The SEC cited eight friends, the tippees, in its complaint and claimed that they had profited by purchasing shares of stock after hearing the inside information that Thayer provided. Later, his friends would sell the shares when public announcement of the merger caused share prices to rise. One tippee, Billy Bob Harris, was the highest paid stockbroker for A.G. Edwards, a St. Louis-based broker. A second, William Mathis, was a broker for Bear, Stearns & Co. in Atlanta. A third tippee, Sandra Ryno, was a former LTV receptionist who, according to the SEC complaint, allegedly maintained a "private personal relationship" with Thayer. The fourth, Julie Williams, an aerobics dance instructor in Dallas, was alleged to have had a similar relationship with Harris. These four, along with four others, made up what *Time* magazine described as "a small circle of high-living Southerners."[7]

In an example cited by the SEC, Thayer spent the weekend of June 25, 1982, in Houston with Ryno, Harris, and Williams (see Exhibit 7). On the following Monday, Harris "contacted a research analyst at A.G. Edwards and suggested to the analyst that Busch was interested in acquiring Campbell Taggart."[8] That same week, Ryno purchased 2,000 shares of Campbell Taggart at $25.75 and $26.375 per share. (See Exhibit 8.) She sold her shares on August 10, after news had come out that the stock was targeted in a takeover attempt and the stock price had risen. In its complaint, the SEC accused the defendants of violating rules 10b-5 and 14e-3 of the Securities Exchange Act and stated that the tippees as a group made illegal profits of more than $1.9 million from the information that Thayer had supplied.[9] Thayer himself did not share in these profits.

Although allegations of insider trading were relatively rare in the early 1980s, equivalent SEC charges were often settled out of court with a "consent decree,"

[6]Grover Heiman, "The Flier Who Kept a Company From Crashing," *Nation's Business*, June 1982, pp. 54–59.
[7]Evan Thomas, "Life with Paul and Billy Bob," *Time*, January 16, 1984, p. 21.
[8]*SEC* v. *Thayer et al*, U.S.D.C. S.D.N.Y. (January 5, 1984), p. 20.
[9]*SEC* v. *Thayer et al*, p. 8.

which saved time and money for both sides. In a typical settlement, the defendant would neither deny nor admit guilt, but agree instead not to break securities laws in the future. If the defendant was later tried and convicted on a new set of charges, the punishment would be more severe, due to the violation of the consent decree. However, during negotiations in late 1983, Thayer refused such a settlement, possibly because it would be tantamount to an admission of guilt.[10] Given Thayer's high-profile position, the political embarrassment would be large. In January 1984, Thayer resigned from the Defense Department in order to avoid further damaging the Reagan Administration and to concentrate fully on defending himself against the SEC charges.

Thayer claimed that the charges were "entirely without merit." Billy Bob Harris, who gave regular stock reports on Dallas television, said that he had proved his innocence by passing a lie detector test.

SUHRE'S DECISION

Suhre realized that Anheuser-Busch faced a sticky decision. Filing a suit against Thayer or some other party might cost several million dollars in legal expenses, with no guarantee of winning. And even if the company could recover part of the damages, press coverage of the suit would be embarrassing to both sides. To sue a former board director was virtually unprecedented, and Anheuser-Busch had no way to gauge how the rest of corporate America would react. To sue some other party—for example, Harris, Mathis, or their employers—had the advantage of increasing the potential size of the final settlement. However, Suhre wondered whether there would be any "fallout" from suing a major Wall Street firm.

Legal action had drawbacks, but so too did inaction. Suhre felt that Anheuser-Busch had a responsibility to initiate proceedings against Paul Thayer. Also, management was keenly aware of company losses from the merger, due both to the insider trading and to the disappointing performance of the Campbell Taggart subsidiary during the two years following the merger. The SEC had a very strong case against Thayer. Suhre was worried that if Anheuser-Busch management did not sue, shareholders might file a "derivative action"[11] suit against Thayer or some other party. In any event, not to sue might be seen as tacit forgiveness for the incident.

---

[10]*Ibid.*

[11]If a corporation sustains significant losses that can be recovered through legal action and the management fails to take such action, shareholders have the right to file "derivative" suit on behalf of, and over the objections of, the corporation. Management may become a co-plaintiff along with the shareholders. The success of such a suit is often interpreted as failure on management's part.

EXHIBIT 1

News Article, The Wall Street Journal, August 10, 1982

ANHEUSER-BUSCH TO BUY CAMPBELL TAGGART INC.
Cash-Stock Offer Is Valued at $570 Million

ST. LOUIS–Anheuser-Busch Co. said it agreed in principle to acquire Campbell Taggart Inc., a Dallas based baked-goods concern, for roughly $570 million in cash and stock.

The brewer, which had disclosed preliminary merger talks last week, said it would pay $36 each for about half of Campbell Taggart's 15 million shares. It would convert the rest into shares of a new Anheuser-Busch convertible preferred stock. Each new share would have a redemption value of $40, bear dividends at a rate of 9% a year, be noncallable for the first 5 years, and be convertible into 0.645 share of Anheuser-Busch common stock. The value of the new preferred stock is uncertain, but the acquisition would total about $570 million if the stock is assigned its redemption value....

Under the terms of the acquisition, Campbell Taggart shareholders may choose cash or stock for each share held, subject to proration if required. Anheuser-Bush said the stock swap is intended to be tax free.

The acquisition requires a definitive agreement and approval of Campbell Taggart shareholders.

Anheuser-Busch said that Campbell Taggart will continue to operate under current management and that its chairman, Bill O. Mead, is expected to be asked to join the Anheuser-Busch board....

Stock market response to the plan has been steady, with Campbell Taggart rising to $30.625, up $1, after the announcement last week and closing $1.75 higher yesterday at $31.75 in New York Stock Exchange composite trading. Anheuser-Busch dropped to $49.625 a share, down $4.375, after talks were disclosed and it closed yesterday on the Big Board at $47.50, down 50 cents....

Emanuel Goldman of Sanford C. Bernstein & Co. said that the acquisition price was reasonable and that it would lead to a 10% decrease in per-share earnings unless Anheuser-Busch could raise the price of its beer.

Source: Reprinted by permission of *The Wall Street Journal,* © 1982 Dow Jones & Company, Inc. All rights reserved worldwide.

EXHIBIT 2

Selected Daily Stock Data for June 1–September 1, 1982

DATE	CAMPBELL TAGGART				ANHEUSER-BUSCH		S&P 500	NYSE
	CLOSING PRICE	VOLUME (000s)	NO. OF INSIDER TRADERS	INSIDER VOLUME (000s)	CLOSING PRICE	VOLUME (000s)	CLOSING LEVEL	VOLUME (MILS)
6/01	$23.250	10.3	0	0	$48.750	126.4	111.68	41.65
6/02	23.500	6.9	0	0	49.250	45.0	112.04	49.22
6/03	23.625	4.2	0	0	50.250	89.3	111.86	48.45
6/04	23.250	1.3	0	0	48.750	132.3	110.09	44.11
6/07	23.750	5.1	0	0	49.125	57.1	110.12	44.63
6/08	23.625	1.8	0	0	49.000	124.4	109.63	46.82
6/09	23.000	18.9	0	0	49.000	76.0	108.99	55.77
6/10	23.000	1.4	0	0	49.625	63.6	109.61	50.95

(continued)

EXHIBIT 2 (cont.)

DATE	CAMPBELL TAGGART				ANHEUSER-BUSCH		S&P 500	NYSE
	CLOSING PRICE	VOLUME (000s)	NO. OF INSIDER TRADERS	INSIDER VOLUME (000s)	CLOSING PRICE	VOLUME (000s)	CLOSING LEVEL	VOLUME (MILS)
6/11	23.625	3.9	0	0	51.125	101.5	111.24	68.61
6/14	23.875	2.5	0	0	49.875	58.4	109.96	40.10
6/15	23.875	21.3	0	0	50.500	18.4	109.69	44.97
6/16	24.000	16.2	0	0	49.875	48.9	108.87	56.28
6/17	24.500	28.7	0	0	49.875	50.5	107.60	49.23
6/18	24.500	2.2	0	0	50.250	65.7	107.28	53.80
6/21	24.125	1.7	0	0	50.250	31.3	107.20	50.37
6/22	24.375	1.5	0	0	50.375	27.0	108.30	55.29
6/23	24.375	7.4	0	0	51.000	114.3	110.14	62.71
6/24	24.750	38.6	0	0	51.125	127.6	109.83	55.86
6/25	24.625	21.4	0	0	51.375	46.9	109.14	38.74
6/28	24.750	1.0	0	0	52.500	40.6	110.26	40.70
6/29	24.875	6.3	0	0	51.750	59.2	110.21	46.99
6/30	25.750	38.2	1	0.1	51.750	46.3	109.61	65.28
7/01	27.000	65.6	9	10.0	51.750	27.4	108.71	47.90
7/02	25.750	46.5	0	0	51.375	27.4	107.65	43.76
7/06	25.875	3.8	0	0	51.125	60.2	107.29	44.35
7/07	25.750	35.2	1	1.5	51.250	17.5	107.22	46.92
7/08	26.000	1.8	0	0	51.125	125.5	107.53	63.27
7/09	25.500	4.7	0	0	52.125	41.6	108.83	65.87
7/12	26.250	28.4	2	1.8	53.625	98.2	109.57	74.69
7/13	26.250	12.2	7	6.9	53.375	50.9	109.45	66.17
7/14	27.000	30.2	3	8.1	53.750	15.6	110.44	58.16
7/15	27.000	10.5	0	0	54.625	94.1	110.47	61.09
7/16	26.750	46.9	0	0	55.750	111.8	111.07	58.74
7/19	26.625	5.2	1	0.3	55.125	35.5	110.73	53.03
7/20	26.375	1.8	0	0	55.000	44.8	111.54	61.06
7/21	26.125	18.1	2	5.0	53.625	81.3	111.42	66.77
7/22	26.750	9.1	8	4.8	53.625	40.7	111.47	53.87
7/23	27.000	32.1	8	12.3	53.125	44.5	111.17	47.28
7/26	27.750	25.2	13	17.4	53.500	12.4	110.36	37.74
7/27	28.250	64.0	10	31.7	53.250	43.7	109.43	45.74
7/28	29.125	90.0	13	20.9	53.000	65.8	107.73	53.83
7/29	28.500	154.1	3	8.7	52.875	83.8	107.72	55.68
7/30	29.000	63.9	7	11.3	53.125	39.6	107.09	39.27
8/02	29.625	128.6	5	29.4	54.500	71.3	108.98	53.46
8/03	30.625	219.0	0	0	49.625	394.6	107.83	60.48
8/04	29.500	215.4	0	0	50.000	197.6	106.14	53.44
8/05	30.000	195.7	0	0	49.500	156.5	105.16	54.70
8/06	30.000	134.6	0	0	48.000	93.0	103.71	48.66
8/09	31.750	360.7	0	0	47.500	215.7	103.08	54.56
8/10	31.625	204.1	0	0	46.500	126.0	102.84	52.68
8/11	31.625	142.7	0	0	45.500	307.1	102.60	49.04
8/12	31.750	119.8	0	0	46.375	216.5	102.42	50.08
8/13	32.625	132.9	0	0	47.500	93.2	103.85	44.72

(continued)

EXHIBIT 2 (cont.)

	CAMPBELL TAGGART				ANHEUSER-BUSCH		S&P 500	NYSE
DATE	CLOSING PRICE	VOLUME (000s)	NO. OF INSIDER TRADERS	INSIDER VOLUME (000s)	CLOSING PRICE	VOLUME (000s)	CLOSING LEVEL	VOLUME (MILS)
8/16	32.750	94.8	0	0	47.750	175.0	104.09	55.42
8/17	33.375	140.2	0	0	49.750	181.5	109.04	92.86
8/18	34.000	238.1	0	0	49.875	300.8	108.53	132.71
8/19	34.000	128.6	0	0	50.000	113.9	109.16	78.27
8/20	34.875	185.9	0	0	52.000	211.0	113.02	95.89
8/23	34.750	34.0	0	0	51.625	115.9	116.11	110.32
8/24	35.125	91.8	0	0	52.750	226.8	115.34	121.76
8/25	35.500	85.2	0	0	54.125	105.4	117.58	106.28
8/26	35.000	262.6	0	0	54.750	155.6	118.55	137.32
8/27	34.625	65.0	0	0	53.500	119.9	117.11	74.41
8/30	35.250	72.8	0	0	54.000	129.4	117.66	59.56
8/31	35.750	89.9	0	0	55.000	106.1	119.51	86.36
9/01	35.000	120.9	0	0	54.875	66.1	118.25	82.83

Note: The midmonth "short interest" in Campbell Taggart for June, July, August and September of 1982 was 255,969 shares, 255,405 shares, 6,300 shares and 100 shares, respectively. The midmonth short interest in Anheuser-Busch for June, July and August of 1982 was 78,522 shares, 118,203 shares and 88,097 shares, respectively. The short interest is the number of shares investors have "sold short", that is, borrowed and then resold.

EXHIBIT 3

Anheuser-Busch Price and Volume

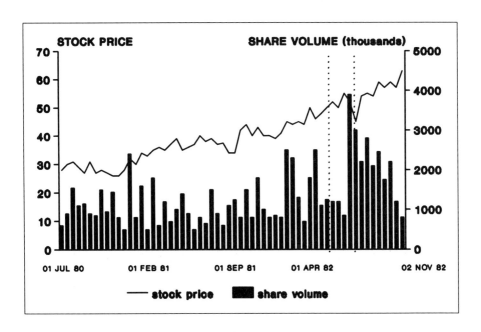

EXHIBIT 4

Campbell Taggart Price and Volume

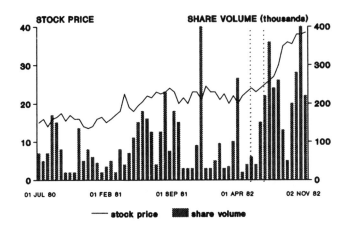

STOCK PRICE   SHARE VOLUME (thousands)

—— stock price   ▮▮ share volume

EXHIBIT 5

ANHEUSER-BUSCH AND CAMPBELL TAGGART
Consolidated Balance Sheets
December 31, 1981
(in millions of dollars)

	ANHEUSER-BUSCH	CAMPBELL TAGGART
Assets		
Current Assets		
Cash and securities	$ 93.6	$ 20.8
Receivables and inventory	376.1	147.1
Other	69.6	12.7
Total	539.3	180.6
Investments and other assets	78.3	42.0
Plant and equipment	2,257.6	292.2
Total Assets	2,875.2	514.8
Liabilities		
Current Liabilities		
Short term debt	$ 29.5	$ 11.6
Accounts payable	209.8	65.9
Accruals and other	254.1	42.3
Total	493.4	119.8
Long-term borrowing	817.3	125.5
Deferred taxes	357.7	21.8
Minority interests	0.0	22.7
Shareholder equity (issued 45,612,716 shares		
and 15,974,687 shares, respectively)	1,206.8	225.0
Total Liabilities and Equity	2,875.2	514.8

EXHIBIT 6

ANHEUSER-BUSCH AND CAMPBELL TAGGART
Consolidated Income Statements
December 31, 1981
(in millions of dollars, except per-share data)

	ANHEUSER-BUSCH	CAMPBELL TAGGART
Income		
Net sales	$3,847.2	$1,257.5
Net cost of goods sold	2,975.5	657.6
Marketing and research	515.0	512.5
Operating Income	356.7	87.4
Other income	0.0	1.6
Net interest expense	31.5	10.7
Taxes	107.8	36.6
Net Income	217.4	41.7
Earnings per share	$4.77	$2.61
Dividends per share	$1.38	$.90
Rank in S&P 500 in 1981	139	334

EXHIBIT 7

Chronology of Events

1/5/82	Paul Thayer is elected a director of Anheuser-Busch.
6/8/82	Anheuser-Busch informs its investment banking firm that it is considering the acquisition of Campbell Taggart.
6/23/82	Thayer attends Anheuser-Busch board meeting, at which Campbell Taggart acquisition is considered.
6/25/82	Thayer travels from Dallas to Houston with friends, returning the next day.
6/28/82	Thayer allegedly tells Harris and others about impending acquisition.
6/28/82	Purchases of Campbell Taggart by defendants begin.
7/6/82	Thayer telephones chairman of Busch's board of directors, then immediately phones Harris.
7/28/82	Thayer attends Anheuser-Busch board meeting and telephones Ryno afterward.
8/3/82	Anheuser-Busch announces merger talks with Campbell Taggart.
8/9/82	Anheuser-Busch announces agreement in principle to acquire Campbell Taggart.
8/17/82	Boards of both companies approve definitive merger agreement.
10/27/82	Campbell Taggart shareholders approve merger agreement.
11/2/82	Campbell Taggart becomes a wholly owned subsidiary of Anheuser-Busch.
12/3/82	SEC notifies Anheuser-Busch that it is investigating "unusual activity" in Campbell Taggart stock. Anheuser-Busch later cooperates with investigation.
12/6/82	President Reagan nominates Paul Thayer to be Deputy Secretary of Defense. The Senate later confirms the nomination.
12/31/82	Thayer resigns his position on Anheuser-Busch board.
1/4/84	Thayer resigns as Deputy Secretary of Defense.
1/5/84	The Securities and Exchange Commission files civil complaint against Thayer, claiming that he leaked corporate takeover plans to eight friends, who made $1.9 million in illegal profits from the information.

EXHIBIT 8

Selected Purchases and Sales of Campbell Taggart by Insiders

DEFENDANT	PURCHASE DATE	SHARES	TOTAL PRICE PAID	SALE DATE(S)
Ryno	6/30/82	100	$ 2,625	8/10/82
	7/1	1,900	50,450	
	7/27	4,000	113,827	
Harris	7/1	3,100[a]	88,200	8/4
	7/27	10,000	284,068	
Mathis	7/7	1,500	38,745	8/4, 8/11 and
	7/14	6,200	168,144	8/24
	7/21	5,000	130,788	
	7/27	2,000	56,800	
	7/30	2,300	65,895	
	8/2	10,000	300,075	
Williams	7/28	2,000	57,251	8/3
Tippee A	7/28	2,000	57,251	8/3
Tippee B	7/28	13,000	383,195	8/3
	7/30	2,000	58,506	
Other Tippees	7/28 and later	31,000	various	various

Note: This exhibit describes a subset of the insider trades documented in Exhibit 2.

[a]Harris purchased this block of 3,100 shares for the account of his father and stepmother.

15

NOTE ON INSIDER TRADING

The purpose of this note is to provide a brief overview of the law concerning insider trading. Insider trading which may attract liability means generally dealing in securities while in possession of material non-public information. Insider trading is defined by a country's securities laws; therefore, what constitutes insider trading differs somewhat between countries.

Insider trading does not relate to all trades made by company management, directors, and large shareholders. These people can trade in company securities and are generally required to disclose such activity publicly.

Whether insider trading is an activity which should be prohibited is a subject of ongoing debate. Proponents of insider trading regulation advance the following arguments:

- Inequality of information, or of access to information, is unfair. Market efficiency depends on equality, because competition depends on equal information. Insider trading is based on inequality of information.

- Insider trading is harmful to the party trading with the insider. Insider trading legislation is necessary to protect investors.

- Insider trading undermines investors' confidence in the integrity of capital markets, and leads to reduced investment and resource misallocation.

Insider trading legislation is generally justified on the above arguments, that is, on fairness.

Those who favour lifting regulations on insider trading rely on the following arguments:

- Insider trading transmits information and helps to move share prices to their "true values." It, therefore, increases efficiency in capital markets.
- Information is a resource belonging to the company. Regulation takes away shareholders' ability to use this resource, for example, in managers' compensation packages.

Regardless of which side of the argument one agrees with, the reality is that many countries regulate insider trading and that prosecution of insiders has gained momentum in the last decade. Managers and those working in securities markets should understand the regulations on insider trading, whatever their personal views on the subject.

Globalization of securities markets has encouraged legislation prohibiting insider trading. This has been driven by two factors. First, growth in global capital movement has increased concern over harmonization of insider trading laws between different national markets. Second, national securities exchanges wish to appear fair and unwilling to tolerate insider manipulation, in order not to lose investment to another exchange which does not condone such behaviour.

The remainder of this Note will outline the regulation of insider trading in the United States, Canada, Japan, Germany, and by the EEC. There are two elements to insider trading regulation: ongoing disclosure requirements for insiders, and a prohibition on certain types of trades, by certain insiders. (The latter only will be referred to as "insider trading.") Most jurisdictions impose reporting requirements on insiders as well as prohibit insider trading. Jurisdictions differ on their approach to insiders who inform others of material non-public information (tippers) and those who are informed (tippees)—some holding both liable for insider trading.

UNITED STATES

The U.S. has seen the largest insider trading scandals ever, with the trial of Dennis Levine, Ivan Boesky, and Mike Milken in the 1980s. The Milken settlement was the largest in history at $600 million in fines and other sanctions. Insider trading regulation in the U.S. has been strengthened in recent years due to the uproar over these cases.

In contrast to Canada, securities regulation in the U.S. is largely a federal matter. The legislation of most relevance to insider trading is the Securities Exchange Act of 1934 (SEA). This act regulates the purchase and sale of securities, and created the Securities and Exchange Commission (SEC) which oversees securities transactions.

There are two concepts underlying the laws prohibiting insider trading in the United States: full disclosure of all material information affecting publicly traded securities, and maintenance of fair and orderly securities markets.[1] Congress views insider trading as unfair and feels that its elimination will maintain investment and confidence in securities markets.[2]

Reporting Requirements

Section 16(a) of the SEA requires disclosure of trades in equities, on a monthly basis, by directors, officers, and shareholders holding more than a 10% interest in the company.

Section 16(b) makes these insiders liable to the company for profit on "short-swing" trades in shares, that is, purchases and sales within six months of each other. There is no requirement that the trade be made on the basis of material non-public information.

Section 10(b) and Rule 10b-5

The two principal provisions of the SEA concerning insider trading, Sections 10(b) and 14(e), are set out very broadly. The U.S. approach is to rely on the courts to define insider trading, rather than adopting a certain definition which could restrict the application of the law and could be subject to circumvention by inventive insiders.

Section 10(b) and Rule 10b-5 enacted under it do not mention "insider trading," but have been interpreted by the courts to prohibit trading or tipping by any person who possesses material non-public information. Material information is characterized as having significance in the deliberations of a reasonable shareholder. The general rule is to disclose the information to the other party to the transaction, or to abstain from trading.

This general prohibition is limited by the requirement that the trader or tipper has a duty to the other party to disclose the information. The duty arises only if the trader or tipper is in a fiduciary relationship with the other side, that is, a relationship of trust and confidence. For example, a financial printer who determined the identity of the target company for a takeover and purchased shares of the target was not liable for insider trading. The printer did not owe a duty to the selling shareholders.[3] (Note that this case was decided before Rule 14e-3 was enacted. Rule 14e-3 is discussed later.)

A fiduciary duty arises where the person can gain access to non-public information about the company as a result of his or her position. This occurs in the following situations:

[1]Gerald Polcari, "A Comparative Analysis of Insider Trading Laws: The United States, The United Kingdom and Japan," *Suffolk Transnational Law Journal*, Vol. 13 (1989), p. 168.

[2]Susan Lorde Martin, "Insider Trading and Rule 14e-3 *After Chestman*," *American Business Law Journal*, Vol. 29 (1991), p. 670.

[3]*Chiarella* v. *United States*, 445 U.S. 222.

- Officers and directors, as well as certain employees.
- Firms retained for a specific purpose and their employees. This includes lawyers, accountants, and investment bankers.[4] Note that in 1989, a lawyer received a criminal sentence of five years in prison, a fine of $332,000, and an order to turn over $350,000 in profit to the government, for using inside information for trading in his clients' stock. He also was required to pay $500,000 in damages in a civil action.[5]

Trading or tipping in company shares using material non-public information is a breach of the person's fiduciary duty to the corporation. A tippee may be liable if the tipper receives some benefit and breaches his or her fiduciary duty to the corporation.

The general prohibition against insider trading has been limited to equities, although the statute does not so limit it. A fiduciary duty has not been recognized as pertaining to bondholders. In addition, the legislation is meant to protect small investors, and most junk bondholders are institutions.[6]

Rule 14e-3

Insider trading regulation in the case of a takeover is quite different. Rule 14e-3, enacted in 1980 under Section 14(e) of the SEA, governs insider trading in the context of a tender offer. A fiduciary duty need not exist between the trader/tipper and the company, and the reach of the law is, therefore, broader.

Persons will be liable during a tender offer if they trade on information, where:

- they know or have reason to know the information is non-public;
- they know or have reason to know it was acquired from certain insiders;
- the insider was an officer, director, or employee of either the target or bidding companies. Also included are persons acting on behalf of either company.

For officers, directors, employees, or advisors of the bidder or target, or their tippees, there is also a prohibition on informing others where it is reasonably foreseeable that the tipping will result in an insider trading violation.

This has been a controversial provision in the United States since its introduction. It has been criticized as creating a new crime, "outsider trading," since this rule will reach those not typically considered insiders.[7]

An example of the reach of this Rule is the decision in *United States* v. *Chestman*.[8] In this case, Ira Waldbaum, the controlling shareholder and president of a publicly traded company, Waldbaum, Inc., negotiated the sale of the company.

---

[4]Joseph McLaughlin and Margaret Macfaclane, *Insider Trading*, edited by Emmanual Gaillard (Deventer, The Netherlands: Kluwer Law and Taxation Publishers, 1992), p. 289.

[5]"Lawyer gets 5 years for insider trading," *Globe & Mail*, Sept. 2, 1989, p. B5.

[6]"The law and the bond-dealer," *Economist*, Vol. 319, April 27, 1991, p. 84.

[7]John C. Coffee, Jr., "Outsider Trading, That New Crime," *The Wall Street Journal*, Nov. 14-A, 16:4, 1990.

[8]947 F.2d. 551 (2d Cir. 1991).

He told his sister to give her shares to him so that he could tender her shares as part of the sale. Mr. Waldbaum told her not to tell anyone of the sale. In response to a question about what she did during the day, the sister told her daughter, Susan Loeb, that she gave her shares to Mr. Waldbaum. She warned her daughter not to tell anyone. Mrs. Loeb told her husband but warned him not to discuss this with anyone. Mr. Loeb told his broker, Robert Chestman, that he had information that Waldbaum, Inc. was to be sold. Chestman, knowing of the husband's relationship with Mr. Waldbaum, purchased shares of Waldbaum, Inc., for himself, Mr. Loeb, and some of his other clients. Chestman was convicted of insider trading under Rule 14e-3. This decision is currently being appealed to the U.S. Supreme Court.

If the law is upheld by the Supreme Court, persons working in securities markets will have to be extremely careful, as "the business of searching for new information will become dangerously entangled with the criminal law."[9]

Employers' Liability for Insider Trading of Employees

Securities firms and other such firms may be liable for unlawful actions of their employees under the SEA or at common law. Corporate liability for employees' insider trades was expanded in the 1988 Insider Trading and Securities Fraud Enforcement Act, discussed later. An employer is generally liable for insider trading by senior management on behalf of the firm or its clients. The employer's liability for trading by more junior employees on behalf of the employer, or for trades on the employee's own account, is more uncertain.

The SEA makes "controlling persons" (such as employers) liable for an employee's own violations of the insider trading provisions. If the employer can show it acted in good faith and did not induce the violation, this section of the SEA will not apply.

While Rule 14e-3 provides for employer liability for an employee's insider trades on the employer's account, there is an exception where the employer can show:

- the employee making the investment decision did not know the material non-public information; and
- the employer had implemented policies to ensure that employees making investment decisions would not violate Rule 14e-3.

Employers can also be liable for insider trading done by employees acting within their scope of employment, under the common law doctrine of "respondeat superior". This doctrine holds employers liable for wrongs committed by their employees, done within their employment. There is some debate as to whether the SEA precludes actions under the common law.

[9]*Ibid.*

Recent Strengthening of Insider Trading Laws

After the scandals of the 1980s, two new tools were added to the fight against insider trading.

a) INSIDER TRADING SANCTIONS ACT.   The first, the Insider Trading Sanctions Act of 1984 (ITSA), expanded the SEC's legal remedies against insider trading. The Act increased the SEC's civil damages on a conviction of insider trading to up to three times the profit gained or loss avoided. Profit gained or loss avoided is statutorily defined, making proof of damages less onerous. (It is the difference between the price at the time of the insider trade and the trading price of the security a reasonable period after public disclosure of the inside information.) The ITSA's civil penalties are in addition to any other remedies the SEC may have. Adding up all the civil penalties, the convicted insider trader may be liable for four times the profit gained or loss avoided.

b) INSIDER TRADING AND SECURITIES FRAUD ENFORCEMENT ACT.   The second recent addition to insider trading regulation is the Insider Trading and Securities Fraud Enforcement Act of 1988 (ITSFEA). This act strengthened the insider trading laws by expanding the criminal and civil penalties, and enacting rules to prevent insider trading by securities firms.

The ITSFEA increased the criminal penalties available for convicted insider traders to up to $1,000,000, and/or up to ten years in prison. The lawyer convicted of insider trading referred to previously was subject to large criminal and civil penalties.

Insider traders were made civilly liable to persons who contemporaneously purchased or sold the same class of securities. Tippers were made liable to the contemporaneous trader jointly with the tippee. Damages can be up to the profit gained or loss avoided by the trader.

The ITSFEA is also significant in that it expands employers' liability for the actions of their employees. The ITSFEA makes a "controlling person" liable where:

- the controlling person knew or recklessly disregarded that the controlled person (the employee) was likely to violate the insider trading laws, and failed to prevent such a violation; and
- the controlling person knowingly or recklessly failed to establish, maintain, and enforce policies to prevent such a violation.

Controlling persons can be subject to a penalty of the greater of $1,000,000, or triple the amount of profit gained or loss avoided by reason of the controlling person's violation of the ITSFEA. (Profit or loss avoided is defined as in the ITSA.)

Registered brokers or investment dealers have a statutory duty under the ITSFEA to establish, maintain, and enforce policies and procedures designed to prevent the misuse of material non-public information, in violation of the insider trading rules. Such policies may include the use of "Chinese Walls," that is, procedures to restrict information flow between departments. These dealers are also subject to having their licenses suspended or revoked by the SEC for violations of the insider trading rules.

CANADA

Canada has not appeared to have its share of highly publicized insider trading prosecutions. This is not because insider trading prosecutions do not take place, but because they are usually settled before the process has been carried too far. The largest insider trading penalty to date was a $550,000 fine and a three year trading ban, in a settlement reached by the OSC and a majority shareholder in a company.[10]

The securities industry in Canada is regulated by both the provincial and federal governments. The provincial securities acts cover public companies (with securities listed on an exchange in the province), and the provincial and federal companies acts cover companies incorporated under them. The Ontario Securities Act[11] will be used as an example for the purposes of this Note; other provincial securities acts are similar. Because the companies' acts are not generally used to prosecute insider trading, these will not be discussed. The provisions in these acts are generally similar to those in the securities acts.

Regulation of insider trading in Canada is based on obtaining information disclosure, and on assuring equal opportunity to access, or equal access to, information which may affect the value of a security.[12]

Reporting Requirements

Generally, insiders are required to report direct or indirect ownership of securities of the company to the appropriate provincial or federal body. Changes in ownership must also be reported, beginning at the time a person becomes an insider. Securities are defined broadly to include shares, debt obligations, options, and convertibles. Once filed, these reports are public. For the purposes of the reporting requirements, "insiders" include directors, senior officers, and major shareholders (those holding more than 10% of the voting shares of the company).

Illegal Trades

Companies falling under provincial securities acts must file a press release of any material change[13] in the business, thereby making the information available to the

---

[10]"Richard Gets Record OSC Penalty," *Financial Post*, 3(80), June 20, 1990, p. 1.

[11]R.S.O. 1990, c. S.5.

[12]"Takeover Bid Issues and Insider Trading Legislation," *Basic Securities Law*, The Law Society of Upper Canada, Toronto, 1991, F-58.

[13]A material change is any change in the business, operations, or capital that could reasonably be expected to have a significant effect on the market price of any of the company's securities. It includes a decision by senior management which they believe the board will confirm. Ontario *Securities Act*, R.S.O. 1990, c. S.5, s. 1(1).

public. There are exemptions from this provision if the company has reasons not to want public disclosure.

Where the company has not disclosed such information, the potential for insider trading exists. Insider trading arises only where a person:

- is in a "specified relationship" with a company;
- trades in securities of the company;
- has knowledge of an undisclosed material fact[14] or material change; or
- informs another person of the material fact or material change.

If such a trade or tip is made but the information will not affect the security's price, this falls outside the insider trading provisions.

Persons at Risk of Insider Trading

Unlike the U.S. SEA, the Canadian statutes define those persons who can be caught by insider trading provisions. Provincial securities law prohibits those in a "special relationship" with a company from trading or tipping in certain instances. This covers a broader range of persons than those insiders required to report ownership of securities.

In addition to including directors, officers, major shareholders, and employees of the company, provincial law holds the following persons to be in a "special relationship" with the company:

- Directors, officers, and employees of another company proposing a takeover or merger.
- A person or company (and its insiders) engaged in or proposing to engage in any business or professional activity for the company. This covers consultants, auditors, investment bankers, lenders, and lawyers.
- Tippees who know or reasonably should know that the tipper is a person in a special relationship with the company. Sub-tippees (a person who learns of a material fact or material change from a tippee) are also included, as tippees themselves are in a special relationship with the company. Thus, insider trading violations can be tracked down a chain of tippees. Tips are not subject to prohibition if they are made in the necessary course of business.

Penalties for Violation

Penalties for violating the insider trading laws are similar to those in the United States. An insider trader or tipper may be subject to criminal and civil penalties. In addition, if the trader or tipper works in the securities industry, he or she may be subject to disciplinary action by the provincial securities commission, including having their registration suspended or cancelled.

---

[14]A material fact is a fact in relation to securities (either issued or proposed to be issued) which significantly affects the market price or value of the security. Ontario *Securities Act*, R.S.O. 1990, c. S.5, s. 1(1).

a) CRIMINAL SANCTIONS.   The insider trader or tipper may be subject to a fine of up to $1,000,000 and/or imprisonment for up to two years. If the person made a profit on the transaction, the person is subject to a fine only, of up to the greater of $1,000,000 or triple the profit realized. Profit is measured against the average price of the securities for twenty days after the information is disclosed.

b) CIVIL.   Insider traders are liable to compensate the person on the other side of the transaction for the person's damages. Tippers are liable to the person who bought from or sold to the tippee. Therefore, a tipper may not trade, but still be liable for damages incurred on the tippee's trade. An example is a consultant discussing a client with a friend who then trades on the information. If the conversation is not in the necessary course of business, the consultant risks liability to the person with whom the friend traded.

Damages are calculated as the difference between the price paid or received on the transaction, and the average price for twenty days after the information is disclosed. The difficulty for the person who may have traded with insider traders or tippees is not proving damages but in identifying the other party to the transaction. This is less difficult in the U.S., where the ITSFEA makes insider traders liable to contemporaneous traders in the same class of securities.

Insiders who trade or tip on undisclosed material information are also accountable to the company for any benefit or advantage received or receivable on the transaction.

Defences Available

If the insider trader or tippee proves he or she reasonably believed the material information had been generally disclosed, there is no civil or criminal liability.

Civil liability can be avoided if the person proves that the other side to the transaction knew, or ought to have known, the material information.

Companies may be liable under the insider trading rules for investment decisions made, where the information known by an officer can be attributed to the company. They can protect themselves from liability by taking appropriate measures to prevent transmission of information, other than in the necessary course of business. Securities firms may use Chinese Walls to segregate trading and research departments.

Conclusion

To demonstrate the different reach of the Canadian and American laws, consider the following fact situation:

> A manager at a company tells her spouse of positive test market results for a new product critical to the company. The spouse buys shares of the company. The next week, the test results are announced and the company's shares rise in value. The spouse's profit is $10,000.

Under U.S. law, the manager would be liable for tipping under Rule 10b-5. She breached her fiduciary duty to the company's shareholders. However, her spouse would owe no fiduciary duty to the company's shareholders and would not be caught by Rule 10b-5. If the information was concerning a takeover bid, then both would likely be liable as no fiduciary duty is required under Rule 14e-3. Under Rule 14e-3, the manager would be liable for communicating material non-public information, if it was reasonably foreseeable that her spouse would trade on the information. Her spouse would be liable for trading while in possession of material information which he knew was non-public and which he knew was acquired from an officer of the company.

Under Canadian law, both would be liable regardless of the existence of a tender offer. The manager was in a special relationship with the company. Her spouse, as a tippee, was also in a special relationship. The manager violated the prohibition against tipping. Her spouse violated the prohibition against trading with knowledge of a material non-public change. Both the manager and her spouse would be jointly and severally liable for the loss of the sellers of the shares. If the manager had received a benefit on the transaction, she would be accountable to the company for the benefit and would have to turn the benefit over to the company.

The American approach to the regulation of insider trading has had great impact on other countries. The Japanese Securities Exchange Act of 1948 contained provisions modelled after the general prohibition against insider trading contained in the U.S. act. U.S. views on insider trading and tightening up of insider trading enforcement may have had an effect on the recent increase in European insider trading regulation.

JAPAN

Until recently, Japan was known by some as "insider's heaven".[15] This can be explained by cultural and regulatory factors.

Bankers, key customers, brokers and others are often given access to otherwise confidential information, as part of the Japanese emphasis on long term business relationships. Tipping of insider information is considered to be an important service of Japanese brokerage firms.[16]

There has also been lax enforcement of the insider trading laws. This is partially due to the law itself: before 1988, insider trading regulations were vague and difficult to enforce. Japanese enforcement also lacked a strong governmental body such as the OSC or SEC. Some also feared that enforcement could block the flow of securities transactions.[17]

---

[15]Tomoko Akashi, "Insider Trading in Japan," *Columbia Law Review*, Vol. 89 (1989), p. 1302.

[16]*Ibid*, p. 1296.

[17]Hideki Kojima, *Insider Trading*, edited by Emmanual Gaillard (Deventer, The Netherlands: Kluwer Law and Taxation Publishers, 1992), p. 329.

In 1988, the Japanese Diet passed an Amendment to the Japanese Securities Exchange Law to strengthen existing law on insider trading. The Amendment was motivated by a number of factors:

- Major insider trading scandals began to emerge. The Tateho Chemical Industries scandal in 1987 involved one of the company's banks, which sold 337,000 shares shortly before the company announced massive losses. The Osaka Securities Exchange investigated but could find no conclusive evidence of insider trading. This led to calls for stronger laws and enforcement. It was felt that if foreign and domestic investors viewed the markets as unfair, it would damage their confidence in the markets.[18]
- Increased interest arose in the appearance of fairness in the markets due to increased numbers of lay investors as well as growth in the global importance of Japanese securities markets.

1988 Amendment

The 1988 amendment strengthened existing law by more clearly defining prohibited conduct.

Persons who gain knowledge of material facts through their connection or position with the company must not trade in the company's securities (including shares, bonds, or options listed on a stock exchange) before public disclosure. Another provision sets out the same prohibition for securities of a target company in a takeover if the person gains knowledge through his or her position with the acquirer.

Japanese law is more limited than U.S. or Canadian law. Insiders must obtain the information in connection with their work for the company. Also, liability does not follow a chain of tippees. The broker in the *Chestman* case would not be guilty under Japanese law.

Penalties are low compared to the sanctions available in North America. Violation of the law can result in imprisonment of up to six months, and/or a fine of up to ¥500,000 (US$4,285 at the time of writing). There is only limited civil liability, and persons who trade with insider traders will have difficulty proving their damages.

The results of the amendment have been poor to date. The first case to go to trial was in September 1992, and the fine was ¥500,000. The only other case investigated settled before trial. Whether the new law has decreased the level of insider trading is doubtful.

Enforcement is still a problem under the new law. The Ministry of Finance (which supervises enforcement) has no legal power to demand access to evidence, as the U.S. has. The staff is also small: 17 people compared to the SEC's 2100, in 1990. The Tokyo police have been assisting in insider trading investigations.

---

[18]*Ibid.*

GERMANY

Germany has a voluntary, contract-based system to regulate insider trading. Pressure has been building for Germany to enact laws regulating insider trading, especially after high profile scandals such as that involving the Deutsche Bank in 1990.

Regulation of insider trading is provided by the Voluntary Insider Trading Guidelines, and the Cope of Procedure, which implements the Guidelines. Companies agree to be bound by the Guidelines, and then individual employees agree with their employers to adhere to the terms of the Guidelines. This is usually part of an employment contract.

Insiders are prohibited from making any transaction in the company's securities, for their own or a third party's benefit, if the transaction uses inside information obtained by virtue of the insider's position. Tipping has only been prohibited since 1988, and tippees are not prohibited from trading. This is less restrictive than Canadian or U.S. law.

Germany has had few insider trading prosecutions, which is expected because the Guidelines are voluntary. Employees who trade with material non-public information are liable to their employer for breach of their employment contract. Penalties are limited to restitution to the corporation of monetary advantage obtained, and are considered to be insufficient to deter the offence.

EEC

The Council of European Communities adopted the EC Directive, coordinating regulations on insider dealing, in November 1989. Its purpose was to harmonize laws in EC member states, in order to increase the "transparency" of securities markets in the EC.[19] Member states were required to amend their existing insider trading laws or enact laws by July 1992 to meet the Directive's provisions. All states except Germany met the deadline.

The Directive applies insider trading law to shares, debt, or options traded on regulated markets. It is less restrictive than U.S. or Canadian insider trading regulations. The nature of the information must be precise, which restricts the type of information covered. The definition of insiders prohibited from trading or tipping is also more limited: the information must arise by virtue of their position or employment as a manager, a shareholder, or a person who has access to company information. Tippees are not prohibited from tipping.

Sanctions are set by member states, and must be sufficient to promote compliance with the Directive.

[19]Isabelle Pingel, *Insider Trading*, edited by Emmanual Gaillard (Deventer, The Netherlands: Kluwer Law and Taxation Publishers, 1992), p. 5.

INTERNATIONAL EFFORTS

National laws clearly apply where a transaction is executed in its entirety within a country. Regulators have difficulty applying and enforcing insider trading regulations where transactions cross national borders. Laws of other states sometimes block regulators' efforts to investigate and enforce insider trading violations.

Regulators have responded to the need to enforce insider trading regulations where trades span national borders with the following:

- Memoranda of Understanding arrived at between national regulators, providing for mutual cooperation. The SEC has such arrangements with several Canadian provinces, including Ontario.
- Mutual Assistance Treaties applying to areas of common law between states. These binding agreements provide for each state to supply help for investigation to the other in the areas of common law.

Despite these actions, detection and enforcement are still a problem. For example, Dennis Levine, the partner of Drexel Burnham Lambert convicted of insider trading in 1987, used an offshore bank account. His trades would have been very difficult to pinpoint had others in the U.S. not followed his trades.

Regulators have not yet found a solution to cross-border insider trading. The European Directive may provide one model for resolution of this problem.

CONCLUSION

Insider trading laws have received increased attention in the last decade. Governments and regulators view such laws as necessary in order to maintain confidence in securities markets.

Managers and those involved in the securities industry should have an understanding of such laws. This Note outlines briefly the U.S. law, as well as describing Canadian, Japanese, and European law. The law as described is simplified in order to highlight the major areas of risk.

16

FINNING TRACTOR AND EQUIPMENT COMPANY LTD.

In mid-July 1982, Vinod K. Sood, President and Chief Operating Officer of Finning Tractor and Equipment Company Ltd. (Finning), was preparing a presentation on dividend policy for the Board of Directors meeting later that week. Two months earlier, because of the depressed economic conditions and poor company earnings, he had postponed the declaration of the second quarter dividend, usually announced in mid-May and paid in early June, until after he had had a chance to analyze the second quarter results. The restraint measures instigated over the past several months had done little to restore profitability and the second quarter earnings received by Sood the previous day confirmed that the company faced ongoing financial problems. Sood's task was to present a comprehensive financial plan to the Board, one important aspect of which concerned dividend policy. The Board would have to approve any change in dividend.

BACKGROUND

Finning was North America's largest distributor of Caterpillar equipment, and as such sold, leased, rented and serviced a wide variety of Caterpillar products through its 23 branches, 9 depots and 19 residences as shown in Exhibit 1. The branches provided full service, parts and service facilities; depots provided service and limited parts supplies; and residences had one or more field service representatives who serviced equipment at nearby customer locations. Some examples of Caterpillar equipment handled by Finning were track type tractors, pipelayers, motor graders, wheel dozers, wheel tractor-scrapers, hydraulic excavators, lift trucks, off-highway trucks, truck, marine, and industrial engines and electric power generating equipment.

The Caterpillar dealership was not Finning's only source of revenue. Finning also held dealership agreements for several other products with companies including Gardner Denver air equipment, JLG and Smith Tool aerial work platforms, Perkins diesel engines, Grove hydraulic cranes, RayGoWagner log stackers, JCB hydraulic excavators and backhoes, DJB Engineering Off-highway trucks and Driltech rotary drills.

Finning extended financing to its customers with leases and conditional sales contracts. Leases were generally operating leases with payments based on a residual value that was Finning's best estimate of the market value of the equipment at the end of the lease term. Financing periods ranged from a few months to seven years, but two to four years was most common. The company could compete successfully with other financing institutions because of its expertise in estimating residual values and its access to Finning Tractor's refurbishing facilities and used equipment market. Finning financed about one-third of its total sales.

COMPANY HISTORY

Finning was incorporated under the laws of British Columbia in 1933 and converted to a public company in September 1969. Considered a growth company by the management, Finning embarked on a series of expansion and acquisition projects, beginning with the acquisition of G.M. Philpott Co. Ltd. (air compressors, rock drills, etc.) in 1971. Any acquisitions were meant to complement the Caterpillar line of products and to achieve a degree of market diversification. The Philpott purchase was followed in 1976 by the acquisition of part of the Northern Commercial Company Ltd., through which Finning became the Caterpillar dealer in the Yukon Territories, in 1977 by the investment of $2.5 million in Dome Petroleum's Beaufort Sea project for .5 percent participation in net earnings, the purchase of Philpott Close Equipment Co. of Seattle/Spokane in 1979, Portland/Springfield in 1980, Percival Machinery and Supply in 1981 and, as of June 1982, the agreement in principle to acquire Bowmaker (Plant) Limited, the Caterpillar dealership for southwest England and Wales.

Exhibit 2 shows that sales, profits and stock price had grown at impressive rates through 1980. In mid 1980, analysts considered Finning stock underpriced and were recommending it as a best buy. Dividends had grown from $.025 per share annually (adjusted for splits), paid quarterly starting in May 1970, to $.30 in March 1980. The stock had split three times since 1969, first in 1972, then in April of

1980 and 1981. Exhibits 3 and 4 show income statements and balance sheets for the years ended 1977 to 1981.

In January 1981, the Series A preferreds were issued to employees as part of a profit sharing plan. The preferreds were convertible into voting shares after January 27, 1983, and before January 28, 1991, at $18.40 per share. They paid a dividend of one-half the prime rate plus one-half percent per annum ((Prime Rate/2) + .5%), effectively giving those employees that borrowed to purchase the stock no after-tax carrying costs.

In May, the common shares were reclassified into class A voting and class B non-voting shares in preparation for the June issue of $65,000,000, 11½ percent convertible debentures. The debentures were convertible into class B shares so that even after conversion the two majority shareholders would maintain their 70 percent voting control of the company.

In July, Canada's financial press was still publishing articles suggesting that British Columbia's economy was expanding, but Finning was showing signs of an approaching downturn. With the majority of its revenues resource-based, 45 percent from forestry, 30 percent from mining and 15 percent from construction, Finning was considered an indicator of B.C.'s economic activity. Sales appeared to continue to climb in 1981 but, adjusted for inflation, they had actually declined. Units sold, total revenue hours and parts sold were all down from 1980. Second and third quarter profits showed a decline that continued into 1982. Exhibits 5 through 8 present the four quarterly reports for 1980 and 1981 and the two quarterly reports for 1982.

In October, when Sood, previously executive vice president, replaced the retiring John Frazee as President and Chief Operating Officer, several restraint measures had already been instigated. New equipment inventories had been cut by $50 million and additional cuts were expected. By year end, employment had been cut by 24 percent from its high of 2,400 in February 1981. Sood, an advocate of active management, believed that the major costs for Finning Tractor were wages and interest and both could be managed so that the equity of the company would be protected throughout recession.

By the end of 1981 the recession had settled in. U.S. housing starts had declined from a seasonally adjusted annual rate of 1.66 million in January 1981, to a low of 863,000 in November. U.S. lumber shipments fell from 2,813 million board feet to 1,637 million board feet over the two year period beginning in January 1979. Copper prices, based on closing prices of May copper futures, dropped 42 percent over the 1981 year. Similar declines could be found in most resource-based areas. It was barely a profitable year for Finning. Bad debts had increased from an average of 0.25 percent of sales prior to 1981 to a staggering 1.5 percent of sales. Interest expense had increased 61 percent from 1980, but with all of the bad news, Finning still had a backlog of orders. Even so, when the 1982 forecast of $550 million in sales was presented, Sood knew it was unattainable.

In January of 1982, Sood requested that market inequities in salaries be removed and the majority of the employees received raises. This was a very unusual move

considering that most other companies were either freezing or rolling back wages. He did reserve the right to return to the employees should the economy deteriorate to a point where alternate salary proposals would be necessary, but Sood strongly believed that salary cuts were very bad for morale and should be avoided if at all possible. The quarterly dividend of $.075 was declared as usual for March 1982. Both of these decisions helped dispel false rumors that Finning was on the edge of bankruptcy and would soon begin to close down some of its branches. These rumors had reached many of Finning's branches, and newspapers such as the *Prince George Citizen* had called for verification on the closures. The revaluation downward of the secured and convertible debt to BB and B from BBB and BB respectively along with the bankruptcy of a major competitor did not help matters.

Sood considered the whole situation ironic since the company's balance sheet had never looked better. Because of the staff layoffs and the inventory and capital expenditure reductions, Finning's short term debt had been reduced to its lowest levels in years. The debenture issue of June 1981 had helped to reduce and stabilize the company's interest costs. The parts and service areas of the company, although affected by the recession, continued to cover all expenses and the company still had substantial lines of untapped bank credit on which to draw. Cash flow had not become a problem. Sood expected that there was considerable pent-up demand for Finning's products, since the forest industry had not had a chance to recover from its strike in 1981 before entering the recession. Several mining and construction projects had been suspended during the economic downturn but would start again as the recession eased.

THE DIVIDEND DECISION

The March 31, 1982, dividend had been the third consecutive dividend declared by the company that was not covered by quarterly earnings. As the mid-May second quarter dividend declaration date approached, Sood thought it would be prudent to postpone any announcement until after the next Board meeting, especially given the unusual environment—low earnings but satisfactory cash flow and an improved balance sheet but rumors of impending bankruptcy. Also, by the July 22nd meeting, he would have had a chance to analyze the second quarter results and ascertain if the recession was easing or if additional restraint measures would be necessary.

As the July Board meeting approached, Mr. Sood knew that several issues could be discussed pertaining to dividend policy including: amount of payment, stock or cash payment, desirable long term dividend policy, preferred dividend policy and effect of dividend policy on stock price. Ultimately, the Board would have to decide on continuation of the current policy or a specific change. The two major shareholders, descendants of the founder, were represented on the Board and each was receiving over $1.5 million a year in dividends from Finning. But the stock price had fallen to half its level of a year ago and a dividend cut might force the price even lower. Eliminating the dividend might affect institutional investors holding the stock, because of the requirement for dividends in acts governing various companies and funds such as Pension Benefits Standards Act (Canada), Pension Benefits Act (Ontario), Supplemental Pensions Plans Act (Quebec), Loan Companies Act (Canada), Foreign Insurance Companies Act (Canada) and the Canadian and British Insurance Companies Act, of which excerpts are shown in Appendix A. In general, if a company paid or earned enough to pay a dividend of at least four percent of the average value of the common stock over the year in four of the previous five years, including the last year, it would meet virtually all statutes. Some exceptions include the Trust Companies Act (Canada), which required the 4 percent rule for every year in the preceding five years, and the Trust Companies Act (Alberta) which required the 4 percent rule apply to earned profits in each of the preceding five years. The Board had always approved dividend changes in a routine way in the past, but they had always been increases. Exhibit 9 shows the weekly stock prices for Finning for the 42 weeks leading up to the meeting.

EXHIBIT 1

FINNING TRACTOR AND EQUIPMENT COMPANY LTD.
Company Locations as of February 1, 1982

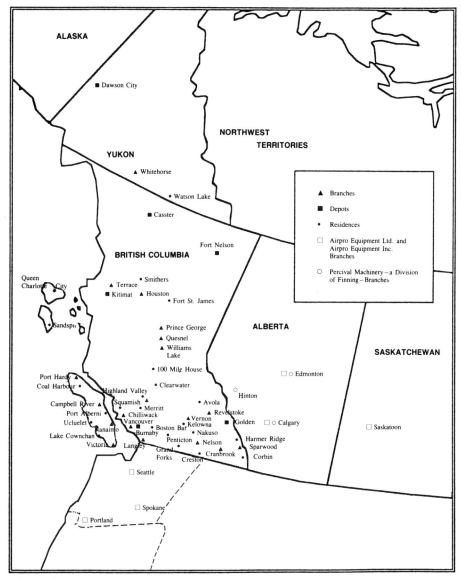

Source: Company records.

EXHIBIT 2

FINNING TRACTOR AND EQUIPMENT COMPANY LTD.

Selected Growth Statistics

(dollar figures in thousands, except per share data)

YEAR	REVENUE	EARNINGS BEFORE TAX	NET INCOME	EPS	STOCK LOW	STOCK HIGH	DIV
1972	$126,622	$ 9,732	$ 5,084	$ .32	$1.53	$ 3.69	$.038
1973	148,157	11,241	5,475	.34	2.19	3.75	.060
1974	162,101	15,424	7,286	.46	1.63	2.88	.070
1975	173,812	15,675	7,942	.50	1.72	2.56	.100
1976	199,795	14,583	8,609	.54	2.19	3.56	.100
1977	246,761	19,625	12,202	.76	2.69	5.13	.125
1978	287,933	24,012	14,769	.93	4.69	7.25	.125
1979	375,417	28,322	19,459	1.23	6.28	9.75	.225
1980	438,327	28,180	18,237	1.15	8.50	17.44	.300
1981	454,377	1,092	3,485	.20	7.50	16.00	.300

Source for Exhibits 2–8: Company records.

EXHIBIT 3

FINNING TRACTOR AND EQUIPMENT COMPANY LTD.
Income Statement
For the years ended December 31

	1981	1980	1979	1978	1977
Revenue	$454,377,077	$438,327,098	$375,417,004	$287,933,418	$246,760,983
Expenses					
Cost of Sales	370,706,718	356,496,469	307,236,286	236,432,076	202,547,062
General and Admin.	32,381,898	22,544,168	18,519,632	16,683,343	15,830,032
Interest	50,196,061	31,106,229	21,338,814	10,805,908	8,731,936
Total Expenses	453,284,677	410,146,866	347,094,732	263,921,327	227,109,030
Income Before Tax	1,092,400	28,180,232	28,322,272	24,012,091	19,651,953
Provision for Income Taxes	(2,392,587)	9,943,564	8,862,804	9,243,416	7,650,353
Net Income	3,484,987	18,236,668	19,459,468	14,768,675	12,001,600
Beginning Retained	95,637,387	82,166,399	66,281,191	53,498,216	43,482,316
Dividends Paid	4,997,072	4,765,680	3,574,260	1,985,700	1,985,700
Net Income	$ 94,125,302	$ 95,637,387	$ 82,166,399	$ 66,281,191	$ 53,498,216

EXHIBIT 4

FINNING TRACTOR AND EQUIPMENT COMPANY LTD.
Balance Sheet
For the years ended December 31

	1981	1980	1979	1978	1977
Assets					
Accounts receivable	$ 61,537,736	72,752,461	55,584,343	42,616,803	30,211,081
Instalment Notes	63,361,092	61,968,696	54,089,792	49,315,241	45,930,381
Income Taxes Refundable	—	591,259	—	—	943,997
Inventories					
Equipment	110,953,365	133,598,453	95,114,682	69,075,396	54,471,698
Parts and Supplies	41,945,998	49,641,113	36,153,273	33,655,018	25,183,978
Total Current Assets	277,798,191	318,551,982	240,942,090	194,662,458	156,741,135
Leased Equipment	90,057,226	97,737,107	78,887,287	51,827,491	40,780,316
Net Land, Buildings and Equipment	54,097,262	47,617,776	40,453,850	29,413,773	21,481,628
TOTAL ASSETS	$421,952,679	463,906,865	360,283,227	275,903,722	219,003,079

180

Liabilities					
Bank Debt	$165,011,604	246,525,775	179,458,055	35,212,147	107,395,310
Accounts Payable	21,509,239	46,023,641	30,391,020	32,212,147	28,722,876
Income Taxes Payable	1,244,699	–	299,764	1,440,982	–
Long Term Debt[a]	28,200,000	28,800,000	29,400,000	30,000,000	153,094
Convertible Debentures[b]	65,000,000	–	–	–	–
Deferred Taxes	35,509,873	37,823,500	29,471,427	25,706,409	20,137,021
Total Liabilities	316,475,415	359,172,916	269,020,266	200,525,969	156,408,301
Equity					
Share Capital[c]	11,351,962	9,096,562	9,096,562	9,096,562	9,096,562
Retained Earnings	94,125,302	95,637,387	82,166,399	66,281,191	53,498,216
TOTAL LIABILITIES & EQUITY	$421,952,679	463,906,865	360,283,227	275,903,722	219,003,079

[a]The long term debt carried several covenants, one of which restricts the declaration and payment of dividends and the reduction of share capital. Under the most restrictive of these provisions, the amount available for dividends was $12,976,296 at December 31, 1981.

[b]The 11.5% convertible subordinated debentures were convertible into class B non-voting shares at $18.00 per share prior to June 24, 1986, and at $18.75 from June 25, 1986, to June 24, 1991.

[c]Share capital in 1981 was divided as follows: Series A Preferred—$2,255,400; Class A Common—$4,544,392; Class B Common—$4,544,170.

181

EXHIBIT 5

FINNING TRACTOR AND EQUIPMENT COMPANY LTD.
First Quarter Report for the Three Months Ended March 31

	1982	1981	1980
Revenue	$ 84,232	$ 119,753	$ 92,224
Cost of Sales, etc.	75,884	101,678	78,715
Interest	8,277	12,287	7,265
Total Expenses	84,161	113,965	85,980
Income Before Taxes	71	5,788	6,244
Provision for Taxes	(589)	1,978	2,185
Net Income	$ 660	$ 3,810	$ 4,059
EPS	$ .04	$ .24	$ .26
Outstanding Shares (adjusted)	15,885,600	15,885,600	15,885,600

Statement of Changes in Financial Position

	1982	1981	1980
Cash Generated			
Net Income	$ 660	$ 3,810	$ 4,059
Depreciation:			
Leased Equipment	6,013	5,551	4,521
Buildings and Equipment	1,316	1,263	1,118
Deferred Income Taxes	(281)	780	1,703
Total Sources from Operations	7,708	11,404	11,401
Cash Used			
Accounts Receivable	(754)	6,473	(20)
Instalment Note Receivable	(4,209)	1,391	(978)
Inventories:			
Equipment	3,010	42,938	24,195
Parts and Supplies	(2,625)	654	2,226
Net Leased Equipment	(1,228)	1,167	5,152
Accounts Payable and Accruals	(8,888)	(4,802)	8,514
Income Taxes	304	(1,019)	(482)
Total Uses from Operations	(14,390)	46,802	38,607
Net Cash Used in Operations	(22,098)	35,398	27,206
Other Uses (Sources) of Cash			
Additions to Land, Buildings, etc.	755	4,621	2,877
Purchase of Secured Debentures	600	300	300
Issue of Preferred Shares	—	(2,519)	—
Redemption of Preferred Shares	92	—	—
Dividends Paid	1,239	1,233	1,191
Total	2,686	3,635	4,368
NET INCREASE IN BANK INDEBTEDNESS	$ (19,412)	$ 39,033	$ 31,574

EXHIBIT 6

FINNING TRACTOR AND EQUIPMENT COMPANY LTD.
Second Quarter Report for the Months Ended June 30

	3 MONTHS			6 MONTHS		
	1982	1981	1980	1982	1981	1980
Revenue	$ 91,983	128,289	118,196	176,215	248,042	210,420
Cost of Sales, etc.	83,802	113,327	101,130	159,686	215,005	179,845
Interest	7,934	13,476	8,858	16,211	25,763	16,123
Total Expenses	91,736	126,803	109,988	175,897	240,768	195,968
Income Before Taxes	247	1,486	8,208	318	7,274	14,452
Provision for Taxes	(379)	87	2,873	(968)	2,065	5,058
Net Income	$ 626	1,399	5,335	1,286	5,209	9,394
EPS	$ .04	.09	.34	.08	.33	.59
Outstanding Shares (adjusted)	15,885,600	15,885,600	15,885,600	15,885,600	15,885,600	15,885,600

EXHIBIT 6 (cont.)

Statement of Changes in Financial Position

	6 MONTHS		
	1982	1981	1980
Cash Generated			
Net Income	$ 1,286	$ 5,209	$ 9,394
Depreciation:			
Leased Equipment	10,918	11,507	9,447
Buildings and Equip.	2,568	2,466	2,234
Deferred Income Taxes	(518)	847	3,770
Total Sources from Operations	14,254	20,029	24,845
Cash Used			
Accounts Receivable	(6,190)	3,997	8,879
Instalment Note Receivable	(5,045)	5,066	3,084
Inventories:			
Equipment	(3,482)	22,762	27,952
Parts and Supplies	(977)	(402)	1,630
Net Leased Equipment	(2,916)	12,168	15,881
Accounts Payable and Accruals	(4,116)	7,748	7,164
Income Taxes	550	(979)	(448)
Total Uses from Operations	(22,176)	50,360	64,142
Net Cash Used in Operations	(36,430)	30,331	39,297
Other Uses (Sources) of Cash			
Additions to Land, Buildings, etc.	1,212	8,276	5,705
Purchase of Secured Debentures	600	300	300
Proceeds on Issue of Debentures	–	(65,000)	–
Issue of Preferred Shares	–	(2,519)	–
Redemption of Preferred Shares	181	47	–
Dividends Paid	1,282	2,488	2,383
Total	3,275	(56,408)	8,388
NET INCREASE IN BANK INDEBTEDNESS	$(33,155)	$(26,077)	$47,685

EXHIBIT 7

FINNING TRACTOR AND EQUIPMENT COMPANY LTD.
Third Quarter Report for the Months Ended September 30

	3 MONTHS		9 MONTHS	
	1981	1980	1981	1980
Revenue	$ 113,682	$ 106,425	$ 361,724	$ 316,845
Cost of Sales, etc.	102,005	93,343	317,010	273,188
Interest	13,570	6,388	39,333	22,511
Total Expenses	115,575	99,731	356,343	295,699
Income Before Taxes	(1,893)	6,694	5,381	21,146
Provision for Taxes	(260)	2,343	1,805	7,401
Net Income	(1,633)	4,351	3,576	13,745
EPS	$ (.10)	$ .27	$ .23	$ .87
Outstanding Shares (adjusted)	15,855,600	15,885,600	15,885,600	15,885,600

Statement of Changes in Financial Position

	9 MONTHS	
	1981	1982
Cash Generated		
Net Income	$ 3,576	$13,745
Depreciation:		
Leased Equipment	18,263	15,302
Buildings and Equipment	4,007	3,216
Deferred Income Taxes	1,956	5,055
Total Sources from Operations	27,802	37,318
Cash Used		
Accounts Receivable	4,264	5,457
Instalment Note Receivable	2,460	3,987
Inventories:		
Equipment	1,080	31,006
Parts and Supplies	(6,748)	3,145
Net Leased Equipment	18,368	23,546
Accounts Payable and Accruals	12,544	5,115
Income Taxes	397	(699)
Total Uses from Operations	32,365	71,557
Net Cash Used in Operations	4,563	34,239
Other Uses (Sources) of Cash		
Additions to Land, Buildings, etc.	9,901	7,490
Purchase of Secured Debentures	600	600
Proceeds on Issue of Convert Deb.	(65,000)	—
Issue of Preferred Shares	(2,519)	—
Redemption of Preferred Shares	99	—
Dividends Paid	3,748	3,574
Total	(53,171)	11,664
NET INCREASE IN BANK INDEBTEDNESS	$(48,608)	$45,903

EXHIBIT 8

FINNING TRACTOR AND EQUIPMENT COMPANY LTD.
Fourth Quarter Report for the Months Ended December 31

	3 MONTHS		12 MONTHS	
	1981	1980	1981	1980
Revenue	$ 92,653	$ 121,482	$ 454,377	$ 438,327
Cost of Sales, etc.	86,079	105,583	403,089	379,041
Interest	10,863	8,595	50,196	31,106
Total Expenses	96,942	114,448	453,285	410,147
Income Before Taxes	(4,289)	7,034	1,092	28,180
Provision for Taxes	(4,198)	2,542	(2,393)	9,943
Net Income	(91)	4,492	3,485	18,237
EPS	$ (.01)	$ .28	$ .22	$ 1.15
Outstanding Shares (adjusted)	15,855,600	15,885,600	15,885,600	15,885,600

Statement of Changes in Financial Position

	12 MONTHS	
	1981	1982
Cash Generated		
Net Income	$ 3,485	$18,237
Depreciation:		
Leased Equipment	24,952	21,234
Buildings and Equipment	5,223	4,657
Deferred Income Taxes	(2,314)	8,352
Total Sources from Operations	31,346	52,480
Cash Used		
Accounts Receivable	(11,215)	17,168
Instalment Note Receivable	1,392	7,879
Inventories:		
Equipment	(22,645)	38,484
Parts and Supplies	(7,695)	13,488
Net Leased Equipment	17,272	40,084
Accounts Payable and Accruals	24,515	(15,633)
Income Taxes	(1,836)	891
Total Uses from Operations	(212)	102,361
Net Cash Used in Operations	(31,558)	49,881
Other Uses (Sources) of Cash		
Additions to Land, Buildings, etc.	11,702	11,821
Purchase of Secured Debentures	600	600
Proceeds on Issue of Convert Deb.	(65,000)	–
Net Issue of Preferred Shares	(2,255)	–
Dividends Paid	4,997	4,766
Total Cash	(49,956)	17,187
NET INCREASE IN BANK INDEBTEDNESS	$(81,514)	$67,068

EXHIBIT 9

FINNING TRACTOR AND EQUIPMENT COMPANY LTD.
Weekly Stock Prices

		CLASS A			CLASS B		
		HIGH	LOW	CLOSE	HIGH	LOW	CLOSE
Week ending							
1981							
October	2	10½	9	10½	10	9	10
	9	10½	10½	10	10¼	9½	9¾
	16	9½	9	9	8¾	8½	8½
	23	8¾	8	8	8½	8	8¼
	30	8	7½	8	8½	7½	8
November	6	10½	8¼	10½	8½	8	8
	13	9¾	8½	9¾	8	8	8
	20	9¼	8½	9¼	8½	8	8½
	27	9¼	8¾	9¼	9¼	8½	9¼
December	4	10¼	9¼	10	10	9¼	10
	11	10	9½	10	9½	9½	9½
	18	10	9½	10	10	9½	9½
	24	10	9¾	10	10	9½	10
	31	10¼	10¼	10¼	9¾	9¾	9¾
1982							
January	8	10½	10	10	10⅜	10⅛	10⅛
	15	10¼	10	10	10	10	10
	22	10½	9¾	9¾	10	10	10
	29	10	9¾	9¾	9	9	9
February	5	10	9¾	9¾	9	9	9
	12	9½	8½	8½	7½	7½	7½
	19	8½	7¾	8½	7¼	7	7¼
	26	8½	8½	8½	8½	7¾	8
March	5	8¼	8	8	8	7¾	8
	12	8	8	8	8	8	8
	19	9	8	8	8	7¾	7¾
	26	8	8	8	8	7¾	7¾
April	2	8	8	8	8	7¾	7¾
	9	8½	8	8½	7¾	7¾	7¾
	16	8½	8	8	7¾	7¾	7¾
	23	8	8	8	8	7¾	7¾
	30	8	8	8	8	7¾	7¾
May	7	7½	7	7½	8	7⅛	7⅛
	14	7½	7⅜	7⅜	7½	7¼	7¼
	21	8¼	7¼	7¼	8¼	7	7
	28	8	7⅜	7⅜	7¼	7	7¼
June	4	7⅛	7	7	7	7¾	7
	11	7	6⅜	6⅜	6¼	5	5
	18	6⅜	5½	5¾	4½	4	4½
	25	6	5	5	5	5	5
July	2	5¼	5¼	5¼	4½	4½	4½
	9	5½	5	5	5	4½	4½
	16	5½	5	5⅜	5	4	4½

Source: Public data.

APPENDIX A
The Canadian and British Insurance Companies Act
(Selected paragraphs)

63. (1) A company may invest its funds or any portion thereof in

(E) the bonds, debentures or other evidences of indebtedness of a corporation that are fully secured by statutory charge upon real estate or upon the plant or equipment of the corporation used in the transaction of its business, if interest in full has been paid regularly for a period of at least ten years immediately preceding the date of investment in such bonds, debentures or other evidences upon the securities of that class of the corporation then outstanding;

(L) the preferred shares of a corporation if

    (i) the corporation has paid a dividend in each of the five years immediately preceding the date of investments at least equal to the specified annual rate upon all of its preferred shares, or

    (ii) the common shares of the corporation are, at the date of the investment, authorized as investments by paragraph (M);

(M) the fully paid common shares of a corporation where during a period of five years that ended less than one year before the date of investment, the corporation

    (i) paid in each of at least four of the five years, including the last year of that period, a dividend upon its common shares, or

    (ii) earned in each of at least four of the five years, including the last year of that period, an amount available for the payment of a dividend upon its common shares, of at least four percent of the average value at which the issued common shares of the corporation were carried in the capital stock account of the corporation during the year in which the dividend was paid or in which the amount was earned as the case may be, but

    (iii) except as provided in sections 64, 65, 90 and 91, a company shall not purchase more than 30 percent of the common shares of any corporation,

    (iv) except as provided in sections 45.1 and 91, a company shall not purchase its own shares,

    (v) if, at the date of a proposed investment, the corporation owns beneficially, directly or indirectly, more than 50 percent of the common shares of one or more other corporations, and if the accounts of the corporation and those other corporations are normally presented to the shareholders of the corporation in consolidated form, a company shall not make an investment under this paragraph unless the requirement in subparagraph (i) or (ii) is met on the basis of the consolidated accounts of the corporation and those other corporations,

    (vi) where the proposed investment is in the shares of a corporation continuing or formed as a result of the amalgamation or merger of two or more corporations, that corporation is deemed, for the purposes of this paragraph, to have dividend and earnings records for any relevant period prior to the date of the amalgamation or merger identical with the dividend and earnings records of the amalgamated or merged corporations determined on the basis of a consolidation of their accounts and,

(vii) except as provided in sections 65 and 90, a company registered to transact the business of life insurance shall not purchase the shares of a corporation transacting in the business of life insurance.

Source: The Canadian and British Insurance Companies Act, 1983.

17

NESBITT THOMSON DEACON INC.—
THE SCEPTRE RESOURCES DEBENTURE

David Gluskin, a vice president of the fixed income area at Nesbitt Thomson Deacon Inc., was sitting in his 21st floor office contemplating the proposal which had been placed before him. It was March 27, 1989, and he had just received a call from Bernie Barth, Senior Vice President of the Bank of Montreal (BOM), requesting that Nesbitt submit a bid for $11 million of Sceptre Resources Ltd. debentures. The Bank of Montreal had originally received the debentures as part of a work-out agreement after Sceptre took over Oakwood Petroleum in a highly leveraged transaction. As one of Sceptre's primary creditors, the BOM already had a large exposure to the company and the sale of the paper was the easiest means by which to reduce this risk. Bernie Barth, who headed the Special Accounts Management Department (i.e., the "work-out" department) at the bank, had been placed in charge of lowering the BOM's exposure to Sceptre.

What made the offer interesting was that this seemed to David to be the first true "junk" bond issue in Canada—the issue had absolutely no covenants protecting the holder. The way it appeared, the paper carried with it significant profit potential for the holder if the company could operate profitably, and of course significant risk if events went in the opposite direction. In order to fully assess the possibilities of the deal, David needed to analyze the state of Sceptre's finances and business,

This case was prepared by Peter Grosskopf under the supervision of Professor Robert W. White for the sole purpose of providing material for class discussion at the Western Business School. Certain names and other identifying information may have been disguised to protect confidentiality. It is not intended to illustrate either effective or ineffective handling of a managerial situation. Any reproduction, in any form, of the material in this case is prohibited except with the written consent of the School.
Copyright 1990 © The University of Western Ontario.

the anticipated demand for such an issue, the fair market value of the paper and the spread which Nesbitt could earn if it was to retail the bonds to other parties. As usual, the time in which to make a decision for a bid was limited; the bank would be going to other possible purchasers within a week.

BACKGROUND ON NESBITT THOMSON

Nesbitt Thomson had been in the investment business since 1924. The firm grew in pace with the investment industry in Canada until the boom years of the business began in the early 1970s. It was then that Nesbitt undertook a series of aggressive acquisitions that propelled it into the top 5 of Canadian investment dealers. When deregulation of the industry occurred in 1987, Nesbitt was purchased by the BOM through a controlling 75% interest. The remaining 25% of the firm was owned by its employees.

Ownership by the bank gave Nesbitt additional capital resources with which to transact its business. This was important, because more and more the investment banks and dealers maintained their profit margins by taking on large market positions. In fact, one of Nesbitt's mandates had been set in 1988 to consistently seek out new avenues to profitably employ increasingly larger amounts of capital. Key Nesbitt financial statistics are presented in Exhibit 1.

BACKGROUND ON SCEPTRE RESOURCES LTD.

Sceptre Resources became a public company in 1977, following a reverse takeover of Decca Resources Ltd. The company's main source of growth had been through acquisitions, a list of which is supplied in Exhibit 2. Over the period 1982 through 1989, Sceptre had acquired over $700 million of assets through share purchases, versus roughly $250 million in capital expenditures. The most recent transaction, as of 1989, was the $275 million purchase of Oakwood Petroleum, through which Sceptre became one of the top ten oil and gas producers in Canada.

Sceptre's single overriding objective continued to be productive asset building through internal development and outside acquisitions. Management at the company had stated its willingness to stick with an aggressive stance to the industry in spite of the industry's volatile nature. For example, efforts in the field continued to lower the average finding and developing costs of Sceptre's oil reserves. In 1989, Sceptre's average development cost was $5.17 per barrel.

While Sceptre's aggressiveness had certainly propelled it to new heights of revenue and production, it had also burdened the company with a large debt load. Sceptre was one of the most highly leveraged Canadian producers, with debt and preferred shares of $495 million, representing over 71% of the company's total capital structure. Financial statistics are presented in Exhibits 3 through 5.

THE OIL AND GAS INDUSTRY

The North American oil and gas producers were driven by pricing issues since the early 1980s. Ever since OPEC forced the price of crude over US$30 per barrel in

1979, U.S. and Canadian producers operated in profit or loss positions mainly due to selling price. After crude prices peaked in 1981, many producers with high production costs were forced out of business, and the industry had achieved rationalization by 1986.

After a modest recovery in 1987, the industry was again plagued by a drastic decline in crude prices during 1988. The North American producers were especially hard hit during the price declines, because their extraction costs frequently made production infeasible with prices under the US$15/barrel benchmark. Compounding the problems in Canada were the rise in interest rates during 1988, and the appreciation of the Canadian dollar against the U.S. dollar, which cost all exporters close to 5% off their margins from March 1988 to March 1989. Exhibit 6 depicts the performance of the TSE oil and gas index, the benchmark of industry performance in the equity market.

On the bright side, 1988 had closed with a reduced production quota among OPEC producers, and crude prices had risen some $4 per barrel since the agreement. In addition, natural gas sales were strong for all Canadian producers, and the governments of both Canada and the U.S. were much more cognizant of industry conditions in 1989 than they were 5 years ago.

THE JUNK BOND MARKET

The term "junk bond" is the street expression for any corporate debt which is not fully secured by assets or a predictable flow of income. Junk bonds are rated BB or below by bond rating services. To compensate for the additional risk, such bonds pay 2.5–7% extra interest per annum. Junk bonds were long marketed as "non-investment grade" or "high yield" securities and became controversial only when Drexel Burnham began to underwrite them in increasingly large amounts to finance risky transactions.

In the U.S., the high yield market underwent a period of tremendous expansion beginning in 1978. By 1986, over $100 billion of this type of debt had been issued, and 1989 estimates placed the total around $225 billion. Due to the large and growing amount of institutional capital in the United States and the attractive yields on junk bonds, most large insurance companies, pension funds and other large investors had become participants in the market for junk by the late 1980s.

The Canadian high yield market had evolved very slowly since its inception in the early 1980s. As is typical with most innovative financial instruments, the Canadian community takes the lead of the U.S. example and even then utilizes the concept mainly for larger investment-grade firms. In addition, the Canadian high yield market had a strong segmentation between small ($5–15 million) private placements and public offerings of the senior firms ($50 million plus). Thus, very few mid-market firms had tapped the subordinated debt market in Canada because their needs most often fall between the two segments. Due to these problems, the outstanding Canadian junk issues totalled only about $3 billion as of March 1989.

THE SCEPTRE DEBENTURE

After the purchase of Oakwood Petroleum in December 1988, Sceptre and its creditors had held a series of meetings in which an acceptable capital structure had been worked out. In the structure of this reorganization, the creditors of Oakwood had agreed to accept $21 million of subordinated debentures as their part in aiding Sceptre with the acquisition of the troubled Oakwood. The arrangement subjected Sceptre to a slightly higher interest rate on the amount, but also provided a small cushion of unsecured debt in the event of a business failure.

The debenture had been structured as an unsecured debenture that was subordinated to the company's senior bank debt. The issue had no financial covenants, which left the holders with very little protection against a decline in Sceptre's business. Should Sceptre decide to pursue further acquisitions, there was nothing to stop the company from issuing debt of equal ranking, or even more senior debt, in order to finance them. However, one point that David was keeping in mind throughout his assessment was that the Caisse de Depot, one of the largest institutional investors in Canada, in combination with Noverco and Soquip, controlled 52% of Sceptre on a fully diluted basis. That made it unlikely that Sceptre's management could undertake purchases in an unduly aggressive manner. Other institutional investors with exposure to Sceptre are listed in Exhibit 7.

The securities were issued with a coupon rate of 10%. In comparison, the current long term Government of Canada yield was close to 10%. Interest would be paid quarterly with the first payment in June of 1989. Term to maturity was 10 years, with the issuing date being listed as January 1, 1989. Complete details of the offering are presented in Exhibit 8.

In evaluating the yield on a comparative basis, David was going to have to look at similar premiums to the government rate both in Canada and the United States. There was one other interesting method through which David could price the issue at its fair value. Sceptre had another two outstanding listed issues of convertible debentures which were easier to price because of their larger volume and higher liquidity. A third convertible debenture issue was traded over-the-counter. These issues, totalling $135 million, were ranked *pari passu* (of equal ranking) with the current debentures. David could thus analyze the conversion premiums by computing a premium for an option with parameters equal to those of the option imbedded in the convertible. This would show the true potential of the issue, since the convertible debentures were, in Nesbitt's experience, a very tradeable and solid bond. In fact, the alternative to this analytically derived price would be to simply use the price on the listed warrants, the only problem being their lack of liquidity. For such a calculation, dilution effects of conversions would have to be taken into account. Prices and details on the various securities are listed in Exhibits 9 and 10. The historical standard deviations of returns on long term (17 years) government bonds was 8.14% and on investment grade industrial bonds was 7.93%.

THE DECISION

The details of the offer by the BOM had been given to David during a 10 minute call. The bank currently held $11 million of the security as their part of the work-out arrangement, and they were interested in selling all of the position as soon as possible. David did not want the paper on Nesbitt's books for a long period of time, so it was important that the bid would give him enough leeway to resell the bonds to an investor at a fair price within the near future.

An important part of David's analysis would be to judge the level for secondary demand for any Nesbitt purchase. He was relatively unsure whether there would be any institutional demand at all, since the other holders of the issue from the work-out had also been interested in getting a bid for their holdings. However, the Nesbitt retail system covered Sceptre and had a moderately enthusiastic outlook at the time. The retail system had also distributed a number of issues with roughly the same size, and demand appeared very strong for higher yielding bonds due to market conditions. Most investment dealers were currently recommending high exposure to bonds because of a probable fall in rates over the next year. Another possibility for distributing the bonds was to sell the excess to other dealers for their own networks.

In weighing all of these factors, David had to act very quickly to get his bid in first. He believed that if the BOM received a reasonable offer from Nesbitt, the deal could be concluded within a matter of days, a positive factor because it exposed Nesbitt to minimal market risk.

EXHIBIT 1

NESBITT THOMSON DEACON INC.
Consolidated Balance Sheet
(thousands)

	MARCH 31, 1988	MARCH 31, 1987
Assets		
Current Assets		
Cash	$ 11,454	$ 15,049
Securities Owned	1,063,960	1,231,975
Accounts Receivable	158,531	318,098
Interest Receivable	5,711	5,858
Other Assets	3,948	6,097
Fixed		
Real Estate	10,577	10,988
Fixtures	9,516	11,410
Long Term Investments		
Intangible Assets	2,857	4,979
	$1,280,027	$1,634,101

(continued)

EXHIBIT 1 (cont.)

	MARCH 31, 1988	MARCH 31, 1987
Liabilities		
Current		
Call and Bank Loans	$ 131,557	$ 550,410
Securities Sold	376,583	389,947
Accounts Payable	572,801	500,978
Taxes Payable	32,216	51,447
Current Long Term Debt	2,162	2,152
Long Term Debt	3,360	12,076
Minority Interests	2,378	
Shareholders' Equity	171,348	124,386
	$1,280,027	$1,634,101

EXHIBIT 2

SCEPTRE RESOURCES LTD.
Acquisitions by Sceptre Resources Ltd.

PetroQuest Resources	1977	$ 11 million
Candecca Resources Ltd.	1981	$ 44 million
Francana Oil & Gas	1982	$107 million
Willowdale Resources	1982	$ 47 million
Soquip Alberta	1987	$191 million
Oakwood Petroleum	1989	$275 million

EXHIBIT 3

SCEPTRE RESOURCES LTD.
Consolidated Balance Sheet
(dollars in thousands)

	JUNE 30, 1989	DECEMBER 31, 1988
Assets		
Current Assets		
Cash	$ 16,214	$ 12,333
Accounts Receivable	42,177	27,727
	58,319	40,060
Fixed Assets, "full cost" method	723,035	430,757
Other Assets	7,558	5,901
	788,984	476,718
Liabilities		
Current Liabilities		
Accounts Payable and Accrued Liabilities	$ 39,817	$ 26,568
Current Maturities on Long Term Bank Debt	11,323	577
Current Amount of Deferred Production Revenue	5,962	4,946
	57,102	32,091

(continued)

EXHIBIT 3 (cont.)

	JUNE 30, 1989	DECEMBER 31, 1988
Long Term Bank Debt	289,031	65,072
Convertible Debentures	135,000	135,000
Subordinated Debentures	21,000	
Deferred Production Revenue	25,785	23,498
Deferred Taxes	6,641	4,431
Shareholders' Equity		
Redeemable Preferred Shares	49,781	49,781
Common Shares	197,336	157,674
Retained Earnings	7,308	9,171
	254,425	216,626

EXHIBIT 4

SCEPTRE RESOURCES LTD.
Consolidated Statement of Earnings
(dollars in thousands, except per share information)

	SIX MONTHS ENDED JUNE 30		THREE MONTHS ENDED JUNE 30	
	1989 (PROJECTED)	1988	1989 (PROJECTED)	1988
Revenue				
Gross Production Revenue	$97,527	$55,974	$48,523	$25,708
Royalties & Mineral Taxes	(19,604)	(10,305)	(9,955)	(4,167)
Net Production Revenue	77,923	45,669	38,568	21,541
Other Income	711	1,309	88	512
	78,634	46,978	38,656	22,053
Expenses				
Production	20,301	11,613	9,922	5,809
General & Admin.	4,812	3,359	2,680	1,172
Interest	22,302	6,719	11,602	3,363
Depletion & Depreciation	31,080	18,762	15,201	8,557
Write-Downs		2,287		2,287
Income Taxes	111	(770)	253	(2,527)
	78,806	41,970	39,658	19,261
Net Earnings	28	5,008	(1,002)	2,792
Preferred Share Dividends	1,891	1,891	946	946
Net Earnings Attributable to Common Shares	(1,863)	3,117	(1,948)	1,846
Net Earnings Per Share	(0.03)	0.05	(0.03)	0.03
Cash Flow Per Share	0.48	0.44	0.20	0.19

EXHIBIT 5

SCEPTRE RESOURCES LTD.
Consolidated Statement of Changes
in Financial Position
(dollars in thousands)

	SIX MONTHS ENDED JUNE 30		THREE MONTHS ENDED JUNE 30	
	1989 (PROJECTED)	1988	1989 (PROJECTED)	1988
Cash Provided by (Used For)				
Operating Activities				
Net Earnings	$ 28	$ 5,008	$ (1,002)	$ 2,792
Adding Non-Cash Items				
Depreciation	31,080	18,762	15,201	8,557
Income Taxes	111	(770)	253	(2,527)
Write-Downs		2,287		2,287
Funds Generated				
Operations	31,219	25,287	14,452	11,109
Changes in Working Capital	(3,689)	(1,214)	(1,842)	(4,383)
Preferred Dividends	(1,891)	(1,891)	(946)	(946)
Other				
Investing Activities				
Fixed Assets	(33,251)	(30,772)	(17,627)	(14,076)
Acquisitions	(280,193)		(195)	
	(313,444)	(30,772)	(17,822)	(14,076)
Financing Activities				
Long Term Debt	234,704	1,993	3,683	4,731
Deferred Revenue	(3,681)	(3,282)	(18)	(272)
Share Issues	39,662	7,331	100	26
Debenture Issues	21,000			
	291,686	5,990	3,765	4,485
Increase (Decrease) in Cash	3,881	(2,561)	(2,393)	(3,811)
Cash at Beginning of Period	12,333	11,597	18,607	12,847
Cash at End of Period	16,214	9,036	16,214	9,036

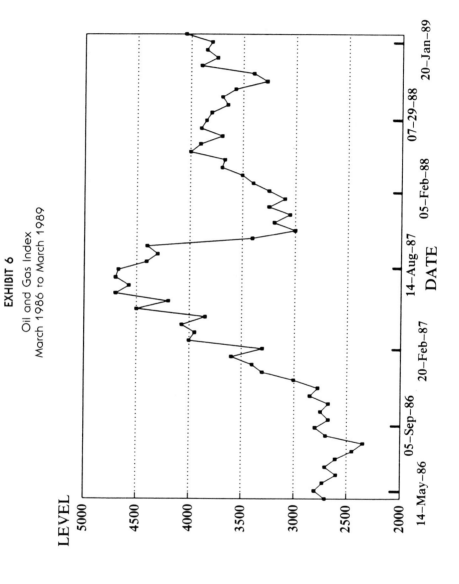

EXHIBIT 6

Oil and Gas Index
March 1986 to March 1989

198

EXHIBIT 7

The Appointment of $192,000,000 Cash
$21,000,000 Principal Amount of 10% Subordinated Debentures and
7,000,000 Common Share Among the Creditors

CREDITOR	LIABILITIES OUTSTANDING AS AT SEPT. 30, 1988	SECURED PORTION			UNSECURED PORTION	
		SECURITY VALUE	CASH^a	PRINCIPAL AMOUNT OF 10% SUBORDINATED DEBENTURES^b	UNSECURED PORTION OF LIABILITIES	NUMBER OF SCEPTRE COMMON SHARES
Bank of Montreal	$120,853,328	$102,781,600	$101,645,133	$11,117,437	$ 8,090,758	535,741
ABC Note-holders						
Series A						
Metropolitan Life Insurance Company	19,883,603	13,190,830	13,044,978	1,426,794	5,411,831	358,353
Great-West Life Assurance Company	7,953,504	5,276,373	5,218,032	570,722	2,164,750	143,342
Series B						
Metropolitan Life Insurance Company	23,657,871	15,694,688	15,521,150	1,697,626	6,439,095	426,375
The Travellers Insurance Company	16,087,371	10,672,401	10,554,395	1,154,387	4,378,589	289,935
The Travellers Life and Annuity Company	2,365,824	1,569,493	1,552,139	169,765	643,920	42,638
The Travellers Insurance Company Account #2	473,135	313,879	310,408	33,951	128,776	8,527
Great-West Life Assurance Company	9,463,167	6,227,887	6,208,472	679,052	2,575,643	170,550
Series C						
Connecticut General Life Insurance Company	15,547,735	10,314,404	12,200,357	1,115,664	4,321,714	280,209
Horace Mann Life Insurance Company	5,979,945	3,967,110	3,923,245	429,105	1,627,595	107,774
Congen Five & Co.	2,391,965	1,586,835	1,569,289	171,641	651,035	43,109
	103,804,120	68,863,900	68,102,465	7,448,707	28,252,948	1,870,812

(continued)

EXHIBIT 7 (cont.)

CREDITOR	LIABILITIES OUTSTANDING AS AT SEPT. 30, 1988	SECURED PORTION			UNSECURED PORTION	
		SECURITY VALUE	CASH[a]	PRINCIPAL AMOUNT OF 10% SUBORDINATED DEBENTURES[b]	UNSECURED PORTION OF LIABILITIES	NUMBER OF SCEPTRE COMMON SHARES
The Royal Bank of Canada	47,225,205	7,302,800	7,222,052	789,912	39,213,241	2,596,565
National Bank of Canada	18,314,617	4,742,800	4,590,358	513,008	13,111,251	868,182
HongKong Bank of Canada	7,911,250	5,227,800	5,169,996	565,996	2,175,786	144,073
Bank of America Canada	7,911	5,227,800	5,169,996	565,468	2,175,786	144,073
Canadian Co-Operative Credit Society Limited	6,347,003	—	—	—	6,347,003	420,277
Saskatchewan Co-Operative	6,347,003	—	—	—	6,347,003	420,277
	$318,713,776	$194,146,700	$192,000,000	$21,000,000	$105,713,776	7,000,000

[a]Without allowance for interest from the Settlement Date to the Effective Date.

[b]Based upon the Security Values set forth above, the Creditors under Specified Credit Facilities entitled to more than 10% of the votes entitled to be cast by all Creditors under Specified Credit Facilities as Secured Creditors are: Bank of Montreal (52.9%) and ABC Note-holders (35.5%); and as Unsecured Creditors are: The Royal Bank of Canada (37.1%), ABC Note-holders (26.7%) and National Bank of Canada (12.4%).

EXHIBIT 8

Schedule "D"
to a Plan of Arrangement
Dated the 12th Day of December 1988

Sceptre Debentures Term Sheet

Issue:	10% Subordinated Debentures (unsecured) of Sceptre Resources Limited (the "Company").
Amount:	$21 million (increased as required for Secured Creditors).
Price:	At par.
Term to Maturity:	10 years.
Redemption:	At the option of the Company at any time at a price equal to the principal amount thereof, together with accrued and unpaid interest.
Ranking:	Subordinate to all secured indebtedness of the Company. There will be no restriction on the Company from incurring additional indebtedness or from pledging its properties to secure any indebtedness.
Events of Default:	The principle of and all interest then due and payable on all the Debentures and all other amounts owing thereunder shall become due and payable:

a) if the Company makes default in payment of any interest due and any such default continues for a period of 60 days;

b) if a decree or order of court is entered adjudging the company or any Substantial Subsidiary as bankrupt or insolvent under the Bankruptcy Act or any other bankruptcy, insolvency or analogous laws, or issuing sequestration or process of execution against the property of the company or any Substantial Subsidiary, or ordering the winding-up or liquidation of its affairs, and any such decree continues in effect for a period of 60 days;

c) if the Company institutes proceedings to be adjudicated a bankrupt or insolvent, or consents with the filing of any such petition or to the appointment of a receiver, or makes a general assignment for the benefit of creditors, or admits to the inability to pay its debts as they become due;

d) if the Company shall neglect to observe any other covenant or condition contained herein and, after notice has been given to the company in writing, the Company shall fail to make good such default within a period of 60 days.

EXHIBIT 9

SCEPTRE RESOURCES LTD.
Convertible Debentures, Common Shares & Warrants
23 Day Trading History

DATE	STOCK	7% CONVERTIBLE DEBENTURES ($4.50 STRIKE)	8% CONVERTIBLE DEBENTURES ($6 STRIKE)	WARRANTS ($5 STRIKE)	
				BID	ASK
03/01/89	$3.95	$ 99.00	$84.000	$2.00	$2.20
03/02/89	3.95	100.00	82.500	2.00	2.20
03/03/89	3.95	100.00	83.000	2.00	2.20
03/06/89	3.95	100.00	83.000	2.00	2.20
03/07/89	3.95	102.00	83.000	2.00	2.20

(continued)

EXHIBIT 9 (cont.)

DATE	STOCK	7% CONVERTIBLE DEBENTURES ($4.50 STRIKE)	8% CONVERTIBLE DEBENTURES ($6 STRIKE)	WARRANTS ($5 STRIKE) BID	ASK
03/08/89	3.90	102.00	83.500	2.00	2.20
03/09/89	3.90	101.00	84.500	2.00	2.10
03/10/89	3.90	101.00	84.500	2.00	2.10
03/13/89	3.90	101.00	84.000	2.00	2.10
03/14/89	4.00	101.00	86.000	2.00	2.10
03/15/89	3.95	101.00	84.000	2.00	2.10
03/16/89	4.10	101.00	87.000	2.00	2.20
03/17/89	4.05	105.00	87.500	2.00	2.20
03/20/89	4.20	105.00	90.000	2.10	2.20
03/21/89	4.20	105.00	90.500	2.10	2.20
03/22/89	4.30	107.00	92.000	2.10	2.20
03/23/89	4.35	108.00	91.000	2.10	2.20
03/24/89	4.35	108.00	92.000	2.10	2.20
03/27/89	4.30	108.00	93.000		

DETAILS OF ISSUES:

Common Shares	57,978,455 outstanding on Dec. 31, 1988
Equity Warrants	5,000,000 outstanding
	Exercise Price $5.00
	Exercise until March 14, 1994
7% Convertible	$15,000,000 in total
Debentures	Maturing March 31, 2002
	Conversion Price $4.50
	Exercise until March 30, 1997
8% Convertible	$80,000,000 in total
Debentures	Maturing Sept. 20, 2002
	Conversion Price $6.00
	Exercise until Sept. 30, 1997
Volatility	25% p.a.

EXHIBIT 10

SCEPTRE RESOURCES LIMITED
Term Sheet
8.75% Convertible Debentures

Issue:	8.75% Convertible Subordinated Debentures.
Amount Outstanding:	$40,000,000.
Date of Issue:	May 22, 1987.
Date of Maturity:	May 31, 1995.
Conversion Terms:	Convertible into common shares at $8.50 until maturity.
Redemption Terms:	At the option of the Company, until January 1, 1990, if the common shares trade at a 125% premium to the conversion price.
Bond Price:	$82.00 (indicative).
Yield to Maturity:	13.13%.
Spread:	***bps. over the 5-year Government of Canada Bond.
Running Yield:	10.67%.
Conversion Premium:	60%.

18

THE RTZ CORPORATION PLC—
RIO ALGOM LIMITED

On June 10, 1992, RTZ Canada Inc.'s investment bank in Canada, Gordon Capital Corporation (Gordon), transmitted a preliminary prospectus to The RTZ Corporation PLC (RTZ PLC). RTZ Canada Inc. was an entity incorporated under the laws of the Province of Ontario, Canada, and was indirectly, a wholly owned subsidiary of RTZ PLC (Exhibit 1). RTZ PLC and RTZ Canada Inc. had decided to divest their 51.5% interest in the common shares of Rio Algom Limited, and Gordon had proposed a unique structuring for this sale. This secondary offering by RTZ Canada Inc. would allow investors to purchase the Rio Algom common shares on an instalment basis. RTZ Canada would proceed according to the advice of RTZ PLC.

BACKGROUND ON THE RTZ CORPORATION PLC

RTZ PLC, based in Britain, was a major international natural resources group with assets and sales approaching £5 billion, and employing 73,000 people. With its worldwide operations, RTZ PLC had an unrivalled spread of metals and minerals

This case was prepared by Kirsten Fear under the supervision of Professor R.W. White for the sole purpose of providing material for class discussion at the Western Business School. Certain names and other identifying information may have been disguised to protect confidentiality. It is not intended to illustrate either effective or ineffective handling of a managerial situation. Any reproduction, in any form, of the material in this case is prohibited except with the written consent of the School.

The writers would like to acknowledge the assistance of David Beatty, Gordon Capital Corporation, and Michael S. Parrett, Rio Algom Limited, in preparing this case.

Copyright 1993 © The University of Western Ontario.

interests. These, and its industrial products, provided a firm base for profitable growth well into the 21st century.

RTZ PLC's strategy was to focus on those business areas where it had a proven track record and where it had a competitive commercial advantage—namely, the development of a diversified spread of world-class mineral resources. RTZ PLC aimed to ensure the consistent high productivity and low operating costs of its mines.

RTZ PLC's assets were predominantly in North America and Australia, with the balance in Europe, Southern Africa and South America (Exhibit 2). Products were sold worldwide and a substantial proportion of group sales were made in the high growth Pacific Rim.

RTZ PLC'S OPERATION ACTIVITIES

RTZ PLC focused on two main areas in terms of the products it offered—natural resources and industrial products. Natural resources was further divided into two categories: Mining and metals, and industrial minerals.

RTZ PLC's mining and metals activities contributed £308 million to 1991 net attributable earnings before exceptional item, exploration and corporate charges in 1991. This represented 72% of total earnings. These activities had been challenged by low metal prices, as supply exceeded demand in the market. In metals, RTZ PLC's interests included copper, gold, iron ore, aluminum, lead, zinc and silver; and in energy, coal and uranium. Exploration for new deposits was an ongoing investment for RTZ PLC, and promising discoveries had been made in the U.S., Australia and South America.

RTZ PLC's industrial minerals businesses contributed £140 million to net attributable earnings before exploration and corporate charges in 1991, representing 33% of total earnings. RTZ PLC's interests included borax, silica sand, titanium dioxide feedstock, zircon, rutile, high purity iron and steel, diamonds, and talc. These markets had been hit quite hard by depressed economies in many areas of the world. The diversity of these assets, in terms both of product spread and of geography, limited RTZ's vulnerability to the volatility of individual metal prices and political upheaval.

RTZ PLC's industrial products businesses contributed £35 million to net attributable earnings before corporate costs in 1991, and represented 8% of total earnings. These products were used in residential and industrial construction, which was affected by the recession in North America. Overall, RTZ PLC had strengthened market share in this division, despite lower margins and intense competition.

RTZ PLC'S FINANCIAL POSITION

Despite the impact of the recession in 1991, RTZ PLC's balance sheet, income statement and cash flow statement remained strong (Exhibit 3). RTZ PLC remained the only mining company with double-A long term credit ratings from Moody's and Standard & Poor's. Thus, RTZ PLC had consistent access to the world's major capital markets. RTZ PLC also enjoyed the highest available short term credit ratings and continued to achieve competitive terms in its US$1.5 billion commercial paper program. During the year, RTZ PLC also launched a Canadian commercial paper programme of up to CA$300 million.

RTZ PLC's normal interest management policy was to borrow at floating rates of interest rather than at fixed rates for long periods of time. As the revenues of the group were largely determined by short term market-related pricing, it was desirable to match this with similarly structured interest costs. World interest rates generally fell in 1991. U.S. dollar short term interest rates, in particular, fell to the lowest level in nearly 30 years. This was of benefit to RTZ PLC, since the bulk of group borrowings was denominated in U.S. dollars.

RTZ PLC's currency exposure management continued to focus on reducing the possible adverse effect of long term currency changes. The focus was on decreasing exposure to key currencies to acceptable levels. First, metal and mineral prices were determined in a basket of currencies, even when they were denominated in U.S. dollars. Second, the broad geographical and commodity spread of RTZ PLC's business diversified its long term exposure among a wide range of currencies. Third, RTZ PLC managed its portfolio of cash and debt to take account of the currencies in which its costs and revenues were incurred.

BACKGROUND ON RIO ALGOM LIMITED

Rio Algom was a North American mining corporation. Its head office was in Toronto, Ontario, and its operations were in Canada, the U.S., Australia and New Zealand. Rio Algom mined minerals including uranium, copper and molybdenum, potash and coal. Rio Algom also invested heavily in development and exploration.

The results of Rio Algom's mining operations in 1991 were (Table 1):

TABLE 1
OPERATING RESULTS
(millions of dollars)

	REVENUE		OPERATING PROFIT	
	1991	1990	1991	1990
Uranium	140.3	266.2	45.4	69.1
Copper/Molybdenum	115.3	132.5	26.1	48.0
Potash	113.5	127.8	6.0	8.7
Coal	41.4	50.5	6.7	18.6
	410.5	577.0	84.2	144.4

(continued)

PRODUCTION/SHIPMENTS
(in thousands)

	PRODUCTION		SHIPMENTS	
	1991	1990	1991	1990
Uranium (lbs)	1529	4491	6134	5539
Copper (lbs)	127004	115069	126419	112609
Molybdenum (lbs)	1289	1342	1403	1192
Potash (tonnes)	1020	1069	1097	1245
Coal (tonnes)	470	447	467	450

Rio Algom's most important growth project was the Cerro Colorado copper mine in Chile. The company estimated ore reserves of 79 million tonnes grading 1.39% copper which would be sufficient for 23 years at a rate of annual production of 40,000 tonnes. Total project costs were forecast at US$290 million, and financing for US$180 million had been completed. Construction was expected to end early in 1994. Full production was expected to be reached by the end of 1994, with the use of low-cost, highly efficient solvent extraction and electrowinning technology.

Virtually all of Rio Algom's uranium production was sold under long term forwards contracts. Rio Algom produced uranium in Ontario and New Mexico.

Rio Algom held a 29.1% joint venture interest in Bullmoose coal mine in British Columbia. Metallurgical coal produced was sold to nine Japanese companies under long term contracts which would expire in 1999.

Rio Algom's potash operations had the unique competitive advantage of being located in both eastern and western Canada, giving exposure to a broader range of markets than regional producers. It also had a transport cost advantage when delivering to certain destinations outside North America through direct access to its own port facility in Saint John, New Brunswick. The company estimated that the underground mine in New Brunswick had a 25-year reserve life at current rates of production, and that the solution mine in Saskatchewan had at least a 40-year life at current rates of production.

Rio Algom was actively involved in exploration and had an exploration program in the range of $15 million annually. One notable project was the Kemess South property in British Columbia. The reserves there had been estimated at 208 million tonnes grading 0.21% copper and .59 grams of gold per tonne.

Rio Algom had faced numerous challenges in 1991. Overall weak economic conditions worldwide reduced demand for most of the minerals it produced, resulting in inventory surpluses and lower prices. This was aggravated by a considerable increase in supply in many mineral markets due to an influx of products from former East Bloc countries. As a result, mineral prices were not high. Also, the high value of the Canadian dollar in 1991 affected revenue and operating profit, as almost all of Rio Algom's mineral production occurred in Canada, while selling prices were determined based on a basket of currencies. Nonetheless, Rio Algom remained profitable and increased its cash flow from continuing mining operations, despite the depressed economic situation (Exhibits 4, 5 and 6).

Rio Algom was also involved in metals distribution activities. This business involved the sourcing, warehousing, processing and distribution of a diverse range of metals products for a wide variety of industrial applications. Rio Algom had 13 facilities in Canada, 15 in the U.S., 14 in Australia, and 4 in New Zealand. The breakdown of operating and financial results is shown in Table 2:

TABLE 2
FINANCIAL RESULTS
(in millions $)

	1991	1990
Revenue		
Mining	410.50	577.00
Metals Distribution	623.40	743.40
Total	1033.90	1320.40
Operating Profit		
Mining	84.20	144.40
Metals Distribution	16.60	37.20
Total	100.80	181.60
Earnings from Continuing Operations	44.80	117.60
Loss from Discontinuing Operations	(20.30)	(30.30)
NET EARNINGS	24.50	87.30
Net Earnings Per Share	0.51	1.93

The decline in the Canadian dollar since the beginning of 1992 favourably affected Rio Algom's first quarter earnings by approximately $500,000 after-tax. Rio Algom was also actively pursuing cost reduction programs, such as rationalizing its workforce and operations.

Rio Algom's common shares were listed on the Toronto and Montreal Stock Exchanges in Canada, and on the American Stock Exchange in the United States (Exhibit 7). Rio Algom's June 5, 1992, closing price (Toronto Stock Exchange) was $16.75, volatility was 21.27% per annum and beta was 1.07.[1]

The dividend policy of Rio Algom was to pay dividends on its common shares in June and December of each year. Rio Algom had sought to pay dividends such that the average dividends over the previous five-year period were approximately equal to 45% of the average net earnings during the same five-year period. Semi-annual dividend payments had been in approximately equal amounts. On June 8, 1992, Rio Algom paid a dividend of $0.40.

RIO ALGOM LIMITED'S RELATIONSHIP WITH RTZ PLC

RTZ Canada Inc. owned approximately 51.5% of the outstanding common shares of Rio Algom Limited. Since RTZ PLC's acquisition of the minerals business of The British Petroleum Company PLC (BP) in 1989, RTZ PLC's activities were heavily focused on North America, where approximately 50% of its assets were

[1]The market risk premium for Canada was 5.38%.

heavily focused on North America, where approximately 50% of its assets were located. RTZ PLC's North American assets were principally held through two wholly owned mining subsidiaries (Kennecott Corporation and United States Borax & Chemical Corporation), a wholly owned Canadian industrial minerals subsidiary (QIT-Fer et Titane Inc.), and a wholly owned industrial subsidiary (Indal Limited). As a result of the 100% ownership of the mineral business formerly owned by BP, the potential for a conflict of interest with Rio Algom in North America had increased significantly.

RTZ PLC, therefore, concluded that it would be in the best interests of its shareholders if RTZ Canada sold the Rio Algom common shares to the public. The board of directors of Rio Algom concurred with this conclusion and considered it to be in the best interests of Rio Algom's shareholders.

RTZ Canada and Rio Algom agreed that the RTZ Group, on Rio Algom's request and on reasonable commercial terms, would continue to provide certain services, technical support and assistance to Rio Algom.

STRUCTURING THE ISSUE

Gordon spent considerable time addressing various alternatives for the secondary offering. The first and most straightforward alternative was a straight equity issue. The success of such an issue rested entirely on the receptiveness of the market to the shares, given the financial performance of Rio Algom, the future prospects for the company, and investor preferences. The type of investors to be targeted was also a consideration.

Secondly, Gordon considered an exchangeable or convertible security debenture. This was basically a straight bond with an option feature, allowing the investor to convert the security into shares depending on the underlying price of this asset. This was an attractive feature for investors because it limited their downside risk, without limiting upside potential. Receptiveness of the market to this security still had to be considered, as did the pricing of the security. The challenge was in determining a price deemed fair by the market and providing RTZ PLC and Gordon Capital with sufficient returns.

Thirdly, a stock and a warrant combination was considered. The warrant was an option to buy a specified number of additional shares of common stock at a specified price during a designated time period. This option provided certain advantages and disadvantages, and pricing was again an issue.

The last main derivative product considered was the instalment receipt. This concept was very new, and the receptiveness of the market to such an untried security was questionable. Pricing, as always, was an added challenge. The description below provides further details on this type of issue.

RTZ Canada began negotiations with bankers at Gordon regarding the possibilities for structuring the issue. Because of the economic environment and its effects on Rio Algom's financial position, it was decided that the terms of the issue would have to be particularly attractive to investors. The North American equity market was not overly receptive to new equity offers. RTZ Canada's objectives were to receive maximum return for the sale of their Rio Algom common shares, and to execute closure of the deal as quickly as possible. They had decided to divest their interests in Rio Algom and were not interested in a lengthy process.

GORDON'S PROPOSAL

Gordon's preliminary prospectus proposed the sale of 22,506,336 common shares of Rio Algom Limited at a price of $16.10 per share, which would be payable on an instalment basis. The first instalment of $5.40 per share would be payable on the closing of the offering. The second instalment of $5.40 per share would be payable in approximately one year, and the third instalment of $5.30 per share would be payable in about two years. The group of underwriters, lead by Gordon, would make the initial instalment payment to RTZ Canada using a "bought deal." The remaining instalments would be paid to RTZ Canada by the registered holders of the Instalment Receipts.

After an investor paid the first instalment, he/she would be issued an Initial Instalment Receipt, evidencing the Rio Algom shares. After paying the second instalment and surrendering the relevant Initial Instalment Receipt, the investor would receive an Intermediate Instalment Receipt. After timely payment of the third instalment and presentation and surrender of the relevant Intermediate Instalment Receipt, the investor would become the registered holder of the applicable Rio Algom common shares.

The Instalment Receipt Agreement would provide that if payment of either the second instalment or the final instalment were not received by RTZ Canada on or before the date due, the Rio Algom common shares, at the option of RTZ Canada, would be accepted by RTZ Canada in satisfaction of the obligations of the investor. RTZ Canada would also have the option of selling these shares to the public. The initial investor in the instalment receipts would then be reimbursed the pro rata portion of the proceeds of the sale after deducting therefrom the amount of the unpaid second and/or final instalment, together with the investor's pro rata portion of the costs of this sale.

By investing in these instalment receipts, an investor would be entitled to certain rights and privileges as outlined in the Instalment Receipt Agreement. In particular, registered holders of Instalment Receipts would be entitled to participate fully in dividends and distributions on the common shares of Rio Algom and to vote at meetings in proportion to the number of Rio Algom Common Shares. Cash dividends would go directly to the instalment holder. However, any "Excess Dividends" declared and paid by Rio Algom would be remitted to RTZ Canada in reduction pro rata of the outstanding instalments payable. Also, any "Stock Dividends" issued by Rio Algom would be held as collateral security for the obligation of the investor to pay the remaining instalments. Upon payment of the second and final instalments, the investor would receive these stock dividends. Lastly, any options sold on the Rio Algom common shares would apply to those bought using instalment receipts. The proceeds from these sales would again be applied pro rata to any outstanding instalments. Instalment receipts were typically listed and actively traded.

The transfer of the Instalment Receipts would be possible at any of the principal offices of the "Custodian" of the issue. For a fee, this organization, usually a bank or trust company, will collect and administer the instalments. The Custodian may also require registered holders of Instalment Receipts to furnish information and documents to ensure that they are in compliance with any fiscal or other laws relating to Rio Algom common shares.

In terms of the tax implications, the gross-up and dividend tax credit rules normally applicable to taxable dividends paid by taxable Canadian corporations would apply to such dividends received by an individual, and such dividends received by a corporation normally will be deducted in computing its taxable income. Tax implications for capital gains or losses on common stock acquisition or sale also apply.

According to Gordon Capital's proposal, 22,506,336 Rio Algom common shares would be issued on an instalment basis. The price of $16.10 per share would result in the amount of the offering totalling $362,352,010. The net proceeds to RTZ Canada after the Underwriters' Fee would be $346,950,924.

THE DECISION

Was this type of issue attractive to investors and why (Exhibit 8)? What was the cost to RTZ of this form of financing, and what were RTZ's returns (Exhibit 9)? The other alternatives considered by Gordon Capital also had certain advantages and disadvantages, which would have to be compared.

EXHIBIT 1
THE RTZ CORPORATION PLC
Organizational Structure

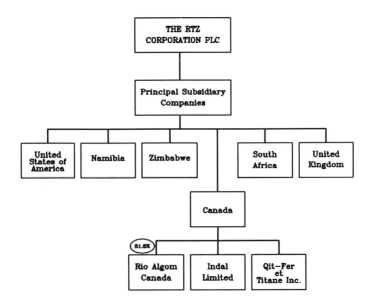

COMPANY AND COUNTRY OF INCORPORATION/PRINCIPAL ACTIVITIES[b]	CLASS OF SHARES HELD	PROPORTION OF CLASS HELD %	RTZ INTEREST %
United Kingdom			
Borax Consolidated Limited	Ordinary £1	100	100
Holding and management company			
Anglesey Aluminium Limited	Ordinary £1	51.0	51.0
Production of primary aluminum			
R.T.Z. Pillar Limited	Ordinary £1	100	100
Holding and management company			
Pillar Building Products Limited	Ordinary £1	100	100
Aluminum, steel and other products for construction			
Pillar Electrical PLC	Ordinary 25p	100	100
Electrical products and systems for buildings			
Pillar Engineering Limited	Ordinary 10p	100	100
Automotive and general engineering; distribution and aviation support			
RTZ Finance plc	Ordinary £1	100	100
Holding of short term investments			
United States of America			
Kennecott Corporation	Common US$.01	100	100
Copper and gold mining, exploration			
United States Borax & Chemical Corporation	Common US$1	100	100
Mining, refining, marketing of borax, exploration and research			
US Silica	Common	100	100
Sand for glass products and metal castings; specialty clays			

(continued)

EXHIBIT 2 (cont.)

COMPANY AND COUNTRY OF INCORPORATION/PRINCIPAL ACTIVITIES[b]	CLASS OF SHARES HELD	PROPORTION OF CLASS HELD %	RTZ INTEREST %
Canada			
Rio Algom Limited	Common	51.5	51.5
Mining of copper, coal, uranium and potash, exploration; metals distribution			
Indal Limited	Common	100	100
Building products, manufacturing and engineering			
QIT-Fer et Titane Inc.	Common CA$100 Class "A" Preferred	100	100
Titanium dioxide feedstock; high purity iron and steel			
Namibia			
Rössing Uranium Limited[c]	"B"R1 "C"10c	53.0 53.5	46.5
Uranium mining			
South Africa			
Palabora Mining Company Limited	R1	64.9	38.9
Copper mining, smelting and refining			
Zimbabwe			
Rio Tinto Zimbabwe Limited	Ordinary Z40c	56.04	56.04
Gold and emerald mining			

THE RTZ CORPORATION PLC
RTZ Principal Associated Companies[a]
At 31 December 1991

COMPANY AND COUNTRY OF INCORPORATION/PRINCIPAL ACTIVITIES[b]	CLASS OF SHARES HELD	PROPORTION OF CLASS HELD %	RTZ INTEREST %
Australia			
CRA Limited	Ordinary A$2	49.0	49.0
Holding, management and exploration company			
Subsidiaries and associated companies of CRA[d]			

Pasminco Limited (40% owned by CRA)		19.6
Lead, zinc and silver mining and smelting		
Kembla Coal and Coke Pty Limited (100% owned by CRA)		49.0
Coal mining and coke production		
Comalco Limited (67% owned by CRA)		32.8
Bauxite mining; alumina production; primary aluminum smelting; aluminum fabrication		
Hamersley Holdings Limited (100% owned by CRA)		49.0
Iron ore mining		
New Zealand		
New Zealand Aluminum Smelters Limited (79.4% owned by Comalco Limited)		26.1
Aluminum smelting		
United States of America		
Commonwealth Aluminum Corporation (100% owned by Comalco Limited)		32.8
Smelting and processing of aluminum		
Chile		
Minera Escondida Limitada		30.0
Copper mining		
Portugal		
Sociedade Minera de Neves-Corvo S.a.r.l.	Esc. 1,000	49.0
Copper and tin mining		
South Africa		
Richards Bay Minerals		50.0
Richards Bay Iron and Titanium Limited	R1	50.5
Tisand Limited	R1	49.0
Titanium dioxide feedstock, zircon and rutile		

[a]The RTZ Group comprises a large number of companies and it is not practical to include all of them in this list. The list therefore only includes those companies which principally affect the profit or asset of the Group.

[b]All companies operate mainly in the countries in which they are incorporated except where otherwise shown.

[c]The Group holding of shares in Rössing Uranium Limited carries 26.5 percent of the total voting rights. Rössing is consolidated by virtue of Board control.

[d]Apart from the subsidiaries of CRA, RTZ's interest in each of the companies shown is held by subsidiary companies of RTZ or their nominees.

213

EXHIBIT 3

THE RTZ CORPORATION PLC
Product Analysis

ASSETS, TURNOVER, PROFIT BEFORE TAX AND NET PROFIT ATTRIBUTABLE TO RTZ SHAREHOLDERS

	1991		1990		1991		1990	
	£m	%	£m	%	£m	%	£m	%
	GROUP OPERATING ASSETS				GROUP TURNOVER			
Mining and Metals								
Copper and gold	1,787	36.7	1,692	35.1	886	18.1	929	18.3
Iron ore	253	5.2	231	4.8	301	6.2	217	4.3
Coal and uranium	595	12.2	585	12.1	376	7.7	387	7.6
Aluminum	297	6.1	316	6.6	438	9.0	465	9.2
Lead and zinc	95	2.0	105	2.2	209	4.3	236	4.6
Tin	–	–	3	–	11	0.2	10	0.2
	3,027	62.2	2,932	60.8	2,221	45.5	2,244	44.2
Industrial Minerals	1,135	23.3	1,112	23.1	938	19.2	954	18.8
	4,162	85.5	4,044	83.9	3,159	64.7	3,198	63.0
Industrial Products	706	14.5	776	16.1	1,726	35.3	1,880	37.0
Total	4,868		4,820		4,885		5,078	

	PROFIT BEFORE TAX				NET PROFIT ATTRIBUTABLE TO RTZ SHAREHOLDERS			
Mining and Metals								
Copper and gold	337	45.9	401	42.6	190	44.4	232	43.0
Iron ore	163	22.2	111	11.8	97	22.6	68	12.6
Coal and uranium	75	10.2	110	11.7	28	6.5	33	6.1
Aluminum	10	1.4	58	6.2	2	0.5	36	6.6
Lead and zinc	(13)	(1.8)	21	2.2	(7)	(1.6)	12	2.2
Tin	(6)	(0.9)	(28)	(2.9)	(2)	(0.5)	(12)	(2.1)
	566	77.0	673	71.6	308	71.9	369	68.4
Industrial Minerals	203	27.6	261	27.7	140	32.7	169	31.4
	769	104.6	934	99.3	448	104.6	538	99.8
Exploration and development	(86)	(11.7)	(70)	(7.5)	(55)	(12.8)	(40)	(7.4)
	683	92.9	864	91.8	393	91.8	498	92.4
Industrial Products	52	7.1	77	8.2	35	8.2	41	7.6
	735		941		428		539	
Exceptional item	(74)				(46)			
Corporate costs	(12)		9		(21)		9	
Net finance charges	(87)		(71)		(53)		(41)	
Total	562		879		308		507	

EXHIBIT 4

RIO ALGOM LIMITED
Consolidated Balance Sheets
December 31, 1991 and 1990
(in thousands)

	1991	1990
Assets		
Current		
Cash and short term investments	$ 182,792	$ 355,253
Receivables and prepaid expenses	158,403	164,992
Inventories and concentrates awaiting shipment	274,637	455,481
	615,832	975,726
Property, plant and equipment	583,153	599,970
Construction in progress, at cost	13,235	10,829
Mining properties and preproduction expenditures	310,997	324,463
Other Assets	67,350	69,653
	$1,590,567	$1,980,641
Liabilities		
Current		
Bank loans and overdrafts	$ 21,073	$ 23,698
Accounts payable and accrued liabilities	101,966	149,400
Income and mining taxes	42,876	50,255
Current portion of long term debt	21,414	19,610
Current portion of site restoration and related obligations	28,328	15,822
	215,657	258,785
Long term debt		
Recourse	32,872	51,435
Limited recourse	100,368	126,052
Advances from Ontario Hydro	284,357	292,982
Non-current site restoration and related obligations	80,128	86,698
Deferred income and mining taxes	210,491	215,903
Minority shareholders' interest in subsidiary corporation	28,899	29,559
Deferred income	6,020	7,310
	958,792	1,068,724
Capital Stock and Retained Earnings		
First preference shares	5,081	5,241
Second preference shares	21,481	21,481
Common shares	68,877	68,877
Contributed surplus	37,725	37,692
Cumulative translation adjustment	(12,633)	(18,585)
Retained earnings	511,244	797,211
	$1,590,567	$1,980,641

EXHIBIT 5

RIO ALGOM LIMITED
Consolidated Statements of Earnings
Years Ended December 31, 1991 and 1990
(in thousands)

	1991	1990
Revenue		
Revenue from mine production and sales of metal products	$1,033,919	$1,320,392
Expenses		
Cost of mine production and metal sales	745,522	940,506
Selling, general and administration	156,295	156,053
Interest expense and other income	3,605	(22,244)
Depreciation and amortization	45,474	56,391
Exploration	18,474	14,920
	969,370	1,145,626
Earnings before taxes, minority interest and discontinued operations	64,549	174,766
Income and mining taxes		
Current	18,677	23,264
Deferred	394	32,994
	19,071	56,258
Earnings from continuing operations, before minority interest in subsidiary corporation	45,478	118,508
Minority interest in net earnings of subsidiary corporation	707	931
Earnings from continuing operations	44,771	117,577
Discontinued operations, net of tax	(20,276)	(30,291)
Net earnings for the year	$ 24,495	$ 87,286
Earnings per common share:		
Earnings from continuing operations	$ 0.97	$ 2.62
Net earnings for the year	$ 0.51	$ 1.93

EXHIBIT 6

RIO ALGOM LIMITED
Consolidated Statements of Changes in Financial Position
Years Ended December 31, 1991 and 1990
(in thousands)

	1991	1990
Operating Activities		
Earnings from continuing operations, before		
minority interest in subsidiary corporation	$ 45,478	$118,508
Depreciation and amortization	45,474	56,391
Deferred income and mining taxes	394	32,994
Decrease in non-cash working capital and other	164,087	67,014
Site restoration and related obligations	(10,165)	(67,471)
	245,268	207,436
Discontinued operations	(12,438)	(10,253)
	232,830	197,183
Financing Activities		
Repayments of long term debt and other obligations	(44,255)	(50,386)
Repayments to Ontario Hydro	(8,625)	(6,720)
Dividends on common shares	(308,336)	(45,915)
Dividends on preference shares	(2,126)	(2,795)
Dividends to minority shareholders	(634)	(1,134)
Purchase and cancellation of preference shares	(127)	(24,090)
	(364,103)	(131,040)
Investing Activities		
Acquisitions	(4,633)	–
Acquisitions of long term investments	–	(9,078)
Disposition of long term investments	–	16,816
Expenditures (net) for plant and equipment, construction		
in progress, mining properties and preproduction		
and development	(33,375)	(32,185)
	(38,008)	(24,447)
Discontinued operations	(555)	(1,668)
	(38,563)	(26,115)
Changes in cash and equivalents during year[a]	(169,836)	40,028
Cash and equivalents, beginning of year	331,555	291,527
Cash and equivalents, end of year[a]	$161,719	$331,555

[a]Cash and equivalents comprise cash and short term investments less current bank loans and overdrafts.

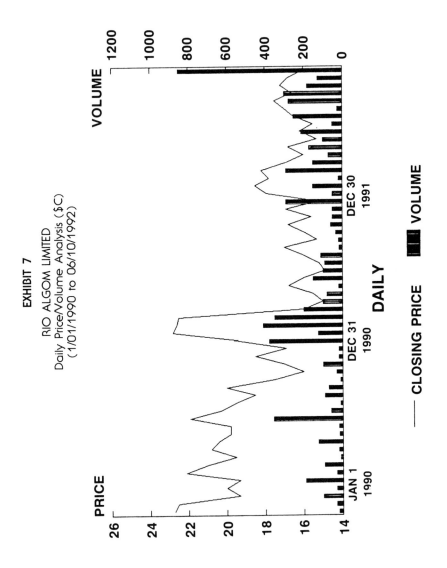

EXHIBIT 7
RIO ALGOM LIMITED
Daily Price/Volume Analysis ($C)
(1/01/1990 to 06/10/1992)

218

EXHIBIT 8

Instalment Receipt Deal Summary

ISSUE DATE	SELLER	ISSUE	SIZE $MM	FIRST INSTAL-MENT	SECOND INSTAL-MENT	TIME IN YEARS	DISCOUNT RATE	PV OF INSTAL-MENT RECEIPT	MARKET PRICE OF STOCK	(DISCOUNT) OR PREMIUM TO MARKET	UNDERLYING STOCK DIVIDEND	INSTAL-MENT YIELD
11/05/92	British Petroleum	BP Canada	$373.5	$4.40 31/05/92	$4.30 31/05/93 $4.30 31/05/94	1.0 2.0	6.95% 7.40%	$12.13	$13.75	−11.8%	$0.00	0.0%
06/03/92	GW Utilities	Interprovincial Pipe Line Inc.	$655.0	$15.00 31/03/92	$11.00 31/03/93	1.0	8.0%	$25.19	$27.75	−9.2%	$2.00	13.3%
04/04/92	Province of Ontario Sun Oil Company	Suncor Inc.	$190.0	$9.50 18/03/92	$9.50 18/03/93	1.0	8.0%	$18.28	Initial Offering	NM	$1.04	10.9%
28/02/92	Oxy Chemical Corp.	Canadian Oxy Petroleum Ltd.	$309.0	$11.75 10/03/92	$14.00 31/12/92	0.8	8.0%	$24.89	$27.50	−9.5%	$0.94	8.0%
24/02/92	British Gas PLC	Consumers Gas	$168.6	$9.50 01/04/92	$7.50 01/04/93	1.0	8.0%	$16.43	Initial Offering	NM	$0.94	9.9%
05/12/91	Province of Alberta	Telus Corp.	$870.0	$7.50 17/12/91	$7.50 08/01/93	1.1	7.3%	$14.45	$15.38	−6.0%	$0.92	12.3%
19/09/90	BCE Inc.	TransCanada Pipelines Ltd.	$637.5	$8.25 01/10/90	$8.25 01/10/91	1.0	12.0%	$15.59	$17.38	−10.3%	$0.68	8.2%

Source: Gordon Capital.

EXHIBIT 9

Selected Financial Information

RIO ALGOM LIMITED

(millions of dollars, except per share data)

	1991	1990	1989	1988	1987
Revenue	1,033.9	1,320.4	1,680.7	1,954.8	1,532.6
Net Earnings	24.5	87.3	73.1	134.4	93.1
Earnings Before Extraordinary Items					
& Discontinued Operations	44.8	117.6	110.7	120.2	93.1
Earnings per Share	0.51	1.93	1.58	3.02	2.12
Dividend per Share	7.05[a]	1.05	0.95	0.70	0.65
Long Term Debt	133.2	177.5	218.4	243.9	270.6
Common Shareholders' Equity	605.2	885.2	846.6	827.4	713.6

[a]Includes special dividend of $6.25 per common share on May 1, 1991; proceeds from sale of a subsidiary.

COMPARABLE CANADIAN MARKET MULTIPLES: 1991

(Integrated, Metal and Non-Base Metal Mines)

COMPANY	PRICE PER SHARE (JUNE 5, 1992)	1991 EPS	BOOK VALUE PER SHARE AT DEC. 31, 91	1991 CASH FLOW PER SHARE (CFPS)	PRICE/ EARNINGS	PRICE/ BOOK	PRICE/ CASH FLOW
Cominco	$22.00	$(0.56)	$12.85	$0.82	NM	1.7	26.8
Noranda	18.63	(1.04)	18.49	1.93	NM	1.0	9.7
Inco (US$)	31.75	0.74	15.70	3.23	42.9	2.0	9.8
Alcan (US$)	21.63	(0.25)	21.17	1.68	NM	1.0	12.9
Metall Mining	12.63	0.35	12.36	0.11	36.1	1.0	NM
Average of Comparables					39.5	1.3	14.8
Rio Algom[a]	15.13	0.51	13.84	1.52	29.7	1.1	10.0

[a]Present value of the secondary offering using a 6.15% one year discount rate and a 6.70% two year discount rate.

CANADIAN INTEREST RATES FOR JUNE 5, 1992

	FRIDAY	PREVIOUS DAY	WEEK AGO	FOUR WEEKS AGO
6 mo. TBill	5.96%	6.05%	6.16%	6.75%
2-year	6.81	6.93	6.94	7.61
5-year	7.23	7.77	7.85	8.31
7-year	8.08	8.18	8.31	8.54
10-year	8.29	8.39	8.40	8.63

Source: Financial Post, June 8, 1992.

PART FOUR · Cost of Capital and Investment Decisions

19. PROCTER & GAMBLE: COST OF CAPITAL
20. THE CONSUMERS' GAS COMPANY LTD.
21. LAWSON MARDON GROUP—CORPORATE ASSET FUNDING FACILITY
22. TANZI PUMP CORPORATION
23. MINNOVA INC.—LAC SHORTT MINE
24. GOLD INDUSTRY NOTE

19

Procter & Gamble: Cost of Capital

Since February 19, 1990, three days previously, Mary Shiller had been looking forward to receiving a reaction from her boss regarding her estimate of Procter & Gamble's (P&G) cost of capital. Ms. Shiller reported directly to Ron Emory, the president of CORPSTRAT, a consulting firm located in Washington, D.C. CORPSTRAT had been successful since its founding in 1980 by providing high-quality analysis for a few large corporate clients. Recently one of its largest clients had revealed that it was considering entering the household-products market and competing directly with P&G, the detergent and soap giant. The client's chief financial officer had stated that his company had become "a highly diversified conglomerate with subsidiaries spanning a host of unrelated businesses" and that "our company's overall cost of capital is neither useful as a benchmark for any of the existing subsidiaries, nor as a hurdle rate for entering new markets like consumer products." Although the CFO's staff had computed its own estimate of the household-products industry's cost of capital, the CFO wanted an independent estimate before taking the plan to the board of directors in March. If the estimated cost of capital was "significantly lower than the expected return" of entering the new market, he fully expected the company to introduce its own brand of detergents, soaps, cleansers, and personal-care products by the end of 1990.

CORPSTRAT had never before been asked to compute a client's cost of capital. The company's real expertise was defining and evaluating the strategic goals of a corporation. Therefore, upon receiving the client's request, Ron Emory quickly assigned the task to Ms. Shiller in order to take advantage of her recent exposure to financial theory in her MBA curriculum. Ms. Shiller decided that she would compute P&G's cost of capital, because P&G was the dominant player in the household-products and consumer-goods markets. Since this was her first project after joining CORPSTRAT, she had spent many hours preparing the first draft of her analysis as a memo to Mr. Emory (Appendix A). Unfortunately, Emory's memo in response to her work indicated that much remained to be done (Appendix B).

APPENDIX A
Mary Shiller's Analysis

TO: Ron Emory
DATE: February 19, 1990
SUBJECT: Analysis of Procter & Gamble's Cost of Capital

I. ASSUMPTIONS

This analysis is based upon the following set of assumptions:

A1. The cost of capital is a market-value concept. Whenever possible, market values rather than book values are used in the calculations, and only current market rates of return are relevant to the estimation process.

A2. Management makes investment decisions with the goal of increasing the wealth of the company's investors. The objective of computing a cost of capital is to determine the minimum rate of return that adequately compensates the company's investors for the risk of investing in the company. Thus, only those projects that are expected to return profits in excess of the cost of capital are acceptable.

A3. The bond and stock markets are reasonably efficient and, therefore, provide an ideal vehicle for extracting the market's assessment of the company's cost of debt and cost of equity.

A4. P&G's employee stock ownership plan (ESOP) and the capital-structure changes associated with it are not relevant to the calculation of the company's cost of capital. P&G management states in the 1989 Annual Report that ESOP debt should not be considered part of permanent capital because "the Company's total cash outflows related to the employee profit sharing plan, with or without the ESOP, are not materially different." The 1989 balance sheet has been reproduced in Exhibit 1 with the effects of the ESOP removed to make it more easily compared to 1988.

II. PROCTER & GAMBLE'S BUSINESS RISK

Procter & Gamble is the leading soap and detergent producer, with annual revenues expected to be approximately $23.5 billion in 1990. Some of P&G's most recognizable detergent and soap brands are Tide, Cheer, Bold, Ivory, Zest, and Coast. The company also produces well-known toiletries like Head & Shoulders shampoo and Scope mouthwash, paper products, including Bounty paper towels and Luvs disposable diapers, foods such as Crisco shortening, Pringles potato chips, and

Folgers coffee, pharmaceuticals, including Dramamine for motion sickness and Vicks cough drops, and a few industrial products such as wood pulp and animal-feed ingredients. For 1989, laundry and cleaning products accounted for 32.5% of corporate sales, personal-care products contributed 45.7%, food and beverages 13.8%, and pulp and chemicals 8.1%.

The personal-care and food-and-beverage segments have risks that are similar to those of the laundry-and-cleaning products segment. Like its competitors, P&G distributes all of its consumer products through grocery stores and other retail outlets such as Krogers, K-Mart, and WalMart. Soaps, detergents, toothpaste, peanut butter, etc., are small-ticket items on the average homemaker's shopping list and are, therefore, relatively insensitive to swings in the economy. By contrast, pulp and chemicals are either sold directly or through jobbers and have had profit margins about double that of the personal-care and laundry-and-cleaning products groups (the food-and-beverage segment had approximately broken even over the past three years). Thus, the industrial-products segment seems to be the only business segment that is of sufficiently different risk to merit having a different cost of capital. On the other hand, since pulp and chemicals made up only 8.1% of 1989 sales, the small influence of the industrial-products segment can safely be ignored in the calculations.

III. THE COST OF DEBT

The cost of debt should represent the cost of refunding the debt on the company's books. The relevant debt is all interest-bearing debt on the books as of the end of fiscal 1989, which according to the 1989 balance sheets (Exhibit 1) is $3,331MM.[1] Most of P&G's debt is privately placed and therefore has no public price information available. The 8¼% coupon issue, however, is traded on the New York Stock Exchange and has a recent market price of $92.50 (see Exhibit 2, Panel D). The yield to maturity (YTM) of 9.18% is very close to February's average yield for Aaa bonds of 9.22% (see Exhibit 3). In addition, the 9.18% is very close to the average coupon rate of the dollar denominated debt on P&G's books.

IV. THE COST OF EQUITY AND THE CAPITAL ASSET PRICING MODEL

The CAPM assumes that beta is the relevant measure of risk for a company. The most recent beta estimate published by *Value Line Investment Survey* is 0.95. This suggests that P&G stock is slightly less risky than the average stock, which has a beta of 1.0. The CAPM is usually written as

$$K_E = r_f + \beta \times (r_m - r_f)$$

where K_E is the cost of equity, r_f is the risk-free rate of interest, β is beta, which measures the firm's systematic risk, and $(r_m - r_f)$ is the expected premium of a

---

[1]Computed by adding the debt due within one year to the long term debt, i.e., $633 + $2,698 = $3,331MM.

market portfolio of stocks over the risk-free return. The interpretation of the model is that the cost of equity is composed of the risk-free rate plus a risk premium equal to the company's beta times the market-risk premium.

Most analysts use the prevailing U.S. Treasury rate for r_f and some sort of historic average for the market premium over r_f. However, there is some debate among academicians as to which risk-free rate and risk premium should be used. The debate centers upon whether it makes more sense to use a short term or long term Treasury rate for r_f. If you believe that the current 90-day Treasury rate is appropriate, then most would argue that the average annual premium of a market index over T-bills should be used for $(r_m - r_f)$. If you like to use a 10- or 30-year Treasury bond rate, then $(r_m - r_f)$ should be the average of the market over long term Treasuries. The table below summarizes the historic market premiums realized over the period 1926–1988 as published by Ibottson Associates:

EQUITY RISK PREMIUM	GEOMETRIC MEAN	ARITHMETIC MEAN
Common Stocks—Bonds	5.4%	7.6%
Common Stocks—Bills	6.2%	8.4%

The two market premiums most frequently chosen are 8.4%, which is an arithmetic or simple average of annual market returns over the Treasury-bill rate, and 5.4%, which is a geometric or compound average of the market over Treasury bonds. Since the cost of debt is measured with YTM, which is a long term, compound rate of return, I have chosen to use the average geometric market premium over long Treasuries to maintain consistency. Using 8.47% for r_f (Exhibit 3), the long term geometric average of 5.4% for $(r_m - r_f)$, and P&G's beta of 0.95 (Exhibit 2, Panel C), we get the following estimate of the cost of equity:

$$K_E = .0847 + .95 \,(.054)$$
$$= 13.6\%$$

V. THE WEIGHTED AVERAGE COST OF CAPITAL

The overall cost of capital is the weighted average of the costs of debt and equity, where the weights are the relative proportions each source represents of the firm's total capital. The formula is

$$WACC = \frac{D}{V} K_D \,(1 - t) + \frac{E}{V} K_E$$

where V is total firm value, equal to the sum of the market value of debt (D) and equity (E), K_D is the cost of debt, K_E is the cost of equity, and t is the corporate tax rate (equal to 34%).

Assuming, as stated in P&G's 1989 Annual Report, that the company's target debt-to-total capital ratio (on a book value basis) is 35% and substituting this into the weighted average cost of capital formula, we get

$$WACC = .35\,(9.2\%)\,(1 - .34) + .65\,(13.6\%)$$
$$= 11.0\%$$

VI. RECOMMENDATION

The *WACC* represents the minimum acceptable rate of return for investing in the consumer-products markets. In a discounted cash flow analysis, the expected after-tax cash flows should be present-valued using 11.0% and compared to the initial investment required to enter the market. If the net present value is positive, the company should proceed with the expansion plans.

EXHIBIT 1

PROCTER & GAMBLE
Balance Sheets for Years Ended June 30
(millions of dollars except per-share amounts)

	1988	1989ᵃ
Assets		
Current assets		
Cash & cash equivalent	1,065	1,448
Accounts receivable	1,759	2,090
Inventories	2,292	2,337
Prepaid expenses & other	477	564
Total current assets	5,593	6,439
Property, plant & equipment	6,778	6,793
Goodwill & other intangibles	1,944	2,305
Other assets	505	675
Total assets	14,820	16,212
Liabilities & Shareholders' Equity		
Current liabilities		
Accounts payable, trade	1,494	1,669
Accounts payable, other	341	466
Accrued liabilities	1,116	1,365
Taxes payable	371	523
Debt due within one year	902	633
Total current liabilities	4,224	4,656
Long term debt	2,462	2,698
Other liabilities	475	447
Deferred income taxes	1,322	1,335

(continued)

EXHIBIT 1 (cont.)

	1988	1989[a]
Shareholders' Equity		
Common stock par $1	169	170
Additional paid-in capital	463	595
Currency translation adjustment	17	(63)
Retained earnings	5,688	6,374
Total equity	6,337	7,076
Total liabilities & equity	14,820	16,212

[a]The effects of a leveraged employee stock ownership plan established in 1989 have been removed to allow comparison of 1988 and 1989.

EXHIBIT 2

PROCTER & GAMBLE
Financial Data

Panel A
Income Statements for Years Ended June 30
(millions of dollars except per-share amounts)

	1987	1988	1989
Income			
Net sales	17,000	19,336	21,398
Interest & other income	163	155	291
Total revenues	17,163	19,491	21,689
Costs & expenses			
Cost of products sold	10,411	11,880	13,371
Marketing, admin., other expenses	4,977	5,660	5,988
Interest expense	353	321	391
Provision for restructuring	805	0	0
Total costs & expenses	16,546	17,861	19,750
Earnings before income taxes	617	1,630	1,939
Income taxes	290	610	733
Net earnings	327	1,020	1,207
Per common share			
Net earnings	1.87	5.96	7.12
Dividends	2.70	2.75	3.00

Panel B
Historical and Expected Growth Information

	PAST 10 YRS.	PAST 5 YRS.	ESTIMATED NEXT 5 YRS.[a]
Sales	7.6%	10.2%	8.0%
Earnings	7.0	5.9	15.5
Dividends	6.5	4.6	11.0

(continued)

EXHIBIT 2 (cont.)

Panel C

Summary Financial Review, 1980–1989

(years ended June 30)

	1980	1981	1982	1983	1984	1985	1986	1987	1988	1989
Net sales ($MM)	10,772	11,416	11,994	12,452	12,946	13,552	15,439	17,000	19,336	21,397
Net earnings ($MM)	640	668	777	866	890	635	709	327	1,020	1,206
Earnings/Net sales (%)	5.9	5.9	6.5	7.0	6.9	4.7	4.6	1.9	5.3	5.6
Earnings/Common share	3.87	4.04	4.69	5.22	5.35	3.80	4.20	1.87	5.96	7.12
Dividends/Common share	1.70	1.90	2.05	2.25	2.40	2.60	2.63	2.70	2.75	3.00
End-of-year stock price	73.75	75.75	83.00	55.13	52.63	57.13	80.13	98.00	77.50	108.38
Beta[b]	0.57	0.63	0.60	0.84	0.88	0.72	1.15	1.23	0.96	0.95

(continued)

EXHIBIT 2 (cont.)

Panel D
Recent Stock and Bond Price Information[c]

	PRICE
8¼% bonds due in 2005, rated Aaa by Moody's	92½
P&G common stock	126¼

[a]*Source: Value Line Investment Survey*, January 26, 1990.
[b]Betas for 1980–1988 are casewriter's estimates using daily stock returns with an equally weighted market-return index. The 1989 beta is taken from *Value Line Investment Survey*.
[c]*Source: Wall Street Journal*, February 23, 1990.

EXHIBIT 3

Current Market Conditions

	1989	1990	
	DECEMBER	JANUARY	FEBRUARY
Money Market Rates (%)			
Commercial paper (3 month)	8.32	8.16	8.22
Eurodollar deposits (3 month)	8.39	8.22	8.24
U.S. Treasury bills:			
3 month	7.63	7.64	7.74
1 year	7.21	7.38	7.55
Prime rate charged by banks	10.50	10.11	10.00
Capital Market Rates (%)			
U.S. Treasury bonds:			
5 year	7.75	8.12	8.42
10 year	7.84	8.21	8.47
30 year	7.90	8.26	8.50
Corporate bonds by Moody's ratings:			
Aaa	8.86	8.99	9.22
Aa	9.11	9.27	9.45
A	9.39	9.54	9.75
Baa	9.82	9.94	10.14

Source: Federal Reserve Bulletin, May 1990.

APPENDIX B
Ron Emory's Memo

DATE: February 23, 1990

SUBJECT: Cost-of-Capital Analysis

I'm on my way out to catch a plane to New York, so I'll outline my comments to save time. I'll take a look at the revised analysis when I get back in town on Monday morning.

I. P&G is only one company in the consumer-products business. However, they have such a dominant market share, I question whether their cost of capital is what a new entrant like our client should expect. I think we should compute the cost of capital for many of the relevant competitors, including Clorox, Colgate-Palmolive, and Church & Dwight. I want you to compute Clorox's cost of capital as a comparison for your P&G estimate. Clorox is much smaller than P&G and should more accurately capture the risks of a new entrant. I've asked Larry Atkins to work on Colgate-Palmolive and Church & Dwight. If your Clorox number ends up being much different from the P&G number, Larry's work may help us resolve which is more reasonable.

II. I get a cost of debt that is slightly lower than what you report. Investors look for yield plus appreciation in their investments. For a bond, the yield is the coupon payment and the appreciation is the difference between current price and par value. If the bond is selling at a discount, the appreciation is positive, and if the bond is selling at a premium, the expected price appreciation is negative, i.e., price depreciation. My estimate of the expected return on P&G's $8\frac{1}{4}$s is:

$$\text{Average yield} = \text{Coupon/Average price} = 8.25/\{(92.5 + 100)/2\} = 8.57\%$$
$$\text{Average gain} = (\text{Par} - \text{Price})/\text{Years to maturity} = (100 - 92.5)/15 = \$0.50$$
$$\text{Average } \% \text{ gain} = \text{Avg. gain/Avg. price} = \$0.50/\{(92.5 + 100)/2\} = 0.52\%$$
$$\text{Total return} = \text{Yield} + \text{Gain} = 8.57\% + 0.52\% = 9.09\%$$

Why are our numbers different?

III. I don't think we can sell the capital asset pricing model to the client. The model's credibility hinges upon the concept that investors value common stocks based upon betas. I'm certain that few, if any, individual investors think in terms of betas. Although stocks are riskier than bonds, investors look for the same two components of return: yield plus capital gains. Leave the CAPM estimates in your report, but add one or two additional estimates for cost of equity that are based on more intuitive techniques like the dividend growth and earnings capitalization models.

IV. Your numbers suggest that the cost of a debt-financed expansion is 9.2%, whereas if the company has to sell stock to finance the expansion, the cost rises to 13.6%. The client's last equity issue was over 30 years ago, and they just recently closed a large private placement of sinking-fund bonds, so we can safely assume that neither stock nor long-term debt will be issued to finance this project. My guess is that they will use retained earnings and short-term bank loans. The bank funds would be borrowed at prime, but I'm not sure how we should estimate the cost of retained earnings. Since retained earnings represent the amount of net income not paid out as a dividend, it would seem logical that the cost would be the capital gains portion of what equity investors demand. Be sure to say how these sources should be factored into the estimation procedure.

V. The CFO has mentioned to me on several occasions that he never uses net-present-value numbers in presentations to the board of directors. The board has some appreciation for a discounted-cash-flow technique, but they prefer to focus on rates of return rather than absolute dollar amounts. Substitute a discussion of internal rate of return for the NPV section in the report.

VI. Clorox has a higher proportion of equity than P&G. Given this difference, will the resulting WACCs for the two firms be comparable? I am having the necessary information on Clorox sent to you separately today [Exhibits A–E]. Clorox has no publicly traded bonds, but I would think that P&G's cost of debt would serve as a reasonable proxy for Clorox's cost of debt.

EXHIBIT A

Clorox: Business Risk

Clorox specializes in detergents and cleansers such as Clorox bleach, Liquid-plumr, Soft Scrub, and Formula 409. Like P&G, Clorox produces other product lines to take advantage of the distribution channels used for its main products. Examples include Kingsford and Match Light charcoal, Hidden Valley Ranch salad dressings, and Fresh Step cat litter. A small percentage of Clorox's sales come from Olympic and Lucite paint brands. Since Clorox's markets are mature, most of the growth has been through acquisitions. For example, since 1986, Clorox has been entering the bottled-water market by acquiring companies such as Aspen Water, Deep Rock Water, and Aqua Pure Water.

EXHIBIT B

CLOROX
Balance Sheets
Years Ended June 30
(000s, except per-share items)

	1988	1989
Assets		
Current assets		
Cash and short term investments	$ 259,278	$ 23,334
Accounts receivable, less allowances	114,697	143,354
Inventories	85,458	110,633
Prepaid expenses	6,353	10,816
Net assets held for sale	0	116,704
Total current assets	465,786	614,841
Net property, plant, & equip.	357,683	410,921
Brands, trademarks, patents, and other intangibles	92,003	99,654
Other assets including investments in affiliates	76,182	87,673
Net assets of discontinued operations	147,665	0
Total assets	$1,139,319	$1,213,089

(continued)

EXHIBIT B (cont.)

	1988	1989
Liabilities and Stockholders' Equity		
Current liabilities		
Accounts payable	$ 86,133	$ 85,798
Accrued liabilities	118,218	142,429
Income taxes payable	12,776	8,303
Commercial paper	78,811	79,580
Current maturities of long term debt	1,838	14,658
Total current liabilities	297,776	330,768
Long term debt & other obligations	29,190	7,051
Deferred income taxes	99,499	89,094
Stockholders' Equity		
Common stock: authorized,		
17,000,000 shares, $1 par	54,044	55,398
Additional paid-in capital	93,240	103,879
Retained earnings	570,163	634,275
Cumulative translation adjustments	(4,593)	(7,376)
Total stockholders' equity	712,854	786,176
Total liabilities and equity	$1,139,319	$1,213,089

EXHIBIT C

CLOROX
Income Statements
Years Ended June 30
(000s, except per-share items)

	1987	1988	1989
Net sales	$1,022,339	$1,153,103	$1,356,294
Costs & Expenses			
Costs of products sold	479,214	524,572	642,141
Selling, delivery, & admin.	204,453	235,629	269,586
Advertising	139,041	161,722	200,696
Research & development	31,049	30,735	37,161
Interest expense	5,377	4,085	7,187
Other (income)	(22,176)	(12,450)	(30,158)
Total costs & expenses	836,958	944,293	1,126,608
Earnings from continuing operations before taxes	185,381	208,810	229,686
Provision for income taxes	80,599	77,884	84,126
Earnings from continuing operations	104,782	130,926	145,560
Earnings (loss) from discontinued operations	117	1,644	(21,416)
Net earnings	$104,899	$132,570	$124,144
Earnings per common share			
Continuing operations	$1.92	$2.37	$2.63
Discontinued operations	0.00	0.03	(0.39)
Total	$1.92	$2.40	$2.24
Weighted-average shares outstanding	54,652	55,127	55,333

EXHIBIT D

CLOROX
Financial Summary Data

Panel A
Summary Financial Review for Years Ended June 30, 1980–1989

	1980	1981	1982	1983	1984	1985	1986	1987	1988	1989
Net sales ($MM)	637	714	804	825	848	932	972	1,022	1,153	1,356
Net earnings ($MM)	33	38	45	66	80	86	96	105	133	124
Earnings/Net sales (%)	5.2	5.3	5.6	7.9	9.4	9.2	9.8	10.3	11.5	9.2
Earnings/Common share	0.72	0.83	0.94	1.34	1.52	1.61	1.77	1.93	2.42	2.24
Dividends/Common share	0.39	0.41	0.43	0.48	0.54	0.62	0.70	0.79	0.92	1.09
End-of-year stock price	10.13	11.63	13.50	33.25	27.25	38.38	55.88	32.88	28.88	40.00
Beta[a]	0.78	0.94	0.96	1.32	1.30	1.36	1.23	1.14	0.91	0.90

Panel B
Recent Stock-Price Information[b]

	PRICE
Clorox common stock	38¼

[a]Betas for 1980–1988 are casewriter's estimates using daily stock returns with an equally weighted market-return index. The 1989 beta is taken from *Value Line Investment Survey*.

[b]Source: *Wall Street Journal*, February 23, 1990.

EXHIBIT E

CLOROX

Historical and Expected Growth Information

	PAST 10 YRS.	PAST 5 YRS.	ESTIMATED NEXT 5 YRS.[a]
Sales	6.6%	8.6%	13.5%
Earnings	13.4	8.1	15.5
Dividends	12.1	15.1	13.5

[a]*Source: Value Line Investment Survey*, January 26, 1990.

20

THE CONSUMERS' GAS COMPANY LTD.

In June 1991, The Consumers' Gas Company Ltd. (CG) filed an application with the Ontario Energy Board (OEB) requesting orders approving just and reasonable rates and other charges for the sale, distribution and transmission of natural gas for the 1992 fiscal year commencing October 1991. One of the more controversial issues involved in the rate-setting process was the determination of a fair rate of return on CG's capital. Several expert witnesses were invited to represent the three major parties: CG, OEB via its own OEB staff, and consumers via a Consumers Coalition (the Coalition). CG requested an equity return of 14.0%. This was, on average, an increase of 0.125% compared to the previous year's recommendation. The OEB staff proposed a return on equity of 12.5–13.0%, citing a marginal diminution of risk since the previous hearing. The Coalition submitted a lower rate, 11.4%, as its recommendation of a fair rate of return for equity. According to the Coalition, its proposal was the most accurate since it did not include unwarranted excess returns due to abuse of CG's monopoly position. The public hearing concluded on November 7, 1991.

This case was prepared by Anh Lo and Dominic Penaloza under the supervision of Professor Robert W. White for the sole purpose of providing material for class discussion at the Western Business School. Certain names and other identifying information may have been disguised to protect confidentiality. It is not intended to illustrate either effective or ineffective handling of a managerial situation. Any reproduction, in any form, of the material in this case is prohibited except with the written consent of the School.

The writers would like to acknowledge the assistance of John Parker, The Consumers' Gas Company Ltd., in preparing this case.

By February 13, 1992, the OEB had reviewed the arguments and evidence put forth by all parties and was preparing to produce its findings and recommendations. The "decision with reasons" document was due on February 14, 1992.

BACKGROUND ON THE COMPANY

As a progressive "newfangled" development, twelve gas lamps were introduced in 1841 as street lighting for the bustling city of Toronto, population 18,000. Fuel for the lights was supplied by Toronto Gas Light and Water, a forerunner of CG. CG was incorporated in 1848 to supply coal-extracted gas for illuminating homes, factories, and a growing system of street lights.

At the time of the 1991 rate application, CG was Canada's largest natural gas distribution utility, serving over one million residential, commercial and industrial customers in the areas of central and eastern Ontario, which included: Metropolitan Toronto and the greater Toronto areas of Peel, York and Durham regions as well as the Niagara Peninsula, Ottawa, Brockville, Peterborough, Barrie and many other Ontario communities. In addition, CG served the areas in and around Hull, Quebec, through its wholly owned subsidiary, Gazifère Inc., and areas in northern New York State, through another wholly owned subsidiary, St. Lawrence Gas Company, Inc. In total, CG distributed natural gas to customers through an underground piping network stretching over 19,200 kilometres serving more than 150 communities. The company employed over 3,200 people.

In addition to its regulated utility operations, CG was engaged in several non-utility businesses which included oil and gas exploration and production in southwestern Ontario and the State of Michigan and energy services in Ontario and the Maritimes.

In February 1992, 100% of the outstanding shares of CG were owned by British Gas Holdings (Canada) Limited, an indirect wholly owned subsidiary of British Gas plc. As a result, only the preference shares of CG were listed on the Toronto Stock Exchange (TSE) and Montreal Exchange. However, British Gas had agreed to reinstate a public float of at least 15% of the common shares of CG no later than September 1992.

In the 1991 annual report, President and CEO, R.W. Martin, predicted a bright future for CG: "Natural gas has the economic and environmental advantages that place it in a pre-eminent position among the energy options. I believe we are at the threshold of another period of substantial growth for the natural gas industry and CG is well positioned to participate in it." Financial statistics are illustrated in Exhibits 1 and 2.

THE RATE-SETTING PROCESS

The OEB was formed in 1960 to provide an impartial formal mechanism for regulating specific aspects of Ontario's natural gas industry. Each natural gas utility sells and transports gas in franchised areas of the province. Competition now exists in the supply of energy: buyers may purchase gas directly from producers or from the distributors, or they may turn to other sources of energy. Since the transportation of gas involves an extensive network of pipelines and storage facilities, a monopoly arrangement is most efficient; it avoids duplication of facilities and the cost increase that would otherwise result.

In setting rates, the OEB tries to strike a balance between the prices to be paid by customers and the rate of return which shareholders of the utilities are allowed to earn on their investment, i.e., to permit utilities to earn a competitive rate of return on common equity so as to be able to attract capital, but not to earn excess returns due to their monopoly position.

In the rate-setting process, the regulatory authority, such as the OEB, determined the cost of providing service and approved a rate structure designed to collect that amount from the various classes of customers. The cost of providing service included gas purchases, depreciation, income taxes, operating and administration costs and the cost of capital used to finance all assets used in the gas distribution business.

The cost of capital was expressed as an allowable rate of return on investment in assets (i.e., aggregate of investment in utility plant less accumulated depreciation and related deferred income taxes—also known as the rate base) used in the regulated business. It was designed principally to meet the cost of interest on long and short term debt, to satisfy the dividend requirements of preference shareholders and to provide common shareholders with an opportunity to earn a fair rate of return on their investment. The determination of a reasonable return to the common share-holders involved a judgmental assessment by the regulatory authority of many factors, including returns on alternative investment opportunities of comparable risk and the level of return which would enable a utility to attract the necessary capital to fund operations. The allowable rate of return was determined as the weighted average cost of the individual components of the capital structure. The application process led to the implementation of new rates which were intended to provide the utility with the opportunity to earn the allowable return.

An ongoing concern of all utilities was the ability, especially in times of rapidly rising costs, to recover the increases in operating costs and cost of capital from their customers. This concern was addressed by the OEB in the mid-1970s, a period of high inflation, when it allowed all regulated Ontario utilities to change from using historic data for rate applications to the "forward test year" method using forecast data. Under the forward test year method of rate making, operating costs and cost of capital were adjusted for the projected effects of inflation and/or increased level of business activity.

NATURAL GAS DEMAND

In 1880–1890, following forty years of increasing popularity, gas faced competition from a new energy source, electricity. Electric lighting eventually triumphed and gas distributors focused on promoting gas for heating and cooking. By 1914, gas appliances were in wide use. In the early 1950s, the costs of producing gas from coal became prohibitive. The Federal Government decided to introduce natural gas from Alberta to Eastern Canada. This was the beginning of a growth period for natural gas distributors in Ontario.

During 1991, recession tightened its grip on Ontario affecting both gas distributors and their customers. New residential construction activity declined. Plant closings in the commercial and industrial sectors reduced gas consumption. Furthermore, in 1990–91, Ontario experienced its mildest winter in over 40 years. The weather was almost 9% warmer than normal and 7% warmer than the same period in 1989–90. As a result of the recession and warmer weather, CG's volume dropped 4.4% in fiscal year 1990–1991.

DETERMINATION OF CG'S RISK

The rate of return allowed on equity is for a future period and is adjusted for risk. If CG's risk has changed materially, then any historical measures of risk should be adjusted to reflect the change. According to CG, the business and financial risk facing CG was essentially unchanged but trending upward. Greater regulatory stringency, forecasting risks, and uncertainty created by industrial restructuring were the main factors behind the risk analysis.

The business risk that CG faced was broken down into five categories; CG's reasoning under each category was:

1. *Market demand risks.* The witnesses felt that the warmer climate and recession had produced noticeable effects on the demand for natural gas. During fiscal year 1990–1991, CG's volumes had declined by 4.4% and profits by 1.5%.

2. *Supply and deliverability risks.* CG had the obligation to always meet user demand at any given time; thus it had a commitment to pay for contracted pipeline capacity whether used or not. The cost of carrying excess capacity had to be compensated.

3. *Gas supply risk.* In a deregulated environment, the use of direct purchase agreements by end users was on the rise. At the time, over half of the gas distributed by CG was under direct purchase agreements. Having an obligation to serve, some extra margin must be kept for direct purchase customers, who may decide to return to CG's system. Keeping such a margin increases the risk of contracting for pipeline capacity that goes unused and hence incurring a financial penalty.

4. *By-pass risk.* Furthermore, customers had the opportunity to physically by-pass CG's physical distribution system in a more deregulated environment. Therefore, the witnesses believed that this phenomenon would occur more frequently in the future.

5. *Regulatory risks.* CG claimed that greater regulatory stringency and greater forecasting risks had been created by industrial restructuring in the province. The witnesses noted that the OEB's more stringent review of CG's rate base, the imputation of an expected labour productivity gain, and a return allowance below that given to other utilities of similar risk had significantly increased CG's risk.

The OEB staff and the Coalition, on the other hand, estimated a marginal diminution of risks since the previous hearing, stating that CG was one of the few high-grade low-risk utilities in Canada.

1. *Market demand risks.* The OEB staff explained that demand was increasing due to several factors. Government policies encouraging the use of natural gas, as well as CG's own marketing efforts, were making natural gas a more popular fuel alternative. Moreover, the concern for the environment had encouraged users to switch to natural gas, since it was a cleaner fuel than most. Lastly, the price advantage of natural gas would make it a more popular choice for users. The Coalition argued that the fluctuations in demand varied with random factors, rather than the business cycle. Therefore, they could not justify an increase in risk due to lower volume demands, as cited by CG.

2. *Supply and deliverability risks.* The OEB staff stated that CG had decreased its supply risks by entering into contracts with various gas producers rather than one seller. CG had more flexibility because it no longer relied on a sole producer and could control the amount of supply that it received by varying the types of contracts that it held. The Coalition concluded that CG faced little risk. As Canada's largest distributor, it could sell its excess transportation and storage services to other gas distributors.

3. *By-pass risks.* Although customers had the choice to buy directly from producers, the OEB staff and Coalition concluded that by-pass risks would remain minimal. CG would find that in a deregulated environment, users would find it more attractive to buy from a distributor who had the economies of scale to offer better rates. The Coalition believed that most customers would still use CG's system; therefore, a monopoly still existed.

4. *Regulatory risks.* The OEB had always worked to compensate for any changes in the environment to ensure that Ontario's regulated industries had viable futures. Additionally, CG had over-earned its equity return over the last eight years; thus the OEB could not have been too stringent.

THE 1992 RATE APPLICATION

Capital Structure

CG proposed a capital structure which remained essentially unchanged from the previous rate application (see Table 1).

TABLE 1
CAPITAL STRUCTURE

	PREVIOUS APPLICATION	1992 PROPOSAL
Long term Debt	55.84%	53.66%
Short term Debt	2.85	5.63
Preferred Stock	6.31	5.71
Common Equity	35.00	35.00
TOTAL	100.00%	100.00%

In the four previous proceedings, the OEB had approved a 35% common equity ratio. To reinforce its argument, CG pointed to evidence showing a marked decline in interest coverage (see Exhibit 3). In CG's opinion, "interest coverage ratios have reached a point where a reversal becomes essential to maintain CG's debt rating and adequate financing flexibility. A prerequisite for such a reversal is a higher return award and/or a higher than 35% common equity ratio." CG's current rating is a high "A". The 35% ratio, as well as the submitted rates for the costs of short and long term debt and preferred shares, was acceptable to all parties involved. See Exhibit 4 for the capital structure ratios of major Canadian utilities.

Cost of Short Term Debt

CG forecasted a rise in short-term interest rates over the 1992 fiscal year as economic recovery strengthened. The cost of unfunded debt was estimated by CG to be 8.72%. This rate was based on CG's latest forecast of the 90-day commercial paper rate, weighted by the monthly borrowing pattern expected to prevail during fiscal 1992. CG employs underground storage in order to satisfy peak loading demands. During the summer they purchase gas for storage for use during the winter. Therefore CG borrows during the summer to finance the inventory. See Exhibit 5 for a summary of financial charges for 1989–91.

Cost of Long Term Debt

↓ coupon

CG estimated the embedded cost of its total long term debt load to be 11.25% during the 1992 test year. The expected all-in yield on cost of a proposed $150 million 20-year debenture issue in 1992 with an estimated coupon of 10.75% was 10.87%.

Cost of Preferred Stock

CG submitted 8.79% as the embedded cost of preferred shares. On June 29, 1991, the closing price for CG's 7.6%, $25 preferreds was $25.

Cost of Common Equity

The three groups differed substantially on the subject of return on equity. Expert witnesses applied various methods for determining the fair rate of return for 1992 as of June 29, 1991. Four methods were used: the comparable earnings test, risk premium test, capital asset pricing model, and discounted cash flow model (see Exhibit 6 for an overview of the approaches). The conclusions are summarized in Table 2. CG proposed an equity return requirement of 14.0%, based on a 35% common equity ratio. This was, on average, an increase of 0.125% on their previous year's request (13.875%). The return on equity actually awarded to CG in FY 1991 was 13.125%.

TABLE 2
SUMMARY OF ESTIMATES OF COST OF EQUITY

	CG	OEB STAFF	COALITION
Comparable Earnings	13.5%	12.6–13.15%	—
Risk Premium	14.5	12.85–13.06	10.95–11.39%
Capital Asset Pricing	—	10.7–11.2	10.75–11.5
Discounted Cash Flow	—	—	10.8–11.9
Recommendation	**14.0%**	**12.5–13.0%**	**11.4%**

CG's EVIDENCE

Comparable Earnings

CG witnesses applied the comparable earnings test by reference to a sample of 33 companies, showing a return of 14.0% for 1983–91. The sample was selected from an initial universe of consumer-oriented industrials, a subset of the TSE 300 companies. The 33 companies were then selected from this group based on stability of book and market returns. The business cycle period used by CG's witnesses commenced in 1983 and ended in 1991.

CG's witnesses compared the cost of attracting capital between the 33 industrials and 5 utility companies. They concluded that during 1983–1991, investors capitalized the earnings of high grade utilities at approximately 50 bp below that of the industrial sample. Therefore an estimate of 13.5% was given for this approach to the cost of equity.

Equity Risk Premium

CG's witnesses undertook two risk premium tests. The first study relied on two samples of utilities: the first, a group of 5 high-grade utilities; the second, an expanded sample of 12 non-diversified utilities, which was used to test for validity of the smaller sample.

Essentially, the CG witnesses estimated the Discounted Cash Flow fair value of return for the two samples going back 15 years (two business cycles). By subtracting the long term Canada bond yield from the estimated annual returns, a history of returns in excess of the risk free rate were determined. Regression analysis was then performed on this series of excess returns and a regression model was developed to predict the risk premium for the two grades of utilities.

In the second test, the witnesses recorded the difference between experienced market returns for the utility stocks and long Canada bond rates. (Utilities rather than the market as a whole were compared since it was felt that utilities offered returns closer to investor expectations and any downward adjustment of risk premiums for CG would be easier to justify.) Differentials were calculated using their own calculations and the study of James E. Hatch and Robert W. White,

Canadian Stocks, Bonds, Bills and Inflation: 1950–1987. CAPM was not deemed valid for this exercise since utility betas only explained 15–20% of utility returns.

CG witnesses concluded that the appropriate risk premium for CG (weighted average of the two methods used), in relation to a projected long Canada yield of 9.75%, was 3.5%, resulting in a "bare-bones" cost of 13.25%. Utilizing the formula: Market/Book Ratio times the "bare-bones" cost divided by (1 plus the retention rate times (M/B − 1)), a cost of 14.5% was arrived at. This adjustment was made to allow for financing flexibility (to permit raising new debt capital and to account for financing costs).

Using the average of the two cost of equity calculations, CG requested that the equity return be raised to 14.0% to improve interest coverage in order to avoid a down rating of its debt and to improve its financing flexibility.

OEB STAFF'S EVIDENCE

Comparable Earnings

The OEB staff selected a sample of 25 firms that were deemed most comparable to Consumers' Gas starting with the companies in the TSE 300 index. They then eliminated companies based on various criteria such as:

- highly contrasting industry accounting reporting requirements
- highly regulated industries to minimize the possibility of a circular argument
- high share price and dividend volatility

The Board staff used two business cycles, one from 1982–1990 and a 16-year period from 1975–1990.

OEB staff submitted that CG's comparable earnings conclusion was 45 bp higher than it should have been were it based on the 1984–1992 full business cycle. Given the full 1984–1992 cycle, CG's average return for its industrial sample would have been 13.55%.

OEB staff submitted that CG witnesses ignored unusual items such as reorganizations in deriving raw equity-return data (in effect, "turned a blind eye"). OEB staff's treatment reflected the idea that within a large sample of industrials, firms are likely, as a group, to be no more or less likely to make investment "mistakes" in the next cycle than in the past. Absent these unusual items, CG reported returns 36 to 116 bp higher than the OEB staff reported for the same firms.

In adjusting for CG's lower risk, OEB staff subtracted 60 bp. CG witnesses testified that this adjustment was "moderate" on the basis of the relative risk data used to quantify the adjustment.

Risk Premium

OEB staff also used two separate risk premium tests. In the first, witnesses determined the difference between average allowed equity returns for Canadian utilities and the long term Government of Canada bond yields in the same year. The test used actual return and interest rate data for a given year. However, CG's witnesses contended that this was an inaccurate measure since, for many utilities, one year's allowed returns are often set on the basis of interest rates that were forecasted to prevail during the subsequent test year (forecasts were made during the latter half of the previous year).

In response to this criticism, OEB staff developed a second version of the risk premium method. In this approach, forecasted interest rates were used to arrive at a recommended risk premium for the coming test year.

The average of the two methods yielded a risk premium of 3.73–3.85%, resulting in a return of 12.85–12.93%. OEB staff had adjusted this initial premium down by 30 bp due to the low risk nature of CG (based on the full range of risk evidence pertaining to Canadian utility firms—calculated in an appendix to the OEB staff recommendation).

OEB staff also submitted that the OEB give some weight to the results of the capital asset pricing model (CAPM) test and little weight to the discounted cash flow (DCF) model on the basis that the latter's applicability to CG was suspect.

CAPM

In its CAPM test, OEB staff, based on a "risk-free rate" of 8.3%, a market risk premium of 5.25–5.75%, and a beta of 0.30–0.35, computed the investors' market required return at 9.9–10.3%. (See Exhibit 7 for betas of similar companies and Exhibit 8 for returns on long term Canada bonds and T-bill rates.) Since these values were market-value based, investment rates of return, while the OEB's responsibility was to determine an allowed accounting rate of return on book equity, it was necessary to make an adjustment to ensure that the accounting return preserved the financial integrity of CG's shares. OEB staff adjusted for financing flexibility to preserve a market/book ratio of 1.15, thus recommending an equity return in the range of 10.7 to 11.2%.

OEB staff's risk-free rate was based on two approaches, with more weight given to the former:

1. Taking the mid-point between current and projected long term bond yields (9.24%) and subtracting a "normal maturity risk premium," 90 bp, for securities at that point in the long term interest cycle resulted in an estimate of 8.34%.
2. Adding to the prevailing U.S. 3-month treasury bill rate (5.1%) a spread of 200 to 220 bp which OEB staff judged to be the equilibrium differential between Canadian and U.S. short term rates in a long-term-stable U.S.–Canadian exchange rate environment resulted in an estimate of 7.1–7.3%.

OEB staff's estimation of the future beta focused on the witnesses' 1988 calculation of CG's future-oriented, utility-only beta at 0.35–0.40. Considering the historical evidence over the 1988–1990 period, the decline in CG's overall riskiness since

1988, and OEB staff's views about risk exposure during its 1992 test year and beyond, the beta was estimated to lie in the range of 0.30–0.35.

To find the equity risk premium required by the market as a whole, OEB staff used the average risk premium from 1961–1990 which was 2.1%. This value was then adjusted upwards to 5.25–5.75% based on outside studies and personal views regarding stock market conditions.

CG's witnesses submitted that the OEB should totally disregard the CAPM results because:

1. No Canadian regulatory board had endorsed the CAPM, essentially because it required reliance on T-Bill rates, which were characterized by wide swings, as amply illustrated during the previous three years.
2. The end result of 10.7–11.2% was almost 200 bp below the average of the OEB staff's results by other techniques, which cast serious doubt on CAPM's validity as a measure of investors' return requirement. Furthermore, a return at this level would barely allow CG to raise debt.

OEB staff argued that the OEB should give some weight to the CAPM test. The reasons for including the CAPM were:

1. CAPM provided a direct reflection of investors' rate-of-return expectations and requirements and, as such, was complementary to OEB staff's other tests;
2. CAPM, "during periods of relative financial market stability . . . was as straightforward and objective as any of the other equity-return models presented for the OEB's consideration"; and
3. the economic environment was conducive for the empirical application of the model.

At the same time, OEB staff limited the weight attached to the CAPM to 10% "simply and only because it focused on a single measure of investment risk, that being beta."

THE COALITION'S EVIDENCE

The Coalition did not present comparable earnings evidence since it was "an accounting return, not an economic return, measured over an arbitrary period and an arbitrary sample of companies. It did not measure the important thing, which is the investor's opportunity cost." However, the Coalition revised the CG witnesses' estimate down to 11.3%. The main criticisms were directed at the sample of firms created and the possible existence of monopoly power within the sample.

The Coalition pointed out that CG used the coefficient of variation, which is the standard deviation of a firm's return on equity divided by its average return on equity, as the main screen to create their sample. The relationship between coefficient of variation and performance is that CG witnesses, in the Coalition's view, were forming samples of high performing firms instead of low risk firms comparable to CG. The Coalition submitted "this is prima facie evidence that CG's sample contains companies with monopoly power, since such firms will tend to be high performing firms, that is, to have high returns on equity given their risk."

Risk Premium

The Coalition obtained a risk premium of 2.2–3.0% over long term Canada bonds, resulting in a return on equity of 10.95–11.39%. In contrast to CG and OEB staff's methods, Coalition witnesses examined the behaviour of market prices with observed excess returns. The Coalition supported an approach which satisfied the criteria of opportunity cost (i.e., a level of returns matching the returns investors might have earned on an alternate investment of corresponding risk).

In criticizing the results of CG, the Coalition contended that the DCF estimate that they used relied heavily on realized historic dividend growth rates over five- and ten-year periods. The Coalition declared that historic rates were only reliable if they passed three diagnostic checks[1], which CG did not use.

CAPM

The Coalition's application of the CAPM employed a market risk premium of 2.2–3.0%, with a beta of 0.34–0.50, resulting in a risk premium for CG of 0.75–1.5%, which, when applied to a long Canada yield of 10.0%, resulted in a cost estimate of 10.75–11.5%.

Although they did not use the CAPM method, CG witnesses performed studies that showed that the preponderance of experts placed the market risk premium in the range of 4.5–5.0%, and betas were an unreliable measure of regulatory risk. They stated "the Coalition's end result of a risk premium for CG of 0.75–1.5% defies common sense."

In rebuttal, the Coalition asserted that, contrary to CG's witnesses, the CAPM did not require the use of the 91-day T-Bill rate. As OEB staff witnesses admitted, the T-Bill rate was not a risk-free return for an investor with a five-year horizon. For this reason, the Coalition and CG witnesses used the long Canada yield as the proxy for the risk-free rate embodied in the CAPM equity return.

The Coalition pointed out that the main area of disagreement between the experts was whether beta was, in fact, the sole measure of risk. CG argued that beta cannot be the sole measure of risk because the R^2 of the regression equations had low explanatory power, and the historic experience had been that the utility sub-index had experienced excess returns much closer to those on the TSE 300 index than a beta of 0.4 or so would indicate. The Coalition answered these criticisms by claiming that low betas go hand in hand with low R^2, in fact a totally riskless company would have an R^2 of zero.

CG replied that "betas are calculated over 5-year historical periods and can provide a distorted view of how investors perceive risk on a forward-looking basis.

---

[1]These checks are used to ensure the simple historical dividend growth rates obtained are not artificially manufactured out of changes in the allowed rate of return or changes in the underlying rate of inflation.

For example, a utility beta covering the period 1981–1985 would be significantly influenced by the stock price movements in 1981–1982, when long term interest rates were at their peak and at their most volatile."

DCF

The OEB staff submitted that while the theoretical underpinnings of the DCF formula were sound, there were a number of well-recognized generic shortcomings associated with the application of the model in the regulatory, rate-setting context. These shortcomings included:

1. The inherent circularity of the approach;
2. The difficulty and arbitrariness of estimating investor growth expectations, especially when these were imputed from an unrelated sample of utilities or industrial companies;
3. The diversified nature of many utilities from which DCF evidence may be gleaned;
4. The implication of a market-to-book ratio of 1.0 in the derivation of the "bare bones" cost of equity; and
5. The disputed necessity and magnitude of the financing flexibility or market-to-book adjustment tacked on at the end of the return-requirement estimation procedure.

Meanwhile, the Coalition believed that the DCF was a suitable test because of CG's relatively high dividend yields and stable growth expectations. OEB staff contended that the DCF model had been used in previous hearings only when CG was an almost pure utility and when market information about CG's share price and dividend yield data was available. The Coalition used historical data in its tests, stating that the stable nature of the utility justified its relevance.

CG disagreed with the data used in the Coalition's DCF study. One of the major disagreements was the imputation of the telephone companies (telcos) DCF cost to CG, without considering whether the DCF cost of energy companies differed from that of telcos. The fact that the dividend yields of CG had been similar to those of the telcos sample was insufficient to draw a reliable inference as to investor expectations. Energy companies had consistently been awarded higher returns than telcos, which, with their similar pay-out ratios, would lead investors to reasonably expect higher growth rates. Therefore, they concluded that the Coalition's "bare-bones" DCF cost was significantly understated.

THE DECISION

The OEB had a difficult decision to make, given the disparity in the determination of CG's common equity rate of return between CG, OEB staff, and the Coalition. The parties did not agree on the degree of risk facing CG and its shareholders. Recommendations from witnesses were the products of combinations of different techniques, resulting in a wide spread of proposed allowable returns. As they pondered the validity of the arguments raised by the three groups, the OEB members remembered how the implementation of their decision would affect the million-plus customers of CG. Financial data for a similar gas utility, Union Energy[2] are presented in Exhibits 9 and 10, and historical risk premium data are presented in Exhibit 11.

[2]A financial research company, Canadian Business Service, in its comparative analysis, pairs Consumers' Gas and Union Energy.

EXHIBIT 1
THE CONSUMERS' GAS COMPANY LTD.
Consolidated Statements of Income
Year ended September 30
(thousands of dollars except per share amounts)

	1991	1990	1989	1988
Gas sales	$1,559,501	$1,612,155	$1,638,146	$1,661,344
Gas costs	1,122,964	1,179,873	1,216,371	1,269,363
Gas sales margin	436,537	432,282	421,775	391,981
Transportation of gas for customers	3,838	6,081	5,704	5,965
Net gas distribution revenue	440,375	438,363	427,479	397,946
Other revenue	123,633	153,727	157,233	146,437
	564,008	592,090	584,712	544,383
Expenses				
Operation and maintenance	207,880	220,447	210,414	197,416
Depreciation and depletion	83,959	79,148	75,482	64,652
Municipal and other taxes	27,684	25,475	22,749	20,272
	319,523	325,070	308,645	282,340
Income before undernoted items	244,485	267,020	276,067	262,043
Financial charges				
Interest on long term debt	109,192	95,016	92,462	90,938
Other interest and finance costs	31,326	37,182	26,666	14,563
Interest recapitalized	(3,113)	(1,884)	(1,597)	(719)
	137,405	130,314	117,531	104,782
Adjustment to write-down of subsidiary in 1990	5,500	–	–	–
Income before income taxes and extraordinary item	112,580	136,706	158,536	157,261
Income taxes				
Current	28,347	39,192	58,497	56,651
Deferred	2,243	1,027	(2,768)	(156)
	30,590	40,219	55,729	56,495
Income before extraordinary item	81,990	96,487	102,807	100,766
Write-down of the investment in Arbor Living Centers Inc.	–	29,000	–	–
Write-down of non-current investments	–	–	–	5,000
Net Income	$ 81,990	$ 67,487	$ 102,807	$ 95,766

(continued)

EXHIBIT 1   (cont.)

	1991	1990	1989	1988
Basic earnings per common				
share (1)	$1.12	$1.36	$1.41	$1.37
Before extraordinary item	$1.12	$0.91	$1.41	$1.30
Net Income				
Times interest earned (2)	1.93	2.44	2.71	2.73
Return on average common				
shareholders' equity				
Before extraordinary item	12.17%	14.82%	15.84%	16.33%
Net Income	12.17%	9.96%	15.84%	15.41%

Notes:
(1) Restated 1988 to 1991 historical data to give retroactive effect to the division of each common share into two shares on February 6, 1992.
(2) For 1991, presented on a pro forma basis (Tecumseh's results are included for a full year).

EXHIBIT 2

THE CONSUMERS' GAS COMPANY LTD.
Condensed Consolidated Balance Sheets
September 30
(thousands of dollars)

	1991	1990	1989	1988
Assets				
Current Assets	$ 558,869	$ 585,827	$ 498,881	$ 517,692
Investments	–	40,031	81,935	73,872
Property, plant and equipment	2,436,175	2,113,525	1,938,126	1,789,497
Accumulated depreciation				
and depletion	628,273	552,491	501,984	451,259
	1,807,902	1,561,034	1,436,142	1,338,238
Other assets and deferred				
charges	95,237	54,051	47,083	32,755
	$2,462,008	$2,240,943	$2,064,041	$1,962,557
Liabilities				
Current Liabilities	$ 684,941	$ 741,014	$ 517,803	$ 530,809
Long term debt	1,013,864	763,968	808,994	730,877
Deferred income taxes	36,146	33,086	31,478	33,337
Shareholders' equity				
Preference shares	107,293	107,651	108,286	108,739
Common shareholders' equity	619,764	595,224	597,480	558,795
	727,057	702,875	705,766	667,534
	$2,462,008	$2,240,943	$2,064,041	$1,962,557

(continued)

EXHIBIT 2 (cont.)

	1991	1990	1989	1988
Capitalization ratios				
Long term debt	58.2%	52.1%	53.4%	52.3%
Preference shareholders' equity	6.2%	7.3%	7.1%	7.7%
Common shareholders' equity	35.6%	40.6%	39.5%	40.0%
Book value per common share (1)	$9.38	$9.13	$9.18	$8.63
Shares O/S (1)	73,206	65,218	51,082	64,776
Share Price (1)	N/A	$16.75	$14.38	$12.07

Note:
(1) Restated 1988 to 1991 historical data to give retroactive effect to the division of each common share into two shares on February 6, 1992.

EXHIBIT 3

Times Interest Charges
Earned Before Income Taxes
for Selected Gas and Electric Utilities

YEAR	CONSUMERS' GAS	CANADIAN UTILITIES LTD.	B.C. GAS[b]	FORTIS INC.	GAZ METRO	TRANS-ALTA UTILITIES	UNION ENERGY
1980	2.35	3.17	3.41	3.46	1.59	3.77	1.87
1981	1.96	3.14	2.71	3.21	1.67	3.28	2.03
1982	2.45	3.80	3.09	3.79	2.28	3.09	2.01
1983	2.40	4.57	2.67	3.72	2.24	3.46	2.59
1984	2.89	4.75	2.03	3.39	2.92	4.13	2.64
1985	2.90	4.35[a]	2.36	3.25	2.30	4.34	2.50
1986	2.68	4.48	1.72	3.13	2.13	3.97	2.55
1987	2.36	3.85	1.65	2.78	2.05	4.56	2.51
1988	2.49	3.43	1.64	2.80	2.18	3.93	2.16
1989	2.33	3.26	1.51	2.51	2.45	3.06	2.00
1990	2.03	2.91	1.54	2.62	2.62	2.93	N/A

[a]Restated from 4.54.

[b]Reflects fiscal year ending June 30 through 1982 and December 31 thereafter.

Note: Times interest charges earned represent the ratio of gross income before the deduction of income taxes to total interest charges.

Source: Annual Reports to Stockholders; Moody's Investors Service, Inc.

EXHIBIT 4

Capital Structure Ratios of Selected Major Canadian Utilities
(in percent)

	DATE	LONG TERM DEBT[a]	SHORT TERM DEBT	PREFERRED STOCK[b]	DEFERRED TAXES	COMMON STOCK EQUITY[c]
Consumers' Gas	9/90	39.5%	23.6%	5.4%	1.7%	29.9%
Gas Distributors and Pipelines						
B.C. Gas	12/90	60.4	11.7	9.2	2.2	16.5
Canadian Utilities	12/90	42.9	3.3	20.4	0.1	33.2
Centra Gas Ontario, Inc.	12/90	50.9	10.6	3.4	3.3	31.8
Gaz Metropolitan	9/90	49.6	0.8	8.3	0.0	41.3
TransCanada Pipelines	12/90	63.4	0.0	8.2	1.6	26.8
Union Energy	3/90	44.6	8.6	7.8	15.4	23.7
Westcoast Energy	12/90	49.2	8.2	4.3	10.2	28.1
Electrics						
Fortis, Inc.	12/90	33.8	11.4	17.0	1.6	36.2
TransAlta Utilities	12/90	42.7	3.3	19.4	1.0	33.6
Telephones						
Bell Canada	12/90	34.4	1.2	5.6	13.4	45.5
B.C. Telephone	12/90	42.8	1.4	4.9	13.4	45.5
Bruncor	12/90	46.2	5.8	3.9	9.5	34.6
Maritime Tel. & Tel.	12/90	42.8	0.0	9.1	12.2	35.9
NewTel Enterprises	12/90	43.0	8.7	9.3	6.6	32.4
Quebec Telephone	12/90	41.1	0.0	2.6	11.7	44.6
Average		45.9%	5.0%	8.9%	6.6%	33.7%

[a]Includes current portion of long term debt.
[b]Includes minority interest in preferred shares of subsidiary companies.
[c]Includes minority interest in common shares of subsidiary companies.

Source: Annual Reports to Stockholders.

EXHIBIT 5
THE CONSUMERS' GAS COMPANY LTD.
Summary of Financial Charges[a]

	TOTAL FINANCIAL CHARGES ($ MILLIONS)	SHORT TERM DEBT BALANCE ($ MILLIONS)	AVERAGE SHORT TERM DEBT COST RATE (%)	LONG TERM DEBT BALANCE[b] ($ MILLIONS)	AVERAGE LONG TERM DEBT COST RATE (%)
1991	137.4	266.4	11.4	925.4	11.8
1990	130.3	258.2	12.8	805.2	11.8
1989	117.5	197.5	11.0	785.6	11.8

[a]The comparative figures in Exhibits 1 and 2 have been reclassified to conform with the presentation adopted in 1992, consequently, the figures in this exhibit, taken from testimony, may not correspond exactly.
[b]Excluding the interest costs and debentures of Tecumseh Gas Storage Limited, since this subsidiary's operating results are presented on a net contribution basis on CG's consolidated statements of income.

EXHIBIT 6
Approaches for Determining Required Rates of Return on Equity

COMPARABLE EARNINGS

The comparable earnings test is a test of fairness and financial integrity for utility gas returns. The comparable earnings test involves three principal issues:

1. The selection of samples of industrials of reasonably comparable risk to utilities.
2. The selection of an appropriate time period over which returns are measured in order to estimate prospective returns.
3. The magnitude of downward adjustments to the "raw" comparable earnings results for the relatively lower risk to utilities and for potential monopolistic elements.

RISK PREMIUM

The risk premium is a market related test, intended to estimate the cost of attracting capital. It assumes that investors are risk-averse. In order for investors to buy a certain security with a risk component, they would have to be compensated a risk premium over the risk-free securities. Various components of the risk premium test include:

1. The determination of the risk-free rate. Generally, the average long-term Canada bond yield is appropriate.
2. Comparison of the rate of return allowed to other utilities (or other control group) over a certain period of time.
3. Calculation of the premium required for a company to attract capital from investors (actual return achieved minus the risk-free rate). This is then arithmetically averaged over the appropriate time horizon.

Certain factors such as inflation rate expectations and historical inflation, dividend payout and ROE trends over time of the various utilities are factored in, since these factors will have an impact on the risk premium required by investors.

EXHIBIT 6 (cont.)

DISCOUNTED CASH FLOW

The DCF is based on the fact that the theoretical share price is the present value of future stream of expected dividends (cash flow). The discount rate is the cost of equity for the issuing company. The standard formula for estimating the cost of equity assumes that investors expect that dividends will grow at a constant rate g forever. The estimation of the expected dividend growth rate is often done by looking at historical growth rates of CG as well as other comparable companies. The cost of equity is calculated using the following formula:

$$k_e = (((d \times (1 \div g)) + p) + g$$

where k_e = cost of equity, d = current dividends per share, p = current share price and g = constant growth rate in dividends expected by investors.

CAPM

The Capital Asset Price Model assumes that the only risk that is priced in the market is systematic or non-diversifiable risk, that risk that investors cannot avoid. An individual securities' non-systematic risk is measured by its beta. The investor's required rate of return, CG's cost of equity, based on the CAPM is the sum of the rate on long term risk-free bonds plus a risk premium equal to CG's beta times the expected risk premium for the market.

EXHIBIT 7

Stock Price Betas for Selected Canadian Utilities

COMPANY	FIVE YEAR BETAS FOR NON-DIVERSIFIED UTILITIES FOR PERIODS ENDING						
	1984	1985	1986	1987	1988	1989	1990
B. C. Gas	0.23	0.13	0.08	0.49	0.52	0.54	0.53
B. C. Telephone	0.48	0.54	0.51	0.32	0.32	0.27	0.29
Canadian Utilities	0.52	0.47	0.47	0.25	0.37	0.39	0.38
Consumers' Gas	n/a	n/a	n/a	0.26	0.30	0.33	0.27
Fortis	0.67	0.60	0.52	0.19	0.26	0.21	0.17
Island Telephone	0.34	0.38	0.43	0.30	0.26	0.27	0.22
Maritime Electric	0.43	0.44	0.41	0.35	0.34	0.33	0.35
Maritime Tel & Tel	0.48	0.50	0.56	0.44	0.34	0.34	0.36
NewTel	0.53	0.58	0.48	0.35	0.41	0.42	0.36
Pacific Northern Gas	0.23	0.23	0.10	0.35	0.32	0.27	0.35
Quebec Telephone	0.23	0.29	0.44	0.35	0.32	0.28	0.22
TransAlta	0.56	0.61	0.55	0.22	0.18	0.20	0.24
MEDIAN	0.48	0.47	0.47	0.33	0.32	0.30	0.32
AVERAGE	0.43	0.43	0.41	0.32	0.33	0.32	0.31

EXHIBIT 7 (cont.)

GAS DISTRIBUTORS AND PIPELINES

YEARS	B.C. GAS		CONSUMERS' GAS		NOVERCO		PACIFIC NORTHERN GAS		TRANSCANADA PIPELINES		UNION ENERGY		WESTCOAST ENERGY	
	BETA (1)	R-SQ. (2)	BETA (3)	R-SQ. (4)	BETA (5)	R-SQ. (6)	BETA (7)	R-SQ. (8)	BETA (9)	R-SQ. (10)	BETA (11)	R-SQ. (12)	BETA (13)	R-SQ. (14)
1975–79	0.81	27.5	n/a	n/a	0.81	23.6	n/a	n/a	1.05	53.9	0.86	44.2	0.79	39.2
1976–80	0.53	25.3	n/a	n/a	0.85	23.6	n/a	n/a	0.82	51.4	0.58	28.0	0.79	37.7
1977–81	0.48	16.8	n/a	n/a	0.77	20.1	0.57	10.9	0.78	40.3	0.60	31.3	0.75	35.4
1978–82	0.31	5.3	n/a	n/a	0.58	15.8	0.30	6.3	0.87	48.1	0.63	39.0	0.87	34.4
1979–83	0.33	6.0	n/a	n/a	0.49	12.2	0.34	5.5	0.88	45.2	0.62	36.0	0.81	29.9
1980–84	0.23	3.2	n/a	n/a	0.44	10.8	0.23	3.9	0.22	36.2	0.68	29.5	0.49	22.2
1981–85	0.13	0.8	n/a	n/a	0.27	5.7	0.23	4.9	0.85	20.1	0.69	35.2	0.40	15.2
1982–86	0.08	0.3	0.42	10.5	0.28	5.2	0.10	0.8	0.89	28.0	0.50	20.3	0.30	7.0
1983–87	0.49	23.4	0.28	8.0	0.39	14.1	0.35	14.5	0.57	18.3	0.44	19.0	0.41	13.2
1984–88	0.52	22.5	0.30	13.8	0.45	18.8	0.32	12.4	0.61	18.0	0.41	17.6	0.45	16.1
1985–89	0.54	22.7	0.33	15.5	0.49	20.5	0.27	8.2	0.58	17.2	0.41	17.9	0.58	23.0
1986–90	0.53	29.1	0.27	10.0	n/a	n/a	0.38	12.2	0.54	18.2	0.34	14.9	0.55	24.6

EXHIBIT 8

Trend in Outstanding Bond Yields and Interest Rates

YEAR	CHARTERED BANK PRIME RATE[a]	3-MONTH TREASURY BILLS[b]	GOVERNMENT OVER 10 YEAR BONDS[c]
1990 Jan	13.50%	12.34%	10.04%
Feb	14.25	13.16	10.64
Mar	14.25	13.26	10.91
Apr	14.75	13.55	11.54
May	14.75	13.67	10.86
Jun	14.75	13.58	10.72
Jul	14.75	13.23	10.78
Aug	14.25	12.67	10.83
Sep	13.75	12.40	11.54
Oct	13.75	12.36	11.15
Nov	13.25	12.01	10.70
Dec	12.75	11.47	10.51
1991 Jan	12.25	10.48	10.22
Feb	11.25	9.72	9.89
Mar	11.25	9.67	9.88
Apr	10.75	9.24	9.91
May	9.75	8.81	9.91
Jun	9.75	8.66	10.36

[a]*Source: Bank of Canada Review*, series B14020.
[b]*Source: Bank of Canada Review*, series B14007.
[c]*Source: Bank of Canada Review*, series B14013.

EXHIBIT 9

UNION ENERGY
Consolidated Statement of Income
For the year ended March 31,
(thousands, except per share amounts)

	1991	1990
Revenues		
Gas sales	$1,517,040	$1,612,636
Transportation and storage of gas	100,247	80,621
Exploration and production	81,000	67,283
Other	59,027	54,920
	1,757,314	1,815,510
Expenses		
Cost of gas sold	1,200,487	1,295,216
Operating, maintenance and administration	224,436	213,339
Depreciation, depletion and amortization	107,335	95,333
	1,532,258	1,603,888

(continued)

EXHIBIT 9 (cont.)

	1991	1990
Operating Income	225,056	211,622
Interest on short term borrowings	21,494	17,596
Interest on long term borrowings	109,347	98,044
Interest deferred	(9,550)	(4,398)
	121,291	111,242
Income before income taxes	103,765	100,380
Income taxes	43,277	44,224
Income including minority interest	60,488	56,156
Minority interest	12,194	10,986
Net Income	48,294	45,170
Preference share dividend requirement	6,816	5,432
Income attributable to common shareholders	$ 41,478	$ 39,738
Weighted average number of common shares outstanding	37,510	37,225
Earnings per common share	$ 1.11	$ 1.07
Share Price	$ 12.88	$ 12.38

EXHIBIT 10

UNION ENERGY
Consolidated Balance Sheet
As at March 31,
(thousands)

	1991	1990
Assets		
Current Assets		
Accounts receivable	$ 250,930	$ 236,596
Inventories	86,102	85,439
	337,032	322,035
Investments	56,088	65,981
Property, plant and equipment		
Utility plant	1,496,630	1,303,449
Exploration and production properties	544,902	520,205
Pipelines	10,863	6,224
	2,052,395	1,829,878
Deferred charges and other	65,868	64,586
	$2,511,383	$2,282,480

(continued)

EXHIBIT 10 (cont.)

	1991	1990
Liabilities and Shareholders' Equity		
Current Liabilities		
Short term borrowings	$ 119,728	$ 132,429
Amounts payable	249,512	277,406
	369,240	409,835
Long term borrowings	996,994	874,833
Deferred income taxes	368,691	337,733
Minority interest	278,044	224,951
Shareholders' Equity		
Capital stock (Note 1)	388,340	347,265
Retained earnings	110,074	87,863
	498,414	435,128
	$2,511,383	$2,282,480

NOTE 1
CAPITAL STOCK

The Company is authorized to issue an unlimited number of Class A Preference Shares, Class B Preference Shares, Class 1 Preference Shares, Series 1, Class 1 Preference Shares, Series 2, and Common Shares.

	1991	1990	1991	1990
	(ISSUED SHARES)		(THOUSANDS)	
Class A				
Preference Shares	1,328,000	1,328,000	$ 16,600	$ 16,600
Class 1				
Preference Shares,				
Series 1	50	50	50,000	50,000
Class 1				
Preference Shares,				
Series 2	40	—	40,000	—
Common Shares	37,511,094	37,411,094	281,740	280,665
			$388,340	$347,265

EXHIBIT 11

Historical Mean Realized Rates of Return and Risk Premiums[a]

	ARITHMETIC AVERAGE	GEOMETRIC AVERAGE	STANDARD DEVIATION
Short Term Treasury Bill Returns			
(Statistics Canada series B14007)			
1950–1990	6.37%	6.29%	3.15%
1950–1970	3.34%	3.33%	1.50%
1971–1990	9.55%	9.49%	3.55%
1986–1990	10.34%	10.32%	3.23%
1989	11.95%	11.95%	3.52%
1990	13.30%	13.30%	3.94%
Long Term Government Bond Returns			
(Statistics Canada series 14013)			
1950–1990	6.00%	5.58%	9.83%
1950–1970	2.68%	2.49%	6.30%
1971–1990	9.47%	8.92%	11.53%
1986–1990	9.87%	9.67%	6.67%
1989	16.47%	16.47%	1.98%
1990	4.10%	4.10%	3.31%
Market Value Weighted Equity Total Returns[b]			
1950–1990	11.80%	10.47%	12.84%
1950–1970	11.31%	10.10%	11.70%
1971–1990	11.73%	10.86%	13.84%
1986–1990	5.72%	5.13%	11.18%
1989	16.01%	16.01%	4.15%
1990	−14.00%	−14.00%	4.49%

	ARITHMETIC AVERAGE	GEOMETRIC AVERAGE
Difference in Means of Equity Total Returns		
and Long Term Government Bond Returns		
1950–1990	5.80%	4.89%
1950–1970	8.63%	7.61%
1971–1990	2.76%	1.94%
1986–1990	−4.17%	−4.54%
1989	−0.46%	−0.46%
1990	−18.10%	−18.10%

[a]Supplied by case writer, yields from Bank of Canada Review.
[b]Based on all available Canadian common equities in the TSE/WBS data base.

21

LAWSON MARDON GROUP LIMITED— CORPORATE ASSET FUNDING FACILITY

In May 1989, Carl Galloway, Treasurer of Lawson Mardon Group Ltd. (LMG) was reviewing the company's current financial structure in light of an innovative financing alternative that had recently become available in Canada. It was Carl's objective to continue to pursue a financial strategy that provided the maximum flexibility for the company in terms of ability to raise funds in all financial markets under the most favourable terms. Carl had recently begun to investigate the possibility of asset securitization as a way to better utilize the company's existing asset base. More specifically, a proposal for the ongoing securitization of a portion of LMG's accounts receivable had been presented by Citibank Canada. Benefits held out in the proposal to LMG included lower financing costs, an improved return on assets and a reduction in leverage.

BACKGROUND ON THE COMPANY

LMG was formed on August 30, 1985 when LMG acquired the predecessor to Lawson Mardon and Lawson and Jones in a leveraged buyout (LBO) acquisition from BAT Industries, plc for an aggregate amount of $559.1 million. The acquisition was financed by $28.5 million of common equity, $98.3 million of subordinated

This case was prepared by Bill Quinn under the supervision of Professor Robert W. White for the sole purpose of providing material for class discussion at the Western Business School. Certain names and other identifying information may have been disguised to protect confidentiality. It is not intended to illustrate either effective or ineffective handling of a managerial situation. Any reproduction, in any form, of the material in this case is prohibited except with the written consent of the School.

debt and $432.3 million of secured bank debt. Approximately $80 million of the bank debt was hedged with an interest rate swap. The ownership of the company included management (20%), Roman Corporation (49%), the Lawson family (12%), Prudential Insurance (17%) and the Bank of Nova Scotia (2%).

LMG was an international company with manufacturing facilities in Canada, United Kingdom, United States, France, West Germany and Ireland. It should be noted that approximately 72.8% of LMG's revenues originated in the U.K. and Europe and 27.2% in North America. The company's corporate head office was located in Mississauga, Ontario. A fundamental aspect of LMG's strategy was to organize into five business groups: Flexible Packaging—Europe; Rigid Plastics and Metals—Europe; Folding Cartons—Europe; Graphics—North America; and Packaging—North America. LMG was a major supplier of packaging to the consumers good industry in the U.K. and Canada. A sample of the company's major customers is included in Exhibit 1. All businesses that did not fit with the core business were divested. LMG divested assets of $92.8 million within 15 months of completing the LBO and a further $22 million in fiscal year 1987.

LMG's successful divestiture program allowed it to renegotiate its banking lines on more favourable terms. In December 1986, LMG agreed to a new 5-year revolving term facility. The key improvements were in rates (LIBOR[1] and Bankers' Acceptances margins were reduced by approximately 75bp to 75bp) and the release of all security previously held by the Banks. An additional feature negotiated by LMG was a Multi-Option Facility (MOF) to be utilized in the United Kingdom.

The MOF, as the name suggests, provided a borrower with multiple financing options. In the case of LMG, borrowings might be denominated in dollars, sterling, and other major European currencies. Also, borrowings might be based on either LIBOR or Bills of Exchange[2] (similar to Canadian Bankers' Acceptances). The MOF had a third feature that was called a "tender panel." The tender panel was comprised of a group of financial institutions including syndicate members that bid on an uncommitted basis for unrated LMG short term notes usually less than 6 months.

Because the tender panel consisted of a closed group of bidders, rates were not as attractive as those available in commercial paper markets. The issuer was willing to pay a higher rate because the tender panel members bid for the paper on a consistent basis whereas this was not necessarily the case for commercial paper programs. As recently as August, 1988 LMG was paying a weighted average cost of LIBOR + 22bp on tender panel advances. Commercial paper would have cost approximately LIBOR + 5bp. In addition, the issuer continued to pay a standby fee

---

[1]LIBOR is the acronym for London Interbank Offered Rate and represents a series of borrowing rates available in London by major banks from around the world. LIBORs may be quoted in various currencies and for different time periods. LIBOR is a base rate for comparison in most financial markets for short term rates.

[2]A Bill of Exchange is a short term promissory note issued by a corporation accompanied by an unconditional guarantee of payment by a commercial bank. The notes are issued on a discounted basis and typically have maturities of up to 90 days.

of 0.125% p.a. on the unused portion of the committed facility. The standby fee can be viewed as an insurance premium on maintaining availability of the facility.

In May 1987, taking advantage of its improved balance sheet and profit levels as noted in Exhibit 2, LMG raised $216 million ($205 million net of fees and commissions) through an initial public offering of 49.46% of its equity. The stock offering included tranches in Canada, the United States and the United Kingdom. Through the use of multiple voting shares the original shareholders retained 73% voting control of the company. The stock was listed initially on the Toronto Stock Exchange (TSE), the Montreal Stock Exchange (MSE) and the American Stock Exchange (AMEX). In the spring of 1988 the stock was listed in London.

The improved balance sheet position allowed LMG to approach its bankers in December 1987 for further concessions. The loan margins were reduced by a further 25 bp and the per annum standby fee on the unused portion of the loan was reduced to 0.125% p.a. from 0.25% p.a. This pricing was consistent with the pricing received by companies of similar risk in the U.K. market. LMG also negotiated the removal of certain restrictive covenants and an increase in the sterling tranche of £15 million to £100 million. This provided LMG with greater flexibility to make significant acquisitions conditional on the financial covenant pattern being adhered to. This was important to the company as LMG had hoped to make acquisitions in the U.S. to balance its revenue between North America and Europe. Potential acquisitions of two to three times the size of LMG were being contemplated. It was management's view that an unrestricted and significant debt capacity would assist the company if an opportunity presented itself.

SECURITIZATION OF ASSETS

Generally, securitization was a process of disintermediation whereby high-cost providers of credit were displaced at a lower cost by institutional investors and the public capital market. Visible examples of this process were the loss by the commercial banking industry of high-quality corporate customers to the commercial paper market and the loss of middle-market borrowers to the speculative grade "junk" bond market.

The securitization of assets referred to the direct financing of pools of corporate assets in the institutional and public capital markets. The first major market in securitized assets was created in the early 1970s when the U.S. government, through agencies and quasi-agencies such as the Government National Mortgage Association (GNMA), the Federal Home Loan Mortgage Corporation (FHLMC) and the Federal National Mortgage Association (FNMA), developed marketable securities based on pools of residential mortgages.

Residential mortgages had traditionally been long term, illiquid financial instruments. The small dollar amount of each mortgage and the cumbersome documentation required to transfer title and service the loans had resulted in little investor interest by institutions and the public. As a result, residential mortgage capital was supplied by commercial banks and thrift institutions who originated, funded and administered the loans. To broaden the sources of mortgage capital, the agencies purchased mortgages from traditional lenders and issued marketable securities backed by the mortgage pools and the guarantee of the respective agency.[3] The popularity of mortgage-backed securities in the U.S. had grown rapidly, as evidenced by the estimated 1988 market size of U.S. $680 billion. In Canada, mortgage-backed securities were introduced for the first time in 1986 and it was estimated that new issues of pass-through securities totalled $400–$500 million in 1987.

In 1989, a wide variety of assets were being securitized. Securities backed by automobile loans dominated new issues with an estimated 70% of the market for securitized assets. Bonds backed by credit card receivables, a recent innovation, comprise an estimated 25% of new issues. Other assets being converted into marketable securities included unsecured consumer loans, computer and equipment leases, life insurance policy loans, and trade receivables.

ASSET-BACKED COMMERCIAL PAPER

LMG had been presented with a proposal by Citibank to securitize a portion of the company's accounts receivable through an asset-backed commercial paper program. Asset-backed commercial paper programs had been in use in the U.S. since the early 1980s, however, due to differences in tax and accounting regulations, they had only recently been adapted for use by Canadian corporations.

In an accounts receivable-backed commercial paper program, a single purpose corporation was established to purchase accounts receivable from participating companies and issue commercial paper in the public debt markets on an ongoing basis (see Exhibit 3). As the cash flow from the purchased assets did not directly correspond with the cash flow of the commercial paper issued, payments on the accounts receivable could be applied to the repayment of maturing commercial paper or be used to purchase additional accounts receivable from the participating companies. In many cases maturing commercial paper was refunded with new issues.

To obtain the highest commercial paper rating possible, the special purpose corporation was structured to be bankruptcy remote with the sole business of the corporation being the financing of accounts receivable. To protect against credit losses, credit enhancement was usually required. This took the form of either over-collateralization, third-party guarantees or recourse to the originator of the accounts receivables. In addition, the special purpose corporation usually maintained a liquidity line of credit with a commercial bank to support payment to holders of maturing commercial paper. This line of credit would only be utilitized in the event

---

[3]In the most popular form of mortgage-backed instrument, a pass-through security, the issuer places a pool of mortgages of similar term, interest rate, and quality in trust with a bank. Pass-through certificates, representing pro rata ownership interests in the pooled mortgages, are then sold to investors by the issuer. The trustee holding title to the pooled mortgages distributes principal and interest flows from the mortgages, less servicing and guarantee fees, to the investors.

that maturing commercial paper cannot be "rolled over" or if the bankruptcy of one of the originators interferes with the cash flow from purchased accounts receivable.

Under the Citibank proposal, LMG would enter into a five-year agreement to sell accounts receivable to Corporate Asset Funding Company (CAFCO), a special purpose corporation established in 1985 for the sole purpose of financing accounts receivable. CAFCO, a Delaware-based corporation, would issue commercial paper in the U.S. market. A maximum amount for accounts receivable purchased from LMG would be established; however, as accounts receivable were repaid, CAFCO would purchase additional accounts receivable from LMG to ensure that the maximum amount was constantly utilized. The agreement would have an "evergreen" feature which provided for an annual one year extension of the term of the agreement and an increase in the maximum amount of accounts receivable purchases, if necessary, to accommodate LMG's growth. LMG would continue to service and collect all accounts receivable sold to CAFCO and in turn would receive a nominal servicing fee. LMG's customers would not be aware that the accounts had been sold.

Participation in the CAFCO program was conditional upon an actuarial analysis of LMG's accounts receivable portfolio, including loss experience and concentration risk. This review would determine the amount of over-collateralization required for the acccounts receivable sold to CAFCO by LMG. For example, LMG might be required to provide additional accounts receivable as collateral in the amount of 5% of all receivables sold to CAFCO. In addition, LMG was required to maintain a level of credit worthiness equivalent to a BBB rating as determined by Citibank. A summary of industrial bond rating classifications is presented in Exhibit 4. If LMG experienced financial difficulty and dropped below a BBB rating, Citibank would step in to purchase the accounts receivable from LMG at a significantly higher cost than under the CAFCO program. This ensured that LMG would have a continual source of accounts receivable financing without jeopardizing the credit ratings of the CAFCO program. No other financial covenants or restrictions on LMG would exist under the program.

By restricting participation in the CAFCO program to credit worthy companies and by closely monitoring the quality of the accounts receivables purchased, CAFCO had been able to obtain Standard & Poor's and Moody's highest commercial paper credit ratings of A-1+ and P-1 respectively. These favourable ratings enabled CAFCO to access the commercial paper market at the lowest possible cost. A historical comparison of CAFCO funding costs with short term interest rate indexes is shown in Exhibit 5.

Proceeds paid to participants for accounts receivable sold to CAFCO are calculated on a discount basis. The discount rate is based on the cost of funding for CAFCO, including commission on commercial paper, liquidity line of credit fees and program operating costs. In addition, each participant pays a program fee based on the credit worthiness of the company. Although Carl had not finalized the program fee for LMG, he expected that the all-in cost of funding through the CAFCO program would be in the range of LIBOR + 25bp to LIBOR + 50bp. LMG would also be required to pay a one-time fee of up to 1% of the total amount of the agreement when the program was established.

Once the accounts receivable had been sold to CAFCO, LMG could remove the assets from the company's balance sheet. No further recourse to LMG existed. The discount paid on the sale of the accounts receivable was deductible by LMG for tax purposes.

LMG'S DECISION

Carl realized that some of the benefits of an accounts receivable-backed commercial paper program were obvious. Participation in the program provided an alternate committed five-year source of funding. The CAFCO program did not impose any additional financial restrictions on LMG beyond the maintenance of a BBB equivalent credit rating. Under LMG's existing banking agreement the company was free to sell its accounts receivable without the approval of the banking syndicate. In addition, the administration of the CAFCO program did not appear to necessitate any additional costs to LMG. LMG would continue to service and collect on all accounts receivable as it had done in the past.

Carl was, however, less certain of some of the other purported benefits of the program. LMG could remove the accounts receivable from its balance sheet. This would reduce the company's assets and liabilities if the proceeds of the sale were used to repay outstanding debt. In addition, the cost of the CAFCO program could be treated as deferred discount expense for accounting purposes, thereby reducing the company's reported interest expense. The reduction in accounts receivable would, in general, result in a lower current ratio. Carl wondered if the improved return on assets, reduced leverage and increased interest coverage resulting from this off balance sheet financing would result in an increased debt capacity for LMG.

Carl was also uncertain as to how the cost of the CAFCO program compared to LMG's existing sources of financing. As the CAFCO program actually removed assets from LMG's balance sheet, less equity financing was required to maintain a constant debt-to-equity ratio. LMG's target capital structure is long term debt to total capitalization of less than 50%, net of goodwill. LMG's cost of equity and debt were approximately 20% and 10%, respectively. Carl wondered if it would be more appropriate to compare the cost of funding under the CAFCO program to LMG's weighted average cost of capital, to a short term debt cost[4], or to a long term debt cost. Carl knew that all the firm's assets were supported by a mix of debt and equity. The CAFCO program seemed to provide quasi-equity because it could be used to fund 100% of the assets taken off the balance sheet.

In preliminary discussions with members of LMG's senior management, Carl had encountered some resistance to the idea of selling company assets as a source of additional financing. Carl felt that this resistance arose from the perception that LMG would be "factoring" its accounts receivable, a high cost financing technique

[4]The current rates on 1, 3 and 6 month LIBOR were 9.87%, 10.0% and 10.06%, respectively.

traditionally used only as a last resort by companies in financial difficulty. However, LMG's corporate strategy was growth via acquisitions. LMG's ability to respond quickly to potential acquisitions was dictated, in part, by their financial capacity, and an asset-backed commercial paper program could contribute significantly to the company's financing flexibility. Carl realized that to make a sound recommendation on the Citibank proposal he had to first clarify the benefits and costs in his own mind.

EXHIBIT 1

LAWSON MARDON GROUP LIMITED
Sample Customer List

NORTH AMERICA

Kraft	Chesebrough-Pond's
J.E. Seagram & Sons	Avon Canada
John Labatt	Imperial Tobacco
General Foods	Lowney's Nabisco
Playtex	Smith & Nephew
Brooke Bond	Johnson & Johnson
Shulton Canada	Charles of the Ritz
Canada Starch	Warner-Lambert
RJR MacDonald	Rothmans
Brown & Williamson	Eaton's
Woolco	Hudson's Bay
Robert Simpson	Paul Masson
Coca-Cola	Nestlè
Carnation	Quaker Oats
Consumers Distributing	Procter & Gamble

U.K.

Mars	Kellogg
Imperial Group	British Tissues
United Biscuits	Beecham
Nabisco Brands	Gallaher
Dalgety Spillers	Tate & Lyle
R.H.M.	Bass
Reckitt & Colman	Davies Brook
Unilever	Allied Lyons
Rowntree Mackintosh	ICI
Assoc. British Foods	Nestlè/Findus
Grand Metropolitan	Reed International
B.A.T. Industries	Hiram Walker
Cadbury Schweppes	St. Regis Packaging
HM Government Distillers	Paterson Zachonis
	General Foods

EXHIBIT 2

LAWSON MARDON GROUP LIMITED
Financial Statements
Balance Sheets
($000s)

	YEAR ENDED DECEMBER 31			
	1988	1987	1986	1985
Assets				
Current Assets				
Cash	$ 533	$ 6,848	$ 3,709	$ 2,928
Accounts Receivable	171,513	174,853	137,492	127,036
Inventory	129,800	137,241	104,964	99,720
Prepaid Expenses	6,617	5,681	8,752	5,751
Due from Associated Companies	2,331			
	310,794	324,615	257,917	235,435
Long Term Assets				
Fixed Assets	278,530	286,137	219,985	211,490
Investments	16,663		12,898	20,534
Other	6,235	6,728	10,822	48,400
Pension Excess	52,277	32,408	14,244	
Goodwill	165,191	181,817	169,805	173,726
Total Assets	$829,690	$831,705	$679,004	$689,585
Liabilities and Shareholders' Equity				
Current Liabilities				
Bank Indebtedness	$ 11,983	$ 7,414	$ 10,003	$ 8,736
Accounts Payable and Accruals	204,619	233,657	185,381	150,765
Dividends Payable		5,769		
Income Taxes Payable	7,851	15,816	1,281	5,554
Current Portion of Long Term Debt	8,444	3,520	4,089	3,557
	232,897	266,176	200,757	168,612
Long Term Liabilities				
Income Taxes Payable	1,178	3,593	7,894	650
Long Term Debt	129,848	118,316	197,014	258,207
Subordinated Debt	98,164	104,042	164,569	170,591
Deferred Taxes	41,590	42,954	42,198	48,379
	270,780	268,905	411,675	477,827
Shareholders' Equity				
Share Capital	250,072	250,080	43,700	35,771
Retained Earnings	74,424	41,127	19,235	4,794
Cumulative Translation	1,517	5,057	3,657	2,581
	326,013	296,264	66,592	43,146
Total Liabilities and Shareholders' Equity	$829,690	$831,705	$679,004	$689,585

EXHIBIT 2 (cont.)

LAWSON MARDON GROUP LIMITED
Income Statement
($000s)

| | YEAR ENDED DECEMBER 31 | | |
	1988	1987	1986
Sales	$1,110,533	$1,034,699	$890,974
Operating Expenses			
Cost of Sales and Operating Expenses	855,601	810,808	703,210
Selling and General Expenses	132,814	103,973	85,066
Depreciation	38,969	33,050	29,111
	1,027,384	947,831	817,387
Earnings From Operations	83,149	86,868	73,587
Other Income (Expenses)			
Interest Expense	(33,608)	(37,390)	(48,737)
Amortization of Goodwill	(4,649)	(4,511)	(4,537)
Income from Associated Companies	(97)		1,652
Unusual Items	8,750	(3,073)	—
Earnings Before Taxes	53,545	41,894	22,145
Income Taxes	11,597	14,233	7,704
Earnings	$ 41,948	$ 27,661	$ 14,441
Earning per share	$1.45	$1.20	$0.94
Weighted average number of shares outstanding (000's)	28,838	22,978	15,295

EXHIBIT 3

Structure of an Asset-Backed CP Programme

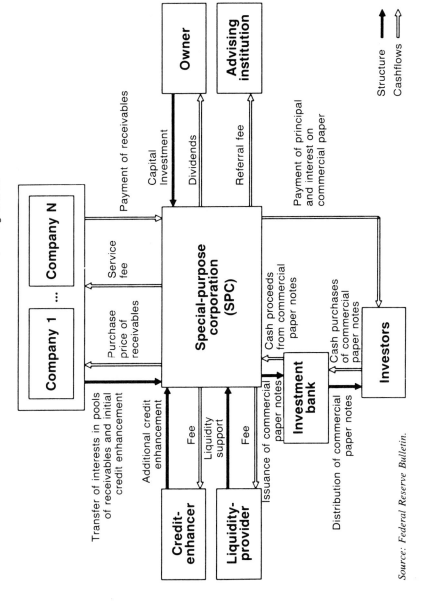

Source: Federal Reserve Bulletin.

EXHIBIT 4

Summary of Industrial Bond Rating Classifications
Financial Measurement and Statistics
Median Values 1987

Measurements	Aaa/AAA	Aa/AA	A/A	Baa/BBB	Ba/BB	B/B
Measurements						
Interest Coverage	14.07X	8.44X	5.61X	3.64X	2.07X	1.73X
Interest Coverage (Inc. Rents)	8.17X	5.59X	3.49X	2.41X	1.70X	1.41X
After Tax Coverage	10.05X	5.81X	3.87X	2.54X	1.85X	1.40X
After Tax Coverage (Inc. Rents)	6.46X	3.98X	2.53X	1.85X	1.51X	1.27X
LTD/LT Capitalization	10.73%	20.36%	29.35%	34.52%	48.10%	48.72%
Total Debt/Total Capital	19.80%	31.24%	35.03%	38.64%	50.71%	51.85%
Long Term Debt/Net Plant	16.99%	29.39%	47.14%	54.96%	69.10%	102.21%
Net Tangible Assets/LTD	767.54%	431.27%	285.08%	242.63%	178.80%	191.84%
Net Tang. Assets/Total Debt	420.93%	299.39%	232.79%	202.62%	172.30%	170.00%
Total Liabilities/Stock Equity	78.31%	127.35%	119.03%	147.75%	186.89%	181.23%
Cash Flow/Short Term Debt	343.09%	318.43%	382.65%	418.62%	425.58%	218.83%
Cash Flow/Total Debt	103.10%	70.88%	48.65%	35.37%	30.55%	14.77%
Working Capital/LTD	348.89%	122.92%	78.01%	70.00%	50.24%	83.69%

Current Ratio	2.00X	1.45X	1.67X	1.54X	1.81X	2.04X
Cash Flow/Current Liabilities	64.24%	45.00%	48.52%	42.81%	48.97%	32.19%
Net Cash Flow/Capital Expend	149.65%	149.46%	125.51%	117.04%	123.40%	74.03%
Return on Equity	18.46%	18.63%	14.67%	11.68%	10.69%	9.11%
Return on Assets	17.78%	15.53%	12.99%	10.72%	10.03%	7.19%
Return on Permanent Capital	14.83%	20.35%	16.79%	14.21%	13.86%	9.31%
Statistics						
Cash and Equivalents	1148.20M	519.93M	112.00M	72.60M	48.36M	36.88M
Net Plant	1948.00M	2554.00M	891.20M	531.90M	397.00M	102.16M
Total Assets	6922.60M	6181.00M	2398.24M	1599.08M	1123.60M	385.41M
Long Term Debt	435.00M	762.60M	473.02M	347.49M	315.40M	140.17M
Stockholders' Equity	3882.40M	2629.07M	1008.51M	588.24M	308.76M	101.56M
Net Sales	6170.30M	8258.40M	2898.06M	1703.53M	1514.43M	328.93M
Net Income	906.40M	480.00M	148.16M	52.44M	35.00M	8.21M
Capital Expenditures	344.10M	486.63M	179.75M	99.49M	79.30M	20.38M
Funds From Operations (FFO)	1049.80M	796.79M	305.47M	140.84M	116.95M	20.60M
Number of Companies	11	36	109	64	41	66

Source: *1987 Financial Measurement Handbook for Industrial Companies*, First Boston, 1988.

EXHIBIT 5

Historical Comparison of CAFCO Funding Costs[a]

1984 AVERAGES	DISCOUNT BASIS			INTEREST IN ARREARS BASIS				
	PROGRAM	FED INDEX[b]	SPREAD	PROGRAM	DMMB[c]	SPREAD	LIBOR	SPREAD
January	9.34%	9.21%	0.126%	9.44%	9.81%	-0.372%	9.74%	-0.297%
February	9.50	9.39	0.107	9.62	9.97	-0.355	9.96	-0.346
March	9.91	9.80	0.106	10.04	10.37	-0.328	10.34	-0.298
April	10.27	10.16	0.113	10.38	10.72	-0.343	10.71	-0.330
May	10.68	10.46	0.217	10.80	11.24	-0.440	11.13	-0.321
June	10.93	10.78	0.143	11.08	11.48	-0.405	11.40	-0.328
July	11.25	11.06	0.190	11.39	11.79	-0.402	11.67	-0.284
August	11.29	11.16	0.123	11.47	11.87	-0.401	11.80	-0.331
September	11.15	11.07	0.081	11.30	11.69	-0.392	11.61	-0.313
October	10.11	10.04	0.071	10.24	10.63	-0.394	10.57	-0.330
November	9.04	8.98	0.061	9.14	9.49	-0.359	9.38	-0.242
December	8.65	8.58	0.078	8.74	9.08	-0.338	9.02	-0.279
1984 Averages	10.18%	10.06%	0.118%	10.30%	10.68%	-0.377%	10.61%	-0.308%

1985

January	8.05%	7.99%	0.063%	8.12%	8.45%	−0.329%	8.33%	−0.208%
February	8.51	8.46	0.049	8.57	8.92	−0.349	8.77	−0.204
March	8.81	8.75	0.053	8.88	9.20	−0.320	9.07	−0.184
April	8.34	8.30	0.037	8.41	8.76	−0.342	8.62	−0.207
May	7.85	7.82	0.029	7.90	8.23	−0.330	8.10	−0.199
June	7.38	7.34	0.042	7.43	7.75	−0.317	7.67	−0.238
July	7.61	7.59	0.022	7.66	7.97	−0.311	7.92	−0.260
August	7.75	7.73	0.025	7.80	8.13	−0.332	8.00	−0.198
September	7.86	7.83	0.036	7.92	8.25	−0.325	8.17	−0.232
October	7.85	7.81	0.038	7.90	8.20	−0.299	8.10	−0.204
November	7.87	7.84	0.030	7.93	8.19	−0.257	8.16	−0.231
December	7.90	7.86	0.040	7.96	8.27	−0.313	8.27	−0.312
1985 Averages	7.98%	7.94%	0.039%	8.04%	8.36%	−0.319%	8.27%	−0.223%

[a]All rates exclude dealer commissions. The Program, FED Index, DMMB and LIBOR rates are for comparable maturities (usually 30 or 60 days).

[b]Federal Reserve Index of AA rated, industrial company, commercial paper issuers.

[c]Domestic Money Market Bid rate (CDs including reserves and FDIC expense).

22

TANZI PUMP CORPORATION

In January 1987, Sophia Ferrara, marketing vice president of Tanzi Pump Corporation, was faced with a significant sales management challenge involving capital investment by the company's customers. During 1986, the company reported pump sales of $177 million, primarily to the petroleum refining and chemical industries. Sales were organized through a system of salaried sales representatives who sold directly to industrial users. These representatives were highly knowledgeable about the specifications and uses of the company's pumps. For many years they had performed effectively on the basis of engineering competence, well-developed contacts with purchasing agents and a strong service organization.

INTRODUCTION OF A NEW PUMP

In 1986, the research and development department of Tanzi made a significant technological breakthrough which had dramatic implications for the future growth of the company. Specifically they had developed a large, powerful, computer-directed switching pump for petroleum refiners and chemical plants which, it appeared, might make obsolete many other pumps in their hydraulic pump line. The new pump, called Tanzi-Power III, had been tentatively priced at $260,000 per unit. The advantage of the new pump was that it required significantly less labour, including maintenance and monitoring, than was the case with other combinations of pumps. This had the effect of reducing labour costs by an amount equal to $52,000 per year. In addition, some savings in the electric power bill of customers could be expected with the more efficient Tanzi-Power III pump. Total labour and electricity savings the first year were estimated to be $60,000, and, with inflation, these savings were expected to increase at a 5 percent compound rate per year. In other words, year 2 expected savings would be $63,000, year 3, $66,150, and so forth. For calculation purposes, it was assumed that the pumps Tanzi-Power III replaced had no salvage value or further remaining depreciation.

The new pump had an economic life of eight years. At the end of its useful life, year 8, it was expected to have a value of $30,000. Ms. Ferrara assumed that all of the company's customers used the cost recovery system under the 1986 Tax Reform Act, the features of which are described in the subsequent note. The pump falls into the 5-year property class with respect to cost recovery (depreciation). Any expected salvage value at the end is ignored when figuring the cost basis for depreciation. However, as the pump will be fully depreciated after five and a half years, the salvage value realized at the end of eight years must be treated as a recapture of depreciation for tax purposes. As a result, the estimated salvage value will be taxed at the ordinary income tax rate. For purposes of analysis, Ms. Ferrara assumed that customers of Tanzi paid an effective corporate tax rate (federal and state) of 38 percent. Finally, all cash flows were assumed to occur at the end of the year whereas the initial outlay was assumed to occur at time 0.

MARKETING THE PUMP

The challenge facing Tanzi and its sales management was that virtually all of their existing pumps were priced under $40,000 and were purchased by plant manager customers without the nuisance of a full capital expenditure analysis. With a $260,000 purchase, however, most customers had to prepare a full "capital expenditure analysis" which was then sent to headquarters for approval. (A sample is shown in Exhibit 1.) Since the plant managers that Tanzi sales representatives met were uncomfortable with these reports, they tended to shy away from "big ticket" items such as a new pump. Instead, they had a preference for less expensive equipment which did not necessitate formal justification. The feelings of many customers were summarized by one fertilizer manufacturing superintendent in Bakersfield, California, who told the Tanzi sales representative:

> Vinny, that new pump of yours is terrific. I sure could use it, but I am reluctant to try and sell the idea to our headquarters. Frankly, I have never been able to understand how to deal with the analysis they require on investments over $100,000. They want everything justified in terms of discounted cash flow, in addition to the standard payback and ROI calculations we use at the plant level. Unless you can help me with the financial side of the deal, I can't consider a purchase.

This new development meant that Tanzi's sales representatives had to be trained in capital investment analysis, to supplement their technical skills, contacts, and service ability. Ms. Ferrara was faced with the challenge of bringing the company's sales representatives "up to speed" in capital budgeting as quickly and as simply as possible. Otherwise they would be at a loss in trying to sell the new pump.

THE DISCOUNT RATE AND PRICING

Another consideration was whether the price of the new pump should be adjusted downward from the tentative price in order to meet the prevailing return requirements of 13 percent after taxes in the petroleum and chemical industries. Prices of new Tanzi products had traditionally been "cost determined." That is, a desired profit margin was added to the cost per unit. In the case of the Tanzi-Power III pump, management wished to experiment with a "market determined" price, based on the value of the product to the customer. One member of the marketing department even thought that the tentative price of $260,000 should be increased if the actual rate of return was greater than the 13 percent target rate of many customers. However, others were concerned with leaving customers some profits, while yet another worried that all customers might not adjust upward for inflation-expected savings in year 2 and beyond.

TANZI-POWER III PUMP

1. Cost:	$260,000.
2. Life:	8 years.
3. Depreciation:	Declining-balance and straight-line methods described in Note.
4. Labour and electricity savings:	$60,000 the first year, which increases by 5 percent per year through year 8.
5. Salvage value:	$30,000 assumed at the end of year 8.
6. Tax rate:	38% of pre-tax profits.
7. Required rate of return:	13% after taxes.

NOTE ON DEPRECIATION

Under the 1986 Tax Reform Act, there are seven property classes for cost recovery (depreciation) purposes. The property category in which an asset falls determines its depreciable life for tax purposes.

> *3-year class.* Includes property with a midpoint life of 4 years or less. The midpoint life of various types of assets under the asset depreciation range (ADR) system is determined by the Treasury Department.

> *5-year class.* Includes property with an ADR midpoint life of 4 to 10 years. Included in this class are most machinery, automobiles, light trucks, most technological and semi-conductor equipment, switching equipment, small power production facilities and research and experimental equipment.

> *7-year class.* Includes property with an ADR midpoint of 10 to 16 years, and railroad truck and single purpose agriculture structures.

> *10-year class.* Includes property with an ADR midpoint life of 16 to 20 years.

> *15-year class.* Includes property with an ADR midpoint of 20 to 25 years, and municipal waterway treatment plants and telephone distribution plants.

> *20-year class.* Includes property with an ADR midpoint of 25 years or more, other than real property discussed below.

> *$27\frac{1}{2}$-year class.* Includes residential rental property.

For the 3-year, 5-year, 7-year and 10-year property classes, the method of depreciation is the 200% declining balance method. This method switches to straight line in the year which provides the quickest writeoff. Moreover, a half-year convention is used in the first year and in the year following the last year. For the 15-year and 20-year property classes, 150% declining balance depreciation is used with subsequent switching to straight line. Finally, for the $27\frac{1}{2}$-year class, straight-line depreciation is used throughout.

To illustrate for the 5-year property class, assume an asset costing $10,000 is acquired at the start of the year. The formula for the declining balance method is $(m \times (1/n))$ where m is the multiplier and n is the number of years in the property category. For our example, $2 \times (1/5) = 40$ percent. However, in the first year the one-half year convention is employed so first year depreciation is 20 percent, or $2,000. At the end of the third year, it is favourable to switch to straight-line depreciation. Thus, the depreciation schedule is:

YEAR	DEPRECIATION	DEPRECIATION	BALANCE
0			$10,000
1	0.2 × $10,000	$2,000	8,000
2	0.4 × $8,000	3,200	4,800
3	0.4 × $4,800	1,920	2,880
4	2,880 ÷ 2.5 years	1,152	1,728
5	2,880 ÷ 2.5 years	1,152	576
6	2,880 × 0.2	576	0

At the beginning of the fourth year, the balance remaining is divided by the remaining life to get straight-line depreciation. The remaining life is $2\frac{1}{2}$ years, owing to the half-year convention in the sixth year. Finally, in the sixth year the remaining balance is $576, or one-fifth of the balance at the end of the third year.

Instead of making such calculations, the Treasury publishes depreciation percentages (to 2 decimal points) of original cost for each property class. For the 5-year property class, they are:

YEAR	PERCENTAGE DEPRECIATION
1	20.00%
2	32.00
3	19.20
4	11.52
5	11.52
6	5.76

These percentages correspond exactly to the numbers employed above, and should be used.

EXHIBIT 1
Sample Cover Sheet of Capital Expenditure Analysis

Division _____

Location _____

Date _____

Project Name _____   Location _____

Project Sponsor _____ (individual's name and location)

Project Description (summary):

Project Type:
△ Cost Reduction
△ Extension of Existing Business or Product Line
△ New Business or Product
△ Supplement or Overrun for an Approved Project
△ Replacement of Existing Assets
△ Environment of Safety
△ Other _____

Project Priority:*
○ High priority
○ Required
○ Deferrable

*Sponsor's Judgment

Project Economics (summary): Payback Period _____   Average ROI _____

DCF Rate of Return _____ NPV _____ Life (years) _____

Project Investment ($000):

_____

Breakdown of Investment:
Fixed Assets   _____
Working Capital   _____
Capitalized Expense (if any) _____
Transferred Investment   _____
    Total Invesment   _____ (authority
                                               limit)

Project Timing:
Commitment Quarter (Q) _____ (year and quarter of start of investment)
Expenditure Forecast: Quarter   Q   _____   Q + 4 _____
                                         Q + 1 _____   Q + 5 _____
                                         Q + 2 _____   Q + 6 _____
                                         Q + 3 _____   Q + 7 _____
                                                            Beyond 2 years

23

MINNOVA INC.—LAC SHORTT MINE

In early June 1988, John Carrington, Senior Vice President at Minnova Inc., was preparing a presentation for the Minnova Board of Directors. He had just received from the Lac Shortt Mine manager the preliminary data necessary for him to decide whether to recommend an extension of the Lac Shortt gold mine from its present 500 metre depth to 830 metres. With this information Carrington wanted to determine if the estimated $19.425 million investment met the company's proposed rate of return and, at the same time, to consider any other business factors relevant to the decision.

THE MINING INDUSTRY

Mining was a highly capital-intensive business with a cost structure made up mainly of fixed components. In establishing a mine, significant up-front exploration costs, preproduction and development expenditures, and large investments in fixed assets were necessary. Because most mines were located in fairly remote areas, preparation for production was often a long and expensive process (for example, roads to the site might have to be built, large equipment would have to be transported in, etc.). As well, hiring the necessary labour force was usually a time-consuming task.

This case was prepared by Rhonda L. English under the supervision of Professor Claude Lanfranconi for the sole purpose of providing material for class discussion at the Western Business School. Certain names and other identifying information may have been disguised to protect confidentiality. It is not intended to illustrate either effective or ineffective handling of a managerial situation. The case was funded through the Plan For Excellence, with a research grant from the Society of Management Accountants of Ontario. Any reproduction, in any form, of the material in this case is prohibited except with the written consent of the School.

Selected mining terminology is defined in Exhibit 1, while Appendix A briefly describes the gold mining process.

MINNOVA INC.

The history of Minnova Inc. dated back to 1928 when Ventures Limited and Falconbridge Nickel were established. These two companies conducted mine exploration and development around the world through an organization of associated companies. The merger of Opemiska Copper Mines (Quebec) and Lake Dufault Mines in 1971 created Falconbridge Copper, which later became Corporation Falconbridge Copper (CFC). In August 1986, Kerr Addison Mines Limited, which was controlled by Noranda Mines, acquired just over 50% interest in CFC and changed the name to Minnova Inc.

Minnova was a natural resource company involved in the exploration, development, and mining of copper, zinc, gold and silver. Exhibit 2 details the extent of Minnova operations throughout Canada and the United States. Exhibit 3 highlights Minnova's financial position for fiscal 1987 and the first three months of 1988. Although the company reported a positive net income for financial purposes, accumulated writeoffs in the form of Capital Cost Allowance (CCA) provisions and deferred exploration expenditures resulted in Minnova not being taxable currently, nor was it expected to be in the near future. In 1988, the company had a statutory tax rate of 47%.

While a mine was producing, Minnova would conduct exploration within a large area surrounding the site. The objective was to find another ore body which could be brought on stream by the time the original was exhausted. If a nearby ore deposit were discovered, costs could be greatly reduced since existing mine facilities and labour could then be utilized. As a result of this strategy, much time and money were dedicated to ongoing exploration and, as long as a mine was producing, the search would continue. Maximizing returns from mining and processing, and locating new ore deposits to replace exhausted ones, were essential factors to the continued profitability of a mining company.

THE LAC SHORTT MINE

Background

Located in Gand township, Quebec, the Lac Shortt Mine cost roughly $51 million, including exploration, to bring into production. It began operations in December 1984. Ore reserves between the surface and the 500 metre level, including a 15% dilution factor, were estimated at 2,239,596 tonnes with a head grade of 5.30 grams of gold per metric tonne. Annual production capacity was 400,000 tonnes per year, resulting in a mine life of about 5.6 years. By June 1, 1988, 1,338,198 tonnes of ore at 4.99 grams per tonne had been mined, producing 198,773 ounces of gold. Exhibit 4 summarizes historical production data at Lac Shortt.

To extend the life of the mine and replace the depleted ore, exploration of the area surrounding the mine site was ongoing. Although to date no other major ore reserve deposits had been located, important showings had been found and there remained significant opportunity for discovery in the unexplored areas.

Once mining from the 500 metre level in the original mine began in January 1988, extension of the ore limits below that level was possible, and therefore explored. A vertical longitudinal section of the mine is illustrated in Exhibit 5. As outlined, exploration drilling from a northwest crosscut was undertaken, intersecting the ore zone as deep as the 800 level. For each exploratory drill point the grams of gold per ore tonne and the width in metres of the ore body at that point were determined. Since the drill intersections cut the ore zone diagonally, the metre figures were converted to a horizontal distance across the ore body. Minimum requirements of 3 grams of gold per tonne with a horizontal width of at least 2 metres were being sought.

From the drilling results, it appeared that the reserves below 500 metres were open to the east and beneath, although the width of the ore body seemed to be decreasing with depth. Diluted ore reserve estimates between 500 and 800 metres were 885,000 tonnes with a head grade of 4.6 grams per metric tonne. This head grade was equivalent to 0.148 ounces of gold per tonne of ore. A 93% recovery rate from the milling process was expected.

The Proposed Development

Following analysis of several alternative methods of deepening the mine, conventional shaft sinking and simultaneous ramping down were decided upon, mainly due to shorter and more flexible scheduling. As indicated on Exhibit 5, the project involved:

- driving a decline from 500 metres to 830 metres;
- developing the 800, 750, and 700 levels and facilities;
- deepening the shaft to the 830 metre point;
- installing loading facilities and developing two stations at the 800 and 700 levels;
- installing a crusher on the 800 level and a conveyor to transfer ore to the shaft; and
- increasing the capacity of the existing tailings pond and developing an appropriate effluent treatment system.

Lac Shortt personnel would complete the ramping and lateral development, while the shaft deepening was to be subcontracted out to the lowest tender.

The $19.425 million investment consisted of preproduction costs and fixed asset costs. The former, amounting to $14,467 million, were composed primarily of shaft deepening, ramping, and developing the underground levels/facilities. For tax purposes, these capital expenditures fell into CCA Class 12 which had a 100% CCA rate. The fixed assets included both surface ($2,250 million) and underground ($2,708 million) equipment, all of which could be written off under CCA Class 41 at 25% per year. Exhibit 6 details the breakdown of expenditures between the two classes for 1988, 1989, and 1990, at which time the extension would be complete.

Mining would begin in 1990 with expected production that year of 330,000 tonnes of ore. Production of 360,000 and 195,000 tonnes was forecast for 1991 and 1992, respectively, at which time the estimated reserves would be exhausted.

The market price of gold was expected to average US$450 per ounce with an exchange rate of US$1 equal to CA$1.22. Historical gold prices and exchange rates are documented in Exhibit 7. Operating costs were calculated on a per tonne of ore mined basis and were expected to decrease as follows, over the three years of production:

> 1990—$50.05/tonne
> 1991—$48.05/tonne
> 1992—$40.74/tonne

CONCLUSION

Minnova Inc. used a range of hurdle rates in assessing investment proposals. These rates were set at 12% for no risk projects (e.g. equipment replacements), 15% for marginal risk projects, and 20% for highly risky investments. Carrington decided that the Lac Shortt proposal fell into the 15% category. Given the uncertainty involved in a number of the factors used in the analysis, he wanted to ensure that he would be prepared to answer any questions the Board might have regarding the sensitivity of the projected return. If the Board rejected the investment proposal, Carrington would be faced with deciding whether to keep the Lac Shortt mine open to continue further exploration projects in the area.

EXHIBIT 1

Glossary of Mining Terms

Ore Reserve Grade. The estimated amount of gold, in grams per tonne of ore, derived from calculations, based on geological interpretation and drill intersection results.

Estimated Head Grade. The estimated amount of gold, in grams per tonne of ore, which will enter the mill for processing. Generally, this will be lower than the ore reserve grade due to dilution and other mining losses.

Head Grade. The actual amount of gold, in grams per tonne of ore, which enters the mill, based on detailed sampling of the mill feed.

Dilution. The reduction in the ore reserve grade caused by waste or low grade ore outside the reserve being incorporated into the actual mining method, and therefore included in processing.

Recovery. The percentage of gold actually retrieved from processing the ore. As described in Appendix A, the gold must be on the surface of the crushed particle to be retrievable.

Tailings Pond. A repository for all liquid and solid wastes from the milling process.

Mill. The place where the ore is ground to a slurry and mixed with cyanide to dissolve the gold. Subsequently, the gold is recovered from the cyanide solution as bullion.

EXHIBIT 2

OPERATION LOCATIONS

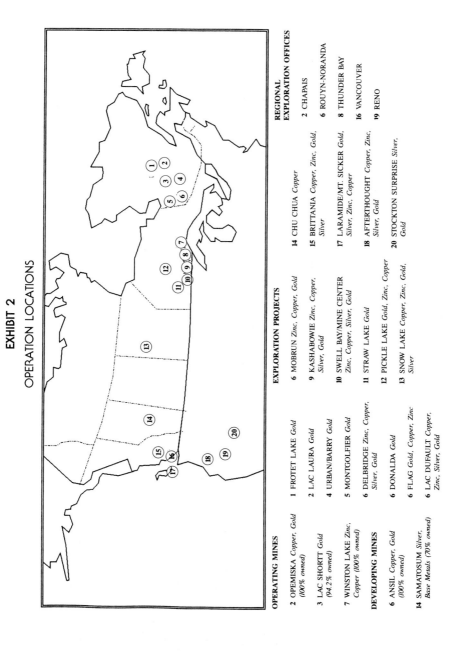

OPERATING MINES

2 OPEMISKA *Copper, Gold (100% owned)*

3 LAC SHORTT *Gold (94.2% owned)*

7 WINSTON LAKE *Zinc, Copper (100% owned)*

DEVELOPING MINES

6 ANSIL *Copper, Gold (100% owned)*

14 SAMATOSUM *Silver, Base Metals (70% owned)*

1 FROTET LAKE *Gold*

2 LAC LAURA *Gold*

4 URBAN/BARRY *Gold*

5 MONTGOLFIER *Gold*

6 DELBRIDGE *Zinc, Copper, Silver, Gold*

6 DONALDA *Gold*

6 FLAG *Gold, Copper, Zinc*

6 LAC DUFAULT *Copper, Zinc, Silver, Gold*

EXPLORATION PROJECTS

6 MOBRUN *Zinc, Copper, Gold*

9 KASHABOWIE *Zinc, Copper, Silver, Gold*

10 SWELL BAY/MINE CENTER *Zinc, Copper, Silver, Gold*

11 STRAW LAKE *Gold*

12 PICKLE LAKE *Gold, Zinc, Copper*

13 SNOW LAKE *Copper, Zinc, Gold, Silver*

14 CHU CHUA *Copper*

15 BRITTANIA *Copper, Zinc, Gold, Silver*

17 LARAMIDE/MT. SICKER *Gold, Silver, Zinc, Copper*

18 AFTERTHOUGHT *Copper, Zinc, Silver, Gold*

20 STOCKTON SURPRISE *Silver, Gold*

REGIONAL EXPLORATION OFFICES

2 CHAPAIS

6 ROUYN-NORANDA

8 THUNDER BAY

16 VANCOUVER

19 RENO

281

EXHIBIT 3

MINNOVA INC.
Financial Highlights
($000s)

	YEAR ENDED DEC. 31 1987	3 MONTHS ENDED MARCH 31 1988
Net Sales	$ 55,030	$14,729
Cost of Production	37,349	10,626
Net Income	3,257	415
Earnings Per Share	$0.24	$0.03
Current Assets	$107,754	$82,041
Net Plant and Equipment	13,085	42,935
Net Preproduction and Dev't Costs	6,477	42,826
Properties Under Dev't	98,674	63,080
Current Liabilities	16,227	14,330
Retained Earnings	116,958	115,068

EXHIBIT 4

Lac Shortt Historical Production Data

	1984[a]	1985	1986	1987	1988[b]
Tonnes milled	61,431	315,565	399,647	395,747	165,808
Grade (grams per tonne)	4.03	5.62	5.32	4.53	4.48
Recovery (%)	90.6	90.0	93.7	93.2	93.4
Total ounces[c]	7,215	51,300	64,031	53,889	22,338
Direct Operating Costs (dollars per tonne)	—	53.01	46.57	48.26	52.42
Operating Costs Incl. Exploration	—	53.78	49.65	53.99	57.08

[a]Preproduction.

[b]To June 1, 1988.

[c]Total ounces = tonnes milled × grade × recovery ÷ 31.1 (difference in actual ounces and formula result is due to rounding).

EXHIBIT 5

MINNOVA INC—DIV. LAC SHORTT

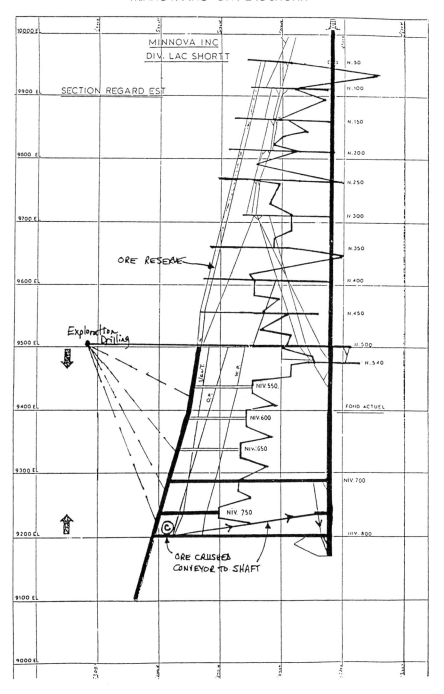

EXHIBIT 6

Investments by CCA Class

	1988	1989	1990	TOTAL
Preproduction Costs (CCA 12)	$2,674,100	$11,599,500	$193,800	$14,467,400
Fixed Assets (CCA 41)	1,377,900	2,950,900	629,000	4,957,800
Total	$4,052,000	$14,550,400	$822,800	$19,425,200

EXHIBIT 7

Historical Gold Prices and Exchange Rates

YEAR	GOLD US$/OZ.	EXCHANGE	GOLD CA$/OZ.
1980	$612.56	1.1968	$733.11
1981	459.71	1.1989	551.15
1982	375.79	1.2338	463.65
1983	424.18	1.2324	522.76
1984	360.44	1.2951	466.81
1985	317.26	1.3655	433.22
1986	367.51	1.3895	510.65
1987	446.47	1.3260	592.02

APPENDIX A
The Mining of Gold

Once an orebody has been located and the mine prepared for production, the mining and processing of the ore containing the gold can be initiated. The ore is drilled, blasted and transported to an underground crusher where it is crushed to approximately 6 inches in size. Once hoisted to the surface, it undergoes further crushing and grinding in water, to the consistency of a very fine slurry. To this slurry is added cyanide which attacks and dissolves any exposed gold on the surfaces of the ground ore particles. The recovery rate in the milling process reflects the efficiency of the dissolving capacity of the cyanide as well as the fineness of grind—the finer the grind, the greater the amount of gold that appears on the surface of an individual ore particle. The gold in the cyanide solution is separated from the ground ore slurry which goes to a tailings pond for final deposition. The cyanide/gold solution is subsequently sent through large steel cylinders which contain numerous racks of activated carbon. The gold in the solution is attracted to and deposits itself on the carbon as it passes over the racks. The final process is the burning off of the carbon, leaving the pure gold bullion.

24

GOLD INDUSTRY NOTE

BRIEF HISTORY OF CANADIAN GOLD MINING INDUSTRY

More than 400 years ago Jacques Cartier came to the New World searching for gold and precious metals but he returned to France with a ship full of "fool's gold" (iron pyrite). What Cartier never got to see was the New Land full of minerals, enough to give Canada second place in terms of metal-producing countries and to establish itself as one of the world's most diversified mining resource countries with over 60 different minerals. As immigrants came to Canada and developed vast means of transportation, explosive opportunities emerged for prospectors and the mining industry. In fact, it was the blasting for the construction of the Canadian Pacific Railway that unearthed the great nickel–copper deposits of the Sudbury Basin. From this, numerous more discoveries were found including the Klondike, coal in Nova Scotia and British Columbia, copper and lead in Newfoundland, asbestos in Quebec and copper, silver and iron in Ontario.

Today, the Canadian mining industry has matured into a world leader in nickel and asbestos production, ranking third in the output of gold and silver. The North American Gold Industry is made up of approximately seventeen large mining companies and numerous medium and small companies. The largest capitalization

This note was prepared by Linda Atkinson and Tom Johnston under the supervision of Professor Robert W. White for the sole purpose of providing material for class discussion at the Western Business School. Certain names and other identifying information may have been disguised to protect confidentiality. It is not intended to illustrate either effective or ineffective handling of a managerial situation. Any reproduction, in any form, of the material in this case is prohibited except with the written consent of the School.

companies include (in descending order): Newmont Gold Company, Placer Dome, Echo Bay Mines, Homestake Mining, American Barrick and Hemlo Gold Mines.[1]

BRIEF REVIEW OF MINE DEVELOPMENT

In this section, we shall consider the various steps involved in developing a deposit from prospecting to production.

- *Geological surveys.* A preliminary survey of a favourable environment, by use of geological mapping, geophysics, and/or geochemistry will usually result in the location of a certain number of prospects. If one of these prospects locates a mineralized zone, the next step is to verify the existence of the mineralization and to provide a qualitative description of it, using wide area sampling methods. The first estimations will tend to be more qualitative than quantitative, as will the geologists' image of the deposit.

- *Systematic surveys and sampling.* Usually consists of drilling on a large and more or less regular grid, covering the mineralized zone, to evaluate the overall *in situ* reserves by tonnages and mean grades. Some in-fill drilling (reducing the grid size) or drilling in adjacent zones may be required. At this point the geologist and engineer are faced with two problems: to determine if the deposit is economically viable and to express the confidence that can be given to the estimations. A substantial amount of drilling is often needed before a full-fledged sampling campaign takes place due to the large expenses incurred once drilling begins.

- *Define technological/economic framework for exploitation.* The total *in situ* resources of a deposit are seldom entirely mineable both for technological reasons (depth, accessibility) and for economic reasons (mining cost, recoverable grades). Detailed sampling-and-analysis work is completed to get further knowledge of such characteristics as the distribution of rich- and poor-grade zones, the variability of thickness and overburden, and the various grade correlations (economic metals and impurities).

- *Mine planning.* To define what type of mining will result in maximum profit from the deposit involves choosing the method (underground or surface techniques), the mining equipment, type of haulage, requirements of stockpiling and blending, mill planning, etc. These choices are conditional, all or in part, upon the geological structures of the of the ore deposit.

- *Development.* Construction of the infrastructure required to exploit the deposit. The extent of the construction depends upon the mine planning carried out previously. This may include access roads, site logging, powerlines, town sites, mine offices, mill structure, water right-of-ways, disposal sites, other support systems as well as development for the actual mining of the deposit.

- *Production.* Actual mining of the ore and overburden. The crude ore is transported to the mill facilities for processing. Different metallurgical operations are then applied depending on the nature of the ore. The most popular technique for recovering gold from crude ore is called solvent extraction. A cyanide solution is used to dissolve the precious metal from the ore. Then the gold is precipitated out of the solution and refined under extreme heat by use of additional chemicals. To get the precious metal to its final form the process of smelting is used. Smelting consists of a number of techniques to up-grade the metal-bearing concentrate to its purer form. The precious metal is then separated for further treatment in a refinery, such as the Royal Canadian Mint.

[1]*Canadian Gold Review,* Wood Gundy, July 1989.

The time required to accomplish all these steps ranges from 2 to 15 years, with the typical timeline being about 5–7 years. From experience, the mine operator knows that, after mining, the actual product will differ from the estimations of the geologist. In general, the tonnage is underestimated and, more importantly, quality is over-estimated. Given the size of present day mining projects and the cost of their investments, the risks of incorrect evaluation of deposits are huge.

RECENT DEVELOPMENTS IN THE PRICE OF GOLD

Gold prices have recently turned bullish. Since moving toward a bottom in early October 1989, at US$360 per ounce, gold has moved steadily to over US$400. The latest positive run seems to have been triggered by economic and political uncertainty, namely the following events: the October stock market crash; the collapse of the junk bond market; the weak U.S. economy; as well as the unprecedented reform movements taking place in Europe.

The price of gold is also related to supply and demand. On the supply side, it is believed that gold loans (a loan of gold advanced in actual ounces of gold and repaid in gold) and forward sales (an agreement to buy or sell an asset at a certain future time for a certain price) constituted a major source of gold last year; American Precious Metals Advisors estimated this supply at 466 tonnes.[2] If this had been absorbed by the market, it would have been equivalent to 20–22% of the total supply from traditional sources. Gold loans and forward sales are sometimes referred to as a type of accelerated supply because they involve the delivery of physical gold not yet mined. Prior to the recent surge in gold prices, a number of gold mining companies have been purchasing gold on the open market to repay their gold loans early at a lower price. It is believed that the availability of bullion generated by gold loans and forward sales peaked in mid-1989.[3] As well, there is talk of the Soviet Union moving towards a gold-backed ruble. If this were to take place, supply would be reduced as large amounts of gold would be pulled out of circulation.

A recent survey of fifty North American gold producers indicated that supply in North America will also slow over the next few years. The survey stated that while mine output will continue to increase, the year-over-year rate of growth in output will actually slow. Production will peak at 13.6 million ounces annually in 1992, with an average cash cost of production estimated at $253 per ounce.[4]

On a worldwide scale non-communist countries have increased production to 970 tonnes last year from 560 tonnes in 1985; whereas the South African gold production has remained relatively stagnant since 1985 at about 620 tonnes per year (information from Kilborn Engineering, Kilborn Update 1989). In the United States, production has increased from 80 tonnes to 245 tonnes, a multiple of roughly three times. This is in part due to the success of the Nevada Heap Leach mines (including Nevada's Carlin mine, owned by American Barrick and Newmont Mining). In

[2]*World Gold Review,* September 1989, Volume 5, Burns Fry Ltd.
[3]*Financial Post,* November 20, 1989, page 31.
[4]*World Gold Review,* Burns Fry.

Canada, production has risen by 49 tonnes from 90 tonnes in 1985 to the present 139 tonnes mined.[5]

On the demand side, strong East Asian economies and growing affluence are expected to keep gold demand strong for 1989 and 1990. Additionally, demand for gold is very strong in Japan, up 23% in the last year. The recent Japanese government ruling to allow property and casualty insurers to hold up to 3% of their assets in gold will also create further demand for gold. Manufacturing demand for jewellery has risen 8% in 1989 and over threefold in the past decade. Record low prices for gold demand will also keep demand strong. For example, the yen price of gold is at its lowest level since 1979.[6] Thus, demand on a worldwide scale will likely improve.

BRIEF HISTORY OF GOLD LOANS

Bullion lending denominations in gold and silver have been around since 1962. Around this time Canadian gold producers began using short term forward sales techniques. Gold loans were developed as a beneficial way to combine price protection of inventory or production with the low financing costs of bullion loans as compared with their dollar equivalent.

A mining company with a need for cash to develop its project obtains cash by borrowing gold from a bank or lending institution and immediately sells the gold into the spot market to convert the gold to cash. This cash is then used to finance the project. The loan is repayable in ounces of gold on an agreed upon schedule. The production levels of the gold producer during future periods are expected to exceed the amounts required to meet any repayment requirements. A multi-option facility allows the mining company to convert back and forth between dollars and gold depending on the expected market conditions.

Gold loans became even more functional by use of the COMEX, which opened its doors in 1975. Additionally, two regional banks in the New England states introduced gold loans to the jewellery industry, paving the way for additional bullion lending usage. By the 1980s bullion loans were used for project financing on a long term basis and at larger and larger values.[7]

Only a few years ago gold loans were almost nonexistent; today they are a way of business for most mining companies and their uses are numerous. These uses include: mine development and expansion; debt refinancing; balance sheet management[8]; and acquisitions. Mine development can include the financing of capital expenditures from new shaft development to expansion of existing production. Some recent project financing has amounted to over $200 million for maturity over more than 10 years.[9] Gold loans can also be used to establish lower debt costs; an example

[5]*World Gold Review*, Burns Fry.
[6]*Canadian Gold Review,* Wood Gundy, July 1989.
[7]*Recent Developments in Bullion Financing*, David Turner, The Bank of Nova Scotia, June 1988.
[8]CICA Emerging Issues Committee, Gold Loans, EIC-32, November 1991.
[9]*Recent Developments in Bullion Financing*, David Turner, The Bank of Nova Scotia, June 1988.

being Newmont Gold's refinancing that used a consortium of banks to provide a loan of one million ounces. Mining companies use gold loans to lock in their future production and are able to use the cash generated to create flexibility for further investment opportunities. One concept currently being developed is the use of bullion loans to finance acquisitions.

REFERENCES

1. American Barrick Resources Corporation, Annual Report, 1988.
2. The Blue Book of CBS Stock Reports, "American Barrick," May 1989.
3. Brock, Horace W., "The Future World Price of Gold," Strategic Economic Decisions, Inc., Menlo Park, California.
4. Burns Fry, *World Gold Review,* Volume V, September 1989.
5. Cousineau, Eric and Richardson, Peter, "Gold: The World Industry and Canadian Corporate Strategy," Centre for Resources Studies, Queen's University Kingston, Ontario.
6. *The Financial Post,* "American Barrick Resources Corporation," November 25, 1989.
7. Green, Alan, "Productivity and Price: The Case of Gold Mining in Ontario," Working Paper No. 32, Center for Resource Studies, Queen's University, Kingston, Ontario.
8. Merrill Lynch, "Presentation to the Association of Mining Financial Professionals at the Petroleum Club," Daniel A. Rolling, First Vice President, June 22, 1989.
9. Nesbitt Research, "American Barrick Resources Corporation," Egizio Bianchini, August 17, 1989.
10. Prudential-Bache Securities Research, "American Barrick Resources Corporation," Barry Allan, March 30, 1989.
11. Wood Gundy, *Canadian Gold Review,* Don McLean, July 1989.
12. Journel, A.G. and Huijbregts, ChJ, *Mining Geostatistics,* Academic Press, 1978.
13. *CICA Handbook,* "EIC-32, Gold Loans," Emerging Issues Committee, November 1991.

PART FIVE · Long Term Financing Vehicles and Decisions

25. THE REDHOOK ALE BREWERY
26. TRI-TECH COMPUTER
27. BELL CANADA
28. ROGERS COMMUNICATIONS INC.
29. THE MULTI-JURISDICTIONAL DISCLOSURE SYSTEM
30. ROBOTICS, INC.
31. COLUMBIA RIVER PULP COMPANY INC.— INTEREST RATE HEDGING STRATEGY
32. EXPORT DEVELOPMENT CORPORATION— PROTECTED INDEX NOTES (PINS)
33. AMERICAN BARRICK RESOURCES CORPORATION
34. CITIBANK CANADA LTD.—MONETIZATION OF FUTURE OIL PRODUCTION
35. COLUMBIA PINE PULP COMPANY, INC.

25

THE REDHOOK ALE BREWERY

Paul Shipman, president and co-founder of the Redhook Ale Brewery, raised his beer mug in a toast with Redhook's treasurer and financial officer, David Mickelson. Sales at the Seattle-based microbrewer had increased at an average rate of 53% per year since 1984, and September 1990 had been another record month. After eight years of operations, Redhook's ales and porters had captured 50% of the increasingly competitive microbrewery market in the Pacific Northwest. Demand was projected to exceed, in two years, the 40,000-barrel annual production capacity of the company's single brewery. As a result, current plans called for the construction of a similar-sized brewery in the Bay Area of northern California. There were also plans to introduce a lager brand which would require the construction of a third, larger brewery in the Puget Sound region of western Washington. Expansion on this scale would require significant outside financing. Shipman and Mickelson were seeking a $5 million equity infusion from a well established European brewery with an interest in entering the North American market. In addition to the new equity, $6.5 million of new bank financing would be required for the planned expansion. Mickelson's next challenge would be to negotiate an acceptable credit arrangement with Redhook's bank to provide the required debt financing.

Copyright © 1991 by the President and Fellows of Harvard College.
Harvard Business School case 9-291-025.
This case was prepared by Research Associate Susan L. Roth under the direction of Professor Scott P. Mason as the basis for class discussion rather than to illustrate either effective or ineffective handling of an administrative situation. Reprinted by permission of the Harvard Business School.

THE RE-EMERGENCE OF MICROBREWERIES

Though regional microbreweries were the norm in 19th-century America, the post–Prohibition era saw a number of fundamental changes in the structure of the brewing industry. Most striking was the significant consolidation in the number of independent breweries and brand names. From this consolidation emerged a small number of dominant firms, characterized by their national marketing scope and utilization of large-volume, cost-efficient breweries.[1] While the current brewing industry was characterized by scale, other factors argued for the re-emergence of microbreweries. Most important, in the early 1970s, sales of imported beer began to grow rapidly, evidencing a shift in American consumers' taste toward higher-quality products. But imports were vulnerable from a number of perspectives. Product freshness and the high cost of shipping relative to the value of the product argued in favour of regional breweries producing specialty products. By knowing their local markets and giving a local character to their brews, microbreweries were re-emerging as a significant factor in sectors of the American brewing industry.

In 1975 there was one microbrewery in the United States; by 1989 there were 300, up from 50 in 1985. While the U.S. domestic beer market had experienced flat sales growth in 1988 and 1989, microbrewery sales were growing at an estimated 30–50% per year. This growth came largely at the expense of imports, whose sales had declined 7.9% in 1989 and were down 2.7% in the first eight months of 1990. These trends were expected to continue, although a drop in consumption was forecast if legislators approved higher beer taxes. Health concerns were also negatively impacting alcohol consumption, although Redhook believed moderation would encourage the switch to beer, and more full-bodied brews in particular.

THE COMPANY

In May 1981 Paul Shipman and Gordon Bowker founded Redhook Ale Brewery in Seattle, Washington. Their decision to start a regional microbrewery was influenced not only by the promising growth in the national import beer market but also by the fact that local per-capita consumption of draft beer was the highest in the country. The combination of these factors indicated to them that the region would be highly receptive to fresh, locally made beers in the European tradition.

Shipman's original vision for Redhook was to produce beers that would compete with well-known imported brands from Europe and Canada. Targeting the import-drinker, Redhook was committed to producing a quality brew that surpassed imports in freshness and offered consumers a more full-bodied flavor. In addition to imports such as Bass and Fullers, Redhook's ales would compete with regional breweries like Anchor Steam and Sierra Nevada, niche microbrewers like Grant's, Hart, and Thousand Oaks, and contract brewers like Samuel Adams.

[1]In 1989 the five largest U.S. commercial brewers had a 91% market share in the U.S.

The Ballard area of Seattle was chosen as the site of the initial brewery because of its existing light industrial facilities and because the surrounding community still retained strong European traditions. To purchase equipment and provide working capital for operations, $350,000 in equity capital was raised from Seattle-area investors. Redhook's 1990 ownership and management are described in Exhibit 1.

Redhook began as a draft-only brewery. On August 11, 1982, the first pint of Redhook Ale was sold. Blackhook Porter was introduced in June 1983 and immediately established a loyal following. The biggest boon for the brewery came with the introduction of Ballard Bitter in the spring of 1984. The immense popularity of this new offering also brought problems as demand began to far outstrip production capacity even with the addition of a bottling line in mid-1985.[2] It became apparent that a larger facility was necessary.

In keeping with Redhook's commitment to the city of Seattle, management chose to move the brewery to the old Fremont (Trolley) Car Barn. This old home of the Seattle Electric Railway not only had historical significance but kept the company in the middle of the community that had supported it from the beginning. The 26,000-square-foot car barn building provided space for expanded brewing capacity up to 40,000 barrels, as well as a brewpub, named the Trolleyman to commemorate the history of the building.

After extensive research, a 110-year-old German company, Anton Steinecker Maschinenfabrik GmbH, was chosen to design and build Redhook's state-of-the-art brewing equipment for the Fremont brewery. The acquisition of this new technology positioned Redhook as the most technically advanced craft brewery in North America and ensured product quality and consistency. No other brewery of comparable size had made such an investment in equipment and technology to date.

As a condition to the commencement of the 18-month process of designing and building the Fremont brewery, Anton Steinecker Maschinenfabrik GmbH required Redhook to have financing in place. In 1987 Shipman raised nearly $1 million in equity and was granted a $1 million, ten-year, Small Business Association (SBA) 504-Program loan through Old National Bank. Operations commenced at the Fremont brewery in October 1988.

BUSINESS STRATEGY

Redhook was committed to producing fresh brews with a more full-bodied flavor than its competitors had. To produce this more full-bodied flavor, all Redhook ales were brewed in accordance with the *Reinheitsgebot,* a German purity law that mandated just four ingredients: malted barley, hops, yeast, and water.

"We are not a yuppie beer, and we won't try to sell to them," asserted Mickelson. The brands were built by informative salesmanship and close work with the distribution network. Redhook products were not advertised, though the lager brand would possibly be an exception. Instead, the marketing mix emphasized point-of-

[2]In 1989 sales were approximately 55% draft and 45% bottle.

purchase displays and publicity. Word of mouth was a significant source of publicity for Redhook. The Seattle/Puget Sound area was the focus of the marketing, and geographical identity as a Northwest brewery was a marketing plus. Over 35% of revenues were earned in a 50-square-mile area around northern Seattle; the remainder came from sales in other regions of Washington state and an expanding distribution network serving Alaska, Oregon, California, Idaho, Montana, and Colorado.

Within the Seattle area the company used its own four-person distribution team to deliver Redhook products. Distributing its own product kept Redhook in touch with the local market. Redhook emphasized top-quality service for its retail licensees. Part of this service was the delivery of fresh beer within a half-hour of a vendor's order. Outside of this area, Redhook used middlemen to distribute the products. The company chose to align with only the strongest distributors.

Redhook had 20 full-time employees, including the four-person distribution team. Shipman prided himself on having a close working relationship with his employees and hoped to build a "family" of Redhook management and employees. Employee turnover at the brewery had been low and all new hires had to meet with approval from everyone in the department according to Shipman's collegial hiring process. Redhook's management is described in Exhibit 1.

Production volumes continued to grow with the move to the Fremont brewery. To manage this growth, a sophisticated computer system was designed to track deposits, keg floats, ingredient inventories, and other specialized brewery functions. The system was also used to project income and set production volumes. The accuracy of these projections allowed raw materials to be purchased on a just-in-time basis. Redhook had long-standing relationships with its primary suppliers and used competitive secondary sources, when necessary, to insulate production from interruption.

Increasing profitability and projected growth told Shipman and Mickelson that the timing was now right for a significant expansion in capacity and product line. Shipman believed a lager product would complement Redhook's existing product line of ales and porters and provide significant growth opportunities for the brewery. Lager beer, a lighter, more "thirst-quenching" brew, appealed to a much broader population of people than ales and porters. Ales and porters were a small niche product while lagers accounted for the bulk of the malt beverage market. The market size for lager was estimated to be greater than ten times the size of the ale market. "It's a huge market, even in the premium segment," said Mickelson. The size of the high-priced lager market in the Northwest alone was estimated at approximately $145 million. The premium lager market in California was estimated to be over $1 billion. With Redhook's outstanding reputation for premium brews, a distribution network in place, heavy advertising, and no domestic competition in their target niche, Shipman and Mickelson believed they would penetrate this market quickly. Shipman saw Redhook lagers eventually becoming the company's lead brand with projected sales of $25 million. It was estimated that constructing the two additional breweries would provide Redhook with sufficient capacity to grow into the late 1990s.

The construction of a larger brewery in the Puget Sound region of western Washington would allow Redhook to develop high-quality lager brands to compete against higher-priced imported lager beers such as Heineken, Beck's, Corona, and Molson. In the strong Pacific Northwest market with its tremendous local pride and demand for locally produced products, there were no locally based participants in this segment. The consolidation of regional breweries by the large national breweries and subsequent closing of many smaller facilities had created an absence of quality regional lager breweries. Redhook's lagers would fill this void in the marketplace and bring the brewery closer to meeting its ultimate objective: to dominate the regionally produced specialty beer industry in the Pacific Northwest and California.

FINANCIAL STRATEGY

Redhook's conservative financial strategy focused on maintaining the flexibility to grow and seize opportunities as they arose. Management was not comfortable with high leverage and set a target debt-to-equity ratio of 1:1. Shipman and Mickelson agreed they wanted to be able to take on additional debt as needed, saying "We don't ever want to be up against a limit and begging."

"We hate to be in a position of needing them," responded Mickelson when asked how he felt about commercial banks. When Mickelson joined Redhook in November 1987, his first task was to refinance the SBA-guaranteed loan, which carried a rate of prime plus 2% and restricted Redhook's ability to take on further indebtedness. Though the loan facility had not been used, funds would be needed to pay for equipment and leasehold improvements for the Fremont brewery. With experience as a lending officer at Barclays Bank, PLC, in Seattle, Mickelson was well aware of financing alternatives and their costs. He strongly believed that cheaper, less restrictive sources of financing were available.

In early 1988 Mickelson prepared a business plan and financing proposal and sent it to seven financial institutions. Only one institution turned down the deal: a $750,000, five-year term loan, with a balloon payment at maturity and a $100,000 line of credit. With U.S. Bank of Washington offering the most favorable terms, Mickelson refinanced the SBA loan at a cost of prime plus 1%, with no personal guarantees. The interest rate was adjusted annually in January, based upon the current prime rate, and interest was payable monthly. The loan was collateralized by all the company's equipment and leasehold improvements. Fewer restrictions on the assumption of further indebtedness, a required debt-to-equity ratio of 1.25:1, and the option to prepay the debt were the key terms of the deal. The line of credit was to be collateralized by the company's receivables and inventories. Interest on any borrowings under this arrangement would be payable monthly at prime plus 1%.

Redhook had maintained a good relationship with U.S. Bank of Washington in Seattle, where the account was covered by a senior loan officer. In 1989 the loan was increased to $865,000 to purchase additional equipment.

U.S. BANK OF WASHINGTON

U.S. Bank of Washington, a wholly owned subsidiary of U.S. Bancorp of Portland, Oregon, was the fourth largest commercial bank in Washington at December 31,1989. The bank was created in February 1988 by the merger of Peoples National Bank of Washington and Old National Bank of Washington. This subsidiary was progressing in asset quality and profitability as the parent company implemented better expense controls and the lending philosophy, policy, and guidelines of the Oregon bank. U.S. Bank's network of 138 branch locations created a substantial base for gathering new business, a primary goal of its parent company. To ensure high-quality service for customers and asset quality for the bank, lending authority and accountability had been placed in the field.

U.S. Bancorp was the largest financial services holding company headquartered in the Pacific Northwest, based on total assets of $17.0 billion at December 31, 1989. Financial statements are given as Exhibit 2. Using its extensive distribution network, U.S. Bancorp sought to establish itself as a source for meeting all the financial needs of its customers. A shift toward relationship banking in 1990 was aimed at accomplishing this goal and would allow the bank to offer some non-traditional banking products and services, including asset management, investments, insurance, and financial planning.

U.S. Bancorp's success was largely attributable to the vitality of the Pacific Northwest, its primary operating territory. Oregon and Washington were national leaders in employment growth in 1989. Industrial strength and its location as the gateway to trade with Pacific Rim countries were driving the region's economic growth. Asset quality had been improving, and further reduction of nonperforming assets to 1% of total loans and real estate owned was an important goal for 1990. The bank had reduced its level of nonperforming assets to 1.73% of total loans at year end 1989 from 2.27% at year end 1988. The company's loan portfolio was 56%, concentrated in commercial loans and well-diversified between Washington and Oregon and between industry segments within these economies. Only a small portion of the loan portfolio originated outside the bank's primary operating territory. With adequate reserves and improvement in the quality of the loan portfolio, capital was sufficient and met all regulatory guidelines. However, consistently strong asset growth over the past several years had eroded U.S. Bancorp's capital position.

FINANCING THE EXPANSION

Mickelson pored over the plans for expanding Redhook's operations. As the main source for growth in the Pacific Northwest, and with capacity to produce a new lager brand, the company was proposing to build a 100,000 barrel brewery with expansion potential to 200,000 barrels in the Puget Sound region of western Washington. This larger brewery would serve as a backsource of ale for both the Pacific Northwest and California. Redhook would also build another brewery, similar to the Fremont facility, in the Bay Area of northern California. The purpose of this brewery would be to provide local identity to the highly populated California market.

Total investment in property, plant, and equipment would approximate $15 million. Exhibit 3 details the investment, and Exhibit 3a estimates the timing of cash outlays. A cash deposit of $1 million would be required on October 1, 1990, and would be applied against the first progress payment due in July 1991. Anton Steinecker Maschinenfabrik GmbH would design and build the breweries and would again require that Redhook have secured adequate financing prior to the commencement of their work.

To determine the financing requirements for the new brewing facility, Mickelson forecast financial performance and cash flows to estimate the timing and amount of the company's financing needs. In addition to the investment in property, plant, and equipment, the significant increase in production would add further strain on cash flow. Shortfalls in cash were not standard operating procedure for Redhook, a company determined to avoid the costs of last-minute financing. Historical financial statements appear in Exhibits 4 and 4a, recent financial performance in Exhibit 4b, and financial statement projections in Exhibits 5 and 5a. The assumptions underlying these projections are included in Exhibit 6. These financial projections would be critical to the bank's evaluation of Redhook's creditworthiness.

Mickelson's ability to secure adequate financing was critical to the brewery's expansion plans. A strong regional economy and the growing U.S. microbrewery industry made this an ideal time to expand Redhook's brewing capacity and product line. Mickelson worried that debt funding requirements might exceed Redhook's creditworthiness. Without a lager product in the market, he knew the bank would focus on Redhook's track record in order to assess its ability to produce and distribute a successful new product. Redhook had thus far been a good credit risk for the bank.

Shipman and Mickelson were anxious to move forward with the expansion. But they would remain patient and secure financing that fit with the company's philosophy. Having established a good relationship with U.S. Bank of Washington, Mickelson hoped to secure financing through them.

EXHIBIT 1

Management and Ownership

One of Redhook's principal competitive advantages was a strong management team and patient, committed investors. An overview of management and ownership is summarized as follows:

MANAGEMENT

Paul Shipman (37), co-founder, president, and CEO. After earning his MBA from the University of Virginia's Darden School of Business in 1978, Mr. Shipman went to work as a strategic planner for Chateau Ste. Michelle winery outside of Seattle, Washington.

Gordon Bowker, secretary, director, and co-founder. Mr. Bowker is an entrepreneur. He has founded multiple companies in the Seattle area. He is the founder and chairman of Starbucks Coffee Company and a director of Sasquatch Publishing.

Pamela Hinckley, marketing manager. Ms. Hinckley has eleven years of experience in the hospitality and alcoholic beverage industry. This experience includes employment with DeLaurenti as a Manager for specialty beer and wine procurement.

David Mickelson, treasurer and CFO. Mr. Mickelson graduated from the University of Washington in 1981 and joined Barclays Bank PLC in Seattle. He began as a credit analyst and was promoted to assistant treasurer and later marketing director. After leaving Barclays in 1985, Mickelson joined Certified Foods, Inc., as their controller.

Allen Triplett, brewmaster and operations manager. Mr. Triplett's management experience includes work as an oil drilling supervisor. He has pursued microbiological studies at U.C. Davis' Seibel Institute.

OWNERSHIP

Redhook was owned by a group of 30 individuals holding approximately 34,000 shares. Six individuals, five of whom served on the board of directors, held 65% of the shares. The stock, whose current value was estimated to be between $105–115 per share, was privately held though liquidity did exist. Owners, including Paul Shipman, were not opposed to raising additional equity to partially finance the expansion; however, the company sought owners who were interested in the long term growth and success of the business. The majority of shareholders resided in Redhook's primary distribution territory.

EXHIBIT 2

U.S. BANCORP AND SUBSIDIARIES
Consolidated Balance Sheet
As at December 31
(in thousands)

	1989	1988
Assets		
Interest Earning Assets		
Money market investments	$ 484,095	$ 623,228
Investment securities (market value 1989–		
$2,221,124, 1988–$1,541,142)	2,211,898	1,565,867
Trading account securities	121,800	79,816
Mortgages held for sale	214,048	78,363
Loans (net of unearned income)[a]	11,409,464	9,676,101
Total interest earning assets	14,441,305	12,023,375
Allowance for loan losses	(153,557)	(126,227)
Cash and due from banks	1,324,717	1,261,763
Premises, furniture and equipment	283,219	280,596
Other real estate owned	47,892	64,003
Customers' liability on acceptances	413,039	371,015
Other assets	618,767	508,877
	$16,975,382	$14,383,402

(continued)

EXHIBIT 2 (cont.)

	1989	1988
Liabilities		
Interest Bearing Liabilities		
Deposits	$ 9,002,799	$ 7,844,640
Federal funds purchased and security		
repurchase agreements	2,570,281	1,603,546
Commercial paper	406,174	279,989
Other short term borrowings	278,635	195,506
Long term debt	602,975	624,770
Total interest bearing liabilities	12,860,864	10,548,451
Noninterest bearing deposits	2,429,387	2,323,090
Accrued income taxes	55,645	56,861
Acceptances outstanding	413,039	371,015
Other liabilities	162,706	140,158
Total Liabilities	15,921,641	13,439,575
Shareholders' Equity		
Preferred stock	—	—
Common stock	249,475	206,777
Capital surplus	361,447	148,474
Retained earnings	444,922	590,720
Less: treasury stock	(2,103)	(2,144)
Total Shareholders' Equity	1,053,741	943,827
	$16,975,382	$14,383,402

[a]U.S. Bancorp's loan portfolio consists of the following loans:

Commercial	$6,371.2
Real estate construction	765.2
Real estate mortgage	1,762.5
Consumer	2,117.6
Foreign	37.5
Lease financing	355.5

Total nonperforming assets at 12/31/89 were $197.8 million or 1.2% of total assets, down from 1.5% of total assets at 12/31/88.

EXHIBIT 2   (cont.)

U.S. BANCORP AND SUBSIDIARIES
Statement of Consolidated Income and Operations Data
Years Ended December 31
(in thousands, except per share data)

	1989	1988	1987
Interest income	$1,436,516	$1,162,964	$976,782
Interest expense	832,932	635,483	529,428
Net interest income	603,584	527,481	447,354
Provision for loan losses	83,765	69,204	57,430
Net interest income after provision for loan losses	519,819	458,277	389,924
Noninterest revenue	235,517	217,590	177,074
Noninterest expense	544,169	503,149	428,739
Income before income taxes and accounting changes	211,167	172,718	138,259
Provision for income taxes	60,385	48,805	38,621
Income before accounting changes	150,782	123,913	99,638
Cumulative effect of accounting changes	—	—	8,834
Net income	$ 150,782	$ 123,913	$108,472
Average number of shares outstanding	49,498	49,237	49,064
Earnings per share			
Before accounting changes	$3.05	$2.52	$2.03
Net income	3.05	2.52	2.21

	1989	1988	1987	1986	1985
Return on average assets	1.00%	0.92%	0.90%	0.69%	0.81%
Return on average equity	15.12	13.78	13.39	10.12	11.74
Equity/Assets	6.21	6.56	6.42	6.44	6.65
Net interest margin	4.96	4.87	4.78	4.70	4.80
Total non-performing assets as a % of total assets	1.2	1.5	1.6	1.6	2.2
Allowance for loan losses to year-end loans outstanding	1.35	1.30	1.31	1.31	1.13

Source: Annual Report, 1989.

EXHIBIT 3

REDHOOK ALE BREWERY
Planned Brewery Construction

Construction of the brewery facilities would commence in mid-1991 and continue until completion by the end of 1993. Projected capital expenditures are highlighted below:

(1) 100,000-barrel brewery in western Washington

    a) Brewhouse:

Plant	$2,500,000	
Installation	350,000	
Filtration	125,000	
		$2,975,000

    b) Fermentation Tanks:

20 @ $50,000		1,000,000
c) Malt System		300,000
d) Boiler		150,000
e) Refrigeration		750,000
f) Keg System		1,000,000
g) Bottling Line		1,300,000
h) Hot/Cold Water Tanks		100,000
i) Leasehold Improvements		350,000
j) Shipping, Duties, Brokerage,		
Construction Management and Misc. Costs		300,000
k) Sales Tax		650,000
		$8,875,000
10% Contingency		887,500
		$9,762,500

(2) 25,000-barrel ale brewery in northern California

    a) Brewhouse:

Plant	$1,250,000	
Installation	250,000	
		$1,500,000

    b) Fermentation Tanks:

10 @ $35,000		350,000
c) Malt System		110,000
d) Boiler		87,500
e) Refrigeration		225,000
f) Keg System		750,000
g) Bottling Line		835,000
h) Hot/Cold Water Tanks		60,000
i) Leasehold Improvements		250,000
j) Shipping, Duties, Brokerage,		
Construction Management and Misc. Costs		200,000
k) Sales Tax		392,000
		$4,759,500
10% Contingency		475,950
		$5,235,450
Total – Both Breweries		$14,997,950

EXHIBIT 3a

REDHOOK ALE BREWERY
New Equipment Acquisition Schedule

The following estimates the timing of payments for the planned brewery construction.

DATE	BREWING EQUIPMENT	FURNITURE & FIXTURES	TRUCKS	LEASEHOLD IMPROVEMENTS
July 1991	$ 2,730,000			
June 1992	2,077,950			$200,000
Sept. 1992	6,660,000			200,000
Nov. 1992		$200,000		
Dec. 1992	2,030,000			200,000
Jan. 1993			$100,000	
April 1993	600,000			
	$14,097,950	$200,000	$100,000	$600,000

EXHIBIT 4

REDHOOK ALE BREWERY
Historical Statements of Operations
For the Years Ended December 31

	1982	1983	1984	1985	1986	1987	1988 (1)	1989
Sales, net of beer taxes	$ 59,345	$259,594	$318,093	$488,151	$702,690	$1,082,589	$1,680,174	$2,676,109
Cost of Goods Sold (2)	67,644	186,962	187,322	250,335	362,766	546,231	1,002,180	1,807,518
Gross Profit	(8,299)	72,632	130,771	237,816	339,924	536,358	677,994	868,591
Selling, General and								
Administrative Expenses	150,189	128,222	131,705	168,541	218,234	286,567	520,079	607,148
	(158,488)	(55,590)	(934)	69,275	121,690	249,791	157,915	261,443
Other Income (Expenses)								
Interest income	9,062	0	18	1,953	505	24,250	14,032	1,724
Interest expense	(699)	(13,155)	(18,526)	(12,502)	(9,054)	(25,646)	(53,863)	(122,211)
Loss on sale of equipment								(9,824)
Other	36	(27)						(7,500)
Income Before Taxes	(150,089)	(68,772)	(19,442)	58,726	113,141	248,395	118,084	123,632
Income Taxes								
Current	0	0	0	0	0	51,018	18,577	46,642
Deferred credit	0	0	0	0	29,132	(6,151)	(12,033)	(27,000)
Net Income	$(150,089)	$ (68,772)	$(19,442)	$58,726	$84,009	$203,528	$111,540	$103,990

Notes:
(1) Redhook commenced operations at the Fremont brewery in October 1988. Annual brewing capacity increased from 8,000 to 40,000 barrels.
(2) Cost of goods sold includes direct costs, defined as beginning inventory, plus purchases, less ending inventory, and an allocation of fixed expenses. Thus as production volumes neared capacity, total COGS generally increased at a slower rate. COGS can be broken down as follows for 1987–1989:

	1987	1988	1989
Cost of Goods Sold			
Beginning inventories	$ 28,141	$ 65,419	$ 160,125
Salaries, wages and taxes	159,084	165,843	282,520
Employee benefits	7,027	13,770	22,700
Professional fees	5,000	5,000	3,903
Rent and common area expense	30,720	94,916	176,891
Real and personal property taxes	5,970	6,392	10,150
Utilities	19,160	39,765	66,746
Insurance	7,734	10,273	16,847
Depreciation	37,127	153,159	252,172
Repairs and maintenance	7,343	7,426	20,581
Purchases	257,795	448,589	717,952
Purchases – promotional items	20,491	29,402	41,029
Brewery supplies and expense	26,058	69,419	90,881
Pub salaries	–	22,982	112,220
Pub operating expenses		29,950	102,496
	611,650	1,162,305	2,077,213
Less ending inventories	65,419	160,125	269,695
	$546,231	$1,002,180	$1,807,518

EXHIBIT 4a

REDHOOK ALE BREWERY
Historical Statements of Financial Condition
As at December 31

	1982	1983	1984	1985	1986	1987	1988 (2)	1989
Assets								
Cash and equivalents	$ 9,151	$ 35,018	$ 28,035	$ 34,583	$ 69,614	$ 192,182	$ 95,220	$ 141,952
Receivables, net	10,866	14,698	14,410	25,781	33,361	57,598	95,157	66,381
Inventories	14,642	13,496	18,565	27,844	28,141	65,419	160,125	269,695
Prepaid expenses	0	0	0	0	1,107	1,591	12,147	4,268
Refundable taxes	0	0	0	0	15,694	0	0	0
Employee advances	0	0	0	0	0	0	1,552	0
Current Assets	34,659	63,212	61,010	88,208	132,223	316,790	379,895	482,296
Equipment and leasehold improvements, net	248,127	305,412	324,061	348,458	552,873	1,018,673	2,568,011	2,465,374
Other assets	10,386	9,552	8,828	5,864	5,089	565,576(1)	41,823	16,888
Total Assets	$293,172	$378,176	$393,899	$442,530	$690,185	$1,901,039	$2,989,729	$2,964,558
Liabilities and Shareholders' Equity								
Accounts payable	$ 30,997	$ 8,693	$ 8,552	$ 2,334	$ 19,713	$ 36,932	$ 249,233	$116,622
Accrued salaries, wages and payroll taxes	10,025	5,924	5,408	7,048	13,361	3,722	5,403	6,747
Accrued taxes	3,840	8,430	8,976	12,412	15,226	19,575	46,244	37,525
Deposits on kegs and neons	14,040	50,732	45,917	61,107	71,435	79,914	92,664	97,410
Other deposits	0	0	0	0	0	0	64,920	0

Accrued interest	330	260	375	765	974	1,769	3,949	5,753
Taxes payable	0	0	0	0	0	51,018	0	22,917
Deferred revenue	0	0	0	0	0	1,666	3,067	2,976
Note payable to individual	0	0	0	0	0	0	0	7,500
Current portion of long term debt	0	32,000	40,750	24,635	40,200	177,624	93,924	104,785
Current portion of capitalized leases	0	0	0	0	0	0	0	5,950
Other	1,208	2,025	2,700	3,375	4,049	0	0	0
Current Liabilities (3)	60,440	108,064	112,678	111,676	164,958	372,220	559,404	408,185
Long term debt, less current portion	32,000	132,000	66,250	60,532	150,603	35,932	852,519	849,873
Capital lease obligation, less current portion	0	0	0	0	0	0	0	19,561
Deferred rent payable	0	0	0	0	0	0	37,260	53,351
Deferred taxes	10,870	10,123	7,424	4,049	29,132	74,829	10,948	0
Shareholders' Equity								
Common Stock, $1.00 par value authorized 50,000 shares, issued and outstanding 34,904 shares	20,915	21,104	22,904	22,904	22,904	34,904	34,904	34,904
Paid-in capital	365,442	372,152	469,352	469,352	469,352	1,326,390	1,326,390	1,326,390
Retained earnings	(196,495)	(265,267)	(284,709)	(225,983)	(146,764)	56,764	168,304	272,294
	189,862	127,989	207,547	266,273	345,492	1,418,058	1,529,598	1,633,588
Total Liabilities and Shareholders' Equity	$293,172	$378,176	$393,899	$442,530	$690,185	$1,901,039	$2,989,729	$2,964,558

Notes:
(1) Includes $547,768 restricted for equipment acquisitions.
(2) Redhook commenced operations at the Fremont brewery in October 1988.
(3) Redhook currently has no contingent liabilities.

EXHIBIT 4b

REDHOOK ALE BREWERY
Recent Financial Performance

Income Statement
For the nine months ended September 30, 1990

Sales, net of beer taxes	$2,867,442
Cost of Goods Sold	1,708,961
Gross Profit	1,158,481
Selling, General and Administrative Expense	637,510
Net Operating Income	520,970
Interest Income	9,052
Purchase Discounts	2,560
Interest Expense	80,406
Income Before Income Taxes	452,177
Income Tax Expense	153,740
Net Income	$ 298,436

Balance Sheet Data
As at September 30, 1990

Assets	
Current assets	$ 782,396
Other assets	106,869
Net equipment & improvements	2,349,311
Total Assets	$3,238,576
Liabilities and Shareholders' Equity	
Current liabilities	$ 490,141
Long term debt	781,566
Other liabilities	69,044
	1,340,752
Total Shareholders' Equity	1,897,824
Total Liabilities and Shareholders' Equity	$3,238,576

EXHIBIT 5

REDHOOK ALE BREWERY
Projected Statements of Income
Years Ended December 31

	1990	1991	1992	1993	1994
Revenues					
Sales—Beer (Draft Ale)	$1,233,000	$1,548,900	$1,989,200	$2,259,500	$2,402,750
Sales—Beer (Draft Lager)				1,205,100	2,166,750
Sales—Beer (Bottled Ale)	2,087,500	3,193,750	4,759,500	5,678,500	6,577,500
Sales—Beer (Bottled Lager)				7,536,000	16,987,400
Sales—Beer (Trolleyman)	480,000	480,000	490,000	490,000	500,000
Gross Sales	3,800,500	5,222,650	7,238,700	17,169,100	28,634,400
Less beer taxes	240,793	336,128	461,380	1,328,007	2,174,617
Net Sales	3,559,707	4,886,522	6,777,320	15,841,093	26,459,783
Cost of Goods Sold					
Direct COGS	925,524	1,221,630	1,626,557	3,960,273	6,614,946
Other	1,336,866	1,477,176	1,667,795	4,870,894	5,545,648
Gross Profit	1,297,317	2,187,716	3,482,968	7,009,926	14,299,189
Selling & marketing expense	280,157	381,063	493,250	1,533,086	2,106,150
General & administrative expense	522,601	674,360	834,593	1,371,525	1,863,322
Total operating expenses	802,758	1,055,423	1,327,843	2,904,611	3,969,472
Net operating income	494,559	1,132,293	2,155,125	4,105,315	10,329,717
Interest income	306,138	663,561	409,549	4,842	126,742
Earnings before interest and taxes	800,697	1,795,855	2,564,674	4,110,157	10,456,459
Interest expense	110,934	95,079	203,982	771,536	600,332
Income before income taxes	689,763	1,700,776	2,360,692	3,338,621	9,856,127
Income taxes	234,519	578,264	802,635	1,135,131	3,351,083
Net Income	$455,243	$1,122,512	$51,558,057	$2,203,490	$6,505,044

EXHIBIT 5a

REDHOOK ALE BREWERY
Projected Statements of Financial Condition
As at December 31

	1990	1991	1992	1993	1994
Assets					
Current Assets					
Cash	$ 50,000	$ 50,000	$ 3,057	$ 50,000	$ 50,000
Short term investments	4,358,209	3,821,464	0	726,327	5,609,474
Accounts receivable – net	214,229	306,788	437,371	1,327,492	2,408,266
Inventory	428,457	613,577	874,742	2,084,912	3,567,349
Total Current Assets	5,050,895	4,791,830	1,315,169	4,188,730	11,635,090
Intangible assets – net	132,159	102,251	72,343	54,435	22,985
Deposits	1,000,000	0	0	0	0
Equipment & leasehold improvements	2,989,160	2,989,160	3,789,160	17,987,110	17,987,110
Less: accumulated depreciation	823,126	1,122,466	1,431,568	2,896,826	4,214,737
Net equipment & leasehold improvements	2,166,034	1,866,694	2,357,592	15,090,284	13,772,373
Plus: construction in progress	0	2,730,000	13,497,950	0	0
Total equipment and leasehold improvements	2,166,034	4,596,694	15,855,542	15,090,284	13,772,373
Total Assets	$8,349,088	$9,490,775	$17,243,055	$19,333,450	$25,430,448

Liabilities

Current Liabilities				
Accounts payable	$ 214,229	$ 306,788	$ 437,371	$ 1,783,675
Accrued liabilities	3,880	4,342	4,430	14,330
Deposits on kegs + neon lights	128,160	158,880	201,720	294,240
Federal income taxes payable	44,799	67,402	69,734	374,027
Current portion—long term debt	129,669	146,620	158,418	196,557
Total Current Liabilities	520,737	684,031	871,673	2,662,829
New term debt	0	0	6,165,000	4,225,000
Other long term obligations	861,689	732,019	585,400	251,243
Total long term debt	861,689	732,019	6,750,400	4,476,243
Less: current portion	129,669	146,620	158,418	196,557
Net long term debt	732,019	585,400	6,591,981	4,279,686
Other liabilities	7,500	10,000	10,000	10,000
Stockholders' Equity				
Preferred stock	0	0	0	0
Common stock	6,361,294	6,361,294	6,361,294	6,361,294
Retained earnings	727,537	1,850,049	3,408,106	12,116,639
Total Equity	7,088,831	8,211,343	9,769,400	18,477,933
Total Liabilities and Stockholders' Equity	$8,349,088	$9,490,775	$17,243,055	$25,430,448

EXHIBIT 6

Assumptions Underlying Financial Statement Projections

1. In recent experience 12% of sales were generated in cash on the premises of the Trolleyman Pub. Over 25% of sales were earned in a 50-square-mile area around North Seattle and paid for upon delivery in cash or check as required by Washington state law. The remaining sales were paid in cash or became accounts receivable. Accounts receivable turnover averaged 20 days. A 30-day aging of accounts receivable is assumed once lager sales commence.

   A shift in the composition of sales, from the current 45% bottles and 55% draft to 75%–80% bottles and the remaining 20–25% in draft over the next few years was forecast. Bottle sales generated a higher contribution per barrel.

2. Costs were projected to remain relatively stable, with gross margins improving as the Fremont brewery reached capacity. Direct costs of goods sold were defined as beginning inventory plus purchases less ending inventory. The remainder of COGS was an allocation of fixed expenses. Thus, as production volume increased and a brewery neared capacity, gross COGS generally increased at a slower rate.

3. Redhook carried on average 40 days' sales as inventory. Raw materials could be converted to finished goods in 10 days and were paid for within 30 days. Accounts payable on average turned over every 20 days.

4. Depreciation charges on brewery equipment, trucks, and leasehold improvements were included in COGS expense. Depreciation of furniture and fixtures was included in selling, general, and administrative expense. No depreciation was expensed until new assets were fully paid for. Projected depreciation expense was $293,640 in 1990 and 1991, $303,402 in 1992, $1,459,557 in 1993 and $1,312,211 in 1994. Projected amortization expense was $21,608 in 1990, $35,608 in 1991 and 1992, $38,608 in 1993 and $37,150 in 1994.

5. On December 31, 1989, the other asset account included net intangible assets as well as an $800 deposit and $8,021 of deferred taxes. Intangible assets include capitalized fees and trademarks. In fiscal year 1990 capitalized fees increased $140,000 and deferred taxes decreased $8,021. The net affect on cash flow in 1990 from the other asset account, including the $1 million equipment deposit paid on October 1, 1990, was a decrease of $1,131,179. It was projected that in 1993 $15,000 was paid to acquire trademarks.

6. Selling and marketing expenses show a dramatic increase in 1993 and 1994, reflecting the rollout of the company's lager product.

7. New Term Debt was expected to have a 7-year term with principle amortization over the term of the loan. Interest expense was calculated using an 11.5% rate on New Term Debt based on the following current market rates of interest:

	8/31/90	8/31/89
Prime Rate	10.00%	10.50%
Federal Funds	8.00	8.875
3-Month T-Bills (yield)	7.67	8.12
10-Year Treasury Notes (yield)	8.80	8.21

   All cash amounts over $50,000 were placed in short term investments earning an annual interest rate of 8.00%.

8. Tax payments were figured at a flat 34% rate.

9. The successful placement of $5 million in new common stock is assumed to have taken place in September 1990.

26

TRI-TECH COMPUTER

In April 1987, financial executives of Tri-tech Computer were meeting to determine the form of a capital issue of $200 million needed for an acquisition that would complement Tri-tech's current business. Financing alternatives available to the company included long term straight debt, convertible debt, and common stock.

Convertible debentures were of particular interest. After a recent visit to Wall Street, "converts" had been touted as overpriced (to investors) by many of the investment banks that Tri-tech had visited. There appeared to be general consensus that the demand for this quasi-equity form of debt was greater than its supply and, therefore, convertible issues were currently selling at a premium. This was attributed to strong interest from institutional investors with limitations on the amount of equity they could hold in their portfolios and their preference for convertible debentures because of the guaranteed minimum return of the coupon payment.

Dick Sutton, the treasurer, began the meeting by saying he thought that convertible bonds were an expensive form of financing for a high-growth company like Tri-tech because the market would not give an appropriate premium for potential appreciation of the equity base. Doug Jenner, the assistant treasurer, had yet another concern: "We've got to keep in mind that investment bankers are salespeople first and financial consultants second. I don't think of them as giving impartial advice so much as trying to sell a hot product." The chief financial officer, Eric Stone, thought that convertibles were securities issued for companies with weak credit, but he wanted to review the analysis of each financing alternative before making a final decision.

COMPANY BACKGROUND

Tri-tech Computer (incorporated in 1972) designed, developed, manufactured, sold, and serviced a compatible family of small- and medium-size computer systems primarily for use in retail sales and financial applications. Located in Boston, the firm had 7,400 employees at year end 1986 with approximately 83% of sales to end users through its own worldwide sales force. Forty percent of sales were non-U.S. and 27% of these were in European markets.

With sales approaching $1 billion, Tri-tech was quickly gaining ground on some of its larger competitors in the computer systems industry. It was considered a pioneer in the application of several advanced technologies (including circuitry and system-based diagnostics) and many analysts believed the company's technological lead was widening. In 1986, product revenue accounted for 81% of the total; the remaining 19% represented service and other revenue. During the 5-year period from 1982 through 1986, service and other revenue growth (39%) outpaced the product revenue growth rate (23%), largely because of the expanding installed- customer base. Total revenues over the period grew at a 25.2% rate. Net profit margin fluctuated considerably but was 8.3% in 1986, its highest margin since 1982 (Exhibit 1).

Consistent with the income statement, Tri-tech's balance sheet (Exhibit 2) and statement of changes in financial position (Exhibit 3) reflected strong performance. This record was especially impressive given the sluggish domestic economy and stagnant profits that confronted many other computer manufacturers in 1986. Compared to its main competitors, Tri-tech's asset management (return on assets of 19.2%) and return on equity (15.2%) were the highest—even compared to blue chip IBM (Exhibit 4).

It is important to note that although Tri-tech had over $300 million in cash at year end 1986, these funds had been targeted for conversion of operating leases. The company leased its headquarters, field offices, certain equipment, and most of its operating facilities under operating lease agreements, and future minimum lease payments totalled $303.4 million. As a result, the ratio of total liabilities to total assets was deceptively low. Since the major rating agencies would consider such lease payments as part of fixed financial charges, it was important that Tri-tech convert the operating leases before going to the capital markets for $200 million for the acquisition.

Tri-tech had never issued debt through the capital markets but it believed its Standard & Poor's bond rating would be "A." An issue rated "A" was considered to be backed by a strong capacity to pay interest and repay principal, although it was regarded as more susceptible to the adverse effects of changes in circumstances and economic conditions than debt in higher-rated categories. With the exception of Prime Computer, the "A" rating would be somewhat less attractive compared to the bond ratings of Tri-tech competitors (Exhibit 5).

With regard to equity, Tri-tech's performance had been very strong; its 1986 average annualized P/E ratio was 19.0. Most recently, its stock was selling at a P/E ratio of 42, far above any of its competitors (Exhibit 6). Although all of its competitors had recently announced repurchase programs, Tri-tech had not issued equity since its 1980 offering. At the end of 1986, it had 56.7 million shares outstanding; earnings per share were $1.44.

Like many other companies in the industry, Tri-tech did not pay a dividend. The company had no plans to pay out dividends, as it believed strongly that investors invested in Tri-tech to fund the company's future growth and thus earn a higher return than they would have if Tri-tech had given them back their own dollars in the form of a dividend rather than through capital appreciation of the stock.

During the first quarter of 1987, Tri-tech continued its strong fiscal 1986 performance and U.S. revenues were up 33% year-to-year, compared to a 50% gain overseas. The company projected a fiscal 1987 revenue growth plan in the mid-20% range, and Tri-tech had plans to increase its head count by 4% during the first quarter, followed by 5% or better in the second quarter.

In mid-April, at the time of the financing decision, Tri-tech was regarded as a leading-edge technology vendor worldwide and was competing well against IBM and others for their systems applications. Japan was viewed as a very strong market for Tri-tech; one of the applications cited involved trading securities from home through PCs tied to Tri-tech's systems at data centers. Since there were six million PCs in Japanese homes, there was believed to be a potential for tying to one million home PCs.

Competitors were not standing still, however, and IBM's benign neglect of the low-end workstation market ended in April with an announcement to compete actively in the PC market through introduction of the IBM Personal System 2. The effect the IBM decision would have on Tri-tech was uncertain.

Although substantial uncertainty surrounded all attempts to forecast the competitive environment, given its strong hardware/software product flow, Tri-tech was rated as a buy by most analysts. EPS for 1987 and 1988 were estimated to be $2.25 and $3.30 respectively. Value Line estimated Tri-tech sales growth to be 23.7% and net margin to increase to 11.1% in 1990. In general, and without regard to longer-term sustainability, it was predicted that the current relative strength in technology stocks like Tri-tech would continue for some time.

THE SPRING 1987 FINANCING

Tri-tech believed that the computer industry was in a period of consolidation and that competition in the industry would continue to intensify. Moreover, the industry continued to be characterized by a trend toward more frequent product introductions and shorter product life cycles. Tri-tech believed strongly that its ability to compete effectively would be dependent upon continuing to develop and introduce new and enhanced product lines on a timely basis. One way to achieve this objective would be through the acquisition of complementary companies and products.

During the first months of 1987, Tri-tech studied several companies for possible acquisition and selected Automated Designs Company (ADC) as their target. Incorporated in Delaware in 1973, ADC also manufactured small- and medium-size computer systems but served three principal markets not served by Tri-tech. Specifically, ADC's market focus was on engineering and scientific commercial data processing, and on computer-aided design and manufacturing. The acquisition would represent a synergistic approach to broadening Tri-tech's customer base.

Since 1985, ADC had invested heavily in research and development and had difficulty controlling expenses after embarking on a rather ambitious expansion program. It was expected that an acquisition would be well received and that ADC would welcome the strong financial resources of Tri-tech. Tri-tech, on the other hand, expected ADC to grow at a rate of 20%–25% beginning in 1989, with some fluctuations due to general economic conditions. In April 1987, ADC had 11.2 million shares outstanding and was at a low share price of $17. Sales in 1986 were $180 million with net income at 5.4% or $9.7 million; the P/E ratio at year end was 15, with a historic low stock price of $13.

Tri-tech's future financing needs, including the ADC acquisition, were reasonably well defined for the near term. It was felt that the $200 million capital issue would allow for the acquisition of ADC as well as the financial support needed to achieve ADC projected growth rates. No further external financing was needed to sustain Tri-tech's own projected growth.

The possible financing alternatives had been narrowed down to three options: long term debt, convertible debentures, and common stock.

1. Ten-year bonds at 9¼% coupon. One of the major New York underwriters had estimated a public issue of $200 million could be placed that would not be redeemable by the company prior to 1994. There would be no sinking fund requirements, and the restrictions on the issue would be less onerous than on privately placed debt that was likely to have several restrictive covenants.

2. Twenty-five year convertible debentures at 4.75% coupon and a 25% conversion premium. The convertible debentures would be subordinated to all debt obligations of the company outstanding at the date of issue. The sinking fund would commence in year 11 at a rate of 5% annually for an average life of 19½ years. The debentures would be convertible into common stock at a price that would be set at 125% of the price of the common stock on the date that the issue was sold. The conversion price would be adjusted for all stock splits, stock dividends, and stock sales at prices below the conversion price. The debentures would not be callable for 2 years unless the stock price was 150% above the conversion price for 20 out of 30 days. If these conditions were met, the bonds would be redeemable at 105.75% in year 1, declining to par at the end of year 10.

3. Common stock at market price. Clearly the most important consideration in regard to the common stock financing alternative was management's assessment of the firm's current stock price relative to the stock price that might reasonably be expected in a few years. The stock was currently selling at a very high P/E ratio—42. (See Exhibits 6 and 7 for Tri-tech's stock prices and related information.)

CONDITION IN THE CAPITAL MARKETS

In April 1987, an inflationary psychology existed in the capital markets that was fuelled by the continued falling of the dollar and rising commodity prices. It was expected that the Federal Reserve would try to squash these inflationary fears by allowing a rise in short term rates, since failure to act would cause both bond prices and the dollar to weaken further. (See Exhibit 8 for history of yields on corporate bonds.) Such an increase would be short-lived, however, since it would eventually promote slower growth and lower inflation.

Although the April unemployment rate of 6.3% was down almost to its 1978–79 rate, the manufacturing capacity utilization rate of 79% and the married male unemployment rate of 4.1% had recovered only about halfway from their recessionary 1982–83 rates.

Given their contention that the U.S. economy had not yet approached high enough utilization rates for the increase in import and tradable goods prices to trigger a new wage-price spiral, a May 1987 Kidder, Peabody & Co. report had predicted that 30-year government bond rates would continue to fall to about 8.25% by the end of 1987 and to 7.75% by the middle of 1988. After a careful review of the leading economic indicators, Kidder Peabody had concluded that inflation fears were overblown and the principal risk to the inflation forecast was that the Federal Reserve would promote monetary demand growth that would cause inflation.

At the other end of the spectrum were several Wall Street firms that believed inflation was ready to take off and expected bond rates to rise as the economic recovery progressed.

As to convertible debentures, the new-issue market during 1986 topped 1985, which was the previous record year. In the first half of 1986 alone, there were 163 issues totalling $8.8 billion. During the same period in 1976, there were only 17 issues worth $1.0 billion.

Coupon rates of convertibles followed the corporate bond market, and this relationship had remained relatively constant through the years. Typically, convertible bond coupon rates varied from 2% to 5% below non-convertible bond coupon rates of similar quality. The level of conversion premiums, however, had not remained constant and had been moving upward. During the second quarter of 1986, conversion premiums averaged 23.3%, the highest in past years. At the same time, the average coupon rate had been decreasing and the conversion premium of new issues had been increasing; this trend caused some investors to conclude that the new-issue convertible market was overpriced and therefore should be avoided.

The counterargument viewed the trend in conversion premiums as merely reflecting market sentiment. In a bullish environment, the enthusiasm of the market had lead to an increase in premium levels, especially of investment grade (rated BBB or better by Standard & Poor's). It was expected that when the market sentiment changed, premium levels would shift very rapidly. Even this view agreed that the new-issue market seemed to be overpriced by historical standards and cautioned investors about the purchase of convertible bonds at these high prices.

THE FINANCING DECISION

Prior to the April 1987 meeting of Tri-tech's financial executives, Doug Jenner had compiled data on new issues of convertible debentures (Exhibit 9). He had studied this information as well as his analysis on the cost of each of the financing alternatives. He would make his recommendation to Dick Sutton and Eric Stone on how Tri-tech should fund the $200 million needed for the ADC acquisition.

EXHIBIT 1

TRI-TECH COMPUTER

Consolidated Statement of Income

For the Five Years Ending December 31, 1986

(in thousands, except per share amounts)

	1986	1985	1984	1983	1982
Revenue					
Product revenue	$797,681	$664,491	$578,708	$464,572	$351,641
Service and other revenue	192,772	140,647	108,372	75,012	51,022
Total revenue	990,453	805,138	687,080	539,584	402,664
Costs and Expenses					
Cost of revenue	319,754	309,792	278,243	217,633	141,003
Research and development	111,731	92,334	67,743	50,527	43,398
Marketing, general and administrative	422,256	338,408	275,174	207,219	165,750
Total costs and expenses	853,741	740,534	621,160	475,379	350,151
Operating income	136,712	64,604	65,920	64,205	52,513
Interest expense	(2,553)	(3,104)	(3,408)	(3,620)	(1,247)
Interest income	13,523	11,192	10,094	4,561	9,030
Income before income taxes	147,682	72,692	72,606	65,146	60,296
Provision for income taxes					
Current period	(65,424)	(28,350)	(29,768)	(25,408)	(21,782)
Benefit of DISC tax reversal	0	0	12,513	0	0
Total provision for income taxes	(65,424)	(28,350)	(17,255)	(25,408)	(21,782)
Net income	$ 82,258	$ 44,342	$ 55,351	$ 39,738	$ 38,514
Earnings per share	$1.44	$0.82	$1.04	$0.76	$0.76
Weighted average shares outstanding	57,019	53,877	53,405	52,611	50,595

EXHIBIT 2

TRI-TECH COMPUTER
Consolidated Balance Sheet
For the Five Years Ending December 31, 1986
(in thousands)

	1986	1985	1984	1983	1982
Assets					
Cash and cash investments	$309,367	$165,992	$137,852	$120,616	$ 32,013
Accounts receivable, net of allowances	254,979	210,758	188,781	154,230	127,465
Inventories	82,855	101,861	119,164	110,837	130,722
Prepaid expenses and other	22,581	13,862	9,027	15,190	21,946
Prepaid income taxes	0	4,715	0	0	0
Total Current Assets	669,782	497,188	454,824	400,873	312,146
Total property, plant & equipment at cost	363,941	311,334	247,364	171,276	138,631
Accumulated depreciation and amortization	(138,163)	(104,162)	(64,826)	(43,848)	(23,323)
Net Property, Plant & Equipment	225,778	207,172	182,538	127,428	115,308
Other Assets	13,922	8,164	10,054	7,748	7,748
Total Assets	$909,482	$712,524	$647,416	$536,027	$435,202

Liabilities and Stockholders' Investment

Accounts payable	$ 65,491	$ 43,056	$ 46,892	$ 36,068	$ 29,564
Accrued liabilities					
Wages, payroll taxes and employee benefits	44,030	36,373	29,060	18,164	11,498
Income taxes	27,954	0	5,728	6,413	9,205
Other accrued liabilities	27,673	23,457	13,973	8,078	7,980
Current portion of long term debt and capital obligations	7,700	9,094	19,381	4,303	2,658
Total Current Liabilities	172,848	111,980	115,034	73,026	60,905
Long term debt and capital lease obligations	8,419	16,011	22,130	30,905	27,222
Deferred income taxes	38,478	42,207	26,345	30,915	23,300
Common stock, $.025 par value, authorized 200,000,000 shares, outstanding 56,655,195 in 1986	1,416	1,335	1,309	1,276	1,214
Additional paid-in capital	373,379	308,307	294,257	266,915	229,309
Retained earnings	314,942	232,684	188,341	132,990	93,252
Total Stockholders' Investment	689,737	542,326	483,907	401,181	323,775
Total Liabilities and Stockholders' Investment	$909,482	$712,524	$647,416	$536,027	$435,202

EXHIBIT 3

TRI-TECH COMPUTER
Consolidated Statement of Changes in Financial Position
For the Five Years Ending December 31, 1986
(in thousands)

	1986	1985	1984	1983	1982
Funds (Cash and cash investments) at beg. period	$165,992	$137,852	$120,616	$32,013	$115,850
Funds provided from operations					
Net income	82,258	44,342	55,351	39,738	38,514
Items not requiring current outlay of funds					
Depreciation and amortization	55,782	45,945	29,336	24,298	13,153
Deferred income taxes	(3,728)	15,862	(4,572)	7,615	12,797
Net book value of property, plant and equipment sold or retired	11,277	17,815	8,533	18,587	2,763
Total Provided from Operations	145,589	123,964	88,648	90,238	67,227
Funds Used for Operations					
Increase in accounts receivable	44,221	21,976	34,551	26,765	36,299
Increase (decrease) in inventories	(19,006)	(17,303)	8,327	(19,885)	60,362
Net change in prepaid expenses and non-debt current liabilities	(58,258)	2,316	(33,091)	(17,233)	9,154
Investment in property, plant and equipment	83,864	87,163	92,260	54,466	84,907
Increase (decrease) in other assets, net	7,560	(659)	3,046	517	7,747
Total Used for Operations	58,381	93,493	105,093	44,630	198,469
Net Increase (Decrease) in Funds from Operations	87,208	30,471	(16,445)	45,608	(131,242)
Provided from (Repayment of) External Financings					
Increase (decrease) in long term debt and capital lease obligations, net	(8,986)	(16,408)	6,306	5,328	26,350
Sale of common stock under employee stock options and stock purchase plans	58,362	12,999	21,918	32,290	15,801
Tax benefit from employee transactions in common stock	6,791	1,078	5,457	5,377	5,254
Total Provided from (Repayment of) External Financings	56,167	(2,331)	33,681	42,995	47,405
Funds (Cash and cash investments) at end period	$309,367	$165,992	$137,852	$120,616	$ 32,013

EXHIBIT 4

1986 Competitive Analysis: Tri-Tech Computer

	TRI-TECH	DEC	IBM	NCR	PRIME
Fiscal Yr. End Income Data					
Sales (mill.)	990.5	7,590.4	51,250.0	4,881.6	860.2
−5 yr. growth rate	25.2%	18.3%	10.5%	8.5%	18.5%
Net Income (mill.)	82.3	617.4	4,789.0	336.5	46.9
Net Profit Margin	8.3%	8.1%	9.3%	6.9%	5.5%
R&D/Net Sales	11.3%	10.7%	10.2%	6.6%	10.7%
Per Share Data					
E.P.S.	$1.44	$4.81	$7.81	$3.42	$0.97
−% increase (5 yr.)	100.0%	27.9%	5.7%	56.2%	−2.0%
Div. per share	nil	nil	4.40	0.91	nil
Balance Sheet Data					
Cash (mill.)	309	1,911	7,257	670	88
Current Ratio	3.87	4.90	2.18	2.01	2.94
Quick Ratio	3.40	3.79	1.55	1.47	2.28
Total Assets (mill.)	909	7,173	57,814	4,015	687
Return on Assets	19.2%	9.7%	9.1%	8.5%	7.8%
Long Term Debt	8	333	4,169	129	14
Common Equity	690	5,728	34,374	2,396	438
Total Cap.	737	6,090	45,071	2,763	541
LT Debt/Total Cap.	1.1%	5.5%	9.2%	4.7%	2.6%
Debt/Total Assets	24.2%	20.1%	40.5%	40.3%	36.3%
Return on Equity	15.2%	13.6%	15.0%	14.5%	12.2%
Sustain. Growth Rate	15.2%	13.6%	6.5%	10.6%	12.2%

EXHIBIT 5

Bond Ratings and Related Information of Selected Computer Companies

	TRI-TECH	DEC	IBM	NCR	PRIME
S & P Rating (April, 1987):					
Senior	*a	AA+	AAA	AA	*a
Subordinated	−	−	−	−	−
Convertible	−	−	AAA	−	BB+
1986 total liab./total assets	24.2%	20.1%	40.5%	40.3%	36.3%
Times Interest Earned:					
3 yr. avg.	35.2	9.8	25.1	15.9	49.1
1986	58.9	10.7	18.7	18.4	46.5
1985	24.4	6.3	27.2	15.0	30.4
1984	22.3	12.4	29.5	14.2	70.3

[a]Not rated.

EXHIBIT 6

Stock Ratings and Related Information of Selected Computer Companies

	TRI-TECH	DEC	IBM	NCR	PRIME
S & P Rating (April, 1987):					
Stock	B	B+	A+	A	B
Beta	1.65	1.25	1.05	1.30	1.35
Most Recent Activity:					
Date	None (in 6 yrs)	11/86	11/86	5/85, 5/86	8/86
Type of Debt		Repo	Repo	Repo	Repo
Amount		5MM shares authorized	5MM shares authorized	8MM shares authorized 6MM bought	2.4MM shares authorized
4/6/87 Stock Price	$73¾	$170⅛	$149⅜	$69¾	$21½
4/6/87 P/E Ratio	42	26	19	20	22
1986 Avg Ann'l P/E Ratio	19.0	14.2	18.0	14.1	20.9

EXHIBIT 7

Comparative Stock Data for the Years 1982 Through 1986

	1986	1985	1984	1983	1982
S & P 400 Industrials					
Year-end Price	$270	$235	$186	$186	$158
Earnings per share	$3.60	$3.81	$4.50	$3.68	$3.30
Dividends per Share Paid	$2.04	$1.94	$1.86	$1.84	$1.80
P/E Ratio (Yr. End Close)	19	15	10	13	12
Industrial Composite, Computer & Business Equipment					
Year-end Price	$196	$219	$178	$180	$145
Earnings per share	$2.76	$3.88	$3.80	$3.28	$2.76
Dividends per Share Paid	$1.43	$1.44	$1.37	$1.29	$1.22
P/E Ratio (Yr. End Close)	18	16	12	14	13
Tri-tech Computer					
Year-end Price	$34¼	$22¼	$19½	$35⅛	$25⅜
Earnings per share	$1.44	$0.82	$1.04	$0.76	$0.76
Dividends per Share Paid	nil	nil	nil	nil	nil
P/E Ratio (Yr. End Close)	24	27	19	46	33

EXHIBIT 8

Standard & Poor's Corporate Bond Yield Index—by Ratings

YIELDS ON OUTSTANDING INDUSTRIAL CORPORATE BONDS[a]

	AAA	AA	A	BBB
As of April 15, 1987	8.89%	9.54%	9.49%	10.31%

[a]These figures compare to weekly yields on U.S. Treasury Issues as follows: long term: 8.47%; intermediate: 7.93%; short term: 7.07%.

YIELDS ON OUTSTANDING INDUSTRIAL CORPORATE BONDS

	AAA	AA	A	BBB
Jan.–March 1987	8.46%	8.98%	8.99%	9.71%
1986 (yr. avg.)	9.02%	9.57%	9.66%	10.37%
1985 (yr. avg.)	10.94%	11.44%	11.54%	12.19%
1984 (yr. avg.)	12.43%	12.81%	13.12%	13.84%
1983 (yr. avg.)	11.45%	11.71%	12.04%	12.76%
1982 (yr. avg.)	13.03%	13.42%	14.02%	15.60%

EXHIBIT 9

Analysis of Recent Issues of Convertible Debentures

COMPANY	ISSUE SIZE	DATE	S & P RATING	COUPON	EFFECTIVE INT. COST	MATURITY	USE OF FUNDS	DEBT/TOTAL ASSETS PRO FORMA
Computer Assoc	$100MM	1/27/87	B+	5.75%	5.88%	2/01/12	repay bank indebtedness and for working capital	1.9%
Prime Computer	$350MM	1/28/87	BB+	5.75%	5.84%	2/01/12	fund acquisitions	39.0%
Masco Corp.	$225MM	2/12/87	A	5.25%	5.32%	2/15/12	gen'l corp. purposes, inc. repayment of debt	n/a
Price Company	$175MM	2/13/87	BB+	5.50%	5.57%	2/28/12	acquire land	38.2%
Sun Microsys.	$100MM	2/19/87	B	5.25%	5.38%	2/15/12	gen'l corp. purposes	41.5%
Compaq Comp.	$150MM	2/24/87	B+	5.25%	5.42%	3/01/12	expansion of business	28.2%
Union Carbide	$300MM	3/18/87	BB–	7.50%	n/a	4/15/12	realign balance sheet after takeover attempt	n/a
Reynolds Metal	$200MM	4/01/87	B–	6.00%	n/a	4/01/12	refinance l.t. debt	50.5%
Atari	$75MM	4/07/87	*a	5.25%	n/a	2002-Euro	expansion of business	42.2%
VLSI	$57MM	5/01/87	B–	7.00%	n/a	5/01/12	construct new wafer fabrication facility & other gen'l purposes	39.4%

aNot rated.

n/a – not available.

27

BELL CANADA

In late summer of 1985, Fred Andrew, Treasurer of Bell Canada, was evaluating which of several financing alternatives for raising $200 million in a contemplated December 1985 offering to recommend to Wes Scott, Bell Canada's Chief Financial Officer. It was expected that Bell Canada would require approximately $625 million of external financing during the remainder of 1985 and through 1986 in order to meet an unprecedented demand for telecommunications services. The remaining $425 million would be raised in three separate issues in 1986. Implicit in this decision were the considerations of what target capital structure would be appropriate to insulate Bell Canada's operating mandate from capital market conditions and what financial objectives would be the most consistent with achieving the chosen target. Extraordinary advances in technology, increased levels of competition, changes in the regulatory environment and rising expectations of customers were all working to reshape the telecommunications industry.

BACKGROUND ON THE COMPANY

Incorporated in 1880 on the basis of Alexander Graham Bell's original telephone patent, Bell Canada was the nation's largest supplier of telecommunication services providing advanced voice, data, image, radio and television transmission and other sophisticated telecommunications services to nearly 7 million customers in the provinces of Ontario and Quebec and in the Northwest Territories. For more than a century, Bell Canada had been a world leader in ascertaining and anticipating customer needs, creating services to fulfill those needs, exploiting technology to build and manage networks to support those services and managing the entire process to ensure superb customer service.

Through its wholly owned subsidiary, Tele-Direct (Publications) Inc., Bell Canada was also engaged in the sale of telephone directory advertising (representing 70% of the Canadian market), and in the publishing of White and Yellow Pages directories. In addition, Bell Canada had a 24.6% minority interest in Telesat Canada, which was engaged in the provision of satellite communication services between locations in Canada. To seek new business opportunities, manage new telecommunications ventures, and consolidate non-regulated activities, Bell Canada Management Corporation (BCMC) was established in early 1985 as a wholly owned subsidiary. Some of BCMC ventures included the marketing of distributed data processing equipment through Bell Data Systems Inc., the retail sales and servicing of computers and related products through Computer Innovations Distribution Inc., and the provision of cellular mobile telephone services through Bell Cellular Inc.

At its inception, Bell Canada's telephone system comprised fewer than 2,000 telephones. Over the next 103 years, Bell Canada's corporate family grew into more than 80 separate companies including Northern Telecom, in 1987 the world's leading manufacturer and pioneer of fully digital telecommunications systems and a significant supplier of integrated office systems; Bell Northern Research (BNR), in 1987 the largest private industrial research and development organization in Canada; and Bell Canada International (BCI) which provided technical, operational and managerial expertise to telecommunication administrations throughout the world.

The operating, research and production synergies of the vertically integrated tri-corporate structure of Bell Canada, Northern Telecom and BNR made the whole greater than the sum of the parts. Their world leadership arose from an inherent ability to identify the service needs of diverse customers, to direct the R & D of the technology, products and services to fulfill those needs and to manufacture the appropriate equipment—all within the same overall organization. The refinement cycle continued as Bell Canada transformed the technologies and products into reliable services and fed back valuable operating information that lead to continual improvement and the identification of even more sophisticated needs and applications. BCI was able to draw from this resource base to assist telecommunications and information-handling organizations throughout the world. During 1984, BCI worked on 58 projects in 32 countries, including a $1.6 billion project in Saudi Arabia.

For its first 103 years, Bell Canada functioned as both an operating company and as a holding company, with its energies divided between tactical operating considerations for the telecommunications operating company, and strategic planning issues for the entire portfolio of businesses in the Bell group of companies. Following a detailed and lengthy study, the Board of Directors concluded that the creation of a separate holding corporation was needed to provide the Bell group of companies with the same degree of structural and operational flexibility as their competitors in order to compete successfully in global markets.

Telecommunications systems and services were becoming an essential element in a nation's economic infrastructure as the developed world shifted towards an information economy. Traditional voice services and rapidly increasing requirements for data transmission were outstripping the ability of existing networks to meet the competitive pressures of global business needs and the growing demands of society. In response to these pressures, many developed countries, most notably the United States, Britain and Japan, were implementing major structural changes to their telecommunications industries through competition and deregulation in various markets and through the privatisation of state-owned monopolies. As governments throughout the world singled out telecommunications as a major priority for development and modernization, the global market for telecommunications equipment and associated services was forecast to reach $300 billion by the year 2000, a growth rate unrivalled by any other industry.

Deregulation and divestiture in the United States were transforming the telecommunications industry into a competitive free-for-all; telecommunications services were becoming a commodity business with price as the distinguishing feature. The technological blurring between the high growth markets of data processing and data communications had encouraged vendors to migrate from one area to the other. In addition to its one-third interest in Satellite Business Systems, a specialized common carrier, computer giant IBM acquired ROLM, a telecommunications equipment manufacturer, and established an alliance with the number-two carrier, MCI Communications. Similarly, AT&T moved into data processing by developing an operating system for mid-size machines called Unix and by forming alliances with Convergent Technologies and Olivetti to manufacture a line of personal computers. In the minds of many industry observers, AT&T and IBM would eventually square off against one another in the new and fast-growing industry of "compunications"—the result of the confluence in the telecommunications and computer industries.

Final federal approval was received on April 28, 1983, and with the support of its shareholders, Bell Canada carried out a reorganization of the Bell group which aligned the various corporate entities around the major business areas and established Bell Canada Enterprises Inc. (BCE) as the parent company (see Exhibit 1). Bell Canada became almost exclusively a telecommunications operating company, while BCE was to concentrate on creating and developing its portfolio of businesses in the most effective configuration to support continuing initiatives within intensely competitive international markets.

As a result of the reorganization, BCE became the owner of all common and preferred shares of Bell Canada outstanding on the effective date of the reorganization on which the former common and preferred shareholders of Bell Canada became owners of equivalent shares in BCE. The mechanics of the transaction involved transferring the investments in subsidiary and associated companies to BCE in exchange for the Second Preferred Shares, Series One and Two, payable by BCE to Bell Canada. Series One had a stated value and redemption price equal to the historical cost of the investments to Bell Canada ($478,743,000), while Series Two was equal to the excess of the net realizable value over the historical cost ($1,624,073,000). Upon reorganizing, BCE redeemed all outstanding Second Preferred Shares, Series Two, and Bell Canada simultaneously paid a dividend on its common shares in an aggregate amount equal to, and therefore offsetting, the redemption price of the preferred shares. As of December 31, 1984, BCE had redeemed $175 million of the Second Preferred Shares, Series One. Exhibits 2 to 4 present financial statements for the years 1983 and 1984.

INDUSTRY CHARACTERISTICS

Technologies and Markets

Like that of other industrialized countries, Canada's shift from an economy based on manufacturing and natural resources to one based on service industries was swift and ubiquitous. By 1985, telecommunications networks were fast becoming the basic infrastructure of an information-based economy as information intensive industries including banking and other financial services, broadcasting, and publishing became increasingly reliant on telecommunications for nationwide distribution of their products and services. Broad technological and economic factors stemming from the growing demand for conventional and advanced telecommunication services and the merger of telecommunications and computer technologies permitting the introduction of a vast range of new products, services and markets were fuelling change within the industry.

The telecommunications, data processing and office equipment industries historically developed as distinct entities along separate paths. When data processing and office equipment were built from single transistors wired together on circuit boards and telephone calls were switched electromechanically, the three industries had little in common. However, since the early 1970s there has been an increasing confluence of the technologies of these industries and the lines of distinction between them began to blur as telecommunication systems, computer data processing systems and integrated office equipment became increasingly similar in function and design. This convergence taking place was driven by advances in digital technology, semiconductors and software resulting in a new information management industry. As the new telecommunications systems became a product of the computer revolution, telecommunications equipment began to evolve as fast as computers. Price–performance characteristics improved as well, and new markets were created as suddenly and as unpredictably.

For most of its first 100 years, the systems and equipment used in the telecommunications network were largely analog. With analog technology, voice or sound signals are converted into electrical waves of varying amplitude and frequency.

When these waves travel over a distance, they may be affected by noise or distortion. Although the human ear can make appropriate adjustments, computers cannot; distortions in data and other non-voice signals can render a uniform electrical code meaningless.

With digital technology, voice signals are coded electronically in the form of binary "on" or "off" pulses in varying sequence through a technique called "pulse code modulation." Transmitted through the network, these codes can be easily and accurately converted back into the original voice signals. A microchip, called a coder–decoder circuit or *codec* chip, has been tailored specifically for this purpose. The inherent advantage is that data and images, as well as voice, can be transmitted with equal ease over digital networks because every signal is handled in the same way as bits of identical characteristics.

On average, every year of the prior 20 years had seen the computing power of semiconductors double while prices were cut in half, leading to a proliferation of mainframe, mini- and micro-computers of increasing power and flexibility. With more information digitized for processing and storage or readied for network transport, along with businesses becoming increasingly dependent on the effective management of their information resources for competitive purposes, the capacity of the public telecommunications network became of increasing concern.

Service markets in the telecommunications industry, encompassing voice, data and image communications, had traditionally been segmented interactively by technology and regulation, resulting in a complex structure of fragmented markets with each designed to achieve a different set of public interest goals. However, customer demands in the marketplace were breaking down the regulatory segmentation driving towards a single set of objectives for all service markets.

As objectives mandated for single-supply service markets were gradually giving way to the objectives of competitive suppliers in an integrated market, Bell Canada began taking major steps to evolve its networks into an integrated digital form. The integrated services digital network (ISDN), to be commercially available in 1990, would allow residential and business users to plug telephones, data terminals and personal computers into ISDN and have access to voice, data, image, facsimile and graphics transmission over an in-place telephone line as easily as placing a regular phone call. By arranging the services as a flexible transmission pipe of varying bandwidth, ISDN would allow customers to tailor services purchased to their actual needs in ways not possible in 1987. The efficiencies and economies of scale of an integrated network allowed these services to be offered at lower cost than if they were provided separately on different physical lines.

Regulation

Bell Canada was subject to the jurisdiction of the Canadian Radio–Television and Telecommunications Commission (CRTC), an agency of the Canadian government, in various respects including its rates, costing and accounting procedures. Although there was no statutory requirement for the CRTC to establish a rate base and provide for an equitable rate of return on that investment, the law required that all rates be just and reasonable. The CRTC established the level of revenue requirements by developing a permissible rate of return on average common equity after taking the costs of debt and preferred equity into account. In a decision dated September 28, 1981, the CRTC concluded that an appropriate rate of return on average common equity as determined for regulatory purposes should be 14.5%, with a permissible range between 14.25% and 14.75%.

From the outset, the pattern of telephone rate-making was based on the premise of making high quality telephone service at low cost available to as large a proportion of the public as possible. The Government of Canada considered an efficient national telecommunications network, responsive to the needs of Canadians, essential to Canada's international competitiveness and to its future economic and social development as a nation. The idea that universal service was socially desirable stems from the notion that each additional subscriber increased the value of the telephone system to other subscribers and was necessary to bind society together. Therefore, in order to serve the prevailing public policy goal of universal telephone service, a rate structure had evolved over the years whereby the prices of most services bore little resemblance to the actual costs of providing the services. Current long distance rates were kept artificially higher than their costs, while conversely, local service rates had been held lower than their associated costs in order to keep access to basic telephone service affordable. Bell Canada's Engineering Economics Department concluded in a comprehensive cost analysis, that it cost Bell Canada $1.93 to generate $1.00 of local service revenue, versus $0.32 to generate $1.00 of long distance revenue.

Another dimension of cross-subsidization was technological. By and large, within any given segment of the network, the equipment in use for the same service could typically be of varying degrees of technological evolution, age and operating costs. Furthermore, the technology was advancing continuously. The foremost consideration of integration, of a technological nature, was that different generations of the technology had to work together so that a technological breakthrough in one area could be employed to enhance productivity and service without negatively affecting service in any other areas. Under this flexible system, the national network developed and flourished as new discoveries, such as electronic switches and fibre optics, were mixed compatibly and worked in tandem with equipment installed 50 years earlier.

Competition

The elaborate rate structure, replete with cross-subsidization, was being fractured by selective competitive entry: competition was being superimposed on regulation. On November 23, 1982, the CRTC confirmed the basic elements of an interim decision issued on August 5, 1980, which mandated that a liberalized terminal attachment policy be followed, allowing the connection to Bell Canada's facilities of subscriber-owned terminal equipment. Since the interim decision in 1980, Bell

Canada had faced substantial competition and had experienced an ensuing loss of market share.

A CRTC decision issued on May 17, 1979, ordered that CNCP Telecommunications, a partnership of the respective telecommunications divisions of the Canadian National Railway Company and Canadian Pacific Limited, be allowed access to Bell Canada's public switched telecommunications network for data communications and certain restricted types of private line voice communications.

With sophisticated communications technologies, including microwave, satellite and fibre optics, widely available in the marketplace, the threat of large companies and institutions constructing their own private networks to bypass the diseconomies inherent in the conventional telecommunications network loomed quite large. From a societal point of view, this would be undesirable since fewer large customers would remain on the network to provide a contribution towards local service costs.

On October 25, 1983, CNCP filed with the CRTC a request that Bell Canada be required to interconnect CNCP's microwave and fibre optics network with the public switched network at selected points in order to compete in providing long distance voice services. Initially, this alternate service would be available to subscribers in Quebec City, Montreal, Ottawa–Hull, Toronto, Vancouver and Victoria at rates 20% lower than those provided by existing carriers. The filing was already under consideration by the CRTC in a generic hearing on the subject of interexchange competition. Major issues underpinning the discussions included the relationship between rates for local and toll services and whether and how much competitors should support local service prices. Moreover, the Federal Department of Communications was conducting its own review of national telecommunications policy, with the objective of promoting competition within the industry. In order to send the right signals to the marketplace and to encourage the adoption of fair and effective competition with the regulatory framework, Bell Canada prepared a proposal to rebalance rates to more closely reflect the underlying costs of providing the services through a gradual five-year adjustment process that would leave total operating revenues unchanged. The rationale underlining this initiative was threefold: lower long distance rates benefit the Canadian economy through new cost effective business applications for long distance services; costs are shared more equitably among customers; and a more rational environment is created in which to face competitors.

The CRTC decision, which would have a profound influence on the future structure and quality of the industry in the years to come, was due within a few weeks.

Construction and Financing Needs and Capital Structure Policy

In order to meet the growing demands of new services and to replace the analog network of mechanical switches and copper wires with an intelligent network based on digital switches and high capacity optical fibres, Bell Canada faced a continuing need to raise large amounts of capital. Selected financial and operating information is presented in Exhibit 5. The impact of inflationary price increases was removed, since the level of construction expenditures had remained relatively unchanged during the 1975 to 1980 period and decreased during the 1981 to 1983 timeframe, largely because of the economic downturn.

Reflecting unprecedented demands for service following the strong economic recovery, Bell Canada had forecasted capital expenditures of $9 billion in the six years between 1985 and 1990. Approximately 75% of capital spending would meet service demands of new and existing customers while the remainder would be used to modernize network facilities, improve operation efficiencies and replace worn out plants.

Bell Canada's debt and dividend policy was predicated on stability and placed a premium on financial integrity as evidenced by its double A credit rating. Since Bell Canada's external financing requirements were large relative to the size and depth of the Canadian market and were largely non-deferrable, it was vital to maintain continued uninterrupted access to global markets at acceptable terms, even during periods of severe financial dislocation. A study conducted by a leading U.S. investment banker noted that although the Euromarket was almost always available at attractive rates to triple and double A issuers, lower rated credits frequently had limited access during periods of adverse market conditions. It went on to add that "perhaps the single most immediate advantage of maintaining double A rating is that in difficult markets the Euromarkets may be effectively closed, or at a minimum not competitive on a spread basis with the U.S. market, for single A or lower-rated issues." With respect to issue size, both U.S. and Canadian data show that the average size of debt capital decreases with lower credits.

DEBT RATINGS AND THE CHOICE OF FINANCIAL OBJECTIVES

Standard & Poor's Criteria

In its February 25, 1985, issue of *CreditWeek,* Standard & Poor's Corporation published its revised benchmarks for the telecommunications industry to reflect the increasing magnitude of business risk faced by most industry participants. Exhibit 6 presents the full text of the article. Standard & Poor's rated operating telephone companies have shown the following capital ratio trends in the past:

TABLE 1
AA RATED TELEPHONE COMPANIES

	1980	1981	1982	1983	1984
Debt	45.2%	43.3%	43.1%	42.7%	44.8%
Preferred	1.0	0.8	0.9	0.8	0.8
Common	53.8	55.9	56.0	56.5	55.2

Bell Canada's average capital structure for 1980 to 1984 and its capital structure in 1984 are summarized below:

TABLE 2
BELL CANADA
CAPITAL STRUCTURE

	AVERAGE (1980–1984)	ACTUAL 1984	CURRENT OBJECTIVE
Debt	48.3%	47.3%	Max. 45%
Preferred	5.3	4.2	5
Common	46.4	48.5	Min. 50

Moody's Criteria

Moody's issued a Corporate Credit Report on Bell Canada in October 1984, and commented on its capitalization:

> The target debt ratio, set in the range of 45% to 50%, appears quite appropriate for the amount of business risk that the company is now facing.

Since the publication did not contain explicit quantitative criteria, Bell Canada's finance group inferred the range of appropriate capital structures from the senior debt ratings and capital structure choices exhibited by closely comparable U.S. telephone companies of similar operating risk profiles.

The AT&T family was made up of 22 local operating companies which were spun off into seven completely independent regional corporations in accordance with the provisions of the antitrust settlement. Each of these holding corporations, now known as Regional Bell Operating Companies (RBOC), had issued their own public debt at some point in time over the prior ten years. It was appropriate from an operating standpoint to compare Bell Canada to its equivalent, the RBOC.

For purposes of comparison, the Aa2- and A2-rated RBOCs were selected based on the ratings issued by Moody's on June 30, 1985. Exhibit 7 summarizes the findings of the comparative credit analysis and specifies reasonable ranges of variation of the key financial ratios that define the capital structures.

Standard and Poor's downgraded Bell Canada in June 1969 from AA to A, citing a market drop in Bell's key ratios over a sustained period. In March 1975, Standard and Poor's restored the rating to AA in view of stable and adequate key ratios.

SELECTING A TARGET CAPITAL STRUCTURE

Exhibit 8 illustrates the interaction of the rate of return measure against various scenarios of interest charge coverage and debt ratio assumptions. The target coverage ratios are a significant factor in determining a target capital structure.

Regulatory Considerations

It was unclear what rate of return the CRTC would allow in the next rate case proceeding since interest rates and inflationary expectations had decreased while the level of systematic risk increased, owing to a heightened level of competition.

Exhibit 9 compares Bell Canada's regulated rate of return and current capital structure vis-à-vis those of other regulated utilities in different industries. A systematic difference across capital structures is evident.

Fall 1985 Financing Proposals

Exhibit 10 presents a pro forma financial structure analysis which displays the impact of the $200 million preferred equity (P), debt (D) or common equity (C) financing alternatives on Bell Canada's credit statistics and reported financial results. The option of an early redemption (ER) of $154 million in the Second Preferred Shares, Series One, payable by BCE to Bell Canada is also included. Financing for 1986 and 1987 was similar for each alternative.

During the 17 month period between April 1984 and September 1985, Bell Canada issued $500 million in debt, of which $375 million, spread equally over three issues, was sold in Canada.

Prevailing market conditions for the three conventional financing alternatives were mixed. Bell Canada's investment bankers indicated that $150 million of long term debt could be readily absorbed by the market, and possibly upwards of $175 million if market conditions were good at the time of issue. However, it was unlikely that a $200 million financing requirement could be met in the Canadian debt market on attractive terms. Estimates of the after tax, all-in cost of issuing $125 million in different markets is outlined in Table 3.

TABLE 3
ALL-IN COST OF ISSUING $125 MILLION

	10 YEAR	15 YEAR
Canadian Public	5.75%	5.73%
USA Public	5.64	5.72
EuroCanadian	5.85	5.94

Issuing common equity would have involved selling additional shares to BCE. A common equity injection by BCE would be taken by the markets as a sign of commitment to Bell Canada and as an indication of satisfaction with current equity returns. Exhibit 11 provides market-to-book ratios for representative Canadian telephone companies. Since Bell Canada's common equity was not traded publicly, and hence did not have an established market value, such shares would have to be issued at book value. The opportunity of issuing above book value with its positive impact on earnings growth was not available to Bell Canada in a practical sense.

In 1987 a lack of good quality preferred instruments in the market was opening a window for a promising reception of a $200 million bought deal or conventionally syndicated preferred issue. This also represented one of the infrequent times in the early 1980s when "permanent" preferred stock financing was available with a relatively long life that could be controlled by the issuing corporation.

Accelerating the redemption of $154 million in BCE Series One Preferreds also offered attractive features. This uncomplicated transaction did not require regulatory approvals, underwriting fees, commissions or other associated expenses and could be implemented in minimal time. However, BCE's approval would be required and would have a negative impact on BCE's financing requirements. Moreover, if implemented, redemption would no longer be available as a future contingency financing option and would provide only short term relief inasmuch as the issue would mature in the near future in any event.

THE DECISION

The ten years from 1975 to 1985 had wrought fundamental changes in Bell Canada's businesses, culminating in the landmark CRTC hearings that would have far-reaching implications for the state of the industry in the years to come. These changes both mandated and provided the opportunity for a fundamental reassessment of Bell Canada's capital structure and financing policies. The rating agencies' application of increasingly stringent rating criteria underscored the importance of determining and committing to a movement towards the stated goals and objectives underlying the choice of capital structure policy.

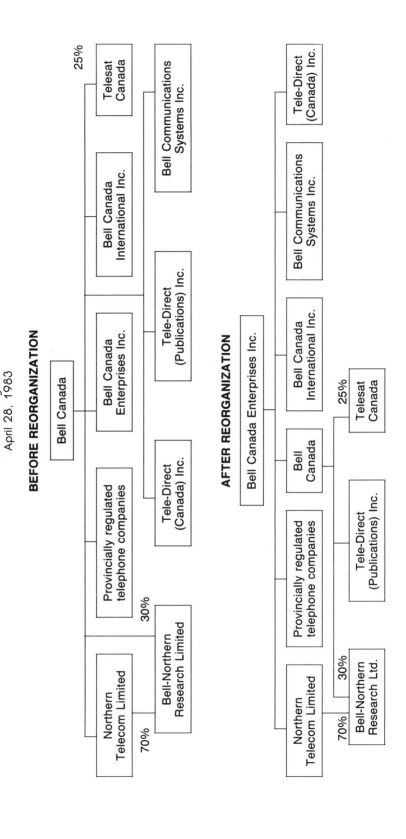

EXHIBIT 1

BELL CANADA
Restructuring Plan
April 28, 1983

BEFORE REORGANIZATION

AFTER REORGANIZATION

EXHIBIT 2

BELL CANADA
Consolidated Income Statement
For the Years Ended December 31
(millions of $)

	1984	1983
Telecommunications operations		
Operating revenues		
Local service	$2,198.5	$2,130.4
Long distance service	2,594.1	2,349.4
Directory advertising and miscellaneous – net	498.0	332.6
Total operating revenues	5,290.6	4,812.4
Operating Expenses	3,808.2	3,481.5
Net revenues – telecommunications operations	1,482.4	1,330.9
Contract operations		
Operating revenues	–	–
Operating expenses	–	–
Net revenues – contract operations	–	–
Total net revenues	1,482.4	1,330.9
Other income		
Dividends		
Parent company	31.3	24.7
Subsidiary and associated companies	–	28.7
Allowance for funds during construction	20.5	21.1
Miscellaneous – net	33.3	36.6
Total other income	85.1	111.1
Interest charges	402.3	378.1
Income before underlisted items	1,165.2	1,063.9
Unrealized foreign currency losses	21.1	12.1
Income before income taxes	1,144.1	1,051.8
Income taxes	517.4	461.2
Net income	626.7	590.6
Dividends on preferred shares	46.0	52.3
Net income applicable to common shares	$ 580.7	$ 538.3

EXHIBIT 3

BELL CANADA
Consolidated Balance Sheet
As at December 31,
(millions $)

	1984	1983
Assets		
Current Assets		
Cash and temporary cash investments		
due from parent company	$ 78.9	$ 89.9
Accounts receivable	724.0	638.2
Other (principally prepaid expenses)	92.4	93.9
	895.7	822.0
Investments		
Parent company — at cost	303.7	378.7
Associated companies — at equity	53.7	45.0
	357.4	423.7
Telecommunications Property — at cost		
Buildings, plants and equipment	13,897.6	13,130.7
Less accumulated depreciation	4,592.2	4,187.9
	9,305.4	5,942.8
Land	88.7	88.5
Plant under construction	224.1	264.6
Material and supplies	66.8	72.0
	9,685.0	9,367.9
Other assets		
Long term receivables	124.4	47.0
Deferred charges — unrealized foreign		
currency losses, less amortization	257.0	164.3
— other	55.9	55.7
	437.3	267.0
Total Assets	$11,375.4	$10,880.6

(continued)

EXHIBIT 3 (cont.)

	1984	1983
Liabilities and Shareholders' Equity		
Current Liabilities		
Accounts payable	528.9	539.5
Advanced billing and payments	85.0	82.7
Dividends payable	117.7	113.5
Taxes accrued	122.9	95.3
Interest accrued	103.2	97.1
Debt due within one year	377.1	142.5
	1,334.8	1,070.6
Long term debt	3,823.9	3,817.9
Deferred credits		
Income taxes	1,478.5	1,395.9
Other	57.4	60.2
	1,535.9	1,456.1
Share capital amortized		
Non-convertible preferred shares (redeemable)	92.7	96.4
Convertible preferred shares (redeemable)	283.3	327.7
Common shareholders' equity		
Stated capital of common shares	1,842.0	1,797.6
Premium on share capital	1,033.5	1,033.5
Retained earnings	1,429.3	1,280.8
	4,304.8	4,111.9
Total liabilities and shareholders' equity	$11,375.4	$10,880.6

EXHIBIT 4

BELL CANADA
Consolidated Statement of Changes in Financial Positions
For the Years Ended December 31,
(in millions $)

	1984	1983
Sources of cash		
Operations		
Net income	$ 626.7	$ 590.6
Add expenses not requiring cash		
Depreciation	879.5	807.1
Deferred income taxes	83.3	97.7
Other items	(32.7)	(20.8)
Deduct income not providing cash		
Allowance for funds used during construction	(20.5)	(21.1)
Total cash from operations	$1,536.3	$1,453.5
Changes in working capital	(55.1)	(26.2)
External financing		
Proceeds from redemption of investment in the parent company	75.0	100.0
Proceeds from long term debt	246.4	—
Issue of common shares		
Under the dividend reinvestment and stock purchase plan	—	50.9
Under the optional stock dividend program	—	7.0
Upon conversion of convertible preferred shares	44.4	94.6
Proceeds from issue of preferred shares	—	—
Increase (decrease) in notes payable and bank advances	34.1	60.7
	399.9	313.2
Total sources of cash	1,881.1	1,740.5
Application of cash		
Capital expenditures (net)	1,185.8	1,116.5
Long term receivables	77.4	47.0
Investments	6.7	9.6
Repayment of long term debt	143.1	65.9
Conversion of preferred shares	44.4	94.6
Miscellaneous	(43.5)	(25.3)
Dividends declared	478.2	459.2
Total application of cash	1,892.1	1,767.5
Cash and temporary cash investments		
Decrease	(11.0)	(27.0)
At beginning of year	89.9	116.9
At end of year	$ 78.9	89.9

EXHIBIT 5

BELL CANADA

Selected Financial and Other Data

(in millions $)

	1984	1983	1982	1981	1980
Income Statement Data					
Telecommunications operations—operating revenues	$ 5,290.6	$ 4,812.4	$ 4,359.3	$ 3,845.1	$ 3,203.1
Contract operations—operating revenues	—	—	469.1	493.2	453.6
Total revenues	5,290.6	4,812.4	4,828.4	4,338.3	3,656.7
Net income	626.7	590.6	521.4	476.0	365.9
Dividends declared	478.2	459.2	419.8	356.0	313.1
Balance Sheet Data					
Total Assets[a]	$11,375.4	$10,880.6	$10,620.0	$10,004.7	$ 9,228.8
Long Term Debt[a] (including current portion)	4,088.3	3,881.8	3,936.8	3,877.6	3,596.9
Preferred Shares[a] (redeemable)	376.0	424.1	522.4	361.6	454.1
Gross capital expenditures	1,178.9	1,140.9	1,417.2	1,401.5	1,297.0
Financial Ratios					
Percent return on average total capital	11.8	11.4	10.9	10.9	9.5
Percent return on average common equity	13.9	13.5	12.7	13.1	10.6
Interest as a percent of total average debt	9.6	9.4	9.2	9.0	8.5
Debt as a percent of total capital[a]	47.3	46.6	47.7	50.2	49.6
Interest coverage	3.84	3.78	3.55	3.64	3.38
Other Statistics					
Network access services[a] (thousands)	6,823.4	6,574.0	6,416.2	6,348.2	6,174.5
Long distance messages (millions)	847.8	787.8	746.9	747.9	699.3
Number of employees[a]	51,167.0	54,423.0	55,761.0	58,659.0	57,267.0

[a]As at December 31.   Net Cash Flow as % Debt % 27.7%

343

EXHIBIT 6

Standard & Poor's Credit Week[a]
Credit Comment

TELECOMMUNICATIONS FINANCIAL RATIOS REVISED

S&P is revising the financial benchmarks for the regulated segment of the telecommunications industry to reflect the increasing business risk faced by most industry participants. While the new benchmarks are effective immediately, the rating process is prospective in nature, and few, if any rating changes are expected to result in the near term. These new benchmarks reflect a range of risk expectations that are evolving with the rapidly changing character of the industry. Initially, financial ratios of many Bell and independent operating companies are expected to fall short of the new tightened benchmarks for fixed charge coverage, debt leverage, and cash flow adequacy. S&P expects that the financial performance and condition of operating companies can steadily improve during at least the next few years to meet these new standards. The principal near-term risks to such improvement include restrictive regulation and an absence of management resolve to curtail debt leverage.

Debt ratings for regulated telecommunications companies are based on the prospective evaluation of 10 qualitative and quantitative criteria areas, rather than just a few financial ratios calculated at one point in time.

BUSINESS RISK

Companies are analyzed on the basis of their ability to provide creditor protection as ongoing enterprises. Implicit in that process is an assessment of business risk. Business risk is defined here as both the staying power of market demand, as well as the integrity of the revenue streams from the various products and services offered to that market. The nature and level of business risk is specifically evaluated for each telecommunications company and then used to determine the financial benchmark levels for credit evaluation. Naturally, these become more stringent as risk increases.

Economic and technological competition are now the primary forces behind business risk in the telecommunications industry. At the present time, switched telephone service appears to be the most efficient, rapid, and flexible form on nonvisual communications between any two parties. However, technology has already provided many viable alternatives, such as optical fibre, cellular radio, and direct microwave transmission, which are fully competitive in certain applications. Pervasive and increasing economic competition, too, is being promoted by a public policy shift to competition.

RISK ANALYSIS

To facilitate its business risk analysis, S&P has divided the regulated services sector of the telecommunications industry into four basic groups.

Group I includes the small to medium-sized, rural local exchange companies that account for the bulk of some 1,400 U.S. telephone companies, the smallest portion of total access lines and little publicly rated long term debt. Competition is not presently expected to materially affect these companies' customers. Consequently, business risk

---

[a]February 25, 1985.

(continued)

EXHIBIT 6   (cont.)

should be little changed from that which existed prior to the start of the new competitive era.

Group II represents the medium to large-sized, rural–suburban local exchange companies, the majority of the traditional independent systems subsidiaries, and a substantial portion of the 22.3 million non-Bell access lines. Many of the companies have publicly rated long term debt outstanding. The majority face actual and potential competition from the inter-exchange carriers, as well as their own customers. This raises level of business risk for Group II companies to points presently somewhat higher than the historic industry average level.

Group III consists of the large metro-suburban local exchange companies, including the Bell operating companies, the bigger companies of the GTE Corp. system and the large non-affiliated independents. These companies own about 85% of all of the access lines and have substantially all of the publicly rated long-term debt. Because most of the access lines are concentrated around major metro areas, already present competition is increasing. As a result, business risk continues to climb from levels that are already well above the earlier industry average level.

Group IV includes the inter-exchange carriers, AT&T Communications, and the so-called other common carriers, such as MCI Communications Inc. and GTE Sprint. Competition is rampant and business risk levels in Group IV are significantly higher than those found in the Group III companies. In fact, levels are approaching those of industrial companies. Presently, only MCI, Western Union Co., and AT&T Communications have publicly rated debt. AT&T's debt rating is at the corporate level.

S&P's prior system of benchmarks has been replaced by four sets of criteria ranges, keyed to the four business risk classes. These ranges are deliberately wide to allow for business risk variations within the classes.

FIXED CHARGED COVERAGE

S&P traditionally uses pretax fixed charge coverage as its primary test for earnings adequacy. To reflect the changes in the business risk classes, benchmark coverage ranges are increased for companies in Groups II, III, IV by 10% to 88% and reduced slightly for Group I companies.

	I	II	III	IV
	PRETAX FIXED CHARGED COVERAGE (X)			
AAA	4.0 or more	4.7 or more	5.6 or more	8.5 or more
AA	3.5–4.7	4.0–5.5	4.5–6.5	5.5–9.5
A	2.7–4.0	3.0–4.5	3.5–5.5	4.5–8.0
BBB	2.0–3.0	2.3–3.4	2.7–4.0	3.5–5.5
BB	2.3 or less	2.6 or less	3.0 or less	4.0 or less

DEBT LEVERAGE

Benchmark levels for total debt as a percentage of capitalization, the primary measure of financial leverage, are also revised to reflect changes in business risk. They are adjusted downward by 2% to 38% for Groups II, III, and IV companies and upward by 8% for Group I companies.

(continued)

EXHIBIT 6 (cont.)

TOTAL DEBT/TOTAL CAPITALIZATION (%)

	I	II	III	IV
AAA	45 or less	40 or less	35 or less	25 or less
AA	45–50	40–45	35–40	25–35
A	50–60	45–55	40–50	30–40
BBB	60–70	55–65	50–60	40–50
BB	70 or more	65 or more	60 or more	50 or more

CASH FLOW ADEQUACY

Over the last several years, the telecommunications industry has moved to hold down spending programs as a result of slowing growth rates and improved capital expenditure productivity. In addition, companies strengthened cash flow by aggressive pursuit of higher depreciation rates. As a result, S&P found that the cash flow adequacy measure previously used, net cash flow (after all dividends) as a percentage of capital expenditures increasingly failed to differentiate credit strength. Instead, net cash flow will now be measured against long term debt in order to improve cash flow adequacy evaluation.

NET CASH FLOW/LONG TERM DEBT (%)

	I	II	III	IV
AAA	35 or more	40 or more	50 or more	65 or more
AA	25–35	30–40	35–50	45–65
A	15–25	20–30	25–35	30–45
BBB	12–20	13–20	15–25	20–30
BB	12 or less	13 or less	15 or less	20 or less

Last year was the first post-divestiture year for the Bell operating companies. For all telecommunications companies it was the first under the access charge system rather than the traditional toll revenue settlements. For these reasons, any historical trends established prior to Dec. 31, 1983 may well be suspect. At the same time, 1984 results could indicate the future direction with long-term debt ratings. S&P expects to comment on 1984 operating results, when available, in the context of both new and old financial benchmarks.

JOHN A. HARDY

EXHIBIT 7

Comparative Credit Analysis

STATISTIC	AVERAGE (1975-1984)			CURRENT POSITION (1984)		
	Aa2[a] RBOCs	A2[b] RBOCs	BELL CANADA	Aa2[a] RBOCs	A2[b] RBOCs	BELL CANADA
Debt Ratio (%)	41.2	41.9	49.0	42.0	42.9	47.3
Preferred Stock Ratio (%)	–	–	6.0	–	–	4.2
Common Equity Ratio (%)	58.8	58.1	45.0	58.0	42.0	48.5
Total Capital	100.0	100.0	100.0	100.0	100.0	100.0

[a]Aa2 rated companies:
Bell Pennsylvania
Diamond State Telephone
Illinois Bell
Indiana Bell
Michigan Bell
New Jersey Bell
Ohio Bell
[b]A2 rated companies:
Chesapeake & Potomac of West Virginia
Chesapeake & Potomac (DC)
New York Telephone
Southwestern Bell

EXHIBIT 8

BELL CANADA
Coverage Ratios
Rate of Return Versus Debt Ratio Scenarios

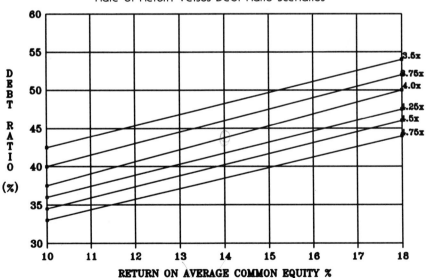

RETURN ON AVERAGE COMMON EQUITY %

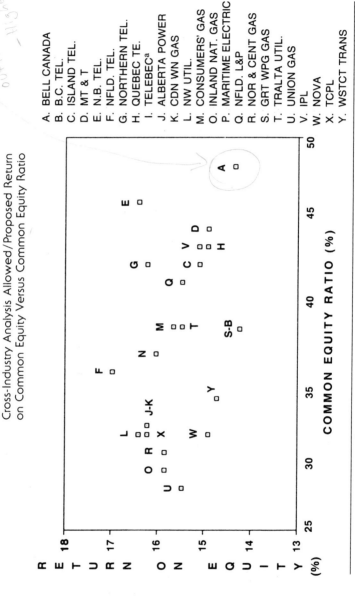

EXHIBIT 9

Cross-Industry Analysis Allowed/Proposed Return
on Common Equity Versus Common Equity Ratio

A. BELL CANADA
B. B.C. TEL.
C. ISLAND TEL.
D. MT & T
E. N.B. TEL.
F. NFLD. TEL.
G. NORTHERN TEL.
H. QUEBEC TE.
I. TELEBEC[a]
J. ALBERTA POWER
K. CDN WN GAS
L. NW UTIL.
M. CONSUMERS' GAS
O. INLAND NAT. GAS
P. MARITIME ELECTRIC
Q. NFLD. L&P
R. NOR & CENT GAS
S. GRT WPG GAS
T. TRALTA UTIL.
U. UNION GAS
V. IPL
W. NOVA
X. TCPL
Y. WSTCT TRANS

COMMON EQUITY RATIO (%)

[a]No allowed return given for Telebec which is excluded from the graph.

348

EXHIBIT 10

BELL CANADA
Pro Forma Financial Structure Analysis[a]

	1983	1984	1985				1986				1987			
			P	D	C	ER	P	D	C	ER	P	D	C	ER
Consolidated Return (%)	13.50	13.90	13.79	13.81	13.78	—	13.62	13.62	13.64	—	13.77	13.77	13.70	—
Regulated Return (%)	13.57	13.94	14.16	14.18	14.14	14.15	14.00	14.00	14.00	14.00	14.00	14.00	14.00	14.00
Coverage (X)	3.78	3.84	3.90	3.89	3.90	3.90	3.99	3.78	4.06	3.89	4.03	3.82	4.08	3.85
Gross Payout Ratio (%)	75.60	74.40	74.40	74.30	75.10	—	74.70	74.60	74.80	—	74.30	74.20	74.30	—
Debt Ratio (%)	46.60	47.30	45.50	47.60	45.50	46.50	46.20	48.30	46.20	47.90	44.70	46.60	44.60	46.60
Preferred Ratio (%)	5.00	4.20	5.90	3.80	3.80	3.90	5.50	3.40	3.40	3.40	5.10	3.20	3.20	3.20
Common Ratio (%)	48.40	48.50	48.60	48.60	50.70	49.60	48.30	48.30	50.40	48.70	50.20	50.20	52.20	50.20
Internally Generated Funds	89.10	89.20	86.00	86.00	85.70	—	80.10	80.20	80.60	—	87.10	87.10	87.60	—
Net Cash Flow/Long Term Debt (%)	26.00	27.70	28.00	26.80	27.90	28.00	26.70	25.60	26.90	27.20	28.30	27.10	28.60	28.60

[a]P = $200 million preferred in 1985.
D = $200 million debt in 1985.
C = $200 million common stock in 1985.
ER = Early redemption of remaining ($154 million) BCE preferred.

EXHIBIT 11

Comparative Ratios of Market Value of Equity
to Book Value of Equity

COMPANY	1980	1981	1982	1983	1984
B.C. Telephone	1.08	0.93	1.02	1.23	1.19
Island Telephone	0.93	0.91	1.00	1.22	1.22
MT&T	0.97	0.88	1.01	1.23	1.40
Bruncor	0.97	0.88	1.08	1.36	1.38
Nfld. Tel.	1.10	0.93	1.12	1.31	1.29
Quebec-Tel	0.91	0.80	0.93	1.24	1.33
Composite	1.00	0.88	1.01	1.23	1.25
BCE[a]	0.97	0.88	1.08	1.36	1.31

[a]1980–1982 data for Bell Canada Consolidated.

28

ROGERS COMMUNICATIONS INC.

It was 3:00 P.M. on Friday, March 29, 1991, as Graham Savage, CFO of Rogers Communications Inc. (Rogers or the Company), leaned back in his chair and thought about his upcoming meeting with his boss, Ted Rogers, President, CEO and the controlling shareholder of Rogers. Graham was scheduled to meet with Ted in an hour when he would recommend which type of financing method Rogers should use to fund its ongoing capital requirements. Graham had postponed completing a major financing for the last twelve months, given the tight market conditions and the recession. However, Rogers was rapidly approaching the point where fund-raising could no longer be delayed.

Graham's decision had become somewhat more complex because of the increasing globalization of financial markets. As Graham reflected on the pros and cons of issuing various securities in different markets, his eye caught yet another article in the newspaper commenting on the movement towards the integration of the disclosure and reporting requirements of the securities regulatory agencies in Canada and the U.S., namely the proposed Multi-Jurisdictional Disclosure System (MJDS). Graham pondered how the movement towards MJDS might play a part in his decision.

This case was prepared by Graeme Falkowsky and Kathryn Montgomery under the supervision of Professor Robert W. White for the sole purpose of providing material for class discussion at the Western Business School. Certain names and other identifying information may have been disguised to protect confidentiality. It is not intended to illustrate either effective or ineffective handling of a managerial situation. Any reproduction, in any form, of the material in this case is prohibited except with the written consent of the School.

The Western Business School would like to acknowledge the assistance of Graham Savage of Rogers Communications Inc. in preparing the case.

DESCRIPTION OF OPERATIONS

With a market capitalization of $2.4 billion in March 1991, Rogers Communications Inc. was a major player in the Canadian communications industry. Through its subsidiaries and affiliates, Rogers was involved in four primary areas of activity: cable television, broadcasting, mobile communications and telecommunications. Rogers believed it was unique among North American communications companies in that it had major interests in several areas of the Canadian communications industry, making it less dependent on a single communications service or technology.

Rogers prided itself on being creative and innovative. This was largely a reflection of its controlling shareholder, Ted Rogers, who was extremely visionary, entrepreneurial, innovative and creative himself. Ted valued these traits and tried to instill them in his employees. An organizational chart outlining the reporting relationships between Rogers' key executives is contained in Exhibit 1.

Prior to 1986, Rogers' main business had been cable television operations in Canada and the U.S. Since that time, Rogers had significantly developed its business by entering into cellular mobile communications and telecommunications. Ted Rogers had been in radio and television broadcasting since 1959. These operations were purchased by the public company in the mid-1980s. In 1989, Rogers sold its remaining U.S. cable television operations and embarked on a major capital expenditure program to upgrade and rebuild its Canadian cable television operations.

Rogers was organized as a holding company with four primary operating units as follows: cable and pay television through Rogers Cablesystems Limited (including a videocassette rental operation); broadcasting (including a home shopping TV network) through Rogers Broadcasting Limited; mobile communications through Rogers Cantel Mobile Inc.; and telecommunications through a 40% interest in Unitel Communications Inc. (formerly CNCP Telecommunications). An organizational chart outlining the corporate structure of Rogers' four principal operating groups is contained in Exhibit 2.

Substantially all of Rogers' business activities were regulated by the Canadian Federal Department of Communications (DOC) and the Canadian Radio-television and Telecommunications Commission (CRTC). Regulations governed licensing, the rates that Rogers was allowed to charge for its cellular telephones, cable television and telecommunications services, the operation and ownership of its communications systems and the ability of Rogers to acquire interests in other communications systems. Changes in such regulations, including decisions by regulators affecting Rogers' operations (such as the granting or renewal of licenses or decisions as to the rate Rogers could charge its customers), or changes in interpretations of existing regulations by regulators, could adversely affect Rogers' operations.

Cable Television

Rogers Cablesystems Limited (Cablesystems) operated all of Rogers' Canadian cable television businesses as well as a pay television business, a converter rental business, a local telecommunications business, and a videocassette rental business. Cablesystems had provided cable television to the Canadian market for over 30 years and management believed that it was the technical and service leader in the industry.

Cablesystems was the largest cable television company in Canada, serving approximately 1,800,000 basic cable subscribers who represented approximately 23% of Canada's total cable subscribers. Cablesystems also owned and operated a chain of 66 video cassette rental stores under the trade name Rogers Video. Rogers Video was the second largest video store chain in Canada in terms of revenue, and operated within the metropolitan areas of Toronto, Ottawa, Calgary, Edmonton and Vancouver.

Under new CRTC rate regulations, Cablesystems expected to receive a rate increase of CPI less two percentage points; however, there was no assurance as to the future level of rate increases that Cablesystems might obtain. Due to the relatively late introduction of television to Canada and a more restrictive regulatory regime whose mandate was to protect Canadian Broadcasters, pay television penetration and revenue per subscriber were both considerably lower in Canada than in the United States. Cablesystems did not expect the recession to significantly affect its cable television revenues.

Although the CRTC allowed only one cable television operator to serve any given area, Cablesystems faced competition and potential competition from alternative forms of television signal distribution, such as satellite master antenna television systems (SMATV), direct broadcasting satellite systems (DBS), and multi-point distribution systems (MDS). Only SMATV systems were currently available in Rogers' Canadian markets. No DBS systems were licensed in Canada although Cancom, Telesat Canada, First Choice Canadian Communications Inc. and others offered quasi-DBS service to a few subscribers mainly outside of cable licensed areas.

Broadcasting

Rogers Broadcasting Limited (Broadcasting) owned and operated Canada's only licensed multilingual television station, located in Toronto (CFMT-TV), and 13 radio stations in Canada including CFTR-AM and CHFI-FM in Toronto. Broadcasting also held a 93.2% interest in CHSN, a publicly listed company which operated a nationally televised shop-at-home service that was delivered by Canada's cable operators, including Cablesystems. Other interests included a 25.4% holding in YTV, a youth television programming service, and 24.9% of Viewers Choice Canada, a newly licensed pay-per-view service.

Broadcasting's television station and radio stations competed for audience with other television and radio stations in the Vancouver, Victoria, Calgary, Edmonton, and Toronto markets. Broadcasting's home shopping service competed across Canada with discount and mail order retailers.

The economic slowdown had lowered profitability and redistributed the advertising revenues among the leading radio and television stations. Several of Rogers' stations had been negatively affected.

All of Broadcasting's operations were subject to licensing and renewal by the CRTC. All of the licenses for Broadcasting's radio stations were due for renewal in 1992, with the exception of CFTR and CHFI which had received renewals in October 1990.

Mobile Communications

Rogers Cantel Inc. (Cantel) operated the largest cellular telephone network in Canada and was the only company authorized to provide service nationwide, offering cellular telephone service to areas where over 22 million people representing 82% of Canada's population resided (Exhibit 3). Cantel's network consisted of some 500 geographical areas known as cells and 15 switches linked by microwave and fibre optic transmission systems. By March 1991, Cantel served over 350,000 cellular telephone subscribers who were able to use their cellular telephones in all parts of Canada covered by Cantel's system. In addition, Cantel had begun a paging service in July 1989 which served 21,000 subscribers as of December 31, 1990.

Cellular telephone service had been commercially available for approximately six years in Canada. Despite the rapid growth of the industry, the commercial feasibility of cellular systems had not been proven over a long period of time. The cellular telephone industry was highly capital-intensive, requiring significant capital to construct cellular systems and to fund initial operating losses.

Since its inception, the Canadian cellular industry had been a duopoly in each service area regulated by the DOC and the CRTC. Although Cantel was the only cellular telephone network authorized to provide service nationwide in Canada, there were 13 other cellular telephone companies operating in Canada, each of which provided cellular service in a specified non-overlapping market. These other cellular telephone companies were wireline telephone companies that provided local telephone service in their respective markets. Competition for subscribers between Cantel and the wireline telephone companies in each market was principally on the basis of services and enhancements offered, the technical quality of the system, coverage, capacity and price. Such competition was intense.

The 1990 recession affected both Cantel's operations and the Canadian cellular industry as a whole through lower usage and higher bad debt expense. The impact was noticed late in the year and extended into 1991. New technologies that were continuing to be developed could be seen as a threat to traditional cellular telephone systems. Cantel was deciding whether to adopt this new technology and had committed to spending 2% of its cellular revenues on research and development.

Telecommunications

Rogers held a 40% interest in Unitel Communications Inc. (Unitel), a national Canadian telecommunications carrier, which had fibre optic networks and digital and analog microwave networks across Canada that provided data transmission services, and private-voice telephone services. Unitel offered substantially the same services as a long distance telephone company except for public-voice long distance services, which Unitel was currently seeking regulatory approval to provide.

Long distance public-voice service (approximately $7 billion annual revenue) was a monopoly service provided by the wireline telephone companies. In May 1990, Unitel had filed an application with the CRTC to enable it to offer public-voice long distance telephone transmission services in seven Canadian provinces. The CRTC's decision was expected in 1992.

Unitel was dependent on the continued development of telecommunications products and the growth of existing products to achieve continued revenue growth and eventual profitability. To meet the level of service required by its customers and to improve profitability, Unitel continued to follow its program of extending its facilities, converting older analog technology to the latest digital technology and increasing the network's capacity by using fibre optic lines in high volume routes. Unitel's main competitors were the member companies of Telecom Canada who provided private-voice telephone and data transmission services.

During the last twelve months, Cantel, Cablesystems and Unitel had begun realizing certain operating efficiencies through coordinated operations. Cablesystems and Cantel shared fibre optic paths, microwave sites and towers, a data centre built in 1990 and the provision to Unitel of transmission services from Cablesystems. Rogers had made significant capital expenditures in building its cellular network, establishing its other mobile communications services and increasing the capacity and reliability of its cable television network. One of the main operational objectives over the next few years was to seek to achieve greater operating efficiencies of this nature. As a result, high levels of depreciation, amortization and substantial interest expense were expected to continue.

FINANCIAL POSITION

Selected financial information pertaining to Rogers is contained in Exhibit 4. The Company had participated in new communications initiatives that required large initial capital expenditures. Interest and depreciation expenses had increased substantially as a result of these capital expenditures and the significant amount of debt used to finance them, causing net losses for all but one period since September 1985. Rogers was highly leveraged and its earnings were generally inadequate to meet its interest commitments. However, Rogers was able to meet its interest commitments since its operating income before depreciation and amortization exceeded its interest expense in all periods. Not surprisingly, Rogers' credit rating was below investment grade.

OWNERSHIP STRUCTURE

Rogers' common stock consisted of two classes of shares—Class A voting shares and Class B non-voting shares—both of which were listed on the Toronto, Montreal, Vancouver and Alberta Stock Exchanges. Although the Class B non-voting shares were widely held, Ted Rogers had virtual control over the Company, holding directly and through associated companies, 89.3% of the Class A voting shares and 19.3% of the Class B non-voting shares in March 1991.

In order to comply with the regulations of the CRTC pursuant to Canada's federal Broadcasting Act, Rogers was precluded from allowing more than 20% of its voting rights or paid-up capital to be controlled, directly or indirectly, by non-Canadians. If foreign ownership of the Company increased to a level above 20%, Rogers' cable television, radio, television broadcasting, cellular and paging licenses could be revoked. In August 1987, Rogers had begun barring foreigners from buying its stock, as a way to reduce its non-Canadian ownership to more acceptable levels. Such controls were extremely effective, and just last week, Rogers had lifted its self-imposed ownership restrictions. Foreign ownership of voting shares and paid-up capital was currently at 2% and 3%, respectively. Although Rogers had removed its foreign ownership restrictions for the time being, it would continue to require buyers of its stock to provide declarations of citizenship to its transfer agent, enabling Rogers to monitor ownership levels. The market had reacted positively to the news, sending Rogers' Class B non-voting shares up by $1.375 the day after the announcement.

FINANCING REQUIREMENTS

For many years, regular significant financing requirements were needed by Rogers to fund its capital expenditures and investments in new communications businesses. Forecasts showed that Rogers and its subsidiaries would continue to require additional financing in the future to fund planned capital expenditures and investments, particularly for Cantel and Unitel. Cantel would require high initial capital investments and high initial marketing expenditures, and capital expenditures over the next several years were expected to be significant.

TRADITIONAL FUNDING SOURCES

In the past, Rogers had relied primarily on traditional bank financing to fund its capital requirements. Rogers' policy was to deal closely with a very few banks. Rogers felt that a close, almost partnership type of relationship with three or four banks offered the Company much more flexibility, and it valued its close, almost informal relationships with its bankers. Due to the quickly changing nature of Rogers' business, the Company would routinely visit its banks and often restructure its loans to reflect these changes. A banking syndicate, comprised of three or four banks that had been very close to Rogers and had been for some time, was able to effect changes much more quickly than would a large, say 50-member, consortium.

Most of Rogers' outstanding bank debt imposed restrictions on the Company's activities and reduced its financial flexibility by requiring Rogers to maintain certain operating and financial ratios, and by posing restrictions on additional investments, capital expenditures, sales of assets and cash distributions.

As a holding company, substantially all of Rogers' business activities and assets were operated or held by subsidiaries. Rogers' ability to meet its financial obligations was primarily dependent upon the receipt of cash dividends, advances and other payments from its subsidiaries, primarily Cantel and Cablesystems. Rogers endeavoured to structure its debt instruments so that borrowings for each of the business groups and for general corporate purposes were generally secured by the assets of the respective entities within each group. Rogers avoided debt financing that required cross-collateralization between groups or parental guarantees.

Although most of Rogers' capital requirements were funded by traditional bank financing, it had raised equity when necessary. For example, in 1989, Rogers had issued $200 million of 7.5% convertible subordinated debentures. In hindsight, that transaction had been particularly timely, as the securities had been issued when Rogers' share price was at its peak. Other financing methods used in the past included tax shelter partnerships in the U.S., equity and convertible debt issues and a subordinated private placement for Cablesystems.

CURRENT BANKING ENVIRONMENT

Unfortunately for Rogers, there was a tremendous lack of liquidity in the banking systems around the world. Most countries, including Canada, the U.S., Australia and Japan, were in the middle of a recession. A global credit crunch was occurring, particularly in the banking industry. The outlook was fairly dismal, and there was a great sense of nervousness on the part of most banks. Several events had led up to the current state of the global banking environment:

1. *BIS Capital Adequacy Guidelines.* In August 1990, it had become apparent that many banks around the world were pulling in their reins, partly in reaction to the capital adequacy guidelines recently established by the BIS (Bank of International Settlement). The BIS was managed by several central banks around the world and had established reserve requirements, increasing the amount of equity each bank was required to have in relation to its assets. Consequently, most banks had increased their threshold parameters when considering new and existing business.

2. *Withdrawal of the Japanese Banks.* The Japanese banks, in particular, were having great difficulties meeting the BIS capital adequacy guidelines and were out of play. This had major ramifications for the availability of credit. In the past, Japanese banks had always acted as lenders of last resort. Their absence from the market made it difficult for ordinary companies to find bank financing.

3. *Savings and Loans Failure in the U.S.* The problems faced by the savings and loans industry in the U.S. in 1990 put a real strain on the U.S. banking system. The near demise of the junk bond market in 1990 forced U.S. banks to classify previous loans that had been made as part of leveraged buyout transactions as HLTs (highly leveraged transactions), causing their credit ratings to nosedive.

4. *Conservatism on the Part of European Banks.* Because of the problems afflicting many banks around the world, European banks were zealously protecting their AAA credit ratings by adopting extremely conservative lending policies. The three main Swiss banks (Union Bank of Switzerland, Swiss Banking Corporation and Credit

Suisse) were developing a fortress-like mentality and lending little to any entity that didn't have a top credit rating.

The result of these events that were happening simultaneously was that most banks were extremely skittish about lending. This nervousness was transferred to Rogers. Since it was next to impossible to borrow bank funds on reasonable terms, Rogers was forced to look further afield for other types of financing.

ROGERS' PARAMETERS

The tight market conditions coupled with Canada's recession had forced Rogers to postpone satisfying its funding requirements. Although Graham had been able to postpone a major financing for the last twelve months, Rogers' pent-up demand for funding meant that major financing could no longer be avoided.

In addition to funding Rogers' ongoing capital requirements, Graham was eager to refinance two particular loans whose restrictive covenants and pledges were hampering Rogers' financial flexibility:

1. $135,000,000 loan from Canadian Pacific Limited (CP). As a last resort, Graham had recently borrowed monies from CP at prime + 1.50% per annum repayable in February 1992. The loan was secured by a pledge on the shares of Unitel that Rogers owned. Rogers had also been required to provide a guarantee. Graham wanted to repay the loan as soon as possible so that the pledge on Unitel's shares would be removed.
2. $113,200,000 note issued to First City Financial Corporation Ltd. (First City). In addition to charging a high coupon (14.5% per annum) and setting several restrictive covenants, First City had a minority interest in certain equity securities of Cantel which were pledged as security for the note. This lien restricted Rogers from using Cantel as a fund-raising vehicle.

Graham's ideal financing method would be one that: (1) had limited or no servicing requirements; (2) would improve Rogers' financial flexibility, allowing it to take advantage of opportunities that might arise in the future; and (3) could be completed relatively quickly.

ALTERNATIVES

Considering the current environment, there were few alternatives that would provide Rogers with reasonable cost financing. Rogers was precluded from completing a financing in Europe. The European market was driven by name recognition rather than credit ratings, which would bode well for Rogers since it was a non-investment grade credit. However, Rogers had no name recognition in Europe. In addition, European banks were unfamiliar with cash flow companies and telecommunications companies. The cellular market was only six years old, and European banks were unwilling to lend to companies operating in industries that had a limited operating history.

An issuance of straight common equity would certainly strengthen Rogers' highly leveraged financial position; however, given the recent performance of Rogers' share price (Exhibit 5), Graham was reluctant to proceed along this route.

Over the last few months, Graham had been approached by several investment banks suggesting various ways to obtain capital. Of the numerous proposals he had received, Graham was considering the following:

1. *The issuance of $50–75 million of Special Convertible Preferred Shares, as proposed by ScotiaMcLeod.* Such shares would be entitled to receive a dividend equal to 5% of that paid on Rogers' Class B non-voting shares, and each preferred share would be convertible into the number of Rogers' Class B shares having a market value of $48.91 at the end of five years. Rogers had a cash call option of $48.91 at the end of five years—meaning it could elect to pay cash to the preferred shareholders instead of Class B shares. Rogers would have the right to force early conversion beginning at 30 months from the issue date at a conversion premium of about 58%, and rising at 60 months to almost 100%. Exhibit 6 lays out the proposed terms and conditions of the Special Convertible Preferred Shares in more detail.

Since Rogers was not currently paying out any dividends on its Class B shares, there would be *no* cash servicing requirement on the Special Convertible Preferred shares. These securities essentially behaved like a zero-coupon debt instrument with a five-year term. Within the investment banking community, there were mixed views on how receptive the Canadian market would be to such a unique instrument. Although it would be a tougher sell than other more standard securities, ScotiaMcLeod was confident it could achieve a timely, successful distribution. Wood Gundy concurred with this view. However, several investment banking houses, including Burns Fry and RBC Dominion Securities, were less enthusiastic and questioned how the Special Convertible Preferred Shares would be received. They were not prepared to go forward. W. David Wilson, Deputy Chairman and Director of ScotiaMcLeod, sat on Rogers' board of directors.

2. *The issuance of Liquid Yield Option Notes (LYONs).* In May 1990, Graham had been approached by Merrill Lynch Canada with a proposal to issue a new hybrid security that Merrill Lynch had developed in the U.S. A LYON was essentially a zero coupon convertible debenture that provided investors with a put option at five-year intervals.

Investors would purchase the zero-coupon bonds at a large discount from the face value and receive no interest payments until maturity (typically 15 to 20 years) when the bonds were redeemed at face value. Similar to convertible bonds, LYONs could be converted into common stock at a fixed price. Although the face value of the LYON accreted with the yield-to-maturity, the conversion ratio remained fixed over the life of the instrument, thus increasing the conversion premium. The put option allowed the holder to sell the bond back to the issuer starting at several fixed dates.

The idea behind LYONs was to combine the tax benefits accruing to the issuer of a zero-coupon bond with the lower interest rates accepted by the investor in return for the conversion option. Corporate issuers could deduct interest payments over the life of the bond even though they were actually back-ending the payments, and the interest rate was lower than straight debt because of the conversion option. The corporation might never pay the interest. Information on Canadian and U.S. interest rates is contained in Exhibits 7 and 8. An example of a term sheet for an issuance of LYONs appears in Exhibit 9.

Although LYONs were popular in the U.S. (Exhibit 10), this innovative structure had never been issued in Canada. If Graham chose this option, he would have to decide if the securities should be issued in Canada, the U.S., or both. Merrill Lynch believed that the Canadian institutional market could absorb a $75–$100 million LYONs issue. This could increase substantially if Graham decided to tap the U.S. market. The Walt Disney Company had recently completed a successful US$2.34 billion dollar LYONs transaction. Given the control considerations, Graham wondered which class of shares the LYONs should be convertible into and whether the foreign ownership restrictions would cause problems.

Graham's thoughts were interrupted as his secretary buzzed him to say that it was five minutes before four o'clock. No doubt Ted Rogers would be waiting for Graham's recommendation as to which financing method Rogers should proceed with.

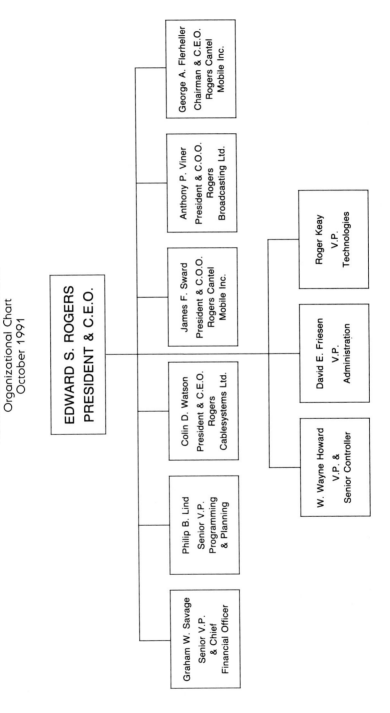

EXHIBIT 1
ROGERS COMMUNICATIONS INC.
Organizational Chart
October 1991

EDWARD S. ROGERS
PRESIDENT & C.E.O.

Graham W. Savage
Senior V.P.
& Chief
Financial Officer

Philip B. Lind
Senior V.P.
Programming
& Planning

Colin D. Watson
President & C.E.O.
Rogers
Cablesystems Ltd.

James F. Sward
President & C.O.O.
Rogers Cantel
Mobile Inc.

Anthony P. Viner
President & C.O.O.
Rogers
Broadcasting Ltd.

George A. Fierheller
Chairman & C.E.O.
Rogers Cantel
Mobile Inc.

W. Wayne Howard
V.P. &
Senior Controller

David E. Friesen
V.P.
Administration

Roger Keay
V.P.
Technologies

EXHIBIT 2

ROGERS COMMUNICATIONS INC.
Corporate Structure

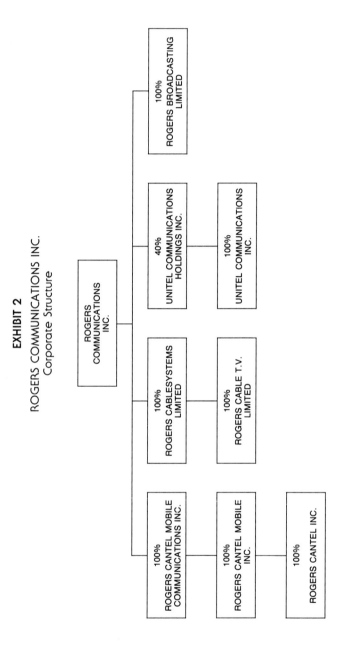

EXHIBIT 3

ROGERS COMMUNICATIONS INC.
Cellular Mobile Communications Network

CELLULAR MOBILE COMMUNICATIONS
■ Existing Coverage Area
CABLE TELEVISION
||
TELECOMMUNICATIONS
∷ Fiber Optic System
— Digital Microwave
BROADCASTING
▲

EXHIBIT 4

ROGERS COMMUNICATIONS INC.
Financial Statements
Consolidated Income Statement
(thousands of dollars, except per share amounts)

	16 MONTHS ENDED DECEMBER 31, 1990	YEAR ENDED AUGUST 31, 1989
Revenue	$1,128,340	$600,839
Operating, general and administrative expenses	847,464	420,747
Operating income before the following	280,876	180,092
Depreciation and amortization	183,137	82,532
Interest on long term debt	216,362	99,483
Other interest	2,918	1,260
	(121,541)	(3,183)
Share of income (losses) of associated companies	(20,598)	878
Investment income	23,037	13,264
Reduction in the carrying value of Canadian Home Shopping Network (CHSN) Ltd.	–	(25,774)
Other income (expense)	(987)	10,964
Loss before income taxes	(120,089)	(3,851)
Income taxes		
Current	3,469	85
Deferred (reduction)	(10,436)	13,869
	(6,967)	13,954
Loss before the following	(113,122)	(17,805)
Minority interest	–	4,156
Loss from U.S. operations	–	(12,190)
Loss before extraordinary items	(113,122)	(25,839)
Extraordinary items	–	728,672
Net income (loss) for the period	$ (113,122)	$702,833
Earnings per share		
Basic		
Loss before extraordinary items	$ (1.51)	$ (0.49)
Net income (loss) for the period	$ (1.51)	$ 6.67
Fully Diluted		
Net income for the period	N/A	$ 5.15

Fully diluted earnings per share are not disclosed for the sixteen months ended December 31, 1990, as they are anti-dilutive.

EXHIBIT 4 (cont.)

ROGERS COMMUNICATIONS INC.
Consolidated Balance Sheets
(thousands of dollars)

	AS AT DECEMBER 31, 1990	AS AT AUGUST 31, 1989
Assets		
Fixed assets	$1,510,014	$ 833,595
Subscribers and licences	826,087	787,478
Goodwill	128,782	79,800
Investments	531,829	183,172
Accounts receivable	107,174	59,720
Inventories	19,728	15,040
Prepaid expenses	10,323	7,834
Other assets	76,804	35,961
	$3,210,741	$2,002,600
Liabilities and Shareholders' Equity		
Liabilities		
Long term debt	$1,871,795	$ 755,418
Operating bank loans and bank advances	49,965	37,014
Accounts payable and accrued liabilities	234,332	183,140
Prepayments for services	41,201	35,007
Deferred income taxes	205,835	210,532
Minority interest	1,026	1,026
	2,404,154	1,222,137
Shareholders' Equity		
Capital stock	699,170	485,401
Reorganization surplus	6,235	6,235
Retained earnings	554,982	732,320
	1,260,387	1,223,956
Deduct the cost of shares of the Company held by subsidiary companies	453,800	443,493
	806,587	780,463
Total Liabilities and Shareholders' Equity	$3,210,741	$2,002,600

EXHIBIT 4 (cont.)

ROGERS COMMUNICATIONS INC.
Five-Year Financial History
(thousands of dollars)

	1990 (16 MONTHS) DEC. 31	1989 AUG. 31	1988 AUG. 31	1987 AUG. 31	1986 AUG. 31
Income & Cash Flow					
Revenue	$1,128,340	$ 600,839	$ 358,426	$273,587	$237,884
Operating income	280,876	180,092	151,110	115,975	95,840
Income (loss) before the undernoted	(113,122)	12,125	8,863	2,133	(932)
Loss from U.S. operations	—	(12,190)	(7,411)	(10,590)	(32,357)
Reduction in the carrying value of CHSN	—	(25,774)	—	—	—
Income (loss) before extraordinary items	$ (113,122)	$ (25,839)	$ 1,452	$ (8,457)	$ (33,289)
Cash flow from operations	$ 105,534	$ 116,763	$ 86,530	$ 92,849	$ 61,264
Capital expenditures	$ 776,061	$ 420,249	$ 121,699	$ 62,042	$ 45,056

Balance Sheet					
Fixed assets	$1,510,014	$ 833,595	$ 498,841	$259,621	$237,928
Goodwill, subscribers and licences	954,869	867,278	229,782	121,645	121,549
Investment in U.S. operations	—	—	163,328	101,914	114,578
Investments	531,829	183,172	135,259	138,046	121,710
Other assets	214,029	118,555	85,296	32,001	43,834
	$3,210,741	$2,002,600	$1,112,506	$653,227	$639,599
Long term debt	$1,871,795	$ 755,418	$ 899,499	$320,975	$284,533
Accounts payable and other liabilities	325,498	255,161	173,606	72,093	70,866
Deferred taxes	205,835	210,532	31,778	12,920	548
Minority interest	1,026	1,026	20,602	3,554	3,341
Shareholders' equity (deficiency)	806,587	780,463	(12,979)	243,685	280,311
	$3,210,741	$2,002,600	$1,112,506	$653,227	$639,599
Average Shares					
Outstanding (thousands)[a]	115,956	102,186	125,062	183,246	175,994
Per Share					
Loss before extraordinary items[b]	$ (1.51)	$ (0.49)	$ (0.11)	$ (0.12)	$ (0.25)
Cash flow from operations	$ .91	$ 1.14	$ .69	$ .51	$ 0.35

[a]Net of shares owned by subsidiary companies and adjusted for seven-for-one share split effective April 6, 1990.

[b]Net of dividends on preferred shares.

EXHIBIT 5

ROGERS COMMUNICATIONS INC.
Historical Share Prices
August 1989–August 1991

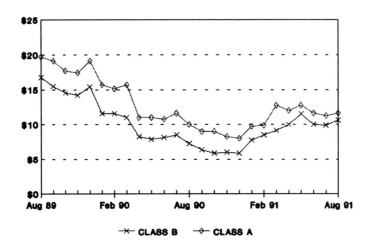

—✕— **CLASS B**   —◇— **CLASS A**

EXHIBIT 6

Special Convertible Preferred Shares
Issuer Base Equity

[Assume Rogers Communications Inc. Class B shares trade at $5.75]

Issuer:	Rogers Communications Inc.
Issue:	Preferred Shares Series XIII (the shares).
Issue Price:	$25 per share.
Issue Size:	2–3 million shares ($50–$75 million).
Issue Type:	Underwritten issue qualified by prospectus in all provinces of Canada.
Share Provisions:	(1) *Voting Rights:* non-voting.

(2) *Dividends:* 5% of the dividend declared on one Class B share of the issuer (with anti-dilution provisions in the event the issuer's Class B shares are consolidated or subdivided).

(3) *Rights on Liquidation:* Each share shall be entitled on the dissolution, liquidation or winding up of the issuer to receive the amount set out in the table in (7) below before any amount is paid or any assets of the issuer are distributed to the holder of any shares ranking junior to the shares.

(4) *Retraction Features:* none.

(5) *Redemption Features:* All but not less than all the shares will be redeemable at the option of the issuer at $48.91 15 days before the conversion date in (6).

(continued)

EXHIBIT 6 (cont.)

(6) *Conversion:* Unless the board of directors of the issuer has given notice to shareholders as provided in (7) below, on the day following the fifth anniversary after issue, the holder of share will be entitled to convert each share into that number of Class B shares of the issuer which have a market value of $48.91, and for such purpose, the market value of the Class B shares of the issuer on such date shall be deemed to be the weighted average price at which the issuer's Class B shares have traded on The Toronto Stock Exchange for the five trading days immediately preceding such conversion date.

(7) *Early Conversion:* At any time prior to the 57th month following the issue date, the board of directors of the issuer may announce an acceleration of the conversion date for the shares by notice mailed to all registered holders and by advertisement in the financial press, and from 15 days following such notice (the first conversion date) to the day following the fifth anniversary of issue, the holder of a share will be entitled to convert each share into that number of Class B shares of the issuer as set out in the table below.

IF FIRST CONVERSION DATE IS AFTER (MONTHS AFTER ISSUE)	AND FIRST CONVERSION DATE IS BEFORE (MONTHS AFTER ISSUE)	VALUE IN CLASS B SHARES
0	30	$39.43
30	36	$41.56
36	42	$43.69
42	48	$45.29
48	54	$46.89
54	60	$48.91

(8) *ITA Part VI.1 Tax:* The shares are taxable preferred shares for the purpose of the Income Tax Act (Canada) as a result of the liquidation preference accorded under the class provisions relating to the shares. The issuer will elect under section 191.2 under the Income Tax Act (Canada) to pay refundable Part VI.1 tax at the rate of 40% of dividends paid on the shares.

Consequences to Issuer:

(1) *Economic:* If the issuer's Class B shares trade at $5.75, then raising $25 by issuing shares can be compared to issuing 4.34783 Class B shares. Since the Class B shares pay no dividend, the issuer would have raised permanent equity at a cost lower than issuing Class B shares today as long as $48.91 is less than the expected market price of 4.34783 Class B shares on the conversion date, or $11.25 per Class B share. A $11.25 Class B share price represents a compound annual growth rate of about 13.65% per annum from today's Class B share price.

(2) *Redemption:* In the event the issuer redeemed the shares if it felt that its Class B shares were at that time trading at an unusually low value, the excess of the redemption price over the issue price ($23.91 = $48.91 − $25.00) would be a deemed dividend under ITAs.84 and the issuer would be liable to pay the 40% tax under proposed ITA Part

(continued)

EXHIBIT 6 (cont.)

VI.1 on such excess. In the event the issuer never recovered the Part VI.1 tax, the cost to the issuer would be approximately 17.36%, and in the event all Part VI.1 tax were recovered, the cost to the issuer would be approximately 13.65%.

(3) *Short Term Preferred Shares:* The shares will not be short term preferred shares within the meaning of the proposed definition in ITAs.248(1) so long as, at the time of issue, the issuer would not be considered likely to exercise its redemption privilege. [This qualification, if a concern, may be eliminated by extending the redemption beyond five years.]

Investor Yield: The shares should behave and trade like a zero coupon bond since they will have a market value of $48.91 at the end of five years. However, because the shares are not debt obligations, the interest accrual rules in the ITA will not apply. Because the shares have a liquidation preference, the shares are not prescribed shares within the meaning of ITAs.110.6 and an investor who sells his shares in the market will not be entitled to claim the lifetime capital gains exemption.

Under the following assumptions:

(1) no dividend is paid on the issuer's Class B shares;

(2) the investor is an individual resident in Ontario;

(3) the investor has a marginal tax rate of 48.23% (Ontario) and dividends are taxed at an effective marginal rate of 32.58%;

(4) the investor holds his shares as capital property;

(5) 75% of capital gains are included in taxable income;

(6) the investor disposes of his shares in the market on or about the fifth anniversary of issue at not more than a 4% discount to $48.91 including share disposal costs;

then the investor will receive an after-tax yield (quarterly compounding) as follows:

IF CONVERSION AND SALE OCCUR (MONTHS AFTER ISSUE)	AFTER-TAX YIELD
30	11.51%
36	10.89%
42	10.40%
48	9.78%
54	9.28%
60	9.00%

An investor who holds the shares as capital property and exercises the conversion privilege will be entitled to rollover treatment pursuant to the provisions of ITAs.51.

In the event the issuer redeems the shares under the redemption provision, the investor will be deemed to have received a $23.91 dividend under ITAs.84 and the individual investor in Ontario who held

(continued)

EXHIBIT 6 (cont.)

the shares from the date of issue will receive an after-tax yield of approximately 10.08%. An individual who purchased his shares in the market at a price considerably in excess of $25 would sell shares in the market to realize a capital gain rather than incur a deemed dividend and a capital loss unless the individual had capital gains to offset the capital loss.

Listing:	On closing, the shares would be listed on The Toronto Stock Exchange.
Underwriter:	ScotiaMcLeod Inc.
Underwriting Fee:	$1.00 per share (4%).

EXHIBIT 7

Canadian Prime vs. U.S. Federal Fund Rate

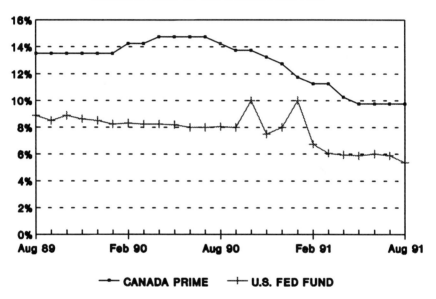

CANADA PRIME ━━ U.S. FED FUND

EXHIBIT 8

Interest Rates, March 28, 1991

MONEY MARKET RATES

CANADA		U.S.	
Bank Rate	9.92%	Discount Rate	6.0%
Prime Rate	11.25	Prime Rate	9.0
Call Loan Average	9.00	Fed. Funds	6.0
T-Bills			
1 Month	9.60	1 Month	5.75
3 Month	9.68	2 Month	5.73
6 Month	9.67	6 Month	5.76

CANADIAN & U.S. GOVERNMENT BOND YIELDS

CANADIAN		U.S. TREASURIES	
2-year	9.28%	2-year	7.01%
5-year	9.41	5-year	7.73
7-year	9.52	7-year	7.94
10-year	9.54	10-year	8.05
25-year	9.77	20-year	8.24
		30-year	8.23

Source: Financial Post, March 29, 1991.

EXHIBIT 9

Summary of Terms
for a Proposed Issuance of
Liquid Yield Option Notes (LYONs)

Issuer:	Rogers Communications Inc.
Securities Offered:	Approximately US$150,000,000–US$200,000,000 gross proceeds (US$720,000,000–US$960,000,000 aggregate principal amount at maturity) of LYONs due on June *, 2011. There may be an additional US$108,000,000–US$144,000,000 aggregate principal amount issued subject to the Underwriter's over-allotment option. There will be no periodic interest payments on the LYONs. Each LYON will have an issue price of US$189.22 and a principal amount due at maturity of US$1,000.
Coupon:	0%
Yield to Maturity:	8.50% per annum (computed on a semi-annual bond equivalent basis) calculated from June *, 1991.
Conversion Rights:	Each LYON will be convertible, at the option of the holder, at any time on or prior to maturity, unless previously redeemed or otherwise purchased by the Company, into Class B non-voting shares at a conversion rate of 19.870 Class B non-voting shares per LYON (assuming an initial conversion premium of 15%, a share price for the Class B non-voting shares of C$9.50 and an exchange rate of C$1.00/US$0.87). In certain circumstances, the Company may arrange

(continued)

EXHIBIT 9 (cont.)

	to pay non-Canadian holders cash in U.S. dollars in an amount equal to the market value of the Class B non-voting shares into which the LYONs are convertible in lieu of the conversion into Class B non-voting shares. The conversion rate will *not* be adjusted for accrued Original Issue Discount, but will be subject to adjustment upon the occurrence of certain events affecting the Class B non-voting shares.
Original Issue Discount:	Each LYON is being offered at an Original Issue Discount for U.S. federal income tax purposes, which is expected to equal the excess of the principal amount at maturity of the LYON over the amount of the issue price. Although there will be no periodic payments of interest on the LYONs, accrued Original Issue Discount will be includible, periodically, in a holder's gross income for U.S. federal income taxes prior to conversion, redemption or maturity of such holder's LYONs. Payments made by the Company to U.S. holders will *generally* be exempt from Canadian withholding taxes.
Sinking Fund:	None.
Optional Redemption by the Company:	The LYONs will not be redeemable by the Company prior to June *, 1993, unless the closing sale price of the Class B non-voting shares equals or exceeds 150% of the initial conversion price, for at least 20 of 30 consecutive trading days ending within five trading days before notice of redemption. Subject to the foregoing, the LYONs are redeemable for cash in U.S. dollars at any time at the option of the Company, in whole or in part, at redemption prices equal to the issue price plus accrued Original Issue Discount to the date of redemption.
Purchase at the Option of the Holder:	The Company will purchase any LYON, at the option of the holder, on June *, 1996, June *, 2001 and June *, 2006, for a purchase price of US$286.90, US$435.00 and US$659.55 (issue price plus accrued Original Issue Discount to each such date), respectively, representing an 8.5% yield per annum to the holder on such date computed on a semi-annual bond equivalent basis. The Company may, at its option, elect to pay the purchase price on any such purchase date in cash in U.S. dollars or in Class B non-voting shares or any combination thereof, subject to certain restrictions on non-Canadian ownership of the Company's shares. In addition, upon a change in control of the Company occurring on or prior to June *, 1996, holders have the right to require the Company to repurchase the LYONs for an amount equal to the issue price plus accrued Original Issue Discount.
Underwriter:	Merrill Lynch
Underwriting Fee:	3% on discount price.

EXHIBIT 10

Previous LYON Issues

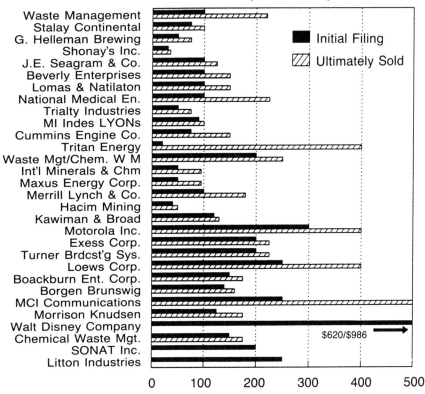

Gross Proceeds (US$ millions)

Percentage Distribution: 45% Retail and 55% Institutional.
Total Proceeds—US $6.5 billion.
Merrill Lynch Underwritings Only.

29

THE MULTI-JURISDICTIONAL
DISCLOSURE SYSTEM

INTRODUCTION

On July 1, 1991, the Multi-Jurisdictional Disclosure System (MJDS) came into effect in Canada and the United States. Canadian securities commissions and U.S. regulators had been working together for over six years on the U.S. Securities and Exchange Commissions (SEC) initiative of an eventual creation of a single North American capital market. This "milestone" agreement makes it substantially easier for eligible Canadian issuers to access U.S. capital markets. Canadian CFOs who intend to raise capital now have easier access to the large American market. Numerous additional financial techniques and alternatives now become available.

MULTI-JURISDICTIONAL DISCLOSURE SYSTEM

Background

Prior to MJDS, whenever an issuer of securities had considered issuing a financial product in a foreign capital market, numerous impediments were encountered. The major complication with a cross-border offering was the requirement to comply with the unique disclosure and reporting requirements of the foreign country. This

This note was prepared by Graeme Falkowsky and Kathryn Montgomery under the supervision of Professor Robert W. White for the sole purpose of providing material for class discussion at the Western Business School. Certain names and other identifying information may have been disguised to protect confidentiality. It is not intended to illustrate either effective or ineffective handling of a managerial situation.

was costly in terms of time and money. The issuer needed to retain both American and Canadian accountants and legal counsel. As well, the "window of opportunity," that is so many times present in public offerings was bypassed because of the additional time required to fully comply with the disclosure and reporting requirements of both the Canadian and U.S. securities regulators. It soon became evident that issuers were bypassing issuing securities in any jurisdictions that required extra disclosure. In response, both the U.S. and Canadian securities regulators were going to great lengths in order to facilitate significant cross-border transactions. The SEC had extended relief from some of its disclosure requirements to issuers undertaking large multinational offerings such as European privatizations. Canadian regulators were granting relief on a case-by-case basis by exempting particular U.K. privatization related offerings from the onerous disclosure and reporting requirements. Even with the flexibility displayed by the Canadian and U.S. regulators, numerous organizations still felt the disadvantages and time commitment required were a deterrent to issuing in a foreign jurisdiction. The SEC concluded that the U.S. market was being continually excluded by foreign issuers, thus precluding U.S. investors from participating in unique investment opportunities. This prompted the SEC to take the initial steps to reconcile this problem.

Alternatives Considered for MJDS

MJDS was initiated in 1985 with the SEC's Concept Release entitled "Facilitation of Multinational Securities Offerings." This release explored two alternative concepts in an attempt to facilitate and simplify cross-border financings between Canada and the U.S. The SEC solicited public opinion on the following alternatives.

COMMON PROSPECTUS APPROACH.   This approach would require the creation of a new international prospectus which would be common to all participating jurisdictions. Some commentators, including the SEC, felt that the uniformity of disclosure standards was attractive, presuming that the benchmark standard would be based on the U.S. SEC standards. It soon became evident that difficulties were arising upon these particular disclosure standards. This approach was eventually abandoned in favour of a system of mutual recognition of disclosure requirements.

RECIPROCAL APPROACH.   Under this type of a system, assuming all eligibility criteria were met, a reciprocal approach would permit an issuer to prepare its disclosure documents under the guidelines of its home jurisdiction. These documents, which would have already been prepared by companies who had issued in their home market, would simply be submitted to satisfy the filing requirements of the foreign jurisdiction. The SEC was initially concerned that the disclosure standards would be lower for Canadian issuers. Extensive research was provided to the SEC on the high level of required disclosure under Canadian law. During this research process several key reforms were undertaken by Canadian authorities in order to harmonize Canadian disclosure requirements with U.S. standards. It may be said that the real benefit to Canadian issuers is not the MJDS but the changes that have occurred in order to facilitate this agreement. These changes would include the Canadian "shelf system" (Appendix A) which is modeled very closely after the U.S. This system provides for a reduction in the cost and time involved for qualified issuers in a public offering. Many qualified issuers who may have never considered financing in the U.S. will still benefit from the positive impact of MJDS through their use of the shelf system. The relative ease of implementation, combined with the efficiencies in time and cost, resulted in the reciprocal approach being adopted as the base to MJDS.

In 1985 the MJDS concept was to include the participation of the United Kingdom, Canada and the United States, however it was subsequently narrowed to focus only on Canada and the U.S. Canadian disclosure requirements were already similar to those of the U.S.; therefore, some harmonization toward common standards had already taken place. This narrower, and somewhat simpler arrangement, was seen to be a "logical first step" toward a broader system which may eventually include numerous countries. The MJDS system was seen as an extension to the case-by-case relief presently granted by the authorities. This increase in flexibility towards issuers reflects the realization that securities regulators had to adapt to the constantly increasing internationalization of the securities markets.

Initially the major force behind the development of MJDS was the rapid internationalization of debt markets. However, the present system has been expanded much further to include the use of reciprocal prospectuses for numerous cross-border financial instruments.

MULTI-JURISDICTIONAL DISCLOSURE SYSTEM MECHANICS

In order for a Canadian issuer to be eligible to utilize the new MJDS system and issue securities in the U.S., the issuer must:

- be incorporated or organized in Canada;
- be either a "foreign private issuer" or a "crown corporation";
- have a three year reporting history with one or more of the provincial securities authorities in Canada (one year in the case of crown corporations);
- be in compliance with Canadian reporting obligations; and
- meet the minimum public float requirements specific for the type of security issued.

MJDS encompasses a wide variety of cross-border securities transactions.

Eligible Canadian issuers are able to issue both debt and equity securities in the United States using a Canadian prospectus. Reconciliation of financial statements to U.S. GAAP is required for equity securities and non-investment grade debt and preferred shares but this requirement is subject to a sunset provision and may expire in 1993. This provision was included to enable investors, who are likely to assess competing investing opportunities, to make direct comparisons. The Canadian prospectus will not generally be reviewed in the U.S. by the SEC, thus allowing the issuer to commence action once the Canadian regulatory review is completed.

Comparable procedures have been enacted for U.S. issuers entering Canadian capital markets.

Investment Grade Debt and Preferred Shares

Investment grade debt or preferred shares can be issued in the United States using a Canadian prospectus. There is no need for any reconciliation of the financial statements to U.S. GAAP or, for U.S. issuers, no need for reconciliation with Canadian GAAP. The Canadian issuer must have a market value at least CA$180 million and a public float of CA$75 million.

Equity and Other Securities

MJDS is also available for all securities other than investment grade debt and preferred shares. Public float requirements remain at CA$75 million but the market value of securities outstanding increases to CA$360 million.

The MJDS is not available to "investment companies" which would include Canadian banks and certain other financial institutions.

Rights Offerings, Take-Over Bids, Exchange Offers and Business Combinations

Previously, Canadian investors have routinely been excluded from participating in foreign rights offerings and take-over bids, given the reluctance of foreign issuers to submit to U.S. and Canadian securities laws. Under MJDS, all eligible Canadian and U.S. issuers will now be able to extend rights offerings to investors in other jurisdictions.

Under MJDS, take-over bids may also be made to investors in other jurisdictions. A take-over offer must be made on the same terms as to all holders in both Canada and the U.S.

Issuers will also be able to use MJDS to facilitate other cross-border transactions such as the exchange of securities and various business combinations. Appendix B illustrates and contrasts a cross-border securities offering before and after MJDS.

IMPACT ON THE SECURITIES INDUSTRY

The adoption of the MJDS has had an impact on several areas of the securities industry.

U.S. Issuers' (and U.S. Investment Banks') Perspective

U.S. issuers and investment banks will now have the ability to add a Canadian tranche onto their offerings with little additional paperwork or expense. This will increase the number of potential investors that will have the ability to participate in an offering therefore increasing the likelihood of a successful offering.

Canadian Issuers' Perspective

As with U.S. issuers, Canadian companies will have the opportunity to extend Canadian offerings into the U.S. with little additional expense. Qualified Canadian issuers will now only have to prepare one set of documents.

MJDS may be seen as having a larger impact on U.S. issuers than Canadian issuers. There are far more organizations that meet the minimum public float and market value requirements required under MJDS. Further, in respect to Canadian investment banks, the impact may be minimal. This is due to deregulation in the late 1980s which allowed Canadian commercial banks to buy ownership of investment dealers. Now these Canadian commercial banks/investment dealers will have to comply with the Glass–Steagall Act in the U.S., which excludes commercial banks from engaging in securities underwriting. Finally, and maybe most importantly, the applicability of the U.S. civil liability and anti-fraud provisions will continue and apply to Canadian issuers in the U.S. Thus, Canadian issuers using MJDS are subject to potential liability under U.S. law if their registration statements, prospectuses, circulars or any disclosure filings contain material misstatements or omissions. The highly litigious environment in the United States will no doubt be a consideration for Canadian issuers.

BENEFITS OF ACCESSING U.S. DEBT MARKETS.   The U.S. debt markets offer Canadian issuers several benefits including:

- Currency hedge for Canadian corporations with U.S. operations or products priced in U.S. dollars.
- Coupon/economic savings as interest rates historically have been lower in the United States.
- Ability to expand a corporations' investor base.

BENEFITS OF ACCESSING THE U.S. EQUITY MARKETS.   Further, advantages exist for Canadian issuers in U.S. equity markets:

- If a corporation's capital requirements are too large to be satisfied in the Canadian market alone, the huge U.S. market will allow a greater degree of financial flexibility.
- A U.S. equity issue will raise the international profile of the issuer. This could be import for future financings.
- The ability to broaden shareholder constituency to include a wider range of institutional and individual investors results in a more attractive pricing for issuers.

Canadian investment bankers indicate that initially MJDS will have minimal impact for Canadian issuers since: (1) the vast majority of Canadian companies can meet their capital requirements by tapping into markets in this country; (2) bought deals for equity are increasingly popular in Canada but not permitted in the U.S.; and (3) Canadian companies are generally not well-known to U.S. investors and it could take a long time to raise their profiles before a cross-border offering is possible. James Dannis, a partner with the New York law firm Cleary, Gottlib, Steen &

Hamilton, states the new system "was never intended to cause a stampede of Canadian corporations to U.S. markets." It is seen as more a proactive approach to dealing with the ever increasing world of global financial markets. Clay Horner, managing partner of the New York office of Olser Renault Ladner states "The New Canadian shelf system and MJDS make it easier for Canadian and other issuers to decide where to raise funds on a basis which focuses almost exclusively on the economics of the transaction, as opposed to the mechanics."

THE FUTURE OF MJDS

The creation of the MJDS system was a major achievement, given the number and levels of securities authorities involved. The question now arises as to if and when additional countries are going to be brought into the system. The SEC is currently working with securities regulators in the United Kingdom, Japan and Mexico. However, it is unlikely that the present negotiations will result in many other participants being added in the near future due to the following reasons:

- MJDS requires a delegation of a regulatory authority's review to the regulatory authorities of the foreign country. In order for this to take place, the host regulatory authority must be satisfied that the foreign disclosure is up to an appropriate level. This requires a great deal of research.
- In regard to the specific accounting disclosure, the SEC seems to be reluctant to accept the fact that financial statements prepared under foreign regulation provide a similar level of investor protection as provided by U.S. GAAP.
- Finally, MJDS is based upon reciprocity and the U.S. and Canadian authorities will not add other jurisdictions unless foreign authorities grant equal treatment to U.S. and Canadian issuers. This process takes a great deal of lengthy negotiation.

After the SEC becomes more comfortable with the recent system it will give consideration to lowering the various eligibility thresholds and expanding the system in other respects. The Canadian authorities are attempting to make further changes to harmonize the Canadian and U.S. systems such as new market stabilization rules and a review of disclosure or executive compensation.

CONCLUSION

MJDS was a milestone in the internationalization of regulation of capital markets. The result was the ability of both U.S. and Canadian companies to offer securities into a North American market. The combined U.S. and Canadian capital markets will result in a pool of approximately $4.2 trillion in equity capital available to both U.S. and Canadian issuers. This will be the largest such market in the world. MJDS may be seen as an initial step towards the integration of capital markets between countries which, as mentioned, may include the United Kingdom, Japan and Mexico. It is assured that these countries will be watching and closely assessing the Canadian–U.S. MJDS developments.

Canadian CFOs should become familiar with MJDS and evaluate their global financing strategies accordingly. There are new opportunities for Canadian issuers, large and small, to raise capital in the United States with increased efficiency and reduced regulatory complications.

APPENDIX A
Canadian Shelf System

A shelf system was considered in Ontario in 1986, as it was already present in the U.S., but was not implemented as underwriters were given the right to solicit expressions of interest 48 hours prior to filing a preliminary prospectus. However, the implementation of MJDS between Canada and the U.S. provided the catalyst for the initiation of such a shelf system in Canada. The shelf system, which has been modeled closely after the U.S. system, was developed to allow issuers to offer securities of a basic type (i.e., debt, preferred shares, common shares) on either a continual basis or a series of delayed offerings over a two year period.

Under this type of a system, a qualified issuer will file and clear a prospectus containing all the required information other than information regarding the specific security or distribution plan. Then when the market opportunity arises, the specific terms of the offering can be determined and the securities can be brought down "off the shelf" through a supplement. The preparation of the supplement can usually be done fairly quickly with little, if any, regulatory approval. This type of system allows issuers to react quickly to opportune market conditions and provides enhanced flexibility in tailoring securities to particular market opportunities.

Eligible U.S. issuers will be able to issue securities under their U.S. shelf prospectus and supplements and likewise Canadian issuers may issue securities in the U.S. under their Canadian documentation.

The implementation of the shelf system in Canada is seen as a major sideline benefit to MJDS as issuers who may never issue in the U.S. can still benefit.

APPENDIX B
Illustration of Canada/U.S. MJDS

Situation: A Canadian issuer has not previously made a public offering in the U.S. or sought any U.S. listing or quotation for its securities.

CURRENT U.S. TREATMENT	U.S. ACCOMMODATIONS UNDER MJDS
• issuer must use long form U.S. prospectus;	• short-form Canadian prospectus satisfies U.S. requirements;
• full U.S. disclosure req.;	• full U.S. GAAP reconciliation until July 1, 1993;
• U.S. shelf procedures not available;	• Canadian shelf rules may be used in U.S.;
• full SEC review of prospectus (generally 4-6 weeks);	• generally no SEC review;
• as result of public offering issuer must file 10-K, 10-Q and 8-K reports;	• Canadian continuous disclosure documents satisfy U.S. requirements;
• full U.S. proxy rules apply if common shares are registered in U.S.;	• complete exemption from proxy rules;
• full U.S. insider reporting and profit recovery rules apply if common shares are registered in the U.S.	• complete exemption from U.S. insider reporting and profit recovery rules.

Source: Blake, Cassels & Graydon.

30

ROBOTICS, INC.

On Tuesday afternoon, March 5, 1985, Ms. Katherine Dawson, financial vice president of Robotics, Inc., was gathering her thoughts about the merits of a proposal recently received from an auto leasing company to lease Robotics a fleet of 100 vehicles. Since this was a major financial commitment, Ms. Dawson wanted to be reasonably assured that she was pursuing the most cost effective course for the company. Further, she realized that if she did recommend to management that a lease agreement be signed, she would have to justify it vigorously because there were several individuals in the company who were generally hostile to the leasing concept. They preferred ownership, perhaps largely as a matter of tradition. Ultimately she felt even these individuals would accept a lease, however, if the financial benefits were persuasive.

Robotics, Inc., located in Southfield, Michigan, was founded in June 1981 by Franklin Williams and a group of venture capitalists to manufacture state-of-the-art robots for sale largely to the automobile assembly business (see Exhibit 1 for balance sheet information). While many felt that U.S. manufacturers were falling behind their Japanese competition in the use of automated manufacturing techniques, the reality was that robot technology in the U.S. was proceeding at an exceedingly rapid pace, especially in some heavy industrial applications. The Robotics Corporation had been a major player in that growth with nearly a fivefold increase in sales in the last two years (Exhibit 2). Presently the company enjoyed a leadership position in the industrial robot field, but intense competition was expected as more aggressive firms entered the market.

The issue of leasing vehicles at Robotics arose due to a large expansion in sales and service personnel as the company grew. Currently there were 70 full-time salespeople and 30 service people in 7 regional offices throughout the U.S. Each sales representative and maintenance engineer drove his/her own vehicle while being reimbursed by Robotics for mileage.

Mr. Williams, chairman and chief executive officer, recently decided that it would be to the company's benefit if the sales and service personnel were provided company vehicles. Reasons for his decision included the feeling that company-owned vehicles would be more consistent with the "Robotics image," i.e., the make and model of the vehicles driven would be subject to more corporate control. Further, Mr. Williams felt that the purchase, sale, and maintenance of personal vehicles for company use was an unnecessary burden on the sales force. Finally, it was felt that a good "company car" was a way to motivate employees in a manner that had preferential personal tax consequences.

BUY/BORROW OR LEASE PROPOSAL

Once the decision had been made to acquire 100 vehicles, the best method of acquiring them became the object of Ms. Dawson's attention. There were two basic alternatives: one was simply to purchase the vehicles from the fleet sales department of a local dealer; the second was to lease a fleet of cars from the Midwest Leasing Corporation, a major independent leasing corporation headquartered in Chicago.

The lease proposal was straightforward and appears in Exhibit 3. Equal quarterly payments to the leasing company of $67,776 were required under the lease, with Robotics being responsible for the ending value (residual) of the vehicles at 40% of the original cost. If Midwest took responsibility for disposing of the vehicles at the term of the lease, usually at a used-car auction, any deficiency in the residual value would be paid to Midwest Leasing, while any excess value would be paid to Robotics.

The ownership option appears in Exhibit 4. That option essentially substitutes a bank term loan for the contractual lease payments. Ms. Dawson felt that it would be possible for Robotics to borrow the full amount of the purchase cost at a 12% fixed rate for the three-year life of the loan. Of course, under the ownership option, the company would be able to depreciate the vehicles. The loan option would involve a payment schedule designed to amortize the loan down to the approximate after tax residual value of the vehicles (Exhibit 5).

One major uncertainty facing Ms. Dawson was the impact of the Investment Tax Credit (ITC) on the calculations. Robotics was only recently emerging from its start-up phase with the result that earnings were still minimal, and it was unclear whether the ITC of 6% would be of any value to the company. If Robotics could not use the ITC, there was a question whether they could negotiate a more favorable lease by "passing it on."

Finally, the issue of maintenance and record keeping for the vehicles was not included in the calculations because a fleet maintenance program was available if the cars were purchased, and a similar cost would be expected to be added to the lease if it was signed. Thus, fleet maintenance was not a variable in the financial considerations of the alternatives.

Ms. Dawson was hoping to be able to present a convincing analysis of the two alternatives to Mr. Williams at their regularly scheduled Wednesday afternoon meeting. To be as precise as possible, she felt she should focus on five key issues.

1. Assuming Robotics can use the ITC, what is the present value cost of the purchase option vs. the lease option. How would this change without the ITC?
2. What is the appropriate discount rate to use in the present value calculation?
3. What rate of return on equity is the leasing company making on the lease, with and without the ITC, assuming they are leveraged 8:1?
4. What other considerations should apply, especially as they pertain to the financial reporting of Robotics, Inc.? Under which alternative will Robotics' reported earnings be the greatest?

EXHIBIT 1

ROBOTICS, INC.
Balance Sheet
As at December 31
($000s)

	1982	1983	1984
Assets			
Cash	60	98	144
Receivables	16	26	38
Inventories	138	223	328
Prepaid expenses	15	24	36
Total current assets	229	371	546
Net plant, equipment	882	1,428	2,100
Total Assets	1,111	1,799	2,646
Liabilities & Net Worth			
Accounts payable	124	201	296
Accrued taxes	21	33	49
Other payables	26	41	61
Total current liabilities	171	276	406
Mortgage loan	34	54	80
Total liabilities	205	330	486
Common stock & capital surplus	1,142	1,842	2,405
Retained earnings	−236	−373	−245
Total Liabilities & Net Worth	1,111	1,799	2,646

EXHIBIT 2

ROBOTICS, INC.
Income Statements
As at December 31
($000s)

	1982	1983	1984
Net Sales	1,310	2,452	6,124
Less: Cost of sales	1,191	2,101	5,420
S.G. & A. expenses	355	488	576
Profit before tax	−236	−137	128
Tax	0	0	0
Profit After Tax	−236	−137	128

Note: There are no taxes due in 1984 because of the accumulated losses of prior years. The balance remaining of the loss carry forwards by the year in which they expire are:

1987	$108,000
1988	137,000
Total	$245,000

The tax effects of the loss carry forwards have not been recorded as an asset on the balance sheets shown in Exhibit 1. The accounting convention is not to capitalize such losses unless it is "nearly certain" that they can be used. These losses can be used to reduce future taxable income up to, and including, the fiscal year in which they expire.

EXHIBIT 3

Proposal from Midwest Leasing Company to Lease 100 Vehicles

1. Number of vehicles (Oldsmobile Cutlass 4-dr)	100
2. Quarterly Lease Cost per Vehicle	$677.76
3. Total for 100 vehicles	$67,776 qtr.
4. Payment timing	Arrears
5. Terminal Rental Adjustment	Yes
6. Number of Payments	12
7. Residual Assumption	40%

EXHIBIT 4

Purchase Option for 100 Vehicles

1. Total cost of 100 Oldsmobile Cutlass 4-dr sedans including dealer allowances and special equipment, $1,000,000.
   Sales tax of 6½% was additional.

2. Terms: Cash.

3. Full amount of purchase price to be borrowed from bank @ 12% interest. Loan amortized to $216,000 balloon payment in third year equal to approximate after tax terminal value of vehicles. See amortization schedule attached. Loan payments are quarterly in arrears.

4. Depreciation under ACRS Accelerated Method:
   Yr. 1 = 25%; Yr. 2 = 38%; Yr. 3 = 37%.

5. Investment tax credit of 6%.

6. Tax rate 46%.

7. Automobiles are sold at end of 12th quarter for 40% of original cost.

EXHIBIT 5

Loan Amortization Schedule
$1,000,000 @ 12% Interest
Level Payment of $85,242

		PAYMENT	INTEREST	PRINCIPAL	BALANCE
Loan	$1,000,000				$1,000,000
Qtr.	1	$ 85,242	$30,000	$55,242	944,758
	2	85,242	28,343	56,899	887,859
	3	85,242	26,636	58,606	829,253
	4	85,242	24,878	60,364	768,888
	5	85,242	23,067	62,175	706,713
	6	85,242	21,201	64,041	642,672
	7	85,242	19,280	65,962	576,710
	8	85,242	17,301	67,941	508,770
	9	85,242	15,263	69,979	438,791
	10	85,242	13,164	72,078	366,712
	11	85,242	11,001	74,241	292,472
	12	301,242	8,774	292,468	4

Note: Rounding error accounts for the $4 ending balance.

31

COLUMBIA RIVER PULP COMPANY INC.— INTEREST RATE HEDGING STRATEGY

Andrew Tharle, Chairman of Columbia River Pulp Company (CRP), sat back in his chair and looked at the jumble of lines, numbers and formulas, in three different colours, on the chart board. It was now 5:15 P.M. and he had spent the last five hours in a crash course on interest rate swaps, caps, floors and collars given by two capital markets professionals of the Toronto-Dominion Bank (TD). Andrew now felt reasonably comfortable with the various products for hedging interest rate risk and had calculated the debt schedule that needed to be covered. The market in New York would be closing in about ten minutes and if he wanted to execute the transactions, he had to give the final nod to the bankers sitting anxiously across the table.

However, several issues were still unclear in Andrew's mind. The first was the question of the interest rate "collar." Was this innovative hedging structure really "free" as explained by the bankers and would a collar give CRP a better hedge than a swap? Second, should CRP hedge all of its floating rate debt, or only the amount required under the loan agreement? Andrew also wanted to be sure that he understood the "all-in" interest costs to CRP after executing the hedging transactions. Whatever

This case was prepared by Graham Carter under the supervision of Professor Robert W. White for the sole purpose of providing material for class discussion at the Western Business School. Certain names and other identifying information may have been disguised to protect confidentiality. It is not intended to illustrate either effective or ineffective handling of a managerial situation. Any reproduction, in any form, of the material in this case is prohibited except with the written consent of the School.

The writers of the case would like to acknowledge the assistance of Derek Cathcart, Toronto-Dominion Bank.

the correct answers were, Andrew knew that his company was about to become a much more sophisticated borrower than it had been the day before.

BACKGROUND ON THE COMPANY

Columbia River Pulp Company owned and operated a world class kraft market pulp mill located in Longview, Washington. The mill began production in 1980, after a two year construction period, and had a rated annual capacity of 385,000 metric tonnes of bleached hardwood and softwood pulp. Output from the mill was sold to paper products manufacturers in the United States, Mexico, Europe and Japan. CRP was recognized as having a favourable cost structure, reliable production record and excellent quality of output. In April 1987, a major consulting firm to the forest products industry estimated the mill's replacement value at $400 million, based on the depreciated value of a 10 year old facility.

Kraft market pulp was a principal input in the manufacturing of high quality paper products, including writing paper and envelopes, boxboard and tissue. The "kraft" process involved cooking or "digesting" wood chips in a chemical solution of caustic soda and sodium sulfide at high temperature and pressure. The resulting pulp, which looks similar to brown porridge, was then bleached to a bright white colour using a five-stage chlorine process. The chemical breakdown of the wood fibres in the kraft process, as opposed to a mechanical grinding breakdown, produced a longer, stronger fibre required for high quality paper.

Kraft market pulp producers, such as CRP, sold their output on the open market, as compared to captive or integrated producers who shipped output to affiliated paper mills. Kraft pulp was a global commodity with price being a function of overall economic activity, industry capacity and the amount of output "dumped" on the market by integrated producers. Price levels for market pulp were extremely volatile and caused dramatic swings in the earnings and cash flow of industry participants, as shown in Exhibits 1 and 2.

1988 REFINANCING OF TERM DEBT

In March 1988, CRP approached TD to refinance $200.0 million of long term debt. The debt was held by a group of U.S. insurance companies that had financed the original cost of the mill in 1978. Cumulative operating losses of CRP totalling $39.1 million over the 1982–86 period had made the insurance companies nervous about the quality of their loans. Kraft market pulp prices had hit a 10-year low of $390 per tonne in 1985. In addition, CRP had experienced technical difficulties relating to its high pressure recovery boiler process. CRP was in default of certain financial covenants and was unable to meet the repayment schedule on the debt. The insurance companies wanted out.

The forest products group at TD conducted a detailed analysis of the CRP operation, including market forecasts for kraft pulp and projected earnings of the mill. Derek Cathcart, a forest products specialist in TD's Corporate Finance group, was convinced that this mill was indeed a low cost producer and would generate significant cash flow as kraft pulp prices continued to rise. After receiving credit approval from the TD Board, Derek's team worked on structuring a $200.0 million, seven-year reducing, revolving term facility and a $25.0 million operating facility which was eventually syndicated among six international banks. The credit agreement, which totalled over 300 pages, was signed on July 21, 1988. The tombstone is presented in Exhibit 3.

The term and operating credits were based on floating rate debt in U.S. dollars. The floating rate borrowing options and bank lending margins, or "spreads," are shown below[1]:

TABLE 1
INTEREST RATE MARGINS

BORROWING OPTION	YEARS 1–3	YEARS 4–7
A. 1,2,3,6 and 12 month LIBOR[2]	+ 1¾%	+ 1⅞%
B. 30,60,90 and 180 day CDs[3]	+ 1⅞%	+ 2%
C. TD Prime[4]	+ 1¼%	+ 1⅜%

The use of floating rate debt to finance fixed assets represents a significant risk to both the lender and borrower if interest rates increased. This risk can be offset, however, through the use of interest rate hedging transactions employing derivative securities, such as interest rate swaps, caps and collars. The market for derivative securities, both in terms of dollar volume and number of participants, had grown dramatically in the past five years. The International Swaps Dealers Association (ISDA) estimated that over $575 billion of interest rate and currency swaps were completed during the first six months of 1987.

In order to partially hedge the floating rate risk on the CRP loans, the bank syndicate had included a positive covenant in the credit agreement which effectively forced the company to lock in fixed rates of interest on its debt. This covenant stated the following:

Within 90 days after closing, the Borrower will arrange interest rate swaps or similar hedging arrangements so that a total of $100 million of debt has a term of at least 3 years and an interest rate not to exceed 12%.

[1]Under the multi-availability facility, CRP takes down the loan with TD. The loan is then prorated to the members of the loan syndicate. Stand-by fees of 37.5 basis points per annum and 50 basis points per annum are charged on the unused portions of the operating and term facilities, respectively.
[2]LIBOR is the acronym for London Interbank Offered Rate and represents a series of borrowing rates available in London by major banks from around the world. LIBORs may be quoted in various currencies and for different time periods. LIBOR is a base rate for comparison in most financial markets for short term rates.
[3]CDs, certificates of deposit, are non-redeemable, registered, transferable, interest bearing notes.
[4]Rate at which the Toronto-Dominion Bank lends to its most favoured customers.

The $200 million term credit, which was fully drawn down on the closing date, was to be repaid over a seven-year period as per the following wording in the loan agreement.

SCHEDULED PRINCIPAL REPAYMENTS:

Scheduled Principal Repayment shall occur in 28 quarterly instalments as outlined below and commencing one quarter after July 21, 1988.

Instalments	1–20	1.75% each
Instalments	21–27	5.00% each
Instalment	28	30.00%

MANDATORY PREPAYMENTS:

Within 120 days of the Borrower's fiscal year end in the amount of 50 percent of the Borrower's Net Cash Flow from Operations and shall be applied in inverse order of Scheduled Principal Repayments.

The terms of the loan agreement also permitted CRP to "prepay" borrowed funds if excess cash flow were available in a given year. This option would allow the company to potentially reduce debt at a faster rate and thereby reduce interest costs. Based on the projected rise in kraft pulp prices, Andrew was confident that CRP would be able to prepay between $11.0 and $23.0 million in each of the next seven years, which would effectively pay off the total loan by the end of 1994. Scheduled repayments of $14.0 million per year and estimated prepayments are shown in the company's financial projections in Exhibit 4.

DEVELOPING A HEDGING STRATEGY

On Monday, July 18, Andrew Tharle, Chairman, and Sara Able, VP and Treasurer of CRP, met with Lawrence Vassallo, TD Capital Markets, and Graham Carter, TD Corporate Banking, to discuss the company's interest rate outlook and to structure an appropriate hedging strategy. Andrew was particularly interested in learning more about the risks/benefits and mechanics of interest rate swaps, caps and collars. The meeting was held in CRP's New York office over an exceptional lunch of poached salmon.

The meeting began with a general discussion of interest rates in the United States and the market outlook for the next 2–5 years. Most analysts were calling for an upturn in rates based on recent inflationary pressure. Capacity utilization in the manufacturing sector remained very high, commodity prices were continuing to climb and the U.S. Government deficit was still a major concern to the financial markets. Exhibit 5 shows the interest rate and inflation forecast of the TD Bank at the time. Andrew's own view of the market was that interest rates would rise significantly over the next 12–18 months. His interest rate outlook, shown in Exhibit 6, projected the three-month LIBOR to increase from the current rate of 8.375

percent to approximately 10.75 percent by January 1990, and then fall back to approximately 9.0 percent. The TD bankers didn't believe that interest rates would go up quite so quickly, but agreed that a 2.0 percent rise over the next two years was likely. This general consensus as to interest rate movements provided the basis for structuring a hedging strategy for CRP.

INTEREST RATE SWAPS

Based on the assumption that interest rates would increase sharply in the next year, the TD team recommended "plain vanilla" interest rate swaps as the most attractive hedging mechanism. Interest rate swaps would effectively lock in a fixed rate on CRP's floating rate bank debt at interest rate levels that were attractive to the company. Andrew and Sara had certainly heard of interest rate swaps, but to this point CRP had never borrowed money at floating rates and had no real need for hedging products. Even the LIBOR floating rate borrowing option was a new concept to the company.

Under the terms of a swap, CRP would receive floating rate interest payments from TD and pay fixed rate interest payments to TD. The interest payments were calculated on a "notional" amount of debt and were separate cash flows from interest payments made to the bank syndicate. The floating rate payment that the company received would offset the floating rate interest owed on the bank loan; thus, on a net basis, CRP would have a single fixed rate interest payment. The floating interest payments would be based on the three month LIBOR, reset every three months to match the reset on the loan. The fixed rate payments would be identical for the 2, 3, 4, or 5 year life of the swap and would be paid semiannually. Throughout the afternoon, the TD bankers used boxes and arrows on the chart board to help explain the various interest rate cash flows. One possible structure, a three year swap for $50.0 million which would provide CRP with an "all-in" fixed rate of 11.31 percent, is shown in Exhibit 7.

INTEREST RATE CAP

A possible alternative to using interest rate swaps was to use a ceiling interest rate agreement (cap). As explained by the TD bankers, a cap was similar to buying insurance against a sharp rise in floating rates. For an upfront fee, CRP would be guaranteed that the interest costs on a notional amount of debt would not exceed a certain rate (the "cap" rate or "strike" rate) during a specified period of time. As in swaps, the floating rate index used for caps is LIBOR, and typically three month LIBOR. For example, TD would sell CRP a 10.00 percent, three year cap on $30.0 million for an upfront fee of $411,000 (or 137 basis points times the notional amount of $30.0 million). If the LIBOR moved above 10.00 percent at reset points during the next three years, TD would make a cash payment to CRP equal to the difference between the market rate and the cap rate. If LIBOR remained below the cap level, the company would continue to pay the market rate on its debt. As highlighted by the bankers, a cap would allow CRP to benefit from a decline in floating rates, unlike a swap which locked in a fixed rate for the life of the transaction.

Caps were available to CRP for maturities of 1–5 years, amounts up to $200.0 million and strike levels ranging from 8.375 percent (the current three month LIBOR) to 15.00 percent. Cap rates above 15.00 percent were available, but didn't make sense based on the minimal rate protection provided. Exhibit 8 shows cap pricing for various maturities and strike rates.

Caps sounded quite interesting to Andrew because this product was very simple and easy to structure. CRP would receive protection if rates increased, but would also enjoy the benefit of a downward trend. Andrew's only concern was the large, upfront cash fee to purchase the cap; $300,000 to $600,000 was a substantial premium to pay for hedging $30.0 million of debt. Further, if his interest rate scenario was wrong and interest rates remained the same or declined, the protection might never be needed!

INTEREST RATE COLLAR

The next hedging product unveiled by the bankers—an interest rate "collar"—sounded more attractive to Andrew, in terms of both risk protection and price. One half of the collar transaction was the purchase by CRP of an interest rate cap, exactly as the bankers had just described. The other component of this hedge was an interest rate "floor," which CRP effectively "sold" to the bank. If the floating LIBOR fell below the floor level at the reset point (for example, 8.375 percent), CRP would make a payment to the bank equal to the difference between the floor rate and the market rate. If LIBOR moved above the cap level at the reset point (for example, 10.75 percent), the bank would make a payment to the company. The net effect of the cap and floor was that CRP's interest cost on debt was "collared" between an upper and lower bound.

The feature of this hedge that caught Andrew's attention was that the collar was "free"—no upfront fee was owed. By selling a floor to the bank, which restricted the benefit to the company of a drop in floating rates, CRP would receive the cap protection at no cost. Based on Andrew's rate outlook, the possible opportunity loss resulting from a downward shift in rates seemed minimal. Even if rates did decline, Andrew did not believe they would drop very far over the next 2–5 years and CRP could easily afford interest costs at a floor of 8.00 percent to 9.00 percent.

Collars were also available for maturities of 1–5 years and amounts up to $200.0 million. There were numerous combinations of cap and floor rates, depending on the sensitivity of the company to rate movements and upfront cash fees. A trade-off must be made between the purchase price paid for the cap and the selling price received for the floor. The purchase price of a cap increases as the strike rate is moved lower because the buyer receives greater protection. Conversely, the selling price of the floor increases as the strike rate is moved higher because the seller gives up more of the downside gain.

Andrew's goal was to minimize any cash fees paid by CRP for hedging protection. With this in mind, TD recommended a collar having a 11.00 percent cap and a 8.375 percent floor. The cap and floor prices would offset, resulting in no upfront fees. The collar would be based on a notional principal amount of $30.0 million and have a maturity of three years.

A second collar structure mentioned by the bankers also caught Andrew's attention. This hedge would provide a 10.25 percent cap and a 8.75 percent floor with no upfront fees. The floor of 8.75 percent was set above the current three month LIBOR of 8.375 percent, but the transaction was structured so that the floor would not come into play for a period of three months. By agreeing to a floor above the current market rate, CRP was able to purchase a lower rate cap, thereby getting greater protection against an increase in interest rates. If Andrew's rate scenario was correct, LIBOR would be above 8.75 percent in three months time and CRP would not owe any money to TD on the next rate setting. This structure is shown in Exhibit 9.

"EXECUTION" TIME

Swaps, caps or collars, or some combination? There were definite trade-offs between these hedging products in terms of flexibility, interest rate protection and true cost. Andrew also had to decide on the amounts and maturities of the various transactions. A three-year swap was less expensive than a five-year deal, but CRP might need the longer term protection. (Indicative rates provided by the TD bankers for swaps, caps and collars are shown in Exhibit 8.) To ensure that the terms and rates quoted by TD were competitive, the management of CRP, during the negotiations with TD, were getting quotes on the proposed instruments from other banks in the syndicate. Should he only hedge $100.0 million for three years, as required under the terms of the loan agreement, or hedge all of CRP's floating rate debt on a declining basis? Swaps offered the lowest fixed rate to CRP, but caps and collars appeared to be more flexible if his interest rate scenario proved incorrect. Based on projected debt repayment, he knew that the company's exposure to interest rate risk would decline significantly in a period of three years. After five hours of discussing strategies and structures, it was now time to "execute"!

EXHIBIT 1

Kraft Market Pulp Prices
(US$ per metric tonne)

	1983	1984	1985	1986	1987	1988E	1989E
Year-End Price	$450	$510	$390	$500	$610	$760	$745

EXHIBIT 2

COLUMBIA RIVER PULP COMPANY INC.
Historical Operating Performance
Year Ends March 31
(US$ millions)

	1983	1984	1985	1986	1987	1988
Sales	$121.8	$139.6	$153.1	$107.5	$159.7	$206.4
Operating Profit/(Loss)[a]	(15.3)	(7.0)	4.2	(21.0)	23.0	58.4
Cash Flow from Operations[b]	13.0	4.7	18.4	(3.9)	31.7	60.2

[a]Operating Profit/Loss is before interest expense and taxes.
[b]Cash Flow from Operations is before interest expense, debt repayment and taxes, but reflects changes in working capital and capital expenditures.

EXHIBIT 3

This announcement appears as a matter of record only.

July 1988

Columbia River Pulp Company

$225,000,000

Recapitalization Financing

Funds provided by

The Toronto Dominion Bank
Canadian Imperial Bank of Commerce
The Royal Bank of Canada

Scandinavian Bank Group plc
Midland Bank plc
The Fuji Bank, Limited

Agent

The Toronto Dominion Bank
    Trust Company

The undersigned negotiated the terms and conditions of this facility as part of the overall structure of the transaction, which included the private placement of $90 Million of subordinated debt.

Syndicated and Advised by

Toronto Dominion Bank

TD BANK

EXHIBIT 4

COLUMBIA RIVER PULP COMPANY INC.
Projections of Net Income and Cash Flow
Fiscal Years Ended March 31, 1989–1995
(US$000s)

	1989	1990	1991	1992	1993	1994	1995
Tons Sold (ADMT)	386,210	386,210	401,177	411,155	411,155	411,155	411,155
Price Per ADMT (Avg)	609.84	609.84	559.84	559.84	644.16	709.84	709.84
Gross Sales	235,727	235,527	224,597	230,182	264,851	291,856	291,855
Less: Selling Expenses	26,359	27,019	27,934	29,389	31,902	33,591	34,442
Net Sales	209,168	208,508	196,663	200,793	232,949	258,265	257,413
Cost of Sales	105,715	110,044	116,926	123,354	128,444	133,770	139,308
Depreciation/Amortization	23,145	24,230	25,350	26,505	27,345	28,220	29,130
Operating Profit	80,308	74,234	54,387	50,934	77,160	96,275	88,975
Less: Interest – LTD	33,149	29,997	26,465	23,465	20,489	14,097	11,181
Interest Income	100	505	1,102	1,544	1,979	2,847	4,034
Pre-Tax Income	47,259	44,742	29,024	29,013	58,650	85,025	81,828
Applicable Taxes	16,068	15,212	9,868	9,864	19,941	28,909	27,822
Net Income	31,191	29,530	19,156	19,149	38,709	56,116	54,006

Cash Flow

Net Income	31,191	29,530	19,156	19,149	38,709	56,116	54,006
Add: Depreciation	23,145	24,230	25,350	26,505	27,345	28,220	29,130
Deferred Interest	11,181	11,181	11,181	11,181	11,181	11,181	11,181
Working Capital Change	(9,218)	(346)	159	(878)	(2,659)	(2,183)	(443)
Cash Flow From Operations	56,299	64,595	55,846	55,957	74,576	93,334	93,874
Less: Capital Expenditures – Reg.	10,000	10,500	11,000	11,500	12,000	12,500	13,000
Capital Expenditures – Opt.	5,000	5,000	5,000	5,000	0	0	0
Principal – TD	14,000	14,000	14,000	14,000	14,000	40,000	0
Prepayment – TD	11,025	15,923	11,798	11,604	23,145	16,505	0
Other Permitted Debt	5,000	3,000	2,000	2,000	2,037	0	0
Other Liabilities	250	250	250	250	250	250	250
Available Cash	11,024	15,992	11,798	11,603	23,144	24,079	80,624
Beginning Cash Balance	1,221	6,732	14,692	20,591	26,382	37,963	53,789
Less: Dividends	5,513	7,962	5,889	5,802	11,573	8,253	80,812
Cumulative Cash After Dividends	6,732	14,692	20,591	26,392	37,963	53,789	53,601

EXHIBIT 4 (cont.)

COLUMBIA RIVER PULP COMPANY INC.
Projected Balance Sheets
Fiscal Years Ended March 31, 1989–1995
(US$000s)

	1989	1990	1991	1992	1993	1994	1995
Assets							
Cash and Equivalents	6,732	14,692	20,591	26,392	37,963	53,789	53,601
Accounts Receivable	15,309	15,309	14,599	4,962	17,215	18,971	18,971
Inventories	14,800	15,406	16,370	17,270	17,982	18,728	19,503
Prepaid Expenses & Other Assets	2,481	2,481	2,481	2,481	2,481	2,481	2,481
Total Current Assets	39,322	47,888	54,041	61,105	75,641	93,969	94,556
Fixed Assets	339,791	355,291	371,291	387,791	399,791	412,291	425,291
Less Allowances for Deprec./Amort.	(183,703)	(207,933)	(233,283)	(259,788)	(287,133)	(315,353)	(344,483)
Net Property & Equipment	156,088	147,358	138,008	128,003	112,658	96,938	80,808
Total Assets	195,410	195,246	192,049	189,108	188,299	190,907	175,364
Liabilities							
Accounts Payable	6,343	6,603	7,016	7,401	7,707	8,026	8,358
Curr. Portion–Long Term Oblig.	17,250	16,250	16,250	16,287	40,250	250	250
Total Current Liabilities	23,593	22,853	23,266	23,688	47,957	8,276	8,608
Other Permitted Debt	6,037	4,037	2,037	0	0	0	0
LTD–Toronto–Dominion	160,975	131,052	105,254	79,650	16,505	0	0
Subordinated Debt–Brian Smith	108,409	119,590	130,771	141,952	153,133	164,314	175,495
Other Liabilities	8,063	7,813	7,563	7,313	7,063	6,813	6,563
Total Long Term Debt	283,484	262,492	245,625	228,915	176,701	171,127	182,058
Equity							
Common Stock	2	2	2	2	2	2	2
Capital Surplus	57,299	57,299	57,299	57,299	57,299	57,299	57,299
Retained Earnings	(168,968)	(147,400)	(134,143)	(120,796)	(93,660)	(45,797)	(72,603)
Total Equity	(111,667)	(90,099)	(76,842)	(63,495)	(36,359)	11,504	(15,302)
Total Liabilities & Equity	195,410	195,246	192,049	189,108	188,299	190,907	175,364

EXHIBIT 5

Interest Rate and Inflation Forecast
United States

INTEREST RATES
(Three month Euro-Deposit Rate)

	Q1	Q2	Q3	Q4	YEAR AVG	% CHG CPI
1987	6.38	7.15	7.22	7.96	7.18	3.7
1988	7.0	7.5	8.3	9.0	7.9	4.1
1989	9.0	8.7	8.6	8.5	8.7	5.0
1990	8.5	8.5	8.6	8.6	8.5	4.6
1991	8.7	8.8	9.0	9.0	8.9	4.8
1992	9.2	9.5	9.8	10.0	9.6	5.2

INTEREST RATE & INFLATION
(percent)

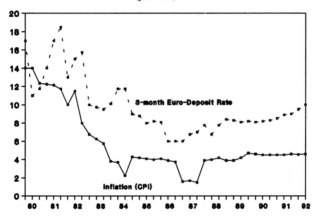

United States short term interest rates continued to move up following the ½ percentage point rise in the Federal Reserve board discount rate to 6.5 percent in early August. The Fed has been maintaining a firm stance against inflation as the U.S. economy has been growing faster than the trend rate of growth of between 2.0 and 2.5 percent. The near-term outlook is for stability or further small increases in short term interest rates. Rates are expected to ease during 1989, remain fairly flat in 1990 and edge up during 1991–92. This forecast assumes that the U.S. Congress and the new Administration will agree on a new deficit-reduction package in 1989. In addition, it is assumed that the U.S. trade deficit will narrow progressively during the forecast period.

The pace of the U.S. economic expansion will be the major factor influencing the path of U.S. short term interest rates. The U.S. economy is likely to remain resilient during the rest of 1988, resulting in some further small increases in inflation and interest rates. Some continued shortages and relatively full employment are likely to result in a further slight increase in price indexes early in 1989. Later in the year, with economic growth slowing down and inflation easing, interest rates should also moderate.

In remainder of the forecast period, 1990–92, growth in the U.S. economy is expected to accelerate gradually, resulting in a gentle uptrend in short term interest rates.

Source: Department of Economic Research, Toronto-Dominion Bank, July 1988.

EXHIBIT 6

COLUMBIA RIVER PULP COMPANY INC.
Interest Rate Outlook

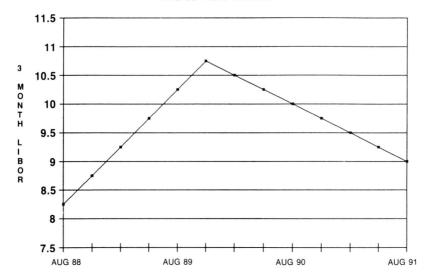

EXHIBIT 7

Interest Rate Swap Proposal
3-Years—$50 Million

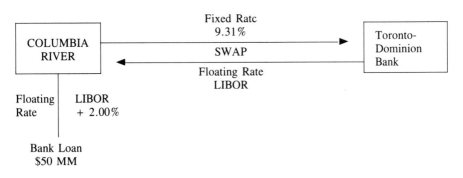

Calculation of Net Fixed Rate:
1. CRP *pays* LIBOR + 2.00% spread on Bank Loan[a]   − (LIBOR +2.00%)
2. CRP *receives* LIBOR on Swap   + LIBOR
3. CRP *pays* fixed rate on Swap   − 9.31
   All-in FIXED RATE ON DEBT   11.31%

---

[a]The 2.00% spread is composed of the 1.75% bank lending margin plus 0.25% in Federal Reserve Bank reserve charges.

EXHIBIT 8

Indicative Market Rates
for Hedging Projects
July 18, 1988

		FIXED RATE[a]		
	MATURITY	TREASURY RATE	SWAP SPREAD	SWAP RATE
I. SWAPS:				
	2 Years	8.36%	+ .75%	= 9.11%
	3 Years	8.43%	+ .88%	= 9.31%
	4 Years	8.55%	+ .89%	= 9.44%
	5 Years	8.71%	+ .86%	= 9.57%

		PRICES FOR CAPS AT VARIOUS STRIKE MATURITY RATES[b]		
	MATURITY	10%	11%	12%
II. CAPS:				
	2 Years	60 bps.	33 bps.	19 bps.
	3 Years	137	84	52
	4 Years	221	143	94
	5 Years	321	219	149

III. COLLARS:

A) Cap Rate:	11.00%	B) Cap Rate:	10.25%
Floor Rate:	8.375%	Floor Rate:[c]	8.75%
Upfront Fee:	$0	Upfront Fee:[d]	$0
Maturity:	3 Years	Maturity:	3 Years

[a]The fixed rate that the company pays on an interest rate swap is quoted as a "spread" over the Government Treasury Bond of the same maturity. The spread rate is a function of supply and demand for swaps in that maturity. This spread applies only to the swap calculation and is unrelated to the bank loan spread.

[b]Upfront cash fees paid by the company. Fees expressed as basis points on the national amount of the cap (for example, 100 basis points on $25 million = $250,000).

[c]Floor would not be effective for the first three months.

[d]The formula for calculating the amortization of arrangement fee is (where **n** is term in years):

$$\text{Annual Arrangement Fee} = \text{Arrangement Fee in \%} \times \frac{\text{Interest Rate}}{1 - (\text{Interest Rate} + 1)^{-n}}$$

EXHIBIT 9

Interest Rate Collar Proposal
3-Years—$30 Million

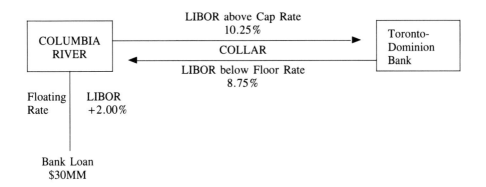

Upfront Fee: CRP pays $0 to TD

Calculation of Maximum and Minimum Collar Rate:

Maximum:

CRP's maximum rate under the Collar equals:

Cap Rate	10.25%
+ LIBOR Spread + Reserves	2.00
+ Amortized Upfront Fee	0.00
All-in RATE	12.25%

Minimum:

CRP's minimum rate under the Colar equals:

Floor Rate	8.75%
+ LIBOR Spread + Reserves	2.00
+ Amortized Upfront Fee	0.00
All-in RATE	10.75%

32

EXPORT DEVELOPMENT CORPORATION—
PROTECTED INDEX NOTES (PINS)

On his daily seven-mile run along the Rideau Canal from his home to the offices of Export Development Corporation (EDC), Clare Marshall, Vice-President and Treasurer, was collecting his thoughts on the presentation he had seen the previous day. Wood Gundy Inc., a Canadian investment dealer, had proposed that EDC use an innovative derivative product called Protected Index Notes (PINS) to raise funds in the Canadian domestic market. PINS are a zero-coupon debt instrument in which the return to investors is tied to the performance in the S&P 500, an index of 500 large blue chip American companies.

Paramount in Clare's mind was the ultimate cost of the issue, the way in which it met EDC's long-term financing needs, and any risks to EDC associated with the issue. Clare believed that giving a quick answer to an investment banker's proposals promoted stronger relationships and increased the number of deals EDC was shown; therefore, he had to decide whether or not to recommend that the board of EDC go with the issue and get back to Wood Gundy within the next few days.

This case was prepared by Christopher Colpitts under the supervision of Professor Robert W. White for the sole purpose of providing material for class discussion at the Western Business School. Certain names and other identifying information may have been disguised to protect confidentiality. It is not intended to illustrate either effective or ineffective handling of a managerial situation. Any reproduction, in any form, of the material in this case is prohibited except with the written consent of the School.

The Western Business School would like to acknowledge the assistance of Clare Marshall of Export Development Corporation and Ed Giacomelli of Wood Gundy Inc. in preparing the case.

EXPORT DEVELOPMENT CORPORATION

EDC was a Crown Corporation established by an Act of Parliament to facilitate and develop export trade by the provision of insurance, guarantees, loans and related financial services. EDC pursued its purpose by providing those services which would best serve exporters of Canadian goods and services through the financial and other powers of the act. The volume of Canadian exports supported and the number of Canadian exporters who purchased EDC's products determined the extent to which EDC was successful in fulfilling its corporate purpose, to facilitate and develop Canada's export trade, and the corporate objectives listed above. In determining its support for individual applications, EDC weighed risk factors and its revenue requirements in order to operate on a *financially self-sustaining basis.*

EDC's financial services helped Canadian exporters to compete effectively in international markets by reducing the financial risks associated with export sales, and by funding foreign buyers of Canadian exports. EDC also offered insurance for Canadian foreign investment, and bonding and surety service for Canadian exporters. In essence, EDC's role was to ensure Canadian exporters of a "level playing field" in competing in foreign markets. In doing so, EDC was filling a gap left by the large chartered banks and insurance companies who did not always supply financing and insurance to this export market. EDC, as the official credit agency of Canada, competed with similar agencies in most industrialized countries.

FINANCING

EDC generally provided export financing for up to 85 percent of the contract value, at both fixed and floating rates of interest, to foreign buyers of Canadian goods, equipment, and services. Funds were disbursed directly by EDC to Canadian exporters on behalf of the borrower, in effect providing the exporter with a cash sale.

EDC offered four basic financing facilities:

Loan. A financing agreement where the terms had been agreed between the foreign borrower and EDC and the funds were disbursed under an agreement between the borrower/buyer, the exporter and EDC.

Line of Credit. A variation of a loan in which the foreign borrower, usually a bank or financial institution, agrees to borrow from EDC for a series of transactions for which neither the exporter nor the buyer had been determined when the line was set up. An allocation occurs when these parties are identified, and approved under the terms of the line of credit.

The Note Purchase Program. The purchase by EDC (usually on a non-recourse basis) of promissory notes issued by foreign buyers to Canadian exporters for the purchase of Canadian goods and services.

Specialized Credit. Available to Canadian entities. Eligible transactions are those for which goods are purchased in Canada by a Canadian buyer that:

will lease such goods to another person for permanent use out of Canada.

will use such goods itself permanently out of Canada.

During 1990, export financing in excess of $1.4 billion helped 105 Canadian exporters and more than 7,000 of their suppliers. This involved 181 transactions in 28 countries (Exhibits 1 and 2). In addition, EDC extended lines of credit of $650 million, bringing the total outstanding in such facilities to $3 billion.

INSURANCE

Canadian firms of any size could insure their export sales against non-payment by foreign buyers. EDC normally assumed 90 percent of the commercial and political risks involving insolvency, default or repudiation, cancellation of a contract by the buyer, blockage of funds, war or rebellion, cancellation of import licenses and the like by foreign countries and cancellation of export permits by Canada. EDC's insurance programs fell into the following categories:

> *Short Term Credit Insurance.* The general insurance of receivables payable in 180 days or less. This was provided on sales worldwide or to those who only sold to specific markets like the United States. In addition to this broad coverage, more specific insurance was available for specific risks in specific markets.
>
> *Medium Term Insurance.* Insurance of receivables over 180 days and specific transactions insurance over 180 days. In addition, policies that protected a member of a consortium against loss resulting from non-performance of a partner and against political risk on equipment in foreign countries were also available.
>
> *Foreign Investment Insurance.* Recognizing the growing importance of foreign investment and joint ventures to Canadian exporters, EDC offered coverage for new investments overseas to protect against the full range of political risks, including the risk of expropriation and repatriation of capital and earnings.
>
> *Performance-Related Guarantees.* Insurance services to protect financial institutions against losses when issuing bid, performance, or advance payments bonds on behalf of Canadian exporters.

In 1990, EDC's export credit insurance supported $5 billion in exports to 1,576 Canadian businesses whose exports were sold in 129 countries worldwide (Exhibits 3 and 4). Almost 200 exporters used specific transaction insurance and guarantees to manage their medium term risks. In addition, EDC insured almost $500 million in Canadian investments abroad. In 1990, EDC paid more than $28 million on 351 claims.

EDC FINANCE AND TREASURY

It was the treasury department's responsibility to fund the operations of EDC. This involved monitoring EDC's current portfolio of liabilities outstanding, refinancing existing debt and financing new business. As a Crown Corporation, EDC enjoyed a AAA rating. It was the government-approved policy of EDC to fund its capital requirements in the international and domestic capital markets through borrowings by any means, including issuing bonds, debentures, notes and other evidence of indebtedness. Debt issuance required approval from both the EDC board and the

Minister of Finance. The department had standing approval to certain limits on debt that had features commonly offered in the public markets. All other borrowings were approved on a case-by-case basis. The basic principles and exposure guidelines, as stated in the summary of corporate plan 1991–1995, are summarized as follows:

- Prudent managing of portfolio interest-rate risk, rather than a matching of individual assets with specific liabilities; this was believed to be the optimal method of maintaining management flexibility and minimizing borrowing costs.
- Endeavouring to match the terms to maturity of its asset and liability portfolios, as well as continuous monitoring and management of the difference between maturing assets and liabilities in light of market conditions.
- Funding when it requires cash, rather than at the time of commitment on lending rates for loan assets, so that it may avoid the cost of negative carry, or cancellation of contingent assets.
- Minimizing of fixed-rate bridge financing or warehousing positions, although sometimes for strategic reasons it would borrow short term to finance loans receivable when rates are high or borrow in advance at fixed rates when interest rates are low.
- Creating liabilities in non-domestic currencies to match those of its loans receivable to minimize foreign exposure.
- Hedging of interest rates and currency movements with respect to its borrowings.
- Viewing equity as residual after the matching of assets and liabilities by type.
- Maintaining its assets and liabilities primarily in U.S. dollars.

EDC was one of the world's most sophisticated borrowers. It had completed well over 100 transactions in the last 10 years. It borrowed in all major international markets through a variety of instruments. In 1990, it completed over $14 billion of foreign currency transactions.

The treasury of EDC had a reputation as an innovative financier. In 1984, EDC, along with Citibank, developed the first putable swap in the world. In 1985, EDC internally developed a short term borrowing program based on various existing programs in both Europe and the United States. These programs included traditional note issuance facilities (NIF), revolving underwritten facilities, tender panels, placements with banks and U.S. commercial paper. This program together with its other treasury operations during the year resulted in EDC being selected the 1985 borrower of the year by *Euromoney Magazine*. In 1989, EDC converted this short term borrowing program to a Registered Claims Program in Switzerland, which allowed EDC to borrow approximately US$1.5 billion at LIBOR minus 70 basis points (bp), compared to top sovereign and corporate borrowers and leading banks at LIBOR minus 20 to 30bp. It was this program that had allowed EDC to set the hurdle rate of its new financing at LIBOR minus 50 bp. EDC's outstanding commitments were approximately $5.5 billion. EDC forecasted that it would need to raise over $1 billion in new funds in each of the next 5 years.

To meet these financing needs at a low cost of funds, EDC had been a proactive borrower. EDC worked actively with the investment banking community, reviewing proposed financing structures on a daily basis, adjusting structures to best meet EDC's needs and taking variations of successful issues to new international markets.

EDC believed that with assets yielding below commercial rates, an aggressive, efficient treasury was essential.

In a discussion as to why EDC had been profitable (Exhibit 5) (the UK equivalent has lost over $2 billion) and might be better suited to service the export market than the traditional banks and insurance companies, *Euromoney Magazine* stated:

> While EDC is selling treasury notes at 10 or 20 basis points over T-bills, the answer must be that EDC raises the cheapest money.[1]

As of the date of the case, EDC had not completed a public issue in Canada. However, EDC had completed private placements in Canada. EDC had yet to find a deal in Canada with sufficient size to meet its hurdle rate, compared to alternatives available internationally. EDC felt this was because Canadian investors expected it to borrow at the same rate as top Provincials (ex. Ontario Hydro). EDC felt that it was a better risk than this and should be priced off treasuries as in the U.S. market. Because of this, EDC and its activities were much better known abroad than in Canada. EDC, however, had actively searched for Canadian deals in order to raise its profile in its home country and provide it with a yet untapped pool of capital. It was not, however, willing to sacrifice cost.

PINS

This security was a U.S. dollar-denominated, S&P-linked note retractable by the holder at any time to maturity at the S&P value of the note. At maturity ($5\frac{1}{2}$ years), the holder received the greater of par value (US $10) or the S&P value of the notes. Initially, a US $75 million offering was thought to be appropriate.

Once the issue was complete, EDC would enter into a swap with the investment dealers in which EDC exchanged its exposure associated with the PINS issue for fixed cost financing at its hurdle rate. The investment dealer then hedged its exposure under PINS using a combination of financial options and futures.

Index-linked notes were not a new instrument. Two recent issues had been completed by the Republic of Austria and Salomon Inc.[2] (Exhibits 6 and 7). Neither of these issues was particularly successful. The generally accepted view was that investors did not find the instrument attractive unless it had a high credit rating and was retractable before maturity, allowing the investor liquidity. The investor would be concerned about the credit rating of the issuer as this gave the investor an indication of the issuer's ability to repay the funds at time of retraction. Also of importance when selling the issue would be the historical performance of the S&P 500 (see Table 1) and the investor's expectations of its future performance.

[1] *Euromoney Magazine,* October 1985.
[2] The majority of Salomon's debt was rated by Moody's as A3. One issue was rated Baa.

TABLE 1
STANDARD & POOR'S 500 INDEX
HISTORICAL PERFORMANCE
OVER ALL 5½ YEAR PERIODS
JANUARY 1980 THROUGH MAY 1991

Average Appreciation	99.5%
Maximum Appreciation	196.7%
Minimum Appreciation	59.7%

The details of the issue that Wood Gundy was proposing are as follows (Exhibit 8):

- Each note will have a principal amount of US$10 with payments with respect to the notes made in US$.
- At maturity the holder will receive the greater of
  a) US$10
  b) Repurchase Price $= US\$10 \times \dfrac{\text{spotS\&Pindex}}{\text{strikeS\&Pindex}}$

  Spot S&P Index is the closing level of the index on valuation date
  Strike S&P Index will be set at 105% of the closing level of the index on the business day immediately preceding the closing date
- The holder has the option to require EDC to repurchase the notes at the repurchase price at any time prior to maturity.
- The notes are RRSP[3] eligible and are not included in the foreign content restriction.[4]
- The notes will be listed on the Toronto Stock Exchange (TSE).

WOOD GUNDY

On the return flight from Ottawa to Toronto, Steve McGirr and Peter Hendrick were considering the issues still outstanding in the PINS transaction. Foremost in their minds were Wood Gundy's role in hedging the issue, an appropriate marketing strategy for the issue, and the timing of the issue in the face of the proposed Petro-Canada privatization. The last point could be especially important if both issues competed for the same investors, used the same distribution network, and were brought to market simultaneously.

BACKGROUND TO THE PINS ISSUE

On February 15, 1991, Steve McGirr attended a closing dinner in New York with David McCutcheon of First Boston Corporation in New York (First Boston). They generally discussed ways of raising capital for Canadian clients using First Boston's sister derivative product company, Credit Suisse Financial Products (CSFP). CSFP

---

[3]Registered Retirement Savings Plan (RRSP)—a plan in which a portion of a Canadian's income can be set aside as retirement savings tax-free. There are certain restrictions on what type of instruments can be held in such a plan.

[4]The foreign content restriction states that only 14% of one's RRSP can hold foreign securities in 1991. The restriction increases by 2% each year until it reaches 20%.

had developed hedging technology which enabled them to hedge an index-linked instrument that was retractable. They had completed several private placements in the U.S. successfully, but a public deal had not yet been attempted. CSFP wondered if any of Wood Gundy's clients would be interested in this structure. Both parties agreed that any prospective issuer would have to be a sophisticated and innovative borrower as they would have to understand the complicated swap and hedging strategy. Working together on the structure seemed advantageous to both firms. EDC seemed a logical choice as it had a growing need for low cost funds, was a knowledgeable borrower, and had a desire to do an issue in Canada. EDC was also very close to Wood Gundy and First Boston.

First Boston were reputed to have the leading derivative group in the world in CSFP. Nine months earlier Peter Hendrick had formed an equity derivatives group within Wood Gundy. First Boston and Wood Gundy agreed that, if Wood Gundy wished, it could share the hedging duties with CSFP. CSFP considered the hedging technology to be proprietary, but agreed to discuss in broad terms how they manufactured the hedge. Paramount in Peter's mind was what the risks were if investors retracted and how that risk could be hedged. Peter considered it an opportunity to work with people of CSFP's abilities but had to consider the risks of undertaking such an innovative hedge with his relatively new group.

Steve McGirr was considering the marketing issues associated with the issue. There were always risks when a structure was attempted for the first time. In addition, he wondered who the end investor would be and what type and level of marketing effort would be needed to sell the issue. A final concern was what the timing of the proposed Petro-Canada privatization would be if this large issue were aimed at the same investors as the PINS issue.

THE DECISION

Clare had been shown similar deals but felt PINS was the first one structured in a way that would be successful in Canada. A problem that bothered him was that EDC was an exempt issuer[5] and, as such, did not fall under the jurisdiction of the Ontario Securities Commission (OSC). Clare had a great deal of political concern about any situation where Canada's position was being judged by a provincial jurisdiction. Wood Gundy felt that due to its innovative structure and the implications to other exempt issuers, the PINS issue might be reviewed by the OSC. This review process could be time-consuming and would involve considerable disclosure. Clare wondered how this should affect his decision. He had to weigh the extent to which the issue met EDC financing requirement against the risks associated with it before recommending it to his board. However, he was confident that Wood Gundy could assist him in solving the problems associated with this issue.

---

[5]As a Crown Corporation EDC was exempt of the normal disclosure procedures required by the Ontario Securities Commission (OSC) when issuing equity or debt. Certain financial institutions, such as banks and trust companies, are also exempt issuers with respect to issuing debt.

EXHIBIT 1

Export Financing by Size of Transaction
($ 000)

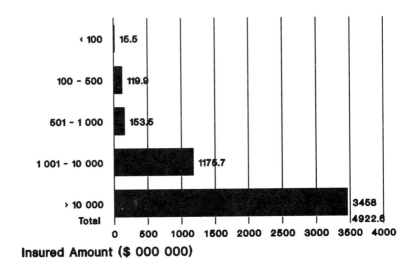

Insured Amount ($ 000 000)

EXHIBIT 2

Export Financing by Geographic Area

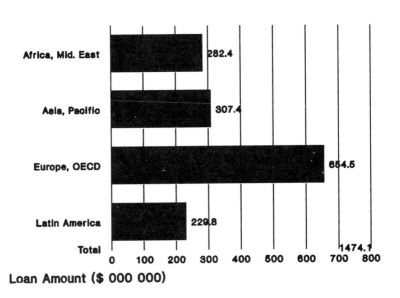

Loan Amount ($ 000 000)

EXHIBIT 3

Export Insurance by Size of Transaction
($000)

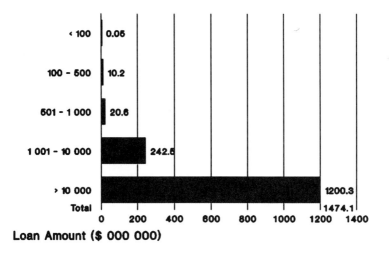

Loan Amount ($ 000 000)

EXHIBIT 4

Export Insurance by Geographic Area

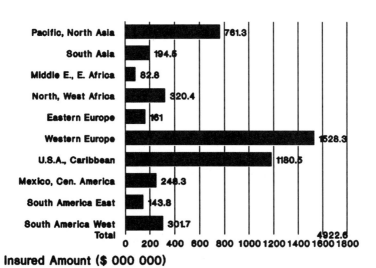

Insured Amount ($ 000 000)

EXHIBIT 5

EXPORT DEVELOPMENT CORPORATION
Balance Sheet
As at December 31, 1990
(in thousands $)

	1990	1989
Assets		
Cash and marketable securities		
Cash and short term deposits	1,127,369	1,175,647
Marketable securities at lower of cost or market	165,427	176,670
Accrued interest	17,907	23,637
	1,310,703	1,375,954
Loans Receivable		
Long term	5,074,395	4,585,653
Current portion of long term	903,502	812,391
	5,977,897	5,398,044
Accrued interest and fees	123,182	131,527
	6,101,079	5,529,571
Less: Allowance for losses on loans	409,513	375,951
	5,691,566	5,153,620
Other		
Recoverable insurance claims	8,318	5,127
Unamortized debt discount and issue expenses		
and other assets	29,608	32,089
	37,926	37,216
	7,040,195	6,566,790
Liabilities		
Loans payable		
Short term	2,195,813	1,975,056
Current portion of long term	708,925	848,376
	2,904,738	2,823,432
Long term	2,950,430	2,649,095
	5,855,168	5,472,527
Accrued interest	179,702	172,423
	6,034,870	5,644,950
Other liabilities and deferred revenues		
Accounts payable	17,700	24,204
Deferred insurance premiums	11,120	9,772
Allowance for claims on insurance and guarantees	46,616	48,659
Deferred loan revenues and other credits	143,750	134,369
	219,187	217,005

(continued)

EXHIBIT 5 (cont.)

	1990	1989
Shareholders' Equity		
Share capital	772,000	697,000
Retained earnings	14,138	7,835
	786,138	704,835
	7,040,195	6,566,790

Undertakings from the Government of Canada on loans receivable
Commitments and contingent liabilities
Approved by the Board of Directors

Charles Diamond	M.D.J. Bakker	R.L. Richardson
Director	Chief Financial Officer	Director

EXPORT DEVELOPMENT CORPORATION
Statement of Income and Retained Earnings
For the year ended December 31, 1990
(in thousands $)

	1990	1989
Loans and Guarantees		
Interest earned	463,325	479,012
Fees earned	39,466	34,394
	502,791	513,406
Provisions for losses on loans	(77,589)	(271,275)
	425,202	242,131
Insurance and Guarantees		
Premiums and fees earned	26,613	25,543
Provision for claims	(18,424)	(12,115)
	8,189	13,428
Investment Interest Earned	112,919	90,913
Earnings Net of Provisions	546,310	346,472
Interest Expense		
Long term	313,431	345,002
Short term	187,211	162,355
	500,642	507,357
Income (Loss) From Operations	45,668	(160,885)
Administrative Expenses	39,365	37,950
Net Income (Loss)	6,303	(198,835)
Retained Earnings		
Beginning of year	7,835	106,670
Add: Transfer from reserve for contingencies	–	100,000
End of year	14,138	7,835

EXHIBIT 5 (cont.)

EXPORT DEVELOPMENT CORPORATION
Statement of Changes in Financial Position
For the year ended December 31, 1990
(in thousands $)

	1990	1989
Operations		
Statement of Income		
Net income (loss)	6,303	(198,835)
Items not affecting cash		
Provision for losses on loans	77,589	271,275
Provisions for claims	18,424	12,115
Accrued interest and fees	22,116	36,321
Other changes	(21,811)	13,450
	102,621	134,326
Assets and Liabilities		
Loans receivable disbursed	(1,394,594)	(853,641)
Loans receivable repaid	851,310	760,610
Items not affecting cash		
Net increase (decrease) in deferred revenue	10,621	(13,746)
Interest rescheduled	(24,856)	(68,452)
Loan interest reversed	(43,978)	(57,475)
	(601,497)	(232,704)
Cash used in operations	(498,876)	(98,378)
Treasury		
Issue of long term debt	1,007,885	741,605
Repayment of long term debt	(860,215)	(523,777)
Increase in short term loans	178,352	152,315
Issue of share capital	75,000	—
Cash provided from financing	401,022	370,143
(Decrease) increase in cash and marketable securities	(97,854)	271,765
Foreign exchange on opening balance of cash	38,333	(27,199)
Cash and Marketable Securities		
Beginning of year	1,352,317	1,107,751
End of year	1,292,796	1,352,317

EXHIBIT 6

Republic of Austria
Summary

The following summary does not purport to be complete and is qualified in its entirety by the more detailed information appearing elsewhere in this Prospectus Supplement and the Prospectus.

On January 28, 1991, the noon buying rate for cable transfers in New York City payable in Austrian schilling, as reported by the Federal Reserve Bank of New York, was 10.4800 schilling per U.S. dollar.

THE OFFERING

Securities Offered:	$100,000,000 Stock Index Growth xxx due August 15, 1996 (the "Notes") (assuming no exercise of the Underwriters' over-allotment option).
Denominations:	$10 per Note and integral multiples thereof.
Price:	100% (par).
Unconditional Obligation:	The Notes are unconditional, direct and general obligations of the Republic of Austria (the "Republic") and the Republic has pledged its full faith and credit for the due and punctual payment of the principal of, and interest, if any, on the Notes.
Maturity:	August 15, 1996.
Interest Payable at Maturity:	At maturity, a holder of a Note will be entitled to receive a contingent interest payment (the "Interest Payment"), which will be equal to 100% of the appreciation (as described below), if any, in the Standard & Poor's 500 Composite Stock Price Index (the "S&P 500 Index") from the date of this Prospectus Supplement to the maturity date of the Notes. If there is no increase in the S&P 500 Index at maturity, or if there has been a decrease in such index, a holder of $10 principal amount of a Note will be repaid the $10 principal amount of the Note, without interest.
	With respect to each $10 principal amount of a Note, the Interest Payment will be equal to the product of (A) the excess, if any, of the "Final Value" over the "Initial Value", divided by the "Initial Value" and (B) $10. The "Final Value" is the unweighted arithmetic average of the closing values of the S&P 500 Index (such values as calculated by Standard & Poor's Corporation ("S&P")) at the market close for the 30 Business Days immediately preceding the second Business Day prior to the maturity date of the Notes. The "Initial Value" is 336.69. See "Description of the Notes—Interest Payable at Maturity" in this Prospectus Supplement.
Redemption:	The Notes are not redeemable prior to maturity.
Listing:	The Notes have been approved for listing on The New York Stock Exchange, Inc., subject to official notice of issuance, under the symbol "SPJ".
Use of Proceeds:	The net proceeds to be received by the Republic from the sale of the Notes will be used for expenditures within the framework of the Republic's 1991 federal budget and to pay for the hedge of its obligation with respect to the Interest Payment on the Notes. See "Revenues and Expenditures—Federal Budget" in the Prospectus.

(continued)

EXHIBIT 6 (cont.)

S&P 500 Composite Stock Price Index:	The S&P 500 Index is published by S&P and is intended to provide an indication of the pattern of common stock price movement. The calculation of the value of the S&P 500 Index is based on the relative value of the aggregate market value of the common stocks of 500 companies at a particular time as compared to the aggregate average market value of the common stocks of 500 similar companies during the base period from the years 1941 through 1943. S&P may from time to time, in its sole discretion, add companies to, or delete companies from, the S&P 500 index to fulfil the above-stated intention of providing an indication of common stock price movement. "Standard & Poor'sXXX", "S&PXXX", and "Standard & Poor's 500" are service marks of Standard & Poor's Corporation and have been licensed for use by Goldman, Sachs & Co. and the Republic of Austria is an authorized sublicensee thereof. See "The Standard & Poor's 500 Composite Stock Price Index" in this Prospectus Supplement.
Special Considerations:	As more fully described below, the Notes are subject to certain special considerations. Investors should be aware that if the Final Value is equal to or less than the Initial Value, holders of the Notes will be entitled to receive $10 in respect of each $10 principal amount of Notes, and no interest, even though the value of the S&P 500 Index as of some interim period between the issue date and the maturity date of the Notes exceeded the Initial Value. The $10 minimum to be received by holders at maturity in respect of each $10 principal amount of a Note does not reflect any opportunity cost implied by inflation and other factors relating to the time value of money. Moreover, securities similar to the Notes have not previously been publicly offered in the United States ("U.S.") and, although the Notes have been approved for listing on The New York Stock Exchange, Inc., subject to official notice of issuance, there is no U.S. precedent as to how the Notes will trade in the secondary market or whether such market will be liquid. It is expected that the secondary market for the Notes will be affected by a number of factors independent of the creditworthiness of the Republic. See "Special Considerations" in this Prospectus Supplement. The Republic is a foreign sovereign government. Consequently, it may be difficult for investors to realize upon judgments of courts in the U.S. against the Republic. See "Special Considerations—Enforcement of Rights Against the Republic" in this Prospectus Supplement. Investors should also consider the tax consequences of investing in the Notes. See "Certain United States Federal Income Tax Considerations" in this Prospectus Supplement.
Form and Settlement:	The Notes will be evidenced by certificates in registered form. Following the issuance of the Notes, the Republic may, at its option, elect to make the Notes eligible for deposit and settlement through the facilities of The Depository Trust Company.
Fiscal Agent:	Citibank, N.A., New York, New York.
Calculation Agent:	Goldman, Sachs & Co., New York, New York.

EXHIBIT 7

SALOMON INC.
S&P Index–Linked Notes Due 1996

USE OF PROCEEDS AND HEDGING

Approximately 50% of the proceeds to be received by the Company from the sale of the Notes will be used for general corporate purposes. See "Use of Proceeds" in the Prospectus. The balance of such proceeds may be used from time to time by the Company or one or more of its subsidiaries in connection with hedging the Company's obligations under the Notes. Depending on market conditions (including the prevailing level of the S&P 500 Index from time to time), in connection with hedging with respect to the S&P 500 Index, the Company expects that it or one or more of its subsidiaries may use dynamic hedging techniques and may take positions in (i) futures contracts on such index or other stock indices on the Chicago Mercantile Exchange, (ii) options contracts on such index on the Chicago Board Options Exchange or in the over-the-counter market, (iii) listed or over-the-counter options contracts on other stock indices and on all or a portion of the stocks underlying the S&P 500 Index (the "Underlying Stocks"). The Company also expects that it or one or more of its subsidiaries may take positions in Treasury Bills, Treasury Notes, futures on Treasury Bonds and Eurodollar futures. In addition, the Company or one or more of its subsidiaries may from time to time purchase or otherwise acquire a position in Notes and may, at their option, hold or resell such Notes, or exercise the Repurchase Option with respect to such Notes. The Company or one or more of its subsidiaries may also take positions in other types of appropriate financial instruments that may become available in the future. Depending, among other things, on future market conditions and the actual amount of Notes outstanding from time to time, the aggregate amount and the composition of such positions are likely to vary over time. Profits or losses from any such position cannot be ascertained until such position is closed out and any offsetting position or positions are taken into account.

DESCRIPTION OF THE NOTES

General

The Notes are a series of Debt Securities issued under the Senior Debt Indenture described in the accompanying Prospectus. Reference is hereby made to the Prospectus for a summary of additional provisions, including the definitions of certain terms used herein, of the Notes and of the Senior Debt Indenture under which the Notes will be issued. Wherever defined terms of the Senior Debt Indenture are referred to, such defined terms are incorporated by reference herein as part of the statement made, and registered form and in denominations of $10 and integral multiples thereof. The Notes are not subject to consequences to Holders (as defined in the Senior Debt Indenture) of the Notes; see "Certain United States Federal Income Tax Considerations" herein.

The Notes will be limited to $ aggregate principal amount. The Company at a later time may, however, issue additional Debt Securities or other securities with similar terms, and such issuances may affect the trading value of the Notes. See "Special Considerations—Certain Factors Affecting Value and Trading Price of Notes" herein.

Except to the extent that the Repurchase Price exceeds $10 upon exercise of the Repurchase Option or at Stated Maturity, interest will not be paid on the Notes. The Repurchase Price will not exceed $10 unless, prior to Stated Maturity, there is an increase in the level of the S&P 500 Index to a level greater than —.

(continued)

EXHIBIT 7 (cont.)

The Notes will mature of February, 1996, the Stated Maturity (as defined in the Senior Debt Indenture) of the Notes. At Stated Maturity, the Holder of a Note will be entitled to receive, with respect to each $10 principal amount thereof, the greater of (A) $10 or (B) the Repurchase Price.

EXHIBIT 8

EXPORT DEVELOPMENT CORPORATION
Summary of the Offering

The following is a summary of more detailed information appearing elsewhere in this Offering Circular.

Issuer: Export Development Corporation (an agent of Her Majesty in right of Canada).

Issue: S&P 500® Protected Index Notes due 1997, linked to the level of the S&P 500 Index.

Currency: U.S. dollars.

Issue Amount: U.S. $75,000,000 (7,500,000 Notes) (subject to increase pursuant to the Agents' over-allotment option).

Issue Price: U.S. $10.00 per Note.

Minimum
Subscription: 100 Notes.

Stated Maturity: January 3, 1997.

Repurchase
Option: A Holder may require EDC to repurchase Notes held by such Holder at the Repurchase Price at any time prior to 10:00 A.M. on the sixteenth Business Day immediately preceding Stated Maturity. If the Holder exercises the Repurchase Option prior to January 3, 1992, the Notes will be repurchased for 95% of the Repurchase Price.

Repurchase at
Stated Maturity: At Stated Maturity, the Holder will receive in respect of each Note held by such Holder the greater of (A) U.S. $10 or (B) the Repurchase Price.

Repurchase Price: U.S. $10 × (Spot S&P Index ÷ Strike S&P Index)

where:

"Spot S&P Index" for a Valuation Date is the closing level of the S&P 500 Index on such date.

"Strike S&P Index" will be set at 105% of the closing level of the S&P 500 Index on the Business Day immediately preceding the Date of Closing (the "Initial S&P Index").

In all calculations, the Spot S&P Index, the Strike S&P Index and the Initial S&P Index will be rounded to four decimal places. The Repurchase Price will be rounded down to the nearest cent.

Breakeven Point: In order for a Holder to avoid a loss on the principal amount of the Notes upon the exercise of the Repurchase Option, the Spot S&P Index must be greater than or equal to 105% of the Initial S&P Index. If the Repurchase Option is exercised prior to January

(continued)

EXHIBIT 8 (cont.)

	3, 1992, the Spot S&P Index must be greater than or equal to 110.53% of the Initial S&P Index. (See "Description of the Notes—Breakeven Point".)
Minimum Repurchase Option Exercise:	100 Notes or integral multiples thereof.
Delivery:	Certificates will not be issued for the Notes. (See "Book Based System".)
Note Agent:	The Royal Trust Company.
Risk Factors:	The trading price of the Notes and the Repurchase Price may vary considerably prior to Stated Maturity owing to, among other things, fluctuations in the prices of the Underlying Stocks, certain characteristics of the S&P 500 Index and factors influencing stock prices generally on the New York Stock Exchange, American Stock Exchange and NASDAQ National Market System, the stock markets on which the Underlying Stocks are traded. Unless the Notes are held until the Stated Maturity, there can be no assurance that Holders will receive the principal amount of the Notes. If the Notes are held to Stated Maturity, Holders will receive the principal but there can be no assurance that they will receive any amount in addition to the return of principal. It is not possible to predict how the Notes will trade the secondary market or whether such market will be liquid or illiquid. (See "Risk Factors".)
Eligibility:	The Notes will qualify for investment under certain statutes, including the Income Tax Act (Canada), by trusts governed by registered retirement savings plans ("RRSPs"), registered retirement income funds ("RRIFs"), and deferred profit sharing plans and Notes will not constitute foreign property for the purposes of such Act. (See "Eligibility for Investment".)
Book Based System:	Registration of interests in and transfers of the Notes will be made only through the book based system of CDS (as hereinafter defined), except as subject to any conditions imposed by any stock exchange on which the Notes may be listed. The Notes must be purchased, transferred and repurchased either directly or indirectly through a participant in the CDS book based system. No Holder will be entitled to any certificate or other instrument from EDC or CDS evidencing the ownership thereof, and no Holder will be shown on the records maintained by CDS except through an agent who is a participant of CDS. (See "Description of the Notes—Book Based System".)
Hypothetical Calculations of Repurchase Price:	The following hypothetical calculations illustrate the Repurchase Price of a Note and the amount payable by EDC at Stated Maturity for various levels of the S&P 500 Index (Spot S&P Index), assuming an Initial S&P Index of 370. (See "Description of the Notes—Repurchase Option".) **EDC and the Agents make no representations as to future levels of the S&P 500 Index. These calculations are for illustrative purposes only.**

(continued)

EXHIBIT 8 (cont.)

INITIAL S&P INDEX	STRIKE S&P INDEX	SPOT S&P INDEX	S&P 500 GROWTH RATE AT STATED MATURITY[a]	REPURCHASE PRICE[b]	PAYABLE BY EDC AT STATED MATURITY
370.00	388.50	200.00	(10.58%)	US$5.14	US$10.00
370.00	388.50	300.00	(3.74%)	US$7.72	US$10.00
370.00	388.50	400.00	1.43%	US$10.29	US$10.29
370.00	388.50	500.00	5.63%	US$12.87	US$12.87
370.00	388.50	600.00	9.19%	US$15.44	US$15.44
370.00	388.50	700.00	12.29%	US$18.01	US$18.01
370.00	388.50	800.00	15.05%	US$20.59	US$20.59

[a]The annual compound growth rate of the S&P 500 for the indicated Spot S&P Index levels.

[b]If the Repurchase Option is exercised prior to January 3, 1992, Holders will receive 95% of the Repurchase Price.

33

AMERICAN BARRICK RESOURCES CORPORATION[1]

Robert Wickham, treasurer of American Barrick Resources Corp., was working late to sort out his hedging plan for the next few days. It was November 17, 1989, and it was again necessary for him to roll the expired portion of the hedges into the future. The recent gold price increase from a low of $360 within the year to a current price of over $394 (see Exhibit 1) was making the roll-over decision that much more difficult than if prices had remained stable. Robert had to decide the quantity of hedges to initiate, the timing of his moves, and the medium through which he could most efficiently make the adjustment.

There were a number of potential alternatives for creating hedges for Barrick. Forward contracts, over-the-counter (OTC) options, and futures were the means through which Barrick could go directly to the market. Gold loans had been used by the company in the past to lock in an effective gold price over a set period. There were several other methods of raising capital based on gold price available to Barrick if they so chose. If this was the right time to hedge, Robert had the

This case was prepared by Peter Grosskopf and Linda Atkinson under the supervision of Professor Robert W. White for the sole purpose of providing material for class discussion at the Western Business School. Certain names and other identifying information may have been disguised to protect confidentiality. It is not intended to illustrate either effective or ineffective handling of a managerial situation. Any reproduction, in any form, of the material in this case is prohibited except with the written consent of the School.
Copyright 1990 © The University of Western Ontario.

[1]All figures except for stock prices are in US$.

choice of rolling over his expiring hedges, adding a percentage to the hedged total, or extending the entire program into a longer time frame. He could also choose any combination of these strategies.

BACKGROUND ON THE COMPANY

American Barrick was founded in 1983 through the merger of Consolidated Summit Mines and Petro Inc. Resources, both of Ontario. The company achieved its early growth through a series of mergers and acquisitions, all of which were financed with a minimum of common equity. Capital to fund these acquisitions was infused through a series of innovative financings, including a 2% coupon gold-indexed note issue, a gold purchase warrant issue and the sale of a gold trust fund which received a percentage of the production from the Renabie mine. In total, these financings raised over $140 million for the company prior to 1985.

Armed with this influx of cash, Barrick purchased a portion of equity in a major international mining concern, Consolidated Goldfields plc, as well as acquiring several smaller companies which had good property but were in poor financial condition. In late 1986, a portion of the stake in Consolidated Goldfields, as well as the bulk of the company's non-gold assets, were sold at a substantial profit.

Once again, Barrick had cash for an acquisition and it wasted no time in choosing the Western States Joint Venture, in combination with PanCana Minerals. This transaction was completed in early 1987 and gave Barrick 100% control of the Goldstrike mine in Nevada, a property that Barrick thought had significant potential. The cost of the ownership amounted to $68 million, which was roughly split between cash and a block of Barrick shares.

As it turned out, Goldstrike proved to be the largest gold deposit in North America, with estimated reserves of over 15 million ounces. Thus, in the five years since Barrick entered the gold mining industry, it had emerged as a leading North American gold producer. The acquisitions had been capitalized on through increased production from 32,000 ounces per year to over 450,000 ounces produced in 1989. Barrick now had direct interests in seven producing gold mines in the U.S. and Canada. Its principal mines were the Goldstrike mine in Nevada, the Mercur mine in Utah and the Holt–McDermott mine in Ontario. In line with properties, reserves had grown from 163,000 ounces at the time of the first acquisition to over 20 million ounces in 1989.

The company policy was comprised of three clearly defined strategic objectives: (1) to become the number 1 North American gold producer; (2) to achieve growth both through development and acquisition; and (3) to be soundly financed and fully protected against exposure to falling gold prices. To add to the final objective, the executive committee had made it clear that Barrick was not in the business of predicting gold prices. Robert knew he would have to balance that wish carefully against the market's perception that the stock of all gold companies contained a significant element of exposure to the underlying price of the bullion.

CURRENT ACTIVITIES

The primary activities of the company included the production of gold and the exploration for additional reserves in various promising areas. Besides Goldstrike, Barrick operated six other producing properties in North America. These mines were expected to produce 550,000 ounces during 1990, and increasing amounts to 1.15 million ounces by 1994. The costs of production averaged $240 per ounce in 1989 and were expected to fall to $225 in 1990. Further operating results are listed in Exhibits 2 through 5.

Barrick's tenfold increase in production had been accompanied by some impressive financial statistics. Pre-tax profits had increased from a deficit of $4 million in 1984 to an estimated profit of $50 million in 1989. Cash flow from operations, one of the more important benchmarks of gold mining companies, was at a strong $40 million for the year. Earnings per share, $0.51 in 1988, were expected to grow to $0.68 in 1989. American Barrick stock, which was trading at $5/share well into 1986 and, as opposed to $16 at the beginning of the current year, had increased to the $28 range at the time the case was written.

Most of the main operating issues the company was facing dealt with the Goldstrike mine. Barrick was facing higher operating costs due to stricter environmental policies, but was also making cost improvements through better technology. At present, there was also a pending lawsuit with Gold Standard Inc. (GSI) over the ownership of a 25% interest in the Mercur mine. The lawsuit was thought to be depressing stock price, but Barrick management and most analysts were of the opinion that GSI's claim would cost Barrick $10 million in royalties in the very worst scenario.

THE GOLD MARKET

Throughout time, gold had come to symbolize wealth and real purchasing power, especially in times of duress, depression, or inflation. By 1989 however, gold prices appeared to be strangely unrelated to world events, as the focus of the investment community switched from caution to achieving real rates of return from paper and other producing investments. During the upheaval of the equity markets in October 1987, gold had only rallied to $28 per ounce. Still, the huge rally of the late 70s was at the back of people's minds and many investors still viewed gold companies, especially juniors, as a leveraged play on a possible gold price increase.

The market itself derived demand from three main areas: investment demand from banks, governments and individuals; industrial demand; and demand from the jewellery industry. Investment demand usually depended on international monetary trends and industrial demand was influenced by the general state of the economy. Jewellery demand, due to its consumer demand base, was fairly insensitive to all factors except for the actual price of the gold. Of these factors, industrial and investment demand were the driving forces behind price due to their size and because of the dramatic decline in the market for gold coins since the mid-80s.

The supply side of the market was also an international affair. Two thirds of the world's gold was still supplied by South Africa. Other major sources of supply were spread out and included Canada, the U.S., the U.S.S.R., and Australia. Since the costs of production in the outdated South African mines approached $340/oz, much output was simply taken off the market at those levels. The average cost of production in a modern North American mine was about $230/oz.

Another important factor in the market was its actual pricing structure. Gold prices in the future were always higher than current prices because of carrying costs and the perpetual possibility of a major international change which might move funds into gold (OPEC, inflation, war, disaster, etc.). The difference in these prices (usually known as the basis in financial markets) was referred to as the contango in the gold market. Gold's contango averaged around 5–6%, and levelled off after about one year (see Exhibit 6).

THE HEDGING STRATEGY

Over the past few years, American Barrick had developed the reputation of being one of the most sophisticated and the most aggressive gold hedgers in the world. This was evident in its 1989 realized gold price, which was approximately 96% hedged at prices far above the market at the time this case was written. Management prided itself on these statistics, and was anxious to remain as an industry leader in this regard. The executive committee had recently decided that hedging was of sufficient priority to extend the process to a five year horizon (providing that it was possible); this was one of the objectives that Robert had to address in any current update of the plan.

When consulting equity analysts on the company, the hedging program seemed to be of considerable importance in comparing Barrick to other major North American gold producers. A survey of companies who had not adopted a system of minimizing the downside received an average of only $384 for their 1989 production. Of course, Robert knew that hedging involved a decision regarding upside potential, and although Barrick avoided forecasting price, he was concerned that with the recent gold price run-up, he might in fact be making the wrong move by hedging now. These thoughts outlined the philosophical discussion of whether a gold company was a miner or a marketer of their product. The conceivable impact on stock price and P/E multiples was the end result of any decision in this regard.

The current hedging program at Barrick involved four segments: forward selling, a min/max strategy, gold loan financing; and other innovative financing techniques. These are broken down in Exhibits 7 and 8. Estimated future production is presented in Exhibit 8. Proven and probable reserve figures are presented in Exhibit 9.

FORWARD SELLING

Forward selling was the most basic form of hedging available to the company. The forward market for gold was fairly liquid, with almost every major commercial bank being able to arrange a contract. Because of their simplicity and acceptance, gold forwards have become competitively bid and their rates incorporated the usual variables—the banks lending rate to the client and the pricing structure in the gold market.

A major advantage of gold forwards was that, just as with the currency and interest rate forward markets, they can be custom designed and adapted to many different situations. For American Barrick, Robert was able to pick specific dates for delivery, going out as far as two full years at which he could hedge at the market price. Several new adaptations in the gold forwards market had recently begun to be marketed by the banks and included forwards which allowed upside price potential, floating rate forwards and pre-deliverable forwards.

Currently, Robert had about 15% of Barrick's production hedged with forwards. There were some problems with hedging further than 1.5 years in that the market does become fairly illiquid and the spread between contango and the realized price tended to widen slightly.

THE MIN/MAX OPTION STRATEGY

When Robert had first taken a look at various option hedging strategies, he had chosen a partial min/max as the optimal strategy to satisfy the firm's objectives. The strategy simply involved buying put options to hedge downside gold price movement, while selling call options to partially finance the puts. The cost of the hedge was then significantly reduced; in fact, it was Robert's guideline to enter the contracts with no net cost to the company. In order to do this he had previously settled for a put to call ratio of 2 to 1 (see Exhibits 7 and 8). That way, he could say that while Barrick's downside was fully hedged on these strategies, they could participate fully in any price increase to the strike prices of the calls, and 50% on any price increase over that. The combination was so successful that roughly 60% of Barrick's nearby production was hedged in this manner.

When Robert decided to hedge more production with the options, his first move was always to choose the time period involved. Next, he would pick a quantity of gold to hedge, along with the optimal strike prices to achieve his objectives. Finally, the choice of the percentage of calls to puts would fall into place.

In order to execute the trades, Robert usually solicited quotes from 3 or 4 investment and merchant banks on his chosen strategy. In some cases the best price won the order, but frequently Robert would spread the business over two or more dealers because liquidity was not ideal in the OTC gold option market. A big problem for Barrick was currently trying to extend the options from a three to a five year horizon. Banks were hesitant to write options much further than two years. The reason for this was that they needed to offset their own risk either through the futures market or through their own portfolio of contracts, both of which became rather illiquid after a two year period. Dealers had very specific option pricing models, most of which were adaptations of Black's or Black–Scholes' option pricing models. Gold price and volatility data are presented in Exhibit 10. Quotations on option prices would undoubtedly include a fair price for the option plus some profit margin for the dealer, based on the credit standing of the client.

GOLD LOANS

Bullion lending, while it had existed in some forms for more than a decade, had seen a phenomenal increase in activity over the past three years. While the activity had recently slowed, gold loans were still regarded as the most lucrative means of project financing for the gold mining industry. The primary reason for this was that gold loans served a dual purpose function—they locked in a future price for the gold while providing an extremely low explicit interest rate for the financing.

Essentially, a gold loan was a loan of gold advanced in actual ounces at a certain time, and paid back in actual ounces over a certain repayment schedule (see Exhibit 11.) The borrower then sold the gold at the market, at the expense of the market price at the time of repayment. For this reason, the gold reserves of the lender and the source of the loan were a concern for the company taking out a gold loan, so that in times of trouble the gold would not be required on short notice. Likewise, the bank extending the loan would always insure that the actual production was imminent. They also frequently included covenants which limited the purchase of call options to a certain percentage of production. The interest charged was the difference between the bank's usual lending rate to the institution, minus the contango present in the market. Thus, gold loans have typically charged an actual annual interest rate of 1.5–4% per annum (see Exhibits 6 and 11).

American Barrick had first utilized a gold loan agreement in 1986, when a facility was set up by the Toronto-Dominion bank to aid in the construction of the Mercur mine. Following this, in October 1987, they contracted with the Union Bank of Switzerland to borrow 267,000 ounces for a total funding of $121 million. This was used for the development of the Goldstrike facility. Barrick's largest loan was executed in March 1989, with a total of over 1 million ounces and a total value of close to $400 million, the largest gold loan completed to that date. The proceeds of this loan were used for further development of Goldstrike, and to pay down the previous loan (see Exhibits 8, 12, and 13 for details on current loans).

While gold loans were typically used for project financing, Newmont Mining in the U.S. had recently used the proceeds from a large bullion loan for the funding of a takeover defense strategy. Robert wanted to avoid further gold loans until a new acquisition or project necessitated one, thereby reserving the strategy for mine development. However, he also realized that with the natural long term hedge it provided, the gold price increase might be creating an opportunity to initiate another loan.

One other point concerning gold loans had just been brought to Robert's attention. It was common practice for mining concerns to carry bullion loans on their balance sheets as items of deferred revenue. This allowed them to be recognized as revenue as they were delivered against and also kept them out of the corporate debt to equity ratio. Interest payments were expensed as a cost of doing daily business. The problem was that the Securities and Exchange Commission in the U.S. was about to conduct a series of hearings on whether or not to classify bullion loans as long term debt. Proponents of this approach argued that the full cost of the loans were not currently being fully disclosed to shareholders for two reasons. First, the deferred revenue approach made no allowance for changes in the current price of gold. If the price was actually higher, an opportunity cost should be incurred. Secondly, a 1.5–4% interest charge did not reflect the true cost of capital. This was argued because the gold price contango should be the future price, and the lender was taking that into account when making the loan. Using a 1.5–4% interest charge in the cost of capital would then be unfair to shareholders, as it would be an inefficient allocation of resources. Robert thought the debate at the SEC would be an intense one, since gold loans as long term debt would involve marking them to market. As a last notion to this, Robert was thinking that if the loans were in fact legislated into debt, any price increases or decreases from that point on would have an impact on the bottom line of the corresponding year.

The pricing structure of gold loans was continuing to change since Barrick had entered its first bullion loan. Specifically, explicit interest rates on the loan had increased from as low as 1.0% to an average 1989 rate of 2.5%. This was due to fluctuations in LIBOR (London Interbank Offered Rate) and physical gold lease charges over the past few years. One method with which to hedge future gold borrowing costs was the newly offered future gold rate agreements (FGRAs), which had been pioneered in mid-1989. Using FRGAs, it was possible for a gold borrower to fix a future gold price in exactly the same manner as an FRA. The pricing of FGRAs was based on the concept illustrated in Exhibit 6.

OTHER FINANCING TECHNIQUES

Prior to having the gold reserves with which to take out gold loans or commit to forward selling, Barrick had utilized a few innovative financing techniques which enabled it to raise funds for additional growth. One of these was the issue of 4 million gold purchase warrants, which entitled the holders to an aggregate of 80,000 ounces at $518/ounce until the end of 1990. This issue raised $4.2 million in 1986. Another example was an issue of $50 million worth of gold indexed notes with a 2% guaranteed coupon. The holders receive the coupon plus any difference in the price of the gold from the time the notes were issued.

Other examples of these financing techniques were the two separate partnerships that had been set up to offer investors participation in various ways to either production, gold price increases, or a combination of the two. Finally, an option that Barrick had at any time was to make a public equity offering, given that it had been over a year since the last one. This would allow Barrick to capitalize on the current bullish environment on both the company and the market. These alternatives were all available to Robert at the present time, although board approval would be necessary for any such move.

THE DECISION

Within the next two days, Robert would have to present his recommendation on the hedging strategy to Barrick's executive committee. The run-up in gold prices was creating a dynamic setting for this meeting, as the investment papers were echoing possibilities that gold had finally broken out of its long bear market. The markets themselves had seen an increase of activity and liquidity as speculators entered the market again, and some smaller companies were even thinking of buying back their gold loans to take advantage of any long term moves. As well, Robert wanted to be cautious that he did not lock in the price on too much of Barrick's future production in case there was a fundamental change in the market over that period of time. It was essential that Barrick retain its identity as a gold producer in order to support its higher P/E ratio.

As to specific features of a revised hedging plan, he was thinking of filling in any un-hedged 1991 production: (1) with forward contracts for near term; (2) by increasing the options positions in later years to a substantial degree; and/or (3) with an equity share offering. Because of the extent of the gold price move, he knew he would have to answer some questions about long term strategy as well. Perhaps now was the ideal time to adjust the program in this context.

EXHIBIT 1

Gold Cash Price History

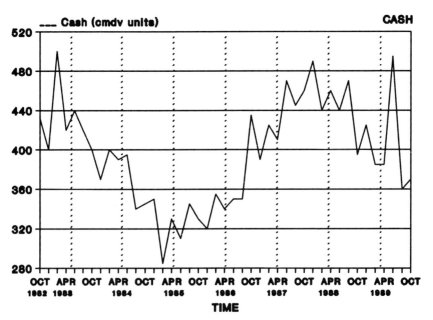

EXHIBIT 2

AMERICAN BARRICK RESOURCES CORPORATION
Consolidated Statements of Income
For Years Ended December 31, 1986, 1987, 1988
(in thousands of dollars, except per share data)

	1986	1987	1988
Revenue	$69,106	$92,127	$147,509
Expenses			
Operating Costs	39,482	48,090	79,545
Administration	4,036	5,547	6,756
Income From Operations	43,518	53,637	86,301
Depreciation, Depletion and Amortization	25,588	38,490	61,208
Exploration and Deferred	(11,868)	(17,383)	(25,681)
Stripping Costs Written-Off	(135)	(3,010)	(501)
Other Income	4,547	18,945	15,369
Interest Expense	(3,844)	(9,985)	(10,671)
Income Before Taxes and Extraordinary Item	14,288	27,057	39,724
Resource Taxes	(546)	(715)	(371)
Deferred Income Taxes	(2,154)	(5,772)	(8,858)
Net Income Before Extraordinary Item	11,588	20,570	30,495
Loss on Non-Mining Properties	–	(1,751)	–
Net Income for the Year	$11,588	$18,819	$ 30,495
Net Income Per Share			
Before Extraordinary Item	$0.28	$0.39	$0.52
For the Year	$0.28	$0.36	$0.52
Fully Diluted Net Income Per Share			
Before Extraordinary Item	$0.28	$0.38	$0.51
For the Year	$0.28	$0.35	$0.51

EXHIBIT 3

AMERICAN BARRICK RESOURCES CORPORATION
Consolidated Statements of Retained Earnings
For Years Ended December 31, 1986, 1987, 1988
(in thousands of dollars, except per share data)

	1986	1987	1988
Retained Earnings Beginning of Year	$(36,444)	$10,476	$24,144
Elimination of Deficit by Reduction in Stated Capital	36,444	–	–
Net Income for the Year	11,588	18,819	30,495
Dividends	–	(2,220)	(4,840)
Costs Incurred in Raising Capital	(1,112)	(2,931)	–
Retained Earnings End of Year	$10,476	$24,144	$49,799

EXHIBIT 4

AMERICAN BARRICK RESOURCES CORPORATION
Consolidated Balance Sheets
As at December 31, 1987 and 1988
(in thousands of dollars)

	1987	1988
Assets		
Current Assets		
Cash and short term deposits	$167,163	$ 51,411
Note Receivable	46,161	—
Accounts Receivable	10,153	16,786
Inventories and Prepaid Expenses	15,946	18,760
Total Current Assets	$239,423	$ 86,957
Investments, at cost	120,005	143,144
Property, plant and equipment	289,304	455,776
Other Assets	27,050	14,958
Total Assets	$675,782	$700,835
Liabilities		
Current Liabilities		
Accounts payable and Accrued Liabilities	$ 24,811	$ 26,209
Current Portion of long term liabilities and deferred revenue	27,807	16,860
Total Current Liabilities	52,618	43,069
Long Term Liabilities	137,010	91,834
Deferred Revenue	24,144	164,300
Deferred Income Taxes	5,612	11,147
Total Liabilities	$337,343	$310,350
Shareholders' Equity		
Capital Stock	315,850	325,562
Retained Earnings	24,144	49,799
Foreign Currency Translation Adjustment	(1,555)	15,124
Total Shareholders' Equity	338,439	390,485
Total Liabilities and Shareholders' Equity	$675,782	$700,835

EXHIBIT 5

AMERICAN BARRICK RESOURCES CORPORATION
Financial Data

FINANCIAL RESULTS (MILLIONS OF U.S. DOLLARS)	1986	1987	1988
Revenue	$ 69.1	$ 92.1	$147.5
Income from Operations	25.6	38.5	61.2
Net Income	11.6	18.8	30.5
Operating Cash Flow	24.5	37.3	61.7

FINANCIAL POSITION (MILLIONS OF U.S. DOLLARS)	1986	1987	1988
Working Capital	$ 22.7	$186.8	$ 43.9
Shareholders' Equity	$108.8	$338.4	$390.5

PER SHARE DATA (FULLY DILUTED) (U.S. DOLLARS)	1986	1987	1988
Net Income			
Before extraordinary item	$0.28	$0.38	$0.51
For the year	$0.28	$0.35	$0.51
Dividends	$0.00	$0.04	0.08
Common Shares (millions)			
Outstanding at Year End	44.3	57.7	58.7
Weighted Average			
Basic	41.4	52.4	58.4
Fully Diluted	44.4	55.2	60.9

EXHIBIT 6

Components of the Contango Rate

LIBOR (London Interbank Offered Rate)	8.00%
− Borrowing Costs of Gold to Lender	3.00%
= MARKET CONTANGO	5.00%
− Margin to the Client	0.75%
= CONTANGO RATE	4.25%

EXHIBIT 7

AMERICAN BARRICK RESOURCES CORPORATION
Summary of Consolidated Hedge Position
As at November 7, 1989

SPOT GOLD $385	OUNCES	PERCENTAGE	AVERAGE PRICE
Gold Loans	4,450	4.3%	$401
Gold Co. of America	1,489	1.4	680
Renabie Gold Trust	128	0	725
	6,067	5.8%	476
Forward Sales	36,275	35%	453
	42,342	41%	456
Put Options			
Barrick	57,000	55%	442
Renabie Mine	1,890	2%	450
Pinson Mine	0	0%	450
	58,890	51%	
Total ounces hedged at minimum	101,232	98%	$448
Under (Over) hedge	2,093	−2%	—
Remaining Production	103,325	100%	

EXHIBIT 8

AMERICAN BARRICK RESOURCES CORPORATION
Consolidated Gold Price Hedge Position
As at November 1, 1989

	1990		1991		1992		1993	
	OUNCES	AVERAGE US$ PRICE	OUNCES	AVERAGE US$ PRICE	OUNCES	AVERAGE US$ PRICE	OUNCES	AVERAGE US$ PRICE
Commitments								
Gold Loans[a]	36,800	$458	32,100	$462	150,000	$422	169,000	$422
Forward Sales	84,000	413	12,600	507	—	—	—	—
Total Commitments	120,800	427	44,700	475	150,000	422	169,000	422
Put Options	409,500	419	431,000	423	510,000	408	120,000	400
Total Hedge	530,300	$421	475,700	$427	660,000	$411	289,000	$413
Estimated Production	550,000		600,000		1,000,000		1,000,000	
Outstanding Call Position								
Call Options Sold to Finance Puts	217,800	$507	250,000	$480	282,600	$415	36,000	$400
Gold Purchase Warrants	80,000	518	—	—	—	—	—	—
5¼% Gold Indexed Note	—	—	94,338	590	—	—	—	—
	297,800	$510	344,438	$510	282,600	$415	36,000	$400

[a]Beyond 1993 the Company will have delivery obligations under its gold loans of approximately 559,000 ounces at an average price of US$400 per ounce.

EXHIBIT 9

AMERICAN BARRICK RESOURCES CORPORATION
Summary Reserve and Operating Data

MINE CONTAINED	TONS	OUNCE PER TON	GRADE OUNCES
Goldstrike			
Proven and Probable:	142,838,000	0.106	15,181,000
Possible:	13,209,000	0.070	928,900
Mercur			
Proven and Probable:	23,079,000	0.056	1,297,100
Possible:	895,000	0.053	47,700
Holt-McDermott			
Proven and Probable:	1,586,000	0.157	249,000
Possible:	3,092,000	0.129	398,900
Camflo			
Proven and Probable:	746,000	0.103	76,800
Possible:	120,000	0.040	4,800
Pinson (26.25% Ownership)			
Proven and Probable:	1,905,000	0.068	129,000
Renabie (45% Ownership)			
Proven and Probable:	457,000	0.215	98,200
Possible:	67,000	0.208	13,900
Valdez Creek (23.125% Ownership)			
Proven and Probable:	444,000	0.116	51,300
Possible:	666,000	0.093	61,800
Proven and Probable			17,082,900
Possible			1,456,000
Total			18,538,900

EXHIBIT 10

Gold Prices
(US$ × 10 i.e., 4072 = $407.20)

DATE	OPEN	HIGH	LOW	LAST	DATE	OPEN	HIGH	LOW	LAST
10/28/88	4048	4124	4048	4124	5/12/89	3779	3810	3769	3779
11/04/88	4126	4220	4110	4215	5/19/89	3749	3756	3663	3666
11/11/88	4212	4235	4190	4216	5/26/89	3607	3670	3632	3660
11/18/88	4201	4257	4174	4174	6/02/89	3655	3692	3621	3686
11/25/88	4169	4200	4158	4200	6/09/89	3668	3810	3565	3581
12/02/88	4245	4335	4207	4317	6/16/89	3595	3695	3590	3651
12/09/88	4313	4320	4190	4229	6/23/89	3646	3785	3659	3785
12/16/88	4215	4220	4120	4140	6/30/89	3780	3830	3731	3746
12/23/88	4140	4190	4128	4185	7/07/89	3763	3838	3784	3836
12/30/88	4186	4195	4082	4100	7/14/89	3851	3846	3708	3708
1/06/89		4108	4063	4063	7/21/89	3711	3726	3683	3724
1/13/89	4025	4049	4023	4023	7/28/89	3724	3763	3658	3670
1/20/89	4016	4085	4022	4048	8/04/89	3665	3570	3670	3678
1/27/89	4087	4078	3961		8/11/89	3678	3678	3620	3652
2/03/89	3951	3962	3888	3931	8/18/89	3642	3708	3647	3681
2/10/89	3925	3980	3882	3888	8/25/89	3675	3686	3607	3607
2/17/89	3870	3876	3800	3808	9/01/89	3610	3680	3599	3624
2/24/89	3843	3925	3830	3911	9/08/89	3588	3616	3590	3594
3/03/89	3923	3905	3835	3866	9/15/89	3594	3639	3592	3639
3/10/89	3881	3951	3880	3943	9/22/89	3611	3662	3612	3662
3/17/89	3925	3962	3898	3936	9/29/89	3687	3698	3665	3672
3/24/89	3956	3965	3928	3928	10/06/89	3660	3676	3628	3637
3/31/89	3913	3920	3815	3815	10/13/89	3631	3643	3610	3633
4/07/89	3860	3877	3815	3834	10/20/89	3710	3710	3668	3673
4/14/89	3814	3930	3810	3860	10/27/89	3664	3783	3670	3783
4/21/89	3853	3862	3828	3849	11/03/89	3788	3810	3742	3785
4/28/89	3839	3882	3775	3779	11/10/89	3803	3888	3815	3868
5/05/89	3749	3790	3765	3777	11/17/89	3898	3946	3885	3946

EXHIBIT 11

Gold Loan

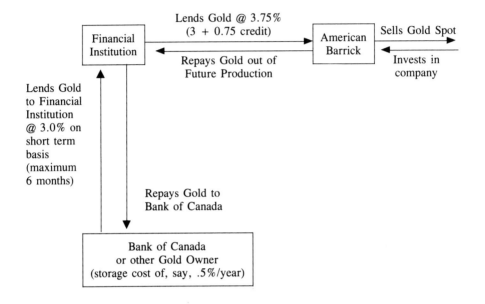

EXHIBIT 12

AMERICAN BARRICK RESOURCES CORPORATION
Deferred Revenue Summary
(in thousands of dollars)

	1987	1988
BULLION LOANS		
Goldstrike	$120,997	$101,635
Mercur	13,273	45,064
Renabie	–	4,592
GOLD COMPANY OF AMERICA	24,441	19,977
GOLD PURCHASE WARRANTS	4,248	4,629
RENABIE GOLD TRUST	3,544	2,893
Total	166,503	178,790
Current Portion of Deferred Revenue	24,400	14,490
Grand Total	$142,103	$164,300

EXHIBIT 13

AMERICAN BARRICK RESOURCES CORPORATION
Summary of Gold Commitments
As at June 30, 1989

1. Gold Purchase Warrants

Company:	American Barrick Resources Corporation
Issue date:	September 25, 1986
Expiry date:	September 25, 1990
Number of warrants:	4,000,000
Entitlement per warrant:	0.02 ounce of gold at US$9.20
Total ounces:	80,000 ounces
Call price per ounce:	US$460 per ounce

2. 5.25% Guaranteed Notes

Company:	Barrick Resources (USA) Inc.
Issue date:	October 31, 1986
Principal:	US$50,000,472
Maturity date:	October 31, 1991
Redemption amount on maturity:	US$55,750,526 (111.5% of issue price)
Number of notes:	29,343
Entitlement per note:	3.215 ounces (100 grams)
Total ounces:	94,338 ounces
Effective call price:	US$590 per ounce

3. 2% Guaranteed Gold Indexed Notes

Company:	Barrick Resources (USA) Inc.
Issue date:	February 26, 1987
Maturity date:	February 26, 1992
Principal:	US$50,000,916
Original issue	
Number of notes:	38,277
Entitlement per note:	3.215 ounces increasing to 3.380 ounces at maturity (100 grams increasing to 105.145 grams)
Total ounces:	122,899 ounces increasing to 129,207 ounces at maturity
Exchange price per ounce:	US$406.84 per ounce decreasing to US$386.98 at maturity
Outstanding at June 30/89	16,152 notes representing 54,600 ounces at maturity

4. Goldstrike Bullion Loan (Union Bank of Switzerland)

Company:	Barrick Goldstrike Mines Inc.
Ounces outstanding at June 30/89:	750,000

Payment Schedule:	Y/E oz.	Payment
1993	735,000	15,000
1994	525,000	210,000
1995	315,000	210,000
1996	105,000	210,000
1997	–	105,000

(continued)

EXHIBIT 13 (cont.)

Interest basis:	Base rate plus 1% (reduced to plus 7/8% when 50% collateralized)

Current interest periods:

Ounces	Interest Adjustment Date	Rate
187,500	July 27/89	2.565%
187,500	Sept. 27/89	2.900%
187,500	Jan. 31/90	3.008%
187,500	Mar. 29/90	3.108%
750,000		2.895%

5. Mercur Bullion Loan (Union Bank of Switzerland)

Company:	Barrick Resources (USA) Inc.
Number of ounces:	105,000 ounces outstanding at June 30/89
	20,000 ounces available
	125,000 total facility

Payment Schedule:	Y/E oz.	Payment
1989	101,562	3,438
1990	75,000	26,562
1991	54,688	20,312
1992	35,938	18,750
1993	17,188	18,750
1994	—	17,188

Interest Basis:	Base rate plus 0.75%
Current Interest rate:	3.700% to July 21/90

6. Gold Company of America

Company:	Barrick Minerals (Canada) Inc.	
Contract Amount:	US$40,126,543	
Contract 1 Commitment:	Total ounces committed	69,287
	Total delivered to June 30/89	40,035
	Outstanding at June 30/89	29,252

1989 Amortization price per ounce:	US$743

34

CITIBANK CANADA LTD.— MONETIZATION OF FUTURE OIL PRODUCTION

On the evening of December 8, 1990, David Hastings and Gordon Williams, of Citibank Canada's (Citibank) Underwriting and Distribution Group, sat back in their chairs to rework their strategy. The success of several months of hard work was now at stake as the pair faced the difficult challenge of privately placing US$125 million of Special Purpose Trust (SPT) paper before December 31. The financing was to fund SPT's forward purchase of a portion of the future oil production of Petrolia Oil Corporation (Petrolia). This structure would allow Petrolia to hedge future oil production at an attractive price and because the forward sale prepayment would be treated as deferred revenue allow Petrolia to lower its debt. Although Citibank prided itself on its creation of innovative financings and the execution of swift transactions, this deal seemed to be pushing their efforts to the limit. With only 3 weeks to complete the transaction and the holiday season at hand, David and Gordon needed to focus their selling effort.

CITIBANK CANADA LTD.

Citibank Canada was a wholly owned subsidiary of Citicorp, North America's largest banking institution. Citibank operated as a Schedule B bank under the Canadian

This case was prepared by Justin Pettit under the supervision of Professor Robert W. White for the sole purpose of providing material for class discussion at the Western Business School. Certain names and other identifying information may have been disguised to protect confidentiality. It is not intended to illustrate either effective or ineffective handling of a managerial situation. Any reproduction, in any form, of the material in this case is prohibited except with the written consent of the School. The assistance of Gordon Carriere, Doug Harvey and David Reese, Citibank Canada Ltd. is gratefully acknowledged.

Bank Act, with operations organized into two divisions: the Individual Bank and Global Finance. The Individual Bank offered retail branch banking services to individuals and small businesses. It also ran the Canadian credit card services operation. Global Finance provided investment banking services to government, corporate, and financial institutions in Canada.

Exhibit 1 illustrates the organizational structure of Global Finance. As members of the Underwriting and Distribution team, David and Gordon worked closely with both the Origination and Structuring groups. Cooperation among this triad was critical to tailoring a deal which satisfied three essential criteria:

> *First*, the issuer's needs must be met. This involved accurately assessing the client's financing needs, timing horizon, market view, and amount of risk they were willing to bear.
>
> *Second*, the issue must be placed in the market. This required targeting specific investor segments, and pricing and positioning the issue to suit their profile. Private placements excluded the traditional distribution channels of public deals and, therefore, required a strong road show and considerable networking with large institutional investors. They were generally not priced as thinly as public issues, but provided the issuer with the advantages of less stringent disclosure requirements and faster execution.
>
> *Third*, the final criterion for a successful issue was sufficient profitability for the intermediary. An explicit fee was usually charged on the principal of the issue. A plain vanilla transaction may cost 25 bps. A sophisticated, cost-efficient structure may cost between 50 and 200+ bps, depending on the demands placed upon the intermediary. Fees were tax-deductible for the issuer on a straight-line basis over the lesser of five years or the life of the issue. Some structures provided additional revenue in the form of spreads on swaps, options, foreign exchange and commodity transactions.

The reconciliation of these three criteria was often an iterative and onerous task. Citibank's Global Finance Group differentiated itself from other Canadian investment banks on what it felt were its three key success factors: innovation, execution, and global reach.

PETROLIA

Petrolia was a large, central Canadian, publicly traded company, engaged in the exploration and production of oil and natural gas in Canada. It was Ontario's largest exporter of crude oil, natural gas liquids, and natural gas and has recently become an international player in the development of frontier discoveries. High provincial royalty rates and higher extraction costs associated with Canadian oil reserves had made the movement toward international development a common trend in Canada. The company employed over 1,000 people in several countries at the time of this case, and had minor subsidiaries in both mining and strategic management consulting. Although its head office remained at the original southwestern Ontario location, most functions were administered from its Yorkville executive office.

Petrolia steadily increased its total liquids sales, despite a continuing decline in both Ontario and western Canadian conventional oil production, by aggressively increasing its international oil reserves with an expanded international drilling program. Petrolia was also involved in both the Hibernia project and arctic offshore drilling development. Increased capital and exploration expenditures were planned to continue. Portfolio asset rationalization had been initiated and was planned to continue, as part of a concerted effort to reduce high debt levels brought on by a series of strategic acquisitions executed on behalf of Petrolia's parent company.

The company was highly sensitive to fluctuations in the volatile oil and gas prices. A $1 change in the WTI (US$) would affect cash generation by $25 million, while a change of ¢10/1000 cu.ft. of natural gas would have an $8 million impact. Although considerable debt retirement had occurred in the previous year from a number of sources, Petrolia remained capitalized with approximately 45% debt. One-third of this was short term (Exhibit 2).

THE OIL MARKET

The year 1990 was proving to be a volatile one, with the effects of the Gulf conflict affecting the price and price volatility of oil (Exhibit 3) and related commodities. Oil price volatility, which typically ranged between 20% and 50%, was over 100% and approaching 200%. The use of hedging instruments was proliferating for crude and refined oil products, as users and producers scrambled to stabilize earnings. Although short and intermediate forward prices (spot to 2 years forward) were extremely volatile since the Gulf outbreak, 5-year forwards reflected only the natural contango of oil.

PETROLIA'S ALTERNATIVES

Petrolia had several alternatives available to raise the required capital and hedge some of its future oil production at currently attractive prices. A traditional forward oil sale to an oil consumer or a group of oil users would provide a natural hedge for both parties, and if prepaid, would provide Petrolia with the capital it required. However, oil producers and refiners had conflicting incentives. Oil refiners were also very revenue-sensitive to oil price fluctuations. Additionally, contract tenors with refiners were more often only 10 days. A forward contract was legally intensive and required risk-sharing documents.

Several U.S. banks were proposing a long term oil swap. The national oil companies of Japan, Singapore and Taiwan had participated in previous swaps and were thought to be ideal candidates, given their current exposure to the oil price shocks inflicted on the markets since the outbreak of the Gulf conflict. However, these countries had not yet expressed any interest in being counterpart to a long term swap and were often not hasty to react.

An oil-linked subordinated bond issue was another possibility. Morgan Stanley had privately placed such an issue for Chevron years earlier, although it was not well received by the market. Denominating the bond in terms of oil would link the entire issue to oil prices. Alternatively, the principal could be denoted in U.S. dollars, with a coupon linked to the price of WTI crude oil. This issue could also be stripped so that the oil-linked portion could be sold separately from the more traditional portion of the security, to improve marketability.

These three alternatives were all dependent on external markets for execution of the transaction. Citibank had reasoned that the use of a captive buyer with the same views as Petrolia would provide a simpler solution with a higher chance for execution before year's end. Additionally, such a structure could provide a longer tenor than otherwise available. A special purpose vehicle could buy forward oil production from Petrolia and prepay the purchase amount to Petrolia, similar to a gold loan. The trust would then sell the oil at spot prices to repay an amortizing loan from a group of lenders. The trust could hedge the future price of oil, leaving the trust subject only to Petrolia production risk and Citibank credit risk.

SPECIAL PURPOSE TRUST

A Special Purpose Trust is a vehicle established as a charitable trust under provincial charter for the sole purpose of facilitating the proposed Petrolia financing. The use of a trust is essential for Citibank to offer such a structure, because U.S. banking laws prohibit banks from taking delivery of oil. As the Canadian subsidiary of a U.S. bank, Citibank must adhere to U.S. banking regulations in addition to Canadian banking regulations. As a charitable trust, SPT provides the benefit of generally being subject to less regulatory scrutiny. As a tax-exempt entity, a charitable trust also provides a modest savings by avoiding the capital tax (20 bps) levied on debt, as the debt burden will be shifted from Petrolia to SPT. The benefactor of any residual in the trust upon the expiry of the transaction was an unnamed charity.

THE OIL MONETIZATION STRUCTURE

A generic swap structure is depicted in Exhibit 4. A prepaid forward oil sale between Petrolia and SPT would provide Petrolia with new capital and a hedge on a portion of its future oil production. A US$ amortizing loan between SPT and a group of lenders would provide SPT with the necessary capital to prepay its forward oil purchase. An oil swap between Citibank and SPT would lock in the prices SPT would receive from the sale of the future oil deliveries from Petrolia.

Petrolia proposed to sell, on a forward basis, *up to* 30,000 bbl/day for 1991 and 25,000 bbl/day for each of 1992 through 1995, for a net present value of aggregate proceeds of up to CA$350 million. SPT would enter into forward contracts to purchase *a portion* of these volumes. The prepayment of the purchase prices under these forward contracts would be funded by the proceeds of the debt issue. SPT expected to borrow approximately US$125 million through an amortizing 24-month facility with an average life of approximately 12 months. As the effective forward oil prices reached attractive levels, Petrolia would be able to enter into *additional* forward contracts with SPT, or other third parties, on a prepaid basis.

Future transactions between Petrolia and SPT would require the consent of the lenders. In terms of delivery risk, the volumes included in the transaction with SPT represent a relatively small portion of Petrolia's net Canadian production (20% for 1991, 12% for 1992). The implementation of the structure was to occur as follows:

1. Formation of SPT.
2. SPT would enter into forward sale contracts with Petrolia, obligating Petrolia to deliver set volumes of oil at set prices, as per a set delivery schedule.
3. SPT would hedge its oil price risk through Citibank.
4. Lenders would fund the trust for the net present value of the future hedged oil deliveries. The discount rate would reflect SPT's cost of capital. The borrowing would be used to fund the prepaid forward contract with Petrolia.
5. SPT would appoint a commodity marketing agent responsible for selling the oil purchased under the forward contracts. Sales would be made at the then prevailing spot price. (The commodity marketing agent could be Petrolia.)

Once established, the structure was to provide ongoing transactions and flows as follows:

1. In each settlement period, Petrolia would deliver oil to SPT.
2. The commodity marketing agent would sell SPT's oil at the then prevailing spot price and pay these funds to SPT.
3. SPT would deliver this payment to Citibank under its swap agreement.
4. Citibank would pay the fixed amount under the swap to SPT.
5. SPT would use the Citibank fixed payment to make principal and interest payments on its amortizing debt obligation.

There were additional benefits to this transaction. One such benefit was the fact that although accounting earnings and operating cash flows were accelerated, income taxes were deferred on production sold forward, no margin requirements were needed for the oil hedge contracts, and no change was required in reported reserves or production.

INSTITUTIONAL INVESTORS

Most of the major types of Canadian institutional investors and their asset/liability characteristics are listed in Exhibit 5. This group accounted for the majority of institutional financial assets in Canada. Other large institutional investors included independent investment counsellors, the Caisse de depot et Placement du Quebec, the Alberta Heritage Fund, and municipal accounts. Specific characteristics of chartered banks, pension plans, trust and mortgage loan companies, insurance companies, credit unions and the caisses populaires are outlined in Exhibit 6.

The rapid evolution of the Canadian financial system had greatly affected institutional investors. Increased institutionalization of savings had been evidenced through the increase in institutional trading volume on the TSE, from 45% in 1978 to over 60%. A greater share of trading was now being executed off-floor. Investors also had available a growing range of derivative products such as synthetic equities, index-linked products, embedded options, dual-currency investments, etc. These sophisticated structures may offer the advantage of being more closely tailored to the needs of issuers and/or investors.

Institutional investment policies varied widely according to the characteristics of their respective liabilities, risk profile, and tax position. Some of the major investing principles were as follows:

- The asset structure should match the structure of their liabilities.
- Institutional investors generally have a very low risk profile, particularly with respect to the risk of loss of capital.
- Institutions reduce risk with diversification of issuers, underwriters, industries, volatility, maturity, duration, and product type.
- Time horizons and liquidity are influenced greatly by liability horizons and liquidity.
- Legislative constraints often contain specific eligibility requirements.
- Tax considerations are strong determinants of investment guidelines.

The management structure of institutional investors also varied widely, but the following general functions were common to most:

- *Senior Investment/Credit Responsibility.* Increasingly a senior internal committee, but sometimes an individual, with the responsibility of setting overall investment policy, asset mix and investment style.
- *Portfolio Management.* Individuals or committees responsible for managing the daily operations within the guidelines established, and to some extent the asset mix. Responsible for selecting specific investments, issuers and underwriters.
- *Research and Analysis.* Responsible for primary credit and earnings research on companies for debt and equity investments, respectively.
- *Economics Department, Technical Analysis.* Responsible for long and short term forecasts, projecting stock and bond market movement for asset mix decisions.
- *Trading.* Responsible for executing trades as per portfolio management requests.

CITIBANK'S PRESENT CHALLENGE

As David and Gordon reflected on the task at hand, they examined the characteristics of the various institutional investors available. They also examined the proposed structure, particularly with respect to its risk profile, and how the investment would be viewed by their target market under various oil price forecasts. Explaining these characteristics would be critical to executing the transaction in the little time remaining to them. Were there too many reasons for investors to reject the deal? Was this structure the best alternative for Petrolia?

EXHIBIT 1

Global Finance Organizational Chart

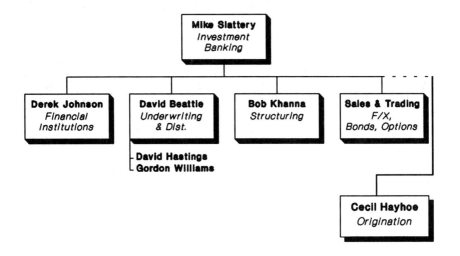

EXHIBIT 2

PETROLIA OIL CORPORATION
Financial Statements
(in $000,000s)

EARNINGS	1989	1988
Revenues		
Net oil & gas	589	511
Contract drilling	56	81
Other	40	57
	685	649
Expenses		
Operating: Production	227	209
Contract drilling	74	50
Exploration	104	119
General & administrative	47	47
Depreciation, depletion and amortization	184	174
Interest expense long term debt	24	34
Other interest expense	76	44
Allocation of interest to discontinued operations	(37)	(11)
Interest capitalized	(21)	(8)
Foreign exchange gains, net	(15)	(4)
Interest income	(31)	(37)
Income tax expense (recovery)	14	(14)
	647	599

(continued)

EXHIBIT 2 (cont.)

EARNINGS	1989	1988
Earnings from continuing operations	*39*	*50*
Discontinued operations	(5)	0
Extraordinary items	0	0
Total period earnings	*34*	*50*
Per ordinary share		
Earnings from continuing operations	($0.23)	$0.00
Total period earnings	($0.26)	$0.00

FINANCIAL POSITION	1989	1988
Current Assets		
Cash	7	76
Accounts receivable	89	107
Materials and supplies	37	44
Other	46	34
	179	261
Investments and other assets	151	338
Property, plant and equipment, net	2,162	2,178
	2,492	2,777
Current Liabilities		
Short term loans	162	418
Accounts payable	104	88
Current portion of LTD	15	17
Other	93	101
	374	624
Long term debt	515	534
Other long term liabilities	58	65
Deferred income tax	174	182
	1,121	1,405
Shareholders' equity – ordinary	1,101	1,101
Senior preferred shares	389	295
Deficit	(102)	(15)
Foreign currency translation adj.	(17)	(9)
	1,371	1,372
	2,492	2,777

EXHIBIT 3

High, Low and Closing Prices of December Crude Oil Futures

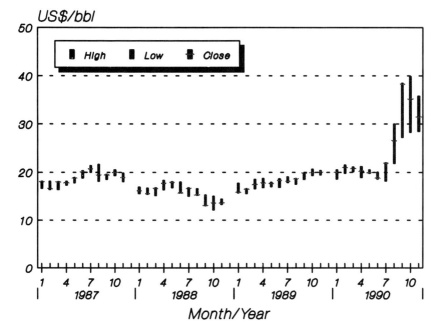

Source: 1991 CRB Yearbook.

EXHIBIT 4

Monetization of Future Oil Production

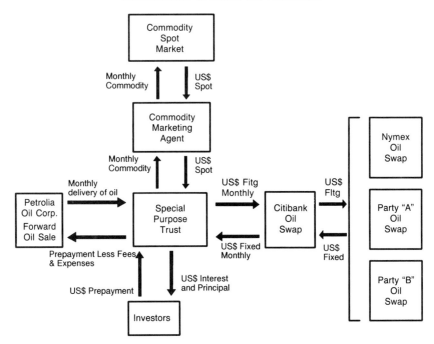

EXHIBIT 5

Assets of Major Canadian Financial Institutions

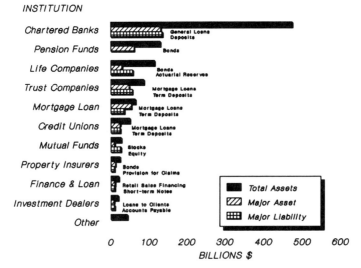

Source: Statistics Canada 61-006, 74-001; 1987.

EXHIBIT 6

An Overview of Major Canadian Institutional Investors[a]

The majority of institutional investment activity in Canada is for the accounts of chartered banks, trusteed and insured pension plans, trust and mortgage loan companies, insurance companies, credit unions and the caisses populaires, and provincial government funds. Municipal government accounts represent an emerging and increasingly sophisticated investor segment which has experienced strong recent growth. Independent investment counsellors are a fragmented group with the 40 largest counsellors managing assets of over $40 billion.

CHARTERED BANKS

Although banks allocate only 1–3% of their assets to provincial, municipal, and corporate securities, this represents an investment of over $12 billion. Investment departments frequently manage their own employee pension plans. With the top six banks now operating an investment bank, some investment management functions in money markets, foreign exchange, and other security trading operations have been melded into a single operation. Banks have recently expanded their investment management operations by soliciting the management of other pension funds, or certain portions of them. The offering of mutual funds and, to a lesser extent, closed-end investment funds (hedge funds, global funds, EAFE funds, Latin America funds, Eastern Europe funds) has also expanded the base of capital under management by the banks' investment departments. Investment committees typically meet each week and may schedule additional reviews if necessary.

In 1980, the Canadian Bank Act was revised to allow the operation of subsidiaries of foreign banks in Canada (Schedule B) under the same reserve requirements and government regulation as the domestic Schedule A banks. Size limitations were imposed limiting the assets of Schedule B banks to 16% of total domestic bank assets. A gearing ratio ceiling limited assets/equity to a maximum of 20 times. As no limitation exists for Schedule A banks, this will be phased out under the Free Trade Agreement. These regulations have resulted in Schedule B banks being selective about taking investments onto their own balance sheets. When underwriting transactions, revenue is generated primarily through explicit fees, and trading and distribution spreads.

Banks are taxed as any corporation, but are subject to more stringent taxation regarding eligibility for capital gains treatment. Additionally, bad debt expenses are not directly deductible, but used in a complex averaging formula which amortizes them over a five-year period. Provinces also levy a capital tax on banks of approximately 2%. Some income, such as small business bonds and Canadian stock dividends, is tax-exempt.

Trusteed Pension Plans

Trusteed pension plans have been an area of rapid asset growth in Canada, with 15% Cumulative Average Growth between 1980 and 1990. The asset mix of this capital has remained largely unchanged with approximately 10% in cash, 43% in equities, and 47% in fixed income. International assets have been capped by law at 10% until recently, but have only ranged between 6% and 8%, most of which is U.S. equity. Recent

(continued)

[a]Parts of this overview are based on information available in *Selling to Institutions,* a publication of the Canadian Securities Institute, the national educational organization of the Canadian securities industry.

EXHIBIT 6 (cont.)

legislation allows a higher ceiling of 16% in 1992, 18% in 1993 and 20% from 1994 on.

The traditional defined benefit plan has been losing favour to the defined contribution, or money purchase plan (MPP), because of administrative complexity and cost, as well as the fact that the MPP avoids potential litigation concerning underfunded plans and plan surpluses. In the case of an MPP, there is little incentive for plan sponsors (the employers) to direct investment counsellors to invest aggressively. Plan sponsors are liable for capital losses and are not compensated for spectacular earnings. In the case of the defined benefit plan, sponsors are responsible for maintaining adequate plan funding. Due to the high degree of conservatism among actuarial approaches, this is not a difficult task and again reinforces a highly conservative investment approach, where the safety of the principal investment is an overriding concern. High levels of inflation have been one of the biggest reasons behind pension fund investments in equity, particularly with in-house pension fund managers. Competition for funds has been a driving force among outside fund managers in their interest for investments promising growth opportunity. The conservative nature of pension funds has resulted in few fund managers outperforming the S&P 500.

Pension plans remain tax-exempt, provided they meet the eligibility requirements of the Federal and Provincial Pension Benefits Acts which include (in Ontario):

- Maximum foreign holdings (16% in 1992 of total pension assets, book value).
- Maximum 10% with any single issuer, except federal or provincial guaranteed issues.
- Corporate bonds are subject to interest coverage tests, stocks to earnings and dividend tests for the past 5 years.
- Not more than 30% of any issuer's securities may be acquired.
- Maximum 7% real estate assets, book value.
- Basket clause—not more than 10% illiquid investments, or 7% ineligible investments.
- May not write options other than covered clearing corporate call options.
- May not purchase more than 10% options, warrants, and rights unless to close out written covered calls.
- Maximum 10% gold or gold certificates; no other commodities are eligible.
- May not purchase or sell forward currency contracts or futures contracts, for the purpose of hedging foreign securities, of more than one year's duration.

TRUST & MORTGAGE LOAN COMPANIES

Trust companies offer, as do chartered banks, a wide range of products including demand deposits, term deposits (TDRs), guaranteed investment certificates (GICs), and RRSP accounts. However, only trust companies may offer trust services and, therefore, pooled pension funds, estate funds, and agency funds comprise a large source of funds for trust companies. Mortgage loan companies, many of which are owned by or affiliated with trust companies, operate principally in the residential mortgage loan business, but may also accept deposits. Typically, a trust company maintains two separate investment groups: the first for company funds (paid-in equity, retained earnings, fees) and guaranteed funds (GICs, TDRs, deposits), and a second for managing estate, trust and agency funds.

With the investment performance of these groups under close scrutiny, investment groups operate in a highly competitive environment. The investment objectives of the

(continued)

EXHIBIT 6 (cont.)

---

two groups are vastly different, given the incentives they face. Some of the larger trust companies have become increasingly aggressive in the investment of company funds. Investment committees typically meet weekly or biweekly.

The taxation of trust companies is similar to that of banks; capital gains and losses on *securities trading* for guaranteed funds and company funds are treated on income account, while company fund *investments* are treated under capital account. As with most Canadian corporations, dividends received from shares of taxable Canadian corporations are tax-exempt. For this reason, many trust companies hold large blocks of preferred shares to improve after-tax portfolio returns.

INSURANCE COMPANIES

Whole, term, and group life insurance policies, annuity premiums, pension and health plans, and interest and dividends make up the chief sources of funds for life companies. Term and group life are two of the largest and fastest growing liabilities for life companies. Canada is a net exporter of life and accident insurance policies, with $330 billion worth of life plans and one-third of all accident plans held outside of Canada. Investment committees meet less frequently than the banks and some trust companies. Life insurance companies are closely regulated and are required by law to meet a list of eligibility requirements for their assets. Eligible investments include:

- Bonds and debentures issued or guaranteed by specific countries.
- Other debt, such as GICs.
- Preferred shares of companies with five years of dividend payout.
- Common shares of companies with a five-year record of defined minimum dividend payment.
- Basket clause—maximum of 7% investments not "legal for life."

Capital gains and losses are generally taxed as income rather than receiving capital account treatment, with the exception of gains/losses on shares, which receive capital account treatment. The earnings from foreign business are not taxed in Canada.

CREDIT UNIONS AND CAISSES POPULAIRES

Membership in these organizations is usually based on a common link, such as an employer. The majority of assets of local credit unions is in loans and mortgages, while central organizations now have a larger position in bonds and equities. Reserve requirements, sources of funds, and eligible assets are generally governed by the respective provincial charters granted to credit unions. Investment departments are typically small and unsophisticated, as the primary business is mortgages and loans.

Taxation of capital gains/losses is treated on capital account, while income is taxed at a rate lower, or equal to, the normal small business tax rate (which is about one-half of the normal corporate rate). Dividends paid out to credit union shareholders are tax deductible and taxed as income in the hands of the shareholders.

35

COLUMBIA PINE PULP COMPANY, INC.

Derek Cathcart, Vice President, Forest Products, The Toronto-Dominion Bank (TD), sat at his desk in early July 1989, reviewing a $525MM funding request from Columbia Pine Pulp Company, Inc. (Pine). As a financial advisor to Pine's sister company, Columbia River Pulp Company Inc. (CRP), Derek had established a strong relationship with Andrew Tharle, Chairman of Pine's Board. In March 1988, CRP had accumulated a negative net worth of approximately $200MM. TD was the lead bank in refinancing CRP. CRP would more than likely have an equity value in excess of $250MM by 1992. The current funding request was for the construction of a proposed pulp mill, Pine, on a site adjacent to CRP in Longview, Washington.

BACKGROUND ON THE COMPANY

Pine and CRP were wholly owned subsidiaries of Whitney & Zeigler Inc. (W&Z). W&Z and its affiliated companies owned and operated North American pulp mills. Through its affiliate, W&Z operated an engineering and consulting group specializing in turnkey projects for pulp, paper and sawmill production complexes.

This case was prepared by Kristina Klausen under the supervision of Professor Robert W. White for the sole purpose of providing material for class discussion at the Western Business School. Certain names and other identifying information may have been disguised to protect confidentiality. It is not intended to illustrate either effective or ineffective handling of a managerial situation. Any reproduction, in any form, of the material in this case is prohibited except with the written consent of the School.

The writers of the case would like to acknowledge the assistance of Derek Cathcart, The Toronto-Dominion Bank.

The W&Z organization had constructed approximately 60 mill projects in 28 countries throughout North and South America, Europe, and Asia.

W&Z was founded in 1853 as a pulp and paper merchant organization and had been privately owned since 1944. In 1978, a group of large U.S. insurance companies financed the capital leasing costs for W&Z's new pulp mill subsidiary, CRP. CRP began production of its bleached kraft market pulp in 1980 after a two-year construction period.

In April 1987, a major consulting firm to the forest products industry estimated the CRP mill replacement value at $400MM, based on the depreciated value of a 10-year-old facility. CRP had invested heavily in emerging technology, including high pressure boilers. In August 1985, these boilers required extensive repairs, removing them from production for $2\frac{1}{2}$ years. CRP spent $37MM on repairs as well as incurring cash flow losses from reduced production efficiency and lost sales. By 1988, the boilers were repaired and CRP's annual capacity was rated at 385,000 mts. One valuation technique was based on five recently completed North American pulp and paper mill transactions. These primary mills sold in the range of 60% to 72% of replacement cost of $1,800 to $2,000 per ton of capacity. CRP would then be valued between $460MM and $613MM. With roughly $275MM in existing senior and subordinated debt at CRP, this valuation implied a residual equity value of $185MM to $338MM.

The Longview site was also chosen for its proximity to available wood and water supply. Pine and CRP owned no timberlands. The timberlands are owned by W&Z. Fibre was supplied by 30–35 local dealers with no single supplier accounting for more than 8% of their needs. Supplier relationships were positive.

Of all the variable costs, those for pulpwood, energy, chemicals and labour played a critical role. CRP operated with a stable non-union labour force and had virtually no turnover. Three previous attempts by unions to organize within the mill had failed.

KRAFT MARKET PULP INDUSTRY

Kraft market pulp is a principal input in the manufacturing of high quality paper products, including writing paper and envelopes, boxboard and tissue. Kraft market pulp is wood cellulose that is in a dried form ready for paper-making. The pulping process breaks wood into individual fibres through a mechanical or chemical process. Chemical pulping results in a longer, stronger fibre which is better for paper production. Pulp made from softwood trees is longer and stronger than hardwood, and somewhat more expensive. In July 1989, hardwood was priced between $745/ton and $765/ton, well below the $830/ton price for benchmark northern bleached softwood kraft.

Kraft market pulp producers, such as Pine, sell their output on the open market, compared to integrated producers who ship output to affiliated paper mills. The largest U.S. kraft market pulp producers were Weyerhaeuser, Georgia-Pacific, and International Paper. In the U.S. and Japan, the production of paper and paperboard is approximately 90% integrated into pulp supply by affiliated companies. In Europe, however, paper mills are basically non-integrated into pulp. As a result, Western Europe continues to be the largest market for kraft market pulp.

Kraft market pulp is a global commodity with price being a function of economic cycles, industry capacity, the amount of output "dumped" on the market by integrated producers, and foreign exchange rates. Price levels for kraft market pulp are extremely volatile and can cause dramatic swings in the earnings and cash flow of industry participants (Table 1).

TABLE 1
NORTHERN BLEACHED SOFTWOOD KRAFT PULP PRICES
IN NORTHERN EUROPE
(US$ PER METRIC TONNE)

QUARTER	1983	1984	1985	1986	1987	1988	1989
First	410	470	420	415	550	670	810
Second	420	540	390	450	590	725	840
Third	425	525	390	475	610	760	840e
Fourth	430	480	390	520	635	760	840e

Performance of the pulp markets over the past year confirmed projections of a tight pulp market in the latter portion of the 1980s through the early 1990s. The outlook for the market pulp business remained favourable despite the likelihood of low economic growth in the developed world, primarily because of strong demand growth in Asia and further expansion of worldwide printing and writing paper demand.

The United States was the largest consumer of wood pulp and it would record its lowest demand growth at 2.8% annually for 1991–2004. This was mostly because of pressure to use more secondary (recycled) fibre.

Worldwide, much of the recent and anticipated future growth in pulp markets came from countries other than the traditional Norscan (Canada, U.S., Sweden and Finland) producers. The decline of total pulp market share for Norscan countries from 83% in 1970 to 64% in 1990 reflected (1) stagnation in Canadian capacity, (2) a long term decline in Scandinavian supply, and (3) growing importance of South American eucalyptus hardwood. Among Norscan producers, only the U.S. industry expanded significantly over the past several years.

These general trends should extend through the 1990s with some modifications. Scandinavians will continue to lose market share as inadequate fibre sources and strong currencies preclude consideration of significant expansion. Canadian producers will shift away from traditional Northern softwood kraft to hardwood kraft and chemo-thermo-mechanical pulp (CTMP), a mechanical/chemical hybrid, production reflecting the developable availability of softwood resources. Most CTMP production had been used in towelling and tissue. Substitution of CTMP for kraft was not likely until significant drawbacks to CTMP were addressed. These included the following: CTMP uses considerably more energy than kraft to produce; CTMP has poor strength and tear properties that reduce its attractiveness to paper-makers; and lower brightness and brightness reversion (fading) make CTMP unacceptable to many in the printing and writing paper market. Continued development of eucalyptus pulp in Brazil was also expected with some radiata pine-based softwood kraft development in Chile (Exhibits 1 and 2).

World demand had grown at 3.6% over the previous 5 years and 3.25% over the previous 10 years. If previous trends continue, this would imply demand growth of 25% through 1995. A number of projects had been proposed (Exhibit 3) and if all of them were built, there would be 33% capacity growth through to 1995, thus implying a capacity utilization of 91%.

Price Forecast

Pulp prices were at an all-time high in 1989, and were expected to remain unchanged through the 4th quarter, and then start sliding in 1990 down to $500 in the second quarter of 1991. Prices were expected to see a strong upturn in 1991–1993, although they should remain 20% lower than their 1988 peak. In 1994, prices are expected to dip lower than 1990–1991, followed by another upswing in 1997–2004.

THE PROJECT

Pine's proposal was to build and operate a bleached softwood kraft market pulp mill which would produce 1,250 air dried metric tons (ADMT) per day, and would operate 345 days per year. The mill would operate with a non-union labour force of 164.

Environmental Matters

Recent concerns developed due to the increased awareness of the environment. One major Canadian bleach kraft pulp mill was delayed a year because the government called for more study on the mill's environmental impact. Pulp and paper mills were one of the major pollutants due to the amount of effluents that were dispensed into water systems. Pine planned to construct and operate the new facility under a current permit for effluent discharge (water permit) and it had an air permit in process. Pine planned to enlist an environmental consultant to prepare the site as part of the Prevention of Significant Deterioration permit. The completed model will be presented to the Department of Environmental Management.

Construction Costs and Funding

Construction was expected to start by October 1989 and to be completed by the first quarter of 1992, with the plant reaching rated capacity in 1993–1994. Future capital expenditures were projected to be $5MM in 1993, increasing to $15MM in 1995, and then escalating at 10%. The applicable depreciation rate was 7%.

Since W&Z would act as both the principal and contractor for this project, it would be able to save $70–90MM in construction fees. White-Brady of Vancouver, Canada, was selected to be the equipment supplier. It was wholly owned by W&Z, and had a strong reputation for producing state of the art technology.

W&Z retained Simons Eastern Engineering of Atlanta to design the mill. Total project costs were estimated at $703MM. W&Z was willing to invest $75MM in cash as well as shared infrastructure and resources estimated at $30MM. A pension fund had agreed to provide deeply subordinated debt valued at $121MM including capitalized interest at a rate of 12%. Repayment would begin in the eleventh year after completion of the project. There was a prepayment requirement out of excess cash at 75% until the debt was paid.

Major financing components are summarized in Table 2. The interest rate on senior debt was expected to be approximately 11.5%, and 11% on a $25MM revolving credit. Excess cash could be invested at 6%.

TABLE 2
SOURCES AND USES OF FUNDS
(US$ MILLIONS)

SOURCES OF FUNDS		
Senior bank debt[a]		$507.0
Subordinated debt[b]	121.0	
Whitney & Zeigler—Cash	75.0	196.0
		$703.0

USES OF FUNDS		
Building and equipment		529.0
Engineering and Management	42.5	
Construction Management	19.0	
Start-up Assistance	1.5	
Contingencies and Escalation	30.0	93.0
Pre-production Expenses		10.0
Capitalized Interest		71.0
		$703.0

aRequested facilities fully drawn.

bActual funding of $100MM, plus accrued interest.

Operating Costs

A comparison of the most modern and efficient U.S., Canadian and overseas pulp mills showed that Pine would be a low cost producer of bleached softwood kraft pulp (Exhibit 4). Pine would enjoy a significant savings in energy costs because it would be largely self-sufficient. "Black liquor," a by-product of processing the wood, would be burned to generate steam, which would turn a turbine to generate electricity. Excess electricity capacity of 83,000 MWH would be sold. This high degree of energy self-sufficiency would result in net energy cost to the facility of $3/ADMT, approximately 10% of the average cost of energy for other producers.

Pine would also enjoy low labour costs because of a high degree of automation, and because some administrative and management services could be shared with CRP.

The tax rates on book income were 34% federal and 5% state.

Marketing Plan

Twenty-six percent of the output was expected to be sold to the Pacific Rim with another 18% to be sold in Western Europe. The remainder (56%) would be sold domestically. Pine would sell all of its pulp through Fraser Pulp Sales Ltd. (FPS) of Vancouver, Canada, a wholly owned subsidiary of W&Z. FPS currently sold the total production of W&Z's mills at West Fraser and Columbia River, as well as pulp from third parties. When Pine was operational, FPS would be the largest seller of kraft market pulp in the world. Projected delivered variable costs from various regions to Northern Europe are presented in Exhibit 5.

Kraft market pulp prices included transportation to the customer. Pine's mill site was well-situated to control freight costs by utilizing various modes of transportation including rail, truck or ship. Furthermore, FPS was the largest single supplier of foreign pulps to Japan, and a large exporter to Europe, thereby gaining advantageous freight arrangements.

FPS had already pre-sold the entire output of the proposed mill for the first 5 years of operation, with the price per ton to be determined by market conditions. Selling commissions of 3% on domestic contracts and 5% on exports were projected. The approximate days accounts receivable outstanding were projected to be: Asia, 10 days; domestic, 28 days; and Europe, 45 days.

The Decision

As Derek put his papers into his briefcase he knew that he would have to make a decision very soon. He had to decide whether to recommend that the TD extend credit to Pine. Furthermore, if he recommended that credit be extended to Pine, Derek would have to decide how to structure a funding package.

EXHIBIT 1

Paper Grade Wood Pulp Demand by Major World Region
(million metric tons, percent share)
June 1989

	1972		1988		2004	
COUNTRY	DEMAND	%	DEMAND	%	DEMAND	%
United States	40.1	39.8	54.5	36.9	71.0	31.8
Other Western Europe	14.9	14.8	20.4	13.8	29.5	13.2
Canada	11.5	11.5	15.2	10.3	21.5	9.6
Nordic Countries	10.5	10.4	16.0	10.8	24.3	10.9
Japan	9.5	9.4	13.0	8.8	20.3	9.1
Eastern Europe & the USSR	7.6	7.6	12.4	8.4	18.2	8.2
Other Asia	2.3	2.3	6.7	4.5	16.9	7.6
Brazil	1.1	1.0	3.1	2.1	7.9	3.5
Other Latin America	1.4	1.4	2.7	2.5	5.5	2.5
Oceania	1.3	1.3	1.9	1.3	4.3	1.9
Africa	0.6	0.6	1.8	1.2	3.7	1.6

EXHIBIT 2

World Market Pulp Capacity
(million metric tons)

	1972	1988	2004
Total	22.1	32.8	56.2
United States	3.4	6.7	10.0
Share	15.6%	20.4%	17.8%
Canada	5.3	8.2	13.5
Share	24.0%	25.1%	24.0%
Nordic Countries	8.0	6.4	7.0
Share	36.5%	19.6%	12.4%
Brazil	0.4	1.7	5.4
Share	1.6%	5.3%	9.6%
Other W. Europe	2.3	4.3	5.7
Share	10.5%	13.1%	10.1%
Japan	1.3	0.8	0.5
Share	5.8%	2.3%	0.9%
Other Far East	0.1	0.5	1.8
Share	0.5%	1.7%	3.2%
Other Latin America	0.2	1.1	4.8
Share	1.1%	3.3%	8.5%
Africa	0.2	0.7	2.1
Share	1.0%	2.1%	3.8%
Oceania	0.1	0.7	3.0
Share	0.7%	2.2%	5.3%
E. Europe & U.S.S.R.	0.6	1.6	2.5
Share	2.9%	4.9%	4.5%

EXHIBIT 3

Major Pulp Expansion Projects
June 1989

	SOFTWOOD		
SPONSOR	TONS (000)	LOCATION	COMMENT
Pine Pulp	420	Washington	Expansion
Weyerhaeuser	420	Mississippi	Expansion
Champion	190	Alberta	Expansion
Howe Sound	125	British Columbia	Expansion
James River	280	Ontario	Expansion
Cariboo	55	British Columbia	Expansion
Weyerhaeuser	(170)	Saskatchewan	Integration
Canadian Pacific	(160)	Ontario	Integration
Procter & Gamble	300	Alberta	Expansion
Pope & Talbot	255	Oregon	Expansion
CMPC	315	Chile	Greenfield
Arauco	265	Chile	Expansion
	2,295		

	HARDWOOD		
Stone Container	235	Georgia	Expansion
Bowater	75	Tennessee	Expansion
Champion	(200)	Michigan	Integration
Daishowa	350	Alberta	Greenfield
Crestbrook	500	Alberta	Greenfield
Aracruz	525	Brazil	Expansion
Bahiasui	350	Brazil	Greenfield
Quatapara	210	Brazil	Greenfield
Riocell	300	Brazil	Expansion
Coperne	350	Brazil	Greenfield
Cenibra	350	Brazil	Greenfield
Macimento	200	Chile	Expansion
Feldmuhle	250	Spain	Greenfield
Portucel	100	Portugal	Greenfield
	3,595		

	CTMP/OTHER		
Cascades	190	Quebec	Conversion
Stone Bathurst	80	New Brunswick	Conversion
Millar Western	210	Alberta	Greenfield
Fibreco	180	British Columbia	Greenfield
Quesnel River	100	British Columbia	Expension
Donohus Matane	210	Quebec	Greenfield
	970		

EXHIBIT 4

Comparative Manufacturing Costs
Bleached Softwood Kraft Market Pulp
on an Air-Dried Metric Ton Basis
(1988 constant dollars)

OPERATING COST	PINE	CRP	SOUTHEAST U.S.	EASTERN CANADA	WESTERN CANADA	SWEDEN
Pulpwood	126	120	110	171	106	199
Chemicals	30	33	40	37	47	35
Energy	3	25	28	20	29	16
Supplies	30	26	25	27	28	18
Labour (Hourly)	32	44	49	32	38	29
General & Admin.	19	37	44	40	53	33
Total Cash Costs	240	285	296	327	301	330

EXHIBIT 5

Average Bleached Softwood Kraft Market Pulp
Delivered Variable Costs to Northern Europe
(per metric ton)

	1972	1988	2004e
U.S. Pacific Northwest	168	344	665
U.S. South	144	366	770
B.C. Coast	172	405	773
B.C. Interior	154	387	727
Eastern Canada	179	379	724
Sweden	175	447	735
Finland	168	480	798
Chile	148	292	603

PART SIX • Measuring the Value Gap and Unlocking Value to Close the Gap

36. THE GOODYEAR TIRE & RUBBER COMPANY
37. NOTE ON THE NORTH AMERICAN TIRE INDUSTRY
38. THE ACQUISITION OF MARTELL
39. BLUE JAY ENERGY & CHEMICAL CORPORATION
40. OCELOT INDUSTRIES LTD.
41. UNION ENTERPRISES LTD.
42. UNICORP CANADA CORPORATION
43. SHERRITT GORDON LTD.—PROXY CONTEST
44. SASKATCHEWAN OIL AND GAS CORPORATION
45. SEALED AIR CORPORATION'S LEVERAGED RECAPITALIZATION

36

THE GOODYEAR TIRE & RUBBER COMPANY

Don Thain sat in his study late in the evening of May 12, 1992. Tomorrow he and the rest of the Independent Committee of the Board of Directors of Goodyear Canada Inc. (Goodyear Canada) would meet to assess the "fairness" of the proposed "Going Private" Amalgamation received from Goodyear Canada's parent, The Goodyear Tire & Rubber Company of Akron, Ohio (Goodyear U.S.).

On February 20, 1992, the Goodyear Tire & Rubber Company offered to buy all the common shares of Goodyear Canada not already owned by them (11.2% of the shares issued were in public hands) for $48.00 Canadian in cash per share. This represented a 22% premium over the closing price on the Toronto Stock Exchange (TSE) on the previous afternoon.

Goodyear U.S. stated the reason for the amalgamation as follows:

> Goodyear believes that the amalgamation is in the best interests of Goodyear and the Company [Goodyear Canada]. Goodyear owns substantially all (over 88%) of the Company's equity and voting shares and almost 70% of the Company's outstanding indebtedness. The Company is a significant part of Goodyear's worldwide operations, substantially all of which are wholly owned. The efficiency of medium term to long

This case was prepared by D. Alasdair S. Turnbull under the supervision of Professor Robert W. White for the sole purpose of providing material for class discussion at the Western Business School. Certain names and other identifying information may have been disguised to protect confidentiality. It is not intended to illustrate either effective or ineffective handling of a managerial situation. Any reproduction, in any form, of the material in this case is prohibited except with the written consent of the School.

The writers would like to acknowledge the assistance of Donald H. Thain, Magna International Professor, of the Western Business School in preparing this case. This case was prepared from publicly available information.

term financial and operational planning for the Company will be improved significantly if the Company is wholly owned by Goodyear. The amalgamation will also enable the Company to avoid the ongoing expense associated with its financial and continuous reporting obligations to Public Shareholders.

The trading market for the common shares of Goodyear Canada was illiquid as a result of the relatively small "public float" and, consequently, was not an efficient outlet for public shareholders to realize value on their investment. The amalgamation was a means of offering all public shareholders an opportunity to realize value for their common shares substantially in excess of market value.

Reflecting on an Independent Director's responsibilities and liability, Don reviewed his notes and tried to decide what position he would take tomorrow and how he would justify it.

THE INDEPENDENT COMMITTEE

All of the directors of Goodyear Canada bear fiduciary responsibilities in respect of the proposed amalgamation. Goodyear Canada is subject to the Business Corporations Act of Ontario (OBCA) which states:

> Every director and officer of a corporation in exercising his powers and discharging his duties shall:
> a. act honestly and in good faith with a view to the best interests of the corporation; and
> b. exercise the care, diligence and skill that a reasonably prudent person would exercise in comparable circumstances.

With respect to conflicts of interest, the OBCA provides, in effect, that notwithstanding disclosure of potential interests, the transaction must be fair and reasonable to Goodyear at the time it is approved by the Board. Failing this, the transaction could be rendered void and any director or officer could be accountable to Goodyear or its shareholders for any profit or gain realized from the transaction.

The proposed amalgamation would be a "going private transaction" as defined by the Ontario Securities Commission's Policy Statement No. 9.1. In a going private transaction, it is prudent for a board of directors to form an independent committee of the board to assist the directors in discharging their fiduciary obligations. An independent committee will not only assist the Board in making a more informed decision, but in an otherwise non-negotiated, non-arm's length transaction, it serves to introduce a more objective element to the board's deliberative process.

After Board approval, the amalgamation has to be approved by a resolution of the public shareholders. Not less than two-thirds of the votes cast at a special meeting of all shareholders must approve the transaction. In addition, a certain percentage of the minority shareholders must approve. The level of support required from the minority shareholders depends on the value or midpoint of a range of values assigned to the common shares by a formal valuation done by an independent valuer. If the $48 offer meets or exceeds the midpoint of the range of values, a simple majority of the votes cast by the minority Goodyear Canada shareholders will be needed to approve the transaction. Otherwise, two-thirds of the votes cast must approve.

BACKGROUND ON GOODYEAR

Goodyear Canada had two main divisions: the Tire Division which manufactured and/or marketed passenger, truck, farm and industrial tires and related products; and the Engineered Products Division which produced industrial rubber, plastics and other products, see Exhibits 1, 2, 3 and 4 for financial information.

In April 1992, Goodyear U.S. announced the proposed sale of its Films Division. This included Goodyear Canada's plant in Etobicoke which produced plastic films.

Tire Division

Tire Division sales amounted to $698MM or 86% of 1991 total sales of Goodyear Canada. Roughly three-quarters of this was sold to the Canadian OE and replacement markets (28% and 48%, respectively) with the balance being sold to Goodyear U.S. via inter-company transfers. Of the total units sold by Goodyear Canada in 1991, 70% were produced in Canada and the rest were imported from Goodyear U.S.

Goodyear U.S. attempted to rationalize production in its plants to maximize efficiency and lower costs by scheduling long production runs. As a result, units were regularly transferred between Goodyear Canada and its parent in order to meet their respective demands for particular tire sizes and types.

Products were distributed to the OE market directly through vehicle manufacturers and to the replacement market through independent tire dealers, franchises, and a chain of company-operated retail outlets. A complete line of mechanical and automotive-related services were also offered through the Goodyear Canada-operated outlets. The company also leased tires to a number of municipal public transportation commissions throughout Canada.

Goodyear U.S. was the largest supplier of original equipment passenger tires in North America with a 37% market share in 1990. Michelin (with Uniroyal Goodrich) had a 32.7% share and Bridgestone (Firestone) had 17%. Goodyear Canada's major OE customers included General Motors, Chrysler, Ford, Honda, and Toyota.

Engineered Products Division

The Engineered Products Division produced a wide range of rubber products such as conveyor belting, hose, and moulded automotive and industrial products in four manufacturing facilities. Engineered Products Division sales were mainly to vehicle manufacturers, industrial end users, resource-based companies, and wholesale distributors of automotive parts. The Engineered Products Division accounted for approximately 14% of Goodyear Canada's 1991 sales.

Manufacturing

Goodyear Canada had three tire manufacturing facilities located in Napanee, Ontario, Valleyfield, Quebec, and Medicine Hat, Alberta.

In 1988, when North American capacity was insufficient to meet demand, Goodyear Canada began construction on a new tire factory in Napanee, Ontario. The plant was officially opened in September 1990 at a total cost of about $320MM. Production levels were delayed from an initial plan of 14,800 tires per day to a level of about 8,000 tires per day because of production start-up problems and weak market conditions during the construction phase. In 1991, the plant operated at about 47% of capacity. Full capacity utilization was not expected before 1995, but Goodyear Canada had announced that the level of production at Napanee would be increased to full capacity by early 1993.

The Napanee plant was designed for long production runs of a limited number of sizes and types of tires. It used the most technologically advanced equipment to produce radial tires for the North American OE market. The plant currently shipped approximately 60% of its production to the OE market and the rest to the replacement market. After 1993, the company expected that 90% of the Napanee production would be for the OE market.

The size of the Napanee property led many industry analysts to speculate that Goodyear Canada planned to increase the capacity of the plant by expansion in the future. Although Goodyear Canada denied such plans, popular figures were doubling, or even tripling, capacity.

Goodyear Canada's Valleyfield, Quebec, plant currently supplied 60% of its production to the OE market. After 1993, 90% of production was expected to be for the replacement market. Capacity utilization was projected to be 91% of this plant's 20,600 tires per day capacity in 1992.

The Medicine Hat, Alberta, facility had a capacity of 7,500 tires per day and was fully utilized. This plant produced convenience spare tires for automobiles and farm tires; 95% of production was shipped to OE customers throughout North America.

Replacement Market Distribution

Goodyear Canada had increased the distribution base for its Goodyear brand products through the acquisition of independently owned tire dealers and through the expansion of its share of franchise and company-owned stores. During 1987 and 1988, Goodyear Canada acquired Sumner Tire and Automotive Ltd., York Tire Ltd., Groupe Réchapex Ltée., and other smaller independent dealers. It also purchased a 49% interest in Fountain Tire Ltd.

Currently, Goodyear Canada was focusing on increasing the efficiency and cost effectiveness of existing locations rather than continued expansion. As a result, several stores and distribution outlets were being closed or amalgamated. The number of retail and commercial outlets was reduced by 11 to 162. The company's strategy included a focus on improving its automotive service business.

Goodyear Canada re-entered the custom brand business in 1991 with the negotiation of a contract with Canadian Tire Corporation Limited. Goodyear Canada had exited this market segment when its capacity shrank in 1987 due to the closure of its Etobicoke plant.

Distribution centres were opened in 1990 in St. Albert, Alberta, and Winnipeg, Manitoba. A new warehouse in Vancouver, B.C., was expected to be completed by the fourth quarter of 1992.

In an attempt to create customer demand for its products and to improve margins, Goodyear Canada introduced four new tires directly into the aftermarket, rather than placing them initially as new tires on cars or trucks. Goodyear Canada was attempting to gain market share and volumes at higher margins before competitors had the opportunity to incorporate the latest improvements in competitive new products.

Raw Materials

The majority of raw materials was sourced on a worldwide basis by Goodyear U.S. and supplied to its affiliates, including Goodyear Canada, in order to maximize economies of scale and ensure stability of supply. Approximately 33% of Goodyear Canada's raw materials was purchased from its parent.

Goodyear U.S. management anticipated that supplies of petrochemical feed-stocks adequate to meet its production requirements for 1992 would be available, generally at a slightly higher price than that in effect at the end of 1991.

Research and Development

The larger tire companies in Canada, including Goodyear Canada, had access to modern technologies through their parent companies. Goodyear U.S. spent US$330MM in 1991 on basic and applied research, and on engineering activities related to design, development, improvement, or modification of new or existing products and to the formulation and design or improvement of manufacturing processes or equipment.

Goodyear Canada paid the parent for research and development through an annual service charge based on 5% of net sales after deducting the cost to Goodyear Canada of all finished products purchased from Goodyear U.S. This fee was paid in consideration of the use of the parent's intellectual property, technical know-how, and management assistance as well as for the overall cost and management efficiencies gained by, for example, centralizing purchasing and production scheduling. According to Goodyear U.S. management, service charges were based on the marginal cost to Goodyear U.S. of providing these benefits to Goodyear Canada.

FINANCIAL NOTES

Tax Loss Carryforwards

Goodyear Canada and its subsidiaries had $106.7MM of operating loss carryforwards which expired at times over the period 1995 to 1998. Management believed that all tax losses were available to offset taxable income in the future, subject to their possible expiration.[1]

Outstanding Debt

On March 31, 1992, Goodyear Canada had $521.1MM in debt outstanding. Outstanding loans and bankers' acceptances amounted to $132.0MM as at March 31, 1992 and included prime base loans and bankers' acceptances covered by revolving credit agreements which were renewed annually. Swaps expiring at various times from October 1992 to June 1995 had been put in place to fix the interest rate on $55.0MM of this floating rate debt. The remaining $77.0MM was due in 1992.

An unsecured credit agreement, entered into by Goodyear Canada on October 1, 1990 with Goodyear U.S., expired on March 31, 1996, and had automatic one-year extensions unless terminated by either party. Up to US$300MM could be drawn under various maturity options as long as Goodyear U.S. owned 67% of Goodyear Canada's common shares. Covenants under the agreement required Goodyear Canada to maintain a current ratio of not less than 1:1 and to maintain consolidated net worth of an amount not less than $75MM at the end of each quarter. Advances under the credit agreement were currently interest-free until June 30, 1992, subject to periodic review thereafter by Goodyear U.S. At March 31, 1992, Goodyear Canada had drawn the entire US$300MM (CA$357.1MM) available under the facility.

Goodyear Canada entered a loan agreement with the Government of Ontario on March 23, 1988, to assist in the funding of construction of the Napanee plant. This loan was unsecured and, providing the company met specific performance criteria relating to capital expenditures and employment levels, would be interest-free. If the capital expenditure criterion was not met, up to $6.7MM of principal would become due on April 30, 1994, with interest accrued from April 1, 1989. At March 31, 1992, $32MM was outstanding under this agreement.

Redundant Assets

Redundant assets are those assets which are in excess of (and, thus, do not affect) the going concern value of the operating assets of a business. These assets are not required in the day-to-day operations of the business.

[1]Canadian tax law allows operating losses to be carried back up to 3 years or forward up to 7 years.

In April 1992, Goodyear U.S. announced the sale of its industrial film business including the plastic films plant in Etobicoke, Ontario. The expected gross proceeds to Goodyear Canada would be approximately $12.0MM.

Production of polyester and nylon fabric materials as reinforcing material in the construction of tires was phased out at Goodyear Canada's 65-year-old factory in Ste. Hyacinthe, Quebec. Overcapacity due to the depressed North American market was the primary reason for the plant closure which occurred in June 1991. An independent appraisal valued these assets at US$2.25MM.

Intercompany Transactions

Historically, there had been substantial amounts of intercompany transactions between Goodyear Canada and Goodyear U.S., including the purchase of raw materials or finished products from Goodyear U.S. and the sale by Goodyear Canada to Goodyear U.S. of finished product (OE and replacement tires or general products). The basis for determining the transfer pricing for tire transactions was[2]:

1. Purchases by Goodyear Canada of tires from Goodyear U.S. are transacted at standard cost (for the particular U.S. plant the tire is sourced from) plus 6.5%.
2. Intercompany sales by Goodyear Canada of tires to Goodyear U.S. are transacted at standard cost (for the specific Canadian plant) plus 7.6%.

According to Goodyear Canada management, cumulative support payments of approximately $119MM were received from Goodyear U.S. from 1987 to 1991. These payments were made to compensate for production allocation decisions made by Goodyear U.S. which, according to discussions with Goodyear Canada management, would not have been economically optimal for Goodyear Canada on a stand-alone basis.

Pension Liability

The Company's obligations for pension benefits arising from service prior to December 31, 1991, were estimated to be $173,878,500. The pension plan assets with a market value of $151,953,950 as at December 31, 1991, were available to meet these obligations.

---

[2]Exceptions to these rules are:

1. From April 1990 throughout the period of management's projections, sales by Goodyear Canada to Goodyear U.S. of radial tires are at standard cost plus 15%.
2. Unisteel tires are purchased by Goodyear Canada from Goodyear U.S. at standard cost less 11.7%. A2 tires are purchased by Goodyear Canada from Goodyear U.S. at standard cost.
3. Kelly-Springfield brand tires are regularly purchased by Goodyear U.S. from Goodyear Canada at standard cost plus 15%. A special program exists whereby up to 1.5 million tires per year may be purchased by Goodyear U.S. from Goodyear Canada at standard cost less $1.00.

FORMAL VALUATION

The provisions of the OBCA and Policy 9.1 require that an independent valuer prepare a formal valuation and that a summary of the valuation be contained in the management information circular which will be sent to the shareholders in connection with the going private transaction (see Exhibit 5 for financial market data, Exhibits 6 and 7 for information on comparable companies and Exhibit 8 for selected tire and rubber acquisition transactions).

The valuation must not contain a downward adjustment to reflect the fact that common shares held by the Goodyear Canada minority do not form part of a controlling interest or the fact that the liquidity of the market for Goodyear Canada shares is affected by Goodyear U.S.'s control position. In preparing the valuation, the valuer should test the valuation through examination of a variety of different appropriate valuation approaches. Furthermore, disclosure should be made concerning the scope of the valuation together with a description of any limitation on the scope of the review and the implications of the limitation on the valuer's conclusion. The valuation approach or approaches relied upon should be described and the reasons for the reliance upon the selected approach over any other approach should be disclosed. The summary of the valuation must also disclose the extent to which any advantage to Goodyear U.S., after completion of the transaction, has been considered in the valuation and the nature of that advantage.

Following this requirement of the OBCA, the Independent Committee had retained the investment firm of Nesbitt Thomson Inc. to perform the formal valuation. Nesbitt Thomson's analysis, summarized in Exhibits 9, 10, and 11, led them to assign Goodyear Canada shares a value of $32–$45 per share.

THE DECISION

Tomorrow the Independent Committee would meet to finalize its report to the Board of Directors of Goodyear Canada. Should they conclude that the offer was fair? If so, should they recommend that shareholders tender their shares?

There was already evidence that some shareholders felt that the stock's value exceeded $70 and considered the offer a gambit by Goodyear U.S. In the face of opposition, Don felt that Goodyear U.S. would simply withdraw their offer. How, he wondered, would Goodyear Canada's Board deal with public relations problems and the inevitable restructuring that would be required after such a move?

EXHIBIT 1

GOODYEAR CANADA INC.
Consolidated Balance Sheet
As at December 31
(dollars in thousands)

	1991	1990	1989	1988	1987
Assets					
Current Assets					
Cash	$ 38	$ 44	$ 52	$ 51	$ 24
Accounts Receivable	103,891	112,024	119,316	103,777	115,983
Due from affiliated companies	53,299	46,777	65,177	58,547	36,814
Inventories:					
Raw materials	15,284	15,476	17,401	19,933	18,762
Work in process	5,574	5,779	8,001	10,498	7,531
Finished product	95,201	122,595	140,062	116,684	97,978
	116,059	143,850	165,464	147,115	124,271
Prepaid expenses	3,897	3,653	4,416	6,295	1,810
Deferred income taxes	–	–	80	374	1,742
Total Current Assets	277,184	306,348	355,305	316,159	280,644
Misc. Investments &					
Other Assets	60,765	57,821	48,110	39,462	11,402
Properties & Plants:					
Gross investment	619,634	608,038	438,539	295,391	283,119
Accumulated depreciation	194,793	180,415	170,088	157,986	179,369
	424,841	427,623	268,451	137,405	103,750
TOTAL ASSETS	$762,790	$791,792	$671,866	$493,026	$395,796
Liabilities & Shareholders' Equity					
Current Liabilities					
Bank indebtedness	$ 7,885	$ 7,002	$ 3,801	$ 31,538	$ 31,806
Accounts payable and					
accrued liabilities	51,911	52,997	88,861	64,706	81,948
Due to affiliated companies	97,049	124,306	72,106	68,077	56,903
Income and other taxes payable	946	2,582	3,178	1,498	4,157
Total Current Liabilities	157,791	186,887	167,946	165,819	174,814
Long Term Loan from Parent	347,379	157,549	–	–	–
Long Term Debt	145,821	297,448	325,557	140,039	56,800
Deferred Income Taxes	250	8,358	16,357	14,416	12,680
Other Long Term Liabilities	6,505	9,202	12,339	17,648	4,497
	657,746	659,444	522,199	337,922	248,791
Shareholders' Equity					
Capital Stock:					
Common shares					
(2,572,600 outstanding)	129	129	129	129	129
Capital Surplus	584	584	584	584	584
Retained Earnings	104,331	131,635	148,954	154,391	146,292
	105,044	132,348	149,667	155,104	147,005
TOTAL LIABILITIES & EQUITY	$762,790	$791,792	$671,866	$493,026	$395,796

EXHIBIT 2

GOODYEAR CANADA INC.
Consolidated Income Statement
As at December 31
(dollars in thousands)

	1991	1990	1989	1988	1987
Net sales	$814,326	$838,171	$886,738	$780,807	$695,534
Income from investments	558	918	1,338	1,375	538
	814,884	839,089	888,076	782,182	696,072
Cost and Expenses					
Cost of goods sold	669,819	678,328	703,322	633,511	547,744
Selling, administrative & general	129,543	135,871	138,864	115,145	87,676
Interest expense	23,892	24,552	25,430	16,398	10,726
Depreciation	18,686	12,280	13,735	12,591	12,775
Restructuring provisions	6,909	7,980	9,137	–	–
	848,849	859,011	890,448	777,645	658,921
Income (loss) before taxes	(33,965)	(19,922)	(2,412)	4,537	37,151
Income taxes (recovery)					
Current	(7,133)	(4,745)	(6,964)	(2,877)	11,827
Deferred					
Current	0	(1,950)	(506)	6	8,991
Long term	(43)	490	6,893	5,102	(4,256)
	(7,176)	(6,205)	(577)	2,231	16,562
Net income (loss) before extraordinary item	(26,789)	(13,717)	(1,835)	2,306	20,589
Extraordinary item	–	–	–	9,394	(8,072)
Net income (loss) for the year	$(26,789)	$(13,717)	$ (1,835)	$ 11,700	$ 12,517
Net income (loss) before extraordinary item per common share	$ (10.41)	$ (5.33)	$ (0.71)	$ 0.90	$ 7.99
Net income (loss) per common share	$ (10.41)	$ (5.33)	$ (0.71)	$ 4.55	$ 4.85

EXHIBIT 3
GOODYEAR CANADA INC.
Selected Segmented Information
As at December 31
(dollars in thousands)

	1991	1990	1989	1988
Tire Division				
Net Sales	$697,718	$721,814	$761,196	$655,363
Operating profit	1,332	25,350	31,077	25,037
Identifiable assets	700,448	735,658	609,024	438,843
Capital expenditures	17,073	169,047	141,811	32,106
Depreciation expense	16,099	9,610	11,060	10,563
Engineered Products Division				
Net Sales	$116,608	$116,357	$125,542	$125,444
Operating profit	4,587	4,706	12,376	10,381
Identifiable assets	58,368	52,414	57,482	47,451
Capital expenditures	1,471	3,300	3,693	6,220
Depreciation expense	2,587	2,670	2,675	2,028

EXHIBIT 4
GOODYEAR CANADA INC.
Selected Financial Information
As at December 31
(dollars in thousands)

	1991	1990	1989	1988	1987
Net Sales	$814,326	$838,171	$886,738	$780,807	$695,534
Net income (loss)					
before extraordinary item	(26,789)	(13,717)	(1,835)	2,306	20,589
Net income (loss)	(26,789)	(13,717)	(1,835)	11,700	12,517
Net income (loss)					
per dollar of sales					
before extraordinary item	(3.3)¢	(1.6)¢	(0.2)¢	0.3¢	3.0¢
Net income (loss) per dollar					
of sales	(3.3)¢	(1.6)¢	(0.2)¢	1.5¢	1.8¢
Taxes & duties, net	6,511	22,421	30,423	46,518	52,766
Current assets	277,184	306,348	355,305	316,159	280,644
Current liabilities	157,791	186,887	167,946	165,819	174,814
Working capital	119,393	119,461	187,359	150,340	105,830
Depreciation	18,686	12,280	13,735	12,591	12,775
Capital expenditures	18,544	172,347	145,504	38,326	22,409
Properties and plants	424,841	427,623	268,451	137,405	103,750
Per common share:					
Net income (loss)					
before e.i.	(10.41)	(5.33)	(0.71)	(0.90)	7.99
Net income (loss)	(10.41)	(5.33)	(0.71)	4.55	4.85
Book value	40.83	51.45	58.18	60.29	57.14
Taxes & duties, net	2.53	8.72	11.83	18.08	20.51
Dividends	0.20	1.40	1.40	1.40	1.40
Employee compensation	207,891	221,273	206,820	197,779	199,861

EXHIBIT 5

Financial Market Data
Recent Trading History on the Toronto Stock Exchange

	HIGH	LOW	VOLUME (SHARES)
1991			
First Quarter	$30	$21.75	80,250
Second Quarter	41	27.50	40,524
July	40	37	3,070
August	39	35	6,700
September	40	36.50	4,916
October	37.50	35	10,718
November	40	37	1,815
December	38	37	5,650
1992			
January	$39	$37.125	1,050
February	50	39	19,320
February 19 (close)		$39.25	
March	50.25	48.75	12,691
April	50	48.50	11,765
May 1 to 12	50	49.25	1,954
May 12 (close)		$49.50	

Money Markets
(rates in %)

	CANADA	UNITED STATES
Bank Rate (Canada)/Discount Rate (U.S.)	6.78	3.50
Prime Rate	7.75	6.50
Call Loan (Canada)/Fed Funds (U.S.)	6.25	3.94
Government Bonds		
2-year	7.49	5.21
5-year	8.25	6.69
10-year	8.55	7.39
T-Bills		
1-month	6.32	3.52
3-month	6.42	3.64
6-month	6.57	3.74
Average Historical Market Premium, $(R_{m,t} - R^L_{f,}{}^t)$, for period: 1950–1991 (Canada); 1926–1991 (U.S.)	5.38	7.40
Corporate Bonds (rating)		
The Bank of Nova Scotia–2001 (AA)	9.80	
John Labatt–2002 (AA)	9.38	
The Goodyear Tire & Rubber Co.–1997 (BB)		8.29
The Goodyear Tire & Rubber Co.–1995 (BB)		8.25

EXHIBIT 6

Information on Comparable Companies[a]
(US$ millions, except per share amounts)

COMPANY	CLOSING SHARE PRICE FEB. 20/92	MARKET EQUITY CAPITAL	PRICE/ EARNINGS	VALUE/ EBIT (3)	VALUE/ EBDIT (4)	VALUE/ SALES (5)	PRICE/ BOOK VALUE
Goodyear Tire & Rubber (1,6)	$63.75	$4,615.5	Neg.	21.9x	9.6x	0.7x	1.7x
Cooper Tire & Rubber Co. (2)	51.13	2,119.7	26.7x	16.8x	13.6x	2.2x	4.8x
Bandag, Inc. (2)	126.00	1,747.5	24.8x	14.6x	12.4x	3.0x	5.9x
Carlisle Companies Incorporated (1)	40.00	304.9	18.4x	11.6x	6.2x	0.6x	1.6x
Goodyear Canada Inc. (7)	39.25	101.0	Neg.	Neg.	55.7x	0.7x	1.0x

Notes:

(1) Financial information based on 12 months ending September 30, 1991.
(2) Financial information based on last 12 months to December 31, 1991, with the exception of depreciation which is estimated for 1991.
(3) Market equity capitalization as at February 20, 1992, plus net book value of debt divided by earnings before interest and taxes.
(4) Market equity capitalization as at February 20, 1992, plus net book value of debt divided by earnings before depreciation, interest and taxes.
(5) Market equity capitalization as at February 20, 1992, plus net book value of debt divided by sales.
(6) Reflects adjustments for common share offering November 13, 1991.
(7) Financial information based on last twelve months to December 31, 1991, in Canadian funds.

^aCooper Tire & Rubber Company—80% of sales to the replacement tire market and the rest to the industrial rubber market.
Carlisle Companies Inc.—principal markets are automotive, electronics, commercial construction, and recreation. Automotive accounts for 34% of sales.
Bandag, Inc.—major manufacturer and supplier to the tire retreading industry. 37% of sales are outside U.S.

EXHIBIT 7

Selected Financial Information
on Comparable Companies
(US$ millions, except per share amounts)

	BANDAG INC.	CARLISLE COMPANIES	COOPER TIRE	GOODYEAR TIRE (U.S.)	GOODYEAR CANADA
Beta	1.00	0.85	1.25	1.15	0.68
Capital Structure (% of total)					
Long Term Debt	2%	26%	11%	43%	
Preferred Stock	0%	0%	0%	0%	
Common Stock	98%	74%	89%	57%	
Shares Outstanding (000's)	27,737	7,622	82,904	70,836	
1991 Income Statements					
Sales	582.9	500.8	1,001.1	10,907	
Operating Margin (in %)	24.4	10.5	16.0	9.5	
Depreciation	21.8	19.4	32.0	441.5	
Tax Rate (in %)	38.0	39.2	36.2	–	
Net Income	79.6	18.2	79.4	31.3	
Cash Flows/Share[a]					
1987	2.51	5.43	0.60	13.86	
1988	2.92	6.01	0.74	12.48	
1989	3.21	5.31	0.99	11.74	
1990	3.62	6.02	1.14	6.44	
1991	3.66	4.93	1.34	6.69[b]	
est. 1992	4.35	5.85	1.60	11.25	
est. 1997	8.35	9.75	2.85	16.40	

[a]*Source: Value Line Investment Survey.*

[b]Based on 1991 capital expenditures of $345.1MM, Goodyear Tire (U.S.)'s 1991 free cash flow per share was $1.818.

EXHIBIT 8

Selected Tire and Rubber Acquisition Transactions

DATE	ACQUIROR	TARGET	TRANSACTION VALUE ($ MILLIONS)	IMPLIED P/E MULTIPLE	TOTAL VALUE/ EBIT (1)	TOTAL VALUE/ EBDIT (1,2)	PRICE/ BOOK	TOTAL VALUE/ SALES (1)	TERMS ($ MILLIONS)
Nov. 1990 (withdrawn)	The Goodyear Tire and Rubber Company	Brad Ragan Inc.	$12.3 for 25%	N.M.F. (3)	36.6x	19.1x	1.0x	0.4x	$12.3 cash
Oct. 1989	Yokohama Rubber Company	Mohawk Rubber Company	$150.0					0.9x	$150.0 cash
Sept. 1989	Michelin Group	Uniroyal Goodrich Tire Co.	$690.0	33.5x	10.8x	7.4x	2.5x	0.7x	$690.0 cash $804.1 net debt
Apr. 1988	Pirelli Group	Armstrong Tire Company (4)	$196.5	19.9x	9.9x	6.2x	N/A	0.4x	$196.5 cash
Mar. 1988	Bridgestone Corporation	Firestone Tire & Rubber Company	$2,522.4	21.0x	10.6x	6.8x	2.1x	0.7x	$2,522.4 cash $433.0 net debt
Dec. 1987	Clayton Dubilier	Uniroyal Goodrich	$225.0 for 50%	38.5x	11.4x	7.0x	0.9x	0.44x	$225.0 cash $459.2 net debt
May 1987	Continental Ag	General Tire (5)	$625.0	15.8x	7.9x	5.4x	N/A	0.6x	$625.0 cash
Oct. 1986 (unsuccessful)	Sir James Goldsmith	The Goodyear Tire & Rubber Co.	$616.6 for 11.5%	26.0x	12.1x	5.5x	1.5x	0.7x	$616.6 cash

Notes:
(1) Total Value is the sum of the transaction price for the equity plus all interest-bearing outstanding obligations of the target company (i.e., short- and long-term debt and preferreds, if any, less any cash or near cash at the time of the acquisition).
(2) EBDIT excludes amortization as well as depreciation and interest expense.
(3) Not meaningful.
(4) Multiples are based on financials for the 12 months ending September 30, 1987.
(5) Multiples are based on financials for the 12 months ending November 30, 1987.

EXHIBIT 9

Summary of Nesbitt Thomson's Preliminary Assumptions

	TARGET WEIGHT	PRE-TAX COST	AFTER-TAX COST	WEIGHTED AFTER-TAX COST
Short term debt	20%	7.40%	4.59%	0.92%
Long term debt	30%	10.84%	6.72%	2.02%
Equity	50%	13.24%	13.24%	6.62%
WACC				9.55%
WACC Estimate Used				10.0%–11.0%

Terminal Value – 8 to 9 times 1999 EBIT

EXHIBIT 10

Nesbitt Thomson's Base Case Results Estimated Value

	TOTAL VALUE		PER SHARE	
	LOW	HIGH	LOW	HIGH
	(MILLIONS)			
Present Value of Future Cash Flows	$ 576.0	$ 612.1	$ 223.89	$ 237.95
Less: Market Value of Debt	(510.2)	(510.2)	(198.31)	(198.31)
Net Value	65.8	101.9	25.58	39.64
Add: Redundant Assets	2.7	2.7	1.05	1.05
Films Division	12	12	4.67	4.67
Equity Value	$ 80.5	$ 116.6	$ 31.30	$ 45.36

EXHIBIT 11

Excerpts of the
Nesbitt Thomson Formal Valuation
of the Common Shares of Goodyear Canada Inc.

VALUATION METHODOLOGIES

This Valuation and Fairness Opinion has been prepared by Nesbitt Thomson in accordance with the requirements of Policy 9.1 and the OBCA. It is based upon the techniques and relevant assumptions that Nesbitt Thomson considers appropriate in the circumstances for the purposes of arriving at an opinion as to the range of fair market values for the Common Shares.

Nesbitt Thomson approached the valuation of the Common Shares by valuing Goodyear Canada on a going concern basis. Nesbitt Thomson concluded that liquidation or "break-up" valuation methodologies were not appropriate in the circumstances.

In Nesbitt Thomson's opinion, the most appropriate valuation approaches in valuing the Common Shares are: (1) the discounted cash flow approach; (2) a comparable

(continued)

EXHIBIT 11 (cont.)

transaction approach; and (3) a comparable companies approach. In Nesbitt Thompson's opinion, the discounted cash flow approach is the most reliable estimate of the fair market value of the Common Shares.

DISCOUNT RATE AND TERMINAL VALUE

The projected future cash flows prior to debt service but after provision for cash taxes, capital expenditures and required changes in working capital investment for the period 1992 to 1999 were discounted at the weighted average cost of capital (*WACC*) for Goodyear Canada. The *WACC* was derived with reference to the risk-free rate of return (10-year Government of Canada bonds) and our estimates of the market risk premiums with respect to the cost and relative weighting of the debt and equity components for Goodyear Canada in the context of other companies operating in the tire and rubber industry.

The terminal value at the end of the 1992 to 1999 projection was based upon a range of 8 to 9 times 1999 EBIT discounted at the *WACC* to present value.

COMPARATIVE TRANSACTION APPROACH

The resultant range for the Common Shares based on 1994 projected EBIT and the . . . EBIT multiples [shown in Exhibit 8] is significantly below the range of values resulting from the DCF analysis. The difference is explained by the anticipated future growth in pre-debt service cash flows in the late 1990s which are not reflected in this analysis but are captured in the DCF analysis. For this reason, Nesbitt Thomson does not regard this comparative transaction approach as an appropriate indicator of value and did not ascribe any weight to this approach in determining the value range of the Common Shares.

COMPARABLE COMPANIES APPROACH

Due to Goodyear Canada's current unprofitability and the high debt component in its capitalization, meaningful comparisons with these companies using current financial performance for Goodyear Canada were not possible.

VALUATION CONCLUSION

Based on and subject to all of the foregoing, Nesbitt Thomson is of the view that the fair market value of the Common Shares is in the range of $32.00 to $45.00 per share.

CONCLUSION AS TO FAIRNESS

Based upon our valuation and subject to all of the foregoing, Nesbitt Thomson is of the opinion that the terms of the Proposed Transaction are fair, from a financial point of view, to the Minority Shareholders.

37

NOTE ON THE NORTH AMERICAN TIRE INDUSTRY

There are two components to the tire industry: the original equipment market (OEM) and the replacement market. In 1989, Canadian companies manufactured roughly 27 million tires of which 30% were sold for original equipment use, with the remaining 70% going to the aftermarket.

Canadian plants produced about 9% of the tires consumed by the North American market, which, in turn, was roughly 34% of the world market for tires. U.S. plants supplied another 71% of the market and the remaining 20% was produced offshore.

The fuel shortages of the 1970s had a dramatic effect on the tire industry. Consumers began focusing on fuel efficiency and bias-ply tires were replaced by the new, longer-lasting and more fuel-efficient radial tires. Fuel efficiency also shifted demand to smaller imported cars, lessening OEM demand as well as increasing demand for foreign replacement tires in the aftermarket. North American producers lost market share.

In the 1980s, there was a worldwide restructuring in the tire industry, which resulted in five major, global tire producers. All of the significant Canadian manufacturers were now part of one of these multinational companies. The major competitors were: Goodyear Tire and Rubber Company (Goodyear U.S.); Compagnie Générale des Éstablissements Michelin (Michelin), which acquired Uniroyal

This note was prepared by D. Alasdair Turnbull under the supervision of Professor Robert W. White for the sole purpose of providing material for class discussion at the Western Business School. The text of this note is drawn largely from the **Fairness Opinion and Valuation of the Common Shares of Goodyear Canada Inc.**, dated May 13, 1992, prepared by Nesbitt Thomson Inc. for the Independent Committee of the Board of Directors of Goodyear Canada Inc.

Goodrich Tire Co. with 15 plants in Canada and the U.S.; Bridgestone Corporation, a Japanese firm that acquired The Firestone Tire & Rubber Company with 6 plants in North America; the German firm Continental Ag. which acquired 4 plants in the U.S. by buying General Tire Inc.; and the Italian-based Pirelli Group who purchased the Armstrong Tire Co. Other competitors included Sumitomo Rubber Industries who owned Dunlop Tire Corp.; Mohawk Rubber Co., owned by Yokohama Rubber Co.; and several Korean tire companies.

This consolidation came about as foreign tire manufacturers sought to acquire well-known brand names, and their market share, in the world's largest tire market: The U.S. globalization led to a need for economies of scale in manufacturing. Although the pace of consolidation slowed, competition was still intense. Tire companies competed on the basis of price, quality, warranty, service, consumer convenience, product design, performance and reputation. Research and development requirements were high and continued to increase, requiring a broad capital base to finance.

CAPACITY UTILIZATION

High levels of new automotive production in 1988 and early 1989 caused the tire industry to operate at capacity and generated backlogs of orders. Reduced demand in the OEM during the latter half of 1989 lowered capacity utilization. During all of 1990 and 1991, there was substantial excess capacity in the tire industry resulting from reduced demand by auto and truck manufacturers and a low growth rate in the replacement market.

THE MARKET

Passenger tires accounted for 77.7% of all tires sold in the U.S. in 1990. Truck tires were another 15.9% and the remaining 6.4% of sales were for farming, industrial, and motorcycle use. Passenger tires were sold either to the original equipment (OE) manufacturer market (24% of all tires sold in North America) or the replacement market.

The OE segment depended on production of high volumes in order to be profitable, given the competitive pricing demanded by OE manufacturers. To achieve long production runs which minimized cost per unit, manufacturers aimed to be the sole supplier of tires on a popular vehicle. Auto manufacturers expected high quality and competitive pricing as well as engineering excellence and consumer appeal.

Tire manufacturers worked closely with OE makers to develop products that functioned well with other elements of the vehicle such as its suspension, braking, and steering. OE tires were manufactured to the highest quality standards and were delivered on a just-in-time basis; engineering changes were done as quickly as possible. In 1992, the OE trend was for a special tire to be designed for each particular model and, on some models, for each particular position on the car.

Despite the need for extremely complex and customer-specific engineering and chemistry, pricing remained the main basis of competition among the major tire makers, particularly when demand for tires was low. Often the OE manufacturers negotiated with tire producers to pass on operating efficiencies in order to lower the cost to the OEM. Benefits of OE contracts included the ability to achieve long production runs to contribute to fixed costs, the lack of advertising or distribution expense, the ability to attract replacement demand when the original tires wore out, and the opportunity to preview vehicle specifications planned by car manufacturers.

The demand for OE tires was related to the number of vehicles assembled in North American plants. The projections in Table 1 were prepared by Goodyear U.S.

TABLE 1
PROJECTED NORTH AMERICAN AUTO SALES

	YEAR	ANNUAL NEW SALES UNITS	YEAR OVER YEAR % CHANGE
Actual	1987	11,309	
	1988	11,599	2.6
	1989	10,760	(7.2)
	1990	10,184	(5.4)
	1991	9,058	(11.1)
Estimated	1992	9,677	6.8
	1993	10,631	9.9
	1994	10,862	2.2
	1995	11,216	3.3

Jacobs, an independent forecasting and strategic planning consultant specializing in the automotive industry, identified demographic trends and the economic outlook as the key factors affecting sales of light vehicles (cars and light trucks). Demand was expected to be affected by the shift in population to age groups that tended to have high new car purchase rates. Pent-up demand for new vehicles was likely to be high following the weak industry sales since 1988. Car sales were expected to improve when the economy recovered.

Jacobs projected that overall light vehicle sales in North America would increase at an average annual growth rate of 4.0% from 1991 through 1997. The passenger car component of light vehicles was projected to grow at 5.9%, with the light truck component growing at 4.5% per annum between 1991 and 1997. Canadian light vehicle sales were estimated to increase from 1.2MM units in 1991 to 1.49MM in 1997, with 4.6% and 1.8% growth rates for cars and light trucks.

Production estimates were influenced by manufacturers' export plans, imbalances between capacity and market demand in a few key segments (e.g., minivans and sports cars) and the trend by Japanese automakers to increase the share of cars produced in U.S. plants. In particular, Canadian production forecasts were affected by cutbacks in production of specific models such as Chrysler minivans at Windsor or full-size cars at Ford in Oakville, if demand did not justify production.

Sales in the replacement market accounted for 76% of all passenger tires sold in the U.S. in 1990. Tires were sold through various channels of distribution for sale to vehicle owners for replacement purposes. The principal method of distribution was a large national network of independently owned tire dealers, franchises, and company-operated stores. Custom brand tires were also distributed through retailers such as Sears, Roebuck and Co. in the U.S. and Canadian Tire Corporation, Limited, in Canada. Sales were also made through mass merchandisers such as discount and warehouse clubs. Table 2 shows the relative sizes of these distribution channels.

The cost of servicing the replacement market was high given the need for consumer marketing and the distribution network required to service the retail customer. On the other hand, pricing was less sensitive than in the OE market although it was affected by raw materials costs and the increasing foreign competition.

TABLE 2
ESTIMATED RELATIVE VOLUME
THROUGH DISTRIBUTION CHANNELS

Tire dealerships	54%
Chain stores and department stores	18%
Tire company stores	13%
Service stations	7%
Warehouse and discount clubs	6%
Auto dealerships	1%
Miscellaneous outlets	1%
	100%

Demand for replacement tires was dictated by the number of vehicles on the road, the durability of tires, the amount and type of driving, and the fact that over the short term, tires were a deferrable expense for the motorist.

Goodyear U.S. management expected North American demand for replacement tires to grow from 201.3MM units in 1991 to 210.5MM units in 1996.

RAW MATERIALS

Synthetic and natural rubber were the main raw materials used in the production of tires. The majority of the raw material inputs used in the manufacture of synthetic rubber was derived from petrochemicals including butadiene, styrene, and carbon black. As a result, raw material pricing was linked to the supply and pricing of oil. The supply of natural rubber was directly correlated to agricultural factors such as crop size. Other inputs included steel wire, fibreglass and nylon, rayon and polyester yarn. Approximately 50% of the manufactured cost of a passenger tire was for raw materials with the remaining 50% going to labour, benefits and plant overhead.

RESEARCH AND DEVELOPMENT

The major technological change in the industry was the replacement of the bias-ply tire with the radial in the early 1980s. In 1992, radial tires accounted for almost 98% of the passenger tire market. Since the development of the radial, which required a fundamental change in the way the industry built tires, several other innovations had been introduced, such as all-season radials and high-performance tires.

Process technology had evolved in order to accommodate production of the radial tire as well as to improve quality, cost, timeliness and flexibility of production. Advances had been made in robotics and automation, raising the cost of construction of a modern tire plant. The larger companies in the industry invested between 3% and 5% of sales annually in research and development.

FREE TRADE

Canadian tariff rates for tires and tubes in 1991 were 10.7% and 10.2%, respectively. The Free Trade Agreement (FTA) will eliminate the tariffs on tires and tubes in ten equal stages ending on January 1, 1998. In the U.S., the corresponding tariffs were 4.0% for tires and 3.7% for tubes.

Tires mounted on finished vehicles traded by manufacturers under the Canada–U.S. Auto Pact or the FTA entered Canada and the U.S. duty-free as part of the vehicles. Most Canadian tire manufacturers imported tires free of duty under a duty remission program which expired in late 1992. Under the FTA, vehicles, parts, and tires exported to the United States were expected to meet a 50% North American rule of origin.

38

THE ACQUISITION OF MARTELL

New Year's Eve 1987 brought with it, in addition to festive good cheer, confrontation among three parties—two of the foremost wine and spirits companies in the world and the government of France over the fate of the prominent French Cognac producer, Martell. Grand Metropolitan plc (Grand Met) and The Seagram Company Limited were on the verge of a bidding war that neither had anticipated, and one which Martell had striven to avoid.

COGNAC

Since the rise of maritime trade during the 17th century, when shipping of "burnt" (distilled) wines proved to be more profitable than shipping bulky wine, the brandy of the Charentes district of western France on the Bay of Biscay had been renown. Though the sour, acidic white wines grown in the district's chalky soils were disagreeable to the palate, when twice distilled and aged in casks made out of Limousin oak cut from the nearby Limoges forests, Charentes white wine was transformed into golden spirits of unparalleled flavour and body. These spirits, blended and bottled locally, were known by the name of the district's principal town, Cognac.

This case was written by Ingo Walter, Professor at INSEAD, Roy C. Smith, Professor at The Stern School of Business, New York University, and Hugh Thomas, Research Assistant. It is intended to be used as a basis for class discussion rather than to illustrate either effective or ineffective handling of an administrative situation. Reprinted with the permission of INSEAD.

By the time Napoleon demonstrated preference for the brandy of Charentes by hauling casks of it around Europe on his military campaigns, purveyors of brandy throughout the western world had taken to calling their liquor "cognac." However, the ire of the Charentes distillers, expressed through the commercial policies of subsequent French governments, succeeded in limiting the use of the term. By the time of the Fifth Republic (the government of France in the mid-20th century) "cognac" was an "appellation contrôlée." The French government insisted that the word be applied only to Charentes brandy, and the world respected its wish.

In 1987, as in the 17th century, the mainstay of commerce in cognac continued to be international trade, with only 8.6% of production sold domestically in France. The United States accounted for 23.9% of sales followed by Great Britain with 12.0%, Japan with 9.9%, France with 8.6%, Germany with 7.9%, East Asia (excluding Japan) with 12.8%, and the rest of the world 24.9%. But shares were not stable. U.S. sales were volatile, being sensitive to changes in the exchange rate, but not exhibiting a noticeable trend, unlike sales of other spirits, whose consumption was in decline.

In Japan and the Far East, in contrast, sales were rising rapidly with increasing affluence. There, cognac was being increasingly regarded as a ceremonial drink of choice, consumed by the tumblerful at weddings and other celebrations, and frequently favoured as a present. Hong Kong residents were already the world's largest consumers of Cognac per capita. The ability to supply cognac was considered critical for any significant distributor of wines and spirits to the Far East.

Although in the 1980s the number of private producers of cognac still numbered in the hundreds (if one counted every farmer who operated a still), most of the 11.5 million cases of cognac shipped annually was accounted for by the large houses Hennessy (21%), Martell (19%), Courvoisier (14%) and Rémy Martin (15%).

In the mid-1980s the Cognac market had been unusually competitive. The stock to sales ratios, which had risen to 6.02 in 1986 before falling to 5.62 in 1987, still remained above their normal level of 5.0. The need for exporting firms to market and distribute worldwide had led to consolidation. Hennessy, a cognac house which dated from an 18th century Irishman who established the firm, combined with the houses of Moët et Chandon in the 1970s and Louis Vuitton in 1987. Courvoisier was bought out by Hiram Walker of the U.S., which was acquired in turn by Allied Lyons of the U.K. Rémy Martin, however, remained private with 51% in the hands of the Heriard family. Although publicly listed on the Paris stock exchange, Martell remained a family concern.

MARTELL

From 1715 to 1987, the house of Martell was largely owned and completely controlled by the members of the founding Martell family, originally merchants from the Channel Islands. However, to meet the requirements for increased capital, the firm went public on the Paris Stock Exchange in 1975. Thereafter, family ownership eroded to 41% of the shares and 57% of the voting rights. The family group comprised some 50 individuals between the ages of 18 and 95, only six of whom were actively involved in the cognac trade.

In 1987 Martell's Chairman was M. René Firino Martell, a member of the eighth generation of Martell to manage the firm. His record was mixed. Analysts gave him high marks for running the cognac business, his strong control over costs, and keeping worldwide staff down to a trim 1,387 employees. Martell's inventory of aging cognac—reportedly the industry's largest with the bulk equivalent of about 100 million bottles aging in oak casks—showed that the firm was planning to increase the proportion of older cognacs in its sales. That inventory and M. Martell's successful introduction of a new top-of-the-line cognac, XO Cordon Supreme, showed his keen insight into market trends.

Under his leadership, however, Martell had tried and failed to diversify away from spirits. The sale in 1987 of the perfumes and cosmetics subsidiary Jacomo marked the end of an attempt started in 1981–82 to penetrate the Middle Eastern market for French perfumes. Prior to and immediately after the sale, Martell's sales by product were as follows:

	FISCAL YEAR ENDED 30 JUNE	
	1986	1987
Cognac	77.3%	81.5%
Other spirits[a]	11.0%	13.4%
Pefumes and cosmetics	9.7%	0.0%
Other products[b]	2.0%	5.1%
Total	**100.0%**	**100.0%**

[a]"Other spirits" consisted primarily of Armagnac and brandies produced by subsidiaries in Mexico, Venezuela and South Africa.

[b]"Other products" primarily comprised boutique leather goods.

In 1987, Martell exported 97% of its cognac to 135 countries, with 44.4% going to other countries of the E.C. (primarily the U.K.), 30.4% to the Far East, 19% to the U.S. and 6.1% to the rest of the world. That summer, under the premise that the outlays for global distribution and marketing were beyond its capabilities, Martell entered into a marketing and distribution agreement with Grand Met, giving that firm exclusive distribution rights to Martell cognac throughout the Far East and the E.C. outside of the U.K. To consummate the alliance, Grand Met with Martell's blessing acquired 10% of Martell stock.

1987 also saw a significant change in the Martell organization. All of the cognac activities were consolidated into a newly established subsidiary, while the listed parent company became a pure holding company. Since the operating subsidiary had not remitted its dividend in the fiscal year 1987 (ending June 30), the financial statements of 1986 and 1987 were not comparable (Exhibit 1); stock market and dividend data are presented in Exhibit 2. Calculated on the same basis as in 1986, 1987 income was only $\frac{1}{2}$% below 1986 income, with losses due to the depreciation of the U.S. dollar, the Hong Kong dollar and the British pound with respect to the French franc being offset by increased sales volumes.

SEAGRAM

Seagram had its origins in the family distilling firm of Joseph E. Seagram & Sons of Waterloo, Ontario, Canada, in 1857. Its rise to maturity as a multinational corporation started in 1928, when it was acquired by Samuel Bronfman. A Russian immigrant who had successfully developed a Canadian liquor mail order business in the early 1900s, Bronfman found his business being undercut in the early 1920s as the provincial governments of Canada took over the sale of alcoholic beverages. Bronfman responded by building a distillery in 1924 at LaSalle, Quebec. His company, Distillers Corporation Limited, was expanded through the purchase in 1928 of Joseph E. Seagram & Sons and Distillers Corporation–Seagrams Limited was born. The company enjoyed a brief association with Distillers Company Limited of the U.K. but Distillers sold its shares when Samuel Bronfman turned his energies to the American market.

With five years left before the repeal of Prohibition, sales of Canadian whisky of all grades were booming. Bronfman capitalized on the demand while simultaneously emphasizing product quality and brand reputation. Moreover, confident that repeal of Prohibition was inevitable, Bronfman built up what became, by 1933, the largest stock of aged rye and bourbon whiskies in the world. Even after repeal he waited 6 months until he could be assured of marketing a quality product before moving into the virgin market. Six weeks after his entry, he commanded 60% of the U.S. market. From the 1930s through the 1980s Seagram led the U.S. whisky market.

By the time Samuel Bronfman died in 1971, Seagram had grown through export sales and acquisitions of well-known beverage producers in Europe, the U.S. and Latin America into one of the foremost spirits companies in the world. The United States, however, continued to be its main market. Seagram brands included Seven Crown, Seagrams VO, Seagrams Gin, Kessler, Paul Masson, Calvert and Chivas Regal. Together, Seagram's brands held one-fifth of the total market share in spirits.

The Bronfman family continued to own a controlling 40% of the shares of Seagram. Samuel Bronfman's sons Edgar (Chairman of the Board and Chief Executive Officer) and Charles (Co-Chairman of the Board and Chairman of the Executive Committee) were the dominant figures in the company. Institutions held a further 21% of the Seagram stock and the remainder of the shares was widely held by the general public.

Notwithstanding the diverse interests of the family, Seagram itself continued to be predominantly an alcoholic beverage company, with the notable exception of large investments in the oil, gas and chemicals industries. Since the 1960s, Seagram had acquired a reputation for diversifying in and out of those industries. As of 1988, the main legacy of that activity was a 22.9% stake in E.I. du Pont de Nemours & Co., the largest producer of chemicals in the U.S. and itself the owner of Conoco, Inc., the ninth largest American oil company. As Exhibit 3 shows, the du Pont investment accounted for about half the assets and over half of the income of Seagram in 1987.

GRAND MET

Started in 1934, Grand Met went public on the London Stock Exchange in 1962 with one hotel as its principal asset. From that base, it capitalized on good management to acquire additional quality hotels in the U.K. and Europe and expanded into related businesses of catering and building management, see Exhibit 4 for financial statement summaries.

The early 1970s saw Grand Met diversifying into brewing, pub management, distribution of wines and spirits, and gambling. Building on its expertise in the promotion of beverages, it launched what became, in one decade, the most popular liqueur in the world, Bailey's Original Irish Cream. The early 1980s saw the significant addition of Intercontinental Hotels, giving it a network of first class hotels throughout the world. Grand Met expanded in the U.S., acquiring Alpo, a large manufacturer of pet foods, and soft drink bottling facilities in South Carolina and California—major bottlers of Pepsi-Cola. In the United States, it also expanded into hospital management and day-care centre management, and, through its 1985 acquisition of Pearle Health Services and Diversified Products Corp., had become the foremost consumer optical service company and manufacturer of physical fitness and exercise equipment in the nation. It pursued further diversification into dairy products, electronics, biotechnology as well as oil and gas.

In 1987 Grand Met celebrated its 25th anniversary of stock exchange listing by reflecting on the route by which it had become the largest hotel, food, and beverage company in the U.K. For the first time, it developed its own logo to complement the many logos, trademarks and brands of its subsidiaries, products and agency relationships. Patterned on a traditional English goldsmith's hallmark, the logo consisted of three block figures in a row—a lion, a sun and an eagle symbolizing, respectively, the U.K., the international market, and the U.S. Grand Met formulated a "mission statement" identifying consumer products in the food, drink and personal services as the chosen fields of activity in which its policy for maximizing shareholder wealth would be "building brands in order to achieve good margins and sustained profitability." It re-confirmed its use of the portfolio approach to managing its companies, allowing them a considerable degree of autonomy in return for acceptable performance.

THE EVENTS OF DECEMBER 1987

The closing months of 1987 found Seagram increasingly profitable, liquid and poised to begin another round of expansion by its favoured method—acquisition. Consequently, few were surprised at the company's announcement on December 17 that it had reached an agreement to purchase from the Martell family all of their 40.1% of the shares of Martell. Through the acquisition, Seagram would bring its stake in Martell to 52%, and management indicated that it intended to buy out the remaining minority shareholders as well. In New York, Seagram's stock traded up by 12½ cents on the day to close at $57.375.

Seagram announced its intention to acquire Martell through its 93%–owned French champagne–producing subsidiary, G. H. Mumm & Co. The price for the shares from the Martell family was FF2,500 ($450) per share and the same was to be offered to other shareholders. The acquisition cost would therefore be FF1.49 billion ($250 million) to the Martell family and an additional $359 million to the minority shareholders for a total of $609 million, an amount within the capabilities of Seagram to raise on short notice. Trading in Martell shares on the Paris Bourse was suspended on December 17 at FF2,390 pending the completion of the acquisition.

The financial press speculated that Seagram's move had been precipitated by the fact that Grand Met had increased its shareholding without the Martell family's consent to 19.9% by buying shares on the open market. By law (see Exhibit 5), all foreign acquisitions of the stock of French companies in excess of 20% had to be approved by the French Ministry of Finance, and it was rumoured that Grand Met had already filed for approval.

The reaction from Grand Met was not long in coming. At its annual press conference held in London on December 17 to discuss year-end results (fiscal year ended October 31) management indicated surprise at the events of the previous day. M. Vernier-Palliez of Grand Met, attending Martell's annual meeting in Paris the same day, questioned the validity of Seagram's buy out agreement and indicated that Grand Met would make a higher offer in compliance with market procedures which required that competing bids be no less than 5% higher than previous bids. Rumours emerged that Grand Met had started lobbying with officials at the Paris Stock Exchange and the French Ministry of Finance to nullify Seagram–Martell agreement. But in Montreal, only a few hours later, Seagram's statement exuded confidence:

> We are delighted that the Martell family chose to deal with Seagram. We are very confident with our agreement and are optimistic that the French Government will approve the transaction.

Seagram declined to comment on rumours that Rémy Martin was also involved in discussions with both Seagram and Grand Met.

The next day Reuters reported that, although Seagram's action was well within the French takeover rules, the fact that most small shareholders were not consulted could prompt political pressure for the government to step in. Speculation continued through the next two weeks. On 30 December 1987 Grand Met announced that it would bid FF2,675 ($482) per share, or $665 million in total, conditional on acceptances from at least 51% of shareholders, with comparable terms to holders of convertible bonds. Grand Met indicated that it had lodged the proposal with the stock exchange authorities on 24 December, and had met on 29 December with the French takeover supervisory committee. Seagram's response reiterated its confidence in its share purchase agreement, and added:

> We continue to be hopeful that the French Government will view this agreement as positively as our two family firms (Martell and Seagram) intend it to be for the further development of the Martell business, for our employees, and for our community.

On New Year's Eve 1987, however, Reuters reported that the Paris Stock Brokers Association gave its opinion that the Seagram bid was improper, and did not respect the requirements of Article 201 of the Securities Brokers' General Regulations requiring that the brokers association must be advised of bids for purchase of the quoted firm's capital sufficient to give it control of the company. The Association stated that, despite need for official authorization for an investment from abroad, this did not mean that the transfer of a block of shares to Seagram was any different from a pure and simple direct sale, and should thus fall under rules for sale of controlling share blocks in quoted companies. Reuters noted that the Paris Stock Exchange Association had no power to block the bid, a power that rested with the Ministry of Finance.

In a public statement that day, Seagram clarified its position. It said that the transaction qualified as an exception to the "transparency" rule requiring consultation of all shareholders because of the complexity and nature of the sale. It was a foreign acquisition contingent on French government approval. Moreover, the transaction was complicated by the various classes of shares, with the shares held by the family having greater voting rights than others. Following the execution of the transaction with Martell, however, Seagram would offer to purchase the shares of all shareholders at the same price regardless of voting class. And the transaction was being carried out according to the wishes of the Martell family, which wanted a private sale to preserve unanimity of the family.

EXHIBIT 1

MARTELL
Financial Statement Summaries
Statement of Income
Years Ended June 30

	MILLIONS OF U.S. DOLLARS[a]	MILLIONS OF FRENCH FRANCS	
	1987	1987	1986
Total Operating Revenues	4.62	28.2	1,333.0
Cost of Goods Sold	0.10	0.6	463.0
Other Direct Costs	0.87	5.3	391.7
Value Added	3.65	22.3	478.3
Absorbed Taxes & Tariffs	0.00	0.0	21.7
Personnel Expenses	0.00	0.0	181.8
Amortization and Depreciation	0.28	1.7	30.5
Other Production Charges	0.13	0.8	1.3
Operating Income	3.24	19.8	243.0
Financial Income	2.51	15.3	32.2
Financial Charges	3.82	23.3	73.6
Current Period Income	1.93	11.8	201.6
Net Loss on Disposal of Assets	1.03	6.8	16.5
Profits Distributed to Employees	0.00	0.0	9.7
Profit Taxes	0.00	0.0	71.0
	0.90	5.5	104.4

[a]Translated at the June 30, 1987, rate of FF6.1055 per US$.
Source: Martell Annual Report, 1987.

EXHIBIT 1 (cont.)

MARTELL
Financial Statement Summaries
Balance Sheet
Years Ended June 30

	MILLIONS OF U.S. DOLLARS[b]	MILLIONS OF FRENCH FRANCS	
	1987	1987	1986
Goodwill	0.41	2.5	2.5
Land	0.00	0.0	6.6
Buildings (net)	4.67	28.5	113.4
Other Fixed Assets	0.00	0.0	149.6
Shareholdings	199.07	1,215.4	226.2
Other Financial Fixed Assets	0.00	0.0	8.0
Total Fixed Assets	204.14	1,246.4	506.3
Raw Materials and Provisions	0.00	0.0	856.0
Goods in Process	0.00	0.0	475.2
Merchandise	0.00	0.0	0.5
Pledged Deposits	0.00	0.0	22.3
Accounts Receivable	0.00	0.0	163.2
Other Receivables	31.89	194.7	104.7
Negotiable Securities & Cash	4.57	27.9	176.7
Total Current Assets	36.46	222.6	1,798.6
Prepaid Expenses	2.80	17.1	32.5
Total Assets	243.40	1,486.1	2,337.4
Share Capital & Issue Premium	58.21	355.4	327.4
Revaluation Discrepancy	2.06	12.6	37.8
Reserves/Regulatory Provision	118.67	724.6	704.1
Carry Forward	8.24	50.3	47.1
Income in Current Year	0.92	5.6	104.4
Total Shareholders' Equity	188.11	1,148.5	1,220.8
Provisions	1.64	10.0	26.2
Convertible Bonds	40.09	244.8	278.9
Bank Debt	2.19	13.4	528.4
Other Debt	9.02	55.1	140.6
Suppliers' Accounts & Payables	0.15	0.9	63.9
Wages Payable	2.19	13.4	78.6
Total Liabilities	53.66	327.6	1,090.4
Total Liabilities and Equity	243.40	1,486.1	2,337.4

[b]Translated at the June 30, 1987, rate of FF6.1055 per US$

Source: Martell Annual Report, 1987.

EXHIBIT 2

MARTELL
Stock Market and Dividend Data

YEAR	NUMBER OF SHARES	DIVIDENDS PER SHARE			PRICE RANGE			DIV. YIELD PER SHARE
		FINAL	INTERIM	TOTAL	HIGH	LOW	CLOSE	
1984	1,053,782	34.00	17.00	51.00	2,075	1,568	1,705	2.99%
1985	1,155,649	37.00	18.50	55.50	1,942	1,310	1,560	3.56%
1986	1,307,408	38.00	19.00	57.00	1,939	1,260	1,592	5.58%
1987	1,381,953	39.00	19.50	58.50	2,269	1,470	1,690	3.46%

Source: Martell Annual Report, 1987.

EXHIBIT 3

THE SEAGRAM COMPANY, LTD.
Financial Statement Summaries
Consolidated Income Statement
12 Months Ending Jan. 31
(US$ millions)

	1987	1986
Sales and Other Income	3,344	2,971
Costs of Goods	2,189	1,941
	1,155	1,030
Selling, General and Administration	962	815
Operating Income	193	215
Interest Expense	84	82
Income Before Income Taxes	109	133
Provision for Income Taxes	6	33
Income from Spirits and Wine Operations	103	100
Dividend Income from du Pont	151	143
Equity in Unremitted Earnings from du Pont	169	76
Net Income	423	319

Source: Seagram Annual Report, 1988.

EXHIBIT 3 (cont.)
THE SEAGRAM COMPANY, LTD.
Financial Statement Summaries
Balance Sheet
Year Ended January 31, 1987
(US$ millions)

Assets	
Cash and Short Term Investments	594
Receivables	590
Inventories	1,250
Prepaid Expenses	48
Wine Company Assets Held for Sale	220
Current Assets	2,702
Common Stock of du Pont	3,330
Note Receivable from Sun Co. Inc	51
Property, Plant and Equipment at cost	843
Accumulated Depreciation	(344)
Net Property, Plant and Equipment	499
Spirits/Wine Co.Investments and Advances	
77 Sundry Assets	228
Total Assets	6,887
Liabilities and Shareholders' Equity	
Short Term Borrowings	460
United States Excise Taxes	61
Payables and Accrued Liabilities	451
Income and Other Taxes	58
Indebtedness Payable within One Year	72
Total Current Liabilities	1,102
Long term Indebtedness	912
Deferred Income Taxes and Other Credits	882
Minority Interest	35
Total Liabilities	2,931
Shares without par value	
1988 – 94.8 million	
1987 – 95.5 million	257
Share Purchase Warrants	28
Cumulative Translation Adjustments	(228)
Retained Earnings	3,899
Total Shareholders' Equity	3,956
Total Liabilities and Shareholders' Equity	6,887

Source: Seagram Annual Report, 1988.

EXHIBIT 4

GRAND METROPOLITAN PLC
Financial Statement Summaries
Statement of Income
Years Ended 30 September

	MILLIONS OF U.S. DOLLARS	MILLIONS OF BRITISH POUNDS	
	1987[a]	1987	1986
Turnover	9,298.3	5,705.5	5,291.3
Trading Profit	931.5	571.6	487.4
Reorganization Costs	15.2	9.3	27.1
Interest Expense	195.9	120.2	101.3
Loss (Profit) on Property Sales	−22.8	−14.0	−8.7
	743.3	456.10	367.70
Tax	195.7	120.1	91.8
Minority Interests	3.7	2.3	2.3
Loss (gain) on Extraordinary Items	−208.3	−127.8	11.7
Net Profit	752.1	461.50	261.90
Ordinary Dividends	168.0	103.1	87.5
Preferred Dividends	0.8	0.5	0.5
Retained Profit	583.3	357.90	173.90
Profits Brought Forward	2,618.1	1,606.5	1,566.6
Plus Gain (−loss) on Forex Translation	−36.5	−22.4	34.5
Net Premium on Share Issues	9.8	6.0	7.8
Minus Goodwill Acquired	−1,062.2	−651.8	−137.7
Minus Bond Issue Capitalized Reserves	0.0	0.0	−38.6
Profits Carried Forward	2,112.4	1,296.2	1,606.5

[a]Translated at rate on September 30, 1987, US$1.6297 per pound sterling.

Source: Grand Metropolitan plc Annual Report, 1986 Moody's International Manual, 1988.

EXHIBIT 4 (cont.)

GRAND METROPOLITAN PLC
Financial Statement Summaries
Balance Sheet
Years Ended 30 September

	MILLIONS OF U.S. DOLLARS	MILLIONS OF BRITISH POUNDS	
	1987[b]	1987	1986
Tangible Assets	4,441.3	2,725.2	2,625.7
Investments	288.8	177.2	129.8
Total Fixed Assets	4,730.0	2,902.4	2,755.5
Stocks	1,195.7	733.7	646.3
Debtors	1,348.6	827.5	731.4
Cash At Banks	184.8	113.4	88.0
Total Current Assets	2,729.1	1,674.6	1,465.7
Less Creditors—Amounts Due in 1 Year			
Borrowings	537.3	329.7	270.0
Other Creditors	1,900.7	1,166.3	979.7
Total Current Liabilities	2,438.0	1,496.0	1,249.7
Net Current Assets	291.1	178.6	216.0
Total Assets Less Current Liabilities	5,021.1	3,081.0	2,971.5
Borrowings	1,861.0	1,141.9	750.8
Other Creditors	168.3	103.3	104.7
Total Creditors: non-current	2,029.3	1,245.2	855.5
Provisions For Liabilities & Charges	114.7	70.4	43.9
Net Assets	2,877.1	1,765.4	2,072.1
Share Capital	718.5	440.9	439.0
Profits Carried Forward	2,112.4	1,296.2	1,606.5
Minority Shareholders' Interest	46.1	28.3	26.6
Total Equity	2,877.1	1,765.4	2,072.1

[b]Translated at rate on September 30, 1987, US$1.6297 per pound sterling.
Source: Grand Metropolitan plc Annual Report, 1986 Moody's International Manual, 1988.

EXHIBIT 5

Mergers and Acquisitions in France

France has come a long distance in relaxing controls over M&A deals, even by foreigners, away from the hopeless difficulties of the 1970s in overcoming often opaque government objections. France has had relatively few explicit barriers to cross-border M&A transactions, with French companies and investment banks among the most active in Europe in M&A deals. In 1987 there were 915 domestic M&A transactions in France worth over about $27 billion, with 156 French acquisitions ($5 billion) by foreign buyers and 196 foreign acquisitions ($8.3 billion) by French buyers.

Ministry of Finance approval is required for non-E.C. bids exceeding 20% of the target company—which is also the limit for non-E.C. ownership of French newspapers—and such bids can be squelched assuming the Ministry can find a matching French bid. The Ministry approval requirement has evidently discouraged many bids. Moreover, many corporate capital structures in France include multiple voting rights and cross-shareholdings or stock purchase options involving friendly interests; the shares of only about 15% of the 1,397 companies quoted on the Paris Bourse in 1988 were actively traded.

Government initiatives have included abolition of concentrated voting rights, mandatory declaration of intentions by anyone with at least a 5% stake in a French company and repeated declarations at the 10%, 20%, 33% and 50% levels, as well as a mandatory tender for all capital of a takeover target that is at least 50% owned. Symptoms of residual barriers to takeover activity are exclusion of French subsidiaries of Rowntree on antitrust grounds in Nestlé's acquisition of the firm in 1988, and government involvement in convincing Peugeot to drop a French auto-parts supplier, Epeda, after it became a de Benedetti target (a French group including Peugeot later bought the firm). Some observers suggest that France will throw up some of the most serious government obstacles to individual crossborder M&A transactions and try to micro-manage domestic ones in the future.

Continued French government interventionism in M&A transactions can perhaps be illustrated by the case of Société Générale, a major bank that was privatized in 1987 under the conservative government of Prime Minister Jacques Chirac, with large shareholdings purchased by political supporters of the government. Following accession to power of the Socialists in 1988, what appears to have been a politically-motivated hostile takeover attempt was initiated by a group led by Georges Pébereau (former head of several large state-owned companies), and backed by the Caisse des Dépôts et Consignations, a state financial institution that already had a significant stake in Société Générale, the effort was interpreted in some quarters as back-door-re-nationalization, in part because it was reported to be overtly supported by Pierre Bérégovoy, the French Finance Minister.

Following a bitter battle, the 10.4% Pébereau stake was sold at a profit of some $100 million to several large institutions. The result was that state-controlled institutions (the Caisse des Dépôts and Rhône-Poulenc) held a combined 22.2% stake, several private-sector institutions (including British and Japanese insurance companies) held 32.5%, the bank's employees held 14.4%, and the general public held 30.9%. The episode was not helpful in clarifying French government policy on M&A procedures, other than to note that the government remains an active observer, and sometimes an active participant, in transactions.

Source: Ingo Walter and Roy C. Smith, *Investment Banking in Europe After 1992* (Oxford: Basil Blackwell, 1989).

39

BLUE JAY ENERGY & CHEMICAL CORPORATION

On February 4, 1988, the Blue Jay Energy & Chemical Corporation's (Blue Jay) President was faced with the most critical decision of his short and highly successful tenure as President and CEO. Only four days had passed since Blue Jay had learned of Calgary-based Eagle Corp.'s $14 per share tender offer for 13 million Blue Jay shares which, if successful, would raise Eagle's voting interest in Blue Jay from 9.7% to 25%. While Eagle's offer represented a 13% premium over Blue Jay's current trading price, Blue Jay's President considered the bid "grossly inadequate" based upon his belief that despite Blue Jay's outstanding recent performance, the company's stock was undervalued on the market. This opinion was supported by the findings of Blue Jay's financial advisor who had estimated Blue Jay's net asset value to be 60–85% higher than its trading price. With Eagle's tender offer set to take place on the Toronto, Montreal and Vancouver stock exchanges on February 22, 1988, Blue Jay's President had little time to devise a defense plan.

Given the undervalued state of Blue Jay stock and the logical strategic fit between the two companies, it was clear that Eagle's offer represented the beginning of a hostile takeover attempt. Blue Jay's financial advisor had provided Blue Jay's President with several viable alternatives which would serve to protect shareholder interests by realizing the full value of the firm. It was now up to Blue Jay's President to decide which alternative would best respond to the Eagle threat.

BACKGROUND ON THE COMPANY

Blue Jay was an integrated petrochemical and petroleum company with an established multinational presence in the production of primary, intermediate and related downstream petrochemicals through Bluebird Limited (wholly owned subsidiary), while maintaining significant operations in the oil, gas and sulphur industries in Canada through Starling Energy Limited (wholly owned subsidiary). An illustration of Blue Jay's corporate organization can be seen in Exhibit 1.

Blue Jay was established in 1971 as the investment arm of the federal government. Through the years, Blue Jay's diverse portfolio came to include interests in petrochemicals, oil and gas, office and industrial automation, venture capital, fishery products and mining. The result of this amalgamation of business interests was a corporate debt level which peaked in 1982 at $4.5 billion and a consistently poor reputation among investors as reflected in the company's stock performance.

When Blue Jay's President joined the company in 1986, he brought with him a new strategic outlook for Blue Jay:

> The strategy we adopted in mid-1986 was to refocus the Company on two core businesses—petrochemicals and petroleum—and sell the rest.

The divestiture of non-contributing assets combined with buoyant prices for the company's petrochemical commodities resulted in an impressive revitalization of the company's financial position. By the end of 1987, Blue Jay had reduced its debt by over $2 billion and had seen dramatic improvements in cash flow and earnings relative to 1986. In 1987, Blue Jay's consolidated revenue and net income were $2.868 billion and $178.1 million, respectively, whereas in 1986, revenue was $2.604 billion with a net loss of $353.8 million. This turnaround earned rave reviews from analysts who referred to Blue Jay's management as "one of the best management teams in the country."

BLUE JAY'S CORE BUSINESSES

Bluebird

Bluebird was an international petrochemical company engaged in the manufacture and sale of basic petrochemicals as well as intermediate and downstream petrochemicals including synthetic rubbers and plastics. It operated through three major divisions: the Basic Petrochemicals Division (BPD), the Global Rubber Division (GRD) and the Plastics Division (PD).

BPD operated a major petrochemical plant in Corunna, Ontario, where it produced ethylene, propylene and butadiene. It also operated a styrene production facility at Sarnia, Ontario. BPD was the second largest Canadian producer of ethylene and styrene and the largest Canadian supplier of propylene. Forty percent of the division's output was consumed by other Blue Jay divisions and a substantial portion of the remaining ethylene production was sold to DuPont Canada and Eagle under long term contracts.

Bluebird, through its GRD, was the largest producer of synthetic rubber in the world. It manufactured both specialty and general purpose rubbers, with a business strategy aimed at increasing production of high margin specialty products. GRD was the world's leading producer of bromobutyl rubber, a high margin product used in radial tires, and the leading producer of nitrile rubber. In general purpose rubbers, GRD was the world's second largest producer of polybutadiene rubber, a commodity product used in tire treads.

Bluebird's PD was a major supplier of polystyrene resin in North America, with a 15% market share. This business was based principally on the former U.S. polystyrene operations of the Monsanto Company, acquired in 1986.

In addition to strong cash flow generation ($265 million in 1987 on sales of $2.4 billion), which was expected to continue as commodity prices remain high, and a tax pool in excess of $1 billion, Blue Jay's petrochemical division also had a tradition of research excellence and product development. Its R&D staff exceeded 400 persons and its budget was among the highest in Canada. As well, the division was well-positioned in an increasingly global chemical industry with plants in five countries.

Starling Energy Ltd.

Starling was a major Canadian producer of oil, gas and sulphur and was involved primarily in the exploration for and the production and marketing of conventional crude oil, natural gas liquids, natural gas and sulphur in Western Canada. Starling was one of the top fifteen crude oil producers in Canada and marketed a portion of its production of crude oil and natural gas to Bluebird for use in the production of petrochemicals. Starling was also Canada's second largest producer and the largest supplier and marketer of sulphur.

In 1987, the operations of Starling were affected by the continued weakness in the world's sulphur market that resulted in reduced selling prices and volumes sold during the year. In addition, Starling substantially reduced the level of its expenditures on oil and natural gas exploration and development. However, Starling had an excellent year in expanding its asset base, replacing all of its 1987 production of oil and natural gas through successful exploration programs and enhanced recovery efforts. As well, Starling made further progress in improving its long term financial position by reducing its debt by $397 million in 1987. In 1987, Starling's revenues and net income were $173.8 million and $15.8 million, respectively. This compares favourably to 1986 figures when revenues were $159.1 million with a net loss of $377.7 million.

A complete summary of the financial performance of Blue Jay and its component business units can be found in Exhibits 2, 3 and 4.

Eagle Corporation of Alberta

Eagle was a major Canadian energy corporation whose operations were conducted primarily in Canada and whose products and services were marketed on a worldwide basis. Eagle's companies, which employed over 7,100 people, were active in petrochemicals, gas transportation and marketing, petroleum, manufacturing and consulting, and research.

Eagle's bid to purchase 13 million shares of Blue Jay came several months after Eagle had initiated discussions with Blue Jay to investigate the possibility of acquiring Blue Jay's petrochemical divisions. Such an acquisition, according to Eagle's chairman, would "make us very strong in the free trade arena," since Blue Jay was one of the few Canadian chemical companies with a multinational presence. Eagle's 1986 and 1987 financial statements can be found in Exhibits 5 and 6.

BLUE JAY'S NET ASSET VALUE

Blue Jay's relationship with its financial advisor dates back to 1986 when the advisor was retained by Blue Jay to aid in the compnay's divestiture program. It was at this time that the advisor's analysis identified the extent to which Blue Jay's shares were underpriced. According to the financial advisor's valuation, Blue Jay's common shares still remained significantly undervalued despite the operating improvements and strong relative share price performance that were achieved in 1986 and 1987. This valuation provided trading values for Bluebird and Starling as separate entities, based on the trading levels of comparable companies, and indicated that Blue Jay's net asset value exceeded its recent share price by approximately 60 to 85% (see Exhibit 7). Thus, Blue Jay as a holding company was trading at a substantial discount to the sum of its parts. Such undervaluation clearly made the company an attractive candidate for restructuring in order to realize the value of the company's underlying assets. More importantly though, this undervaluation made Blue Jay an excellent takeover candidate.

Bluebird

Blue Jay's financial advisor estimated that the fully distributed trading value of Blue Jay's petrochemical assets was $900 to $1,050 million, based on a 6.5 to 7.5 P/E multiple. This multiple reflected the trading levels of comparable companies in the industry, and projected a 1988 net income of $140 million. The trading multiple, which was actually lower than industry comparables, had been adjusted by the advisor to reflect the compnay's relatively high financial leverage and to recognize that the company's 1988 forecasts were based on the expectation of unusually high commodity prices. Exhibit 8 shows market and financial statistics of comparable chemical companies.

Starling

Oil companies generally trade on their projected cash flow from operations, rather than estimated earnings. Therefore, the financial advisor's estimated fully distributed trading value for Starling of $450 to $550 million was based on a 3 to 4 multiple of 1988 projected cash flow from operations (implied by the trading levels of comparable companies; see Exhibit 9). Due to Starling's high degree of leverage, the company's common shares, in effect, represented a leveraged play on the possibility of higher oil prices. In this way, Starling's shares had a significant element of warrant value.

As well, the advisor believed that the acquisition value of Starling would be significantly lower than its trading value due to limitations on the universe of potential purchasers imposed by the Investment Canada regulation concerning the oil and gas industry. In addition, the large amount of debt that a purchaser would be required to assume would also negatively affect any acquisition price. It was the opinion of the financial advisor that these impediments to achieving full value for Starling's assets were exacerbated by the fact that Starling was part of a larger holding company. Therefore, the highest value for Starling was thought to be in the public market. However, "maintenance of ownership" debt covenants required Blue Jay to own more than 50% of Starling's common shares.

POSSIBLE REASONS FOR UNDERVALUATION

A number of Canadian research analysts had proposed reasons for Blue Jay's undervaluation:

> A troubled history has led to numerous disappointments and market scepticism towards pronouncements of a recovery. *Canadian Research*

> In the past, Blue Jay has traded at the large discount to net asset value due to (a) a diverse and complex conglomerate (i.e., "Holding Company Discount"), (b) a large corporate debt load, (c) subsidiaries had difficult industry conditions (Starling). *Canadian Research*

> The company deserves a new group of analysts as an integrated oil or chemical company and a market revaluation to the earnings multiples such companies now receive. *First Marathon*

> The stock has been hit in the past by low commodity prices, high interest rates and a strong U.S. dollar. All these factors are now positive. *First Marathon*

Another possible reason for the undervaluation was simply that the market had not yet fully recognized the substantial improvement in Blue Jay's financial performance.

In addition, while oil companies generally trade on their projected cash flow from operations, chemical companies tend to trade on their projected earnings.

Starling has strong cash flow but negative net income. To the extent that Blue Jay tends to be valued on its earnings, the $450–550 million estimated trading value of Starling may not even be reflected in its parent's (Blue Jay) market valuation.

ALTERNATIVE RESPONSES TO EAGLE'S TENDER BID

Blue Jay and its advisors had devised a number of alternative plans to increase shareholder value by realizing the full value of Blue Jay's assets, when Eagle announced its tender bid. Given the estimated value of the company (see Exhibit 7), it was clear that Blue Jay's President could not recommend Eagle's $14 tender offer as being in the shareholders' best interests.

Blue Jay's President, officers and investment bankers reviewed a wide range of alternatives to induce shareholders to reject Eagle's bid as inadequate and to increase Blue Jay's value in the marketplace. Blue Jay had several options: do nothing and rely on federal government ownership restrictions to prevent Eagle from eventually gaining control; request its investment bank to search for a "white knight" to thwart Eagle's bid; try to increase shareholder value (push Blue Jay's stock price over the Eagle bid) by a spin-off plan; or increase shareholder value by a recapitalization plan.

Do Nothing

Blue Jay possessed an inherent "poison pill." Upon selling Blue Jay to the private sector, the Canadian government restricted the voting ownership in Blue Jay by a single shareholder to 25%. If this restriction was breached, the Blue Jay board had the right to remove the holder's rights and the entitlement to dividends. Thus, effectively, transfer of the ownership of Blue Jay could occur only through an asset sale, approved by the Blue Jay board.

While this by-law would make complete acquisition of Blue Jay by Eagle or anyone else difficult without a long fight with both Blue Jay and the federal government, Blue Jay's President did not eagerly support this alternative. Relying on the poison pill did nothing to generate value for his shareholders and did not release the true value of the firm as estimated by Blue Jay's investment bankers.

White Knight

Blue Jay's President, with the advice of the investment bank, could provide shareholders with an alternative offer by seeking a white knight—a fair and friendly competing tender offer. A friendly white knight that agreed with the valuation could enter the arena with a tender bid higher than Eagle's, thereby thwarting Eagle's "hostile" takeover attempt.

Although the extent of Blue Jay's undervaluation seemed to make the search for a white knight easy, no obvious white knight existed. Selling Blue Jay as one piece would not be easy. Blue Jay consisted of many diverse businesses. Bluebird (Petro-Chemicals) was a highly attractive acquisition candidate. However, the highly leveraged Starling was far less attractive. In addition, restrictions by Investment

Canada on the sale of Canadian Oil & Gas interests (Starling) added to the potential difficulty. Blue Jay's President and investment bank were confident that a white knight could eventually be found; the problem was one of timing. Blue Jay was not sure if an acceptable white knight could be found and in place before the February 22 deadline.

Spin-Off Alternative

The spin-off alternative was designed by Blue Jay's investment bank to create value for Blue Jay shareholders by making Bluebird (PetroChemicals) and Starling separate publicly traded companies, thereby reducing the "holding company" discount. Bluebird would trade on the basis of its projected net income, which would not be reduced by consolidation with Starling's losses. On the other hand, Starling would trade on the basis of its projected cash flow.

In the spin-off alternative, Blue Jay would distribute its Bluebird (PetroChemicals) shares directly to its shareholders, leaving Starling as its remaining asset. The alternative form of spin-off (i.e., distributing Starling) was made impossible because of Starling debt covenants that required that Blue Jay retain control. The spin-off would also involve a series of cash transfers within the company. Prior to the spin-off, $55 million of the $425 million of proceeds from the sale of Blue Jay's latex business (sold to BASF as part of Blue Jay's earlier divestiture program) would be used to pay down Bluebird's long term debt, while the remaining $370 million would be dividended up to Blue Jay.

In addition, some of Blue Jay's corporate obligations would need to be eliminated, since Starling's projected cash flows would be insufficient to service such obligations. Therefore, $125 million of 1983 Preferred Shares (Blue Jay) would be tendered for retirement with $135 million of the $370 million dividended up to Blue Jay. In addition, $300 million of Blue Jay's 1980 Preferred Shares would be called for conversion into additional Blue Jay shares.

The remaining $235 million of net proceeds from the sale of the latex business would be distributed to Blue Jay's shareholders as a special one-time cash payment. Blue Jay's investment banker's total estimated initial value for this alternative was $16.00–20.00 per share. Exhibit 10 shows the transaction diagram for the spin-off alternative. Exhibit 11 provides a pro forma financial impact of the transaction.

The Recapitalization (Recap) Alternative

The recap alternative was designed to create value for Blue Jay's shareholders by making Starling a publicly traded company, and by highlighting the substantial debt capacity of Bluebird. Blue Jay would be viewed as a highly leveraged petrochemical company with a significant investment in the oil company. Such recapitalized companies tend to trade primarily on the basis of cash flow rather than earnings.

Under the recap, Blue Jay would distribute to shareholders the following:

- 49% of its shares in Starling, this percentage being limited by Starling debt covenants that require Blue Jay to retain control of Starling (one share of Starling per Blue Jay share).

- a one-time cash payment of $370 million, funded by the $425 million of net proceeds from the sale of Blue Jay's Latex business.
- proceeds from $130 million of Floating Rate Notes, with a five-year maturity.
- proceeds from $240 million of zero coupon preferred shares (i.e., deferred preferreds) of Blue Jay. This preferred stock, due in 1993, was intended to further leverage Blue Jay's common stock without requiring cash payments for the first five years.

According to the analysis of Blue Jay's investment banker, the total value of this recapitalization to Blue Jay shareholders would fall between $17.00 and $20.50 per share. Exhibit 12 shows a transaction diagram for the recapitalization alternative. Exhibit 13 presents the pro forma financial impact of the alternative.

THE DECISION

As Blue Jay's President examined his alternatives in the face of Eagle's $14 tender offer for 25% of Blue Jay, he knew that he had only a day or two to choose the most appropriate one. Blue Jay's President was convinced of Blue Jay's true value and was determined to realize that value for Blue Jay's shareholders. However, he was concerned that the Canadian marketplace might be slow to react to either the spin-off or recapitalization alternatives. While Blue Jay's investment bank had successfully executed several of these complex restructurings in the United States, Blue Jay would be the first Canadian firm to restructure in this manner.

EXHIBIT 1

BLUE JAY ENERGY & CHEMICAL CORPORATION
Corporate Organization

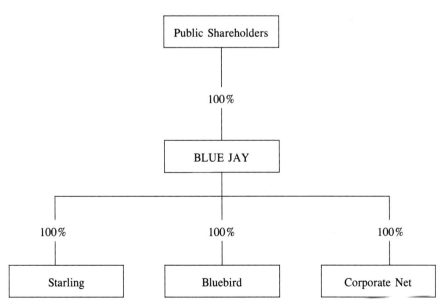

EXHIBIT 2

BLUE JAY ENERGY & CHEMICAL CORPORATION
Consolidated Statement of Income
For Years Ending December 31
(millions of dollars)

	1987	1986	1985
Revenue	$2,868.5	$2,604.7	$2,935.8
Expenses			
Cost & expenses before the undernoted	2,131.6	1,979.0	2,213.1
Depreciation, depletion & amortization	280.0	313.2	280.0
Write-down of property, plant & equipment	—	304.7	—
Interest on long term debt	231.8	312.2	299.7
Other interest	12.4	2.6	31.7
	2,655.8	2,911.7	2,824.5
Income (loss) before the following	212.7	(307.0)	111.3
Income taxes	(76.2)	80.9	(35.2)
Minority interest	(17.2)	(10.6)	(18.3)
Income (loss) from operations	119.3	(236.7)	57.8
Equity in earnings of discontinued operations	0.7	(70.9)	(25.8)
Non-recurring items	107.5	10.8	127.2
Net income (loss)	227.5	(296.8)	159.2
Preferred share dividends	(49.4)	(57.0)	(53.1)
Net income (loss) applicable to common shares	$ 178.1	$ (353.8)	$ 106.1
Per common share			
Income (loss) from operations	$ 1.33	$ (7.73)	$ 0.13
Net income (loss)	$ 3.39	$ (9.31)	$ 2.86

EXHIBIT 3

BLUE JAY ENERGY & CHEMICAL CORPORATION
Consolidated Balance Sheet
As at December 31
(millions of dollars)

	1987	1986	1985
Assets			
Current Assets			
Cash and short term investments	$ 54.1	$ 165.5	$ 70.1
Accounts receivable	510.6	521.7	699.5
Inventories	377.5	359.8	469.0
Other current assets	16.1	11.9	10.0
	958.3	1,058.9	1,249.1
Long Term Investments	245.1	658.8	997.5
Property, Plant & Equipment	3,998.7	4,065.0	4,362.3
Other Assets	243.8	458.9	514.9
	$5,445.9	$6,241.6	$7,123.8
Liabilities			
Current Liabilities			
Short term loans	$ 165.7	$ 162.1	$ 306.3
Accounts payable and accrued liabilities	452.8	368.8	410.4
Long term debt due within one year	144.0	105.4	142.7
	762.5	636.3	859.4
Long Term Debt	2,624.5	3,750.7	3,883.3
Deferred Income Taxes	396.0	254.8	314.9
Interests of Minority Shareholders	268.9	495.3	590.5
	4,051.9	5,137.1	5,648.1
Shareholders' Equity			
Capital Stock			
Preferred	628.5	721.2	765.3
Common	586.8	381.2	352.5
Retained Earnings	178.7	2.1	357.9
	1,394.0	1,104.5	1,475.7
Total Liabilities and Shareholders' Equity	$5,445.9	$6,241.6	$7,123.8

EXHIBIT 4

BLUE JAY ENERGY & CHEMICAL CORPORATION
Summary of Operations by Division
For Years Ending December 31
(millions of dollars, except per share amounts)

	1987	1986	1985	1984	1983
BLUE JAY CO.					
Revenues	$2,868.5	$2,604.7	$2,935.8	$2,790.3	$2,591.5
Total Assets	5,445.9	6,241.6	7,123.8	7,188.3	6,409.7
Total long term debt and redeemable preferred shares	3,665.3	5,054.8	5,348.3	5,484.18	5,331.8
Free cash flow from operations	378.0	186.3	228.8	164.3	102.1
Net income (loss)	227.5	(296.8)	159.2	56.2	(48.7)
Per common share	3.39	(9.31)	2.86	0.29	(2.51)
Fully diluted	2.64	(9.31)	1.99	0.29	(2.51)
BLUEBIRD CO.					
Revenues	$2,464.0	$2,047.6	$2,193.6	$2,218.4	$2,112.3
Total Assets	2,369.9	2,386.3	2,431.2	2,368.4	2,308.7
Total long term debt and redeemable preferred shares	1,287.3	1,637.7	1,572.1	1,365.2	1,331.3
Free cash flow from operations	301.5	89.8	17.4	26.4	11.5
Net income	167.4	18.6	(10.2)	26.3	9.0
Contribution to Blue Jay net income (loss)	172.4	13.0	(17.0)	19.2	2.1
STARLING CO.					
Revenues	$ 452.0	$ 556.6	$ 766.5	$ 628.7	$ 547.0
Total assets	2,922.5	3,278.2	3,748.7	3,458.3	3,180.5
Total long term debt	1,918.7	2,316.0	2,353.5	2,360.0	2,215.2
Free cash flow from operations	119.3	176.3	312.9	181.3	133.1
Net income (loss)					
Before write-down	15.8	(22.2)	85.4	26.1	21.1
Write-down of assets	—	(355.5)	—	—	—
Contribution to Blue Jay net income (loss)					
Before write-down	(17.8)	(10.7)	94.7	30.7	15.7
Write-down of property, plant and equipment	—	(218.0)	—	—	—

EXHIBIT 5
EAGLE CO.
Consolidated Balance Sheet
(thousands of dollars)

| | DECEMBER 31 | |
	1987	1986
Assets		
Current Assets		
Cash and short term deposits	$ 74,207	$ 48,407
Funds on deposit	–	138,050
Receivables	405,449	300,428
Inventories	117,354	110,441
Asset held for sale	–	358,998
Prepaid expenses	8,004	6,931
	605,014	963,255
Long Term Investments	768,308	505,318
Plant Property and Equipment	4,455,908	4,282,265
Less accumulated depreciation and depletion	1,227,425	1,064,734
	3,228,483	3,217,531
Other Assets	83,943	76,848
Total	$4,685,748	$4,762,952
Liabilities and Common Shareholders' Equity		
Current Liabilities		
Bank loans	$ 72,163	$ 76,986
16¼% Unsecured debentures	–	138,050
Accounts payable and accrued liabilities	342,879	312,361
Income taxes payable	4,044	6,022
Dividends payable	29,813	35,186
Long term debt instalments due within one year	76,290	69,884
	525,189	638,489
Long Term Debt	2,358,941	2,390,999
Deferred Income Taxes	103,532	53,583
Deferred Gain	52,879	57,535
Interest of Others in Subsidiaries	13,502	146,731
Preferred Shares – Redeemable	328,908	826,908
Convertible Debentures	150,000	–
Common Shareholders' Equity	1,152,797	648,707
Total	$4,685,748	$4,762,952

EXHIBIT 6

EAGLE CO.

Consolidated Statement of Income

(thousands of dollars, except for share data)

	YEAR ENDED DECEMBER 31		
	1987	1986	1985
Revenue	$2,322,438	$2,680,966	$3,347,236
Operating Costs and Expenses			
Operating expenses	1,603,201	1,819,347	2,288,419
Depreciation and depletion	178,071	292,544	310,180
Petroleum and gas revenue tax	–	(25,620)	52,903
Loss on foreign currency translation	12,968	21,474	22,162
	1,794,240	2,107,745	2,673,664
Operating Income	528,198	573,221	673,572
Other Income (Deductions)			
Interest expense	(242,729)	(284,292)	(315,915)
Allowance for funds used during construction	2,501	3,480	3,171
Equity in earnings (losses) of affiliates	12,789	(15,204)	(7,235)
Loss on investments	(18,146)	(30,125)	–
Miscellaneous income and other (deductions)	(13,410)	(14,312)	1,921
	(258,995)	(340,453)	(318,058)
Income Before Income Taxes, Interest of Others in Income of Subsidiaries and Extraordinary Items	269,203	232,768	355,514
Income Taxes	(74,341)	(61,614)	(155,892)
Interest of Others in Income of Subsidiaries	(15,732)	(63,157)	(65,511)
Income Before Extraordinary Items	179,130	107,997	134,111
Extraordinary Items	–	(7,800)	(216,522)
Net Income (Loss)	179,130	100,197	(82,411)
Less Preferred Share Dividend Entitlement	49,296	84,071	85,511
Net Income (Loss) to Common Shareholders	$ 129,834	$ 16,136	$ (167,922)
Average Common Shares Outstanding (Thousands)	185,321	134,655	128,087
Net Income (Loss) Per Common Share			
Before extraordinary items			
Basic	$ 0.70	$ 0.18	$ 0.38
Fully diluted	$ 0.67	$ 0.17	$ 0.38
After extraordinary items			
Basic	$ 0.70	$ 0.12	$ (1.31)
Fully diluted	$ 0.67	$ 0.12	$ (1.31)

EXHIBIT 7

Blue Jay Net Asset Valuation: Risks and Opportunities

	AMOUNT	PER SHARE
Bluebird[a]	$900–1,050	$11.17–13.04
Starling	450–550	5.59–6.83
Cash from Latex Sale[b]	370	4.59
Corporate, Net[c]	(125)	(1.55)
Illustrative Net Asset Value	$1.595–1.845	$19.80–22.91
Current Trading Value[d]	$997	$12.38

[a]Assuming the conversion of the $300 million of 1980 Preferred Shares and 80.55 million shares outstanding.

[b]Assumes $55 million of the $425 million net proceeds from the sale of the Latex business are used to pay down Bluebird debt.

[c]Assumes that corporate assets equal corporate liabilities.

[d]Share price as of 1/29/88 times 80.55 million shares outstanding.

EXHIBIT 8

Market and Financial Statistics of Selected Chemical Companies (1)
(US$, except Canadian firms)

	MARKET VALUE ($ MM)	P/E MULTIPLE			PRICE/CASH FLOW		MKT CAP/ EBDIT	PRICE/ BOOK	PRICE/ NET PP&E	TOTAL/ DEBT ADJUSTED BOOK CAP (5)	TOTAL/ DEBT CURRENT MARKET CAP (6)	CURRENT DIVIDEND YIELD (7)	MOODY'S/ S&P RATINGS (14)
		LTM	1987(E) (2)	1986(E) (2)	LTM	1987(E) (3)							
CONGLOMERATES													
Dow Chemical	16,281	20.1x	17.5x	14.3x	9.0x	8.1x	8.2x	3.0x	3.0x	43.5%	20.2%	2.6%	A2/A
Du Pont	27,688	17.9	15.9	13.7	6.1	5.6	6.0	2.0	1.8	28.5%	16.4%	2.8%	Aa1/AA
Monsanto	6,465	14.3	14.1	12.2	6.1	5.8	5.3	1.6	2.2	35.6%	25.3%	3.4%	A1/A
Olin Corp.	1,238	17.0	16.0	12.8	6.1	5.7	6.5	1.6	1.7	36.7%	26.0%	3.1%	NR/NR
Average		17.3x	15.9x	13.2x	6.8x	6.3x	6.5x	2.1x	2.2x	36.1%	22.0%	3.0%	
INTERMEDIATES													
Rohm & Haas	3,285	20.9x	17.6x	15.1x	14.7x	12.8x	10.0x	3.2x	5.1x	27.4%	10.7%	1.7%	A1/A
Reichhold	301	16.0	16.5	12.5	9.1	8.9	6.2	1.5	1.5	37.0%	28.4%	2.0%	Baa3/NR
Dexter	638	17.1	16.6	14.6	8.9	8.5	8.4	2.4	3.7	37.5%	20.1%	2.3%	A2/A
Ethyl Corp.	3,751	19.8	19.3	16.8	12.4	11.9	9.6	4.1	6.3	36.0%	12.1%	1.3%	A2/BBB+
Witco	935	14.2	13.2	12.0	7.4	6.9	6.5	2.0	2.5	34.1%	20.9%	2.7%	A2/A
Average		17.6x	16.7x	14.2x	10.5x	9.8x	8.1x	2.6x	3.8x	34.4%	18.4%	2.0%	
BASIC PETROCHEMICALS													
National Distillers	2,130	19.8x	17.7x	12.5x	10.7x	9.7x	12.8x	2.0x	1.5x	52.6%	35.3%	3.3%	Baa2/BBB
Himount (15)	2,922	30.0	16.3	13.7	16.8	11.2	13.6	6.5	7.7	21.0%	3.9%	0.4%	NR/NR
Aristech	741	15.2	12.6	9.9	9.0	8.5	6.0	2.3	2.6	15.6%	7.5%	0.6%	NR/NR
Average		21.7x	15.5x	12.0x	12.1x	9.8x	10.8x	3.6x	3.9x	29.7%	15.6%	1.4%	
LEVERAGED FIRMS													
Union Carbide	3,799	24.0x	12.8x	9.7x	4.3x	3.6x	6.2x	3.5x	0.9x	78.3%	50.7%	5.0%	Baa3/BB+
FMC (11)	1,745	11.5	18.9	13.7	4.2	4.7	2.3	NM	1.3	136.9%	50.3%	0.0%	Ba2/BB
Vista (12)	495	12.2	14.3	10.7	5.1	5.2	5.0	4.0	1.8	65.3%	31.9%	0.0%	NR/NR
Georgia Gulf	500	12.4	11.8	N/A	6.8	6.4	5.7	6.4	4.2	56.5%	16.9%	0.0%	NR/NR
Average		15.0x	14.5x	11.4x	5.1x	5.0x	4.8x	4.6x	2.0x	84.2%	37.4%	5.0%	

CANADIAN
FIRMS (8,9)

Celanese Canada	297	16.5x	12.5x	5.6x	5.1x	5.4x	2.0x	2.5x	0.0%	0.0%	4.6%	NR/NR
C-I-L	404	26.9	21.3	6.4	5.9	5.6	0.7	0.7	32.4%	39.1%	1.4%	A+(low)/A
DuPont Canada (4)	902	15.0	11.8	7.4	4.5	6.1	2.6	3.0	34.2%	16.8%	1.1%	A/BBB(high)
Union Carbide Canada	344	21.5	14.3	6.6	6.0	8.0	1.1	1.3	44.7%	41.8%	1.2%	A(low)/BBB
Eagle	1,308	24.2	11.7	2.3	2.0	4.9	0.9	0.4	65.7%	68.3%	4.6%	A(low)/ BBB (high)
Average		20.8x	16.9x	14.3x	5.7x	4.7x	6.0x	1.5x	1.6x	35.4%	33.2%	2.6%

INDICES

S&PChemicals (10)	65,982	18.5x	16.0x	
TSE 300 (16)	111,068	21.0	20.8	
S&P 400 (13)	1,740,077	23.1	19.6	17.5

Notes:
(1) All multiples are based on closing prices on 6/16/87, current shares outstanding, and financial data for the latest twelve months ended 3/31/87, except where noted.
(2) IBES earnings estimate as of 5/14/87.
(3) Estimated 1987 Cash Flow based on IBES earnings estimate and 7.0% growth of 1986 Non-cash items.
(4) Adjusted for 2-for-1 stock split effective 5/15/87.
(5) Sum of long term debt, short term debt and minority interest divided by the sum of long term debt, short term debt, minority interest shareholders' equity (including preferred stock).
(6) Sum of long term debt, short term debt and minority interest divided by current market capitalization (market value plus total debt).
(7) Dividend Yield from RT-Quotes as of 6/11/87.
(8) Data in Canadian dollars.
(9) 1989 Earnings and Cash Flow multiples based on the average of earnings estimates by Midland Doherty and Richardson Greenshields.
(10) Index multiples based on LTM earnings ended 3/31/87 from *S&P Analyst Handbook*, April 1987, and closing price on 6/16/87.
(11) FMC underwent major recapitalization in 1986 and completed 5.667 to 1 stock split on 5/28/86.
(12) Fiscal year ending 9/30.
(13) Based on IBES earnings estimates as of 5/14/87.
(14) Canadian credit ratings by CBRS/DBRS.
(15) Fiscal year ending 10/31.
(16) Based on Canadian Corporate Earnings Forecasts as of 5/12/87.

EXHIBIT 9

Market and Financial Statistics for Selected Oil Companies (1)
(data through 3/31/87)

	MARKET VALUE ($ MM)	P/E MULTIPLE			PRICE/CASH FLOW		MKT CAP/ EBDIT	PRICE/ BOOK	PRICE/ NET PP&E	TOTAL/ DEBT ADJUSTED BOOK CAP (5)	TOTAL/ DEBT CURRENT MARKET CAP (6)	CURRENT DIVIDEND YIELD (7)	MOODY'S/ S&P RATINGS (8)
		LTM	1987(E) (2)	1988(E) (3)	LTM	1987(E) (4)							
CANADIAN INTEGRATED OILS (w/Chemicals) (2)													
Imperial Oil	11,294	24.6x	18.0x	15.2x	10.6x	6.3x	6.3x	2.2x	1.9x	16.5%	8.3%	2.3%	Aa2/AA+
Shell Oil	3,445	17.8	25.3	20.3	4.7	7.4	5.7	1.3	1.0	23.7%	19.7%	1.5%	A1/AA
Texaco Canada	4,319	15.8	12.6	9.4	10.0	8.1	6.7	1.8	2.2	3.5%	2.0%	3.4%	A++/AA
Ultramar (7)	1,511	NM	–	–	2.9	–	7.1	1.0	0.6	56.6%	55.7%	8.3%	NR/NR
Average		19.4x	18.6x	15.0x	7.0x	7.3x	6.5x	1.6x	1.4x	25.1%	21.4%	3.9%	
US INTEGRATED OILS (9)													
Amoco	22,317	33.0x	20.6x	16.6x	6.5x	5.5x	6.0x	2.0x	1.2x	25.1%	14.6%	3.8%	Aaa/AAA
Amerada Hess	3,065	14.1	13.5	11.5	5.1	4.8	5.1	1.4	0.9	36.8%	30.1%	0.4%	Ba3/B
Phillips Petroleum	3,767	20.4	22.6	13.1	3.4	3.3	4.2	2.3	0.4	78.9%	62.2%	3.6%	Ba1/BB
Unocal	4,539	27.2	23.5	16.7	3.0	2.7	5.6	2.6	0.6	74.8%	53.1%	2.6%	Baa3/NR
Kerr-McGee	1,753	83.1	31.0	21.1	4.2	3.6	5.8	1.3	0.8	37.6%	31.6%	3.0%	A3/A
Average		23.7x	22.2x	15.8x	4.4x	4.0x	5.4x	1.9x	0.8x	50.6%	38.3%	2.7%	

CAN. EXPLOR. &
PROD (2)

Pan Canadian Petroleum	4,122	28.7x	21.2x	15.5x	13.4x	10.8x	10.3x	3.2x	2.2x	6.3%	2.1%	1.7%	A++/AA
Alberta Energy	1,084	19.2	24.4	15.2	5.2	5.4	7.3	2.0	0.6	59.3%	42.0%	1.4%	A(l)/BBB(h)
Norcen Energy	689	12.4	17.8	10.3	3.1	5.6	5.8	1.1	0.4	64.6%	61.4%	2.1%	B++/A(low)
Canadian Occidental (10)	1,261	28.1	21.9	16.1	6.5	5.8	6.9	1.9	1.1	23.3%	13.8%	1.7%	A_/A
BP Canada	1,052	67.9	26.9	13.3	12.1	3.7	18.6	2.4	2.6	22.2%	10.7%	1.1%	NR/NR
Average		22.1x	22.4x	14.1x	8.1x	6.3x	7.6x	2.1x	1.4x	35.2%	26.0%	1.6%	
STARLING CO.	704	NM	NM	NM	4.8x	5.3x	9.6x	1.4x	0.3x	81.8%	76.1%	1.1%	NR/NR

Notes:
(1) All multiples based on closing prices on 6/16/87, current shares outstanding, and financial data for the latest twelve months ended 3/31/87.
(2) Data in Canadian dollars, except where noted.
(3) IBES earnings estimates as of 5/14/87.
(4) Estimated by Canadian Corporate Earnings Forecasts as of 5/12/87.
(5) Sum of long term debt, short term debt and minority interest divided by the sum of long term debt, short term debt, minority interest shareholders' equity (including preferred stock).
(6) Sum of long term debt, short term debt and minority interest divided by current market capitalization (market value plus total debt).
(7) Data through 12/31/86.
(8) Ratings for Texaco Canada and all Canadian E & P companies are by CBRS and DBRS.
(9) Data in U.S. dollars.
(10) Adjusted to normalize $431.2 MM writedown in 1987.

EXHIBIT 10

Transaction Diagram for Spin-Off Alternative

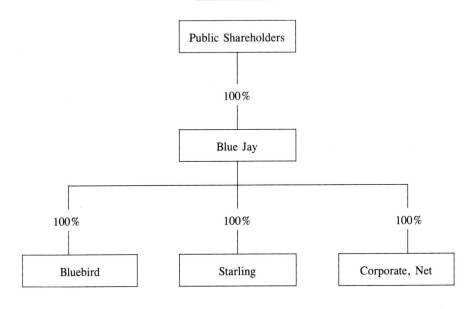

Before Spin-Off

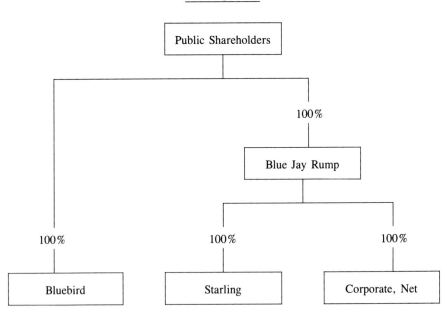

After Spin-Off

EXHIBIT 11

Pro Forma Financial Impact of Transaction

Spin-Off Alternative

(CA$ in millions)

	ACTUAL 11/30/87	ADJUST 11/30/87		BLUE JAY RUMP		PRO FORMA 11/30/87 BLUEBIRD	
		AMOUNT	%	AMOUNT	%	AMOUNT	%
Long Term Debt	$2,717	$2,717	58%	$2,042 (3)	77%	$ 693 (8)	41%
Minority Interest	450	268 (1)	0	0	0	268	16
1980 Preferred	300	300	6	0 (4)	0	0	0
1983 Preferred	125	125	3	0 (5)	0	0	0
1985 Preferred	205	205	4	0 (6)	0	205	12
Common Equity	789	1,069 (2)	23	596 (7)	23	540 (9)	31
Total Capitalization	$4,586	$4,684	100%	$2,638	100%	$1,706	100%
Coupon Bearing Securities/ Capitalization (10)	83%	77%	–	77%	–	68%	–

Notes:

(1) Adjusted for the defeasance of $281MM Bluebird Third Preferred Shares.
(2) Adjusted for $280MM net gain on the sale of the Latex business. Does not adjust for any gain on defeasance of Third Preferred.
(3) Equal to Starling Debt and Corporate Debt before transaction.
(4) Assumed to be converted into common.
(5) Assumed to be repaid with Latex proceeds.
(6) May actually exist on balance sheet but would be offset by matching asset.
(7) Equal to Adjusted Common Equity plus $300MM additional equity from conversion of 1980 Preferred Shares, minus Cash Dividend; where Bluebird basis equals $630MM reported basis, plus $280MM gain, minus $370MM dividend; and cash dividend equals $233MM. Assumed no taxes incurred Blue basis equals $630MM reported basis, plus $280MM gain, minus $370MM dividend; and cash dividend equals $233MM. Assumed no taxes incurred in transaction.
(8) Equal to Bluebird long term debt minus $55MM assumed to be repaid.
(9) Equity equals basis as calculated in Note 7.
(10) Coupon Bearing Securities includes Long Term Debt, Minority Interest, and all Preferred Shares.

517

EXHIBIT 12

Transaction Diagram for Recapitalization Alternative

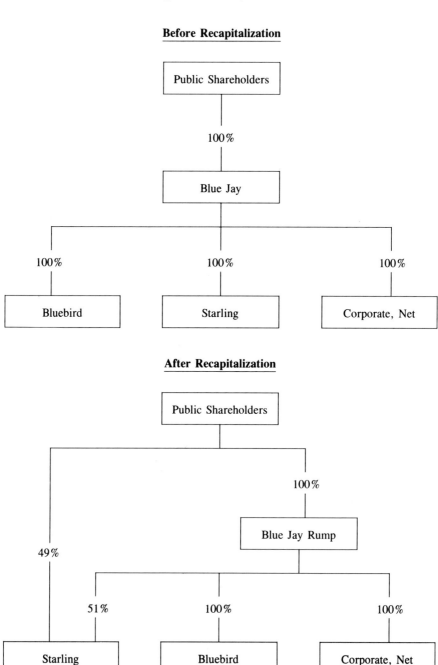

EXHIBIT 13

Pro Forma Financial Impact of Transaction
Recapitalization Alternative
(CA$ in millions)

	ACTUAL 11/30/87	ADJUST 11/30/87		BLUE JAY RUMP (3)		PRO FORMA 11/30/87 BLUEBIRD	
		AMOUNT	%	AMOUNT	%	AMOUNT	%
Total Debt	$2,717	$2,717	58%	$2,662 (4)	58%	$2,662	58%
New Senior Note	0	0	0	130	3	130	3
Minority Interest	450	268 (1)	6	573 (5)	13	573	12
Deferred Preferred Security	0	0	0	240	5	240	5
1980 Preferred	300	300	6	0 (6)	0	0	0
1983 Preferred	125	125	3	125	3	125	3
1985 Preferred	205	205	4	205	4	205	4
Common Equity	789	1,069 (2)	23	629 (7)	14	700	15
Total Capitalization	$4,586	$4,684	100%	$4,564	100%	$4,635	100%
Coupon Bearing Securities/ Capitalization (8)	83%	77%	—	86%	—	85%	—

Notes:
(1) Adjusted for the defeasance of $271 million Bluebird Third Preferred Shares.
(2) Adjusted for $280 million net gain on the sale of the Latex business.
(3) Assumes that Starling will be consolidated on financial statements.
(4) Adjusted for $55 million of debt paid down with proceeds of Latex sale.
(5) Adjusted for $305 million of Starling Minority Interest (49% of $621.6 million basis).
(6) Assumed to be converted into common.
(7) Equal to Adjusted Common Equity plus $300 million from conversion of 1980 Preferred Shares, minus $370 million Cash distribution, $240 million Warrant distribution, and $130 million Senior Note Distribution.
(8) Coupon Bearing Securities includes Long Term Debt, Minority Interest, Notes, Warrant Security and all Preferred Shares.

40

OCELOT INDUSTRIES LTD.

In early June 1991, Brad D. Griffiths, a Director of Gordon Capital Corporation (Gordon), gazed out of the window of his 53rd-floor office and reflected on the proposed re-organization of Ocelot Industries Ltd (Ocelot). In August 1988, following an analysis that concluded that the shares of Ocelot were undervalued, Gordon purchased 3 million Class B shares, or 25% of the outstanding shares of this class. Gordon proposed the re-organization in order to realize the true value of the investment. The proposal, if approved by Ocelot's Board, principal lender, and minority shareholders, would see Ocelot split into two operating units, each of which would be publicly traded. In view of Ocelot's poor financial condition, Mr. Griffiths pondered whether the proposed structure was the only viable option and, if so, were the key stakeholders likely to approve it?

BACKGROUND ON GORDON CAPITAL CORPORATION

Gordon began in 1969 as an institutional stock-trading firm in Montreal. As of 1991, Gordon had evolved into one of Canada's largest independent investment dealers, with offices in Toronto, Montreal, Calgary, Vancouver, Paris, London and New York. It was a member of all four Canadian exchanges, the Investment Dealers

Association of Canada, and, through an affiliate, the New York Stock Exchange, the American Stock Exchange, and the National Association of Securities Dealers Inc.

Gordon was well known for its aggressive approach to principal trading and its pioneering of innovative underwriting techniques. The corporation was actively involved in all aspects of investment banking, and was committed to providing large amounts of capital to facilitate client transactions. Gordon's corporate strategy was based on four key principles:

1. *Distribution and Trading Support.* Gordon had a reputation and a long history as a leader in institutional and corporate placement power and in block trading. The corporation routinely contributed large amounts of capital to facilitate client transactions and to provide liquidity in the secondary market.
2. *Low-Cost Structure.* Limiting manpower growth and keeping fixed overheads low allowed Gordon to price aggressively in both trading and underwriting.
3. *Innovative Transactions.* With a unique organizational structure that encouraged the overlap of Research, Corporate Finance, Currency and the Institutional Equity and Debt functions, the office was a fertile environment for idea generation and speedy customer service.
4. *Institutional Relationships.* Gordon was primarily focused on the institutional buyers of securities. It believed that the resulting market awareness was essential to the success of equity and fixed income underwritings.

It was Gordon's belief that new issues were driven by the institutional market. Accordingly, the institutional capabilities of an investment banking firm were key to an issuer when selecting an underwriter. This belief was supported by the fact that, first, while institutional investors might vary their percentage commitment to the equity markets, it was unlikely that they would abandon it altogether; second, they would have continuing cash flows to invest; and third, their long term orientation necessitated involvement in the equity market to achieve superior returns over cash rates.

BACKGROUND ON OCELOT INDUSTRIES LTD.

Incorporated under the laws of the Province of Alberta on March 11, 1968, Ocelot was a resource development company, operating three distinct business divisions: chemicals, oil and gas, and the petroleum service and supply industry.

Chemicals Division

The principal business of the chemicals division was carried on through Ocelot Chemicals Inc., a wholly owned subsidiary, and consisted of the production and marketing of methanol. The division's principal facilities were located in Kitimat, British Columbia, where it was in close proximity to the natural gas fields of Northern British Columbia and had access to ample amounts of hydro-electric power, both at very favourable rates. The division had 95 employees, 83 who worked in the plant, and 12 who marketed the methanol produced by the plant and who carried out the administrative functions.

Methanol had two primary uses:

1. As a chemical feedstock in the production of formaldehyde and acetic acid.
2. As a component in the production of an octane enhancer called Methyl Tetiary Butyl Ether (MTBE), the demand for which was expected to increase as a result of the passage in 1990 of the Clean Air Act in the United States.

As mentioned above, methanol was a primary liquid petrochemical made from renewable and non-renewable fossil fuels containing carbon and hydrogen. In 1991, 35% of the global production of methanol was consumed in the manufacture of formaldehyde, which was used in the production of resins used in wood, panel-board products and building materials.

The second largest, but fastest growing, use for methanol was as a fuel source. It was used as a component in the production of octane enhancers, MTBE, for existing fuels, and as a cleaner fuel alternative for both transportation and stationary power generation. MTBE usage as a gasoline additive had been shown to reduce carbon monoxide and nitrous oxide emissions into the atmosphere and, therefore, to lessen ozone damage. Consequently, with the passage in 1990 of the Clean Air Act in the United States, there had been a huge increase in demand for MTBE, which, in turn, increased the demand for methanol.

World methanol demand grew at a rate of 4% per annum from 1980–1984, and 7% from 1985–1990. The demand for methanol was inelastic; that is, demand was not affected by changes in price. Demand was inelastic for two reasons. First, there were few cost effective substitutes for methanol. Second, methanol costs typically accounted for a small portion of the value of the final derivative products in which it was used.

World demand for methanol was likely to grow at 5%–6% per year from 1990–1995. MTBE growth would likely account for approximately 39% of new methanol demand, due to increased use in the United States and Europe. MTBE was expected to grow at an annual rate in excess of 15% through 1995, due to the passage of the Clean Air Act in the United States, environmental pressure for lower emissions and increasing demand for additives to improve octane performance.

There were three key costs faced by a methanol producer: natural gas costs, operating costs, and distribution costs. New capacity was, therefore, constructed in locations with low gas costs, in order to offset high production and transportation costs.

The future supply of methanol to 1994–1995 could be forecast with reasonable certainty because:

1. There were no non-operating plants which could resume production of methanol.
2. There was a 3–5 year lead time to plan and construct a new plant, and although several new plants had been announced, there were only two known plants under

construction. As illustrated in Exhibit 1, increased future demand for methanol would create shortages around the middle of the 1990s.

There was, however, significant future opportunity for low cost producers to capitalize on the anticipated imbalance between supply and demand.

As illustrated in Exhibit 2, there had been significant variability in the price of methanol between January 1981 and December 1990. This price volatility was largely due to methanol's inelastic demand. The related impact on Ocelot's methanol cash flows is highlighted in Exhibit 3.

The division's marketing strategy was to develop and maintain a strong customer base in markets which were strategically located to its production facilities, to form direct customer relationships rather than sell to methanol traders and to secure and maintain long-term sales contracts with major end users. For example, in 1990 the division sold 240,000 tonnes of methanol in the United States. Under the Canada–U.S. Free Trade Agreement, Canadian methanol was exempt from the 18% U.S. import tariff. The division had also entered into a 3-year contract with Mitsui & Co., which had agreed to purchase between 150,000–200,000 tonnes of methanol per year from Ocelot at current market prices.

The division was also engaged in the production and marketing of ammonia and the provision of terminalling services for certain chemicals. Ammonia was sold through the wholly owned subsidiary, Kitimat Ammonia Inc.; the primary market for ammonia was fertilizer. The production facilities located at the Kitimat location were constructed specifically to serve the California market for ammonia used either directly or, after upgrading, as fertilizer. Ammonia can be transported by ship from Kitimat to California at costs much lower than ammonia shipped from a U.S. originating port or transported by rail or road from within continental U.S.

Another market now available to Ocelot was the Japanese market. This market, which was previously closed to imports, was now taking ammonia from various foreign suppliers.

Energy Division

Ocelot conducted oil and gas exploration, development and production activities in western Canada. The company's oil and gas reserves were located in British Columbia, Saskatchewan and Alberta, although it should be noted that 80% of these reserves were located in B.C. Exhibit 4 summarizes the company's reserves as of April 1, 1991, and shows the estimated present value of the reserves.

Services Division

The Services Division had three business units: pipeline construction, contract drilling of oil and gas wells, and rental of oilfield equipment.

The pipeline construction business was conducted by O.J. Pipelines Inc., a wholly owned subsidiary, and South Eastern Pipeline Construction, an operating division of the company. These two operations generated approximately 55% of the revenues of the division for the year ended December 31, 1990.

Based in Nisku, Alberta, O. J. Pipelines was one of the major large diameter (14–48 inches) pipeline companies operating in Canada. The subsidiary bid for contracts to construct large diameter pipelines in Canada for customers that owned and operated major gas transmission systems. The firm was recently awarded a contract by a major Canadian gas transmission company for a construction project valued at approximately $95 million.

Based in Medicine Hat, Alberta, South Eastern provided small diameter (3–13 inches) pipeline construction services in southeastern Alberta and southwestern Saskatchewan. Small diameter pipelines were used to link individual wells into central gathering and transmission facilities.

The contract drilling business was conducted in western Canada by Cactus Drilling, and in the Rocky Mountain area of the United States by Cardinal Drilling Company. The contract drilling business generated approximately 38% of the revenues of the Services Division for the year ended December 31, 1990.

Each company was run as a separate unit, with its own head office staff and responsibility for submitting bids and hiring personnel.

Generating about 7% of the division's revenues in 1990, Lynx Tool Company Ltd. conducted oilfield equipment business in western Canada, while Lynx Tool Company Inc. performed this function in the United States. The companies manufactured, sold, repaired and rented a wide variety of oilfield equipment.

FINANCIAL PERFORMANCE OF OCELOT

The consolidated financial statements for Ocelot for the most recent fiscal period, March 31, 1991, are presented in Exhibits 5 and 6. Ocelot had incurred significant operating losses in each of the last 3 fiscal periods due to unstable prices in key product areas, low capacity utilization in the service division's key businesses, and onerous interest payments. The 1990 year-to-date financial performance of the company appeared to be improving; however, this was largely due to the elimination of interest payments owing on long term debt.

In 1990, Ocelot repaid $250 million of bank debt with proceeds raised from the issuance of preferred shares of a wholly owned subsidiary. The preferred shares were subscribed for by Ocelot's principal lender, and were cumulative, non-voting, non-convertible, redeemable and retractable with a term of five years. Ocelot and its subsidiaries had effectively pledged all of their assets as security for the payment of dividends and redemption obligations of these preferred shares. The amount of preferred shares required to be redeemed for the next five years was dependent upon consolidated cash flow from operations from the preceding year, with a minimum redemption of $40 million in 1991. On October 31, 1990, Ocelot's principal lender postponed the $40 million preferred share redemption and temporarily increased Ocelot's operating lines by $12.5 million, in response to operating cash flow deficiencies. The net asset value of the company's energy and services divisions was $177 million.

Despite the poor financial condition of Ocelot, it was widely believed that the management team currently in place was among the best in the industry. The team was young, knowledgeable and aggressive, and had the drive and staying power required to lead Ocelot back to profitability.

The authorized share capital of the company was comprised as follows:

1. 25,000,000 Preferred Shares without nominal or par value;
2. 7,500,000 Class A common shares without nominal or par value; and
3. 25,000,000 Class B subordinate voting shares without nominal or par value.

The Class A and Class B shares ranked equally with one another except that each Class A share carried twenty votes and each Class B share carried one vote. The Class A shares were convertible at any time into Class B shares on a one-for-one basis. As of March 31, 1991, the following shares had been issued:

	CLASS A	CLASS B
Number of Shares	3,700,822	12,761,418
Consideration	$7,573,000	$67,002,000

At this date, 87.9% or 3,103,760 Class A common shares and 0.01% of the Class B shares were either directly or indirectly held by one individual. This individual effectively had full control of Ocelot and its assets.

PRIOR ATTEMPTS TO RE-ORGANIZE

The current proposal was not the first structure to be considered by Gordon. There were two previously proposed structures. The first structure involved locating a private corporate investor who would become a partner and invest approximately $200 million. However, Gordon quickly realized that investors were only interested in very specific business units, not the company as a whole. The bids received reflected these preferences, and as such, were not acceptable to the company. The second structure was very similar to the structure currently under consideration in which Ocelot would issue $55 million in warrants, and retain a well-known U.S. investment bank to sell the Services and Supply Divisions to private investors in the U.S., for a minimum consideration of CA$50 million. Ocelot would net approximately $105 million, which would be used to pay down outstanding bank debt, thereby gaining the Bank's approval to split Ocelot into two publicly traded companies, as currently proposed. The warrants were issued in early 1991; however, the U.S. investment bank was unable to sell the Services and Supply Divisions, and the deal collapsed.

THE PROPOSED RE-ORGANIZATION

The Corporate Finance Team at Gordon was now proposing that Ocelot separate its business into two distinct, publicly traded companies. A new company, Ocelot Energy Inc., would own the oil and gas business and the oil and gas service and supply business of Ocelot, while Ocelot Industries Ltd. (Ocelot new) would continue to own the methanol and ammonia businesses and related assets. Additional assets from a second entity called Lone Pine Resources Ltd., with a net worth of approximately $53 million, would also be absorbed into Ocelot Energy Inc., reducing the volatility of the asset pool and improving the financial position of the new energy company. The suggested re-organization is illustrated in Exhibit 7.

Under this arrangement, each Class A common share of Ocelot (old) would be exchanged for:

1. One New Common Share of Ocelot (new) and
2. One-half of a Class A share of Ocelot Energy Inc.

Similarly, each Class B common share of Ocelot (old) would be exchanged for:

1. One New Common Share of Ocelot (new) and
2. One-half of a Class B share of Ocelot Energy Inc.

The Class A and Class B designations would thereby be removed from the share capital of Ocelot (new); however, the class designations would remain in the capital structure of Ocelot Energy Inc. As a result, the proportionate shareholdings of Ocelot Energy Inc. would be the same as those currently existing for Ocelot (old).

Ocelot Energy would assume approximately $90.33 million of Ocelot's debt and liabilities. Ocelot Energy would also assume approximately $30 million of debt from Lone Pine Resources.

The purpose of the re-organization was to:

1. Address the poor financial condition of the company;
2. Provide greater flexibility in investment decisions for each business segment, ensuring that each firm was more viable in its own right than was Ocelot Industries today, and better able to operate and compete effectively in its respective business environment;
3. Address the security position of the bank, and improve the overall banking relationship; and
4. Satisfy the demands of investors and the market in general by providing an appropriate mix of assets and financial structure. That is, it allowed the investor to choose between a pure methanol "play" and an oil and gas "play."

Exhibits 8 to 11 outline the pro forma statements for Ocelot Industries Ltd. and Ocelot Energy Inc. after the re-organization.

THE DECISION

The question that faced the team now was whether or not this structure was the best alternative, and would it be accepted by the key stakeholders?

EXHIBIT 1

World Supply/Demand of Methanol
(thousands of tonnes)

	1990	1991	1992	1993	1994	1995
Supply @ 90% of Nameplate						
Capacity	20,262	20,757	21,425	21,425	23,415	23,415
Demand						
Formaldehyde	6,900	7,038	7,179	7,394	7,616	7,844
Acetic Acid	1,362	1,507	1,549	1,650	1,750	1,850
MTBE	2,953	3,542	4,041	5,567	5,987	6,279
All Others	6,785	6,989	7,198	7,414	7,637	7,866
Total	18,000	19,076	19,967	22,025	22,990	23,839
Surplus/(Deficit)	2,262	1,681	1,458	(600)	425	(424)
% Capacity Utilization	89	92	93	103	98	102

EXHIBIT 2

U.S. Gulf Coast
Contract Barge Price for Methanol
(U.S. cents/U.S. gallon—average per quarter)

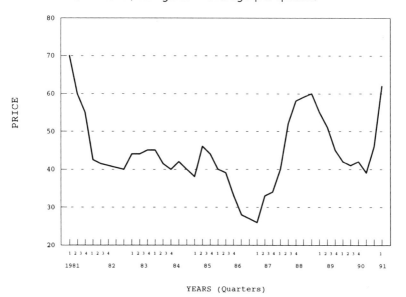

YEARS (Quarters)

EXHIBIT 3

Methanol Price Impact
on Methanol Cash Flows
($ millions)

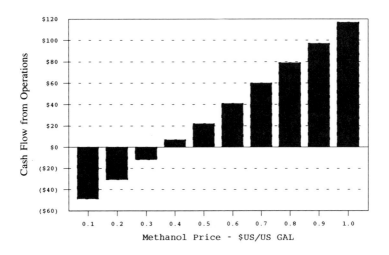

EXHIBIT 4

OCELOT INDUSTRIES LTD.
Total Oil and Gas Reserves

	GROSS RESERVES			NET RESERVES			ESTIMATED PRESENT WORTH VALUE DISCOUNTED AT			
	NATURAL GAS	SULPHUR	PETROLEUM AND NATURAL GAS LIQUIDS	NATURAL GAS	SULPHUR	PETROLEUM AND NATURAL GAS LIQUIDS	0%	10%	15%	20%
	(MMcf)	(MLT)	(Mbbl)	(MMcf)	(MLT)	(Mbbl)		(THOUSANDS OF DOLLARS)		
Escalated Prices										
Proven Reserves										
Producing	94,808	251	122	75,489	194	102	136,691	74,888	59,633	49,109
Non-producing	41,517	61	0	35,012	55	0	91,906	34,692	24,015	17,584
Total Proven	136,325	320	122	110,501	249	102	228,597	109,580	83,647	66,693
Probable Additional	17,862	20	11	14,063	16	11	7,799	3,890	2,861	2,200
Total Before ARTC	154,187	340	133	124,564	265	112	236,396	113,470	86,509	68,893
Alberta Royalty Tax Credit	—	—	—	—	—	—	240	148	132	119
TOTAL	154,187	340	133	124,564	265	112	236,637	113,618	86,640	69,011
Constant Prices										
Proven Reserves										
Producing	94,145	251	122	77,727	194	102	70,308	48,005	41,037	37,705
Non-producing	41,544	68	0	36,349	55	0	40,648	20,094	15,293	12,091
Total Proven	135,689	320	122	114,076	249	102	110,956	68,098	56,330	47,796
Probable Additional	17,862	20	11	14,789	16	11	3,979	2,455	1,908	1,540
Total Before ARTC	153,550	340	133	128,865	265	112	114,935	70,553	58,237	49,336
Alberta Royalty Tax Credit	—	—	—	—	—	—	248	187	165	148
TOTAL	153,550	340	133	128,865	265	112	115,183	70,740	58,403	49,484

EXHIBIT 5

OCELOT INDUSTRIES LTD.
Consolidated Balance Sheet
As at March 31, 1991
(Prior to Re-organization)
(thousands of dollars)

Assets

Current Assets	68,930
Equity Investment	10,467
Property Plant & Equipment	184,759
Other Assets	6,427
TOTAL ASSETS	270,583

Liabilities and Shareholders' Equity

Current Liabilities	
Bank Debt	31,309
Accounts Payable	54,009
Current Maturities on Long Term Obligations	42,112
	127,430
Leases	10,248
Long Term Debt	1,764
Deferred Foreign Exchange	5,927
Preferred Shares of Subsidiary	210,025
	335,394
Shareholders' Equity	
Capital Stock	74,575
Deficit	(159,386)
	(84,811)
TOTAL LIABILITIES AND SHAREHOLDERS' EQUITY	270,583

EXHIBIT 6

OCELOT INDUSTRIES LTD.
Consolidated Statement of Earnings
(Prior to Re-organization)

	($000s) THREE MONTHS ENDED MARCH 31,		($000,000s) YEAR ENDED DEC. 31,	
	1991	1990	1990	1989
Revenue	88.4	46.2	198	173
Costs and Expenses				
Cost of sales and op. exp.	76.4	44.7	187	165
Depletion and depreciation	3.5	3.5	14	13
	79.9	48.2	201	178
Earnings (Loss)				
From Operations Before Undernoted Items	8.5	(2)	(3)	(5)
Interest on long term debt	0.3	6.4	14.4	27.8
Other interest	1.1	1.1	10.0	0.3
Preferred share div. of sub.	4.1	0.0	8.2	0.0
Share of loss of ammonia ops.	(.7)	2.0	0.4	0.9
	4.8	9.5	33.0	29.0
Earnings (Loss) for the Period	3.7	(11.5)	(36)	(34)

EXHIBIT 7

Current Structure

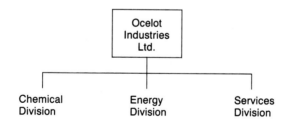

Structure After Proposed Re-organization

EXHIBIT 8

OCELOT INDUSTRIES LTD.
Pro Forma Consolidated Balance Sheet
As at March 31, 1991
(After Re-organization)
(thousands of dollars)

Assets	
Current Assets	16,992
Equity Investment	10,467
Property, Plant & Equipment	72,763
Other Assets	3,187
TOTAL ASSETS	103,409
Liabilities and Shareholders' Equity	
Current Liabilities	
Accounts Payable	15,465
Current Maturities on Long Term Obligations	3
	15,468
Long Term Debt	21,888
Deferred Foreign Exchange	5,927
Preferred Shares of Subsidiary	128,109
	171,392
Shareholders' Equity	
Capital Stock	90,731
Deficit	(158,714)
	(67,983)
TOTAL LIABILITIES AND SHAREHOLDERS' EQUITY	103,409

EXHIBIT 9

OCELOT INDUSTRIES LTD.
Pro Forma Consolidated Statement of Earnings
(After Re-organization)

	($000s) THREE MONTHS ENDED MARCH 31,		($000,000s) YEAR ENDED DEC. 31,
	1991	1990	1990
Revenue	20.0	14.2	65.0
Costs and Expenses			
Costs of sales and op. exp.	13.3	14.3	61.0
Depreciation and depreciation	1.2	1.5	5.0
	14.5	15.8	66.0
Earnings (Loss)			
From Operations Before the Undernoted Item	5.5	(1.6)	(1.0)
Interest on long term debt	0.6	3.3	6.0
Preferred share div. of sub.	2.0	0.0	4.0
Share loss of ammonia ops.	(0.7)	0.0	0.4
	1.9	3.3	10.4
Earnings (Loss) for the Period	3.6	(4.9)	(11.4)

EXHIBIT 10

OCELOT ENERGY INC.
Pro Forma Consolidated Balance Sheet
As at March 31, 1991
(After Re-organization)
(thousands of dollars)

Assets	
Current Assets	50,773
Property Plant & Equipment	111,650
Other Assets	32,936
	195,359
Liabilities and Shareholders' Equity	
Current Liabilities	
Bank Debt	1,158
Accounts Payable	29,325
Current Maturities on Long Term Obligations	2,109
	32,592
Leases	10,248
Long Term Debt	120,330
	163,170
Shareholders' Equity	
Capital Stock	32,189
Total Liabilities and Shareholders' Equity	195,359

EXHIBIT 11

OCELOT ENERGY INC.
Pro Forma Consolidated Statement of Earnings
(After Re-organization)

	($000s) THREE MONTHS ENDED MAR. 31,		($000,000s) YEAR ENDED DEC. 31,	
	1991	1990	1990	1989
Revenue	68.3	25.2	110	84
Costs and Expenses				
Cost of sales and op. exp.	62.3	23.1	100	77
Depletion, depreciation and depreciation	2.2	2.0	8	7
	64.5	25.1	108	84
Earnings (Loss) From Operations Before				
the Undernoted Item	3.8	0.1	2	00
Interest on long term debt	3.0	3.1	14	12
Earnings (Loss) for the Period	0.8	(3.2)	(12)	(12)

41

UNION ENTERPRISES LTD.

Late in the afternoon of Thursday, January 24, 1985, Michael Kordyback, Vice President and Chief Financial Officer of Unicorp Canada Corporation (Unicorp) reviewed the information that he had collected on Union Enterprises Ltd. (UEL). Michael had just learned that GLN Investments Limited (GLN), the owner of 16.3 percent of UEL's common stock, was willing to sell its shares to Unicorp. During January, Unicorp had accumulated 13.8 percent of UEL's common stock as a strategic investment and the successful purchase of GLN's shares would put Unicorp in the position to make a takeover bid for UEL. Michael was scheduled to meet with Unicorp's investment bankers that evening to discuss the possible bid and he wanted to have a clear recommendation on how to proceed formulated for the meeting.

UNICORP CANADA CORPORATION

Unicorp Canada Corporation was an asset oriented management and investment holding company with interests in commercial real estate, energy and financial services (Exhibit 1). Unicorp's founder and Chairman, George Mann, controlled the company through his 68 percent ownership of Unicorp's Class B voting shares.

Prior to 1977, Unicorp's activities were limited principally to real estate holdings, an investment position in Unity Bank, a small Canadian chartered bank, and a controlling investment in United Trust Company. Unicorp took an active management role in the bank and trust company operations. By mid-1977 both the bank and trust company had been merged into larger companies and Unicorp embarked on a strategy of investing its funds in companies which had management in place and did not entail additional day-to-day operational responsibility for Unicorp.

In 1978, Unicorp commenced a major program of real estate investment in the United States through the acquisition of interests in publicly traded real estate investment trusts (REITs). Through its subsidiary, Unicorp American Corporation, Unicorp acquired direct control of the assets owned by three REITs and the assets of a publicly traded real estate company.

Unicorp's activities in real estate were centered around the investment in and management of income producing commercial properties. Real estate assets included high rise office buildings, shopping centres, land under ground lease, commercial and industrial properties and land held for development and sale. Properties were located in 18 different states, Canada, Puerto Rico and the Virgin Islands.

In 1982, Unicorp expanded its acquisition and investment activities to the Canadian oil and gas industry. Interests in one private and two publicly traded junior oil and gas producers were acquired with Unicorp eventually assuming control positions in the three companies. Unicorp's principal activities in the energy field included the exploration for, development, and production of oil and natural gas in western Canada.

Prior to 1984, Unicorp had closely followed a strategy to invest in or to acquire, directly or indirectly, a pool of high quality assets having the potential for long term appreciation. Total assets increased from $56 million at the end of fiscal 1979 to $336 million at the end of fiscal 1983. Much of the growth was financed with debt and, as a result, debt to total capitalization increased from 49 percent to 71 percent in the same period.

Due to the company's high debt levels in a volatile interest rate environment, dependence on capital gains for earnings and large number of significant mergers and acquisitions, net income had been erratic. In 1984, net income of $19 million was generated from $112 million in total revenue. In the previous year, revenue was significantly lower at $58 million and net income was $1.8 million. The strong increases in revenue and net income were the result of $39.1 million in gains on the sale of securities and real estate investments. Historical income statements for Unicorp are presented in Exhibit 2.

The increase in revenue from the sale of investments marked the beginning of another phase in the company's development. Management realized that continued growth would require greater access to the public debt and equity markets. This access would depend, to a large degree, on the ability of Unicorp to generate a more consistent earnings performance. A decision was made to give more emphasis to the realization of values from the investment portfolio through more aggressive management of the company's assets. In addition, Unicorp began to actively search for an investment that would provide a stable base of cash flow and earnings.

The shift in emphasis was reflected in the appointment of James Leech as President to oversee the day-to-day operations of the company. George Mann would continue to investigate future investment and acquisition opportunities in the role of Chairman. During the year, all real estate and energy operations were consolidated into two publicly traded subsidiaries, Unicorp American Corporation and Unicorp Resources Ltd., respectively (Exhibit 1). $109 million in new equity was raised and $62 million in cash was generated from the sale of investments.

The injection of new equity and profitable sale of investments improved Unicorp's financial position significantly. At December 31, 1984, debt to total capitalization was 59 percent, down from 71 percent at the previous year end. Unicorp had $479 million in total assets with over 65 percent of this total in U.S. real estate:

TABLE 1
(CA$, THOUSANDS)

	CANADA	UNITED STATES	TOTAL
Real Estate	$ 9,856	$315,510	$325,366
Energy	70,115	—	70,115
Investments	36,272	28,322	64,594
Other	9,088	10,688	19,776
	$125,331	$354,520	$479,851

The fair market value of the company's real estate holdings was estimated at $467.5 million, $142.1 million in excess of the net book value of $325.4 million. The appraised value of energy assets, assuming no change in oil and gas prices and a 15 percent discount rate, was approximately $62.0 million. Market value of investments at December 31, 1984, was $72.6 million. Historical balance sheets for Unicorp are presented in Exhibit 3 and Unicorp's detailed capitalization is presented in Exhibit 4.

UNION ENTERPRISES LIMITED

Union Enterprises Ltd. was a management holding company with principal investments in the natural gas utility and resource industries. The assets of UEL were comprised substantially of its two wholly owned operating subsidiaries, Union Gas Limited, a regulated gas utility, and Union Shield Resources Ltd., an unregulated resource company (Exhibit 5).

UTILITY OPERATIONS

The predecessor company to Union Gas Limited was formed in 1911 with the amalgamation of three small gas exploration companies into the Union Natural Gas Company. The primary business of the company at that time was the production of natural gas from fields in southwestern Ontario and the distribution of the gas to surrounding communities.

Union Gas grew to the point where, at the end of 1984, it was Canada's second largest distributor of natural gas. The company owned and operated a fully integrated natural gas transmission, storage and distribution system serving 492,000 residential, industrial and commercial customers in southwestern Ontario. Union Gas' unique underground storage capabilities enabled the company to supplement local gas supplies with gas produced in western Canada and the United States. Spent gas wells were refilled with imported gas during the summer months. Stored gas was then used to meet peak customer demand during the winter. In addition, Union Gas provided storage and transmission services to other gas distribution companies in eastern Canada.

Although inherently stable, fluctuations in the demand for gas depended on the individual utility's customer base. Demand from residential and commercial customers, where gas was used primarily as a heating fuel, was dependent on outside temperatures. On the other hand, industrial customers used gas for both heating and manufacturing processes and, as a result, their demand was sensitive to both weather conditions and the level of business activity. Total sales volume of natural gas in Canada declined from 1980 to 1982 as a result of the economic recession; however, sales had recovered in 1984 and 1985 as economic activity increased (Exhibit 6).

Union Gas' customer base was heavily weighted toward industrial users (Exhibit 6). This mix had resulted in greater volatility of gas sales than that experienced by the industry in general. In 1982, the tail end of the economic recession combined with a warmer than average winter in southwestern Ontario resulted in a 12.5 percent decline in gas sales volume from the previous year for Union. In contrast, total industry sales volume decreased by only 5.6 percent in 1982. In 1983, economic recovery prompted a 4.2 percent increase in total industry volume; however, Union Gas' sales volume increased 14.6 percent.

Union Gas had achieved average annual growth in gas sales revenue of 18.5 percent over the past ten years due primarily to strong energy price increases. Gas volume sold, however, had increased only 7.5 percent since 1975. Union Gas had achieved close to maximum penetration of the markets it served and it was estimated that only about 80,000 potential new customers were on or close to the distribution system in the company's service area. Future growth would depend on the stimulation of demand for natural gas in a restricted market area.

Efforts to increase demand for natural gas were concentrated in three areas. First, Union Gas was continually expanding the distribution system within the company's service area. Capital expenditures on utility operations totalled $52.8 million in fiscal 1984 and $62.6 million in the first nine months of fiscal 1985.

Second, the company was promoting the use of natural gas as a fuel for vehicles. This program was in its initial stages; however, public and government interest had been strong. Under a government program, vehicle owners could apply for a $500 grant to be used for conversion of a vehicle from gasoline to natural gas fuel.

Finally, natural gas producers and distributors were lobbying the government for the deregulation of wholesale gas prices. Since 1975, the price of Alberta natural gas sold in eastern Canada and the United States had been established in agreements between the governments of Canada and Alberta. Under this arrangement, natural gas prices were linked to crude oil prices. With oil in short supply and natural gas in abundant supply, the net effect had been to inflate gas prices and reduce its competitiveness versus alternative fuels such as electricity.

The major anticipated impact of price deregulation was increased competitiveness of natural gas versus alternative fuels and therefore increased demand in domestic and export markets. Union Gas felt that increased storage and transportation revenues from the movement of western Canadian gas through the company's distribution system would more than offset the revenue losses from lower prices on its own limited gas production volume.

In export markets, the initial effects of deregulation had already been experienced. In November 1984, the federal government revised its export pricing policy to allow Canadian companies to export gas to U.S. buyers at negotiated prices. Gas exports had increased almost 23 percent since the new policy had become effective.

In the year ended March 31, 1984, Union Gas achieved record sales volume of 7.1 billion cubic meters generating $1.3 billion in revenue. Utility operating income was also a record $174 million. In the first nine months of fiscal 1985, gas sales were 2.3 percent above 1984 levels; however, margins had declined with a reduction in higher profit sales to residential customers caused by a warmer than normal winter. Consolidated income statements for Union Enterprises are presented in Exhibit 7.

As a utility company in Ontario, Union Gas was subject to regulation under the Ontario Energy Board Act (Act). Earnings from utility operations were regulated by the Ontario Energy Board (OEB) on the basis of a targeted return on the rate base for a test year period. In its determination, the OEB applied cost rates to each component of the utility capital structure and set gas rates that would achieve the appropriate return using projected sales volumes for the upcoming year. The company was currently allowed a return on equity of 15.6 percent on a deemed equity ratio of 29 percent.

As the OEB determined the appropriate capital structure for the utility operations, Union Gas had little flexibility to increase equity returns through higher debt levels. The OEB would not allow additional financial risk to be passed along to customers through higher rates. Similarly, the OEB would ensure that debt service ratios were maintained at acceptable levels by restricting the cost of debt that could be passed on to customers through rate increases.

The Ontario Energy Board Act also dealt with the ownership and control of utilities within its scope. In response to the attempted hostile takeover of Union Gas by Consumers' Gas Company in 1969, Bill 109, a tag-on to the 1964 Act, was enacted. This legislation made an OEB hearing mandatory when one gas utility proposed acquiring more than 20 percent of the shares of another. With the new legislation in place the Ontario cabinet, on recommendation of the OEB, vetoed the Consumers' Gas takeover bid. Today, Subsection 26(2) of the Act effectively prevented any individual or company from acquiring more than 20 percent of any class of shares of a regulated utility without the approval of the Ontario government.

RESOURCE OPERATIONS

Until 1968, the production, storage and distribution of natural gas remained the sole business of Union Gas. At that time, the company started to diversify into oil and gas related investments in western Canada in an attempt to expand beyond the regulated utility business. In 1980 Union Gas purchased a 10.7 percent interest in Numac Oil and Gas Limited, later increased to 18.3 percent. In 1981, Union Gas acquired a controlling interest in Precambrian Shield Resources Limited. Both Numac and Precambrian were diversified, Alberta based companies engaged in the exploration for and production of oil and gas in Western North America.

In fiscal 1984, resource operations contributed revenue of approximately $17 million and operating income of $7.5 million to UEL's results. Resource operations accounted for $239 million of the company's $1.4 billion in total assets. At January 23, 1985, the market values of UEL's 65.2 percent investment in Precambrian and 18.3 percent interest in Numac were $93.8 million and $57.2 million, respectively. Consolidated balance sheets for Union Enterprises are presented in Exhibit 8.

The value of oil and gas producing companies in Canada was directly related to the world price of oil (Exhibit 9). A general consensus existed that oil prices would continue to decline over the next two to three years as a result of excess world supply, sluggish demand and the weak position of the OPEC cartel. Low inventories of oil in the U.S. and Japan, a decline in production in the Soviet Union, and continuing political strife in the Mid-East region were expected to moderate the decline and avoid a drop below U.S.$20 per barrel from the present U.S.$28 per barrel price. Longer term forecast indicated a gradual increase in oil prices beyond 1988 (Exhibit 9). Segmented results for Union Enterprises are summarized below:

TABLE 2
(CA$, THOUSANDS)

	UTILITY		RESOURCE	
	1984	1983	1984	1983
Revenue	1,350,873	1,103,072	16,638	11,040
Operating Income	174,389	129,440	7,543	6,176
Identifiable Assets	1,160,232	1,140,295	239,009	231,722
Capital Expenditures	52,807	92,499	28,438	24,609
Depreciation and Depletion	29,588	23,627	4,418	2,172

UNION ENTERPRISES REORGANIZATION

Prior to 1985, all regulated and non-regulated operating activities of the present UEL were carried on by Union Gas Limited. In an effort to simplify the regulation of the utility operation and provide more flexibility to pursue non-regulated activities, Union Gas restructured its business activities effective January 2, 1985.

Under the restructuring, UEL was formed to hold 100 percent of the common shares of two subsidiaries, Union Gas Limited and a newly formed Union Shield Resources Ltd. Union Gas continued to operate the gas utility business while Union Shield Resources operated the company's interests in resource assets. Shareholders of Union Gas became shareholders of UEL in a one-for-one share exchange.

In its information circular dated November 10, 1984, Union Gas stated that after the reorganization, the 20 percent ownership limitation imposed by Subsection 26(2) of the Ontario Energy Board Act would not apply to Union Enterprises. In other words, UEL was no longer protected from hostile takeover.

UNICORP'S INVESTMENT IN UNION ENTERPRISES

In June of 1984, George Mann and James Leech became aware of the impending reorganization of Union. Both men felt that the restructuring would be beneficial to UEL as the company's flexibility to expand into unregulated businesses would be greatly enhanced. Several years earlier, Bell Canada Enterprises Inc., using a holding company structure similar to UEL's, had made the transition from a regulated telecommunications utility to one of Canada's most profitable conglomerates engaging in a wide variety of regulated and unregulated businesses. George Mann and James Leech felt that similar potential existed in UEL. Unicorp purchased 100 common shares of UEL in order to monitor the progress of the reorganization. This was standard practice for the company when evaluating potential investments.

Unicorp saw potential in an investment in UEL for several additional reasons. First, Unicorp was still not well known in the Canadian investment community. Acquiring a large ownership position in a prominent Canadian company would enhance Unicorp's investor profile and possibly improve the company's access to Canadian capital markets. Management, with extensive experience in mergers and acquisitions, could build on the relatively stable earnings and cash flow of the gas utility to generate a more consistent operating performance for Unicorp. Second, Unicorp was becoming more bullish on the business environment in Canada as a result of the policies of the recently elected Progressive Conservative government.

At the end of 1984, 75 percent of Unicorp's assets were located in the United States with the remaining 25 percent in Canada. The company had made a conscious decision to balance the asset mix between the two countries and a large investment in UEL would accomplish this objective. Finally, the reorganization of Union Enterprises would eliminate the 20 percent ownership restriction under the Ontario Energy Board Act. Without this protection UEL was a potential takeover candidate. Arbitrage opportunities might exist for Unicorp.

Upon further investigation, Unicorp determined that the major shareholders of UEL were GLN Investments Limited with 16.3 percent of the common shares and National Victoria and Grey Trustco (NVG) with between 6 and 15 percent. Both companies were represented on the board of directors of UEL. NVG was affiliated with EL Financial. EL Financial's corporate strategy was similar to Unicorp's. No other single shareholder controlled more than 10 percent of the common shares outstanding. GLN Investments Limited was a subsidiary of Great Lakes Group Inc., a private securities underwriting firm controlled by Edward and Peter Bronfman through Brascan Limited. During November, George Mann and James Leech discussed GLN's UEL holdings with representatives of the company and felt confident that GLN would be open to alternatives proposed by Unicorp.

In early December, Unicorp made the decision to acquire a position in Union Enterprises' common stock. As the company saw it, four alternatives were available:

1. Pool Unicorp's investment with one or both of the other large shareholders' to take control of and direct the affairs of UEL.
2. Sell the investment to one of the other large shareholders.
3. Offer the position together with one or two of the other large shareholders' to a third party.
4. Purchase one of the other large shareholders' interests and make a bid for control of UEL.

During January, Unicorp purchased 4,500,000 common shares of UEL, comprising approximately 13.8 percent of the total outstanding shares, at an aggregate purchase price of $58,341,988. The share purchases were financed with a new $60 million line of credit provided by Continental Bank of Canada for this purpose.

THE TAKEOVER BID PROPOSAL

On January 24, George Mann and James Leech met with representatives of GLN to discuss the UEL shares held by GLN. They were told that GLN had decided that its investment in UEL was no longer strategically attractive and it would be willing to sell its 5,290,100 common shares. GLN indicated that it would consider an offer of cash or securities; however, the value of the offer would have to exceed its all-in cost of $12.50 per share. Under Ontario law, a takeover bid was deemed to be in progress when any single shareholder acquired in excess of 20 percent of the voting shares of another company. A successful offer for the shares held by GLN would move Unicorp above the 20 percent takeover threshold and, therefore, an identical offer would have to be made to all remaining shareholders. Based on the January 23 closing price of $13.00, the market value of the approximately 28 million UEL common shares that Unicorp did not own was $364 million.

An outright takeover of UEL by Unicorp would be a "company making" transaction in the words of James Leech. Unicorp would acquire a stable earnings base and an instant following in the investment community. This higher and more traditional profile would provide the company with the capability to raise additional capital and expand its investment activities more quickly.

On the other hand, Michael felt that $12.50 to $13.50 per share represented the full value of Union Enterprises to Unicorp based on the growth prospects of the regulated utility subsidiary and the current value of UEL's oil and gas investments. The UEL share purchases by Unicorp during January had been at an average cost of $12.96 per share; however, UEL shares had been trading consistently below this price in 1984 (Exhibit 10). He had collected comparative information on Canadian gas and electric distribution utilities, as shown in Exhibit 11. Information on stock market indexes is shown in Exhibit 12.

Michael wondered if a bid of $12.50 per share would be sufficiently attractive to shareholders other than a motivated seller such as GLN. He also wondered about the possibility of a competing bid for UEL from a "white knight" and how this should be reflected in Unicorp's offer. Given management's initial strategy for the investment, Unicorp would be willing to sell to another bidder for an adequate premium.

The financing of the bid was a major consideration in the form of offer to be undertaken. Given Unicorp's relatively high leverage and inconsistent cash flow, the company would be unable to borrow the money required for an all-cash offer. UEL presently paid a dividend of $0.80 per common share and generated operating cash flow per common share of $3.90; however, the majority of the company's cash flow came from the regulated utility. Any attempt to increase the dividend pay-out or raise debt directly in UEL would be closely scrutinized by the OEB. The maintenance of adequate interest coverage and equity ratios would be the OEB's primary concerns.

An issue of Unicorp equity in exchange for UEL common shares was another alternative. Great Lakes Group, GLN's parent company, was a major underwriter of and investor in preferred shares, indicating that GLN would find a preferred share component in the offer attractive. Unicorp's investment bankers estimated that a preferred share issue based on Unicorp's credit risk and current market conditions would be priced to yield approximately 10 percent. Similarly, Unicorp could offer non-voting Class A or voting Class B common shares as part of the bid. Both the Class A and Class B shares currently paid dividends of $0.20 per share.

A share issue through the offer would allow Unicorp to raise equity and broaden the company's investor base. Michael realized that any issue of Unicorp non-voting equity in exchange for voting common shares of UEL would possibly be less attractive to UEL's common shareholders; however, dilution of the present Unicorp shareholders was a major concern. The present market capitalization of Unicorp's Class A and Class B shares was a total of $65.4 million in comparison to the $364 million value of the outstanding (and not owned by Unicorp) UEL common shares. In addition, George Mann would not allow his holdings of Class B voting shares to be reduced below 51 percent. Recent trading information for Unicorp shares is shown in Exhibit 13.

Michael felt that the attempted takeover of Union Gas by Consumers' Gas Company in 1969 might provide some insight into strategic issues that should be considered in a contested takeover of Union Enterprises today. In September 1969, Consumers' Gas, a large utility serving the Toronto area, made a bid for 67 percent of Union Gas' common shares. The initial bid was accepted by Union Gas' board of directors on the condition that it was extended to 100 percent of the common shares. Consumers' Gas agreed to the condition at a lower price and the Union Gas board accepted.

While negotiations were occurring between the companies, a citizens committee was formed in Chatham to oppose the takeover on the grounds that it would reduce competition in the industry and result in increased gas costs to customers. This group was quickly joined by the City of Chatham and 15 other southwestern Ontario municipalities.

In response to the political pressure exerted by those groups opposing the takeover, the Ontario government passed Bill 109 prohibiting the acquisition of over 20 percent of a utility by another utility without government approval. As the battle continued, the Union Gas board of directors changed their position from approval to opposition. Eventually, on the recommendation of the Ontario Energy Board, the Ontario cabinet vetoed the takeover attempt.

Michael suspected that political intervention would be a factor again. Union Enterprises played a significant role in the southwestern Ontario economy, employing over 2,200 people. In addition, Darcy McKeough, President and Chief Executive Officer of UEL, had been the Treasurer of Ontario prior to joining Union Gas in 1979. Many members of the Progressive Conservative government with whom he served were still in power in 1985. In addition, UEL had many years of experience dealing with the government on utility regulation issues. On the other side, Unicorp was relatively unknown in the Ontario business community and had not dealt with the Ontario Energy Board in the past.

THE DECISION

If Unicorp could formulate an offer acceptable to GLN, it had the opportunity to control 30.1 percent of UEL's common stock before the tender offer was in the hands of the other shareholders. This would put Unicorp in the position to acquire outright control of UEL or to sell to a third party that was interested in acquiring control.

Michael had to decide on the price, form and conditions of an offer to GLN based on Unicorp's objectives for the investment, its financial resources, the underlying value of UEL, and his assessment of the probability of the possible outcomes of the takeover bid. He then needed to develop a strategy for the presentation of the bid to UEL and the public. The acquisition of Union Enterprises held out great potential for Unicorp but not without significant risk.

EXHIBIT 1
UNICORP CANADA CORPORATION
Organization Chart

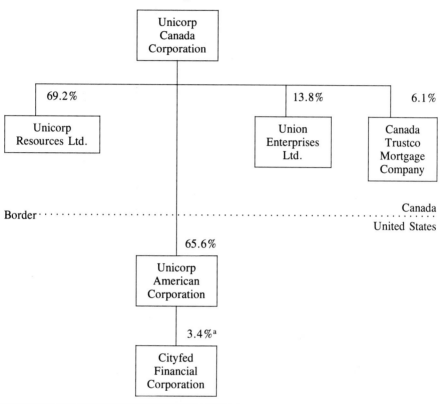

[a]8.2% voting interest calculated on a fully diluted basis.

EXHIBIT 2

UNICORP CANADA CORPORATION
Consolidated Statement of Income
(CA$, thousands)

	YEAR ENDED DECEMBER 31		
	1984	1983	1982
Revenues			
Rental operations	$ 54,087	$47,823	$30,743
Oil and gas	12,391	–	–
Income from short term investments and marketable securities	2,373	2,985	8,238
Gain on sale of securities	18,918	4,975	10,943
Gain on sale of real estate investments	20,245	430	838
Mortgage loan interest and other income	3,545	1,786	1,247
	111,559	57,999	52,009
Expenses			
Rental operations	22,845	19,923	12,799
Oil and gas	3,339	–	–
Depreciation and depletion	14,248	7,050	4,661
Interest on mortgage loans and notes payable	9,007	7,474	6,642
Interest on convertible mortgage bonds payable	6,167	1,396	–
Interest on bank indebtedness	15,750	6,977	11,112
General and administrative	10,189	8,151	4,694
Write-down of long term investment	–	5,266	–
	81,545	56,237	39,908
Income (loss) before the undernoted	30,014	1,762	12,101
Equity in earnings of associated companies	1,654	1,511	993
Minority interest	(6,410)	(1,455)	(4,694)
Provision for income taxes	(7,355)	(12)	(1,550)
Net income (loss) before extraordinary item	17,903	1,806	6,850
Income tax recovery	1,106	–	–
Net income (loss)	19,009	1,806	6,850
Preferred dividend requirement	3,485	751	832
Income attributable to Class A and Class B shareholders	$ 15,524	$ 1,055	$ 6,018

EXHIBIT 3

UNICORP CANADA CORPORATION
Consolidated Balance Sheet
(CA$, thousands)

	DECEMBER 31	
	1984	1983
Assets		
Real Estate Investments		
Income producing properties	$270,738	$230,927
Properties held for and under development	29,218	18,880
Mortgage loans receivable	25,410	3,887
	325,366	253,694
Oil and Gas Properties	70,115	–
Other Long Term Investments	59,837	46,621
Other Assets		
Cash and short term investments	2,588	7,463
Marketable securities	4,757	18,267
Amounts receivable	13,241	8,656
Other	3,947	1,459
	24,533	35,845
Total Assets	$479,851	$336,160
Liabilities and Shareholders' Equity		
Liabilities		
Mortgage loans and notes payable	$ 72,058	$ 70,859
Convertible mortgage bonds payable	49,894	46,758
Bank indebtedness	135,346	102,870
Accounts payable and accrued charges	37,895	24,137
Income taxes payable	1,738	178
	296,931	244,802
Deferred Income Taxes	1,122	614
Minority Interest	93,322	40,493
Shareholders' Equity		
Capital stock	61,825	37,816
Retained earnings	25,934	11,744
Foreign currency translation adjustment	717	691
	88,476	50,251
Total Liabilities and Shareholders' Equity	$479,851	$336,160

EXHIBIT 4

UNICORP CANADA CORPORATION
Capitalization as at December 31, 1984
(CA$, thousands)

	AUTHORIZED	OUTSTANDING
Indebtedness		
Bank Loans		
Unicorp Canada Corporation		
General Lines of Credit		$81,946
Acquisition Lines of Credit[a]		—
Unicorp Resources Ltd.		6,866
Unicorp American Corporation		46,534
Mortgage Loans and Notes Payable		
Unicorp Canada Corporation		2,160
Unicorp American Corporation		69,898
Convertible Mortgage Bonds Payable		
Unicorp American Corporation		49,894
Minority Interest		93,322
Share Capital		
Class I Preference Shares:		
10% Preference Shares, Series C	276,000	5,520
Employee Preference Shares, Series 1	43,525	870
Class II Preference Shares:		
$0.80 Preference Shares, Series A	3,546,870	35,469
Class A Non-Voting Shares	Unlimited	14,176
Class B Voting Shares	20,000,000	5,790

[a]$58,342 was outstanding at January 23, 1985.

EXHIBIT 5
UNION ENTERPRISES LTD.
Organization Chart[a]

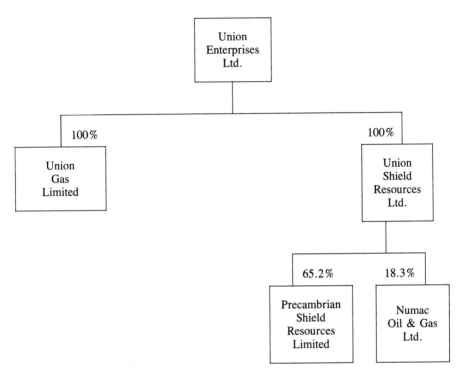

[a]Union Gas has a preference share investment in Union Shield.

EXHIBIT 6

Canadian Natural Gas Industry Sales and
Union Enterprises Sales Composition

Natural Gas Industry Sales

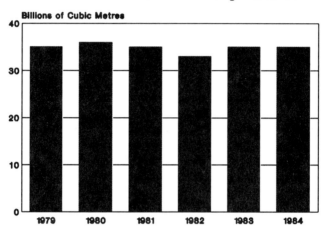

Source: Wood Gundy.

Union Enterprises Ltd.
Annual Volume of Gas Sales

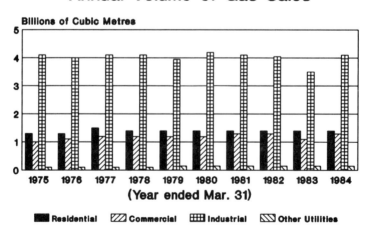

Source: 1984 Annual Report.

EXHIBIT 7

UNION ENTERPRISES LTD.
Consolidated Statement of Income
(CA$, thousands)

	NINE MONTHS ENDED DECEMBER 31	YEAR ENDED MARCH 31	
	1984	1984	1983
Gas sales	$811,586	$1,280,228	$1,037,504
Cost of gas sold	660,404	1,032,145	849,731
Gas sales margin	151,182	248,083	187,773
Transportation and storage of gas	31,402	41,631	36,333
Oil and gas production	18,866	14,663	7,908
Other	25,878	30,989	32,367
	227,328	335,366	264,381
Expenses			
Operating and maintenance	83,175	107,328	92,204
Depreciation, amortization and depletion	28,987	33,159	24,730
Property and capital taxes	10,283	12,947	11,831
	122,445	153,434	128,765
Operating income	104,883	181,932	135,616
Interest Expense			
Long term debt	41,437	53,830	46,648
Short term debt	13,089	16,548	20,780
Interest deferred	(1,740)	(778)	(408)
	52,786	69,600	67,020
Income before income taxes	52,097	112,332	68,596
Income taxes: current	26,245	34,681	15,708
deferred	—	20,346	17,063
	26,245	55,027	32,771
Income before minority interest	25,852	57,305	35,825
Minority interest	1,424	1,089	1,021
Net income	24,428	56,216	34,804
Preference share dividend requirements	10,453	14,111	11,891
Net income attributable to common shares	$ 13,975	$ 42,105	$ 22,913

EXHIBIT 8

UNION ENTERPRISES LTD.
Consolidated Balance Sheet
(CA$, thousands)

	DECEMBER 31 1984[a]	MARCH 31 1984	MARCH 31 1983
Assets			
Current Assets			
Accounts receivable	$	$ 225,938	$ 203,221
Inventories: Gas in underground storage		89,519	169,257
Merchandise, stores and spare equipment		10,414	10,290
	407,441	325,871	382,768
Property Plant and Equipment			
Utility	764,079	724,464	700,420
Resource	247,682	224,633	200,825
	1,011,761	949,097	901,245
Deferred Charges			
Synthetic natural gas supply premium		31,241	26,934
Other		19,423	8,919
	78,171	50,664	35,853
Investments			
Numac Oil & Gas Ltd., at cost (market value at March 31, 1984 – $64,548,200)		70,202	50,362
Other		3,407	1,789
	73,600	73,609	52,151
Total Assets	$1,570,973	$1,399,241	$1,372,017
Liabilities and Shareholders' Equity			
Current Liabilities			
Short term borrowings		68,914	148,100
Accounts payable and accrued charges		132,693	104,263
Dividends payable		8,252	8,714
Income taxes		6,791	11,945
	368,567	216,650	273,022
Long term debt	437,612	447,412	430,337
Deferred income taxes	213,083	188,939	168,601
Minority interest in Precambrian Shield Resources Limited	80,449	80,055	53,772
Shareholders' Equity			
Share capital			
Preference shares	131,303	135,255	137,508
Common shares	233,610	225,059	219,140
	364,913	360,314	356,648
Retained earnings	106,349	105,871	89,637
	471,262	466,185	446,285
Total Liabilities and Shareholders' Equity	$1,570,973	$1,399,241	$1,372,017

[a]Only category totals were available on interim statements.

EXHIBIT 9

TSE Oil and Gas Index vs. Spot Crude Oil Price and
World Oil Price Forecast

TSE OIL & GAS INDEX VS. CRUDE OIL PRICE

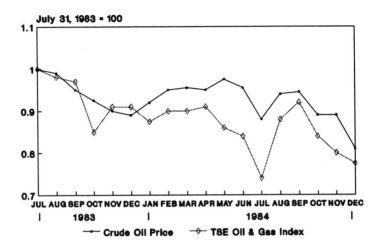

WORLD OIL PRICE FORECASTS

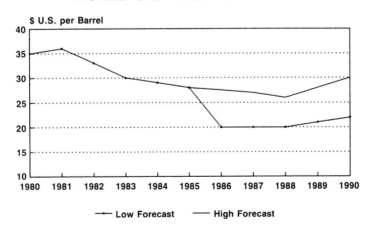

Source: Wood Gundy.

EXHIBIT 10

UNION ENTERPRISES LTD.
Trading in Common Shares

	HIGH	LOW	VOLUME
1984 January	$12.000	$11.000	1,159,524
February	11.875	11.000	441,525
March	11.625	11.125	537,602
April	11.250	10.375	564,844
May	11.000	10.500	452,981
June	11.125	10.625	385,756
July	10.750	9.875	385,201
August	10.750	10.125	1,934,085
September	11.125	10.375	970,378
October	11.375	10.875	473,680
November	11.375	11.000	651,077
December	12.500	11.125	1,130,732
1985 January[a]	13.000	11.875	5,081,800
January 23 Close		13.000	
Beta (UEL) = 0.4			

[a]January 2 to 23.

EXHIBIT 11

Canadian Gas and Electric Distribution Utilities
Selected Ratios

COMPANY	RETURN ON COMMON EQUITY	DIVIDEND PAY-OUT RATIO	MARKET VALUE/ BOOK VALUE	PRICE/ EARNINGS RATIO	INTEREST COVERAGE	INTEREST + PREF. DIV. COVERAGE	COMMON EQUITY RATIO
Canadian Utilities	17.0%	58.0%	1.50	8.3	4.8	1.8	29.1%
Consumers' Gas	16.7%	56.0%	1.23	8.1	2.9	2.3	39.8%
Gaz Metropolitan	17.3%	57.0%	1.19	7.3	2.8	2.2	42.8%
Inland Natural Gas	16.2%	48.0%	0.97	8.3	2.2	2.0	31.8%
Inter-City Gas	11.9%	30.0%	0.85	11.1	1.7	1.6	15.4%
Maritime Electric	16.0%	49.0%	1.19	6.6	3.2	2.2	34.5%
Nfld. Light & Power	15.7%	51.0%	1.22	7.2	3.4	2.3	37.8%
Pacific Northern Gas	14.7%	47.0%	0.98	6.7	2.1	1.9	29.7%
Transalta Utilities	16.0%	50.0%	1.29	7.9	4.1	2.1	37.6%
Union Enterprises	13.2%	60.0%	1.09	11.5	2.6	1.9	28.0%

EXHIBIT 12

Stock Price Indexes for Union Enterprises
and Toronto Stock Exchange Categories

	UNION ENTERPRISES	GAS UTILITIES	OIL & GAS PRODUCERS	TSE 300
1984 January (=100)	100	100	100	100
July	85	86	85	87
August	91	91	102	97
September	94	93	105	97
October	97	93	95	95
November	95	92	93	96
December	106	99	89	97
1985 January 23	111	N/A	N/A	102

Source: Toronto Stock Exchange Review.

EXHIBIT 13
UNICORP CANADA CORPORATION
Trading in Selected Shares

	CLASS A NON-VOTING			CLASS B VOTING			CLASS II PREF. SERIES A		
	HIGH	LOW	VOLUME	HIGH	LOW	VOLUME	HIGH	LOW	VOLUME
1984									
July	$6.500	$5.000	81,088	$6.625	$5.500	8,878	$7.125	$6.375	8,657
August	7.500	6.000	82,842	8.000	6.500	6,499	7.875	6.500	20,587
Sept.	7.000	6.500	7,139	8.250	7.500	2,315	8.000	7.625	10,128
October	6.875	5.375	79,374	7.750	5.375	21,687	7.625	6.500	6,786
November	7.125	5.500	103,570	7.000	6.000	36,650	7.875	7.000	21,147
December	8.250	6.500	64,810	8.250	6.625	7,180	8.125	7.125	11,112
1985									
Jan.[a]	8.125	7.625	26,546	8.750	7.500	13,512	9.125	7.750	20,825
Jan. 23	8.125			8.375			8.375		
Close									

Volatility = 31% p.a.
Beta Class A = 1.0
Beta Class B = 1.1
[a]January 2 to January 23.

EXHIBIT 14

Selected Interest Rates on January 23, 1985
(in percent)

| TERM | GOVERNMENT OF CANADA | | | | | | McLEOD YOUNG WEIR CORPORATION BOND INDEX | |
	3 MONTH	6 MONTH	1–3 YEARS	3–5 YEARS	5–10 YEARS	>10 YEARS	MEDIUM TERM	LONG TERM
Yield	9.50	9.71	10.27	10.46	10.97	11.38	11.58	12.06

Source: Financial Post.

42

Unicorp Canada Corporation

On January 2, 1985, the reorganization of Union Gas Limited was officially completed. The reorganization resulted in the formation of Union Enterprises Ltd. (UEL), a management holding company, to hold 100 percent of the common shares of two subsidiaries: Union Gas Limited, a government regulated natural gas utility; and Union Shield Resources Ltd., an unregulated resource company. The major purpose of the reorganization was to allow the company to expand into new areas of business free from government regulation. UEL was free from government imposed restrictions; however, it had lost the benefit of a law limiting ownership of the shares of a regulated utility by any one person to 20 percent.

During January 1985, Unicorp Canada Corporation (Unicorp), a real estate management and investment holding company, acquired 13.8 percent of the common shares of UEL through open market purchases. On January 31, Unicorp's intentions were made public when the company announced a tender offer for any and all outstanding common shares of UEL. Unicorp offered to exchange one $1.17 Cumulative Redeemable Retractable Class II Preference Share and one-half of a Class A Non-Voting Share Purchase Warrant for each UEL common share. A summary of the tender offer is presented in Exhibit 1. Pro forma consolidated balance sheet and income statement assuming 100 percent acceptance of the tender offer by UEL shareholders are presented in Exhibits 2 and 3.

This case was prepared by Bill Quinn under the supervision of Professor Robert W. White for the sole purpose of providing material for class discussion at the Western Business School. Certain names and other identifying information may have been disguised to protect confidentiality. It is not intended to illustrate either effective or ineffective handling of a managerial situation. Any reproduction, in any form, of the material in this case is prohibited except with the written consent of the School.

559

Disclosed with the offer was the information that GLN Investments Limited (GLN), UEL's largest single shareholder, had agreed to tender its 16.3 percent common share ownership to Unicorp. Unicorp effectively controlled 30.1 percent of UEL before the offer was in the hands of all shareholders.

THE TAKEOVER BATTLE

On February 5, the battle for control of Union Enterprises began on three fronts. First, the board of directors of UEL urged shareholders to reject the Unicorp offer as "unfair and inadequate." The company attacked the proposed takeover with a variety of claims mailed to shareholders in a circular:

1. UEL's investment bankers valued the Unicorp offer at $11.25 to $12.25 per UEL share. UEL described this price as financially "unfair and inadequate."
2. UEL alleged that Unicorp's purchases of 4,500,000 UEL shares for cash in January were part of the takeover bid and, therefore, remaining shareholders were not being treated equally under the terms of the offer now being made.
3. UEL objected to the exchange of voting, fully participating common shares for a non-voting, non-participating preferred share and one-half of a warrant to purchase a non-voting common share. The company claimed that shareholders would be deprived of participation in UEL's future growth.
4. UEL objected to the control of a public utility such as Union Gas by one individual, George Mann. The company declared that it was not in the best interests of Union Gas' customers to have the utility controlled by a single shareholder.
5. Unicorp's brief corporate history, volatile earnings and high leverage were highlighted by the circular. It was asserted that the securities offered by Unicorp were not of "investment quality."
6. UEL believed that Unicorp's present emphasis on investment in the United States indicated that Unicorp would divert UEL's investment activities to the U.S. as well. In addition, UEL implied that Unicorp would siphon off UEL assets and earnings to purchase real estate and service dividend requirements arising from the takeover.

Through the circular and the media, UEL attempted to reinforce the suggestion that Unicorp lacked the expertise to run a utility and the acquisition would financially weaken Union Gas. The possible result would be poorer service and higher gas costs for the utility's customers.

Second, UEL requested that the Ontario Securities Commission (OSC) hold a hearing to review the takeover. The company alleged that Unicorp had, in effect, made a two-tier offer by purchasing the shares of some shareholders for cash while offering only a share exchange to other shareholders. Ontario law required that all shareholders in a specific class of shares be treated equally in a takeover bid. As such, a two-tier offer was clearly illegal.

Finally, the City of Chatham, the location of UEL's head office, began to form an alliance of Southwestern Ontario communities to oppose the proposed takeover. Chatham City Council expressed concern about gas price increases and the possible loss of jobs in the Chatham area. Provincial officials were contacted in an attempt to have the takeover reviewed by the Ontario Energy Board (OEB).

On February 8, the OSC commenced a hearing to examine the circumstances surrounding the takeover bid. The investigation centered on the question of whether or not Unicorp's open market purchases of UEL common stock during January were part of a predetermined bid to acquire the company. UEL alleged that Unicorp was not treating all shareholders of its common stock equally as was required under Ontario law.

During five days of acrimonious hearings, allegations were made that Unicorp's investment bankers had manipulated stock prices and leaked news of the impending takeover offer to institutional shareholders of UEL before the public offer had been made. These allegations were vehemently denied by Unicorp and its advisors.

Under Ontario law a takeover had not commenced until the acquiror crossed the 20 percent ownership level in the target company. On February 15, the OSC ruled that Unicorp had crossed the 20 percent ownership threshold with the same share exchange offer to GLN Investments that was now being made to the other UEL shareholders. Therefore, Unicorp was treating all shareholders equally under the offer. The Unicorp bid could proceed so long as Unicorp extended the deadline for the offer and amended its offering circular to disclose open market purchases made by its investment banker during the bid to cover a short position in UEL common stock.

Unicorp's victory was short-lived. On the same day, the Ontario government announced that the OEB would hold an inquiry into the proposed takeover. Complaints had been received from Union Gas customers, the coalition of southwestern Ontario communities and from UEL itself. The government said it was concerned about concentrated ownership in the utility industry and the effect the acquisition might have on gas prices. Unicorp now faced the possibility that if it continued the takeover bid and took up shares under the offer, it might be forced to roll back its shareholdings to the position existing on February 15.

With the Ontario Energy Board hearings scheduled to commence March 14, the battle shifted to the shareholders. Both Unicorp and UEL conducted expensive media campaigns in an attempt to win shareholders over to their respective positions. Senior management of both companies embarked on extensive tours of southwestern Ontario communities to put forward their positions to shareholders directly. The companies felt that the small shareholders, the "widows of Wallaceburg," would be the key to the success or failure of the takeover attempt and they spared no expense in attempting to gain their support.

On February 14, Dominion Bond Rating Service (DBRS) released its rating of the Unicorp preferred shares offered as P-3 (middle). DBRS said that the preferred shares were "moderately speculative" due to the high dividend payment requirements the new shares placed on Unicorp.[1] This rating supported UEL's contention that the securities offered in exchange for its shares were not of investment quality. In a related move, DBRS placed Union Gas on credit rating alert due to "possible changes which may result from the takeover."[2]

---

[1] *The Globe and Mail,* February 14, 1985.
[2] *The Globe and Mail,* March 1, 1985.

Throughout the takeover bid, heavy trading of UEL's stock fuelled speculation of a possible "white knight" offer for the target company. In a *Toronto Star* article published on February 19, McKeough said "we are having discussions or have been approached by 20 or 30 companies."[3] UEL's board of directors included representatives of several possible white knight candidates including Hal Jackman, Chairman of National Victoria and Grey Trustco, a 6 to 15 percent owner of UEL; and Mervyn Lahn, President and Chief Executive Officer of Canada Trustco.

The possibility of a competing offer for UEL was made less likely by the fact that Unicorp controlled at least 30.1 percent of the common shares. In addition, the impending OEB hearings would deal with the general question of the concentration of ownership in regulated utilities. The board's rulings could impact on the acquisition of UEL by any company.

On March 2, it came to light that UEL had tried to regain the legislative ownership protection that it had lost at the time the holding company was formed. UEL signed an agreement in principal to purchase Haldiman Gas and Oil Wells Ltd., a small natural gas distributor serving 30 customers in Wellandport, Ontario. The Ontario cabinet was asked to approve the acquisition and subsequent amalgamation of the utility into UEL. If approved, Union Enterprises would again fall under the regulation of the Ontario Energy Board and the 20 percent ownership restriction of the Ontario Energy Board Act, however, the cabinet refused to approve the transaction, sending it to the OEB for consideration.

BURNS FOODS LTD. ACQUISITION

On March 7, the most significant event to date in the battle was announced by Union Enterprises. The company had agreed to purchase all outstanding shares of Burns Foods Ltd. (Burns) of Calgary for $125 million in convertible preferred stock. UEL issued 10 million, 8 percent convertible preferred shares with a stated value of $12.50 per share. Each share carried four-fifths of a vote.

The acquisition and related share issue increased the number of UEL votes outstanding from 33 million to 41 million. Unicorp's now estimated 36 percent interest in UEL was diluted to approximately 27 percent. More importantly, Burns was a private company, 100 percent owned by a group headed by Burns' President Arthur Child. The 8 million new votes attached to the convertible preferred shares were controlled by a group friendly to UEL.

Burns Foods Ltd. was a holding company with 13 subsidiaries engaged in a variety of food related businesses (Exhibit 4). The company was taken private by a group of investors in 1978, therefore, little public financial information was available to Unicorp. UEL executives disclosed that pre-tax profits ranged from $26 million to $38 million per year in the 1980 to 1983 period. In 1984 pre-tax profits of $13.9 million were depressed by a strike in the meat packing subsidiary and the

[3]*The Toronto Star*, February 19, 1985.

closing of two plants. After-tax profits in 1984 were $1.5 million on an estimated sales base of $1.1 billion[4]. The major businesses of Burns were as follows[5]:

Burns Meats Ltd. Meat packing operations with estimated 1984 sales of $455 million. The company suffered a prolonged strike in 1984 due to an attempt to cut employee wages. Two plants were closed recently as part of an ongoing attempt to improve profitability in a financially troubled industry.

Palm Dairies Ltd. Largest western Canadian dairy with estimated 1984 sales of $240 million.

Scott National Co. Ltd. Grocery wholesaling and distribution company with 1984 sales estimated at $220 million.

Canbra Foods Ltd. Canola (oil seed) crushing and processing firm with estimated 1984 sales of $135 million. Canola oil is used for margarine, cooking oil and shortening.

Stafford Foods Ltd. A Canbra subsidiary distributing food products to institutional customers.

Unicorp felt that the acquisition of Burns by UEL was a blatant attempt to fend off its takeover bid. Jim Leech publicly criticized UEL's management for not consulting Unicorp, their largest shareholder, on the purchase. Leech also questioned the fairness of the $125 million price paid for Burns, "I think Mr. Child has got an enormous price for his company to the clear detriment of all the common shareholders in Union."[6]

Union Enterprises claimed that the acquisition had been in the planning stages for three years. Burns "is an excellent fit, particularly from an asset and earnings potential point of view, with the utility and resource holdings of Union," said McKeough.[7] With projected net income of $16 million in 1985, Union Enterprises felt that the acquisition was fairly priced; however, no formal valuation had been done by the company's investment bankers.

Unicorp fought to have the Burns Foods acquisition stopped by requesting that the transaction be reviewed by the Toronto Stock Exchange (TSE) and the Ontario Ministry of Consumer and Commercial Relations. Unicorp claimed that UEL had violated TSE listing rules by issuing shares without prior approval from the exchange. In addition, Unicorp alleged that the share issue contravened the Ontario Business Corporations Act as UEL's Certificate of Incorporation did not permit the issuance of new voting stock without the approval of shareholders. In both cases, Unicorp hoped to have the new share issue revoked, thereby increasing Unicorp's percentage ownership in UEL.

THE DECISION

Late in the evening of March 7, Michael Kordyback pondered the events of the past five weeks. The battle for control of UEL had been acrimonious and expensive

---

[4]*The Toronto Star,* March 9, 1985.
[5]*Ibid.*
[6]*The Toronto Star,* March 8, 1985.
[7]*Ibid.*

for both sides. Unicorp now controlled approximately 36 percent of UEL's common shares but only 27 percent of the votes outstanding. Aside from 1.9 plus million UEL shares held by National Victoria and Grey Trustco (NVG), a party apparently friendly to UEL, the remaining common shares outstanding were held by small shareholders. The hard fought battles of the past five weeks had yielded little in the form of additional control for Unicorp if the Burns purchase and associated share issue were upheld by the TSE and the Ontario Ministry of Consumer and Commercial Relations. In addition, the Ontario Energy Board hearings were still to be held and it was possible that Unicorp's share ownership in UEL could be rolled back further.

As a result of the Burns acquisition, Michael wanted to reevaluate Unicorp's strategy for the takeover bid. Assessing the impact of the Burns acquisition on the value of UEL was a difficult matter due to the limited information on Burns available to Unicorp. UEL had paid $125 million for Burns, a company with a book value of $64 million at December 31, 1984. Unicorp felt that a realistic price was in the range of $90 to $100 million. If Michael's estimates were accurate, UEL had overpaid by as much as $35 million for Burns. The per share impact on the value of UEL could be as much as $1.00 per common share.

Since the announcement of Unicorp's tender offer for UEL and prior to the announcement of the acquisition of Burns, UEL shares had declined from $12.75 on January 29 to $11.75 on March 6 (Exhibit 5). In the same period the TSE 300 Index had increased by 2.4 percent. With the Burns announcement on March 7, the shares had declined in value to $11.125, down $0.625 from the previous close (Exhibit 6). If Michael was correct in his assessment of the value of Burns, Unicorp's offer should now be more attractive to UEL shareholders.

Michael had collected information on the market price of Unicorp Class A non-voting stock, the outstanding $0.80 Class II preference shares, and market interest rates in order to assess the market value of the tender offer at the present date (Exhibits 7 and 8). The most recent quarterly dividend paid on the Class A non-voting shares was a dividend of $0.05 per share payable on February 15, 1985. Each Class II preference share paid a quarterly dividend of $0.20 and was convertible into one Class A non-voting share at the option of the holder until December 31, 1985. At that date all remaining Class II preference shares would be automatically converted on the same basis.

Michael felt that Unicorp had several alternatives at this time. It could extend the offer from the present expiry of 12:00 midnight on March 11 in the hope that the Burns acquisition would encourage more UEL shareholders to tender their shares or that the regulatory authorities would overturn the issuance of the additional UEL voting stock. Unicorp could also amend its offer to reflect its assessment of the impact of the Burns purchase on the value of UEL. Finally, Unicorp could abandon its takeover bid and dispose of its shareholdings. Under the offer Unicorp could return the shares tendered to the offer; however, it would have to develop a strategy to deal with the 4,500,000 shares purchased in the open market. Unicorp had to develop a response to UEL's most recent move by morning.

EXHIBIT 1

Summary of Unicorp Tender Offer

1. Unicorp offers to purchase any and all outstanding Union Enterprises Common Shares on the basis of one Unicorp $1.17 Cumulative Redeemable Retractable Class II Preference Share, Series B, and one-half of a Unicorp Class A Non-Voting Share Purchase Warrant for each Union Enterprises share. The preferred shares are redeemable at $13.00 after March 31, 1988, and are retractable at $13.00 on March 31, 1992, and each anniversary date thereafter. Each warrant entitles the holder to purchase one Class A Non-Voting Share of Unicorp at a price of $9.75. The warrants expire March 1, 1987.

2. The offer is not conditional upon any minimum number of shares being tendered.

3. The offer is not being made to holders of Union Enterprises Preference Shares.

4. The offer expires at 12:00 midnight on February 22, 1985. Unicorp reserves the right to extend the termination date for the offer.

5. Tendered shares may be withdrawn at any time up to 12:00 midnight on February 11, 1985. If the offer is changed (other than solely an increase in price), tendered shares may be withdrawn at any time until the expiration of 10 days from the date when the varied offer is mailed.

6. Unicorp will have the right not to take up and pay for any Union Enterprises shares deposited under the offer if a material change in the affairs of Union Enterprises occurs as the result of undisclosed action taken before the offer or action taken after the offer by any person or company (including a governmental or regulatory authority) other than Unicorp.

7. Unicorp will take up and pay for shares deposited under the offer commencing February 12, 1985 or the expiry of the withdrawal period in the case of a varied offer.

8. Unicorp does not intend to purchase Union Enterprises shares in the market during the offer period.

9. If in excess of 90 percent of Union Enterprises Common Shares are tendered to the offer, Unicorp will, pursuant to section 187 of the Business Corporations Act, purchase the remaining Union Enterprises Common Shares outstanding on the same basis set out in the offer.

10. Unicorp presently owns 4,500,000 Union Enterprises Common Shares, comprising approximately 13.8 percent of all outstanding Union Enterprises Common Shares. These shares were purchased in the market during January at an aggregate cost of $58,927,000. The purchase of shares was financed by acquisition lines of credit arranged specifically for this purpose.

11. GLN Investments Limited, the owner of 5,290,100 Union Enterprises Common Shares, is the single largest shareholder of Union Enterprises. GLN has agreed to deposit all its Union Enterprises shares under the offer. GLN is not entitled to withdraw the shares deposited unless Unicorp abandons the offer or fails to take up and pay for the shares in accordance with the offer. As a result of the agreement with GLN Investments Limited, Unicorp will own at least 30 percent of the outstanding Union Enterprises Common Shares.

12. In the opinion of Unicorp counsel, the exchange of a Union Enterprises Common Share pursuant to the offer will result in a tax-deferred rollover of 90.75 percent of the adjusted cost base of the Union Enterprises share. The shareholder will be considered to have disposed of the remaining 9.25 percent of each Union Enterprises share for one-half of a Unicorp warrant on a taxable basis.

(continued)

EXHIBIT 1 (cont.)

13. As at March 31, 1984, the share capital of Union Enterprises consisted of:

113,299	Class A, Series A, 5½% Preference Shares—$50 Par
90,000	Class A, Series B, 6% Preference Shares—$50 Par
92,200	Class A, Series C, 5% Preference Shares—$50 Par
73,000	Class B, Series 2, Variable Preference Shares—$20 Par
1,700,000	Class B, Series 3, 7% Preference Shares—$20 Par
1,751,000	Class B, Series 4, 9⅞% Preference Shares—$20 Par
2,500,000	Class B, Series 5, 14.38% Preference Shares—$20 Par
32,071,314	Common Shares

14. As at December 31, 1984, the share capital of Unicorp consisted of:

276,000	Class I, Series C, 10% Preference Shares—$20 Par
43,525	Class I, Series 1, Employee Preference Shares—$20 Par
3,546,870	Class II, Series A, $0.80 Preference Shares—$10 Par
4,707,883	Class A, Non-Voting Shares
3,238,948	Class B, Voting Shares

EXHIBIT 2

UNICORP CANADA CORPORATION
Pro Forma Condensed Consolidated Balance Sheet
As at December 31, 1984
(CA$, thousands)

Assets	
Current Assets	$ 405,651
Utility Plant	850,610
Real Estate Investments	318,611
Resource Properties	304,898
Other Long Term Investments	132,663
Deferred Charges	66,753
Other Assets	4,052
Total Assets	$2,083,238
Liabilities	
Current Liabilities	$ 506,797
Long Term Debt	612,264
	1,119,061
Deferred Income Taxes	204,040
Minority Interest	307,331
Shareholders' Equity	
Share Capital	426,155
Retained Earnings	25,934
Foreign Currency Translation Adjustment	717
	452,806
Total Liabilities and Shareholders' Equity	$2,083,238

EXHIBIT 3

UNICORP CANADA CORPORATION
Pro Forma Condensed Consolidated Statement of Income
For the Year Ended December 31, 1984
(CA$, thousands)

Revenues	
Utility operations	$1,353,357
Rental operations	54,087
Resource operations	33,256
Capital gains	39,163
Other	40,593
	1,520,456
Expenses	
Operating and maintenance	1,220,350
Depreciation, amortization and depletion	53,239
Interest	107,823
	1,381,412
Income Including Minority Interest	139,044
Minority Interest	21,885
Income Before Income Taxes	117,159
Provision for Income Taxes	66,732
Income Before Extraordinary Item	50,427
Income Tax Recover from Prior Year's Losses	1,106
Net Income	51,533
Preference Dividend Requirement	36,275
Income Attributable to Class A Non-Voting and Class B Voting Shareholders	$ 15,258
Income Per Class A Non-Voting and Class B Voting Share	
Basic	$ 1.92
Fully Diluted	$ 1.34

EXHIBIT 4

BURNS FOODS LTD.
Organization Chart

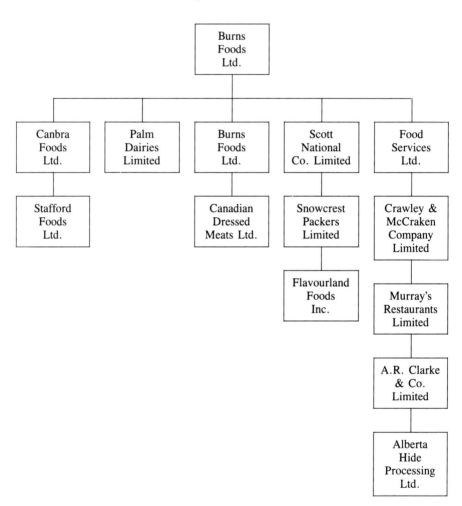

EXHIBIT 5

UNION ENTERPRISES LTD.
Trading in Common Shares

1985		UEL SHARE PRICE			UEL VOLUME	TSE300 INDEX
		HIGH	LOW	CLOSE		
January	29	$13.250	$13.125	$13.250	51,597	2580.06
	30	13.000	12.375	12.750	334,757	2604.02
	31	12.750	12.500	12.625	302,557	2595.05
February	1	12.875	12.375	12.750	197,497	2575.45
	4	12.875	12.625	12.875	142,376	2588.88
	5	12.875	12.500	12.625	221,756	2605.28
	6	12.625	12.250	12.375	172,658	2614.48
	7	12.625	12.375	12.500	338,170	2620.69
	8	12.500	12.375	12.375	103,411	2612.92
	11	12.500	12.250	12.375	205,768	2601.78
	12	12.500	12.250	12.500	417,437	2602.15
	13	12.500	12.250	12.250	139,146	2628.31
	14	12.375	12.250	12.375	119,726	2623.17
	15	12.375	12.250	12.375	69,430	2614.43
	18	12.250	11.750	12.000	94,049	2608.16
	19	12.125	11.875	12.000	184,785	2609.70
	20	12.750	11.750	12.625	1,470,720	2614.72
	21	12.750	12.125	12.375	354,437	2605.76
	22	12.375	12.125	12.250	129,476	2591.21
	25	12.375	12.000	12.000	124,345	2570.92
	26	12.125	12.000	12.000	61,280	2584.75
	27	12.250	11.875	12.125	338,166	2585.40
	28	12.000	11.875	12.000	56,449	2594.98
March	1	12.000	11.875	12.000	53,487	2625.21
	4	11.750	11.500	11.500	42,811	2628.54
	5	11.375	11.375	11.375	284,926	2647.02
	6	11.750	11.500	11.750	205,358	2643.01
	7	11.625	11.000	11.125	118,705	2618.25

EXHIBIT 6

UNION ENTERPRISES LTD.
UEL Common Share and TSE 300 Trading Data
March 7, 1985

	TIME INTERVAL	LAST PRICE UEL COMMON	VOLUME TRADED UEL COMMON	TSE 300 INDEX
Open	10:00	$11.750		2643.01
	10:00–10:59	11.625	23,221	2629.94
	11:00–11:59	11.500	39,770	2630.22
	12:00–12:59	11.500	31,486	2627.42
	13:00–13:59	11.500	8,925	2627.52
	14:00–14:59	11.375	6,578	2621.50
	15:00–15:59	11.125	8,725	2618.25
Close	16:00	11.125	118,705	2618.25

EXHIBIT 7

UNICORP CANADA CORPORATION
Selected Trading Information on Class A Non-Voting
and Class II Preference Shares[a]

1985		CLASS A NON-VOTING	CLASS II PREFERRED
January	2	$7.938[b]	$8.125[b]
	3	7.750[b]	8.000
	4	7.750	7.750
	7	7.750	7.500
	8	7.625	7.750
	9	7.625	7.750
	10	8.000	8.000
	11	7.875[b]	8.000
	14	7.875	8.000[b]
	15	8.000	8.000
	16	7.875[b]	7.750
	17	8.000	8.000
	18	8.000	7.750
	21	7.938[b]	7.750
	22	8.125	8.000
	23	8.125	8.375
	24	8.500	8.500
	25	9.000	8.875
	28	9.000	8.875
	29	8.875	9.250
	30	8.250	8.875
	31	8.500	8.750
February	1	8.500	8.375
	4	8.375	8.375
	5	8.500	8.500
	6	8.250	8.375
	7	8.500	8.500
	8	8.250	8.500
	11	8.250	8.375
	12	8.375	8.250
	13	8.000	8.250
	14	8.000	8.250
	15	8.000	8.375
	18	8.125[b]	8.000
	19	8.500	8.375
	20	8.250	8.250
	21	8.375	8.250
	22	8.125	8.250
	25	8.250	8.250
	26	8.000	8.125
	27	8.125	8.313[b]
	28	8.188[b]	8.313[b]

(continued)

EXHIBIT 7 (cont.)

1985		CLASS A NON-VOTING	CLASS II PREFERRED
March	1	8.250	8.125
	4	8.188[b]	8.250[b]
	5	8.125	8.125
	6	8.250	8.250
	7	8.125	8.250

[a]The annualized standard deviation of price changes for the class A non-voting common was 31%.
[b]Stock not traded, values are mean of bid/ask quotes.

EXHIBIT 8

Selected Interest Rates on February 7, 1985

GOVERNMENT OF CANADA				
Term	3 months	1–3 years	3–5 years	5–10 years	>10 years
Yield	11.56%	11.92%	12.15%	12.22%	12.43%

Source: Financial Post.

43

SHERRITT GORDON LTD.—PROXY CONTEST

On September 19, 1990 Charles Heinrich, President and CEO of Sherritt Gordon Ltd. (Sherritt), called the shareholders' meeting to order. This was a special meeting to vote on a proposal to remove the present directors from office and elect new directors to the board. It had been just over two months since a group called Canada SherGor Enterprises (SherGor), led by Ian Delaney, a Bay Street deal-maker, had purchased 5% of Sherritt and requested the meeting (see Exhibit 1 for a chronology of events). Charles wondered if Ian had generated enough support among the shareholders for his proposal to replace the board of directors. If Ian was successful, this would be the last meeting that Charles would chair at Sherritt.

BACKGROUND ON THE COMPANY

The company was incorporated in Ontario on July 5, 1927, as Sherritt Gordon Mines Limited. On June 1, 1988, the company changed its name to Sherritt Gordon Limited.

In the early 1920s, a portion of the original property at Sherridon, Manitoba was acquired by Messrs. Sherritt and Madole. In 1926–27, J.P. Gordon, Thayer

This case was prepared by David Fear and Marc Lavine under the supervision of Professor Robert W. White for the sole purpose of providing material for class discussion at the Western Business School. Certain names and other identifying information may have been disguised to protect confidentiality. It is not intended to illustrate either effective or ineffective handling of a managerial situation. Any reproduction, in any form, of the material in this case is prohibited except with the written consent of the School.

Lindsley and Robert Jowsey acquired options on the property which totalled 58 claims, following which the present company was incorporated and 3,000,000 vendor shares were issued for the Sherridon claims.

By June 1990, Sherritt was one of Canada's largest natural resource companies. Headquartered in Toronto, Ontario, Sherritt operated through four separate business divisions including Fertilizers, Metals, Special Products, and Technology, with sales totalling $545.9 million in 1989 (see Exhibit 2). Sales and operating profit of each division were as follows:

TABLE 1
SHERRITT'S SALES AND PROFITS BY DIVISION

DIVISION	SALES ($000's)		OPERATING PROFIT ($000's)	
	1989	1988	1989	1988
TOTAL	545,899	545,319	73,926	94,877
Fertilizer	139,487	139,781	20,963	17,939
Metals	364,933	364,278	45,495	65,846
Special Products	33,123	30,877	5,019	6,866
Technology	8,356	10,383	2,449	4,226

Fertilizer Division

Operations of this division were conducted by Sherritt Fertilizer Company (65% owned by Sherritt and 35% by Unocal Canada Limited). The division included the manufacture, distribution and marketing of a broad range of nitrogen and phosphate fertilizers. Production facilities were located in Alberta and included modern world-scale ammonia and urea plants, as well as smaller ammonia, urea, ammonium sulphate and phosphate facilities. Primary markets were in Western Canada and the U.S. Pacific Northwest, where products were distributed mainly through a network of independent dealers and a major distributor. Fertilizers were also sold to offshore markets (see Exhibit 3 for historical fertilizer prices).

Metals Division

This division was comprised of a metals refining business and a rolling mill and coinage products business. The metals refining unit treated nickel and cobalt materials from third parties and marketed the metal output. The nickel refinery had a capacity of 55,000,000 lbs. and the cobalt refinery a capacity of 2,500,000 lbs. Both facilities usually operated at near capacity levels with materials supplied from a number of countries. Nickel was marketed through Sherritt Metals Marketing Co. Stainless steel represented approximately 50% of refined nickel sales; the chemical market, welding rod industry, powder metallurgy and foundries accounted for the balance. Forty percent of nickel sales were made in North American markets, with

Europe and Japan being approximately 30% each (see Exhibit 4 for historical nickel prices).

Special Products Division

This division was comprised of two separate areas of business: the Specialty Metal Products unit which manufactured and marketed a range of proprietary materials for the aerospace, electronic, automotive and mining industries; and the Special Chemical Products unit which manufactured and sold a range of small volume commodity chemicals including water treatment chemicals, sulphuric acid, hydrogen sulphide and carbon disulphide.

Technology Division

Formed during 1989, the Technology Division consisted of the Research Centre, Engineering Department and the External Technology business which previously was part of the Special Products Division. Also included was the new government cost-sharing program in which $140,000,000 was to be spent over 5 years by Westaim Technologies Inc., a subsidiary of the company, to research and develop advanced industrial materials.

TAKEOVER THEORY

Some economists argue that there is a theoretical point at which companies are operating at their "optimal" profitability. This occurs when the company's strategy and management capabilities combine to effectively utilize the company's assets. If the company deviates from the "optimal" point, profitability will fall and the returns to the investors will be below their expected values. It is at this point that the company becomes a takeover target. A raider can exploit this opportunity and create value by restoring the company to the "optimal" point (see Exhibit 5).

Unfortunately, this "optimal" point of profitability is not determined by any simple valuation formula, but is influenced by individual perceptions about what a company is capable of accomplishing. Even if one believes that a company has deviated significantly from the "optimal" point and has become a takeover target, it is difficult to determine the root of the company's problems. Without a clear understanding of the changes necessary to improve performance, the raider will not be able to attain the "optimal" level and create additional value.

The performance of a company is usually synonymous with the performance of the management. However, it is extremely difficult to evaluate the management's performance independent of environmental factors to determine the ability of the company to operate at the "optimal" performance. Sherritt's track record over the previous decade is summarized in Exhibits 6, 7 and 8.

METHODS OF TAKEOVERS

In order to take over a company, the raider must gain voting control of the common stock. Traditionally this had been accomplished by purchasing, either by cash or share offering, the individual shares. This takeover method required strong financial backing.

Throughout the 1980s, large voting blocks could be acquired with the use of high yields bonds. These bonds carried a higher interest rate, in some cases 600–800 basis points over government bonds, in order to compensate the bondholder for the additional risk created by the resulting highly leveraged capital structure. Due to the higher perceived risk of default, these bonds were rated below investment grade quality and became commonly known as junk bonds.

As the junk bond market grew, financing for takeovers became readily available. Many companies, fearful of being selected as takeover targets, took defensive action. One major defense tactic was the implementation of shareholder rights plans, known as poison pills. Such plans increased the difficulty for a raider to gain control of the target company without the approval of the existing management. Between October 1988 and February 1990, 21 poison pills were implemented by Canadian companies.

In 1990, the faltering economy, Wall Street scandals and the alarming increase in high yield bond defaults have effectively eliminated the high yield market for new issues (see Exhibit 9 for junk bonds issued in United States). Without access to such financing, raiders have been forced to seek alternative methods of gaining voting control of corporations.

One of these methods was the use of a proxy contest. Such a takeover tactic would allow the raider to gain effective voting control of a company without purchasing the shares. Such a tactic would also be effective against companies that had shareholder rights plans in place.

SHAREHOLDER RIGHTS PLAN

On November 23, 1989, Sherritt's management implemented a shareholder rights plan (see Exhibit 10). The stated rationale for this plan was to prevent creeping takeover bids or partial bids which might not be fair to all shareholders. Sherritt had no knowledge of an impending takeover bid. Commentators stated that an absence of a majority shareholder had prompted Sherritt to adopt the rights plan. Commentators also suggested that the rights plan was adopted, in part, to defend the company against Trelleborg AB which, it has been speculated, may have accumulated 9% of Sherritt Gordon.

Although the plan was passed by a slim margin of 53.6%, some investors felt that their opportunity to realize the full value of their shares was being inhibited by increasing the difficulty in making a takeover bid. Thus, many investors believed that the plan was implemented only to protect management's interests.

THE PROXY CONTEST

Proxy Contest Overview

Although shareholders have the ability to vote their block of shares, many shareholders do not attend shareholder meetings to vote. As an alternative to attending meetings, shareholders can vote via a proxy. Proxy consent can be given on a particular issue or the shareholders can grant complete voting control to another party (see Exhibit 11).

Fundamental changes in the Canadian business environment have contributed to an increased use of proxies. These changes included:

- Increased concentration of corporate control. The size and economic power of institutional investors had almost doubled over the previous four years. In 1989, the top 40 Canadian pension funds owned $43.4 billion in Canadian equities, versus $23.6 billion in 1985.
- Higher level of shareholder awareness of corporate governance issues. Institutions were no longer indifferent to voting rights and were becoming increasingly hostile towards management.
- Frequent low quorum and low turnout at shareholder meetings had created a high opportunity for active and vocal shareholders to disproportionately influence management.
- The disappearance of the high yield bond market had removed an effective source of capital necessary for tender offer takeovers to gain corporate control.

Proxy contests emerged as a vehicle for either gaining control of a company or for shareholders, particularly institutions, to increase their participation in the corporate decision-making process.

The Proxy Contest Begins

On July 10, 1990, SherGor announced that they had acquired 5% of Sherritt and requested a special meeting of the shareholders to vote on a proposal to replace the current Board. SherGor was recently formed by Ian Delaney and Sprott Securities to bring forth this proposal. Sprott Securities had once placed a 34% interest in Sherritt to its institutional investor clients. Through regular dealings with these investors Sprott determined that there was widespread dissatisfaction with the present management of Sherritt. At this point, both Sherritt's directors and SherGor started their solicitation of shareholder support.

On July 17, Charles Heinrich issued a press statement (Exhibit 12) outlining Sherritt's position regarding the recent events. Sherritt's management followed this press release with an information circular (Exhibit 13) mailed to all shareholders on August 3, which confronted Canada SherGor's allegations. SherGor responded with an information circular (Exhibit 14) on August 29, outlining the problems with the current management.

SherGor's Allegations

Below is a summary of the allegations about Sherritt's current management as voiced by SherGor:

1. Sherritt does not have strong management.
2. "Sherritt needs a new strategic direction" . . . "the Company lacks strategic direction."
3. ". . . the Sherritt Gordon board has not seized the opportunities provided by its strong asset base and sound operating management to increase shareholder value."
4. ". . . we would like to manage the company so that it would not be susceptible to such violent swings with its two basic commodities."
5. Sprott and Delaney criticized Sherritt for "failing to secure enough nickel feed for its refinery in Fort Saskatchewan, Alberta."
6. Sherritt management and board do not have "a sufficient equity interest in the company."

THE SPECIAL MEETING OF THE SHAREHOLDERS

In these final moments of the proxy contest, there were a number of unanswered questions: Was the current management of Sherritt running the company properly? Did the Board have the support of the shareholders? Had Charles Heinrich taken the proper actions to defend the management against this proxy contest? What was best for Sherritt?

EXHIBIT 1

Chronology of Sherritt Gordon Ltd. Proxy Fight

DATE	EVENT
April 20, 1988	Sprott Securities Ltd. buys 34% of Sherritt from Newmont Mining for CA$50.4MM. The shares are re-marketed to institutions (Vencap Equities Alberta buys the largest piece, 11.2%).
August 4, 1989	Sherritt shares rise $7/8$ to $14 on rumours that Placer Dome Inc. is interested in acquiring the company.
November 2, 1989	Trelleborg AB rumoured to own 9% of Sherritt.
November 22, 1989	Sherritt's Board of Directors approves a Shareholder Rights Plan (designed to prevent creeping takeovers). Analysts speculate that this is in response to a rumoured Trelleborg bid.
December 31, 1989	Sherritt's contract with Inco for nickel concentrate expires (Inco supplied 60% of the nickel concentrate processed at Sherritt's Fort Saskatchewan refinery).
January 9, 1990	Charles Heinrich, formerly president of Alcan Pacific Ltd., is named president and CEO of Sherritt.
April 19, 1990	At the Sherritt Annual meeting, 53.6% of those voting favour management's shareholder rights plan.
June 30, 1990	Sherritt's nickel refinery temporarily closes because of lack of feed stock.
July 10, 1990	Ian Delaney (formerly President of Horsham Corp.) and Bruce Walter announce that their company, SherGor, has 5% of the shares of Sherritt and is requesting a special meeting of shareholders pursuant to the Ontario Business Corporations Act. The purpose of the special meeting is to vote on removing the present directors from office and electing new directors.
July 17, 1990	Sherritt calls the special meeting for September 19, 1990, and hires RBC Dominion Securities Inc. to provide assistance.
August 1, 1990	Scotia McLeod Inc. analyst Graham Encott recommends that shareholders vote against the dissident shareholders unless they table convincing business proposals in their information circular.
September 19, 1990	Special Meeting of the shareholders to vote on the removal of the present directors.

EXHIBIT 2

SHERRITT GORDON LTD.
Financial Performance
Consolidated Statement of Income and Retained Earnings

YEARS ENDED	DEC. 31 1989	DEC. 31 1988	DEC. 31 1987	DEC. 31 1986	DEC. 31 1985	DEC. 31 1984	DEC. 31 1983
				$000s			
Revenue							
Metal Sales	364,933	364,278	154,908	148,790	152,806	232,194	217,172
Mining[a]	–	–	–	79,476	100,302	–	–
Fertilizer & Chemicals Sales	139,487	139,871	119,697	138,492	167,300	161,466	114,618
Special Products	33,123	41,260	31,207	21,997	21,623	–	–
Other	8,356	–	–	2,131	3,343	3,504	5,293
Total Revenue	545,899	545,409	305,812	390,886	445,374	397,164	337,083
Operating Costs	433,842	417,558	258,237	320,810	351,482	326,180	277,796
Research & Dev. Expenses	4,542	1,167	1,904	1,588	2,403	1,694	1,774
Exploration Expenses[b]	–	–	–	3,075	2,766	2,622	2,619
Admin., Selling General Exp.	21,347	14,533	11,839	12,184	12,207	10,859	8,868
Interest Expense	8,026	10,167	9,309	25,075	28,438	32,849	18,060
Depreciation, etc.	26,517	23,379	18,115	32,530	39,837	37,693	22,842
Foreign Exchange Loss	–	–	–	247	819	–	–
Income Taxes	19,444	27,373	3,129	(993)	2,790	(6,125)	288

(continued)

EXHIBIT 2 (cont.)

YEARS ENDED	DEC. 31 1989	DEC. 31 1988	DEC. 31 1987	DEC. 31 1986	DEC. 31 1985	DEC. 31 1984	DEC. 31 1983
				$000s			
Minority Interest	—	—	—	(434)	—	—	—
Unusual Items[c]	—	—	—	24,600	19,461	—	—
Discontinued Operations (net)	—	5,259	2,606	—	—	—	—
Net Income, Operations	32,181	56,491	5,885	(27,796)	(14,829)	(8,608)	4,836
Extraordinary Item[d]	—	—	—	—	—	(4,214)	—
Net Income	32,181	56,491	5,885	(27,796)	(14,829)	(12,822)	4,836
Previous Retained Earnings	66,170	56,491	20,987	52,922	74,211	93,928	94,706
Preferred Dividends	2,305	3,742	3,624	4,139	4,377	4,961	4,654
Common Dividends	7,519	7,489	2,338	—	2,083	1,934	960
Retained Earnings	88,527	66,170	20,910	20,987	52,922	74,211	93,928
Cash Flow ($000s)	78,112	97,923	26,014	31,616	46,871	23,920	28,678
Per Share	$3.12	$3.92	$1.17	$1.43	$2.14	$1.11	$1.34
Earnings per Share and Dividends Paid							
Common: Earned[e]	$1.19	$2.27	$0.10	$(1.45)	$(0.89)	$(0.63)	$0.01
Earned[f]	1.19	2.27	0.10	(1.45)	(0.89)	(0.83)	0.01
Paid	0.300	0.300	0.105	—	0.095	0.090	0.045

[a]Combined with metal sales to 1984.

[b]Combined with research and development expense in 1987 and thereafter.

[c]Unusual items comprise the following: in 1986, $24,565,000 write-off of Ruttan mine assets and $16,435,000 provision for Ruttan Mine closure costs, less $16,400,000 future income taxes; in 1985, reduction in carrying value of Ruttan Mine assets of $30,000,000 and write-off of original urea plant of $2,220,000, less $12,759,000 future income taxes.

[d]Investment write-off in 1984.

[e]Before (¹after) extraordinary items.

580

EXHIBIT 2 (cont.)

SHERRITT GORDON LTD.
Financial Performance
Consolidated Balance Sheet

AS AT	DEC. 31 1989	DEC. 31 1988	DEC. 31 1987	DEC. 31 1986	DEC. 31 1985	DEC. 31 1984	DEC. 31 1983
				$000s			
Assets							
Current							
Cash, Short Term Inv.	5,907	62,592	–	–	17,996	–	5,530
Accounts Receivable	78,230	75,021	65,507	62,071	78,931	85,989	53,723
Inventory of Products	84,835	87,380	70,706	68,941	80,107	53,469	48,564
Supplies at Av. Cost	20,493	19,434	18,788	22,766	22,955	21,762	19,912
Prepaid Expenses	9,520	10,485	8,441	6,889	2,821	2,670	1,996
	198,985	254,912	164,442	160,667	202,810	183,890	129,725
Housing Loans Due	–	–	–	6,043	5,313	5,064	5,180
Unamort. Dev. Costs	36,205	38,827	39,995	79,152	49,644	59,875	49,998
Invest. in Other Cos.	–	–	12,197	1,729	1,749	1,746	5,049
Equity S. Metals Mktg.	3,763	7,171	2,619	–	–	–	–
Other Loans & Advs.	8,867	7,860	5,097	–	–	–	–
Patents Less w/o	–	–	–	–	–	–	1,217
Unamort. Exch. Loss	–	–	–	–	–	19,367	4,405
Fixed							
Prop., Plant. & Equip.	544,578	515,044	365,059	457,146	599,537	607,568	601,165
Depreciation	(205,513)	(181,900)	(151,588)	(213,401)	(208,476)	(184,167)	(153,958)
	339,065	333,144	213,471	243,745	391,061	423,401	447,207
	586,885	641,914	437,821	491,336	650,577	673,343	642,781
Liabilities							
Current							
Bank Indebt.	16,372	–	19,969	30,537	30,083	33,490	–
Accts. Payable & Accr.	93,410	113,730	82,102	70,286	84,453	73,897	53,535
Dividends Pay.	–	–	–	–	–	–	1,163

(continued)

EXHIBIT 2 (cont.)

AS AT	DEC. 31 1989	DEC. 31 1988	DEC. 31 1987	DEC. 31 1986	DEC. 31 1985	DEC. 31 1984	DEC. 31 1983
	$000s						
Long Term Debt	—	21,055	11,127	134,270	18,254	15,129	16,140
Inc. Tax & Royal. Pay.	—	—	—	10,510	—	2,105	2,904
Long Term Debt (net)	109,782	134,785	113,198	111,333	132,790	124,621	73,742
Mine Closure Costs	125,831	151,940	105,355	16,435	240,802	254,982	251,185
Deferred Income Taxes	62,583	44,623	20,402	12,408	29,197	37,703	42,746
Deferred Revenue	—	—	—	5,302	2,800	—	—
Minority Interest	48,886	43,696	—	10,144	10,368	—	—
Shareholders' Equity							
Preferred Stock	—	50,000	53,125	56,250	59,735	62,500	62,500
Common Stock	80,108	79,532	53,663	53,039	51,155	48,158	47,512
Contributed Surplus[a]	71,168	71,168	71,168	71,168	71,168	71,168	71,168
Retained Earnings	88,527	66,170	20,910	20,987	52,922	74,211	93,928
	239,803	266,870	198,866	201,444	234,620	256,037	275,108
	586,885	641,914	437,821	491,336	650,577	673,343	642,781
Working Capital ($000s)	89,203	120,127	51,244	49,334	70,020	39,269	55,983
Ratio	1.81	1.89	1.45	1.44	1.53	1.32	1.76
Equities							
Net Worth[b] ($000s)	239,803	266,870	198,866	201,444	234,620	256,037	275,108
Preferred	—	$106.75	$74.87	$71.62	$79.03	$81.93	$88.03
Common	9.57	8.69	6.54	6.55	7.99	9.01	9.96
SHARES OUTSTANDING							
Series A Pref.[c]	—	2,500,000	2,656,250	2,812,500	2,968,750	3,125,000	3,125,000
Common	25,064,079	24,962,954	22,278,662	22,178,657	21,924,093	21,489,188	21,336,383

[a] Consisting of net premiums on shares issued plus cash retained on shares forfeited less commission on sales of shares.

[b] Available for capital stock, based on shareholders' equity. Preferred stock deducted at stated value before calculation of common equity.

[c] Redeemed Jul. 20, 1989.

582

EXHIBIT 3
Historical Fertilizer Prices

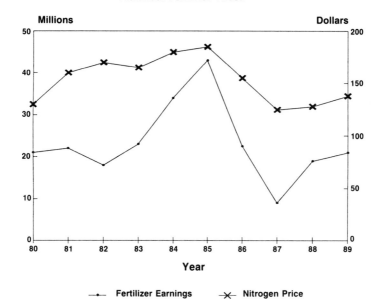

— •— Fertilizer Earnings   —×— Nitrogen Price

EXHIBIT 4
Historical Nickel Prices

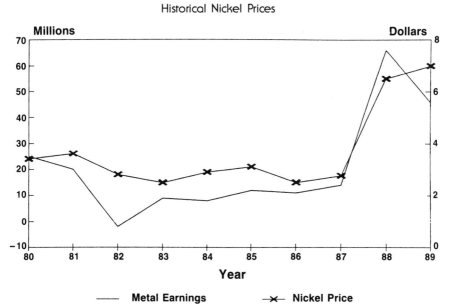

—— Metal Earnings   —×— Nickel Price

EXHIBIT 5

Corporate Value Gaps

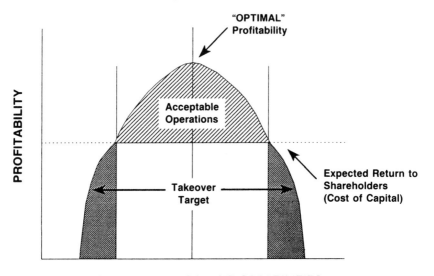

STRATEGY AND MANAGEMENT CAPABILITIES

EXHIBIT 6

Stock Performance Relative to TSE

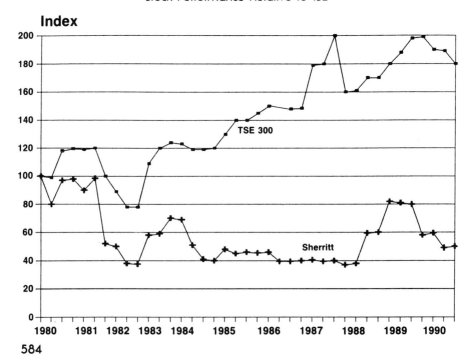

EXHIBIT 7

SHERRITT GORDON LIMITED
Price–Volume (000) Study
(08/01/1989 to 09/13/1990)

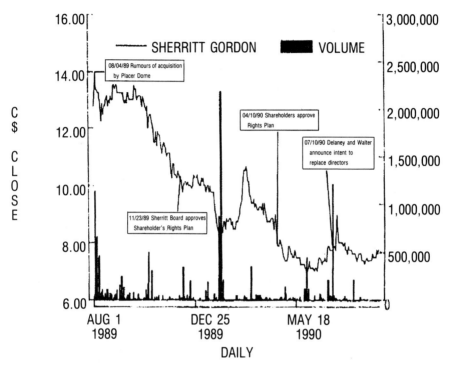

Proxy Contest Announced on July 10, 1990.

EXHIBIT 8

Earnings per Share and Return on Equity

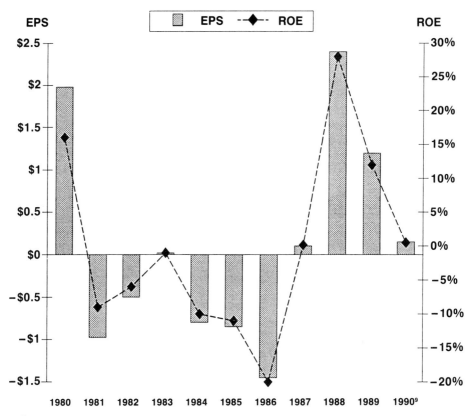

^{9}Six months ended June 30, 1990.

EXHIBIT 9

United States
High Yield Market

OVERVIEW OF THE HIGH YIELD MARKET
Volume of New Public Straight High Yield Debt Issues (1)

(U.S.$ Billions)

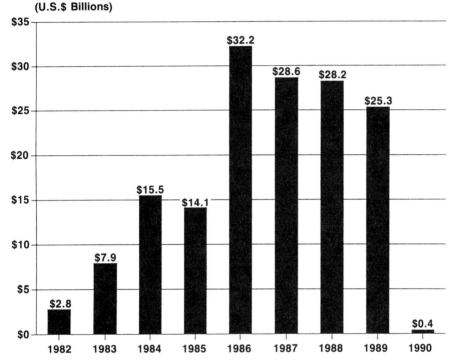

Note: (1) Through August 15, 1990.

High Yield
as % of New
Corporate Issues

| | 5.5% | 17.2% | 15.8% | 18.4% | 21.7% | 25.3% | 23.0% | 20.5% | 0.9% |

EXHIBIT 10

Shareholder Rights Plan

Effective Date:	November 23, 1989.
Flip-In Event:	In the event that a person becomes the beneficial owner of 20% or more of the common shares of Sherritt, other than by way of a Permitted Bid, the rights entitle the holders thereof, other than the acquiror, to purchase common shares of Sherritt at a 50% discount to the market price.
Permitted Bid:	A permitted bid is a takeover bid made to all shareholders for all the shares of Sherritt in accordance with the takeover bid circular requirements of the Securities Act (Ontario). The offeror under the permitted bid may offer cash or securities, but must be approved by 51% of the votes cast by independent shareholders at a special meeting of shareholders called for such purposes.
Separation Time:	The rights will not be exercisable and will not trade separate and apart from the common shares until a person or group of persons acquire, or announce an intention to acquire (in a manner that does not constitute a Permitted Bid), 20% or more of the votes attached to all securities of Sherritt.
Term:	Ten years.
Shareholder Approval:	The rights plan was approved by the shareholders of Sherritt at the annual meeting held on April 19, 1990.

EXHIBIT 11

Proxy Form

THIS PROXY IS SOLICITED BY SPROTT SECURITIES LIMITED AND CANADA SHERGOR ENTERPRISES INC. FOR USE AT THE SPECIAL MEETING OF THE HOLDERS OF COMMON SHARES OF SHERRITT GORDON LIMITED (THE "CORPORATION") TO BE HELD ON SEPTEMBER 19, 1990 FOR THE PURPOSE OF REMOVING FROM OFFICE THE PRESENT DIRECTORS OF THE CORPORATION AND ELECTING NEW DIRECTORS. Management of the Corporation is not soliciting this proxy.

The undersigned holder of common shares of the Corporation hereby appoints Eric S. Sprott, or failing him Ian W. Delaney, or failing him Bruce V. Walter, or instead of any of them

with full power of substitution, as proxy holder to attend, vote and act for and on behalf of the undersigned at the special meeting of holders of common shares of the Corporation to be held on September 19, 1990 in Commerce Hall, Commerce Court, Toronto, Ontario at 11:00 o'clock a.m., Toronto time, and at any adjournments thereof (the "Meeting").

Subject to the directions, if any, made below, and to applicable law, the proxyholder appointed above will have the same powers at the Meeting as the undersigned would have if he or she were personally present. The proxyholder is directed to vote as indicated below:

(continued)

EXHIBIT 11 (cont.)

---

1. FOR ☐ or AGAINST ☐ the removal from office of the present directors of the Corporation.

2. FOR ☐ the election of the following persons as directors except WITHHOLD FROM VOTING FOR any persons whose names are crossed out below.

NEIL CARRAGHER	DANIEL P. OWEN
RALPH S. CUNNINGHAM	ERIC S. SPROTT
IAN W. DELANEY	JAMES G. TEMPLE
FRANK W. KING	BRUCE V. WALTER
EDWARD M. LAKUSTA	

This proxy confers discretionary authority upon the persons named herein to vote as they may see fit with respect to amendments or variations, if any, to matters identified in the notice of meeting and with respect to other matters, if any, which may properly come before the Meeting or any adjournment thereof.

This proxy revokes any prior proxy or proxies given by the undersigned in respect of the Meeting.

PROXIES SHOULD BE MAILED IN THE ENCLOSED ENVELOPE OR DELIVERED SO AS TO REACH SPROTT SECURITIES LIMITED PRIOR TO 1 P.M. ON MONDAY, SEPTEMBER 17, 1990

DATED: _____, 1990

PLEASE SIGN EXACTLY AS YOUR NAME IS PRINTED ON THIS FORM OF PROXY

_____
Signature(s) of Shareholder(s)

_____
(please print name here)

_____
(number of shares)

☐ CHECK HERE IF THIS PROXY REVOKES A PRIOR PROXY GIVEN BY YOU IN RESPECT OF THE MEETING.

EXHIBIT 12

Press Release

---

sherritt   Toronto, July 17, 1990

Dear Shareholder:

I am writing to outline recent events which preceded a requisition from a shareholder for a shareholders meeting.

On July 10, 1990, Messrs. Ian W. Delaney, Bruce V. Walter and Eric S. Sprott initiated a meeting with Mr. E.L. Donegan, Chairman of the Board and me. They claimed to own 5% of the shares of Sherritt and demanded that the Chief Executive Officer and a majority of the Board of Directors be replaced by their representatives. Mr. Delaney would appoint himself as Chief Executive Officer. Most of their 5% holding was not acquired until after that meeting.

By telephone on July 11, they requested a meeting with Sherritt's Board of Directors prior to July 17. They stated there should be no press releases until then and asked that Sherritt not make any public disclosure. On July 13, they issued a press release on the subject and sent a requisition to Sherritt requesting a shareholders meeting.

Sherritt is unclear about the motivation of Messrs. Delaney, Walter and Sprott since they have provided no details regarding their plans. Their company was not a shareholder of record prior to July 10, 1990, and they have made no proposals regarding the business of Sherritt. The Board has received no other complaints or comments from investors evidencing "widespread dissatisfaction" as alleged by Mr. Sprott, nor was there any such indication at the recently held Annual Meeting where all management resolutions were passed.

Despite the premature public disclosure by Mr. Sprott, and various changes in their demands, the Sherritt Board of Directors are willing to meet with Messrs. Delaney, Walter and Sprott this week and have so advised them. It is hoped that this meeting will provide some indication of the specific concerns of these people, whether they reflect the views of any other shareholders and what, if anything, they propose other than taking control of the Board.

One may well ask the question: If these people want to take control of Sherritt, why don't they do it the old-fashioned way with a cash bid to all shareholders?

Sherritt will call a shareholders meeting in response to the requisition within the period specified by the Business Corporations Act, 1982 (Ontario), but regrets the expense and inconvenience of a second shareholders meeting so close to the Annual Meeting.

Sherritt has retained RBC Dominion Securities Inc. to provide advice on this matter.

Yours sincerely,

Charles G. Heinrich
President and Chief Executive Officer

Sherritt Gordon Limited

EXHIBIT 13

Sherritt Gordon—Information Circular

sherritt

August 3, 1990

Dear Shareholder:

As most of you know, Ian Delaney and Bruce Walter, through Canada SherGor Enterprises Inc. have requested a special meeting for the purpose of removing the present directors from office and electing new directors. By this move they are attempting to take control of your Corporation. We believe that it is critical to your investment that their attempt be defeated and that you vote the enclosed proxy AGAINST the resolution to remove the present directors. We are confident that we have the ability to manage your company in your best interests.

Canada SherGor Enterprises Inc. is a private company incorporated by Messrs. Delaney and Walter for the purpose of requisitioning the special meeting. Its shareholding in Sherritt was acquired in July so that it would be able to requisition the special meeting. This shareholding has been hedged to eliminate financial risk to them of share price fluctuation.

Messrs. Delaney and Walter, together with Eric Sprott, met with Sherritt's board to request executive control of Sherritt. They still have not provided Sherritt with any plans or proposals they have beyond removal of the directors and have not even provided the names of nominees other than themselves.

Messrs. Sprott and Delaney have made a number of allegations about Sherritt and its management. These allegations are totally without merit and display a lack of knowledge of the Corporation and its businesses. The enclosed Information Circular responds to each of these allegations.

This letter accompanies a Proxy solicited by management in connection with the special meeting to be held Wednesday September 19 at 11:00 a.m. in Commerce Court on the corner of Bay and Wellington Streets. We sincerely hope that you will be able to attend and vote against the resolution to remove the present directors. If you are unable to attend we strongly urge you to ensure that your shares are voted against the resolution by returning the enclosed blue proxy to us in the enclosed envelope.

Yours sincerely,

E.L. Donegan
Chairman of the Board

Sherritt Gordon Limited
P.O. Box 28, Commerce Court West, Toronto, Ontario M5L 1B1
(416) 363-9241 Telex 06-22195
FAX (416) 363-1624

EXHIBIT 14

Canada SherGor—Information Circular

page 1

Canada SherGor Enterprises Inc 5 Hazelton Avenue Suite 200 Toronto, Ontario M5R 2E1	Sprott Securities Limited Royal Bank Plaza South Tower, Suite 2300 P.O. Box 63 Toronto, Ontario M5J 2J2

To: Holders of Common Shares of Sherritt Gordon Limited

For over a decade, to be a shareholder of Sherritt has not been a rewarding experience. Possessing a solid asset base, the company has been run unimaginatively and without a strategic direction designed to enhance shareholder value. A board of directors with little or no financial stake in the company has been content with an erratic and generally poor earnings performance and poor share performance. In addition, the company has been confronted with serious problems threatening the viability of its core businesses which have not been adequately addressed.

Canada SherGor, with the support of Sprott Securities, has requisitioned a meeting of Sherritt's shareholders in order to give you an opportunity to make a meaningful choice. In a letter to shareholders, Mr. Heinrich, the present President of Sherritt, wrote, "If these people want to take control of Sherritt why don't they do it the old-fashioned way with a cash bid to all shareholders?" Mr. Heinrich misses the point. You have entrusted the present board of directors with setting the strategic direction of the company and managing its businesses. The meeting has been called not to take control of Sherritt from the shareholders of the company, but to give you the opportunity to exercise your control to put in office a new board who will provide strategic direction to increase shareholder value.

We are proposing a new board and executive management who will bring to Sherritt the vision, enthusiasm and commitment needed to revitalize the company and build Sherritt to deliver improved returns to shareholders. Seven of the nine board members will be outside directors. All of them are outstanding businessmen; their experience and records justify complete confidence on the part of shareholders.

The members of the proposed board do not offer a simple short-term solution to the poor performance of Sherritt. No "quick fix" will be attempted. Their collective ability and experience in providing entrepreneurial leadership to operating businesses in a variety of situations will be brought to bear in confronting the serious problems facing Sherritt and enhancing shareholder value.

The present directors of Sherritt are using substantial funds of your company to pay investment dealers to solicit votes on their behalf. We believe this is an inappropriate use of your company's funds. We ask you to read this information circular, then carefully weigh the choice put before you and vote on the merits. Your vote is important to the future of your investment in Sherritt. We hope you will conclude that voting FOR a new board of directors is in your best interest.

(continued)

EXHIBIT 14 (cont.)

---

page 2

We hope you can attend the September 19, 1990 meeting in person. If not, we ask that you complete and return the enclosed GREEN form of proxy in the envelope provided. You may do this even if you have previously signed a form of proxy in support of management; the more recent proxy automatically cancels the earlier one.

If you have any questions in connection with your proxy please call Lorne Graham at Sprott Securities at (416) 362-7485.

Yours truly,   Yours truly,
Canada SherGor Enterprises, Inc.   Sprott Securities Limited

Ian W. Delaney   Bruce V. Walter   Eric S. Sprott
Chairman   President   President & Chief Executive Officer

44

SASKATCHEWAN OIL AND GAS CORPORATION

In the late afternoon of August 27, 1985, David Tate, a Director of Wood Gundy Inc., gazed out of his Calgary office window towards the snowcapped foothills of the Rocky Mountains. Wood Gundy had been selected to lead manage Saskatchewan Oil and Gas Corporation's (Saskoil) privatization by way of an initial public offering (IPO). The underwriters had been asked to submit their recommendations on several issues, including the type of instrument, the size of issue, the pricing, and the marketing strategy. A meeting was scheduled tomorrow morning to discuss these issues with Saskoil's Privatization Steering Committee (PSC). All decisions would be complicated by the fact that Saskoil was a Crown corporation and this first privatization represented a major policy initiative by the Saskatchewan Conservative Government. David knew that every recommendation he made must reflect the objectives of the Province. He also knew that the volatile oil and gas industry was particularly challenging for new issues. The balancing of government goals and market realities was going to make this IPO significantly more complex than a standard stock issue.

BACKGROUND ON THE COMPANY

Saskoil was a Crown corporation that was formed in 1973 to participate in the exploration, development, production and transportation of crude oil and natural gas. Since the company's inception, it had been 100% owned by the Province of Saskatchewan. As a Crown corporation, Saskoil was regulated by the Saskatchewan Oil and Gas Corporation Act. The key consideration that prompted Saskatchewan's NDP government of the 1970s to consider greater involvement in the oil industry seems to have come from the overall role it accorded to three of the Province's mineral resources—potash, uranium, and oil—in fostering economic growth. The government was searching for ways to reduce its dependence on wheat and other grain crops and to develop a larger manufacturing and industrial base. In addition, the Saskatchewan Government intended Saskoil to support its public policy mandate on three fronts: guaranteed energy supply as a response to the first shocks of the world oil embargo, domestic ownership of natural resources, and increased exploration and development within the Province.

Operations were conducted in all three prairie Provinces with a heavy concentration of oil plays in Saskatchewan. Through its undeveloped land holdings and exploration activities, the company had a strong position in heavy oil. This area of activity was considered to have increasing potential as a result of developments leading to significant heavy oil upgrading capacity in Saskatchewan.

In 1976, Saskoil acquired the Saskatchewan properties and field operations of Atlantic Richfield Canada Limited. The acquisition of these oil and gas assets established Saskoil as a major light and medium oil producer in southern Saskatchewan. Saskoil's activities in the late 1970s and early 1980s centred around exploration and development of heavy oil reserves in the Kindersley-Lloydminster region. By 1983, Saskoil had participated in the discovery and development of seven major heavy oil pools in Saskatchewan: Marsden, Neilburg, Senlac, Plover Lake, Court, Luseland and Cactus Lake (see Exhibit 1).

In terms of oil production, in 1985, Saskoil ranked among the top 20 oil companies in Canada. Approximately 98% of Saskoil's revenue was derived from oil production in Saskatchewan, which averaged 14,114 barrels per day in 1984. This amount represented roughly 8% of the total production of crude oil in Saskatchewan. Gas production generated a minor percentage of Saskoil's revenues.

Exploration for Alberta light oil and Saskatchewan natural gas had been expanded in 1984 and 1985 in response to anticipated market opportunities. In addition, enhanced oil recovery methods will also be used as another source of new revenues. Finally, the exploration and production of natural gas, which accounted for roughly 2% of total production in 1985, continued to expand in order to play a more prominent role in the company's activities.

Saskoil's financial results had shown significant improvement from net earnings of $1,568,000 in 1982 to net earnings of $44,033,000 in 1984. During this same period, cash flow from operations increased 158% from $24,528,000 to $63,241,000. Exhibit 2 provides a more detailed look at Saskoil's operating results from 1981 to 1985.

OIL AND GAS INDUSTRY IN CANADA

In 1985 the oil and gas industry was a $20 billion plus per annum industry in Canada. The industry was divided into two types of activities: upstream operations, which include the exploration for, and development and production of, oil and gas; and downstream operations, which include refining, petrochemicals, and marketing. Integrated companies covered the entire spectrum of oil and gas industry activity. Saskoil's activities were concentrated in upstream operations.

Historically, downstream operations were the most profitable of the integrated operations since crude oil was relatively low priced prior to 1973. But downstream operations had since become less profitable as the integrated producers had to contend with a loss of control over crude oil supplies and prices, overcapacity in the industry, and price wars.

In late 1973, the oil embargo created an energy crisis that caused worldwide oil prices to skyrocket. As OPEC cut back oil exports to the western world, oil prices increased in one year from US$2.20 per barrel to US$10 per barrel. In addition, projections for Canada indicated that domestic oil demand would outstrip production as new discoveries in western Canada were decreasing and falling below the rate of consumption.

As a result of the expectations that the price of crude oil would rise to levels of $50 to $75 per barrel during the 1980s, a very significant investment boom took place in the upstream business in the late 1970s and early 1980s to meet demand. At that time, the TSE Oil and Gas Index outpaced the growth of all other industries represented by the TSE 300 Index. Also, the petroleum industry recorded year over year increases in after-tax profits of 53.8% and 31.0% in 1979 and 1980, respectively.

However, by early 1984, oil prices had stabilized at about 1981 levels, demand for crude was down, and OPEC control over supply and price was not as effective as in the past.

PRIVATIZATION

The desire of the Saskatchewan Government to privatize Saskoil resulted from three key events occurring between 1980 and 1984 that changed the original situation existing in 1973. Most importantly, election of a Conservative Government in 1982 resulted in the implementation by Premier Grant Devine of policies which included less government involvement in business, especially in a volatile industry which had caused Saskoil to suffer significant losses in 1981. Secondly, fears of restricted oil supply were subsiding and the original "guaranteed supply" mandate of Saskoil seemed no longer necessary. Finally, the Conservative Government was particularly interested in a program to provide the Saskatchewan people with opportunities to put their considerable savings to work. This huge savings pool provided an opportunity to develop and expand the industrial base in Saskatchewan in an attempt to reduce the significant control from eastern Canada. The program was also intended to introduce investment alternatives to the Saskatchewan residents other than the traditional Canada Savings Bonds.

In order to develop a sense of investor comfort among the traditionally conservative Saskatchewan residents, the government allowed both SaskPower (also a Crown corporation) and Saskoil to issue corporate bonds in 1984. The SaskPower bonds were conventional fixed-yield instruments but the Saskoil bonds had an innovative twist. Each bond had a 10% government guaranteed coupon *plus* a participation component which added .03% for each full $1MM of net sales attained by Saskoil. The $15MM issue, an overwhelming success, was fully subscribed within two days of the announcement.

By the spring of 1985, the Saskatchewan Government was certain that the conditions were right to privatize Saskoil. First, the success of the bond issues demonstrated investor interest in direct participation in a Crown corporation. Secondly, the price of oil currently being realized by Saskoil was holding strong at over $30 per barrel, suggesting at least short term earnings stability for the corporation (see Exhibit 3 for Saskoil's historical and projected oil prices). The Province was politically concerned that the first privatization venture should produce a successful operating company with strong stock performance for Saskatchewan residents. Thirdly, the previous 4 years had seen a newly managed Saskoil generate record-breaking sales and profits. The corporation was healthy and operating efficiently. Management was eager to build on this strength and pursue a growth and expansion phase.

Government's Objectives

The privatization process and issue structure would be affected by a number of key government objectives. The government wished to recoup some of the $145MM of taxpayers' money which had been previously invested. The proceeds would pay back the equity advances provided by the Crown Investment Corporation (CIC), the high-profile holding company of the Government of Saskatchewan, for all of the Province's Crown corporations. The provincial election was a maximum of 2 years away and a record of CIC profits would be a strong, positive indication of the success of Grant Devine's policies. The government was also adamant that the going-forward company start its existence with a strong financial position as a result of the IPO. In addition, the government wanted to effect certain issue restrictions regarding ownership and control, yet it did not want to appear as the managing force behind Saskoil, for fear that investors would shy away from a government-influenced corporation. The final objective for the IPO, that the shares offered would be affordable to all income classes (i.e., 100 shares could be purchased), would allow maximum distribution to the various investor groups in Saskatchewan.

THE CHALLENGE FOR WOOD GUNDY INC.

The Wood Gundy team had been working for two months preparing the analysis papers for Saskoil after having received its initial invitation to present to the Saskoil PSC. Each issue had been carefully outlined but the final recommendations had been left for David to decide. If the presentation did not meet the requirements of the Saskoil PSC, either the privatization would be abandoned or a new lead manager would be selected to do the underwriting. David gazed through the gathering dusk as he ran through the list of topics yet to be resolved.

The Target Market

The target market decision carried implications regarding the type of security to be offered, the size of issue to be undertaken, and the marketing program and method of distribution to be selected. Specific decisions included the degree of priority to be given to "Saskatchewanites," the mechanics of exactly how to market to this group, as well as the residual priority to be given to investors in other parts of Canada and around the world.

One approach was to incorporate into the legislation a provision to offer priority to the residents of Saskatchewan on a "reasonable efforts" basis, similar to the approach taken by the Alberta Government in the privatization of Pacific Western Airlines Corporation in December 1983. This type of priority system would require the investment dealers to undertake an extensive marketing program in all parts of Saskatchewan. Wood Gundy would undertake to direct a larger percentage of the issue to Saskatchewan than would be the case in a normal public offering, and would also undertake to process all "small" orders from residents of Saskatchewan. However, in order to provide a broad secondary market for the issued shares, retail and institutional demand should also be satisfied in the other Provinces across Canada.

Other options included giving no priority to residents of Saskatchewan, or giving even greater priority to residents of the home Province. The system employed by the Alberta Energy Company Ltd. is an example of the latter. The Alberta Energy Company Ltd. Act specified that in any offering of Alberta Energy Company Ltd. shares to the public at large, the company shall allot those voting shares in preference or priority to residents of Alberta. This has been interpreted to mean that a formal system must be in place which ensures that all demand for shares from residents of Alberta will be satisfied prior to any shares being sold to residents of any other

Province or territory of Canada. The resulting system is both cumbersome and expensive.

While satisfying Saskatchewan residents was a priority of the Province, David Tate knew that he must also include investors outside Saskatchewan in order to ensure a successful offering. First and foremost, the liquidity of the capital markets in Saskatchewan was insufficient to accommodate anything greater than perhaps a $50MM issue. Secondly, the addition of sophisticated institutional investors outside of Saskatchewan made selling the issue both easier and less costly per dollar raised. The broader investor group attracted by a wider target market also gave the company a wider following for future financings. Unfortunately, additional time and effort would be required to expand the roadshow and marketing across Canada and/or around the world.

The Market Value

The Wood Gundy team had prepared two preliminary ways in which the market value of Saskoil could be estimated. The first was the net present value of future cash flows. The discount rate used in this type of calculation would be a function of the risks the company was expected to face and the variability of the estimated cash flows. This was a particularly difficult task in Saskoil's case. Cash flow estimates were based on estimating the volume and recovery of reserves in the ground, on forecasting the price and market, and on estimating the impact of the world political situation, especially the behaviour of the OPEC nations. Bill Douglas, President of Saskoil, had sent David a preliminary report from the independent engineering firm Coles Nikiforuk Pennell Associates Ltd., which had been hired to prepare a full analysis of Saskoil's assets. The report had just come in that morning. Refer to Exhibit 4 for an excerpt from the report and Exhibit 5 for an explanation of the net asset calculation.

The second valuation method the Gundy advisors had suggested was the "investment value" approach. This technique assesses the market value of Saskoil's shares that investors should be prepared to pay based on alternative investment opportunities of similar risk. In theory, the price that investors were prepared to pay for common shares of a company was the present value of the future stream of dividends. In practice, however, valuation was expressed in terms of an assessment of a company's growth potential and business risk. This assessment was then translated into a number of comparative ratios such as price/net asset value, price/cash flow, and price/earnings.[1] These ratios form the basis of comparison for publicly traded companies in the oil and gas industry (see Exhibit 6).

---

[1]Price/earnings valuation, although common for industrial analysis, is not considered as useful in the oil and gas industry. All net earnings are essentially re-invested in drilling and development; hence cash flow is the preferred measure of financial performance.

The Amount of Government Ownership and Control

Particularly important factors affecting the size and marketability of the issue were the percentage of ownership to be retained by the Province of Saskatchewan, the board representation and influence of the Province in the day-to-day affairs of the company, and the restrictions on share ownership by individual investors or by groups of investors.

David knew that for the IPO to be successful, the Province would have to reduce its ownership in Saskoil to a level that encouraged broad public ownership of Saskoil's shares, particularly in Saskatchewan. What he did not know was the exact level of ownership that would accomplish this end, especially given the desire to retain control of the corporation in Saskatchewan. The Alberta Energy Company Ltd. and Pacific Western Airlines Corporation IPOs had successfully adopted such a strategy. The Alberta Energy Company Ltd. IPO resulted in the reduction of the Government of Alberta's ownership position from 100% to 50%. The Pacific Western Airlines Corporation IPO resulted in the Government of Alberta's ownership declining from 100% to 15%. The Government of Alberta subsequently reduced its interest in Pacific Western Airlines Corporation to 4% through a secondary offering of common shares.

If the Province elected to retain a majority shareholding in Saskoil, minority board representation less than proportionate to the Province's ownership position would help satisfy investor concerns regarding potential conflicts of interest. Specifically, such a conflict might arise between a normal board member concerned with maximizing returns for all shareholders and the Province's appointed board members who might have non-financial objectives. Provincial board members might even have financial objectives that were unrelated to Saskoil and that might be detrimental to Saskoil's ability to carry on its operations and achieve its profit objectives. If the Province's level of ownership declined to less than 50%, the number of directors that it would be permitted to appoint would be reduced proportionately.

An alternative to this method of determining the board of directors of Saskoil would be to provide to all investors, including the Province, the right to vote to elect directors in direct proportion to their share ownership. The Province would then have the option either to act strictly as a passive investor and not to vote to elect directors, or to vote its shares to elect directors. The Province of Alberta has acted as a passive investor with regard to its shareholding in Pacific Western Airlines Corporation.

Of course, board representation can be taken as proxy for the level of influence the Province intends to exercise in the day-to-day affairs of Saskoil. Before any distribution of shares of Saskoil could be made to the public, prospective investors would require clarification from the Province and Saskoil of the company's corporate objectives, in particular those regarding the priority to be given to earning a return competitive with comparable businesses. Prior to the IPO, it was imperative that the Province convey its intentions to potential investors. Statements in this regard would be made in the legislature, during presentations by the company to the investment community, and in the prospectus. An example of the prospectus wording that might be considered was the following modified version of wording used by the Province of Alberta in the privatization of the Alberta Energy Company Ltd.:

> The Government of Saskatchewan has indicated that it intends to participate in ownership, not management, of Saskoil and that it does not intend to vote its shareholding on resolutions moved at general meetings, although it retains the power to do so.

Other possibilities included the creation of a special class of shares and the absence of restrictions on the amount of voting shares held by Saskoil. The special share approach would require two classes of shares to be created, Class A shares and Class B shares. Class A shares would carry the individual ownership restriction deemed appropriate; the Class B shares would be issued only to the Province. Holders of Class A and Class B shares would be entitled to one vote per share, except that the Province could vote its Class B shares separately as a class on the election of the board of directors. The Province's Class B shares as a class would be entitled to elect a majority of the board of directors, thereby ensuring control over the future direction of the company.

The Province would also be able to elect to retain a "Special Share" of Saskoil, similar to those held by the British Government following various privatizations in the United Kingdom, for example, Amersham International. There was a time-provision written into Amersham's articles of association stipulating that the company could not be taken over for at least five years. The government then retained a newly created "Special Share" of Amersham, giving it the power to prevent any one person from acquiring more than 15% of the company's voting share capital—as well as the right to veto any material disposal of assets or voluntary closure of the business.

A Special Share would allow the Province to ensure that the company maintained an independent board of directors, and would allow the Province to block attempts to dissolve or take over the company. Special Share arrangements have not been used in the privatization of Canadian companies, and it was as yet unclear how the investment community might respond to such a move by the Province of Saskatchewan in the privatization of Saskoil.

Alternatively, if the marketing decision were made to allow foreign investors to participate in the privatization of Saskoil, the decision might still be made as to the extent of foreign share ownership allowed. The Province would still have the option of restricting the IPO to residents of Canada, removing foreign restrictions only on the secondary market and for subsequent primary market transactions of the company.

A restriction on the ownership of the voting shares to holders who were either Canadian citizens or residents would probably not adversely affect the trading performance of Saskoil shares, as demand for the shares would largely be in Canada, particularly in Saskatchewan. However, avoiding such a foreign-ownership restriction might provide Saskoil with future flexibility to market shares in international capital markets. Alberta Energy Company Ltd., Canada Development Corporation and British Columbia Resources Investment Corporation restrict the ownership of their shares to Canadian citizens or residents.

An intermediate alternative that would allow Saskoil limited flexibility to access international capital markets would be to limit the aggregate percentage of voting shares owned by shareholders who were not residents or citizens of Canada to some fixed percentage of the shares outstanding. The Canadian Bank Act, for example, limits aggregate share ownership of chartered banks by non-residents to 25% of the total shares outstanding.

On a related front, the imposition of a maximum individual shareholding would encourage broad public ownership of Saskoil's shares, and help to ensure that effective control of Saskoil would remain in Saskatchewan. Ownership restrictions would also ensure that no shareholder other than the Province of Saskatchewan could accumulate an ominously large percentage shareholding, while at the same time not unduly restricting the ability of institutional investors to buy and hold shares of Saskoil.

A maximum individual shareholding of 4% was the limitation established for Pacific Western Airlines Corporation prior to its IPO of voting shares to the public. Alberta Energy Company Ltd., however, had a 1% limitation on holdings of the company's voting shares. Other companies that have a maximum individual shareholding limitation on their voting shares include Canada Development Corporation (3%) and British Columbia Resources Investment Corporation (1%, but 3% for mutual or pension funds). The appropriate level of restriction would not unnecessarily restrict institutional investors and would allow adequate flexibility in their ability to buy and hold shares of the company.

The Liquidity of the Shares

The stock price has a drastic effect on the size of issue possible in two ways. First, an expensive instrument would be more difficult to sell, especially in Saskatchewan, by reducing the total dollar amount of the offering because of poor saleability. A lower overall dollar offering leads to reduced after-market liquidity. Second, an expensive instrument would reduce the number of shares issued given a fixed dollar amount of the offering. Fewer shares available to trade also leads to reduced liquidity. David realized that given the recent high volatility in the stock markets, investors' interests in new common issues were down. He estimated that the entire Canadian market would absorb a straight common issue of between $50MM and $100MM. A larger issue of common stock could be completed if the issue were priced at an appropriate discount to the estimated fair market value of the shares. Alternatively, an issue of $100–$200MM would be tolerable if a blended issue of units[2] of convertible preferred shares and common shares, or if units of convertible debentures and common shares, were announced.

The Type of Instrument

David considered a number of alternative issue instruments. The simplest alternative would be a straight common stock issue. Straight common shares, however, represent higher risk for the investor than other unit alternatives. These risks include the ability to market a large percentage of the issue in Saskatchewan and the stock market risk of volatile returns that was diminished in an offering that includes a fixed yield instrument. Given the conservative nature of the Saskatchewan residents, David thought fixed yield was an important selling point if the majority of the issue were to be marketed within the Province. The principal advantage of a common share issue was that it results in immediate public ownership of common equity of a known amount. With an issue of units comprised of convertible instruments and common shares, the timing of conversions and the number of securities eventually converted would both be uncertain at the time of the IPO.

Issuing units of convertible preferred shares and common shares, or of units of convertible debentures and common shares, would allow a more sizable issue and be more attractive to the investment community. The ultimate decision as to the type of convertible security that might be offered as part of a unit depended on Saskoil's tax position and the market conditions. David had discovered that morning that the Saskatchewan Government was likely going to provide Saskoil with a substantial tax shield (approximately $385MM) in lieu of built up depletion and depreciation allowances previously not taken as a Crown corporation. The application of this shield would result in no taxes being paid for many years to come. In both cases, however, the units would be lower risk than straight common shares and would provide a steady stream of either dividend or interest income.

A number of additional decisions would have to be made if the unit alternatives were to be pursued. Most importantly, how many convertible securities and how many common shares would constitute a unit, and at what price would the unit be issued? David was concerned that if the units contained too large a proportion of convertible securities, the common share component would not be large enough to maintain a healthy level of liquidity in the after-market. To attract the attention of large institutional investors, the minimum common float size should be in the $50–$60MM range. This amount would give them the assurance that the company was stable, and they could buy and sell in sizable blocks without unduly affecting price.

David had many decisions to make. What interest rate or dividend rate should be recommended for the convertible securities? At what premium above stock price

---

[2]A unit is a combination of instruments sold as a single package, for example, a common share and a preferred share or a common share and a debenture.

(i.e., strike price) would the conversion be set and, therefore, what would be the conversion ratio? How long should the conversion period last and would there be multiple stages, thereby slowly increasing the conversion premium over time? How should the redemption terms be structured? Finally, should the preferred shares be given voting rights?

The Pricing

David knew that the issue had to be priced so that 100 shares could be affordable to most Saskatchewan residents, but he was not sure what was considered "affordable." The research group had suggested that issues priced in the $10 to $20 per share range had sold well and were considered attractive to investors. They had warned David that shares priced too low were perceived as speculative "penny stock" and that a low price also leads to lower earnings per share given a fixed dollar size of issue.

The Method of Distribution

The two basic choices David reviewed were a conventional underwritten issue of shares distributed exclusively by investment dealers, and distribution through banks and trust companies as well as investment dealers. The primary argument in favour of distributing exclusively through investment dealers was that the trained professionals employed as account executives by investment dealers have the knowledge, experience, information and ability to sell securities successfully to the public. If the selling skills of these account executives were combined with a special marketing program designed to achieve broad distribution of shares throughout Saskatchewan, the objectives of the Province would be achieved and risks would be minimized.

Alternatively, the issue might also be partially distributed through banks, trust companies, and credit unions as well as through the investment dealers. The immediate problem was that existing securities laws restricted marketing of securities to investment dealers, and Saskoil would, therefore, require an exemption from the appropriate securities commissions in order to allow banks, trust companies, and credit unions to participate in the issue. A different type of concern was that the use of other financial institutions as agents could result in the shares of Saskoil being sold to individuals who did not have the risks inherent in investments of this type explained appropriately. Such investors might be inclined to sell their shares or be critical of the Province and Saskoil in the event the share price declined soon after the offering date. As an example, Alberta Energy Company Ltd. offered $75 million of common shares at $10 per common share with priority being given to Alberta residents through a group of agent financial institutions in 1975. The shares performed poorly for several months following the IPO, trading as low as $8.50 per common share. One factor underlying this weakness was the use of agent financial institutions in distributing the issue, since this method of distribution meant poorly informed investors were asking poorly informed distributors for explanations of price declines. The proverbial situation of the blind leading the blind might have worsened the price decline.

THE DECISION

The principal decision regarding the mechanics of the offering was whether to do a primary or a secondary share offering. A primary offering would have Saskoil sell treasury shares to the public directly. A secondary offering would require the existing shareholder, namely the Saskatchewan Government in the form of the CIC, to sell its shares to the public. Under normal circumstances, the difference between a primary and a secondary offering would be clearly apparent in the equity section of Saskoil's balance sheet. For example, a $100MM primary issue by Saskoil would increase shareholders' equity by that same amount, but a $100MM secondary offering by CIC would flow exclusively into CIC's accounts, bypassing Saskoil entirely.

It was entirely possible that the Government of Saskatchewan would decide to retain something less than 100 percent of the proceeds. The question of the amount the government would leave in the hands of Saskoil would be dependent on the corporation's investment needs in the foreseeable future, as well as on the issue of whether leaving some funds in the hands of the company would be perceived by investors to connote future growth opportunities.

David knew that this situation was a test of both political and market ingenuity. Since his flight to Regina International Airport would be leaving in less than 12 hours, he had to decide what issues he was going to recommend to Saskoil's PSC regarding the potential privatization of the company.

EXHIBIT 1

SASKATCHEWAN OIL AND GAS COMPANY
Land Holdings and Operations

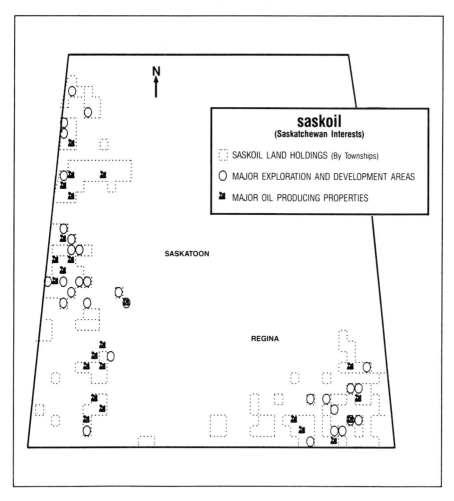

EXHIBIT 2

SASKATCHEWAN OIL AND GAS CORPORATION
Consolidated Statement of Earnings
(thousands of dollars)

	EIGHT MONTHS ENDED AUGUST 31 (UNAUDITED)		YEAR ENDED DECEMBER 31				
	1985	1984	1984	1983	1982	1981	1980
Revenue							
Crude oil and natural gas sales	$104,817	$107,003	$160,935	$136,047	$103,968	$60,014	$59,888
Less: royalties	31,743	33,248	50,251	48,142	37,180	26,210	26,013
Net sales revenue	73,074	73,755	110,684	87,905	66,788	33,804	33,875
Interest & other income	3,584	2,567	4,309	3,247	1,813	729	688
Net operating revenue	76,658	76,322	114,993	91,152	68,601	34,533	34,563
Expenses							
Operating and administrative costs[a]	25,534	21,868	34,681	33,725	31,022	20,461	15,218
Depletion, depreciation and amortization	14,100	12,803	19,162	12,974	11,639	13,111	11,876
Grants in lieu of taxes	9,092	9,409	14,544	10,222	8,536	3,686	–
Interest	2,959	1,531	2,573	3,302	4,548	3,481	3,094
Unusual items	–	–	–	–	11,288	–	–
Total expenses	51,685	45,611	70,960	60,223	67,033	40,739	30,188
Earnings (loss) for period	$24,973	$30,711	$44,033	$30,929	$1,568	$(6,206)	$4,375

Consolidated Statement of Retained Earnings

	1985	1984	1984	1983	1982	1981	1980
Retained earnings, beginning of period	$52,034	$15,606	$15,606	$14,677	$14,677	$20,883	$16,508
Earnings (loss) for period	24,973	30,711	44,033	30,929	1,568	(6,206)	4,375
Dividend	–	–	(6,605)	(30,000)	(1,568)	–	–
Retained earnings, end of period	$77,007	$46,317	$53,034	$15,606	$14,677	$14,677	$20,883

[a] General and administrative expenses for 1983 and 1984 were $10.7MM and $10.3MM, respectively, and were projected to be $11.0MM for 1985.

EXHIBIT 2 (cont.)

SASKATCHEWAN OIL AND GAS CORPORATION
Consolidated Statement of Financial Position
(thousands of dollars)

	EIGHT MONTHS ENDED AUGUST 31	YEAR ENDED DECEMBER 31				
	(UNAUDITED) 1985	1984	1983	1982	1981	1980
Assets						
Current assets						
Cash, including short term deposits	$ 46,963	$ 45,193	$ 16,580	$ 7,907	$ 4,892	$ 8,384
Accounts receivable	25,335	25,927	17,649	21,006	12,986	15,705
Inventories and prepaid expenses	7,269	3,732	2,989	3,889	4,487	4,031
	79,567	74,852	37,218	32,802	22,365	28,120
Property and equipment, at cost less accumulated depletion, depreciation and amortization	211,658	198,462	177,605	165,234	151,221	109,773
Unamortized discount and expense on long term debt	484	575	60	93	126	—
Total Assets	$291,709	$273,889	$214,883	$198,129	$183,712	$139,676

Liabilities and Shareholders' Equity

Current liabilities						
Accounts payable and accrued liab.	$ 22,464	$ 25,199	$ 16,138	$ 21,384	$ 39,535	$ 27,540
Grant payable in lieu of tax	5,411	3,214	2,639	–	–	–
Dividend payable	–	6,605	10,000	1,568	–	–
Long term debt due within one year	25,000	25,000	–	–	–	–
	52,875	60,018	28,777	23,252	39,535	27,540
Deferred gas revenue	327	337	–	–	–	–
Dividend payable	–	–	20,000	–	–	–
Long term debt	15,000	15,000	25,000	35,000	35,000	35,000
	68,202	75,355	73,777	57,952	74,535	62,540
Equity, Province of Saskatchewan						
Equity advances	145,500	145,500	125,500	125,500	94,500	54,000
Retained earnings	78,007	53,034	15,606	14,677	14,677	23,136
	223,507	198,534	141,106	140,177	109,177	77,136
Total Liabilities and Equity	$291,709	$273,889	$214,883	$198,129	$183,712	$139,676

EXHIBIT 2 (cont.)

SASKATCHEWAN OIL AND GAS CORPORATION
Consolidated Statement of Changes in Financial Position
(thousands of dollars)

	EIGHT MONTHS ENDED AUGUST 31 (UNAUDITED)		YEAR ENDED DECEMBER 31					
	1985	1984	1984	1983	1982	1981	1980
Funds were provided from:							
Operations							
Earnings (loss)	$24,973	$30,711	$44,033	$30,929	$ 1,568	$ (6,206)	$ 4,375
Add items not requiring outlay of funds:							
Depletion, depreciation and amortization	14,100	12,803	19,162	12,974	11,639	13,111	11,876
Amortization of discount and expense							
on long term debt	91	22	46	33	33	33	–
Unusual items	–	–	–	–	11,288	–	–
Other	1,454	–	–	–	–	–	–
Funds from operations	40,618	43,536	63,241	43,936	24,528	6,938	16,251
Proceeds from disposal of assets	310	389	773	1,155	462	276	–
Deferred gas revenue	–	337	337	–	–	–	–
Government incentives	2,281	2,230	3,425	3,580	3,629	2,671	3,493

Sale of bonds [net of issue costs]							
Long term debt	—	—	14,439	—	—	—	—
Equity advances	—	—	20,000	—	31,000	40,500	5,000
	43,209	66,492	67,776	48,671	28,619	9,885	39,744
	43,209	66,492	102,215	48,671	59,619	50,385	44,744
Funds were used for:							
Acquisition of property and equipment	31,341	20,803	44,217	30,080	31,031	69,792	45,468
Deferred gas revenue reduction	10	—	—	—	—	—	—
Repayment of long term debt	—	—	—	10,000	—	—	—
Long term debt due within one year	—	—	25,000	—	—	—	—
Dividend	—	—	6,605	—	1,568	—	—
Dividend—1983	—	20,000	20,000	10,000	—	—	—
	31,351	40,803	95,822	50,080	32,599	69,792	45,468
Increase (decrease) in working capital	$11,858	$25,689	$ 6,393	$ (1,409)	$27,020	$(19,407)	$ (724)
Increase (decrease) in working capital components:							
Cash, including short term deposits	$ 1,770	$13,439	$28,613	$ 8,673	$ 3,015	$ (3,492)	$ 8,754
Other current assets	2,945	4,028	9,021	(4,257)	7,422	(3,920)	6,381
Dividend payable	6,605	10,000	3,395	(8,432)	(1,568)	—	—
Other current liabilities	538	(1,778)	(34,636)	2,607	18,151	(11,995)	(15,859)
Total increase (decrease) in working capital	$11,858	$25,689	$ 6,393	$ (1,409)	$27,020	$(19,407)	$ (724)

EXHIBIT 3

Historical and Projected Oil Price

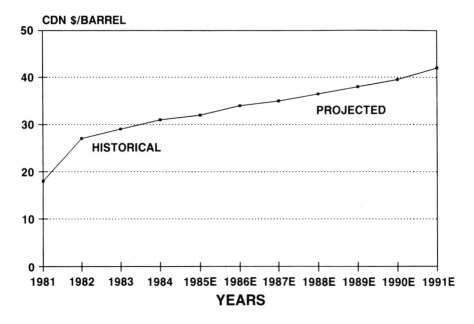

EXHIBIT 4

SASKATCHEWAN OIL AND GAS CORPORATION
Selected Operating Information

	NET (AFTER ROYALTIES) RESERVES		PRESENT WORTH BEFORE TAX OF FUTURE NET PRODUCTION REVENUE			
	CRUDE OIL (MILLIONS OF BARRELS)	NATURAL GAS (BILLIONS OF CUBIC FEET)	UNDISCOUNTED	DISCOUNTED AT THE RATE OF		
				10%	15%	20%
				(millions of dollars)		
Escalating prices						
Proven producing	30.1	2.2	$1,231.2	$399.2	$300.0	$242.8
Proven non-producing	3.6	25.0	259.2	56.6	32.8	20.0
Probable	17.2	9.7	1,129.5	215.1	130.0	87.4
Total proven and probable	50.9	36.8	$2,619.9	$670.9	$462.8	$350.2
Constant prices						
Proven producing	30.1	2.3	$ 612.2	$316.9	$259.0	$220.3
Proven non-producing	3.6	25.4	103.9	32.3	20.2	13.1
Probable	11.0	9.7	395.3	128.1	88.0	64.3
Total proven and probable	43.0	37.4	$1,111.4	$477.3	$367.2	$297.7

(continued)

613

EXHIBIT 4 (cont.)

WELLS	GROSS	NET
Producing oil wells	3,788	791.9
Producing gas wells	33	8.5
Shut-in gas wells	33	6.3
Total	3,854	806.7

LAND INTERESTS	GROSS	NET
Saskatchewan	1,356	656
Alberta	653	157
Manitoba	70	59
Total	2,079	872

The gross appraised value of Saskoil's undeveloped acreage as at August 1, 1985, was $68.4 million. The yields on short, medium and long term Government of Canada bonds in August 1985 were 10.16%, 10.64% and 11.17%, respectively. The yield on AA long term corporate bonds in August 1985 was 11.49%. The average beta for oil producers was 1.4. The excess return on the market was estimated to be 6.4%.

EXHIBIT 5

Net Asset Calculation

This valuation method is particularly used in the oil and gas industry. It is often used instead of the standard discounted cash flow procedure typical of commercial/industrial business analysis.

Net Assets = Net Production Revenue Discounted at Appropriate Risk-Adjusted, Before-Tax Rate + Undeveloped Land Holdings + Non-Oil Producing Assets, Plant and Equipment − Long Term Debt

where:

Net Production Revenue = Gross Production Revenue from Proven Producing, Proven Non-Producing, and Probable Reserves − Operating Costs (Field Costs, Lifting Costs, Transportation, Direct Overhead) − Capital Expenditures − Royalties

EXHIBIT 6

Comparative Statistics for Similar Companies

	PRICE 11-JUL-85	CASH FLOW				EARNINGS/SHARE				NET ASSET VALUE
		1983A	1984A	1985E	1986E	1983A	1984A	1985E	1986E	
PRODUCERS										
Aberford	$8.50	$1.60	$2.10	$2.65	$3.40(+)	$0.30	$0.31	$0.45(+)	$0.75(+)	$17.00(+)
Alberta Energy	$19.38	$3.87	$4.08	$5.10	$5.80(+)	$1.03	$1.22	$1.55	$2.00(+)	$29.05(+)
Asamera(1)	$9.63	$1.21	$1.10	$2.10	$3.00	($0.97)	($0.41)	$0.30	$0.55	$13.75
Bonanza	$3.50	$0.71	$0.82	$1.00	$1.30(+)	$0.13	$0.19	$0.25	$0.33(+)	$6.70(+)
B.P. Canada	$31.50	$3.62	$4.87	$5.75(−)	$6.60(−)	$1.09	$1.79	$2.15	$2.85(−)	$61.20
Bow Valley	$15.25	$1.62	$5.33	$6.00	$7.00	$0.18	$0.83	$1.00	$1.35	$23.94
Canada NW(2)	$22.75	$3.13	$4.08	$3.80	$3.90(+)	$2.24	$2.68	$2.45	$2.48(+)	$32.34
Canadian OXY	$28.50	$4.50	$7.85	$8.40	$8.45(+)	$1.90	$2.75	$3.50	$3.55(+)	$46.63(+)
Chieftain	$11.25	$1.17	$1.34	$1.55	$1.90(+)	$0.42	$0.44	$0.55	$0.75(+)	$15.95(+)
Dome Canada	$6.88	$1.17	$1.53	$2.00	$2.30(+)	$0.08	$0.37	$0.60(+)	$1.00(+)	$12.60(+)
Dome Pete.(4)	$2.90	$0.80	$0.80	NA	NA	($4.72)	($0.84)	NA	NA	NA
Merland	$3.55	$1.19	$1.25	$1.30	$1.45	$0.10	$0.13	$0.15	$0.25	$6.75
Murphy	$20.50	$4.17	$4.13	$4.55	$5.00	$1.69	$1.59	$1.95	$2.45	$29.69
Norcen(3)	$14.75	$3.20	$3.34	$3.75(+)	$4.40(+)	$1.38	$1.62	$1.70(+)	$2.05(+)	$26.90
Numac	$12.50	$1.22	$1.54	$1.90(−)	$2.20(−)	$0.58	$0.60	$0.70(−)	$0.80(−)	$16.00(+)

Oakwood	$7.75	$2.51	$2.00	$2.10	$2.55(+)	$0.06	$0.00	$0.05	$0.20(+)	$14.25(+)
Omega	$8.25	$2.38	$2.31	$2.30	$2.35(+)	$1.34	$1.32	$1.27	$1.35(+)	$17.25(+)
Pancanadian	$31.63	$3.14	$3.76	$4.30	$4.85	$1.93	$2.40	$2.80	$3.00	$44.03
Precambrian	$5.00	$0.36	$0.61	$0.90(-)	$1.15(-)	$0.11	$0.08	$0.15	$0.20	$6.20(+)
Roxy B	$4.80	$0.78	$1.05	$1.35	$1.65	($0.24)	$0.12	$0.30	$0.45	$10.62
Ranger(1)	$4.65	$1.43	$0.63	$0.85	$0.85	$0.61	($0.23)	$0.20	$0.20	$9.17
Sceptre	$5.13	$0.29	$1.21	$1.45	$1.80(+)	($6.67)	$0.26	$0.60	$0.75(+)	$9.45(+)
INTEGRATEDS										
Gulf Canada	$17.88	$3.20	$3.57	$4.00(+)	$4.45(+)	$0.96	$1.35	$1.65(+)	$1.95(+)	$27.55(+)
Husky Oil	$9.88	$2.87	$3.63	$3.05(+)	$4.10(+)	$0.51	$1.06	$1.25(+)	$1.85(+)	$19.11(+)
Imperial Oil	$50.25	$4.97	$6.31	$8.10(+)	$10.50(+)	$2.09	$3.32	$4.30(+)	$6.00(+)	$70.38(+)
Shell Canada	$26.50	$5.10	$5.42	$6.45(+)	$7.10(+)	$0.83	$1.27	$1.70(+)	$2.10(+)	$52.56(+)
Texaco Canada	$32.63	$4.04	$4.82	$5.60(+)	$6.30(+)	$2.74	$3.41	$3.80(+)	$4.45(+)	$47.55(+)
Total Pete.(1)	$17.50	$2.17	$4.05	$5.75(+)	$6.00(+)	($1.97)	$0.23	$1.75(+)	$2.00(+)	$23.34(+)
SERVICES										
Bow Valley Res.	$6.25	$1.67	$4.86	$4.81	$5.43	$0.00	$1.23	$1.08	$1.40	
Bralorne	$4.45	$0.48	$0.63	$0.75	$0.85	($0.40)	($0.11)	$0.00	$0.10	
Computalog	$22.50	$1.31	$2.12	$2.90	$3.70	$0.61	$1.30	$1.95	$2.50	
Nowsco	$20.00	$2.37	$3.09	$3.00(-)	$3.25(-)	$1.19	$1.56	$1.75(-)	$2.05(-)	
Trimac	$4.45	$0.80	$0.98	$1.28	$1.52	($0.07)	$0.16	$0.25	$0.45	

Note: Cash Flow net of preferred dividends and capitalized interest where provided.

NAVPS = Net Asset Value Per Share

(−) or (+) indicates direction of latest revision.

Source: Wood Gundy Inc.

EXHIBIT 6 (cont.)
Comparative Statistics for Similar Companies

| | PRICE | PRICE/CASH FLOW | | | PRICE/EARNINGS | | | P/NET ASSET | RETURN ON AVE. (84) | | DEBT |
	11-JUL-85	1984E	1985E	1986E	1984E	1985E	1986	VALUE	EQUITY	CAP. EMP.	EQUITY
PRODUCERS											
ABERFORD	$8.50	4.0	3.2	2.5	27.4	18.9	11.3	50.00%	4.1%	2.3%	1.22
ALBERTA ENERGY	$19.38	4.8	3.8	3.3	15.9	12.5	9.7	66.71%	13.1%	4.6%	1.15
ASAMERA(1)	$9.63	6.4	3.3	2.3	NA	23.3	12.7	70.04%	-14.1%	-8.6%	0.43
BONANZA	$3.50	4.3	3.5	2.7	18.4	14.0	10.0	52.24%	3.1%	3.1%	0.41
B.P. CANADA	$31.50	6.5	5.5	4.8	17.6	14.7	11.1	51.47%	13.9%	9.6%	0.00
BOW VALLEY	$15.25	2.9	2.5	2.2	18.4	15.3	11.3	63.70%	12.8%	2.5%	4.03
CANADA NW(2)	$22.75	5.6	6.0	5.8	8.5	9.3	9.2	70.35%	26.0%	17.7%	0.24
CANADIAN OXY	$28.50	3.6	3.4	3.4	10.4	8.1	8.0	61.12%	19.7%	13.1%	0.17
CHIEFTAIN	$11.25	8.4	7.3	5.9	25.6	20.5	15.0	70.53%	7.6%	4.4%	0.86
DOME CANADA	$6.88	4.5	3.4	3.0	18.6	11.5	6.9	54.60%	3.4%	2.5%	0.23
DOME PETE. (4)	$2.90										
MERLAND	$3.55	2.8	2.7	2.4	27.3	23.7	14.2	52.59%	11.9%	2.6%	4.07
MURPHY	$20.50	5.0	4.5	4.1	12.9	10.5	8.4	69.05%	14.6%	10.2%	0.03
NORCEN (3)	$14.75	4.4	3.9	3.4	9.1	8.7	7.2	54.83%	15.6%	8.6%	0.52
NUMAC	$12.50	8.1	6.6	5.7	20.8	17.9	15.6	78.13%	10.7%	7.4%	0.39
OAKWOOD	$7.75	3.9	3.7	3.0	NA	155.0	38.8	54.39%	2.5%	1.5%	4.21
OMEGA	$8.25	3.6	3.6	3.5	6.3	6.5	6.1	47.83%	38.6%	21.4%	0.56
PANCANADIAN	$31.63	8.4	7.4	6.5	13.2	11.3	10.5	71.84%	26.5%	16.0%	0.13

	Price										
PRECAMBRIAN	$5.00	8.2	5.6	4.3	62.5	33.3	25.0	60.98%	1.3%	2.8%	0.36
ROXY B	$4.80	4.6	3.6	2.9	40.0	16.0	10.7	45.20%	1.0%	1.5%	0.09
RANGER (1)	$4.65	5.4	4.0	4.0	-14.7	16.9	16.9	50.71%	-6.6%	-1.4%	0.32
SCEPTRE	$5.13	4.2	3.5	2.9	19.7	8.6	6.8	54.29%		6.9%	2.49
AVERAGE		5.2	4.3	3.7				59.55%	10.29%	6.13%	1.04
INTEGRATEDS											
GULF CANADA	$17.88	5.0	4.5	4.0	13.2	10.8	9.2	64.90%	12.6%	7.4%	0.32
HUSKY OIL	$9.88	2.7	3.2	2.4	9.3	7.9	5.3	51.70%	12.9%	5.9%	0.29
IMPERIAL OIL	$50.25	8.0	6.2	4.8	15.1	11.7	8.4	71.40%	12.1%	8.5%	0.26
SHELL CANADA	$26.50	4.9	4.1	3.7	20.9	15.6	12.6	50.42%	6.2%	3.1%	0.45
TEXACO CANADA	$32.63	6.8	5.8	5.2	9.6	8.6	7.3	68.62%	21.1%	16.2%	0.04
TOTAL PETE. (1)	$17.50	3.1	2.2	2.1	55.3	7.3	6.4	74.98%	3.0%	3.8%	2.46
AVERAGE		5.1	4.3	3.7				63.67%	11.32%	7.48%	0.64
SERVICES											
BOW VALLEY RES.	$6.25	1.3	1.3	1.2	5.1	5.8	4.5		18.2%	3.4%	3.65
BRALORNE	$4.45	7.1	5.9	5.2	NA	NA	44.5		-3.0%	.0%	1.06
COMPUTALOG	$22.50	10.6	7.8	6.1	17.3	11.5	9.0		28.2%	25.5%	0.00
NOWSCO	$20.00	6.5	6.7	6.2	12.8	11.4	9.8		21.6%	13.8%	0.40
TRIMAC	$4.45	4.5	3.5	2.9	27.8	17.8	9.9		3.9%	1.8%	1.41
AVERAGE		6.4	5.0	4.3					13.8%	8.9%	1.30

Notes:
(1) EPS & CFPS in U.S. dollars. Multiples reflect $1U.S. = $1.375 Canadian.
(2) Year-end September 30.
(3) Restated.
(4) We are currently restricted from publishing changes to our forecasts.

EXHIBIT 6 (cont.)

Comparative Statistics for Similar Companies

	APRIL 30/85 TSE WEIGHT (% OF OIL INDEX)	RECOMMENDED WEIGHT—% OF OIL PORTFOLIO	RECOMMENDED WEIGHT—% OF TOTAL PORT.	EST. 1-YEAR TRADING RANGE HIGH	EST. 1-YEAR TRADING RANGE LOW	EST. 1-YEAR TRADING RANGE UPSIDE	EST. 1-YEAR TRADING RANGE DOWNSIDE	52-WEEK PRICE RANGE HIGH	52-WEEK PRICE RANGE LOW
ABERFORD	0.0%	0.0%	0.0%	$12.00	$8.00	41.2%	−5.9%	$11.38	$7.75
ALBERTA ENERGY	4.4%	0.0%	0.0%	$22.50	$18.00	16.1%	−7.1%	$23.25	$17.75
ASAMERA(1)	2.7%	0.0%	0.0%	$14.00	$9.00	45.4%	−6.5%	$14.36	$8.63
BONANZA	0.6%	0.0%	0.0%	$4.80	$3.70	37.1%	5.7%	$5.25	$3.65
B.P. CANADA	2.0%	10.0%	1.6%	$45.00	$30.00	42.9%	−4.8%	$36.00	$23.00
BOW VALLEY	3.7%	0.0%	0.0%	$19.00	$14.00	24.6%	−8.2%	$24.63	$14.00
CANADA NW	1.9%	0.0%	0.0%	$26.00	$19.00	14.3%	−16.5%	$33.88	$21.25
CANADIAN OXY	3.9%	7.0%	1.1%	$36.00	$27.00	29.8%	−5.3%	$32.00	$24.25
CHIEFTAIN	0.9%	0.0%	0.0%	$12.50	$9.00	11.1%	−20.0%	$17.00	$10.88
DOME CANADA	2.6%	7.0%	1.1%	$9.50	$6.50	38.1%	−5.5%	$8.25	$4.90
DOME PETE.	5.0%	0.0%	0.0%					$3.65	$2.00
MERLAND	0.3%	0.0%	0.0%	$4.50	$3.25	26.8%	−8.5%	$5.88	$3.50
MURPHY	0.5%	0.0%	0.0%	$27.00	$19.00	31.7%	−7.3%	$25.50	$19.75
NORCEN	4.2%	7.0%	1.1%	$19.00	$14.50	28.8%	−1.7%	$19.25	$14.00
NUMAC	2.3%	0.0%	0.0%	$15.50	$11.00	24.0%	−12.0%	$17.25	$11.00
OAKWOOD	0.6%	0.0%	0.0%	$10.50	$6.00	35.5%	−22.6%	$10.50	$4.65
OMEGA	0.6%	0.0%	0.0%	$10.00	$7.50	21.2%	−9.1%	$11.00	$7.50

PANCANADIAN	3.8%	0.0%	0.0%	$32.00	$42.00	32.8%	1.2%	$36.25	$23.50
PRECAMBRIAN	0.4%	0.0%	0.0%	$4.50	$5.40	8.0%	-10.0%	$6.50	$4.25
ROXY B	0.2%	0.0%	0.0%	$4.25	$5.50	14.6%	-11.5%	$8.40	$4.80
RANGER	2.5%	0.0%	0.0%	$3.90	$5.25	12.9%	-16.1%	$10.25	$3.90
SCEPTRE	1.2%	0.0%	0.0%	$5.00	$7.00	36.5%	-2.5%	$7.25	$5.00
TOTAL PRODUCERS	45.1%	31.0%	4.8%						
INTEGRATEDS									
GULF CANADA	13.0%	7.0%	1.1%	$16.00	$22.00	23.0%	-10.5%	$21.00	$14.25
HUSKY OIL	2.1%	10.0%	1.6%	$9.00	$15.00	51.8%	-8.9%	$13.13	$9.38
IMPERIAL OIL	18.4%	33.0%	5.1%	$47.00	$70.00	39.3%	-6.5%	$55.00	$33.63
SHELL CANADA	4.5%	0.0%	0.0%	$24.00	$31.00	17.0%	-9.4%	$29.88	$19.50
TEXACO CANADA	6.7%	7.0%	1.1%	$30.00	$42.50	30.2%	-8.1%	$41.25	$30.13
TOTAL PETE.	1.4%	4.0%	0.62	$14.00	$23.00	31.4%	-20.0%	$17.38	$10.50
TOTAL INTEGRATEDS	46.1%	61.0%	9.5%						
SERVICES									
BOW VALLEY RES.	0.0%	4.0%	0.6%	$5.75	$12.00	92.0%	-8.0%	$10.13	$6.00
BRALORNE	0.0%	0.0%	0.0%	$3.50	$5.50	23.6%	-21.3%	$6.75	$4.45
COMPUTALOG	0.0%	4.0%	0.6%	$21.00	$30.00	33.3%	-6.7%	$25.00	$10.75
NOWSCO	0.0%	0.0%	0.0%	$17.00	$23.00	15.0%	-15.0%	$26.38	$17.00
TRIMAC	0.0%	0.0%	0.0%	$3.75	$5.00	12.4%	-15.7%	$5.88	$3.65
TOTAL SERVICES	0.0%	8.0%	1.2%						
TOTAL OIL & GAS		100.0%	15.5%						

45

SEALED AIR CORPORATION'S
LEVERAGED RECAPITALIZATION

Shortly after the close of trading on April 27, 1989, Sealed Air Corporation issued a press release announcing a one-time special cash dividend of $40 per share payable on May 11, 1989. (Exhibit 1 contains a copy of the press release.) Over the 30 days prior to this announcement, the stock had been trading between $44⅛ and $45⅞ a share. In its ten year history as a New York Stock Exchange (NYSE) listed firm, Sealed Air had paid quarterly dividends, but never one larger than 18¢ per share.

With 8.245 million shares of common stock outstanding, the total cash payout amounted to $329.8 million or 87% of the total market value of the firm's common stock at $45⅞ per share. With only $54.3 million in cash and short term investments, the company borrowed most of the funds required to pay the dividend. After completing the transaction, Sealed Air would have a debt-to-book value ratio of 1.36 (up from .13) and negative net worth of $160.5 million. The financial press dubs transactions where a firm increases leverage substantially and makes a large cash payout to shareholders "leveraged recapitalizations."

THE COMPANY

Founded in 1960, Sealed Air manufactured and sold a wide variety of protective packaging materials and systems. The company's products included the famous packing bubbles everyone loves to pop, padded mailing envelopes, pads for absorbing moisture in supermarket meat packages, and equipment and supplies used to create customized foam for packaging fragile or unusually shaped items. Its principal packaging products were sold under the following registered names and trademarks: Instapak® foam-in-place packaging systems; AirCap® and PolyCap® Plus air cellular cushioning materials; Jiffy™ padded, Jiffylite® and other specialty light weight shipping mailers; Cell-Aire® polyethylene foam; PolyMask® and Bubble Mask® coated masking materials, Kushion Kraft® cellulose wadding; and Dri-Loc® absorbent pads. Exhibit 2 presents pictures of products from each of Sealed Air's major product lines. Bulky products, such as bubbles and foam, were sold through distributors. Salespeople for these products often made calls on end-users, but always pulled the sale through a distributor. Engineered products, such as Instapak, were sold partly through distributors and partly directly to end-users.

Sealed Air succeeded in growing rapidly during its first 25 years of business. Many of its products had strong patent protection, and so during this period management had emphasized the development of a strong sales force to exploit its revolutionary products. By the late 1980s, however, the necessity of focusing on the manufacturing side of the business was becoming apparent. E.N. "Pete" Funkhouser, Senior Vice-President, International Operations, described Sealed Air's situation:

> We really needed a shakeup in the company, Let me explain why. For the first 25 years, our organization has emphasized developing a sales force to sell a wonderful product. All our products were proprietary. We started with the patented bubbles—they were revolutionary. Then in 1976 we bought Instapak and their patents, then in 1983 we bought Dri-Loc and its patents. We were displacing the old-fashioned way of doing things. We priced our product based on benefit to the customer, and not necessarily cost. We had 45–50% margins. We didn't need to manufacture efficiently, we didn't need to worry about cash. At Sealed Air capital tended to have limited value attached to it—cash was perceived as being free and abundant.

> By the mid-80s it became apparent that things would change. For one thing most of our air cellular patents had run out and we were getting more competition. We had already experienced some of these problems in Europe because in the earlier years we didn't secure strong positions with patents and distributors there.

> We began to put more emphasis on areas we had ignored, particularly manufacturing. Two years ago our factories were underperforming. It took three weeks to get product, we had inventories all over the place, scrap was too high, quality control was inadequate, and process control wasn't working.

T. J. Dermot Dunphy, President and CEO, had known for several years that a change in the strategic direction of Sealed Air would eventually be necessary. He and several other members of senior management believed that manufacturing, which had previously been neglected in favor of sales and marketing, was an essential component of the strategic change they wanted to make. A year before its leveraged recapitalization, Sealed Air launched a program called World Class Manufacturing to promote manufacturing excellence.

WORLD CLASS MANUFACTURING

Jim Lyons, Vice-President, Manufacturing, became excited about the opportunity to improve production efficiency after reading a book by Richard J. Schonberger entitled *World Class Manufacturing: The Lessons of Simplicity Applied*. He saw the World Class Manufacturing Program (WCM) as providing a solution to his manufacturing problems:

> The main lesson of WCM is that if you do it right you can have it all—high quality, low cost, fast and dependable customer service and reduced working capital. There are no trade-offs!
>
> Customer service is at the head of the parade. Inventory is the enemy because it gets in the way of better service and hides quality defects. Reducing inventory also increases cash flow. Quality means lower cost because doing it right the first time costs less.
>
> For production, you want simpler as opposed to complex machinery. The knee-jerk reaction is to get bigger and bigger machinery, making larger and larger capital expenditures. Now we emphasize consistency in machinery. Consistency makes change-over easier and change-over is critical to service—you have to be able to change size and formula. Most manufacturing people like to run a size 8½ shoe factory.

Together, Dunphy and Lyons decided that WCM was the ideal vehicle for achieving their manufacturing objectives. They pressed ahead with a plan to adopt the WCM approach, inviting Schonberger to speak to plant managers and operating personnel. They then began to implement the principles of WCM. In mid-1988 Sealed Air Corporation embarked full-force on its WCM program.

WCM: A YEAR LATER

A year after its implementation, Sealed Air management felt they had made significant progress on their WCM program. The program had revitalized the company and put new energy and creativity into the manufacturing process. Changes were taking place at all of Sealed Air's manufacturing facilities.

Changes at the Packaging Products Division

One manufacturing facility for the Packaging Products Division was located in Totowa, New Jersey. Here the bubble packaging product, as well as polyethylene foam packing, were produced. Hedley Batters, Plant Manager, discussed the effects of the WCM program and the recap on his plant's operations:

> We used to run one product a day. Now we run eight products in a single day. Broadly speaking, what's made today is shipped tomorrow. We try not to produce anything that is not sold. The floor used to be packed with product. Now when a truck pulls up to load only half the shipment is made. The product goes off the line and into the truck. We've had to go to shorter production runs—you get better yields if you use longer runs—so productivity is down, but at least we know where the product is.

There's a lot more pressure now. There's risk of running too close to the wind. We have less margin for error and we could miss some orders this way. For example, if a machine goes down we could have problems. We've had to spend a lot of money on maintenance in the last four months, but we're trying to get operators more involved in maintenance and to participate in company goals.

Changes at the Food Packaging Division

In his capacity as Vice-President, Food Packaging Division, Bruce Cruikshank summarized the changes in the production of Dri-Loc® Pads:

> I've found that it's important to have decisions made at the lowest possible level. The process is 60% science and 40% art—that's where the people come into play. The operator has to constantly adjust. We make billions of pads per year on several machines. The operator needs to make the right decision at the right moment. Only the operator knows if a bearing needs replacement, and can replace it before it breaks. After WCM we took 20 operators and had our first training seminar. They shared ideas and concepts. They were so interested that they stayed at the table talking through the break. Our quality is up, productivity is up, and the level of excitement is up.

> Here's an example of the enthusiasm and participation generated by WCM. We let our operators know that we wanted to improve one of our products. It was a pad for chicken that was marginally profitable. We had been making it largely by hand and we wanted ideas for how to make it on our automated equipment. Within two weeks we had three sample products from our plants. A third shift operator was coming in during his time off to run quality control on the samples.

At all facilities a suggestion system was adopted and the results surpassed all of management's expectations.

Cruikshank explained:

> Before the suggestion system, we seldom thought of manufacturing as an important source of new ideas. New ideas always came from customers, product managers, salespeople, and research and development.

Lyons elaborated:

> Prior to WCM we weren't doing well with training and motivating our hourly employees. Our yields were off. We implemented a suggestion system. I was skeptical about this, now I love it. Even though the employees only win $25 for a top suggestion the ideas were shockingly good. And we keep getting more and more suggestions—we have had over 2,000 so far. We started holding an annual awards banquet where employees making the best suggestions were awarded OSCARs. We want our employees to feel that innovation is a part of their job.

MAINTAINING THE MOMENTUM

Dunphy was enthusiastic about WCM, but he was concerned about the organization's ability to maintain the changes brought about by the program. Previously, acquisitions had acted as catalysts for organizational change. Dunphy stated:

In the past, most of our crises were the result of acquisitions. Our acquisitions were all integrative, none of this we love your management, we'll leave you alone, you'll like our benefits. Every time we made an acquisition we re-evaluated *everyone* and put the best people in the best places.

A year after the implementation of WCM, Sealed Air had $54 million in cash, and Dunphy expected the company's cash balance to more than double in the next year and a half. Dunphy knew an acquisition or new capital project would initiate the shake-up he wanted and the company could certainly afford it, but management was unable to identify profitable acquisitions or expansion projects. Cruikshank explained:

> There were no good acquisitions and we had nothing to do with the cash. Just increasing the dividend over the years is admitting defeat. We don't want to be a public utility.

Dunphy felt strongly that the company shouldn't hold on to the cash:

> Shareholders are not paying me to invest their money in securities. That is not my area of expertise. Once a manager starts worrying about what securities the firm is holding, it's time to give the money back to the shareholders.

He had served on the board of several leveraged buyout companies and had seen the positive effect of leverage on firm performance:

> In my experience as a director and in my personal investments I have seen the benefits of leverage. I wanted Sealed Air to have the discipline of high leverage, but still wanted the organization to grow.

A large payout to shareholders, financed by borrowing, was seen as the best use of Sealed Air's cash flow. It would benefit shareholders and provide the impetus necessary to maintain a momentum toward continued improvement within the company.

THE RECAPITALIZATION

Once the decision to make a substantial payout to shareholders had been made, the management team had to determine how much to borrow and how to pay out the cash to shareholders. In addition to a special dividend, they considered several other alternatives, including an open-market stock repurchase and a tender-offer for their own shares. Management ruled out a leveraged buyout almost before they started considering the options. Cruikshank explained:

> We hadn't yet determined the level of debt we wanted, but the goal was not to take it to the wall. An LBO cuts into the muscle of the firm. We had too good a company to do an LBO.

Dunphy added:

If we had done this as an LBO it would have put the company into play and forced us to leverage to the wall. The special dividend did not put the company into play. Moving from 70% to 90% leverage is a crucial difference between being able to grow and not being able to grow. A financial group can gut the company for the short term. There are companies that should be gutted, but you shouldn't gut a quality company.

In executing the recap, I had two simple objectives in mind: (1) take care of your shareholders and they'll keep you in your job and give you the right to manage the company, and (2) take care of your employees.

Along with other members of the management team, William Hickey, CFO, spent six months determining the optimal amount to borrow, to pay out to shareholders, and the tax effects of the various alternatives. A process of elimination was used to decide what form the transaction would take, using four criteria as a guideline: the transaction must

1. create value for shareholders,
2. be simple,
3. treat all shareholders equally, and
4. not encourage unsolicited offers from outside investors.

The type of financing and the decision on how much to borrow were interrelated, so decisions on these issues were made simultaneously. Unusual financial instruments (such as PIK [Pay-in-Kind] paper and zero coupon bonds) were eliminated quickly because management felt these securities were generally associated with lower quality transactions.

Mary Coventry, Director of Corporate Development, explained:

The decision to keep the transaction simple and eliminate unusual financial instruments was effectively a self-imposed cap on borrowing. We wanted to provide for both debt service and the future growth of the company.

Our upper and lower limits on borrowing were based on cash flow models with varying assumptions about growth. Once we established upper and lower limits on borrowing, we developed a model to project shareholder value. The model was based on discounted cash flows, levels of investment risk, and resultant market multiples. From this model, we made the decision to borrow against our future cash flow stream and declare a $40.00 per share cash dividend.

Hickey described some of the problems he ran into working on the recapitalization plan:

The banks told us that we could not borrow the amount that we needed because we didn't have a track record for managing large amounts of debt. You can't borrow money unless you've borrowed money. In addition, the banks held it against us that we didn't have an LBO partner who understood leverage and could make the tough decisions including getting rid of Dermot, if that was necessary.

Dunphy elaborated:

In selling this deal to the banks we ran into two problems. First, top management got large dividend checks because we owned stock and the banks worried about our commitment. Second, the company ended up with a negative net worth. There was a strong reaction to the negative net worth. A lot of banks can't get a deal with negative net worth past the loan committee. It is really a triumph of form over substance!

In spite of these problems, Sealed Air was successful in financing the special dividend. The company borrowed $136.7 million under a $210 million senior secured bank credit agreement with Bankers Trust Company acting as agent for a syndicate of banks. As of the end of 1989, the weighted average interest rate on borrowings under the credit agreement was 11.5%.[1] Sealed Air also issued $170 million in subordinated bridge notes. The bridge notes were later refinanced through a public offering of $170 million in 10 year senior subordinated notes at $12\frac{5}{8}$%. To finance the balance of the dividend payment, the company used $5.6 million in cash it had received as a dividend from its subsidiaries, liquidated short term investments, and paid the remainder using cash on hand.

The credit agreement required the following principal repayment schedule:

1991:	$15.3 million
1992:	$15.3 million
1993:	$19.6 million
1994:	$26.2 million
1995:	$34.0 million

It also required that the proceeds of any asset sales and, if the firm's cash flow was unusually high, any "excess cash flow" be used to repay principal. Further, the credit agreement restricted additional borrowing and also required that the company enter into swap and interest rate cap agreements to establish a fixed interest rate on $80 million of borrowings under the agreement.

The senior subordinated notes were not subject to any sinking fund requirements. The company could redeem the notes beginning July 1992 at a price starting at 107.9% of face value and declining to 100% of face value by July 1, 1997. Should a change in control of the company occur, Sealed Air was required to redeem the notes at a premium. Financing fees and other expenses associated with the special dividend totalled $20.9 million.

Dunphy announced the completion of the recap to his fellow employees on July 12, 1989. In his President's Newsletter he shared his views on what the transaction meant for the company (Exhibit 3). Sealed Air's management did not view the recap as a purely financial transaction; it was undertaken to strengthen and motivate the organization. When Dunphy announced the completion of the recap, he also announced the adoption of a new set of priorities for the company.

---

[1] The interest rate on the credit agreement was, at Sealed Air's option, the Bankers Trust prime rate plus $1\frac{1}{2}$% or the reserve adjusted Eurodollar rate plus $2\frac{1}{2}$%.

CHANGING PRIORITIES AND INCENTIVES

Following the recapitalization, management focused the attention of employees on a new set of priorities. A cardboard number "1" with a list of five new priorities, in order of importance, on the front and the corporate mission on the back was distributed to employees and displayed prominently throughout the company (Exhibit 4). Sealed Air's stated post-recap objectives were:

1. Putting our customer first,
2. Cash flow,
3. WCM,
4. Innovation, and
5. Earnings-per-share.

A New Bonus Plan

The emphasis on the new priorities was more than verbal. After the recap, Sealed Air adopted a new bonus plan for its managers. Before the recap, Sealed Air based its bonuses on earnings-per-share. After the recap earnings-per-share (EPS) based goals were replaced with goals based on Earnings Before Depreciation, Interest, Taxes, and Amortization (EBDITA), inventory turns, receivables, and working capital. The objective of the new bonus plan was to focus managers' attention on the importance of generating cash flow. Cruikshank explained some of the challenges managers faced in the post-recap environment:

> At Sealed Air our managers never had to manage a balance sheet at the divisional level, and capital expenditures were never really an issue. We just took the wish-list, eliminated the obscure and recommended everything else to the Board.

Moving from EPS to EBDITA caused managers to focus on cash flow from operations. Non-cash accounting expenses, interest expenses and taxes did not affect performance based on EBDITA. Meeting inventory, receivables and working capital goals required that managers become aware of the opportunity cost of cash tied up in these balance sheet items. Exhibit 5 presents excerpts from the firm's financial statements for the year ending December 31, 1990.

Sealed Air continued to pay salespeople a salary plus commission, but did not extend incentive compensation to the shop floor. Lyons explained:

> We didn't adopt incentive pay for our hourly workers because we didn't have a good measure to pay on. We don't have the ruler straight yet. We could use a piece-rate, but the feedback of the system on quality is weak. Salespeople give customers rebates on the spot to adjust for quality problems, but we never hear about it. To do quality control or to pay on quality, the operator has to understand what quality is on that line and has to get consistent raw materials. We don't have either of these yet!
>
> Salespeople's total compensation was about two-thirds salary and one-third commission. Commission varied depending on the product.

Employee Stock Ownership

In addition to the bonus plan, Dunphy planned to place more emphasis on employee stock ownership after the recap. He explained:

> One of the purposes of the recapitalization is to establish a greater identity of interests between shareholders and employees through broader employee stock ownership. This goal will be accomplished over time through our Contingent Stock Award Program and our Profit-Sharing Plan. By the first anniversary of the recapitalization, assuming the Company achieves its financial objectives, it is anticipated that employee ownership, which stood at approximately 7.9% on the date of the recapitalization, will have increased to approximately 16%. My goal is for management and employees to own 18% of the stock by the second anniversary of the recap. It's not a magic number, but I don't want more than 20% management ownership—we don't want to be an employee-owned firm. We want to be publicly owned, and our employees have to take care of the shareholders who are the owners.
>
> The Profit-Sharing Plan, which owned approximately 0.7% of Sealed Air stock on the date of recapitalization, will own approximately 4.7% on the first anniversary and approximately 6.0% on the second anniversary of the recap. The balance of employee stock ownership results primarily from awards of Contingent Stock but also includes stock acquired through other means. The number of employees who had received stock under the Contingent Stock Plan as of the date of the recapitalization was 159; it is anticipated to grow to 194 by the first anniversary and approximately 220 by the second anniversary of the recap. The foregoing number of employees represents approximately 6.5%, 7.7% and 8.5% of the total number of employees at each date.
>
> I want to emphasize that employee ownership was *not* increased as part of the recapitalization. Our recap was structured so that, with the exception of those shareholders who bought and sold in the normal course of business, our shareholder base would be the same the day before and the day after the recap. All shareholders— management, employees and outsiders—were treated identically under the terms of our recapitalization.

Dunphy felt strongly that employee stock ownership improved company performance.

> Stock ownership motivates managers. I can't prove it, but I believe it. But people have to hold onto the stock for it to work. At many firms, people cash in when it vests, but at Sealed Air people don't sell. I take a paternalistic, intrusive approach when employees want to sell their shares. Selling stock defeats the purpose. Of course, people can sell for a good reason—college education for their kids, etc., but I want them to keep 70% of everything they've been awarded.
>
> We revitalized our compensation plan for the benefit of middle and lower management and our outstanding professionals. The older managers made money on Sealed Air stock, but over the two years before the recap our stock was stagnant. It certainly wasn't something that would give you the opportunity to get rich. I had a conviction that we could do better than the current price. The recap made it possible to say to the younger generation "you can make it happen too." Some analysts have suggested that the stock could be back at $50 by 1993.

EFFECTS OF THE RECAP

Assuring the Independence of the Company

Dunphy felt an important outcome of the recapitalization was that it assured Sealed Air's independence without the adoption of anti-takeover devices. Dunphy explained his position on these issues:

> While I want Sealed Air to remain independent, I have an aversion to shark repellents. They protect only the managers and increasingly are clothed as shareholder protection. We have no employment contracts, no golden parachutes. When you act like a shareholder you don't need to go around protecting your job. It's easy to get a high priced lawyer to come in and tell you it is your fiduciary duty to adopt a shark repellent. I like to be exposed to the market place—the discipline is important.
>
> While recapitalization should help us to remain independent in the short run, in the long run, staying independent is the result of doing the right things. We don't pursue profit, we *do* the things that *generate* profit and cash flow.
>
> We had to decide how much of our unutilized borrowing power we wanted to draw on. We wanted to increase the market value of the company. We decided to give as much as we could to shareholders without deterring the company from its growth path. We are right on the growth target—the underlying business is growing at 10%.

In an address to employees Dunphy stated:

> We believe it is important to preserve the Sealed Air culture which for so many years has served its employees and customers so well. We believe that as a consequence of benefiting our shareholders, this decision will help to maintain the Company's independence.
>
> For the 18 years that I have been President of Sealed Air, I have said, "As long as we continue to reward our stockholders with increased earnings, I believe that we will remain independent and not have to endure the anxiety of being taken over by a larger corporation that might not have Sealed Air's high standards of concern for people."

Investors' Response

In the financial markets of 1989, there was much concern about the apparent general increase in corporate borrowing, and financial analysts' reactions to Sealed Air's recap were mixed. Oppenheimer issued a buy recommendation for Sealed Air's common stock. Dun & Bradstreet issued a report that described Sealed Air's condition as "unbalanced," and summarized the trend as downward. The report emphasized the company's negative net worth.

On the day after the announcement of the recap, there was an imbalance of orders for Sealed Air's stock on the NYSE and trading didn't open until 11:00 A.M. The opening price was $53 and the stock closed at $50½—up $4⅜ for the day. The $40 dividend was distributed to shareholders of record on May 8, 1990, and the stock went ex-dividend on May 12, 1990. On May 11, Sealed Air stock closed at $50¾, and on the following day the stub share closed at $12½. Over the rest of the year the stub share's closing price increased steadily, reaching a high of $23 and ending the year at $20⅜. (Exhibit 6 presents a history of Sealed Air's stock price performance.)

After the recap, management observed what was essentially a complete turnover of Sealed Air's shareholder base. Cruikshank noted that many institutional investors had sold their holdings following the recap. They were replaced by what management called "cash flow" investors.

> The big hang-up is our negative net worth. I don't understand why traditional investors are so bothered by it. Our customers and employees don't see it as a problem at all.

Coventry elaborated:

> The institutional investors who held our stock prior to the recap were more conservative. Their goals were to invest in companies with consistent growth, a "solid" financial situation, and limited downside risk. Investment managers whose investment policies required market capitalization in excess of a certain level were required to sell their holdings in Sealed Air after the special dividend was declared. Pension funds whose policies required them to hold dividend paying stocks had to sell as well, because our stock would not pay a dividend after the recap. Other institutional investors who sold their shares were negative toward leverage and deficit net worth.

> One money manager, a long-time Sealed Air shareholder, called us up to tell us he was sorry to have to sell our shares *before* the special dividend was paid. He was evaluated solely on capital gains.

> Now our institutional investors are more speculative investors looking for significant gains in profitability. They are willing to look beyond the negative equity and focus on cash flow projections. Limited partnerships, such as the Tiger Management Company, and wealthy private investors are important new shareholders for Sealed Air.

Binding Debt Covenants

As part of the debt covenants with the banks, Sealed Air agreed to the following capital expenditures/capitalized lease obligations schedule:

1990:	$ 7.0 million
1991:	$ 8.0 million
1992:	$ 9.0 million
1993:	$10.5 million
1994:	$12.0 million
1995:	$12.5 million

Capital expenditures were restricted to $7 million in 1990, down from $13.4 million in 1989. Dunphy explained:

> The only short term negative, and it's a real psychological stumbling block, is the severe restrictions placed on capital spending by the bank agreement. We can spend $7 million next year for the whole company—we've been spending that much in Europe. It was the only overly aggressive assumption that we can identify in our planning of the

recapitalization. The banks wanted a restriction, but didn't demand this low number. I was too pessimistic about our sales growth and how that related to the capacity of multiple plants. We will probably renegotiate the covenant later this year. The constraint has forced us to prioritize capital expenditures, however, and to restructure our formal capital budgeting process.

Cruikshank described the constraint as:

Tough—but do-able. We've never really revved the place up—we could go three shifts, seven-days-a-week. I don't think the capital expenditure constraint has forced us to have too short term a focus—we've just had to learn to prioritize our expenditure decisions.

ASSESSING THE TRANSACTION

By the end of 1989, Sealed Air's strong cash flow allowed the company to repay $30 million of bank debt and $5.1 million of its notes payable. This put the company a year ahead of the principal payments required by the banks—no additional principal repayment was required until 1991! Looking back, Dunphy assessed Sealed Air's leveraged recap:

The significance of strong balance sheets has changed greatly over the past 10 years. They are no longer so significant as symbols of financial strength. Cash flow has become recognized as the more important measure of financial strength and Sealed Air is enormously strong on that score.

The recapitalization, in addition to its financial objectives, was planned as a reinforcer and re-energizer of a change in strategy and culture that was initiated in late 1988. We planned our recapitalization with the purpose of using the Company's capital structure to influence and even drive a change in strategy and culture which had already been initiated with the adoption of WCM as a way of doing business.

There is no doubt that we executed a successful financial transaction. The danger is that it is only that—a financial transaction.

EXHIBIT 1

Press Release Announcing Sealed Air Corporation's Leveraged Recapitalization

for release:

Contact: Bruce Cruikshank   April 27, 1989

FOR IMMEDIATE RELEASE

SEALED AIR CORPORATION • PARK 80 EAST, SADDLE BROOK, NEW JERSEY 07662-5291

SEALED AIR CORPORATION
DECLARES SPECIAL DIVIDEND
OF
$40 PER SHARE

Saddle Brook, New Jersey, April 27, 1989—Sealed Air Corporation (NYSE-SEE) announced today that its Board of Directors has declared a special cash dividend of $40 per share of Common Stock, payable, subject to certain conditions, to holders of record as of the close of business on May 8, 1989.

In order to provide funds necessary to pay the special dividend, refinance certain existing indebtedness, pay related fees and expenses and provide working capital, the Company has entered into a $210 million senior secured bank credit agreement with Bankers Trust Company and a $170 million subordinated securities purchase agreement with an affiliate of Donaldson, Lufkin & Jenrette Securities Corporation.

Payment of the special dividend will be made as promptly as practicable after the record date and the satisfaction of the conditions to borrowing under the financing agreements and receipt of certain solvency related opinions. Although no assurances can be given, it is currently expected that the special dividend will be paid on or about May 11, 1989.

Commenting on the special dividend, T. J. Dermot Dunphy, President, stated "The special dividend will enable all of the Company's stockholders to realize in cash a significant portion of the current value of their shares, while at the same time allowing them to retain their equity interest in the Company.

"Our corporate strategy has emphasized worldwide leadership in protective packaging. Through a combination of new product developments and acquisitions intended to be consistent with our corporate strategy, the Company has a strong record of growth in net sales and earnings.

(continued)

EXHIBIT 1 (cont.)

"Over the past several years, we have generated more than sufficient cash flow from operations to support the growth in our operations, our capital expenditure needs and our acquisition program. With the substantial capital investments that the Company has made over the past few years, we believe that the Company has adequate manufacturing capacity to meet increased demand for its products during the next several years without significant additional capital expenditures.

"We also believe that it is unlikely in the current market environment that we will be able to find opportunities for significant acquisitions at an acceptable price that would be consistent with our corporate strategy.

"In light of these circumstances and other factors, the Board determined that it was an appropriate time to realize value for the Company's stockholders. Unlike many recapitalizations, the special dividend was not made in response to an acquisition proposal by any third party.

"The Company expects to service the indebtedness incurred in connection with the special dividend without the sale of significant assets or business units. We will, however, discontinue our quarterly cash dividend of the foreseeable future and take certain other appropriate steps to reduce expenses and improve cash flow to service this indebtedness."

Although it is not possible to calculate until after December 31, 1989, the Company anticipates that a portion of the special dividend will not be treated as a dividend for Federal income tax purposes.

Based on discussions with the New York Stock Exchange, the Company understands that its stock will begin to trade ex-dividend on the day following the payment date and will trade with due bills from May 2, 1989 through the payment date.

The Company intends to mail to its stockholders an information statement providing further information concerning the special dividend, which information statement will be filed with the Securities and Exchange Commission as a Current Report on Form 8-K.

Sealed Air manufactures and markets a complementary line of specialized protective packaging and process protection materials and systems that protect products from hazards of their environment. Sealed Air also manufactures and markets selected food packaging and recreation and energy conservation products.

* * *

EXHIBIT 2

Products from Each of Sealed Air Corporation's Major Product Lines

Our Products Protect Your Products.®

Sealed Air Corporation manufactures and markets a wide variety of materials and systems to protect products from damage caused by shock, vibration, abrasion, and electrostatic discharge.

For the 90's, we will continue our tradition of leadership by providing solutions — not compromises — through technological development and innovation.

Our Environmental Commitment

Sealed Air is committed to sound business practices based on the most current environmental information available. We have adopted a program that encompasses specific lines of action:

1) **Source Reduction:** In our twenty packaging labs worldwide, we are continually striving to reduce the amount of packaging material needed to ensure adequate product protection.

2) **Recycling:** Sealed Air recycles over 100 million pounds of paper and plastic each year.

3) **Reusability:** Products are designed for maximum reuse.

4) **Disposal:** Sealed Air® products are efficiently and safely incinerated, or take up minimal landfill space.

Our Products Are Supported By:

- **Consultative sales reps** who will work with you to determine the most cost-effective packaging method.
- **Package design and testing** at no charge to you.
- **Training** to ensure your personnel are using our products effectively and economically.
- **Local full line distributors** providing complete sourcing for all your packaging needs.
- **Multiple shipping points** throughout the U.S.
- **System installation and service** by local Sealed Air Representatives.
- **Worldwide availability** for those customers with multi-national requirements.

PACKAGING PRODUCTS DIVISION:
AirCap®, and PolyCap®R Barrier Bubble Cushioning Products, **Instasheeter**™ High-Speed Converting Systems, **Jiffy Packer**® Paper Packaging Systems, **VoidPak**™ Inflatable Packaging, **Kushion Kraft**®, **Custom Wrap**™ and **Void Kraft**™ Paper Packaging Materials, **Jiffy Mailer**® Products, **Shurtuff**® Durable Mailers and Static Control Products.

POLYETHYLENE FOAM PRODUCTS DIVISION:
Polylam® Laminated Plank, **Sealed Air**® **Plank**, **Cell-Aire**® and **Cellu-Cushion**® Polyethylene Foam Products.

ENGINEERED PRODUCTS DIVISION:
Instapak® Foam-in-Place Packaging Materials and Systems.

OUR PRODUCTS PROTECT YOUR PRODUCTS®

Sealed Air Corporation, 19-01 State Hwy. 208, Fair Lawn, NJ 07410 (201) 703-5500

INTERNATIONAL
Canada, England, France, Germany, Holland, Hong Kong, Italy, Japan, Malaysia, Mexico, Singapore, Spain, Sweden, Taiwan.
INTERNATIONAL LICENSEES AND DISTRIBUTORS
Australia, Korea, New Zealand, Peoples Republic of China.
® Reg. Pat. Off. © Sealed Air Corporation 1993. All Rights Reserved.

D-86 REV 9/93
Printed in U.S.A. on Recycled Paper

EXHIBIT 2 (cont.)

DRI-LOC® PAD

Meat, Fish and Poultry Absorbent Pad

The Leading Edge
In Consumer Satisfaction

1. Reduce Rewraps

With Dri-Loc® Pads you'll be wrapping up higher profits, instead of rewrapping your products.

- Superior performance and retention.
- Drier Packages.
- Eliminates leaking.
- No plies to separate.
- Reduced packaging and labor costs.

*Complies with USDA regulations. Dri-Loc® Pads are available in a variety of sizes and absorbencies to meet your specific packaging requirements.

Sealed Air Corporation

Food Packaging Division
Patterson, N.C.

2. Keeps Meat, Fresher Longer

Dri-Loc® Pads keep your ribs at their prime.

- Absorbs only from bottom of pad.
- Absorbs naturally released juices (no wicking)

- One-way valves and sealed edges lock-in free flowing juices.

3. Cleaner Display Cases

Dri-Loc® Pads assure cleaner, more attractive display cases.

- Attractive display means more impulse purchases.
- Reduced paper towel and poly bag use at meat counter (secondary packaging).
- Maximum absorbency, superior retention.
- Downgrading and spoilage greatly reduced.

4. Greater Customer Satisfaction

Dri-Loc® Pads mean no more customer beefs about your meats.

- Drier, more attractive packages.
- Fresher meat.
- Continued benefits after sale, eliminating mess on car seat, in refrigerator, and on kitchen floors and counters.
- Easy peeling from meats with no tearing, shredding or sticking, even when frozen.
- Customer satisfaction means repeat purchases.

EXHIBIT 3

Dunphy's Letter to Fellow Employees
Announcing the Completion of the Leveraged Recapitalization

President's
Newsletter

July 12, 1989

Dear Fellow Employee:

Sealed Air has just completed an extremely successful offering of senior subordinated notes to complete the financing of the recapitalization that I have been telling you about for the last couple of months.

We financed the original dividend, which was paid to holders of Sealed Air stock (including Fund C of the Company's Profit-Sharing Plan), partly out of excess cash that we had accumulated, partly from bank borrowings that we will pay down over the next several years, and with a short term loan known as "bridge notes" which was arranged through our investment banker. These bridge notes were at a very high interest rate and were, in any event, only intended to be short term. These notes have now been replaced by ten-year senior subordinated notes at the extremely attractive interest rate for this kind of financial security of $12\frac{5}{8}\%$.

On June 29 when the underwriting of these notes became effective, no fewer than 152 major insurance companies, mutual funds and other financial institutions wanted to buy Sealed Air's $170 million offering. The total of the notes that all of these institutions wanted to buy far exceeded $170 million and thus our investment banker was able to negotiate a relatively low interest rate in the process of allocating the number of notes to be sold to each enthusiastic buyer.

Bill Hickey and Bruce Cruikshank did a superb job in the extensive preparation necessary for making this sale and in presenting the Sealed Air story to the prospective buyers of our notes. Bob Grace did his usual very professional legal job and a lot of other Sealed Air people participated in what was ultimately, in the best Sealed Air style, a team effort.

At the same time, the Company's stock has been performing exceedingly well and is now at an all time high, demonstrating that our recapitalization has been well received and that investors are confident the company will continue to perform well.

WE CAN NOW PUT ALL OF THIS FINANCING BUSINESS BEHIND US AND CONCENTRATE ON THE PRIORITIES OF OPERATING SEALED AIR.

Along with this President's Newsletter is a new "Priorities Card" which I hope you will put in your pocket for regular reference. It emphasizes that our No. 1 priority continues to be *putting our customer first*. This is consistent with the everyday efforts of our sales,

(continued)

EXHIBIT 3 (cont.)

customer service and manufacturing people throughout the company. It is highlighted by the OSCAR competition and has recently been demonstrated in the considerable improvements that we have achieved in reducing the lead time from receipt of customer order to shipment of the order.

No. 2—*Cash Flow*—is a new priority for Sealed Air. You will be receiving a lot of new information defining our cash flow objectives, which from now on are more important than the so-called "bottom line"—the earnings per share (E.P.S.) that has been such a major goal of Sealed Air for so long. However, although the Accounting Department will define cash flow more accurately for you than I can in this Newsletter, it is really nothing more than common sense applied to business. As the Priorities Card shows, we need simultaneously to increase sales and margins, have less inventory, less capital expenditures and faster collections.

Most of you are already familiar with our 3rd priority, *WCM*—which really makes the first two priorities possible. Our entire manufacturing organization at all levels and at all locations is dedicated to achieving *World Class Manufacturing* through total quality (TCQ), just-in-time inventory (JIT), total material usage (TMU), total preventative maintenance (TPM) and employee involvement (EI).

Our 4th priority is *Innovation*. Putting our customer first and WCM will automatically stimulate innovation throughout the company, and I am looking forward to a steady flow of new products and new ways of operating our business and serving our customers.

Our 5th objective is the familiar *earnings per share* (*E.P.S.*). Although cash flow takes priority, our shareholders will always be interested in E.P.S. and improvement in E.P.S. will continue to be an important Sealed Air goal. Because of the recapitalization, E.P.S. in 1989 will be significantly less than 1988, and E.P.S. may be more volatile for the next few years because of our interest expenses arising from the recapitalization. Also, we expect that the costs of the recapitalization will result in Sealed Air's reporting a loss in the second quarter in terms of E.P.S. However, from that point on, we expect our earnings performance and cash flow to show steady improvement as we work to meet our priorities.

The back of the card states our *Corporate Mission*. It is the cumulative effect of all 2000+ employees of Sealed Air continually finding ways to do their job a little better that has made us the worldwide leader in protective packaging and that will keep us there!

Our *Code of Conduct* speaks for itself, and we are making it stronger than ever throughout the Company.

Issue No. 89-4
Attachment

EXHIBIT 4

SEALED AIR CORPORATION'S NEW PRIORITIES CARD
Distributed to All Employees with the President's Newsletter of July 12, 1989

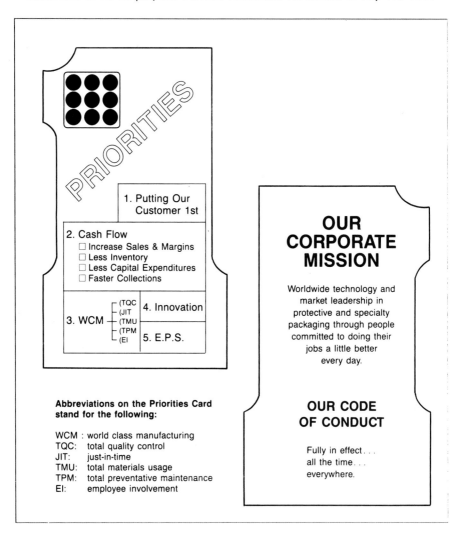

PRIORITIES

1. Putting Our Customer 1st

2. Cash Flow
   ☐ Increase Sales & Margins
   ☐ Less Inventory
   ☐ Less Capital Expenditures
   ☐ Faster Collections

3. WCM ┬ (TQC
        ├ (JIT
        ├ (TMU
        ├ (TPM
        └ (EI

4. Innovation

5. E.P.S.

Abbreviations on the Priorities Card stand for the following:

WCM : world class manufacturing
TQC: total quality control
JIT: just-in-time
TMU: total materials usage
TPM: total preventative maintenance
EI: employee involvement

**OUR
CORPORATE
MISSION**

Worldwide technology and market leadership in protective and specialty packaging through people committed to doing their jobs a little better every day.

**OUR CODE
OF CONDUCT**

Fully in effect . . .
all the time . . .
everywhere.

EXHIBIT 5

Excerpts from the Financial Statements of Sealed Air Corporation
For Fiscal Years Ended December 31
($ in millions)

	1989	1988	1987
Selected Income Statement Data			
Net Sales	$385.0	$345.6	$302.7
Cost of Sales	(250.5)	(230.2)	(199.3)
Gross Profit	134.5	115.4	103.4
Net Earnings	7.2	25.3	20.5
EBIT	53.7	43.6	36.1
(Earnings Before Interest and Taxes)			
EBDITA	69.9	56.5	48.2
(Earnings Before Depreciation, Interest, Taxes and Amortization)			
"Cash" EBDITA	74.7	59.3	
EBDITA adjusted for the effects of all non-cash revenues and expenses			
Cash Flow Data			
Interest Outlays (Net)	(17.1)	(1.7)	
Income Tax Outlays	(12.9)	(14.3)	
Capital Expenditures (Net)	(13.4)	(20.5)	
Proceeds from Borrowings Associated with the Leveraged Recapitalization	306.7	—	
Dividend Received from Subsidiaries	5.6[a]	—	
Cash Dividends Paid to Stockholders	(329.8)	(4.7)	
Financing Fees	(20.9)	—	
Proceeds from Other Long Term Borrowings	3.5	7.8	
Total Principal Repayments	(38.1)	(8.5)	
Proceeds from the Sale of Short Term Investments	28.9	(5.6)	

[a]As a part of financing the $40 special dividend to Sealed Air's common stockholders, the company's subsidiaries borrowed and paid the net proceeds to the parent company in the form of a special dividend of $5.6 million.

(continued)

EXHIBIT 5   (cont.)

Excerpts from the Financial Statements of Sealed Air Corporation
For Fiscal Years Ended December 31
($ in million)

	1989	1988	1987
Selected Balance Sheet Data[b]			
Current Assets			
Cash	$ 25.5	$ 28.1	$ 25.9
Short Term Investments	—	27.0	20.7
Receivables	58.8	58.1	48.3
Inventories	25.9	36.2	31.3
Prepaid Expenses	2.0	1.7	1.1
Non-Current Assets			
Property Plant & Equipment – Net	85.1	83.7	78.5
Patents and Rights – Net	7.4	7.6	5.4
Deferred Financing Costs	12.9[c]	—	—
Other Assets	12.6	14.9	17.0
Total Assets	$230.2	$257.3	$228.2
Current Liabilities			
Notes Payable	4.6	9.7	10.1
Current Portion of Long Term Debt	4.9	4.8	3.3
Accounts Payable	21.6	24.4	21.6
Accrued Interest	12.7	0.2	—
Other Accrued Liabilities	24.9	21.2	18.3
Income Taxes Payable	8.2	5.1	4.3
Non-Current Liabilities:			
Long Term Debt (less Current Portion)	301.6[d]	19.0	21.0
Deferred Credits	12.2	10.6	8.5
Shareholders' Equity	(160.5)	162.3	141.1
Total Liabilities and Shareholders' Equity	$230.2	$257.4	$228.2

[b]Balance sheet data were modified slightly from the original to undo the effect of currency translation on cash balances.

[c]In financing the special dividend, the company incurred expenses of $20.9 million. Of this amount, $6 million was charged to 1989 income as an expense and the rest was capitalized as an asset. Also in 1989, $2 million of amortization expense associated with this asset was charged to income, hence the net asset amount of $12.9 million.

[d]Includes $110.4 million in borrowings under the senior secured credit agreement, $170 million in senior notes, and $26.1 million in other long term debt, less current portion of $4.9 million.

EXHIBIT 6

Historical Stock Price Performance of Sealed Air Corporation
New York Stock Exchange Ticker SEE

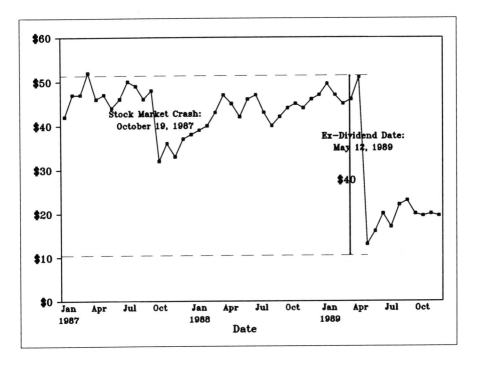

INDEX OF CASES

The Acquisition of Martell   484
American Barrick Resources Corporation   421
Anheuser-Busch and Campbell Taggart   148
Altantic Lumber Traders   57
Bell Canada   327
Blue Jay Energy & Chemical Corporation   498
Cambridge Nutrition Limited Financing Growth (A)   25
Citibank Canada Ltd.—Monetization of Future Oil Production   439
Columbia Pine Pulp Company, Inc.   452
Columbia River Pulp Company Inc.—Interest Rate Hedging Strategy   388
Columbia River Pulp Company Inc.—Recapitalization   66
The Consumers' Gas Company Ltd.   235
Dow Europe   124
Export Development Corporation—Protected Index Notes (PINS)   403
Fantastic Manufacturing, Inc.   109
Finning Tractor and Equipment Company Ltd.   172
Gold Industry Note   285
The Goodyear Tire & Rubber Company   462
John Labatt Limited   2
Kitchen Helper Inc.   14
Lawson Mardon Group Limited   94

Lawson Mardon Group Limited—Corporate Asset Funding Facility   258
Maschinenbau Arrau A.G. (A)   116
Minnova Inc.—Lac Shortt Mine   277
Morley Industries, Inc.   20
The Multi-Jurisdictional Disclosure System   375
Nesbitt Thomson Deacon Inc.—The Sceptre Resources Debenture   190
Note on Insider Trading   159
Note on the North American Tire Industry   479
Note on Value-Added Taxes   39
Ocelot Industries Ltd.   520
Procter & Gamble: Cost of Capital   222
The Redhook Ale Brewery   292
Robotics, Inc.   383
Rogers Communications Inc.   351
The RTZ Corporation PLC—Rio Algom Limited   203
Saskatchewan Oil and Gas Corporation   594
Sealed Air Corporation's Leveraged Recapitalization   622
Sherritt Gordon Ltd.—Proxy Contest   572
Sophisticated Petites   45
Tanzi Pump Corporation   272
Tri-tech Computer   313
Unicorp Canada Corporation   559
Union Enterprises Ltd.   535
Warner-Lambert Canada Inc.   84